Borges

A LIFE

Borges

A LIFE

Edwin Williamson

VIKING

VIKING

Published by the Penguin Group
Penguin Group (USA) Inc., 375 Hudson Street, New York, New York 10014, U.S.A.
Penguin Group (Canada), 10 Alcorn Avenue, Toronto, Ontario, Canada M4V 3B2
(a division of Pearson Penguin Canada Inc.)
Penguin Books Ltd, 80 Strand, London WC2R 0RL, England
Penguin Ireland, 25 St. Stephen's Green, Dublin 2, Ireland (a division of Penguin Books Ltd)
Penguin Books Australia Ltd, 250 Camberwell Road, Camberwell, Victoria 3124, Australia
(a division of Pearson Australia Group Pty Ltd)
Penguin Books India Pvt Ltd, 11 Community Centre, Panchsheel Park, New Delhi – 110 017, India
Penguin Group (NZ), Cnr Airborne and Rosedale Roads, Albany, Auckland, New Zealand
(a division of Pearson New Zealand Ltd)
Penguin Books (South Africa) (Pty) Ltd, 24 Sturdee Avenue, Rosebank,
Johannesburg 2196, South Africa

Penguin Books Ltd, Registered Offices: 80 Strand, London WC2R 0RL, England

First published in 2004 by Viking Penguin, a member of Penguin Group (USA) Inc.

1 3 5 7 9 10 8 6 4 2

Excerpts from the writings of Jorge Luis Borges are used with permission.

PHOTOGRAPH CREDITS:
Photographs 1–10, 13, 17–19: courtesy of Colección Jorge Luis Borges,
Fundación San Telmo; 11, 14–16: Susana Lange; 12: from *Martín Fierro,* December 12, 1926;
20: © Ferdinando Scianna/Magnum Photos; 21: © Kelly Wise; 22: María Kodama;
23, 24: Amador Martínez-Morcillo

LIBRARY OF CONGRESS CATALOGING-IN-PUBLICATION DATA

Williamson, Edwin.
Borges, a life / Edwin Williamson.
p.   cm.
Includes bibliographical references and index.
ISBN 0-670-88579-7
1. Borges, Jorge Luis, 1899–1986   2. Authors, Argentine—20th century—Biography.   I. Title.
PQ7797.B635Z953 2004
868'.62—dc22
[B]   2004041290

This book is printed on acid-free paper. ∞

Printed in the United States of America
Set in Minion
Designed by Francesca Belanger

In memory of H.W.,
and for Susan, Louise, and Phoebe

Preface

FOR THE GREATER PART of his life, Jorge Luis Borges worked in obscurity, or at least the relative obscurity that living in Buenos Aires imposed on a writer so far removed from the established centers of literary culture. Fame was thrust upon him in his early sixties, when he was awarded the International Publishers' Prize in 1961, and even then a split jury required that he share it with Samuel Beckett. Still, grudging as fate had been toward Borges, it now lavished favors beyond imagining—recognition swiftly blossomed into an extraordinary renown, and within a few years he was being acclaimed as one of the great writers of the twentieth century and acknowledged as the most influential writer in the Spanish language of modern times.

Borges had a seminal influence on twentieth-century Latin American literature, whose richness and vitality were being celebrated worldwide at around the time he came to prominence. Subsequently, he was to have a remarkable impact on a rising generation of writers in Britain, the United States, Italy, and France, for his work extended the range of serious fiction in surprising ways, encouraging writers to depart from the character-based psychological or social realism of the postwar novel and embrace fiction as a self-conscious, rhetorical artifact, susceptible to unashamed fantasy and to overtly intellectual, and even philosophical, concerns. Additionally, his stories and essays were perceived to have anticipated some of the principal topics of modern critical theory. His subtle reflections on time and the self, or on the dynamics of writing and reading, had generated texts that embodied ideas such as the arbitrariness of personal identity, the decentered subject, the "death of the author," the limitations of language and rationality, intertextuality, or the historically relative and "constructed" nature of human knowledge (viz. Borges's elliptical "histories" of abstract concepts, such as infamy, eternity, or angels).

Borges rejected what he saw as the intrinsic fraudulence of realism—the novelist pretending to hold up a mirror to "reality" when in fact he knew as little as his readers about the way the world actually worked. There was no point in disguising the artifice of fiction, he believed—a story was an *orbe autónomo,* a self-contained realm of the imagination that the author was free to shape at will so long as he could persuade the reader to lend it an appropriate degree of "poetic faith." Not only did Borges throw off the constraints of realism, he called into question the preeminence of the novel in the hierarchy of modern literature. He was drawn to modes of storytelling that had long preceded the novel—fable, epic, parable, and folktale. Favored also were contemporary modes that had been relegated to the category of subgenres by the towering prestige of the novel—Gothic fantasy, tales of adventure, science fiction and, best of all, detective stories, which he admired for their highly wrought, "teleological" plots. Not that he felt bound by categories of any sort. Nothing was proof against the spell of fiction—a book review, an obituary, a scholarly essay or a footnote could just as soon be touched by the magic of the storyteller. Even metaphysics and theology, as he famously observed, could be regarded as branches of the literature of fantasy.

Borges's writing was rooted in his childhood reading of adventure stories by authors like Robert Louis Stevenson, Rudyard Kipling, Alexandre Dumas or the Argentine Eduardo Gutiérrez, but his imagination was equally stirred by the philosophy of Berkeley and Hume, Schopenhauer and Nietzsche. From Berkeley and Hume he took his basic premise—the subjective nature of all knowledge and experience; from thinkers like Schopenhauer and Nietzsche he derived a sense of the fragility of personal identity, as likely to be the product of self-assertion as a mere conceit of some cosmic intelligence. Lacking objective truth, man was condemned to play in a game of no fixed rules and no specific end, for if the existence of beings other than oneself was uncertain, the presence of God or a hidden demiurge could not be ruled out. The act of writing was a paradigm of existence: the author might invent characters and plots, but was he the true source of his inventions, or did they simply reflect patterns repeated endlessly throughout universal literature? In the face of such radical uncertainties, the reader was invited to question personality, meaning, and, ultimately, objective reality itself.

Other than poetry, Borges's favorite medium was the *ficción*—a short story or prose text whose brevity allowed him to condense mental play into reverberating images and situations. The early *ficciones* were metaphysical fantasies in which, for instance, the universe was compared to a well-ordered but limitless library that refused to disclose its overall design, or the play of chance and necessity likened to a lottery run by a sinister panel of judges, or a novel held to represent the labyrinths of infinite time. An obsessive theme was the duel, the clash for supremacy between two rivals—Borges chose mostly hoodlums or adventurers, but he could also write teasingly about contests between theologians, society ladies, and even the two great South American liberators, Bolívar and San Martín, at their enigmatic encounter in Guayaquil. The duel became a metaphor for the yearning to assert identity by eliminating a rival, though Borges often liked to show how the victor might in the end be no more than a mirror image of his victim.

Borges's pronounced metaphysical concerns fostered the view among critics that his writing belonged in an ideal, timeless space, a kind of literary utopia, and this perception was underscored perhaps by the blindness that afflicted him a few years before he became famous, which lent him the aura of an otherworldly, sightless bard, capable of reaching into the vast storehouse of world literature and making present to us the eternal forms of a fading heritage. This impression of timelessness was further reinforced by the hazy chronology of his output. He had a habit of appending additional texts to later editions of his books, texts that had often been written years before, or indeed after, those books had first been published. He also continually revised the poems of his youth, purging them of local color and even omitting a good number altogether from successive editions of his collected works. In the case of three books of essays from the 1920s, he opted for outright suppression, steadfastly refusing to have them reprinted in his lifetime and claiming that he had done his best to buy up all extant copies and consign them to the flames.

Little wonder, then, that Borges's career appears to be so full of gaps, discontinuities, reversions, and turning points. Why did he try to disguise or conceal his youthful writings? Why did he abandon poetry at the age of thirty? Why did he cease writing stories in 1952 to take up poetry once more? And why, when he started telling stories again, did his writing appear to lose so much of the abstract, metaphysical quality that was so notable in his earlier *ficciones*? If there is a thread that runs through that maze of questions, it is Borges's conviction that writing, ultimately, is a form of autobiography. At the height of his fame, he confessed to an interviewer,

> I have felt my stories so deeply that I have told them, well, using strange symbols so that people might not find out that they were all more or less autobiographical. The stories were about myself, my personal experiences.[1]

He was, in fact, restating a belief first expressed in one of the youthful books of essays he wanted to suppress. In an essay called "A Profession of Literary Faith," he had written, ". . . All literature is autobiographical, in the last instance. Everything is poetic inasmuch as it confesses a destiny, inasmuch as it gives us a glimpse of one." The "autobiographical substance" of a work, he conceded, might at times be rendered invisible by the "accidents" that embodied it, but it subsisted all the same, "like a heart beating in the depths."

The career of Borges was a quest to discover what it meant to be Borges, and it is this search for a destiny that I would invoke as justification for my undertaking a biography of so elusive a writer. My attempt to get a sense of this hidden search has taken nine years—roughly twice as long as I had anticipated. As might be expected in an enterprise of this length, there have been frustrations and setbacks, but if there was anything that sustained me through these difficulties, even at the cost of prolonging the enterprise itself, it was the discovery of new material—in the form either of fresh sources or of new insights—that lit up further reaches of the autobiographical hinterland of Borges's oeuvre. Chronology turned out to be the key, for only by reconstructing the sequence of events in the life and relating these as far as I could to the order of composition of the work was it possible to discern the contours of personal experience and finally take the pulse of the "heart beating in the depths" of the writing.

Fairly early on in my research, I was able to glimpse the elements of a story that held the promise of drawing together the seemingly disparate parts of Borges's life. I began to suspect that his insistence on amending or erasing his youthful writings was motivated not so much by an aversion to his early poetics as by a wish to cover up some matter that had caused him particular pain. In due course I was able to gather evidence that revealed that he had indeed undergone an experience in his mid-twenties that had driven him to the brink of suicide and almost destroyed him as a writer. Borges never directly spoke of this experience, but it became evident that it had been pivotal to his development, for it was as a result of that trauma that he ceased being a poet, and it was largely on account of it that he discovered the kind of writing that would eventually make his name. In one of Borges's most famous stories, "The Garden of Forking Paths," a character asks another, "In a riddle whose subject is chess, what is the one word that is forbidden?" And the reply is, "The word *chess.*" Likewise, the one subject that was never openly declared by Borges in fact haunted the work of his middle years and was encrypted in signs, symbols, and motifs virtually everywhere in his texts. Only when love was finally revealed to him was he able to exorcise the ghosts of the past and arrive at the serenity, and indeed happiness, that characterized the last two decades of his life.

Needless to say, the myriad inventions and subtleties of literature cannot be reduced to the circumstances of mere biography, but a writer's life is the seedbed of his work, and from this biographical study, I would contend, there emerges a fuller, more human, more richly faceted Borges than the anemic bibliophile of legend would suggest. Borges was a man riven by inner conflicts, a man who, far from holding himself aloof from the great issues of his time, was deeply imbued with a sense of history. The fact that he was Argentine was critical in this respect. According to Borges, Argentina had come into being as an act of faith in the possibility of inventing a nation, and for the whole of his life he remained seized by the dream of building the *patria*, but even though he had been born at the height of Argentina's golden age, when the country was among the most prosperous in the world, it fell to him to witness its appalling descent into violence and disarray. Borges's fears over the destiny of the nation ran parallel with the quest for a destiny of his own, and not the least of his achievements was to have made his readers recognize themselves in that predicament—he converted the anxiety of being an Argentine, as it were, into an emblem of a universal condition, for in brilliant, lucid, powerful writings, he was to imagine the dissolution of the self and insinuate the horrors that might attend on its passing.

Edinburgh,
December 2002

Acknowledgments

As with any book, the writing of this biography has been a journey of discovery. I wish to record my gratitude to the people who made that journey possible.

I would like to thank the staff of several institutions for making available documents, books, and material that were vital to my research. In Buenos Aires: Biblioteca Nacional; Biblioteca del Congreso; *La Nación; La Prensa; Clarín;* Fundación Internacional Jorge Luis Borges; Fundación Antorchas; Fundación San Telmo. In the United Kingdom: Edinburgh University Library; University of London Library; Taylor Institution Library, Oxford. In the United States: Stanford University Library; Harvard University Archives, Pusey Library, Cambridge, Massachusetts; Widener Library, Harvard University; Special Collections Department, Alderman Library, University of Virginia. I am also grateful to the Leverhulme Trust for a Research Fellowship (1995–96); to the British Academy for a Research Leave Award (1997) and two research travel grants; and to the University of Edinburgh for a period of leave and a research travel grant.

A number of people helped me get the project off the ground. I greatly benefited from John King's extensive knowledge of Argentine culture and of Borges's circle in particular. I would like to thank him for the personal contacts he provided and for his unfailing encouragement. I am grateful to Jason Wilson, who also provided me with fruitful contacts and helped me become acquainted with Argentina. Elsie Rivero Haedo was always hospitable and opened many doors for me in Buenos Aires. Isabel Quesada lent me her apartment at a propitious time. Ezequiel de Olaso became a reliable guide and intellectual companion but sadly passed away before we had a chance to discuss the book. María Gabriela Mizraje taught me more about the barrios and byways of Borges's native city than I could ever have discovered for myself.

The following, whom I list in alphabetical order, collectively assisted me in all sorts of ways: Carlos Alberto Andreola, Raúl Antelo, Patricia Artundo, Marta Barbato, Ana María Barrenechea, José Luis Boquete, Jorge Calvetti, Alberto Casares, José María Castiñeira de Dios, Fermín Chávez, William Chislett, Edgardo

Cozarinsky, Nigel Dennis, Mercedes Dipp, Javier Fernández, Annette Flynn, Germán García, Ian Gibson, José Gilardoni, Norman Thomas di Giovanni, Nigel Glendinning, Mariano Goñi, Andrew Graham-Yooll, Peter Graves, Francis Korn, Andrés Lema-Hincapié, Eduardo Paz Leston, Rafael Arráiz Lucca, Francisco Márquez Villanueva, Gabriela and Pino Marrone, Xavier Martini, Daniel Martino, Graciela Melgarejo, Carmine Mezzacappa, Ian Michael, María Esther de Miguel, Jorge Moentack, Adolfo de Obieta, Miguel Alfredo Olivera, Herman Pálsson, Alicia Parodi, Mora Pomares de Pezzutti, Ricardo Piglia, Cristina Piña, Patricio Randle, Ted and Judy Riley, Jeremy Robbins, Luis Alberto Romero, Horacio and Graciela Salas, Raúl Salinas, Beatriz Sarlo, Jorge Schwartz, Ed Shaw, Marcela Solá, Philip Swanson, Nicholas Tozer, Jon Usher, Luisa Valenzuela, David Viñas, Lita Vogelius, Julio Woscoboinik, Héctor Yánover, Irma Zangara, Wally Zenner.

I was very fortunate to have been given access to unknown, forgotten, rare, or (at the time) unpublished sources. I am grateful to Nicolás Helft, the director of the Colección Jorge Luis Borges at the Fundación San Telmo, for letting me see primary sources, for sharing with me his extensive knowledge of the bibliography by and on Borges, and for providing several photographs to illustrate the book. I am grateful, too, for the help I received from Susana Lange, who made some rare material and photographs available to me. I would like to thank Mariana Eppinger de Helft, Jorge Helft, Wáshington Pereyra, and Alejandro Vaccaro for allowing me to work on manuscripts, letters, contemporary magazines, and other original sources that were of vital importance in the early phase of my research. Also invaluable were the sources, photographs, and other material provided by Eduardo Alvarez Tuñón, Fermín Chávez, Uki Goñi, Alicia Jurado, Denah Lida, Amador Martínez Morcillo, Fedra Petit de Murat de Suárez Boedo, Alastair Reid, Horacio Salas, and Donald Yates.

I am indebted to a number of people who were good enough to share their memories of Borges and others with me: Gloria Alcorta de Girondo, Adolfo Bioy Casares, Norah Borges, Estela Canto, Betina Edelberg, Mercedes Gini de Mills, Alicia Jurado, Norah Kildal Lange, Susana Lange, Jack Macrae, Lila Mora y Araujo, Olga Orozco, Fedra Petit de Murat de Suárez Boedo, Alastair Reid, Miguel de Torre, Donald and Joanne Yates, and Esther Zemborain de Torres Duggan.

I owe a particular debt of gratitude to María Kodama, Borges's widow, for her kindness and generosity toward me. I would like to thank her for granting permission to quote extensively from Borges's writings and for providing original material but, especially, for her willingness to share with me much new information about her relationship with Borges, which served to transform my understanding of his life and work.* I should point out, however, that this is

*All quotations from Borges's writings have been translated into English by the author, as well as quotations from foreign language sources, unless otherwise indicated.

not an authorized biography and the interpretations and judgments on which it is based are entirely my own.

I would like to thank my editors at Penguin for their patience and trust over so many years: Andrew Kidd in London, who worked with me until very near completion, and Michael Millman in New York; also, Kate Barker, who took over from Andrew. I remember with affection the late Giles Gordon, my agent, who believed in the project at the outset and offered me his advice and encouragement through to completion of the typescript, but who, alas, did not live to see the book published. My greatest personal debt is to my family: Louise was a young girl when I first talked to her about Borges, and she has been taken with the story ever since; Phoebe was too little at the time but her hand would seek mine whenever I came home from Buenos Aires; without my wife Susan's support and forbearance, I could not have seen the thing through to the end.

Contents

PART ONE

The Sword
and the Dagger
(1899–1921)

CHAPTER 1

Family and Nation

THE ANCESTORS of Jorge Luis Borges were among the first Europeans to arrive in America. Explorers, conquistadors, founders of cities, and rulers of provinces, they were builders of the vast empire that Spain was to establish in the New World. Gonzalo Martel de la Puente followed Pizarro in the conquest of Peru, Domingo Martínez de Irala won Paraguay for the Spanish Crown, Jerónimo de Cabrera founded the city of Córdoba in Tucumán, while Juan de Garay secured the settlement of the remote township of Buenos Aires. However, Borges himself was indifferent to these connections: "The Iralas, the Garays, the Cabreras and all those other Spanish conquistadors who founded cities and nations, I have never dreamed about them. . . . I am quite ignorant about their lives. They were people of very little intelligence—Spanish soldiers, and from the Spain of those times!"[1]

The ancestors Borges dreamed about were the men who had broken with Spain and had fought to create the Argentine nation. On his mother's side, Francisco de Laprida was president of the congress that declared the independence of the "United Provinces of South America." General Miguel Estanislao Soler commanded a division in the patriot army that the great Argentine liberator, San Martín, led across the Andes to free Chile and then Peru from the Spanish yoke. On his father's side, Juan Crisóstomo Lafinur was one of the first poets of Argentina and a friend of Manuel Belgrano, a founding father of the nation. Among Borges's papers there survives a postcard depicting Lafinur (proudly identified with a cross by the young Jorge Luis) standing in the foreground of the picture as General San Martín is being received by the National Assembly of the new republic.[2]

The most romantic of all Borges's ancestors was undoubtedly Isidoro Suárez, a great-grandfather on his mother's side. At the age of twenty-four, Suárez led the cavalry charge that turned the tide of battle at Junín, the second-last engagement in the liberation of South America. The battle took place on August 6, 1824, high up in the Andes of Peru, and the lofty silence of the snow-capped peaks was broken only by the clash of lance and sword, for no guns were used in combat by either army, and the patriots defeated the Spaniards in little under an hour. Suárez's heroism won the praise of Simón Bolívar himself, who declared that "when history describes the glorious Battle of Junín . . . it will be attributed to the bravery of this young officer."[3] And it was Bolívar who promoted Suárez to the rank of colonel after the young officer again distinguished himself at Ayacucho, the battle that finally put paid to the rule of Spain in America.

Borges conceived of the War of Independence as a "rupture in the continuity of the bloodline," a "rebellion of sons against their fathers."[4] His family, after all, took great pride in being criollos, people of pure Spanish descent born in America, but the meaning of independence, in Borges's view, lay in the fact that the criollos had "resolved to be Spaniards no longer:" they had made "an act of faith" in the possibility of creating a national identity distinct from that of Spain, and it followed that if the Argentines did not persevere in the struggle to forge this new identity, "a good many of us" would "run the risk of reverting to being Spanish, which would be a way of denying the whole of Argentine history."[5]

The movement toward independence in the area now comprising modern Argentina was spearheaded by Buenos Aires. An important reason for the city's historic role is to be found in the strategic position it occupies on the estuary of a mighty river system that reaches right up into the heart of South America. This huge estuary was first discovered by Spanish explorers searching for a westward passage to Japan. In 1536 the first settlement, called Santa María de los Buenos Aires, was established on its right bank, but it succumbed to Indian raids, and it was not until 1580 that the town was founded on a permanent basis by the conquistador Juan de Garay. By this time the estuary was known as the Río de la Plata, the "River of Silver" (distorted since in English to "River Plate"), thus called because the Spaniards believed that deposits of silver could be found on its shores. No silver was discovered, however, and for the next two hundred years, Buenos Aires was to languish as an outpost of empire in a forgotten corner of the Americas.

The tiny settlement was all but engulfed by vast plains, empty save for herds of wild cattle and horses that roamed the pampas, as these plains were called. These herds were hunted by tribes of nomadic Indians and plundered for their meat and hide by freewheeling horsemen of Spanish descent called gauchos. Otherwise the colony subsisted on the illegal exchange of silver from Peru for African slaves imported from Brazil. Only in the late eighteenth century, when advances in shipbuilding made it economical for Spain to communicate directly with the region, did it become possible to exploit the strategic position of Buenos Aires, and in 1776 the city was made the capital of the new viceroyalty of Río de la Plata. This relatively sudden promotion of Buenos Aires transformed the geopolitics of South America—all the Spanish territories (except Venezuela) that lay to the east of the Andes were obliged to sever a connection with Peru that went back 250 years and deal thenceforward with the upstart port city to the south. In this historic wrench lay the fundamental cause of the bloody conflicts that would bedevil the area for most of the nineteenth century.

After the first revolt against Spain in 1810, Buenos Aires would struggle to maintain its authority over the provinces comprising the former viceroyalty. It failed to prevent Bolivia, Paraguay, and Uruguay from going their separate ways, and even though the remaining provinces came together to declare independence from Spain at the Congress of Tucumán in 1816, there followed a long period of instability as the interior provinces continued to challenge the authority of Buenos Aires. The basic dispute was between the liberal *unitarios,* who sought to create a centralized state led by Buenos Aires, and the more conservative *federales,* who favored a confederation of provinces that would preserve as much local autonony as possible. The lack of effective nationwide institutions led to endless power struggles between caudillos, or provincial chieftains, of both conservative and liberal persuasion, who employed gaucho cavalry (*montoneros*) to further their own ends. Both sides of Borges's family were *unitarios,* and in his celebrated "Conjectural Poem," he recalled the murder of his ancestor Laprida, onetime president of the Congress of Tucumán, by the *montoneros* of Felix Aldao, a caudillo of the province of Mendoza.

Eventually there appeared a caudillo strong enough to impose some order on this chaos. In 1829 Juan Manuel de Rosas, a wealthy landowner and a strong advocate of *federalismo,* became governor of the huge province of Buenos Aires, and over the next six years he acquired enough power to become the effective leader of the "United Provinces." In the city of Buenos Aires, a bastion of liberalism, Rosas instituted a reign of terror designed to wipe out the *unitarios.* He created a secret organization known as La Mazorca that recruited servants to spy on their masters and formed death squads to root out opponents. Rosas also enlisted the support of the clergy, who preached blind loyalty to the caudillo and allowed his portrait to be displayed in the churches. He gained immense popularity with the lower classes, and a hysterical personality cult came into being—the color red, the color of the *federales,* was worn on sashes and banners, and slogans such as "Long live the Federation! Death to the filthy, savage *unitarios!*" became tokens of loyalty to the supreme leader. After Rosas achieved total power in 1835, those liberals he did not manage to eliminate he drove into exile abroad.

The privations endured by Borges's family under the dictatorship of Rosas were indeed horrible and outrageous. Colonel Suárez, the "Hero of

Junín," was forced into exile in Uruguay, where he died in 1846. One of the colonel's brothers was shot against the wall of the Recoleta Cemetery in Buenos Aires by agents of the Mazorca. The man's eleven-year-old son was forced to watch the execution, after which the boy had to find work in a tavern, since there was no one to look after him.[6] Thanks to Rosas, the family of Borges's grandfather, Isidoro Acevedo, lost their estates in the north of the province of Buenos Aires near the town of Pergamino. Isidoro's father joined a rebellion against Rosas but was taken prisoner and put to work in the tyrant's stables for nine years. One night the Mazorca raided the family home, horsewhipped Isidoro's mother and sacked the house. The two oldest daughters managed to escape but lost touch with their family for several years and ended up living in Brazil. Isidoro's mother took her three remaining children to Buenos Aires, where she was forced to earn a living as a seamstress mending trousers for Rosas's soldiers. Grandfather Isidoro used to tell a gruesome story about how, as a boy of ten, he came across a cart covered by a tarpaulin and, taking a peek inside, found the bloody heads of dozens of men killed by the Mazorca. He was so shocked that he was unable to speak for several hours after he got home.[7] When he grew up, Isidoro became an *unitario* like his father and joined the struggle to overthrow Rosas.

The tyrant was finally deposed in 1852, when his many enemies united to defeat him at the Battle of Caseros. But the victor of Caseros was yet another caudillo, General Urquiza, the boss of the rival province of Entre Ríos, who managed to topple Rosas with the support of Brazil, Uruguay, and the exiled *unitarios*. Being himself a *federal*, Urquiza passed a new constitution providing for a confederation of provinces, though under a strong presidentialist regime. The *unitarios* refused to accept this federal arrangement, but they were defeated by Urquiza at the Battle of Cepeda in 1859. Two years later the *unitarios* rebelled again, and this time their leader, Bartolomé Mitre, overthrew Urquiza at the Battle of Pavón, and Buenos Aires was at last accepted by the provincial caudillos as the de facto capital of the nation.

With Buenos Aires at its head, Argentina was set upon the road of stability and modernization. In the course of the 1860s and 1870s, successive liberal presidents, Mitre, Sarmiento and Avellaneda—all former *unitario* leaders—put in place the machinery of a modern nation-state: an integrated judicial system, a central bank, a professional army, a system of public schools and libraries, an academy of science and other technical institutions. The Argentine economy was geared toward the export of wool, meat, and wheat for the industrial centers of Europe, and this required the progressive privatization and enclosure of land in the pampas. Successive governments actively promoted European immigration with the aim of developing a rural middle class to replace the gauchos and the Indian hunters on the open range. Foreign capital was invested in the construction of a modern infrastructure of communications and transport. The British in particular would build new docks in Buenos Aires and a railway network across the pampas designed to consolidate the export economy by linking up the hitherto fractious provinces to Buenos Aires and, through the port city, to the world outside.

Domingo Sarmiento, who became president in 1868, was a prominent liberal intellectual and the author of one of the most influential books in Argentine history, *Facundo: or, Civilization and Barbarism,* a book in which the liberal vision of the nation's destiny was most fully expressed. Originally published in 1845, at the height of the struggle against Rosas, *Facundo* takes the form of a biography of Facundo Quiroga, a famous caudillo who pursued a violent career in the aftermath of independence until he was killed in 1835, almost certainly on Rosas's orders. Sarmiento argued that Argentina could be saved from this chaotic "barbarism" only by adopting the modern "civilization" of the European Enlightenment.

By "barbarism" Sarmiento meant the lack of stable government based on legitimate authority. He argued that barbarism was rooted in the pampas because the great plains were so underpopulated that the people who lived there lacked the habits of social coexistence that provide the basis for civilized values. In this sense the gaucho was a barbarian because he led a life of anarchic individualism in which he resorted to force in order to assert his will. This made him the ideal tool for the ambitions of regional caudillos, whose power struggles had led to the anarchy that had engulfed the entire viceroyalty of the Río de La Plata in the aftermath of independence.

How could this barbarism be tamed once more? There were two forms of civilization available to the rulers of Argentina: there was the clerical civilization of Catholic Spain, which had been successful in ensuring order during the colonial period, and the civilization of the Enlightenment. The former, in Sarmiento's view, was incapable of turning back the tide of barbarism. He portrayed the inland city of Córdoba, a bastion of Hispanic traditionalism, as a somnolent relic, its venerable buildings reflected on the stagnant waters of an ornamental lake. By way of contrast, he described the vitality of Buenos Aires, standing at the mouth of the river system of the Plata, a thriving port equipped to trade in goods and ideas with the world at large. Having initiated the wars of independence, Buenos Aires could claim a historic right to lead the nation toward modernity.

The plight of Argentina was encapsulated by Sarmiento in the vivid image of a gaucho's dagger stuck in the heart of liberal Buenos Aires. But even in *Facundo* one encounters an ambivalence toward the gaucho, for when Sarmiento wrote about the gaucho's skills as horseman, tracker, and wandering troubadour, he could not help but display a certain admiration for this authentic son of the native soil. The fact was that even though the gaucho might have been a "barbarian," he also represented whatever distinctive identity the young republic could claim to possess in relation to Spain. And yet, by the logic of his own argument in favor of progress and modern civilization, Sarmiento had to accept that the gaucho's traditional way of life was condemned eventually to disappear.

It was during Sarmiento's term of office as president that a book appeared which was to become the other great classic of Argentine literature. Published in 1872, *The Gaucho Martín Fierro* is a narrative poem by José Hernández written in a style based on the gaucho dialect. It tells the story of Martín Fierro, an innocent gaucho press-ganged into the army to serve in a frontier garrison against the Indians of the pampas. After being mercilessly exploited by the authorities, Fierro deserts and roams the pampas as an outlaw, killing a black gaucho in a senseless brawl and later claiming another victim. Pursued by the police, he is forced eventually to seek refuge with the Indians.

Hernández conceived the poem originally as a critique of Sarmiento's *Facundo* and as a protest against a modernizing government that had broken faith with the gauchos. However, by the time a sequel was published seven years later, Hernández himself had bowed to the inevitability of modernization. Accordingly, in Part II, Martín Fierro is repelled by the barbarism of the Indians and decides to return to Christian "civilization," but he finds that nothing has changed, and all that society can offer him is work as a hired hand on an *estancia*. Caught as he is between white "civilization" and Indian "barbarism," Fierro has nowhere to go, so the narrative draws to an inconclusive end with the protagonist riding off into the unknown, a rootless fugitive at the mercy of chance.

The two classic books of the nineteenth century, *Facundo* and *Martín Fierro*, represent a division that would become ingrained in the Argentine psyche. *Facundo* expressed the desire of the Argentines to build a modern liberal nation, while *Martín Fierro* crystallized an ambivalence about modernity, for even though the march of progress appeared to be unstoppable, there lingered a fear that the country might lose its soul to the devil of new ideas and foreign commerce. The figure of the gaucho thus came to embody the unresolved question of national identity, a question that would gnaw away at the Argentine conscience and would resurface periodically in a violent impulse to hold on to or to retrieve some vital essence that might be lost as Argentina acquired the trappings of a modern nation.

As a triumphant Buenos Aires monopolized the resources of the young republic, the interior provinces entered a long-term decline that has lasted to this day. Even so, there remained pockets of resistance to this rapid modernization. In the 1860s and 1870s, Indian raids on white ranches on the pampas became a menace that threatened further development, and there occurred also several rebellions of gauchos, particularly in the province of Entre Ríos after its caudillo Urquiza was defeated by Buenos Aires in 1861.

Borges's grandfather, Colonel Francisco Borges, played a leading role in the suppression of these vestiges of provincial "barbarism." In 1870 he commanded the troops sent by President Sarmiento to suppress the gaucho rebellion in Entre Ríos. After defeating the rebels, he was appointed commander of the garrison at Junín on the Indian frontier and in 1872 led his troops at the Battle of San Carlos, a major encounter that served to contain the Indian threat on the pampas. The following year he defeated a second rebellion in Entre Ríos. The colonel's brilliant career, however, was cut short in 1874, when he met his death on the field of battle. This untimely end was to rob his family of the fruits of his exploits, for the armed forces of Buenos Aires, under the command of General Julio Argentino Roca, would five years later embark on the "Conquest of the Desert," a full-scale campaign to expel the Indians from the pampas once and for all, and in a matter of months, the pampas of west-central and southern Argentina were cleared of Indian nomads.

The Conquest of the Desert was to be a decisive turning point in the history of Argentina. The defeat of the Indian tribes released vast tracts of land for conversion into *estancias,* massive ranches for the production of meat and wheat for export to Europe. A feverish boom ensued as established landowners, army officers, speculators, financiers, merchants, even some canny immigrants, acquired land and began to form a new oligarchy of *estancieros* that would rapidly overshadow the old patrician elite that had secured the independence of the republic. This land boom was shortly followed by a tremendous acceleration in the rate of immigration. Attracted by high wages, huge numbers of foreigners came to Argentina. In 1870 the population was less than 2 million, but over the following fifty years approximately 3.5 million immigrants would settle in the country.

The Conquest of the Desert made General Roca the strongman of Argentina. Anxious to avoid the instability that had plagued the country since independence, he created a political machine that secured power through systematic electoral fraud for the next thirty years. The criollo republic thus never evolved into a genuine democracy, passing instead into the hands of a ruling class of landowners, led by political caudillos, who controlled the burgeoning export economy in association with foreign business interests. Those criollos who had been excluded from the bonanza of progress denounced the materialism of the new elite. Former presidents like Mitre and Sarmiento lamented the corruption of the civic virtues of the early republic. The rule of

President Juárez Celman—a stooge of General Roca's—was especially resented, and when Baring Brothers, a British investment bank, crashed in 1890, Roca's opponents staged an armed uprising in Buenos Aires.

Although this "Revolution of 1890" was defeated, out of it grew the Radical Party, which would become the major party of opposition, largely representing the urban middle classes. Both the Acevedo and the Borges families would give their allegiance to the new party, not least because its founder, Leandro Alem, was a close friend of Isidoro Acevedo's. The watchword of the Radicals was "Intransigence," which meant that they rejected electoral deals as a means of gaining power, preferring instead to mount armed rebellions. The Radicals rose against the government in 1892 and again in 1893, but the political machine created by General Roca held fast, and there was no stopping the new money, the new men, even the new races, that came flooding into the country to change the face of the old criollo republic beyond recognition.

In the course of the 1880s and 1890s, the new plutocratic elite would transform Buenos Aires into one of the most modern cities in the world. Public services were revolutionized with the electrification of public lighting, the creation of modern water-supply and sewerage systems, the mechanization of horse-drawn tramways, the construction of an underground railway, as well as one of the largest suburban railway networks in the world. At the same time, the elite embarked on a hugely ambitious plan to redevelop the entire center of Buenos Aires. The pattern of the original Spanish settlement still determined the shape of the city, which amounted to little more than a tight grid of narrow streets extending from the central square of the conquistadors to form a warren of low houses and dim churches. But the modern aspirations of the elite could no longer be contained within this ancient layout; the new ruling class sought to burst out of the confines of its Spanish colonial heritage and remake Buenos Aires in the image of Paris.

A primary aim of the project was to arrange the great buildings of state so as to reflect the separation of powers that constitutes the ideal balance of liberal government—a new palace would be built for the president, and another great building would house the congress, and each would stand within sight of the other at either end of a grand avenue. The transformation began with the enlargement of the central square—now called the Plaza de Mayo—that had formed the heart of the city since its foundation. The old fortress, which had once housed the Spanish viceroys, had already been demolished in 1853, after the defeat of Rosas, but this further enlargement would involve the demolition of La Recova, the old arcaded market. The new presidential palace, known as the Casa Rosada, was situated at the far end of the enlarged square. Another huge square was created to the west and a vast neoclassical edifice built there to house the National Congress. The two squares, designated respectively for the executive and legislative branches of government, were joined up by a splendid thoroughfare known as the avenida de Mayo, which required the demolition of several streets and the controversial mutilation of the Cabildo, one of the oldest colonial buildings in the city. When the avenida de Mayo was inaugurated in 1894, it was something of an architectural wonderland, its lofty buildings topped with extraordinary confections in concrete—a proliferation of whorls, pinnacles, turrets, and spires, set among dozens of little cupcake domes.

The avenida de Mayo represented a new line of demarcation between the old Buenos Aires and the new. Since the epidemic of yellow fever in 1871, there had been a drift of better-off families from the center to more salubrious higher ground toward the north. In the 1880s this area was refashioned as the Barrio Norte, and it remains the favored area of the middle classes to this day. Once more it was Paris that provided the inspiration. The innovations undertaken in the French capital by Baron Haussmann were much admired, and his ideas were adopted in the planning of the new district. Entire streets were sacrificed to spacious boulevards. The Frenchman Charles Thays designed several Gallic-style squares and parks, including the imposing Plaza San Martín. The boulevards were graced with trees native to the River Plate—notably the jacarandas that blossom in November, brightening the Barrio Norte with splashes of blue, and *palos borrachos,* whose large pods put out creamy yellow flowers in February. The grandest families built mansions in the style of Parisian *hôtels,* complete with domes, mansard roofs, and heavy wrought-iron gates. The giant pile that now accommmodates the Círculo Militar on the southwest corner of the Plaza San Martín is one of the largest and most impressive of the mansions of the Argentine belle époque; it was designed by a Parisian architect as a town house for José C. Paz, founder of the great newspaper *La Prensa.*

Still, it was not just the wealthy classes who were to change the face of Buenos Aires toward the end of the nineteenth century. The huge numbers of foreigners who came to work in Argentina also contributed to the reorganization of the city. They settled around their places of work—the stockyards, tanneries, and meatpacking plants that serviced the booming export economy. These new immigrant settlements were very modest indeed, not much better than strips of one-story houses grouped into geometrically exact blocks and fanning out into the countryside along the routes of the tram lines or the suburban railway. The historic limits of the city were breached by the growth of new districts like Almagro, San Juan, and Boedo. The new suburbs pushed westward, too: immigrant communities like La Paternal, Villa Ortúzar, Villa Urquiza sprang up beyond the railway line that served the cemetery of La

Chacarita in the northwest. In a matter of a decade or two, pleasant little towns like Flores and Belgrano would be threatened with absorption by the relentless expansion of the capital.

As different ethnic groups gravitated toward particular areas, these raw proletarian barrios soon became the focus of communal loyalties. The largest group by far were the Italians, known derisively as "gringos" by the criollos. But they, too, tended to congregate according to their region of origin. The Genoese settled in La Boca, at the mouth of the Riachuelo, a river that debouches onto the estuary of the River Plate. A Neapolitan barrio, suitably called Nueva Pompeya, grew around the Corrales, the great stockyards on the south side of the city. The barrio of Palermo in the northwest attracted immigrants from Calabria and Sicily. Jews from Eastern Europe gathered around the Plaza del Once to the west, where a garment industry began to thrive. To a lesser extent, Armenians, Turks, Arabs, and many others who flooded in from the Old World formed their own communities in different areas of the city and its environs.

The historic center of Buenos Aires, where the old criollo families had lived for centuries, was increasingly left in a social limbo, suspended between the elegant Barrio Norte and the new immigrant barrios. Once-respectable districts in the city center, especially those to the south of the avenida de Mayo, like San Telmo or Barracas, degenerated into decrepit slums. There were many large, historic mansions that turned into overcrowded warrens known as *conventillos,* as the rich abandoned their houses and subdivided them into tiny apartments for rental to poor immigrant families.

On the other hand, those patrician families who had failed to profit from the land boom of the 1880s were effectively demoted in the new pecking order that was emerging in Argentina. Borges's mother cited in her memoir the case of Micaela Soler, a kinswoman of hers on the Suárez side, who lived on the income from the pensions that her father, the illustrious General Miguel Estanislao Soler, had been awarded by no fewer than three South American countries for his services in the wars of independence. Doña Micaela was just about able to keep up the grand style in which she had been raised—there was nothing she loved better than to have a coach with a liveried driver draw up outside her house—but even so she had been obliged to move to rented accommodation, and this was a circumstance with which she could not fully come to terms: whenever her Italian landlord had the effrontery to ask for rent on the first day of the month, she would reach into her wardrobe for her papa's sword and brandish it in the face of the startled man until the wretched gringo finally learned that he must wait for his rent until somewhat later in the month.[8]

There was, of course, no hope of turning back the tide of change. The new leaders of society—the great *estancieros*—rapidly developed a cosmopolitan outlook. Even though the Argentine economy depended overwhelmingly on British capital, it was France that set the style and tone for the beau monde that came into being in the course of the 1880s and 1890s. Men with pretensions to culture subscribed to the *Revue des Deux Mondes* to keep abreast of developments in Paris. At the Club del Progreso, which occupied the marbled halls of the Palacio Muñoa, champagne flowed liberally at sumptuous receptions, and its dining room served haute cuisine prepared by chefs brought over from France. The best families engaged French governesses so that their children might learn to speak French fluently. The ultimate cachet was reserved for those magnates who could afford to take their families, with maids, chauffeurs, and all, for a sojourn of several months in Paris, the Ville Lumière, the "City of Light."

By the end of the nineteenth century, Argentina was one of the richest countries in the world, almost as rich as the United States and incomparably richer than Spain, the old mother country. The criollos of the River Plate had good reason to be proud of their achievements, for theirs was one of the great postcolonial success stories. In 1910, the centenary year of the first revolt against Spain, the government chose to commemorate the birth of the nation with a series of extravagant celebrations to which distinguished foreign statesmen, scientists, writers, and artists were invited. But despite the official triumphalism, there remained unruly elements that threatened to disrupt the smooth progress to modernity envisaged by the elite. The Radical Party, for one, resented its exclusion from the fruits of office. In 1905 it had organized yet another uprising under its new leader Hipólito Irigoyen, the nephew of the founder Leandro Alem. A more dangerous threat to the status quo came from an emerging sector of society, the industrial workers, most of whom were immigrants who had brought with them political ideologies such as anarchism and socialism that had never been heard of before by the criollos. The first decade of the century saw an explosion of industrial action organized by the anarchist-controlled labor unions—in 1896 there had been 26 strikes in Buenos Aires, but by 1910 the number had shot up to 238. Strikes were a relatively new phenomenon in Argentina, and the ruling class became alarmed by the violence of these disputes. In 1909, just a year before the centenary celebrations, the chief of police of Buenos Aires was assassinated by a Russian-Jewish anarchist, an outrage that provoked a furious backlash from upper-class criollo youths of the newly formed Patriotic League, who unleashed the first pogrom in Argentina against the *rusos,* as East European Jews were called.

Argentina's tremendous economic advance stirred up anxieties once more about its national identity. By the early twentieth century, Buenos Aires was teeming with people of a bewildering variety of nationalities. Many of these foreigners would settle in Argentina, but others continued to migrate seasonally from Europe. Fears grew that such high levels of immigration would destabilize the country and might even swamp the culture and identity of the criollos. Had the nation lost its soul to foreign commerce? Were the Argentines in danger of becoming pseudo-Europeans or, worse still, some mongrel race with no inherent qualities of its own? What, indeed, did it mean to be an Argentine? The political establishment turned for an answer to its most famous poet, Leopoldo Lugones, who in 1913 delivered a series of lectures at the Teatro Odeón in Buenos Aires, which was attended by the president of the republic and several cabinet ministers. His subject was the significance of the gaucho in Argentine history. He argued that the political liberty of the River Plate had been won by the gauchos, who had formed the backbone of the patriot armies in the wars of independence. The gauchos had thus provided the foundation of the national identity, and José Hernández's *Martín Fierro* should be regarded as the national epic of Argentina because it expressed the essential spirit and character of the people of the River Plate as embodied in the gaucho. Lugones's argument contradicted Sarmiento's classic liberal thesis that the gaucho represented the barbarism of the pampas and must therefore be made to submit to civilization. But Lugones was involved in a new ideological operation—he was trying to offer the criollos a distinctive identity that would act as a bulwark against the waves of immigrants who were flooding the country. To this end he wanted to create a spurious continuity between the past and the present by rehabilitating the gaucho in the eyes of the millionaire ranchers who had actually thrown him off the land.

Lugones's insistence on the cultural supremacy of the criollos within Argentina was inherently reactionary and would shortly take him in the direction of fascism, for the social and political realities on the ground did not permit such an elitist vision of the nation; there were millions of people in the country other than the criollos, and they, too, would have to be accommodated in the Argentine self-image. Indeed, a few years after Lugones gave his famous lectures on the gaucho, the political voice of the masses who had been ruled out of account by Lugones made itself heard when the leader of the Radical Party, Hipólito Irigoyen, was elected president in 1916. There followed an upsurge of popular demands for reform, which the new president tried to satisfy by creating jobs and increasing public spending. His term of office, however, was plagued by high inflation and mounting industrial unrest, raising fears in the political establishment of a return to chronic instability. Irigoyen's successor in 1922 was a patrician landowner who attempted to steer the country back on its usual course of export-led growth under the control of the *es-*

tancieros and foreign investors but a revolution of expectations had been unleashed among the urban classes and demands for political reform and a better distribution of wealth could no longer be ignored. When Irigoyen stood for the presidency again in 1928, there was another great upsurge of popular enthusiasm at the prospect of dismantling the conservative political machine once and for all. And one of Irigoyen's keenest supporters was none other than the twenty-eight-year-old Jorge Luis Borges, who formed a group of young intellectuals within the Radical Party in order to campaign for the reelection of the great Radical champion of the people.

Borges's vision of the nation was directly opposed to that of Leopoldo Lugones. By this time Lugones was peddling a theory of Argentina as a social hierarchy in which the criollos must be accorded a preeminent position, guaranteed, if necessary, by military force. But Borges rejected this elitist nationalism and contested Lugones's interpretation of *Martín Fierro* as the epic of the criollos. In fact, in everything Borges would write about *The Gaucho Martín Fierro,* there would run an implicit argument against Lugones's mystification of the poem. It was not an epic, he would contend, not least because Fierro was hardly exemplary; he was a murderer and a deserter, and as such he had more of the contradictory qualities of a character in a novel than of an epic hero.

In 1928 Borges delivered an address to a group of young nationalists in which he argued that the criollos must "sacrifice" their pride in their ancestry for the sake of the greater honor of the nation:

> In this house which is America, my friends, men from various nations of the world have conspired together in order to disappear in a new man, who is not yet embodied in any one of us and whom we shall already call an "Argentine" so as to begin to raise our hopes. This is a confederacy without precedent: a generous adventure by men of different bloodlines whose aim is not to persevere in their lineages but to forget those lineages in the end; these are bloodlines that seek the night. The criollo is one of the confederates. The criollo, who was responsible for creating the nation as such, has now chosen to be one among many.[9]

Whereas Lugones wanted to fix the Argentine identity in the past, Borges had a dynamic vision of nationhood and urged his fellow criollos to look to the future. Independence, as he saw it, had been a revolt of sons against their fathers, an "act of faith" by the criollos in the possibility of being different from the Spanish. However, at the turn of the century, the realities of immigration had ruptured the criollo bloodline once again, and in order to persevere in the venture of building the nation, it was necessary to extend and renew the original act of faith so as to include all the people who had settled in Argentina since independence.

Borges held to this vision with extraordinary conviction, and it shows in the tropes he used—"bloodlines that seek the night," the "confederates" (or "conspirators," since the word *conjurados* admits either meaning in Spanish) aiming to create a "new man" in Argentina. The fact was that he had a personal stake in the question of national identity. His own ancestry was mixed—his mother was a pure criolla, while his father was half English—but the story of Argentina had so thoroughly permeated the consciousness of his family that he had come to regard the destiny of the nation as a wider mirror of his own.

CHAPTER 2

Mother and Father

Leonor Acevedo

BORGES'S MOTHER, Leonor Acevedo, was the granddaughter of Colonel Isidoro Suárez, the young officer who led the Peruvian Hussars to victory at the Battle of Junín. Although Suárez saw action in many of the major battles of the war of independence and the later war against Brazil, he would always be remembered in his native land as the "Hero of Junín." In the latter years of his life, however, he was forced into exile in Uruguay on account of his *unitario* sympathies. It was there he married Jacinta Haedo, who came from an old Uruguayan landowning family, and settled in the town of Mercedes. But these were turbulent times in the whole area of the River Plate, and during a routine visit to Montevideo, Suárez found himself suddenly trapped in the city when it was besieged by forces allied to the Argentine dictator Rosas. His wife made several desperate efforts to free him, but he fell ill and died in Montevideo in 1846 at the age of forty-seven, leaving five children, the eldest of whom was only nine. His family suffered considerable hardship after his death—their estates and most of their property were impounded to pay off their debts. Eventually Suárez's widow moved to Buenos Aires with her children and a few of the family's black slaves and bought the house at calle Tucumán in which Jorge Luis Borges was born.

In 1861 one of Colonel Suárez's daughters, Leonor, married Isidoro Acevedo, a young man from another criollo family. The Acevedos had owned *estancias* at San Nicolás in the northwest of the province of Buenos Aires. Isidoro's mother was a Laprida, and the niece of Francisco Narciso de Laprida, the man who had signed the declaration of Argentine independence in 1816. But like the Suárezes, the Acevedos, being *unitarios,* had suffered badly under Rosas. They forfeited their estates after Isidoro's father, Judas Tadeo Acevedo, joined a revolt against Rosas and was taken prisoner. His wife was forced to abandon the family home by Rosas's Mazorca and moved with some of her seven children to Buenos Aires, where the family lived in much-reduced circumstances. As a youth Isidoro Acevedo became a supporter of the *unitario* cause, saw action against Rosas in Caseros, and subsequently fought in the battles of Cepeda and Pavón against Urquiza.

Although their respective families had come down in the world, Isidoro and Leonor were comfortably off after their marriage. Isidoro found employment in the police department, and when Leonor Suárez's mother died in 1869, the couple moved to the house on calle Tucumán and rented out another property they owned at calle Azcuénaga. The genial Isidoro knew everyone in Buenos Aires, or so his daughter claimed in her memoirs.[1] However, when Isidoro Acevedo married Leonor Suárez in 1861, this self-contained little world of the old criollo families stood on the threshold of a drastic process of change, for in the same year as their wedding took place, Buenos Aires finally emerged as the leading city of Argentina, and the country was to enter a long period of relative stability and rapid economic growth.

Isidoro and Leonor threw themselves into the social whirl of the burgeoning metropolis. A handsome woman, Leonor Suárez had a passion for dressing well: she loved going to the opera, the theater, and the music hall, and since the couple had no children, she could afford to indulge her expensive tastes. Isidoro did well for himself in the police department, rising to become the commissioner responsible for the markets in the Plaza del Once, where all the produce that supplied the city was brought by cart from the country to be sold wholesale. He was to garner considerable influence through his post at the markets and through the contacts he had made as an activist in the *unitario* cause. When one of his sisters-in-law lost her husband, Isidoro petitioned Congress for a pension to be granted to one of the daughters of Colonel Isidoro Suárez, the Hero of Junín. He received a magnificent response from deputies and senators, and even his old friend Nicolás Avellaneda, a former president of the republic, turned up to vote.

The couple had been married for fifteen years when Leonor Suárez was surprised to find herself expecting a baby at the age of forty. Born in 1876, the baby girl, Leonor Rita Acevedo, was doted on by her parents. She was installed in a four-poster brass bed with a statue of a guardian angel over the headboard, and when they took her out, she would be dressed in long, lacy robes and covered in a gauze veil to protect her against the flies and mosquitoes of the city streets. As an only child, Leonorcita had few friends, so her mother found her a little Indian girl called Dominga as a playmate. One fine day, however, Dominga was wrapped up in a cloak and taken away in a coach never to be seen again. Several years passed before Leonorcita was told that little Dominga had in fact died of pneumonia.

It was her mother who became her closest companion in childhood. When she was tucked in at night, there was nothing she liked better than for Mama to climb into the bed with her and talk about the family's golden age,

when they owned *estancias* and black slaves. Leonorcita learned about the illustrious career of her grandfather, the Hero of Junín, whom her mother pas-
sionately adored and whose picture she kept in a gold locket. But it caused her
mama exquisite anguish to recall the time when the family had suffered its
most cruel privations at the hands of Rosas. The tyrant was a class traitor,
Leonorcita was informed by her mother—he hated the *gente bien,* people of
good family like themselves, even though he belonged to one himself. In fact,
Rosas and Colonel Suárez were distantly related to each other, but Mama's
dear father became a bitter enemy of the tyrant and was therefore publicly denounced as "a disgusting, filthy, savage *unitario.*"

All of this Leonorcita took in—all these distressing yet romantic stories of
battles won and lost, of confiscated lands, of exile and murder. So strongly did
she identify with the dispossessed heroes of the family that even as an old lady
she would proudly describe herself as a "savage *unitaria,*" dismissing anything
that reminded her of the tyrant Rosas—gauchos, caudillos, the provinces, or
the ways and habits of the lower orders—as *guarango,* or "common," the most
damning term in her vocabulary.

There survived customs in the family that reinforced Leonorcita's impression of being special. The water from the tank in their patio, for instance, was
so greatly appreciated in the neighborhood for its sparkling freshness that
friends would send their maids around to draw some before lunch and dinner.
She grew accustomed to the attentions of servants: her mother had the habit of
picking flowers from their patio and placing them on a silver tray to send
around as gifts for the neighbors. When she was a little older, she was often
taken by Mama to see the animals at the zoo in Palermo Park in a hired coach
driven by a black man in livery, called Epifanio. (That family memory of the
black coach driver was potent enough to appear in Borges's novella *The Congress.*) And yet, even when she was still quite little, she had some measure of her
family's fall from grace, for only a couple of blocks from the Acevedos' house
on calle Tucumán there were a number of streets where, Leonorcita noticed,
the shutters were always closed, and when she asked an older girl why this was
so, she was told that those were houses of ill repute. Nevertheless, in her bed at
night, Leonorcita would lie back and gaze at the little brass crown that clasped
the white muslin on the canopy above her four-poster bed, and which, as she
recalled, inspired in her countless dreams of grandeur.

Leonorcita was fourteen when the Revolution of July 26, 1890, took place,
after the collapse of the Baring Brothers bank. Her mother, who was always
greatly enthused by politics, followed with enormous excitement the events
leading up to the outbreak of hostilities. The insurgents set up their barricades
in the Plaza del Parque (now called Libertad) just three blocks away from
where the Acevedos lived, so her father Isidoro, ever keen to do his bit, had

only to get out of bed in the morning and walk up the road to join the revolution. Leonorcita, however, was confined indoors and spent four anxious days hearing bullets whistling past the house. Suddenly it was all over—the revolutionaries had forced the resignation of the president, and the government had collapsed. There was general rejoicing—Leonorcita could remember the opera singer Tamagno leading the crowds in a rendition of the national anthem from a balcony on calle Florida. But this famous victory soon proved to be a false dawn, since the ruling oligarchy lost no time in rigging elections once again through its network of local bosses.

After the Revolution of 1890, families like the Acevedos had no option but to accept the fact of their decline. Not that the genial Isidoro seemed to mind much—he would wrap himself every night in his dramatic Spanish cape and go off to play cards or billiards at the Club Católico or the Cercolo Italiano, both entirely respectable institutions, of course, but hardly in the same league as the Club del Progreso, not to speak of the Jockey Club, the exclusive preserve of the new *estanciero* elite. And one could still rely on Isidoro to pull a few strings, if necessary. Even after his retirement, the house at calle Tucumán attracted a stream of visitors seeking favors—a job, a permit—in return for a chicken or a clutch of eggs.

It was Isidoro's wife and daughter who did their best to uphold the values of the past. Trips were organized to visit the Acevedos' former estates at San Nicolás, and they much appreciated it whenever they were paid a visit by the descendants of the black slaves the family had once owned. And as for Buenos Aires itself, well, they really could not get along with all those newfangled street names, much preferring the old appellations—"La calle del Temple," "Las Cinco Esquinas," "La Plaza del Parque." They reserved a special place in their hearts for Uruguay, which they still called "La Banda Oriental" (the "Left Bank" of the River Plate) and never "Uruguay" as such, a name Leonor Suárez regarded as unpleasant and offensive, and one used only by *guarangos*. Their attachment to this anachronism may be explained perhaps by the fact that the Uruguayan branch of the family, the Haedos, had done rather better in holding on to their wealth than had the Acevedos or the Suárezes. Every summer Leonorcita would be taken to spend three months with the Haedos in their large villa at Paso del Molino on the outskirts of Montevideo or at their estates near Fray Bentos, a practice she would continue with her own children. These summer holidays at Paso del Molino and the *estancias* of her cousins on the Uruguay River and the Río Negro were among Leonorcita's most treasured memories.

Leonor Acevedo grew up in a period of great ferment and change in Buenos Aires, and she prided herself on the fact that her father knew deputies, senators, and government ministers. She had vivid memories of being taken for Sunday lunch at the Café de Paris or the Restaurant Charpentier, the smartest French establishments in Buenos Aires. She recalled the men wearing stiff collars and gold cuff links, their top hats hanging on hooks around the marble pillars, as she and her father entered the room to be greeted from all sides by Isidoro's many friends, his former comrades calling him "Captain," the younger men (including Carlos Pellegrini, a future president of the republic) addressing him as "Uncle." Men would come up to their table and kiss her on the cheek, though she much preferred it when they just shook her by the hand because it made her feel important.

Leonorcita, however, was not allowed to encroach upon the male sphere of politics and free thought. She was confined instead to pursuits that were deemed suitable for young ladies—singing, piano playing, and the reciting of verse. The Acevedos and Suárezes, in any case, were not much taken with the life of the mind. The girl was brought up in the narrow Catholicism reserved for the womenfolk of the old criollo families, and she would remain a strictly observant Catholic all her life. Catholic piety, too, served as a shibboleth of social distinction. During Holy Week, for instance, she and her mother would dutifully observe the Stations of the Cross, putting on their best dresses for this purpose, but on Good Friday, Mama, following the convention of the time, wore no jewelry and dressed entirely in black.

Leonorcita was an exceptionally pretty girl, and her pale complexion was enviably set off by dark, lustrous hair. Her best asset, she thought, was her eyes—bright, dancing buttons of light, of an emerald green that drew from male admirers a stream of compliments, which she lapped up with undisguised relish. She also inherited her mother's taste for elegant clothes, and together they used to patronize a dress shop run by a French lady where all the outfits and hats came from Paris. One of her dresses caused a sensation among the girls at school—the fact that it had been tailor-made certainly set them talking, she recalled. Among her most treasured possessions was a beautiful doll with long blond hair, which had been brought over specially from Paris; she also loved a mechanical peacock given her by a wealthy relative: it was almost life size and, when wound up, would walk about majestically, opening and closing its tail like a fan.

One senses a deep frustration in Leonor Acevedo. She clearly realized early on that she was talented and clever, but her head had been stuffed full since infancy with dreams of her family's former grandeur, and the ruling passion in her life, as a result, became the desire to restore the family to what she felt was its rightful place in the world. She was trapped, however, by the expectations of the age in the submissive role of the middle-class lady, and so this spirited, highly intelligent woman with a will of iron was forced to look to the men in her family—to her husband and later her son—to realize that overwhelming social ambition on her behalf.

Even so, she remained obscurely aware of the restrictions to which her family had subjected her. There was a cousin of her mother's whom the rest of the family thought of as crazy (*loco*), but this was, she suspected, because the little money he had was spent on books and works of art. She used to enjoy listening to him, because he used to talk to her about things that were different from the usual topics of conversation. He called her "Nena" and brought her sweets and books, including an illustrated book of Greek mythology that entertained her for a long time. This *"loco"* was called Hamilton Otálora, and, curiously, this was the surname that Leonor's son, Jorge Luis Borges, would give to the protagonists of two of his most important stories, both clearly alter egos of the author himself—Benjamín Otálora in "The Dead Man" and Javier Otárola [*sic*], the old Colombian professor in "Ulrica." Perhaps Borges may have wished to recall those qualities of his mother's that had been repressed by her upbringing and which, had they been allowed to flourish, might have altered the destiny of the family as a whole.

Still, Leonor Acevedo did once break through the restrictions in which her spirit had been immured by her social conditioning. At the age of twenty-two years, she met a handsome youth of great charm who had just graduated in law from the University of Buenos Aires. His name was Jorge Guillermo Borges, and he was the younger son of a fallen hero, Colonel Francisco Borges, who had been a friend of her father's before his tragic death on the field of battle. The Acevedos and the Borgeses had not seen each other since that unhappy episode, but they met again in 1898 when the elder son, Frank Borges, returned from exile in Montevideo after having taken part in the unsuccessful Radical revolution of 1893. Colonel Borges's English widow, Fanny Haslam, invited the Acevedos to tea at her house, and from the renewed friendship between the two families, Leonor would observe in her memoir, was born the love at first sight that would bind her to Jorge forever.

Jorge Guillermo Borges

THE BORGES FAMILY was of more recent vintage in Argentina than were the Acevedos or the Suárezes. They derived their surname from Francisco de Borges, a lieutenant in the Portuguese navy, about whom very little is known, though he may have come to the region of the River Plate while serving the Portuguese crown in Brazil. In 1829, Borges married María del Carmen Lafinur, a member of an illustrious criollo family from the city of Córdoba. They had a son, Francisco, and the fact that he was born in Montevideo in 1833 suggests that the family had *unitario* sympathies that may have forced them to leave Córdoba and go into exile in Uruguay. At the age of nineteen, young Francisco served with an Uruguayan division at the Battle of Caseros against Rosas, and three years later he offered "his arm and his sword to the government of the state of Buenos Aires."[2]

As a professional soldier, he fought for Buenos Aires in several battles against the *federales,* including Cepeda and Pavón against Urquiza, as well as in the Paraguayan War (1864–1870). By 1868 he had been promoted to the rank of colonel, and two years later he was sent to relieve Paraná, the capital of the province of Entre Ríos, which was under siege by the gaucho troops of the federalist caudillo Ricardo López Jordán. It was here that he met an Englishwoman, Frances Haslam. His grandson gave a romantic account of that first encounter: "Borges, riding at the head of his regiment, commanded the troops defending the city. Fanny saw him from the flat roof of her house; that very night a ball was given to celebrate the arrival of the government relief forces. Fanny and the Colonel met, danced, fell in love, and eventually married."[3]

Colonel Borges's English bride, Frances (Fanny) Haslam, was born in Hanley, Staffordshire, though the family had originated in Northumberland. Her father, Edward Young Haslam, was a schoolmaster. Family legend had it that he could not afford Oxford or Cambridge, so he went to Germany and eventually obtained a doctorate from the University of Heidelberg, "going through the whole course in Latin."[4] His marriage to Jane Arnett produced four children, three of them girls. The family was Methodist, and deeply religious— Haslam's father, William, having been a Methodist minister of some repute in the Midlands. When Jane Arnett died in 1853, Edward was left to bring up the children, the eldest girl, Caroline, being fourteen and the youngest, Agnes, only four.

The Haslam family's initial connection with Argentina came through Caroline's marriage to an Italian-Jewish engineer called Jorge Suárez, a naturalized British subject. Sometime in the 1860s, Caroline and her husband emigrated to Paraná, the capital of the province of Entre Ríos, which was then ruled by the caudillo Urquiza, the man who had defeated Rosas some ten years earlier. There Suárez embarked on a number of business ventures—he was an agent for the Siemens company and also invested in the construction of bridges, viaducts, and new docks on the river Paraná. In 1869 he obtained a licence from Urquiza to set up a horse-drawn tramway, the first in Argentina, which was to run from the city center to the port. Toward the end of the 1860s, Fanny Haslam, accompanied by her father, came to live with her sister Caroline and her husband in Paraná. It is not known what prompted this move to Argentina, and nothing is known either of the whereabouts of the other two younger siblings, Edward and Agnes, who would have been in their early twenties. During his time in Argentina, Edward Haslam taught English in various schools in Buenos Aires and Paraná and wrote for English-language newspapers like The *Southern Cross,* the *Buenos Aires Herald,* and the *River Plate Times.*

The wedding of Fanny Haslam and Colonel Borges took place in the cathedral at Paraná on August 14, 1871. Later that same year, Borges was posted to Junín, a garrison town in the pampas, as commander-in-chief of the three frontiers—the northern and western frontiers of the province of Buenos Aires and the southern frontier of the province of Santa Fe. His mission was to contain Indian incursions into territories incorporated in the Argentine republic. At Junín his English wife, Fanny, would live on the very edge of the South American wilderness, or the "Desert," as it was called by the Argentines. On June 3, 1872, Fanny gave birth to a son, Francisco, but by the time the second son, Jorge Guillermo, was born on February 24, 1874, the family had returned to Paraná, where the colonel had been sent to deal with another uprising by the gauchos of López Jordán.

Despite the hardships of life on the Indian frontier, there can be little doubt that a lower-middle-class English girl like Fanny Haslam had made an excellent marriage to a young officer like Colonel Borges, whose prospects were exceptionally good, for in a few years' time, the army would embark on the Conquest of the Desert with the aim of driving the Indians off the pampas altogether and claiming massive new territories for Argentina. After the Conquest of the Desert, a commander of a frontier garrison would have been eligible for a land grant of eight thousand hectares, and Colonel Borges, as commander in chief of three frontiers, would have stood to receive a grant of that size at the very least.[5] However, in October 1874, Borges became involved in a political dispute over the succession to the presidency at the end of Sarmiento's term of office. Sarmiento had done a deal to ensure that he would be succeeded by Nicolás Avellaneda, but a rival candidate, Bartolomé Mitre, raised a revolt in the army, which Colonel Borges decided to join. Sarmiento wrote to Colonel Borges exhorting him to remain loyal to the government. Borges responded by pledging his loyalty until October 12, the precise date on which Sarmiento's term was due to expire. Unfortunately, Mitre brought forward the date of his uprising, and Borges was put in a quandary, which he resolved by surrendering to President Sarmiento, as the official head of state, the troops under his command—one infantry and three cavalry regiments—and then resigning his post to join the rebellion. This pleased no one, for Sarmiento saw Borges's defection as treachery, while Mitre resented the handing over of valuable troops to his enemy. Mitre's attempted coup d'état was put down at the Battle of La Verde on November 26. Colonel Borges died two days later as a result of being struck by two bullets as he was giving orders to a subordinate officer during the fighting.[6]

After only three years of marriage, Fanny Haslam found herself a widow with two infant sons and very limited means, not much more than her war widow's pension and a sum of money raised in her benefit by her husband's comrades. She returned to her family in Paraná, but only four years later misfortune struck again when her father, who must have provided her with some financial assistance through his teaching, died unexpectedly in 1878 from a severe attack of bronchitis. Dr. Haslam had become a respected member of the British community in Argentina: an obituary in the *Southern Cross* described him as "the best English writer in the Plate," "upright and honourable in all his dealings," "a thorough gentleman," and "a man of deep religious feelings."[7]

A few years later, the family was to suffer yet another misfortune when Fanny's brother-in-law, Jorge Suárez, went bankrupt. He had tried to assist General Urquiza in the modernization of Entre Ríos by developing the port of Paraná, but the rise of Buenos Aires downriver became irresistible after Urquiza's death, and the rebellions raised by López Jordán inflicted further damage on the economy of the province. By the mid-1880s, Fanny and her two boys were living in Buenos Aires in a house at calle Libertad 1346, where she supplemented her meager income by taking in English-speaking young ladies as lodgers. Her sister and her husband also moved to the capital, and there Caroline Haslam made a career for herself as a teacher, becoming in due course the head of the English department at the School of Modern Languages, a prestigious teacher-training institution.

Fanny brought up her two sons in what was to all intents and purposes an English household, especially while her father was still living. They all spoke English at home, and as a great reader herself, Fanny encouraged the boys to read English books. A patriotic Englishwoman, living far from her homeland, she must have told the boys nostalgic stories about her childhood in Staffordshire and the family's roots in Northumberland. Certainly the younger son, Jorge Guillermo, grew up with a strong awareness of his Englishness and would, in consequence, always feel something of a misfit in Buenos Aires and unsure of his relation to Argentina.

This uncertainty was compounded by the emotional impact on the family of Colonel Borges's tragic death. Jorge Guillermo was only nine months old when his father was killed in battle, and as he grew up, a sensitive and dreamy boy, the figure of the father whom he had never known would loom large in his imagination. Everything the boy learned about his father was inevitably filtered through his widowed mother, and Fanny had good reason to lament the death of her husband—if he had lived, she could have become the mistress of a great *estancia*—but what must have been particularly galling was the fact that he had not even been killed in a glorious cause; he had died in a failed power struggle between rival caudillos. Perhaps to mitigate her grief, she embroidered the facts of Colonel Borges's death into a romantic account that has come down to us in the version given by her grandson, Jorge Luis, who heard it directly from her, and which must therefore have been the account she gave her two sons.

In this version General Mitre had ordered his troops to retreat from the battlefield even though Colonel Borges informed him that the enemy was running out of ammunition. When Mitre insisted on retreating, Borges, who was wearing a white poncho, mounted his white charger and rode out toward enemy lines, his arms folded across his chest. He fell under a hail of bullets and was carried by his men in a cowhide to a neighboring *estancia*, where he died from his wounds. His last words were said to have been, "I have fallen in the belief of having fulfilled my duty and my convictions, and for the same principles that I have fought all my life."[8] Even though the historical record shows that Colonel Borges died from wounds sustained during the battle and not as a deliberate act of suicide,[9] it is understandable that his widow should have preferred to find some meaning in his otherwise quite senseless death and grasped for this by elaborating a myth of her husband's choosing death rather than submit to an unnecessary defeat.

There is little doubt that the bereft Fanny passed on to her sons an exaggerated image of her late husband's heroism. The effect upon Jorge Guillermo of this glorification of Colonel Borges was to make him doubt his own worth. The boy grew up under the oppressive image of a father he had never known and whom he could never know other than indirectly, through his mother. It must have been impossible for him, therefore, to question, let alone rebel against, that mythical father without experiencing a strong sense of guilt. All the subsequent evidence points to Jorge Guillermo's having developed an indecisive and self-critical personality, forever vacillating between his wish to respect his mother and an urge to assert his own independence.

Jorge was enrolled at the Colegio Nacional in Buenos Aires when he was thirteen, but he hated school, and his academic performance was mediocre. In a novel whose protagonist is a transparent alter ego, he would describe the Colegio Nacional thus: "Absurd days: masters either pedantic or grotesque. His schoolmates irritated him. There was something which made him different from the others: an excessive sensitivity. He was too self-conscious. He suffered a good deal, stupidly and unnecessarily. He found no one poor or humble enough to want to become his friend."[10] He did, nonetheless, make a lifelong friend at the school, a boy called Macedonio Fernández, who in time would befriend his son, too. Macedonio came from a very different background. His family was of patrician criollo stock and had once owned *estancias*. However, what may have created a bond between the two boys was that Macedonio, like Jorge, had never really known his father, who had died when the boy was only three years old. Unlike Jorge, who performed indifferently at school, Macedonio was effortlessly brilliant at his studies. The two friends went on to read law at the University of Buenos Aires and became involved in the anarchist movement. Macedonio used to hold a regular discussion group at his house, which was attended by some of the brightest young intellectuals in Buenos Aires, such as Juan B. Justo, who would go on to found the Socialist Party of Argentina; José Ingenieros, later an eminent sociologist; and Leopoldo Lugones, who edited an anarchist journal with Ingenieros but who would become famous as a poet and cultural commentator a few years later. After his third year at university, Jorge Borges dropped out of full-time study, and for the fourth and fifth years of the course, he was registered as an *alumno libre,* an external student. This may indicate a lack of commitment to his legal studies, or perhaps a need to work to support his mother. At any rate, his grades deteriorated in the latter years of the course, but in the end he managed to complete his degree with a dissertation on a legal aspect of naval finance, which he dedicated to Fanny Haslam.

Still, even though Jorge Borges tried to please his mother by becoming a lawyer, he continued to regard himself as a social rebel. He was tempted by the idea of withdrawing from capitalist society altogether and experimenting with alternative lifestyles. After graduating in 1897, he and Macedonio Fernández, together with a group of friends, set about planning to found an anarchist commune in Paraguay, where the family of their comrade Julio Molina y Vedia had acquired land during the Paraguayan War. There they proposed to create a model for a new society in which private property would be abolished and bourgeois morality replaced by free love and complete equality between the sexes. However, early in 1898, when plans for the commune had not yet been finalized, Jorge Borges met Leonor Acevedo and fell head over heels in love with her. Theirs would be a whirlwind romance, for Jorge decided to drop out of the scheme for the anarchist commune in Paraguay and marry his new sweetheart instead. The wedding took place on October 1, 1898, just a few months after the couple had been introduced to each other at the house of Fanny Haslam.

Jorge and Leonor

ON THE FACE of it, Jorge and Leonor were an ill-matched couple. She was Catholic, bourgeoise, and obsessed with her criollo pedigree. He was an outsider, the anarchist son of an English widow. Nevertheless, each possessed attributes that met a need in the other. The self-doubting Jorge was drawn to Leonor's strength of character, while Leonor may have sensed that, through Jorge, she might develop those latent qualities that she had only glimpsed as a girl, thanks to Hamilton Otálora.

After their marriage Jorge took a modest administrative job as a lawyer in the secretariat of the civil law courts. In Argentina a person with a law degree is conventionally addressed as "Doctor," a sign of the high esteem accorded the profession. In the case of Dr. Jorge Guillermo Borges, however, the legal system was held in utter contempt. The law, he would write in his novel *El Caudillo,* was based on everything that was "conventional and dead," and its purpose was to protect "the narrow interests of society, its desire for profit, and the petty concerns of family, nation, state." As his career stagnated in the bureaucratic routine of the law courts, he took a second job teaching psychology to middle-class young ladies at the School of Modern Languages, the teacher-training institution where his aunt Caroline was head of the English department. Yet even there he was dissatisfied—he was such a skeptic, his son would say, that he doubted the existence of the subject he was employed to teach.[11]

Jorge eventually returned to his old pursuits in the company of his friend Macedonio Fernández, who had returned to Buenos Aires after the failure of the anarchist commune in Paraguay. That experiment had been predictably short-lived—the comrades, who were all city boys after all, very soon got fed up with the heat and the mosquitoes and began to feel terribly bored, cut off as they were from the usual stimulants of bohemian life in Buenos Aires. The fact was that Jorge Borges and his friends, for all their anarchist ideas, were inveterate womanizers and loved to fritter their time away in cafés, taverns, and brothels, playing *truco,* the typical criollo card game, discussing literature and politics, reciting poetry, and playing traditional music on their guitars. Jorge's companions were mostly minor writers on the fringes of the literary world, such as his cousin Álvaro Melián Lafinur, a poet and literary journalist; Marcelo del Mazo, also a poet and a cousin of Macedonio's; and Charles de Soussens, a Belgian writer of somewhat invisible means known to his friends as Charles de "Sans Sous." It was hardly the social circle Leonor Acevedo would have wished for a husband of hers, but as a dutiful Catholic wife, there was not much she could do but put up with Jorge's errant ways.

After a few years, Leonor would have realized that there was no hope of Jorge's ever restoring the social standing of the family, while Jorge must have accepted that he had failed to induce his wife to give up her bourgeois prejudices. Both had been unable to overcome their backgrounds: Leonor remained obsessed as ever with her family's former grandeur; Jorge was still haunted by the ghost of his father. Disappointed in love, Jorge took up writing and would attempt novels, poems, and plays, but he would tear up most of what he wrote, and among the compositions he destroyed was a play about "a man's disappointment in his son," to which he gave the title *Hacia la nada*— whose meaning might be conveyed as *Heading Nowhere*.[12]

The one novel that Jorge Borges did eventually complete, at the age of forty-six, was published at his own expense in 1920. Although weak as fiction, it is nevertheless of great value as a biographical source, not just because it affords insights into Jorge Guillermo Borges's personality but more so because it was to have a far-reaching influence on both the life and the work of his son Jorge Luis. Entitled *El Caudillo,* it is set in Dr. Borges's native Entre Ríos, at a time when the province was recovering from the ruinous conflicts caused by the rebellions of the *federal* chieftain Ricardo López Jordán. The eponymous Caudillo is Andrés Tavares, one of the minor chieftains who had supported López Jordán's first uprising but who now accepts that *federalismo* is a lost cause and economic interests dictate acquiescence in the rule of Buenos Aires. He has formed a commercial partnership with a cosmopolitan Jewish-Italian capitalist, known as El Gringo, a character modeled on the author's uncle, Jorge Suárez. The characters are ranged in opposite camps: there are those who favor tradition, like the Caudillo's wife and several of his associates, and others who are willing to accept progress, like El Gringo, the provincial governor, and the Caudillo's son. The matter at issue is whether the Caudillo himself will finally opt for progress or revert to the federalist cause of provincial autonomy. That issue is symbolized by a bridge that El Gringo has persuaded the Caudillo to build across a river that divides his *estancia* from the estate belonging to a Frenchman who lives in Buenos Aires.

The theme of building bridges is developed through the love affair between the Frenchman's son, Carlos Dubois, and the Caudillo's daughter, Marisabel. An alter ego of the author, Dubois is a man of cosmopolitan outlook—he was born and bred in Buenos Aires and has also lived in Paris, but he is a disappointment to his father, having kept bad company and failed his law examinations. By way of punishment, and in order to break up an affair with the unsuitable Lina, Carlos is sent to the country to manage the family *estancia,* at which, of course, he is hopeless, preferring to spend his time reading and wandering in the woods with his dogs. This fecklessness earns him the contempt of the Caudillo and his cronies, who attribute such odd behavior to his being of French descent, to the "foreign flaw" he carries in his blood.

The Caudillo's daughter, Marisabel, is a forceful young woman who is crying out to be liberated from her tyrannical father. There is "a mystical flaw" in her that impels her toward adventure and uncertainty. She falls for the cosmopolitan Dubois, but the latter cannnot make up his mind about her: "Like all weak personalities he blamed himself without really being sure of his own guilt." A crisis is precipitated when Dubois is recalled to Buenos Aires by his father, who has decided to accept his son's marriage to Lina. At this point Marisabel takes the initiative and arranges a meeting with Dubois by the bridge. However, a huge storm blows up, and the river bursts its banks, forcing Marisabel to take refuge in Dubois's house. There her passion sweeps away all Dubois's inhibitions, and he yields to the "enormous reality of sex," imagining that Marisabel will give him the happiness that he lacks the strength to achieve for himself. But the Caudillo is outraged to learn that his daughter has spent the night in Dubois's house, and when the waters subside, he sends his men to the ranch where the lovers have sheltered from the flood. Dubois is hacked to death, the rebellious daughter disowned. The Caudillo renounces progress and joins the rebellion of López Jordán's gauchos instead.

In the character of Marisabel, one might see the strong-willed Leonor Acevedo, who, although the offspring of a deeply rooted criollo family, also, like Marisabel, possessed a "mystical flaw"—a certain openness to passion— which Jorge Borges must have hoped would induce her to rebel against the ancestral prejudices of her clan in order to venture with him in bridging tradition and progress, the criollo and the foreign, the past and the future. That dream of reconciliation would have seemed possible during the long honeymoon enjoyed by Jorge and Leonor on the Haedo estate in Uruguay, where they must have experienced the "enormous reality of sex" that crowns the love affair of Dubois and Marisela in *El Caudillo*. Jorge Borges was to describe the passionate lovemaking of his protagonists in mystical terms as an orgasmic union with the spirit of the cosmos:

> He felt transformed, free, perfectly free of any particular goal, of all vain disputes. . . . He felt himself fall, fall deep into the womb of time, the centuries slipping away, until he reached the very beginning. Dissolving in that primordial clay, which the ages have kneaded and worked with pain, and fear and hunger, he found himself before the gods who had made him. He could not see their faces, but in spasms of ravished bliss he felt their tremendous power strike each of his cells like lightning, and he felt the woman's body tremble with equal joy.

This transcendent passion would not be sustained for long, however, once Jorge and Leonor fell into the routine of married life in Buenos Aires. The denouement of *El Caudillo* shows the probable cause of that failure—Jorge felt overwhelmed by the power of "the Caudillo," the imaginary spirit of that perfect, heroic father he had never known; and Leonor Acevedo, despite her strength of character, was unable to rebel against "the Caudillo" either: she could not finally reject the shadow of her ancestors and succumbed once more to her fear of betraying the honor of her patrician criollo family. The flood-waters of tradition, as it were, rose up and encircled Jorge and Leonor, and, like Dubois and Marisela, they were eventually forced apart.

The lovers would nevertheless hold on to the memory of that early passion. Leonor would retain for the rest of her life a strong sense of the romantic love that had swept her off her feet as a girl—she would always wear a ring Jorge was to give her in Geneva, a large emerald that he described to her as containing "water from the Rhône."[13] Jorge, for his part, would not discount the hope of recovering that first experience of happiness, although he believed it would be impossible to find it again in Argentina. Still, just as Carlos Dubois had dreamed of settling somewhere in the Old World with his first sweetheart, Lina, in a place of refuge where he would write a book, "a very personal book, one that was very much his own," so, too, did Jorge cling to the notion of taking Leonor to Europe, where they might both find release from the power of "the Caudillo" and rekindle the passion they had once known.

Meanwhile, Jorge and Leonor would look to their son to fulfill their divergent aspirations. Leonor wished him to restore the family to its former social importance, and she would, as it were, brandish before him the ancestral sword of honor, the very sword that, ironically, had severed her from her husband and from her heart's desire. Jorge's demands on his son would be more complex and intangible—the boy should come to grips with the ghost of the hero or else fulfill the literary destiny that he had himself been denied.

Still, Jorge Luis Borges had once been the object of quite different hopes. Born within a year of the marriage, he embodied the first flowering of the passion that had brought the ill-starred lovers together. "My parents engendered me for the risky and beautiful game of life, for the earth, and the water, and the air, and the fire."[14] In due course Borges would take it upon himself to see that his parents' youthful will was done, if only vicariously, by seeking to fulfill in his own life the dream that had eluded the early hopes of Jorge and Leonor.

CHAPTER 3

Childhood

(1899–1914)

AFTER THEIR MARRIAGE Jorge Borges and Leonor Acevedo went to live with Leonor's parents at calle Tucumán 840 in the center of old Buenos Aires. Their first child was born in this house eight months later, on Thursday, August 24, 1899, in the early hours of a chilly winter's morning. The boy was named after his father and also after each of his grandfathers, Francisco Borges and Isidoro Acevedo. He duly appeared in the Civil Register as Jorge Francisco Isidoro, but when he was baptised at the Church of San Nicolás de Bari on June 20, 1900, the name Luis was added, the only one he could call his own of the four he had been given.

Shortly after the birth of his son, and with the help of his wife's parents, Jorge Borges bought two adjacent plots of land for thirteen thousand pesos in the barrio of Palermo next to the house on calle Serrano where his mother, Fanny Haslam, lived with her widowed sister, Caroline. Although Palermo is today one of the most desirable residential districts in Buenos Aires, it was then an outlying barrio on the very edge of the city—only a few yards from the calle Serrano flowed the Maldonado River, little more than a muddy stream, which marked the northwestern limits of Buenos Aires. (It has since been covered over and now runs under the avenida Juan B. Justo.) Beyond that there was open country, with only the odd smallholding here and there until one eventually arrived at the town of Belgrano.

Palermo had an unsavory reputation at the time. Inhabited by large numbers of poor Italian immigrants, mostly from Calabria and Sicily, it was known as the haunt of petty criminals and pimps—on the other bank of the Maldonado from where the Borgeses lived, there was a seedy area of taverns and dance halls, where girls could be hired to dance the tango. Just south was the notorious "Tierra del Fuego," an area around the huge state penitentiary that was the stomping ground of some of the most feared knife fighters in all of Buenos Aires. Even so, Palermo was slowly attracting more respectable people as tracts of land were divided up into single plots and sold off at auction for the construction of private dwellings.

Dr. Borges paid for the land in monthly installments of one thousand pesos, and over the year or so it took to make these payments, he had a house built in the fashionable art nouveau style. In the course of that year, Leonor became pregnant with their second child, and before the new house was ready, she gave birth on March 4, 1901, to a girl, Leonor Fanny (Norah), in Fanny Haslam's house at calle Serrano 2135.[1] When their own house was completed sometime later that year, the family moved into Serrano 2147 on the corner of calle Guatemala. The Borgeses' new home was relatively grand for the barrio: it had two stories and a large enclosed garden with several trees and a windmill pump. There were still many vacant plots all around and only one other two-story building, a blacksmith's, on calle Serrano, the remainder being low brick dwellings that typically housed the immigrants in the marginal suburbs of the city.

The Borgeses secluded themselves in their large house and had little contact with their neighbors. Borges was to recall that he "lived essentially indoors" and the family did "its successful best" to ignore what went on in the barrio; many people were "ashamed" of saying they lived in Palermo and "spoke in a dim way of living on the north side."[2] A patrician criolla like Leonor Acevedo certainly felt like a fish out of water among all the southern Italian gringos in the area. "I remember that my mother used to tease Norah for having been born in Palermo. She would say to her: 'Aren't you ashamed of having been born in the *orillas*? You're a true *orillera, caramba!*' That joke of my mother's left poor Norah totally confused."[3]

Theirs was a close-knit family: the house in which Fanny Haslam lived with her sister Caroline was separated from their own by a low wall, and the children would be taken on frequent visits to their maternal grandparents, the Acevedos. When grandfather Isidoro died in 1905, his widow, Leonor Suárez, rented out her house on calle Tucumán and came to live with her daughter's family in Palermo. The children had few other social contacts and no friends to speak of, so Georgie and Norah spent virtually all their time in the house, playing together in their large garden. Norah, the more high-spirited of the two, took the lead in the games they devised to amuse themselves, and they invented two phantom playmates, whom they called Quilos and the Windmill and who became as real to them as the people they knew; eventually, when they grew bored with them, they told their mother that their friends had died.[4]

In summer the whole family would go to Adrogué, a new town some twenty-five miles south of Buenos Aires that had been designed as a resort for the middle classes of the big city. Adrogué's pleasant parks and tree-lined promenades provided a welcome relief from the stifling heat of the austral summer. The Borgeses used to rent a villa called La Rosalinda on calle Macías, only a few blocks away from the railway station. Borges would grow very fond of Adrogué; as an adult the smell of eucalyptus trees would take him back to those summer days of his childhood, and he would often go there to unwind from the pressures of city life.

In February, the hottest month, they would cross the River Plate to Uruguay, where they stayed at Paso del Molino, on the northern outskirts of Montevideo, with their wealthy cousins, the Haedos, who lived at Villa Esther, a well-appointed mansion with extensive grounds, a swimming pool, and a large summer pavilion. There the children were able to play with their cousin Esther and her older sister, Aurora. Sometimes they would take a trip to the Haedos' country estate on the Uruguay River, near the town of Fray Bentos, where they enjoyed a more active, open-air life, swimming in the river, which Georgie greatly enjoyed, and riding, at which the boy, always physically clumsy, was never much good.

For most of the year, however, Georgie and Norah were confined to the isolated, hothouse atmosphere of the family home in Palermo. Here it was the womenfolk—Mother, their English "Gran," and, to a lesser extent, their maternal grandmother, Leonor Suárez—who were responsible for their early education. Their father was a distinctly remote figure who was content to leave the affairs of the family and the day-to-day running of the house to his wife, while he pursued his interests elsewhere with his bohemian friends. Spanish was normally spoken in the family, but since Fanny Haslam had never learned to speak the language properly, they used English with her. Leonor had a smattering of English, which she picked up from her husband so as to communicate with his mother, but Norah did not take to English very well. With Georgie it was different: Fanny took the boy under her wing at a very early age, and he developed a strong emotional bond with her; he was soon bilingual to the extent of not being entirely conscious of the differences between English and Spanish, other than having a vague awareness that he must employ a different mode of communication with Gran from the one he normally used with the rest of the family. Still, Spanish was Borges's mother tongue without a doubt, and his lightly accented English would never lose a certain stilted, bookish quality.

He was first taught to read in Spanish by his mother,[5] but he retained more vivid memories of learning to read with his beloved Gran. With her he worked through passages in English from what he called a *leccionario* (a childish pun crossing "reading book" with "lesson" to form "lessonary"), which was a large volume of selected extracts from classic authors—the Brothers Grimm, Kipling, Stevenson, Poe, Victor Hugo, Dumas, Walter Scott, and so on. It was Fanny Haslam who awakened in him an enduring love of English prose. As a good Protestant, she would keep the King James Bible at her bedside and could quote from it chapter and verse. Once he was able to read on his own, probably by the age of four, the little boy would spend hours lying on the floor with his head stuck in a book. One of the first novels he read right through was *Huckleberry Finn,* and soon afterward he plunged into the books beloved of Edwardian boys—adventure stories by Captain Marryat, H. Rider Haggard, Robert Louis Stevenson. In Spanish he liked Eduardo Gutiérrez, a writer of popular books, and especially his *Croquis y siluetas militares (Military Sketches and Profiles)* because it gave a melodramatic account of the heroic death of his grandfather, Colonel Borges.

However, far more than reading, what molded the character and imagination of the young boy were the tales he was told by his mother and grandmothers. Leonor Acevedo relayed to her son the stories she herself had heard as a little girl from her own mother. He learned about the family's days of glory— the *estancia* in San Nicolás that the Acevedos had once owned, and the black slaves who bore their family's name. She told him about Colonel Suárez leading the cavalry charge that turned the tide of battle at Junín, as well as his subsequent exile and death in Uruguay on account of Rosas's tyranny. He learned about the confiscation of their estates, about the beatings and executions the tyrant had inflicted on the family. "She would speak about the time of Rosas as if she had been a contemporary of the Mazorca."[6] That ancient quarrel still determined an absolute social divide as far as Leonor was concerned—anything associated with Rosas was common, vulgar, *guarango,* and she detested gauchos to the extent of forbidding her son to read *The Gaucho Martín Fierro* because its author, José Hernández, had been a *federal.* As Georgie would eventually come to recognize, there was something absurd in the intensity of such emotions. He would recall how, many years later, he asked his mother how she was feeling just after the old lady had undergone an operation, and heard her murmur in reply, "Savage *unitaria!,*" an old slogan from the period of Rosas, as a signal to him that she was all right. "It made no sense at the time to speak of *unitarios* and *federales,*" Borges observed, "but she was still faithful to the cause."[7]

Leonor Acevedo was indeed wedded to the past. She would reminisce about her childhood, communicating to her son a nostalgia for that older Buenos Aires that she was just old enough to remember, a Buenos Aires that was little more than a large village before it was subsequently ruined by the nouveaux riches who had taken over the republic. Leonor would describe the house on calle Tucumán where she had been raised and where he had himself been born. Her memories of its two patios, its water tank and modest porch, would find their way into his poems. He learned from her the traditional topography of the city, the street names and layout of the historic center before everything changed; there were streams called *terceros* that flowed through the city when it rained—there was a *tercero* in the north side, with a footbridge at calle Florida, and another in the south, with a bridge of its own, too.

These secondhand memories of better times were to inspire in Borges a fondness for the run-down barrios on the south side of Buenos Aires. These were the areas abandoned by those criollo families who could afford to move to the fashionable districts of the Barrio Norte, when the north side of Buenos Aires was being redeveloped along Parisian lines. Those areas of the city to the south of the Plaza de Mayo were left to molder away, and as a result the neglected Barrio Sur was to retain a faded ambience of yesteryear. Borges would always enjoy strolling along the streets of districts like San Telmo or Barracas, whose dilapidated buildings, with their crumbling masonry, narrow vestibules and Spanish patios, preserved something of the flavor of what the city had been like in the early decades of the previous century. These streets were to form the seedbed of many of his poems and stories, evoking within him an elegiac sense of the passing of a simpler, more noble age, in which the criollo families of Buenos Aires had endeavored to create a *patria* of their own. When he dedicated his *Complete Works* to his mother in 1974, he thanked her for having given him her "memory and within it the memory of our ancestors."

Yet while Mother fostered his awareness of the family's criollo antecedents, he was influenced, too, by the tales he heard from Fanny Haslam. Her nostalgic account of life in her native land conveyed to him a sense of England as a second, spiritual home. Indeed, Fanny was as proud of her English blood as Mother was of her criollo pedigree. Young Georgie once asked his Gran if she had any Scottish blood, and her reply could not have been more emphatic: "I haven't a single drop of Scotch, Irish or Welsh blood in me, thank goodness!"[8] Georgie loved to hear about the Haslams' origins in Northumberland, and, being susceptible to the romance of history and to the bonds of genealogy in particular, he was taken early on with the epic battles between Saxon, Viking, and Celt that formed the remote beginnnings of the English nation, a childhood interest he would revive as a grown man in his study of Anglo-Saxon and Norse literature.

Fanny Haslam's sense of displacement as an Englishwoman living on the edge of the civilized world came through powerfully in these stories. She would tell him about her life in Entre Ríos at the time of the uprisings of López Jordán and his gaucho cavalry, and about life in the garrison town of Junín on the Indian frontier. Fanny claimed to have met Indian chieftains with strange names, like Simón Coliqueo, Catriel, Pincén, and Namuncurá. She had come across Indians so uncivilized that they had never before seen a door. The story that made the greatest impression on young Georgie was the one about the English girl who had been abducted by Indians. Fanny had offered to help her escape, but the captive girl showed no interest at all in returning to civilization. And yet the thought that his grandmother might have suffered a fate similar to the English girl's would have brought a frisson of horror to the timid boy. But his dear Gran, of course, had been protected from the Indian savages by the heroic Colonel Borges. It was he who had stood between civilization and barbarism. And so, to his mother's stories about Colonel Suárez's exploits in the wars of independence was added the memory of the other great family hero, Colonel Borges, the scourge of the wild Indians and gauchos of the great plains of South America.

In their different ways, Fanny Haslam and Leonor Acevedo converged upon the same theme in their respective accounts of the family's history: they had been robbed of their just deserts by some cruel fate, and there remained, therefore, a lack, a void, that was crying out to be filled so that they could all find their rightful place in the world once more. Leonor blamed Rosas for having inflicted so many injustices on the Suárezes and the Acevedos. Fanny's grievance was more nebulous, more metaphysical, as she pondered the misfortune of having lost her husband so pointlessly during General Mitre's failed rebellion.

Young Georgie would certainly be haunted by the tragic significance of Colonel Borges's demise. In the course of his life, he would write a total of five poems evoking that loss, and for the most part his public references to his grandfather's death would repeat Fanny Haslam's romantic tale about her husband's choosing suicide as the only honorable way out of an impossible dilemma.[9] As late as 1968, he would write, "Borges mounted his horse and, accompanied by several of his loyal soldiers, slowly rode out, arms across his chest, toward the enemy lines. The revolt failed, Mitre was imprisoned for several months, but his life was spared. Borges died from his wounds two days later. In his last words, he said, 'I have fallen in the belief of having fulfilled my duty and my convictions, and for the same principles that I have fought all my life.'"[10] At the time of writing, Borges would almost certainly have been apprised of the historical truth of the matter—that the colonel just happened to have been hit by two bullets in the heat of battle—but the version he learned as a boy from his grandmother, with its fateful conflict between honor and betrayal, was still too powerful to resist. He had grown up to believe that Colonel Borges was "a character of epic and legend," and that his last action possessed "a grandeur that has disappeared in our day," for "defeat," after all, "is more poetic than victory. It is there one finds the essence of ancient tragedy."[11]

The figure of the ancestral warrior—a composite of Colonel Suárez and Colonel Borges—would cast a very long shadow over Georgie. The swords of the two heroes were displayed like sacred relics in the family home in Palermo, and on a table in the drawing room were laid out a silver basin and a silver-trimmed *mate* gourd that Colonel Suárez had brought back from the wars of independence. Portraits of the dead heroes hung on the walls of the house, and their noble features were preserved also in daguerrotypes mounted on silver frames or clasped yet more intimately in treasured lockets. Wherever he looked, Georgie was confronted by the ghosts of his venerable ancestors, holding aloft, as it were, the sword of honor that had conferred such distinction upon them all.

Young Georgie, however, felt overwhelmed by the force of this collective female yearning to recover the glories of the past. It transmitted to him an expectation that he somehow take up the hero's sword once more and fill the void at the heart of the family's self-esteem. In his "Autobiographical Essay," Borges was quite explicit about the effect upon him of this ancestor worship: "As most of my people had been soldiers—even my father's brother had been a naval officer—and I knew I would never be, I felt ashamed, quite early, to be a bookish kind of person and not a man of action."[12] The sword of honor undermined his faith in himself to such a degree that he felt he could not be truly loved by his parents: "Throughout my boyhood, I thought that to be loved would have amounted to an injustice. I did not feel I deserved any particular love."[13] His birthdays filled him with shame, because everyone heaped gifts on him when he thought he had done nothing to deserve them; it made him feel, he wrote, "that I was a kind of fake."[14]

The boy was a worry to his parents. Like many premature babies, he was weak and sickly, his eyesight was poor, and when he started to talk, he distorted words so badly that his mother became concerned that his hearing might not be normal.[15] He was also an extremely anxious child who suffered from frequent nightmares. The terrors that seized the boy seem to have been connected with the sense of inadequacy that afflicted him as a child. He used to have bad dreams about peeling off his face and finding someone else's beneath it, or of taking off a mask only to discover that he was wearing another. Similar anxieties invaded his waking life, too: He was frightened of mirrors, even shrinking from his own image when he saw it reflected on the polished mahogany of the furniture in his bedroom; at times he imagined he could see someone else's face staring back at him and he hated having to look in the mirror anyway, as if his own reflection threatened to rob him of a sense of who he really was: "As a boy I used to fear that the mirror / might reveal to me another face, / or a blind, impersonal mask doubtless hiding /some atrocious being."[16] This horror of reflections would lead to his perverse fascination as an adult with doubles, reproductions, copies, facsimiles, translations—with anything, indeed, that could undermine the uniqueness of an object or a person by dint of repeating it. In one of his poems he would call a mirror "the stuff of magic," because "you dare multiply the number of things / we are and which define our lot. After I am dead, you shall copy someone else / and then another, and another, and another, and another . . ."[17]

If the self might hide another person, so, too, might reality conceal some alien world: "I feared also that the silent time of the mirror / might diverge from man's daily round of hours, and harbour / within its vague, imaginary confines, / new beings and forms and colours."[18] It was as if anything and everything might turn out to be other than it appeared or else a dreamlike projection of his own consciousness, for his inner life transpired in a state of acute solipsism: there were no clear limits between self and world, and no center even within that boundless self, since the "I" that seemed to anchor his personality was itself a suspect quantity, shifting and receding and changing in the hall of mirrors that passed for objective truth.

The other memory that stood out from his childhood was his passion for tigers. From the earliest, he worshipped tigers with great "fervor"; tigers were "delicate and fatal, charged with infinite energy"; they seemed to possess a mysterious power, for "only men of war, riding in a castle mounted on an elephant" could confront them.[19] After his reading lessons with Gran, he would ask her to talk to him about "ferocious tigers,"[20] and when he read Kipling's *Jungle Books*, "I was unhappy that Shere Khan, the tiger, was the enemy of the hero."[21] Encyclopedias and books of natural history were judged by the quality of their illustrations of tigers, and he would often lie on the floor making drawings of tigers himself.[22]

This obsession with tigers was the one issue that caused overt conflict in his childhood. One of his favorite treats was to be taken to see the Bengal tiger in Palermo Zoo, which was a short walk from their house. He would contemplate the tiger at the zoo for ages and would keep his mother standing at the cage until the sun went down. Leonor would lose patience with Georgie and try to drag him away, but the boy would refuse to move. It was a battle of wills significant enough for Leonor herself to recall it in a memoir: "He had a passion for animals, especially wild animals. Whenever we went to the zoo, it was difficult to get him to leave. And I, being so small, was afraid of him, since he was big and strong. I was afraid he might lose his temper and hit me."[23] He once threw such a terrible tantrum that his mother locked him up in a room as a punishment and told him he would not be let out until he admitted that he had defied her "without meaning to." But Georgie simply would not give in and kept screaming, "I did mean to do it," until Leonor was forced to relent.[24] *

The fact was that this very timid boy concealed a violent temper beneath

---

*His willfulness comes across far more strongly in Spanish because he countered the normal idiom used by Mother, *sin querer*, "without meaning to," with his own ungrammatical *con querer*, literally, "*with* meaning to."

a placid exterior, and there was nothing that would bring out the rage and aggression locked within more than his being deprived of the sight of the Bengal tiger. But his mother found a way to quell his rebelliousness: "Whenever he didn't want to give in, I would take his books away: it never failed."[25] It was an infallible remedy without a doubt, for what would Georgie have done without his books? Reading gave him license to roam beyond the confines of the house in which he was normally cooped up, so his mother's threat, in effect, spelled a kind of death of the imagination for the young boy, and he had little choice but to submit to her authority. However, when he was only five, he scrawled a string of words—"Tiger Lion Papa Leopard"—on a piece of paper. The curious interpolation of "Papa" in that sequence rings out like a cri de coeur from the boy to his father at a time when the tiger had become the object of a battle of wills with his mother.

Georgie, in fact, associated his father in a very particular way with the mysterious power of the tiger. Dr. Borges used to tell his son about a visit he once made to an *estancia* where he met a man whose job it was to kill jaguars that preyed on the cattle. The *tigrero*, or "tiger man," would get his dogs to force the jaguar out of his lair, and then, dagger at the ready, he would wait for the beast to jump at him before killing it with a sharp upward thrust into its belly.[26] The tale of the tiger man took root in the boy's imagination—here was a man who could confront the "infinite energy" of the tiger and master it with nothing more than a knife. So if the tiger represented a raw, elemental power, then a man capable of vanquishing the tiger had to possess a degree of self-assurance that was the precise opposite of the myriad doubts to which Georgie himself was prey. And what made his father's story even more intriguing was that nobody thought of the tiger man as a hero; "he was a specialized workman."[27] Such workaday courage stood in stark contrast to the glory of Georgie's heroic ancestors, which so oppressed him with feelings of unworthiness and inadequacy. And so, in order to offset the forbidding grandeur of his ancestor's sword of honor, Georgie would fetishize the dagger of the tiger man as a symbol of a vital power that could surpass even that of the tiger itself.

His father's association with tigers was further reinforced by an antique Spanish dagger he kept in a drawer of his writing bureau. This weapon exerted a magnetic attraction on Georgie. He would picture it lying among his father's papers, "dreaming a simple dream of killing its tiger."[28] Whenever he saw his father showing it to his friends, he yearned to be allowed to handle it, too: "You can tell they had been longing to hold it in their hand; they grip the handle, which has been lying there waiting for them, and the blade, compliant and powerful, slips in and out of its sheath with deadly precision."

.   .   .

When Georgie was six or seven years old, the time came for Jorge and Leonor to make a decision about their son's education. The nearest primary school was on calle Thames, but it was a rough place, attended mainly by the poor boys of Palermo, and Georgie was such a sickly boy that his parents were concerned that he might be exposed to the many contagious diseases, not the least of which was tuberculosis, which were common at the time. In the end Dr. Borges decided that it would be best if the children were educated at home for as long as possible, and an English tutor, a Miss Tink, was engaged to come to the house to provide classes for Georgie and his sister, Norah.

Well meant though it was, this decision to keep Georgie from attending school cut the boy off from his peers for most of his childhood. Instead of friends, Georgie would be given books, for Dr. Borges accorded his son the privilege of unrestricted access to his personal library of over a thousand volumes. This collection of mostly English and French books was arranged on glass-fronted shelves and kept in a room of its own, and here Georgie would become a voracious reader, reveling in the freedom books afforded him to venture in strange, faraway lands—England, Scotland, India, Africa, China, Arabia. Father's library, in effect, became his playground, and all the energies of a growing child were channeled into an imaginary world that soon became more real to him than the circumscribed little domestic world around him. His nearsightedness reinforced this illusion—his eyes were so bad that he was better able to see "small and minute things" like print than he could see other people.[29] And he discovered that the books he read could at times mirror his worst nightmares. He was terrified by Alexandre Dumas's story *The Man in the Iron Mask.* From one of the illustrations in the edition he read, he retained the poignant image of the man parading sadly along a terrace overlooking the sea, wearing his mask of iron. It reminded him of *Lalla Rookh,* a poem by Thomas Moore about the Prophet of Khorassan, who kept his face veiled in order to conceal his disgusting leprosy. "Both images were associated with one another and they used to make me very frightened."[30] H. G. Wells's *The First Men on the Moon* also induced the kind of terror he used to feel in his nightmares: what scared him was the fact that the narrator had betrayed his friend and abandoned him on the moon.[31] Perhaps he saw an analogy with his own predicament, for his father had given him the run of his library but had then abandoned him to his fate, as it were, in the satellite world of books.

"If I were asked to name the chief event in my life, I should say my father's library," Borges would write in his "Autobiographical Essay."[32] Indeed, he would come to regard his father's library as a metaphor for the solipsism that afflicted him for most of his life. The library, after all, was a mixed blessing— on the one hand, it helped him preserve a certain freedom of the imagination against the oppressive authority of the sword of honor, but, on the other, his prodigious reading served to aggravate his self-absorption and reproduce the dreamlike subjectivity from which he so desperately wanted to escape.

While young Georgie languished at home with his books, Dr. Borges spent a good deal of his time in the company of his friends. On Sundays they would go to the races at the Palermo course, and they would all come afterward to the Borges house for dinner and conversation, often staying on till dawn. At first Georgie resented his father's bringing his friends around after the races, and he knew that his mother disliked Macedonio Fernández and Charles de "Sans Sous," but one Sunday evening his attitude was to change dramatically when he heard a young man called Evaristo Carriego recite a long poem "in an exaggerated manner": "I didn't understand any of it, but poetry was revealed to me, because I saw that words were not just a means of communication, they also contained a sort of magic."[33] After this revelation Georgie liked to stay up to listen to Carriego recite his own verse, and, as his mother recalled, "he would stand there, his eyes wide open. . . ."[34] Young Georgie would come to idolize Carriego, to the point where he became a kind of father surrogate for the boy.

Still in his twenties, Carriego was considerably younger than Dr. Borges and his cronies, but in about 1908 he had been taken up by Charles de Soussens, who had been impressed by his talent as a poet. Carriego, in fact, was a fairly disreputable character who inhabited a netherworld of drink, dope, and general dissipation. He fancied himself a kind of *poète maudit,* and at the time he joined Dr. Borges's group of friends, he would have just published, or been about to publish, his first book, to which he gave the suitably blasphemous title of *Las misas herejes (The Heretical Masses)* and in which he sang the delights of forbidden fruit in a self-consciously Baudelairean manner.

Carriego worked as a journalist for *La Protesta Humana* and a number of other anarchist publications. As an anarchist he tended to glorify social rebels like the gaucho Juan Moreira, a Robin Hood figure who had roamed the pampas as a bandit in the previous century. He also retained a romantic attachment to his native province of Entre Ríos, even though his family had moved to Buenos Aires when he was four years old, because it was the last of the provinces to succumb to the political authority of Buenos Aires. One day Carriego observed to Dr. Borges in his usual bombastic manner, "Here we are, both natives of Entre Ríos!," and Dr. Borges wearily replied, "Yes, and like all the natives of Entre Ríos who can get out, here we are in Buenos Aires."[35]

But it was precisely this romantic idealism that drew young Georgie to the ardent Carriego, who lived not far away in a modest one-story dwelling on the calle Honduras. And it was through Carriego, too, that the boy was to get some inkling of life outside the family domain. Carriego was an aficionado of the popular culture of the outlying *arrabales* of Buenos Aires. These areas were known as the *orillas*, or the "shores," of the great metropolis, and here country folk mingled with the masses of immigrants from the Old World. By the turn of the century, the *orillas* had produced a vibrant subculture of their own that was virtually unknown to the middle classes. Rustic speech had become inflected with new words to create distinctive urban dialects that have now melded into the Buenos Aires slang called *lunfardo*. *Sainetes*, or plays about local characters or legendary heroes like the gaucho Juan Moreira, were performed in tents at local fairs. Folk songs and stories celebrated the feats of knife fighters like Juan Muraña, the most feared *cuchillero* of Palermo. And then, of course, there was the tango. The country music of the gauchos continued to thrive in the *orillas*, but over time native genres such as the *milonga* had begun to interact with styles brought over by the immigrants, and by the 1890s the primitive tango had been born in the rough-and-ready brothels and dance halls of the *orillas*. Its lyrics were peppered with double entendres referring to the grossest sexual practices, while the dance that accompanied it seemed to mimic the act of copulation itself. No decent woman of any class would have anything to do with the tango, for it was the music of prostitutes and their clients, and it was not uncommon for a couple of men to perform the dance with each other while waiting their turn at the whorehouse or outside the *esquinas*, the street-corner taverns, which were typical of the *arrabales*.

From an early age, Carriego had developed a fascination with the *cuchilleros* of Palermo who worked as bodyguards for political bosses or as bullyboys to help deliver the vote at elections. The most colorful of these low, urban types was the dandified *compadrito*, a gaucho turned city slicker with a weakness for sharp suits and flashy jewelry, and whose jeering, effeminate tone of voice belied a tremendous ferocity when roused to combat. Carriego was not yet fifteen when he sought out Don Nicolás Paredes, the godfather of the Palermo underworld. According to Borges, he made his way "through the thugs in tall hats who served as the the the caudillo's praetorian guard" and introduced himself to Paredes, who welcomed him and eventually "loved and cared for him like his own son"; it was thus that Carriego came to "rub shoulders with *compadritos* and delinquents of all kinds, addressing those killers in the most familiar terms."[36]

The world described by Carriego acquired the allure of the forbidden for the young boy. One of his favorite books was the popular novel *Juan Moreira* by Eduardo Gutiérrez, which related the adventures of the eponymous gaucho bandit and also mentioned his own grandfather Colonel Borges, the scourge of gauchos and Indians. However, as Borges was to tell Victoria Ocampo, "I would have preferred to have been the grandson of Moreira rather than of Borges."[37] He took to reading *The Gaucho Martín Fierro* in secret, lapped up gauchesque poetry, became an aficionado of the tangos and *milongas* that his father's cousin, Álvaro Melián Lafinur, used to play on his guitar on Sunday evenings after the races and found out all he could about the *compadritos* of Palermo, discovering that even his own dear Miss Tink, the English governess, had a cousin who was a hoodlum known as Juan Tink, el inglés.

Carriego's "cult of courage," his interest in the exploits of *compadritos* and gauchos, brought to life a world quite as exciting as any Georgie had read about in the adventure stories he found in Father's library, except that he could imagine it going on all around him beyond the walls of the garden. And when he was allowed to venture outside the library, especially when the family went on its summer holidays to the cousins' estates in Uruguay, Georgie would look out for real gauchos. He first saw some while staying at the Haedos' summer villa in Paso del Molino. He had only ever seen pictures of them before, "but when I saw real gauchos I was deeply moved."[38] He tried riding horses on his uncle's *estancia* near Fray Bentos and was once allowed to accompany some gauchos on horseback as they herded cattle to a river.[39] He claimed to have become a "passable horseman," but admitted that he had fallen off horses on several occasions, which is what one would have expected of a boy who was so physically inept.[40]

Carriego, then, was the conduit through which Georgie first learned about the folklore of the *orillas,* but, needless to say, young Georgie's new-found enthusiasm for the common people was not shared by his mother. The patrician Leonor Acevedo had no time for gauchos and *compadritos,* let alone the tango, which had such unpleasant associations. Nor was she much impressed with Carriego's poetic talent, even though the effusive young bard was gallant enough to dedicate his poem "Vulgar Sinfonía" ("Popular Symphony") to her, commending in his verse dedication the literary aspirations of her son, "who can sense already upon his brow, / the first yearnings for the laurel crown."[41] But Mother's disapproval served only to increase Georgie's admiration for Carriego, since it was Carriego who offered him what he had initially sought from his father: the means to overcome the inadequacy he felt at being unable to live up to his mother's lofty expectations. Carriego validated what one might call the emotional logic of Borges's imagination: whatever was forbidden by Mother—tigers, gauchos, *compadritos*—was by that token life-enhancing; and whatever she approved of—the ancestor's sword of honor—was oppressive and "unreal." Following this logic, therefore, rebellion against Mother was the key to independence and self-fullfilment.

.   .   .

The time finally came when Dr. Borges decided to send Georgie to school. Borges would always be fairly guarded about his schooldays: he claimed to have first attended school when he was nine, which would mean that he had started in March 1909.[42] In fact, the only record of his attending primary school that has been found states that he was registered at the local school on calle Thames 2321 in Palermo on March 2, 1911.[43] This was the time that Norah Borges first went to school, having "just reached the age of 10."[44] If Georgie had started in 1909, it seems unlikely that Norah, who would have been of school age by that date anyway, would have continued to be taught at home by Miss Tink for another two years. It is almost certain, therefore, that Borges was not sent to school until March 1911, when he was eleven and half years old. He was placed in the fifth grade at first but a few days later was transferred to the fourth,[45] which suggests that the school authorities found his education lacking, no doubt because he had been kept at home until such a late age.

There were forty-five pupils in the fourth grade that year, mostly boys from the poor families of that shabby neighborhood. Georgie, of course, was one of the few middle-class exceptions, and his mother, who was conscious of just how different her son was from the common herd, made sure everyone would instantly recognize this fact and sent her Georgie to school in a jacket and tie. Little wonder that this terribly shy, stammering boy, who wore thick spectacles and an "Eton collar and tie," as he described it, felt intimidated by the other boys.[46] As might have been expected, he faced a rude awakening to the world outside Father's library. There was only one other middle-class boy in the fourth grade, Roberto Godel, and the other children, as Borges recalled, "never forgave" the two outsiders[47] and made them "pay a high price" for their presumed superiority.[48] They were constantly "jeered at and bullied"[49] and Georgie was introduced to "the rudiments of *lunfardo*," the plebeian slang, and to "ten or fifteen obscene synonyms" that he had "never heard at home."[50]

Georgie, nevertheless, managed to complete fourth grade, and at the start of the following academic year, in March 1912, he was enrolled in Grade 5B, but Roberto Godel, his one friend, was sent by his parents to another school, leaving Georgie to stand up to the other boys on his own.[51] There was to be no respite in the bullying Georgie had to endure; he took part "in several fistfights," but he did this "out of cowardice, because I was forced to by the other boys."[52] A few weeks after the beginning of the school year, he must have been involved in a particularly violent episode of bullying, and this, I believe, was the incident Borges had in mind when he wrote "The Maker" ("El hacedor"):

> Another boy had insulted him and he had gone to his father and told him what had happened. The latter let him speak, acting as if he was not listen-

ing or could not understand him, and he took down from the wall a bronze dagger, beautiful and charged with power, which the young lad had furtively coveted. He held it in his hands now and the surprise of possessing it canceled the insult he had suffered, but the voice of his father was saying: *Let them know you are a man,* and there was a command in that voice.[53]

This account rings true as a memory from Borges's own childhood: it is described as a "lost memory that shone like a coin in the rain." His father had converted the fight with the bully into a test of manly honor, and this may be why Borges, many years later, gave these violent encounters with his tormentors an almost chivalrous gloss: "Well, my eyesight was bad, I was very weak, and I was generally defeated. But it had to be done. Because there was a code and, in fact, when I was a boy, there was even a code of dueling."[54]

Just over a month after the beginning of the new term, on April 19, the boy was withdrawn from school by his parents. The reason stated in the school records was that the family would be leaving Buenos Aires for an unspecified period,[55] but Georgie was never to return to the school on calle Thames, and no evidence has come to light that the Borges family was absent from Buenos Aires for any significant length of time at this point. The most likely explanation for Georgie's sudden withdrawal from school is that the bullying had become serious enough to persuade his parents that their son, like Roberto Godel, should no longer be exposed to the persistent violence of his classmates. The memory of that violence would remain with Borges for the rest of his life—one of his recurrent nightmares as an adult was of being tormented by dwarfs and little boys.[56]

But even more potent than the memory of the bullying itself was his memory of Father's handing him the dagger and telling him to be a man. This would become a compelling motif in his stories, for, in handing him the dagger, Father was effectively inviting Georgie to be as brave as the *tigrero* confronting the tiger. Borges would remember the intoxicating sense of power he felt when he held the dagger in his hand. He attempted to put it into words in "The Maker":

Clutching the dagger to his breast, feeling in it a magic power, he went down the steep slope that encircled the house and ran to the seashore, dreaming that he was Ajax and Perseus, and filling the salty darkness with wounds and battles.[57]

It was "the precise taste of that moment" that really mattered to him; "he didn't care about the rest: the insults of the challenge, the clumsy fight, his coming back with the bloodstained blade." And yet the fact remained that he had been defeated by the other boys; his parents had withdrawn him from school; he had ventured out into the world but had been driven back and forced to take refuge once more in the unreal domain of Father's library.

After he left the school at calle Thames, Georgie would receive no formal schooling until he entered secondary school in March 1913. There remains no record of what exactly happened in the intervening period, but it is almost certain that he spent the time at home, probably receiving instruction from a private tutor. Father, however, also took a hand in educating his son. Borges, for instance, retained a particular memory of his father's expressing anarchist ideas to him: "Once he told me that I should take a look at soldiers, uniforms, barracks, flags, churches, priests, and butcher shops since all these things were about to disappear, and I could tell my children that I had actually seen them."[58] But more than politics, what Dr. Borges taught his son were certain basic ideas of philosophy. Borges remembered how Father first awakened his sense of wonder at the strangeness of living: "'What a queer thing,' he said, 'that I should be living, as they say, behind my eyes, inside my head; I wonder if that makes sense?'"[59] Georgie, who had spent most of his life peering out helplessly at the world through the garden gate, "pounced" on that idea, because "I knew what he was saying." He also recalled his father demonstrating to him the paradox of Achilles and the tortoise by using the pieces on a chessboard. Zeno's famous paradox, which proved that the fleet Achilles would never catch up with the tortoise, encapsulated for Borges "the earliest fears and wonders" of his childhood—"being afraid of mirrors, being afraid of mahogany, being afraid of being repeated."[60] He was also introduced to the basic notions of philosophical idealism. Father held up an orange and demonstrated to Georgie how none of its attributes could lead the perceiver to a certain knowledge of its objective existence. And Father explained Plato's theory of forms, according to which there existed a truer world beyond the senses, where things subsisted as pure archetypes.

Such notions would have confirmed Georgie's preexistent impression of the "unreality" of the world around him. And if the reality of the world was unreachable in the present, so, too, was it in the past. Father told him that he found it impossible truly to recall the time when he first came to live in Buenos Aires as a child. He illustrated the point by placing a few coins on top of each other: "The bottom coin would be the first image, for example, of the house of my childhood. Now this second would be a memory I had of that house when I went to Buenos Aires. Then the third one another memory, and so on."[61] This meant that there were no true memories of youth, for each memory was distorted by successive repetition, and "if in every repetition you get a slight distortion, then in the end you will be a long way from the issue." Young Georgie found that "a very saddening thing."

Dr. Borges became a contradictory figure to his son. On the one hand, he had given Georgie a dagger, urging him to be a man, while, on the other, he kept the boy from engaging with the world, confining him instead to the library. The enigma his father represented became the central concern of a brief play Georgie wrote around this time about the legendary Spanish knight Bernardo del Carpio.[62] Handwritten on five sheets, it consists of three very brief scenes. The first has Bernardo del Carpio calling for his sword before setting off to pay a ransom for his father, who is being held prisoner by a wicked king. In scene 2, Bernardo agrees to surrender the ancestral castle of Carpio in exchange for his father's liberty. In the final scene, Bernardo hands over the keys of his castle, offering the king everything in it except for an old dagger and a piece of yellow paper. The king asks what these are worth; Bernardo replies that the dagger belonged to his father and on the yellow paper is inscribed the last thing his father had written. The king now invites Bernardo to meet his father at the door; Bernardo runs to greet him, crying out "Father!" only to discover two servants bearing his dead body. Outraged by this treachery, Bernardo draws his sword, challenges the king to a duel, and puts him to death.

In this little play, Georgie tried to explain his father's contradictory behavior toward him by imagining that he was the captive of a treacherous king. Already certain key ideas have taken root in Borges's imagination—the topic of the duel, the contrast between dagger and sword and, strangest of all, the motif of an internecine trinity, which first appears in this play in the triad of father, son, and king. Notable also is the son's readiness to surrender everything to the king in order to set his father free, except, curiously, his father's dagger and a sample of his writing. It was as if Georgie had intuited that dagger and pen together represented a special bond with his father that he could not bear to lose. The link between the dagger and writing, which is still somewhat vague in this text, would prove to be of great significance for Borges. The dagger had become a symbol of energy and passion through its association with the tiger, but here it was juxtaposed with a piece of yellowing paper on which his father had written his last words.

As is evident from this play, Georgie no longer believed that his father could help him recover the magic power of the dagger. Instead it was to Evaristo Carriego that the boy would turn to lead him out of Father's library and into the reality of the world beyond, for Carriego had achieved what Borges's father had not—he had become a successful author, writing about the world he lived in and winning the acclaim of an enthusiastic public. Indeed, by 1912, at exactly the time that the young Borges had been taken out of school, Carriego was basking in the glory of a considerable reputation as the author of poems about the proletarian barrios of Buenos Aires. His poetic sketches of the typical life of the *orillas* appeared in *Caras y Caretas,* a hugely popular magazine of the day, and his play *Los que pasan (Passersby)* was being performed at the National Theater that year.

There was, nevertheless, something desperate about Carriego's concern with his literary reputation. He would recite his poems in the cafés of Buenos Aires at the first opportunity and would keep referring to "my talent" in conversation, belittling the work of other poets and claiming that only his poetry would last because it was a "document" of everyday life.[63] He reserved an especial loathing for Lugones, a hostility that may not have been unconnnected with the fact that his book, *Las misas herejes,* had been overshadowed by his rival's work. The truth was that Carriego was so hungry for fame because he was suffering from tuberculosis and knew that he had very little time left. He died on October 13, 1912, when he was not yet thirty, leaving one book of symbolist verse and a slim body of poems about the people of the *orillas* of Buenos Aires, which his brother would later collect in a posthumous volume called *La canción del barrio (The Song of the Barrio)*.

Still, this meager legacy was to bear unexpected fruit some fourteen years later, when his young admirer, Jorge Luis Borges, found a rich source of inspiration in Carriego's discovery of the *orillas* as a literary subject. But Carriego's influence on Borges was, I believe, yet more subtle and profound. It was Carriego's revelation of the "magic" of poetry to the young Georgie that encouraged Borges to capture with his pen the magic power he had felt at "the precise moment" he grabbed the dagger his father had offered him. The pen, in short, would become a surrogate for the dagger, which was the weapon of the gauchos and *compadritos* that Carriego so admired. From this seminal connection, Borges was to conceive of an ideal of writing as expressive of the thrill that a tiger man or a *compadrito* might have felt as he drove his knife into the body of an adversary; it was an ideal of writing as rapture, as the simple, unreflective joy of pure being.

In March 1913, less than five months after the death of Carriego, Georgie was sent to secondary school, having passed the entrance examination to the prestigious Colegio Nacional Manuel Belgrano. The boys in his class were roughly his own age, and, unlike those in his primary school, many of them were middle class. Even so, he would not do well at this school; his marks would be below average, and he would perform particularly badly in French, drawing, and geometry.[64] This lack of achievement may well have been due to his delayed and interrupted education so far.

Not long after starting at the Colegio Nacional, he published a story called

"The King of the Jungle" ("El rey de la selva") in the school magazine.[65] Written between March and August of that year, it began by describing the killing of a black panther by a mighty tiger (the king of the jungle of the title). The great tiger is "excited to a frenzy by the smell of blood," but sometime later he is surprised in his lair by an "audacious" creature who shoots an arrow into "its striped fur":

> The King of the Jungle crouched, fixed his ferocious gaze on the intruder, gathered up all his strength, and leaped. Ten paces separated the adversaries, another arrow sank into the broad chest of the King of the Jungle, who let out a terrible roar: the roar of a vanquished beast. And he fell . . . a bloody corpse, at the man's feet.

Georgie was clearly reworking his father's account of the *tigrero* into a fantasy of self-assertion. And in the blood-soaked frenzy felt by the tiger, the boy was attempting to put into words the sensation of power he felt when he held the dagger his father had given him after he had been bullied at school.

Even so, there are traces of self-doubt to be found in the text. Borges dwells on the tiger's ecstatic bloodlust after killing the panther, but the account of the man's victory over the tiger is comparatively muted; it is almost outside the frame of the story, and the weapon employed is not a dagger but a bow and arrow, thus reducing the man's physical contact with his prey. Finally, the *tigrero* remains nameless, and this anonymity is compounded by the curious fact that when the story was published in the school magazine, Georgie chose "Nemo" as his nom de plume, as if this wild fantasy of self-assertion had been undercut by its author's fears that he might turn out to be a nobody after all.

In my view "The King of the Jungle" was Georgie's homage to Evaristo Carriego, given that it was written so soon after the death of the man who had opened his eyes to the connection between the magic of the dagger and the pen. But the hints of self-doubt in the text may be evidence of Georgie's fear that the death of his hero had left him vulnerable to the mysterious passivity that afflicted his father. Perhaps also they reflected his own difficulties in adapting to life at school. Indeed, the period of his attendance at the Colegio Nacional is cloaked in mystery. Borges himself never mentioned it; the few available references to this period come by way of his mother and sister, and they relate to an accident Georgie apparently suffered on his way to school sometime in 1913.

The Colegio Nacional was located about two miles down the avenida Santa Fe from where the Borgeses lived in Palermo, so Georgie used to travel by tram, often accompanied by Roberto Godel, his friend from primary school. Norah Borges was to describe how a police officer turned up at the house one day to report an accident in which Georgie had been involved.[66] Her brother appeared two hours later with a bandaged head and doing his best not to cry. It seems that he had lost his footing as he was trying to board a tram and narrowly missed being run over by the second car. His glasses had been smashed in the fall, and he had suffered two broken teeth and a severe cut to the side of the head.[67] These injuries, however, are consistent with those he might have sustained in a fight with other boys, and, bearing in mind his experience of bullying in primary school, it may be that the bullying did not stop at the Colegio Nacional, which may account for the involvement of the police and his subsequent reluctance to mention this phase of his school career.

Georgie's accident (or a second episode of violent bullying, if such it really was) brought to a head a matter that Dr. Borges may have been mulling over for some time. Borges père seems to have been in a state of considerable gloom in this period. In March 1913, the very month that Georgie started at the Colegio Nacional, he published three sonnets in the respected literary journal *Nosotros*.[68] Under the common title "Momentos" ("Moments"), these poems form a progressive sequence on the theme of love lost through the passing of time. The first expresses the author's anguish at the "grim silence" of his lover, who is "mute" and "numb" to his pleas for love, while he reflects upon his life "in the painful mirror of the past." In the second he bemoans the fact that "the blue night, the hushed garden," "the jasmines whiter than the moon," have been swept away by time, and he wonders whether happiness can be "resurrected." Fearing that "the past never returns," he ends on a note of anguished doubt: "Did I love you? Was it the truth or just a dream?" In the third sonnet, he concludes that, since everything in this life is mutable, "I too should withdraw to other places," yet he extends his hand to his lover, "for the sake of the night that had no orange blossom, / and for the kiss that never found your lips."

Dr. Borges's regret at the passing of time may be explained by the fact that he was approaching the age of forty, and as middle age set in, he missed the passion he had once shared with his young bride, Leonor. The anxiety that time was running out for him would have been sharpened by other factors. The recent death of his young friend Carriego so soon after he had managed to achieve recognition as a writer would have led him to reflect on his own unrealized literary aspirations. And such anxieties could not have been helped by his rapidly deteriorating eyesight, the result of a long-standing problem with cataracts. His eyes were so weak by now that he could scarcely make out the documents he worked on at the law courts.

There were grounds also for his feeling disillusioned with the political situation. An electoral law passed in 1912 was designed to consolidate the vote for the ruling coalition of conservative parties and reinforce the electoral dominance of the oligarchy's political machine. If an anarchist like Dr. Borges had entertained hopes of radical change in Argentina thanks to the rising political agitation of the first decade of the century, the revolutionary moment now appeared to have passed. The renewed complacency of the oligarchy was epitomized by the lectures on the gaucho delivered at the Teatro Odeón by Leopoldo Lugones only a few months after the death of Carriego. Jorge Borges might well have reflected on the irony that Lugones had been a friend and fellow anarchist in his university days but had since become the darling of the ruling class. It would have been particularly galling to observe Lugones pressing the gaucho into service as a national symbol for the liberal establishment and eclipsing the unfortunate Carriego's more populist view of the gaucho as social rebel and hero of the people. In these circumstances Argentina must have seemed an uncongenial place for foreigners and social outsiders like the half-English Jorge Borges, whose "foreign flaw" had always troubled him and led him to question his relation to the country of his birth. Probably, like Carlos Dubois in *El Caudillo,* he was already tempted by the thought of leaving the country altogether and settling with Leonor somewhere in Europe, where he could live in anonymity with his books and even write "a very personal book" of his own.

In 1913 he decided that he would take his family to live in Europe for an indefinite period of time, and possibly for good. He must have arrived at this decision no later than November, since his plan would have involved extensive preparations: he had to obtain extended leave of absence from the School of Modern Languages before the end of the academic year in December, apply for early retirement from the law courts and organize a long-term rental for the family house in Palermo.

In his "Autobiographical Essay," Borges gave the following reasons for the family's decison to leave Argentina:

> The idea of the trip was for my sister and me to go to school in Geneva; we were to live with my maternal grandmother, who traveled with us and eventually died there, while my parents toured the Continent. At the same time, my father was to be treated by a famous Genevan eye doctor.[69]

This account, I believe, retrospectively condenses a more complex set of factors. The chief reason for the trip, as Borges himself indicates, was to give the children a European education. Dr. Borges had a poor opinion of Argentine schools: "My father used to say that Argentine history had taken the place of the catechism, so we were expected to worship all things Argentine. We were taught Argentine history, for example, before we were allowed any knowledge of the many lands and the many centuries that went into its making."[70] Borges would say that his father had wanted him "to become a citizen of the world, a great cosmopolitan," as in the case of Henry and William James, who had been sent to Europe to be educated "so that they would not be . . . well, provincial, let us say."[71] However, it is unlikely that Geneva would have been Dr. Borges's first choice for this purpose. To begin with, the children had little French, if any, whereas the family was fluent in English, and the children had been educated at home for several years by an English governess. Dr. Borges, in any case, "was proud of his English blood,"[72] as was attested by the impressive collection of mainly English books which he had built up over the years. If the aim was to give the children a good education, the most likely destination by far, in the opinion of Borges's nephew Miguel de Torre, would have been England, and probably London.[73]

Another important motive for the journey, according to Miguel de Torre, was Dr. Borges's wish to tour the Continent with his wife.[74] He must have envisaged this tour à deux as a means of revitalizing their relations, given his regrets at the fading of love as expressed in the sonnets he published in *Nosotros* earlier that year. And there was also the matter of finding some remedy for his failing eyesight, but, in Miguel de Torre's view, he would most probably have considered going to London or Paris in the first instance to consult an eye specialist. So why did they go to Geneva? In Borges's own account, the choice was a fairly arbitrary one: his father knew nothing at all about the city, but he chanced upon a photograph showing the Old Town, the Alps, and the Rhône and rather liked the look of the place.[75] He may also have regarded its location as a convenient base to leave Georgie and Norah with their grandmother while he and his wife went on their Continental tour before sending the children to school in England in the autumn of 1914.

On the most plausible configuration of the available evidence, one can outline the following hypothesis: The Borges family's departure from Argentina in 1914 was the result of the decision of a disillusioned man undergoing a personal crisis as he approached the age of forty. According to Borges, his father "was such a modest man that he would have liked being invisible";[76] he "wanted to live in a city in which he would be totally unknown."[77] It is even possible he had a mind to leave Argentina for good, if things went well for them in Europe. The initial plan may have been to settle in London, where his children might receive a better education than he believed to be available in Buenos Aires. But first he and his wife would go on a tour of the Continent, leaving the children with their grandmother in Geneva. Shortly after the family arrived in Geneva, however, a European war broke out, and they decided to remain in neutral Switzerland for the duration.

The Borges family began a decade of wandering early in 1914. Leonor, the children, and their Argentine grandmother, Leonor Suárez, found themselves uprooted from their native soil and driven from place to place by Dr. Borges's inner restlessness. They would live in hotels and rented apartments in a number of different cities; the children's schooling would be broken and their lives disrupted several times over by arbitrary changes of plan. The fact was that Dr. Borges was a fugitive from his own failure to live up to the imaginary memory of the heroic father he had never known, and when he took himself off to Europe with his family, he hoped to compensate for that failure by achieving success as a writer and by recovering, if he could, the passion he had once known with Leonor.

CHAPTER 4

Geneva

(1914–1919)

THE BORGES FAMILY departed Buenos Aires on February 3, 1914, aboard the *Sierra Nevada,* a German ship bound for Bremen. About three weeks later, they arrived at Boulogne and went straight to Paris, where they spent their time sightseeing and visiting museums. In Paris, however, they were detained for several weeks longer than planned on account of a road accident they were involved in on their way to Versailles in an open motorcar in which Leonor Suárez suffered a dislocated arm. Once the old lady had sufficiently recovered, the family traveled on to Geneva, arriving probably in April. On the twenty-fourth of that month they moved into a rented apartment at 17 rue Malagnou (today it is 9 rue Ferdinand Hodler) in the Old Town. This was to be their home until 1918.

Over the next few weeks, Leonor set about equipping the apartment and getting it ready for the children to live in with their grandmother over the summer months while she and her husband went traveling in Europe. Dr. Borges and his wife set off on their tour toward the end of July, but they had not got much farther than Munich when, in the first week of August, they found themselves in the middle of a continent that had gone to war. They managed to get back to neutral Switzerland, but it was clear that they must revise their plans regarding the children's education, since it would have been unwise in the circumstances to take them to London. They therefore decided to stay in Geneva and send the children to school there.

The school chosen for Georgie was the Collège de Genève, which had been founded by John Calvin in 1559 and was a short walk away from where they lived. As for Norah, there were fewer concerns about getting her into a school, and she appears to have been educated at home, where she spent much of her time painting, until she was eventually admitted to the École des Beaux-Arts at the age of fourteen. The question of Georgie's schooling did not prove straightforward. There was a problem about his age: he had turned fifteen that August and was too old for admission to the first year at the Collège de Genève. Dr. Borges resolved this problem by pretending his son was a year younger, giving

Georgie's date of birth as August 24, 1900. Then there was the not inconsiderable problem of Georgie's having little if any French. It was urgent, therefore, that he learn enough of the language to cope when he started school a few weeks later. He was found a teacher in the neighboring town of Annemasse, where he would cycle every day for his French classes that summer.

It could not have been easy for Georgie, with his experience of constant bullying in Buenos Aires, to start at a school in a foreign city whose language he had not had the time to master and knowing, moreover, that he had got in under false pretenses regarding his age. He would never be particularly happy at school. He was put in a class of forty-three boys, most of whom were up to four years younger than he was. (Only one boy had been born in 1900; the rest had dates of birth between 1901 and 1903.)[1] Despite being so much older than most of his classmates, he did not shine in any way at his studies, largely because of his difficulties with French and also, no doubt, because of the belated and interrupted schooling he had so far experienced. Although he was not bullied at the Collège de Genève, he found it hard to get on with the other boys. About half the class were Genevois, and most of the others came from various Swiss cantons and turned up at school in their regional dress. But, as he soon found out, it was "very difficult to have a Swiss friend," and it was with the foreign boys, those who were refugees from the war, that he felt most at ease.[2] In Geneva, then, Georgie felt as cut off from other people as he had been in Buenos Aires, only it was all so thoroughly unfamiliar that he was homesick for Argentina. To his former schoolmate Roberto Godel, he wrote that his constant wish was to return to Buenos Aires,[3] and in several letters to his adored grandmother, Fanny Haslam, he wrote of the things he missed about home.[4]

As ever, he took refuge in books. He no longer had the run of his father's library, but he plunged nevertheless into the aimless reading he had become used to and would never really give up. The family had brought over a few Argentine and English books, and when his French improved, he took out a subscription to a circulating library and lapped up melodrama and tales of high adventure, such as the novels of "Gyp," the Comtesse de Martel, who wrote about star-crossed aristocratic lovers; he remembered weeping over Gyp's *Une Passionette*, the story of a baroness who commits suicide after being deserted by her lover. Another of his favorites was Alphonse Daudet's *Tartarin de Tarascon*, a comic novel about a man who keeps telling tall stories about his extraordinary adventures and then has to try to back them up in real life. He was to graduate to more serious reading, however—Zola's *Rougon-Macquart* novels, Maupassant, Victor Hugo, whose poetry he greatly preferred to his fiction, and Flaubert, for whom he retained a lifelong admiration.

If Georgie found it hard to settle in Geneva, his sister, Norah, rapidly acclimatized to the new environment—too rapidly, if anything, the rest of the family thought. In March 1915, Georgie complained to Godel that Norah kept using French words when speaking Spanish in the family. She even started to dream in French, and one day Mother found her cowering behind the curtains crying, *"Une mouche! Une mouche!"* having got hold of the French idea that flies were dangerous. Dona Leonor was not impressed. "You come out of there," she scolded, "you were born and bred among flies."[5] But the girl was clearly thriving—not only doing extremely well at her art but also writing poetry. She was to put together a little volume of eight poems, with accompanying drawings, and call it *Notas lejanas* (*Notes from Afar*).

There is no evidence of any writing by Georgie at this time, however. And he continued to perform indifferently at school. His grades were unimpressive in the examinations at the end of his first year, in June. He did best in Latin and well enough at history, natural sciences, and bookkeeping; he scraped through in German, failed in drawing and physical education, and for music (which largely involved singing) he was given a mark of zero.[6] But, crucially, he failed in French, and this meant that he would not be allowed to proceed to the second year of the course, so he faced the embarrassing prospect of having to start the first year of secondary education all over again at the age of sixteen. Even though Georgie had made few friends, his classmates nevertheless came to the rescue and wrote to the headmaster requesting that he be admitted to the second year in consideration of the enormous effort involved in having to work at all his other subjects through the medium of French, a language he had not had time to learn properly. So he passed into the second year, but he would never be the most assiduous of students, and his grades were never remarkable. Having got used to following his own interests since he was very young, he found that the reading he did at home was far more stimulating than the routine of studying his school subjects. The one exception was Latin, at which he was quite good. He retained a fondness for reading passages of Virgil, Tacitus, and Seneca. He also mentioned keeping a copy of Tacitus's *Germania* in the original and in English translation on the shelf of his bedroom at home.[7]

Georgie continued with his lonely, book-ridden existence in the bosom of his family. At the end of 1915, their number increased to six when Fanny Haslam arrived in Geneva, having braved the German U-boats during the long sea voyage. She must have arrived in time to spend Christmas with them, for on January 19, 1916, she had already received her *permis de séjour* in Geneva.[8] Fanny had remained in Buenos Aires to be with her sister, Caroline, but on the latter's death in July 1915, she joined her son and his family in Europe. In the first months of the New Year, they received a visit from some Argentine relatives, and there is a photograph of Georgie surrounded by the women of the family, including their female visitors Jacinta, Dayla, and Clara Mendoza Haedo, handsome, bright-eyed, nubile girls. Georgie was now fifteen and a half, and there certainly were erotic stirrings—he mentioned keeping a book "on the sexual customs of the Balkans" hidden in his bedroom, but if he had any romantic feelings for any of the girls, he kept them to himself.[9]

The most significant event in his bookish life was his discovery of Thomas Carlyle, the first in a series of writers whom he would hero-worship in his youth. Through Carlyle he encountered Schopenhauer and the idea of the will as a creative force in an otherwise illusory world of appearances. He was to say of Schopenauer, "If the riddle of the universe can be stated in words, I think these words would be in his writings."[10] He decided to teach himself German in order to read Schopenhauer in the original. He had done two years of German at school, though he was not terribly good at it, but he acquired a concise English-German dictionary and threw himself in at the deep end, choosing Goethe's *Faust* and Kant's *Critique of Pure Reason,* no less, as primers in the language. He was soon floundering and turned to Heine's *Lyrisches Intermezzo,* which he could manage much better. Once his command of the language was good enough, he began to "read and reread Schopenhauer in German."[11] He would persevere with his reading in philosophy, building on what his father had taught him as a boy. A favorite sourcebook was Fritz Mauthner's dictionary, which was "really a collection of essays on different subjects, such as the soul, the world, mind, consciousness, etc.," which he "consulted with the greatest pleasure."[12]

During his first three years in Switzerland, the young Borges and his sister led a sheltered existence with mostly their family for company. Norah, who started at the École des Beaux-Arts in 1915, recalled their routine: "We used to go to bed early because we had to get up early to go to school. We had to be there by eight and in winter it was very cold. . . . In the evenings we would stay at home either doing our homework or playing together, and Georgie would always think up things to do to pass the time."[13]

This dearth of social contacts affected the whole family. The Swiss had a "certain disdain for the foreigner," Borges would tell an interviewer, Antonio Carrizo, and "one always remained something of a tourist."[14] It may have been the tedium of this secluded existence that eventually took its toll on the relationship between Dr. Borges and his wife. After a while the handsome Jorge Guillermo Borges returned to his errant ways: he appears to have frequented prostitutes and liked to pick up pretty women in the street, and it is also very likely that he had one or two mistresses during his years in Geneva—Borges would tell a friend that his father had conducted an affair with the wife of a painter who lived in one of the apartments above theirs.[15] Indeed, Leonor Acevedo used to tell a curious story about her wayward husband's philandering in Geneva. A man came up to her once in the street and started to proposition her; she looked round and saw it was none other than her husband, whose sight was so poor that he had failed to recognize his own wife. "Why, Jorge," she exclaimed, "won't you even leave me alone!"[16]

In 1917, after he had lived in Switzerland for nearly three years, Georgie's isolated existence at last came to an end when he got to know another youth his own age, Maurice Abramowicz. What sparked their friendship was their common interest in literature, and it may have been Abramowicz who introduced him to the French symbolist poets whose work he first read in an anthology published by *Le Mercure de France*. He claimed to have learned Baudelaire's *Les Fleurs du mal* by heart with Abramowicz, as well as Rimbaud's *Le Bateau ivre*, which he could recite almost word-perfect decades later.[17]

At about this time, he told his parents that he wanted to become a writer, and he began to write poetry, mostly sonnets in French and English. One of his earliest compositions was a little symbolist poem called "Pièce pour être récité avec un accent russe," which included the line "La petite boîte noire pour le violon cassé," and he also wrote some "poor imitations of Wordsworth."[18] He even tried his hand at writing verse in Latin with the help of Guicherat's *Gradus ad Parnassum*.[19] But as far as we know, he wrote nothing in Spanish, which might be taken as a sign of his deracination after three years or so living away from his native land. He tried to establish some bond with his father through their common interest in literature, but Dr. Borges once again showed a curious indifference to his son's aspirations. "I wanted to show my manuscripts to my father, but he told me he didn't believe in advice and that I must work my way all by myself through trial and error."[20]

Possibly through Abramowicz, he got to know another boy, Simon Jichlinski, who shared their interest in writing. These two boys, who were roughly his own age, became the first real friends he ever had, and the fact that they were Jewish may explain his enduring affection for the Jews and their culture. He would go swimming and recite poetry on the banks of the Rhône with his new friends, and he began to stay out late at night, visiting alehouses and wandering the streets, "discussing everything and nothing," a habit he was to keep up for most of his life.[21] He taught his Swiss friends to play the Argentine card game *truco*, and they were such quick learners that he was left without a centime at the end of their first session together.

The bond of adolescent comradeship he had established with Abramowicz and Jichlinski helped him loosen his ties to his overprotective family. In 1917 he became more conscious of the European war. He read Henri Barbusse's antiwar novel *Le Feu*, about life in the trenches and the carnage that was taking place on the Western Front. Through his discussions with his two friends,

Georgie was able to appreciate the broader political issues thrown up by the terrible European war. Another author he read was Romain Rolland, through whom he may have first encountered socialist ideas. He recalled that in 1917 people used to say that Rolland's novel *Jean Christophe* was "the password of the new generation."[22] And it was this sense of belonging to a new generation that led him to reject the society that had made possible the calamity of the Great War. A word that crops up from time to time in his correspondence in these years is *occidentalismo*—Georgie and his friends were opposed to the capitalist system of the West and were drawn to revolutionary ideas, especially the belief that it was their generation that must put an end to an unjust and corrupt social order. They looked eastward to Russia: the abdication of the czar in February 1917 appeared to herald the birth of a new society. Georgie and his friends followed with avid interest the revolutionary events that were unfolding and called themselves "maximalists," because, like Lenin and the Bolsheviks, they believed in the total overthrow of capitalism.

Borges's opposition to militarism and his support for revolutionary socialism led him to make one of the most important literary discoveries of his youth: he came across German expressionism, whose impact on his aesthetic ideas would be decisive and long lasting. Expressionism was an avant-garde movement that had emerged in Germany in the first decade of the century. The expressionists broke with the conventions of naturalistic representation in literature or the visual arts and sought to convey their individual response to the physical world by refracting sense experience through feeling and imagination. The movement flourished during the First World War in reaction to the senseless carnage and became associated with an antibourgeois, revolutionary spirit. It was to endure in the German-speaking countries after the war, but it spread widely in Europe and would exert a multifaceted influence on the modern art movement of the twentieth century. German expressionism appealed to Borges as a budding writer in Geneva because it was in accord with certain profound intuitions that he had harbored as a child. The intense emotionalism of the expressionists corresponded to his sense of the magic of poetry, of writing as rapture. And since it conceived of art as an interaction between the individual and the world, expressionism also validated his sense of the pen as a weapon, like the tiger man's dagger, through which the writer could connect with reality.

Toward the end of 1917, he wrote to Roberto Godel in Buenos Aires that he had been reading the young writers of Germany—Johannes v. Becher, Franz Pfemfert, Otto Ernst Herre, Max Pauluer, Gustav Meyrink, Franz Werfel, Hasenclever, and many others, who were all opposed to militarism, as much as Godel was himself.[23] Forsaking Thomas Carlyle, Borges now adopted the German expressionist Johannes Becher as his literary hero and would describe him thus: "the greatest poet in Germany, and one of the leading poets of the pluricordial (*pluricorde*) European epic. Crucified on the mutilated torso of Europe, he sang, in hymnals full of oceanic resonances, the epic of war and revolution, of agony and resurrection. . . . His poems reach us from the barricades of Berlin—flexible bridges of steel brightened by the loftiest banners of metaphor."[24] However, Becher's preeminence in Georgie's literary pantheon would not last long: he was shortly displaced by Walt Whitman, whom Borges discovered through the expressionists. He first read *Leaves of Grass* in a German translation but sent off to London for the English original. Thereafter Whitman would become a model of the ideal writer for Borges, since he regarded Whitman's poetry as the supreme example of writing as rapture, possessing, as he saw it, a passion and vitality that he would pursue in his own writing for most of his life.

The year 1917 would be a watershed for Georgie. His friendship with Abramowicz and Jichlinski, his interest in socialism and expressionism, were causing him to break out of the protective cocoon his family had spun round him. His impatience to cut free is evident in his decision to drop out of high school after his third year, with two more years of the course to go before completing his *baccalauréat*. But he would turn eighteen in August, so if he stayed on at the Collège de Genève, he would not finish his secondary education until he was twenty. He decided instead to enroll at an institute in September, and, as he explained to Godel, he proposed to cram the two remaining years of the *baccalauréat* into one.[25]

This was to be a momentous autumn for Georgie. In October the Bolsheviks seized power in Russia, while the situation in Germany, too, seemed to be moving toward another revolutionary crisis, as political agitation, mutinies, and riots threatened to overturn the monarchy. Even in his personal life, he was to experience a revolutionary upheaval of sorts. Shortly after starting at the institute, he met a young Czech woman from Prague called Adrienne, who, at twenty-five, was several years older than he, but thanks to her he discovered what he called the "Great Theme," by which he meant the delightful business of falling in love, albeit unrequited in this case.[26] This amorous "crisis," as he called it, was to last some three months, and he would inquire of his friend Roberto Godel whether he had ever been in love, whether he had tossed and turned in bed thinking about a girl, prepared compliments he could not bring himself to utter, blushed whenever he saw her.[27] The fortuitous combination of love and revolution made for a heady brew, and when he wrote to Godel on December 4, 1917, he was bursting with optimism about the possibility of a revolution in Germany.[28] His hopes had been raised by some recent events—the attempted uprising in the navy, the riots in Berlin, and, of course, the glorious Russian Revolution. He desired a revolution with all his heart, he told Godel, and assured his friend that the young German intellectuals would welcome such a revolution with enthusiasm.

The political awakening that Georgie and his two Genevan friends underwent in 1917 was to stay with them for the rest of their lives. Abramowicz and Jichlinski would remain Communists, although Borges's trajectory would be more tortuous, partly because of the idiosyncrasies of his upbringing, but also on account of the very checkered political history of Argentina during his lifetime. Even so, he never lost sight of the legacy of 1917: he would always retain a strong sense of the political responsibilities of the writer and would never quite abandon his belief in the need for a radical transformation of society. Indeed, that belief would be dramatically reborn at the very end of his life, when he was to embrace once more the antimilitarist and revolutionary spirit of his early youth in Geneva.

The winter of 1917–18 was particularly hard: the snow came early, and they all suffered badly from the cold in their gloomy apartment. To make things worse, food was in short supply as the Swiss authorities introduced strict rationing to cope with the shortages occasioned by the war. More than ever Switzerland seemed cold and inhospitable. Possibly on account of Adrienne's lack of interest in him, he felt low, and he complained to Godel that he and his family were dragging along with their boring lives; he was on the lookout for a new girlfriend, but it was hard going, because even though easy girls were two a penny, he was shy with women, and, in any case, not only were the girls of Geneva exceptionally ugly, they also stank to high heaven.[29]

Much of his time was spent reading Russian novels—*Crime and Punishment,* he told Godel, was the best novel he had ever read; he was also trying his hand at writing what he called parables, and by the spring he had produced a couple of these parables, entitled "The Prophet" ("El profeta") and "The Hero" ("El héroe"), which he sent to a popular magazine in Buenos Aires called *Caras y Caretas,* although there is no record that they were ever published, and are no longer extant.[30]

That winter the Spanish influenza epidemic began to sweep across Europe, taking a terrible toll of lives. Leonor Suárez, who was an old lady of eighty-one, fell victim to it and became very ill. Doctors advised that she would fare much better in a warmer climate, and the family decided it was safe enough to take her to Spain for a while. Georgie was very keen to visit Spain, the homeland of his ancestors and his race, as he described it to Godel, but he welcomed the prospect also because he had wasted a lot of his time and was scared of taking his exams; he had in any case conceived a hearty loathing of Switzerland: it was terribly bourgeois, a place of hotels and chocolate factories.[31]

The family planned to leave Geneva for Spain in the middle of June, and they gave notice to their landlord that they would quit their apartment in the first week of that month. Leonor Suárez's condition, however, became very grave: she developed a high fever and kept lapsing into unconsciousness. The whole family was distraught—they gathered around the bed, stroking her face and holding her hand. "There we all were, standing over her, touching her, weeping, not knowing what to say or do, when, in a rare moment of lucidity, my grandmother opened her eyes, looked at us and said in a faint but quite clear voice, 'Oh, *carajo,* why don't you just let me die in peace.'"[32] They were amazed that the old lady should have uttered this obscene expletive, except for Dr. Borges, her anarchist son-in-law, who observed, "Well, that's not bad for the daughter of Colonel Suárez."

Leonor Suárez died on June 6, after a long and painful illness. Her death meant that the family's trip to Spain had to be abandoned, and they were detained in Geneva indefinitely in order to sort out probate and other legal matters. Since they had already given notice to quit their apartment, they moved to a hotel, where it was at least warmer than at the rue Malagnou. Then another unforeseen complication arose when they heard from the Argentine consulate in Geneva that Georgie had been called up for military service by the Ministry of War in Buenos Aires.[33] However, they persuaded the Argentine authorities to delay Georgie's call-up pending a medical examination to determine his fitness for military service on account of his extreme myopia.

Although Georgie had been looking forward to leaving Geneva for Spain, he would change his mind a few weeks later when he met a Swiss girl called Emilie and fell in love with her. This time his feelings were reciprocated, so that by the early summer of 1918, Georgie had at last found his first sweetheart. Hardly anything is known about this girl. In an undated letter to Roberto Godel, written from Lugano not too long after his nineteenth birthday, Georgie refers to a girl in Geneva with whom he was falling seriously in love, and in the next letter he wrote to Godel, there is a passing reference to a girl called Emilie.[34] A fuller picture of her can be found in a prose poem called "An Interlude of Passion" ("Paréntesis pasional") that is set in Geneva, though actually written in Seville in 1920.[35] Here she is referred to as the Beloved (La Amada), and Borges describes taking her to a *bierkeller* one evening where they drink wine before making passionate love that night. (This was almost certainly a wishful fantasy, although there must have been some vigorous sexual contact.) She has green eyes, a "glowing mane" of red hair and a "dazzling body." There are hints that she comes from a humble background—the "Beloved" mentions a "workshop" and a "cabin." This impression of her lowly social status is reinforced by an allusion to a red-haired girl that can be found in a letter written in about March or April 1922 by Borges, who was by then in Buenos Aires, to a Spanish friend, Jacobo Sureda, who was living in Switzerland: "Have you been lucky enough to meet up again with that laundress of the flaming red hair with whom I thought I was in love a very long time ago?"[36]

In the summer of 1918, as he approached his nineteenth birthday, Georgie was a young man enjoying his first experience of mutual love. However, he must have been aware that his relations with Emilie would lead to conflict with his mother, for if Georgie's sweetheart belonged to the working class, there can be no doubt that she would have been regarded as totally unsuitable by Leonor Acevedo, proud granddaughter that she was of Colonel Suárez, the Hero of Junín. If anything, the likelihood of Mother's disapproval appears to have whetted Georgie's desire for the girl. Emilie's red hair was emblematic of forbidden fruit, for the color red was powerfully symbolic in the context of family tradition—it was the color of the *federales* and the tyrant Rosas, the color, in other words, of barbarism. And yet in "An Interlude of Passion," Borges revels in the forbidden color—the girl's tresses are as red as the wine they are drinking; his palate is "a red yoke" that "straddles" the "red flame" of her tongue. Emilie must have personified for him the freedom he had tasted in 1917, her red hair signifying a combination of passion and rebellion, so that through his love for her he would feel strong enough to defy the will of Mother and attain to that invigorating self-possession he had once envied in the tiger at Palermo Zoo.

Strangely enough, though, in the letter he wrote his friend Sureda in 1922, Borges would recall red hair in somewhat negative terms, associating it with misfortune: "In Spanish the word *bermejía* is used to describe that bad luck which people with red hair [*bermeja* = vermilion] can sometimes bring us. But why am I giving you this pedantic information?"[37] The reason may well have been that, nearly four years after he had left Geneva, he still associated the red-haired Emilie with unhappiness and bad luck, and he must surely have had in mind in this regard the personal crisis he underwent only a matter of weeks after he had found his first girlfriend.

At around the time of Georgie's nineteenth birthday on August 24, Dr. Borges asked his son whether he had ever slept with a woman, and when Georgie replied that he had not, Father resolved to do something to help the youth negotiate the usual rites of passage to manhood. It was the custom in Argentina for fathers or uncles to arrange for the initiation of adolescent males with a prostitute in a brothel,[38] and so, in accordance with this practice, Dr. Borges gave Georgie the address of a flat on the place du Bourg-de-Four, which was in the red-light district not too far from where they lived, and told him that a woman would be waiting there.[39] Most young men approach their first experience of sexual intercourse with considerable apprehension, and when Borges finally reached the woman's flat, he was in a state of high anxiety. As it turned out, it appears that he was too precipitate in his approach and did not fully go through with his initiation. This unsurprising adolescent setback, however, seems to have been exceptionally traumatic for Georgie—in a poem written over thirty years later, he would refer to this encounter in what he called a mercenary bedroom in Europe, with excessive, self-punishing shame.[40]

Norah Borges had some memory of the upset her brother experienced as a result of this episode, though she was not aware of its cause at the time.[41] Father was evidently at a loss to understand what had gone wrong. The matter appears to have been discussed with Mother, which must have caused Georgie considerable embarrassment, since the subject of sex had hitherto been completely taboo in the family. He was taken to see a doctor, who diagnosed a weak liver and prescribed a course of treatment to beef him up.[42] A change of climate was also recommended, as well as fresh air and exercise.[43] In the circumstances Dr. Borges decided to take the entire family to Lugano, which was close to the Italian border, possibly so that Georgie might better recover his strength in the milder climate of southern Switzerland. But this decision was nothing short of a disaster for Georgie, of course, since it meant that he would be parted from Emilie only a few months after they had fallen in love.

In Lugano the family stayed at the celebrated Hotel du Lac, which overlooked the lake and afforded wonderful views of the surrounding mountains. Georgie, however, was too upset to derive much benefit from his surroundings. In a letter written to Roberto Godel from Lugano,[44] he acknowledged the magnificent beauty of the place—the blue lake, the high mountains forming a sort of amphitheater around the city, the houses on the waterfront, everything indeed was beautiful, and yet, such beauty served only to fill him with disgust. He told Godel that, as the fortunate denizen of flat lands, he could scarcely imagine how depressing it was to be near high mountains—they seemed to cast an eternal shadow, besieging, oppressing, annihilating, pulverizing, stifling, and crushing one's spirit. He couldn't stand the people of Lugano: they were so Italian, so common, so loud, such show-offs; hearing them made him think he was back in Argentina. The girls of Lugano were very dark and quite vulgar; odd as it might seem, brunettes had always given him the impression of being dirty. No doubt Godel would think this bad mood of his had deep and unknown roots, but the reason for it was very simple: he had left a girl in Geneva with whom he was beginning to fall seriously in love. The family's trip to Lugano had forced him to leave her suddenly. Still, they were writing to each other all the time, and he had promised he would be back soon. Borges's anger was rattling away inside him, but he managed—just—to prevent his bad temper from boiling over into the letter he was writing his Argentine friend. Clearly he was tempted to confide in someone, and yet he was embarrassed to disclose the roots of his foul humor. Instead he told Godel that he was suffering from a terrible headache.

The encounter with the woman at the place du Bourg-de-Four had undermined his self-confidence. In arranging for his son's initiation, Father must have seemed once more to be placing a dagger in Georgie's hand and ordering him, as in the case of the bullies at school, to *"let them know you are a man."* However, Borges would later tell friends that, as he made his way to the place of assignation, he was struck by the thought that if his father had given him the address of the woman, he might well have had relations with her himself.[45] The encounter thus created a psychological difficulty for Borges in reconciling love with desire. Ever since his tantrums before the tiger's cage at the zoo, he had seen defiance of Mother's authority as the key to his own freedom, but the assignation in Geneva appears to have induced a sense of having colluded with Father in an indirect betrayal of Mother. Rebellion was one thing, betrayal quite another. Henceforward, rebellion against Mother would smack of infamy and dishonor, and never more so than in his relations with the opposite sex.

Borges, indeed, would experience an intense ambivalence toward women. On the one hand, he regarded love as the gateway to personal fulfillment and as entailing, therefore, a rebellion against the oppressive authority of the sword of honor: he would be drawn, in consequence, to women of whom Mother would not approve, and these women would be idolized as "goddesses" who had the power, he fancied, to bring him unutterable happiness. On the other hand, he was wary of putting himself to the test with these forbidden "goddesses," because desire was so strongly associated with degradation and shame that sexual activity could be conducted only in the illicit obscurity of the brothel. This extreme dissociation of love and sex placed him in a double bind—if he loved fully, he would betray Mother, yet if he did not, he would betray his heart's desire.

Georgie's bad mood lasted the whole time the family spent in Lugano. He would shut himself up in his room to read instead of taking fresh air and exercise. From time to time, he would be persuaded to take his sister out on the lake, and Norah remembered him declaiming Baudelaire and Rimbaud as he rowed her along in a boat.[46] At last in November they learned that the war was over. Georgie had gone out for a walk with his father when they caught sight of a billboard announcing the German surrender. They rushed back to the hotel to tell the others, and the whole family rejoiced that the war had ended in a victory for the Allies. Finally they were free to travel as they pleased. They decided to spend several months touring Spain, after which they would return to Switzerland so that Georgie could finish his high school education and Dr.

Borges resume treatment for his failing sight. But first the family went back to Geneva to prepare for the journey, and in January or February of 1919 they left for Spain on a train that took them across the South of France to Barcelona, where they would stay for two or three months.

Georgie left Switzerland with a heavy heart. He no longer wanted to go to Spain: he wrote to Godel from Barcelona that he was sad to leave Geneva—and when he had said good-bye to Emilie, the poor thing had looked terribly sad, too.[47] He observed to Godel that there was nothing more common in Geneva than to see couples in parks going about arm in arm or wrapped around each other, embracing and kissing with wonderful audacity.[48] No one found this shocking, no one mocked or complained; people just minded their own business. In Barcelona, by contrast, he had yet to see a single couple since he arrived.

The young Borges must have reflected on the possibility that, if his budding love affair with Emilie had not been unwittingly disrupted by his father, if he had been able to embrace and kiss the girl with the openness other couples were allowed in Geneva, he might have found the emotional fulfillment he so much desired. The taste of that first, all-too-brief experience of innocent love with Emilie would never be forgotten. Geneva would linger in Borges's memory as a place of unrealized promise, a place where he had glimpsed, and then lost, the chance of happiness.

CHAPTER 5

Spain

(1919–1921)

BARCELONA FAILED to make much of an impression on Borges—he was put off by the dirt and the noise.[1] The family may have stayed in the city for a couple of months, but after a time they decided to visit Majorca "because it was cheap, beautiful, and had hardly any tourists but ourselves."[2] Again, not much is known about this first sojourn of the Borges family in Majorca in 1919, not even the length of their stay, which may have extended to about six months. What is certain is that they found the island highly congenial after having endured the long years of the war in cold, damp Geneva, not to speak of the more recent trauma of Leonor Suárez's death. In Palma they stayed in a hotel opposite the little Church of San Miguel in the heart of the old town. They were enchanted by the city, especially by the historic quarter, with its stately cathedral and the old Moorish castle of La Almudaina overlooking the sea. And, unlike in Geneva, they found it easy to meet people. In the beautiful mountain village of Valldemosa, they got to know the Sureda family, one of the wealthiest on the island, who lived in a Moorish palace near the monastery where George Sand had wintered with Chopin. Don Juan Sureda and his wife, Pilar Montaner, a leading painter, liked to entertain interesting foreign visitors to Majorca. They had twelve children, the eldest of whom, Jacobo, was living at home, having been forced to give up his studies at Madrid University after contracting tuberculosis. A painter like his mother, and a budding poet, Jacobo was roughly the same age as Georgie, and the two young men soon became friends.

Borges's father was captivated by the sensuous delights of life on this Mediterranean island. Majorca certainly lit a creative spark, and he was to embark on a Spanish verse translation of Edward Fitzgerald's classic English rendering of the *Rubáiyát* of Omar Khayyám. The Persian love poet's hedonism strongly appealed to Dr. Borges: "Omar's philosophical attitude is very simple. All is contained in the present moment, which is the shadow of the past and rushes forward into nothingness. One must embrace in the present the brief pleasures afforded by time."[3] He also made a start on *El Caudillo,* the novel he was to regard as his life's work. Indeed, there is evidence to suggest that during this springtime in Majorca, he rediscovered with his wife Leonor the kind of passion he had been seeking when he left Buenos Aires in 1914. In a poem glossing the biblical Song of Songs, he cast himself as the lover to whom the Shulamite returns after she has spurned the great King Solomon himself. Her beauty is dark as the night, and on her breath there "burns" a "nuptial song"; her mouth is the "ember" that love has ignited "to acclaim the triumph of the hours in siestas swollen with passion."[4]

Georgie, too, felt inspired to write in Majorca, and he was to produce the first poems he would feel confident enough to publish. Like his father, he wrote about the awakening of the senses, employing terms and images that echo the older man's exultant hedonism. The transports of joy that bring his father's "Song of Songs" ("El cantar de los cantares") to a close—"Oh tower of ivory! Oh flame of gold . . . ! Oh lamp of silver in my night!"—would resonate in his son's memory down the years. Half a century later that serial exclamation— "Oh! . . . . Oh! . . . . Oh!"—would resurface in *The Congress* (*El Congreso*), a novella Borges wrote to mark the resolution of the conflicts that his father had done so much to sow. But in Majorca young Georgie's erotic dreams remained stubbornly unfulfilled. His poem "The Flame" ("La llama") is a lament for those like himself who long "to be dazzled and lose ourselves in feasts of passion—in the crucifixion of quivering bodies," but for whom life is like "an ember of a fire that went out centuries ago—the last echo of an extinguished voice."[5]

Georgie sought relief in swimming, always a deeply satisfying activity for this awkward boy. In Majorca, what was more, he found he could "astonish the natives" with his "fine swimming," having learned "in swift rivers, such as the Uruguay and the Rhône, while Majorcans were used only to a quiet, tideless sea."[6] And it was in the sea that he would come closest to the sensual abandon of his parents. In his "Hymn to the Sea" ("Himno del mar") he portrays himself "athletic and naked," surrendering to his "brother Sea" and savoring an "instant of magnificent plenitude," which he strives to capture in images of wild abandon—the sun "flutters like a scarlet banner over the waters," the sea kisses "the golden breasts of virginal beaches," hurling "blasphemous cries to the wind"; he and the sea "have known each other for centuries": he has "emerged from the sea" and plunges into it once more to experience that glorious "instant" in which he can forget everything in the past, for "only you exist"—"Brother, Father, Lover!"[7] Years later he would observe about his "Hymn to the Sea" that he had tried his hardest to be Walt Whitman, and he dismissed this style of writing, in Arnold Bennett's phrase, as "the third-rate grandiose."[8] Even so, it was the first time he had managed to put into words what was in fact the driving force of his will and imagination: the urge to transcend his inveterate conflicts and become one with the world in the sweet oblivion of true being.

The Borgeses left Majorca in the early autumn, by which time Georgie's friendship with Jacobo Sureda had become so close that he found it very hard to part. What made leaving so painful for him was the thought that Jacobo's tuberculosis was terminal and he would probably never see his friend again. Georgie felt that the young Spaniard's "soul was full of suicide," and, with a typically adolescent sense of melodrama, rather "envied" that death wish, since he was feeling so miserable himself.[9]

Before embarking on the next leg of their Spanish tour, they visited Ibiza and then crossed to the mainland at Valencia, traveling down the coast to Granada and Málaga. Finally they arrived in Seville in the late autumn and decided to stay in the city, possibly until Christmas. "After that," Georgie wrote to Abramowicz, "we shall leave for Córdoba and Madrid. Then we return to Geneva via Barcelona."[10] One of the reasons for the length of their stay in Seville may have been that both Georgie and his father were able to make certain contacts in the literary world there and saw an opportunity to have their work published for the first time. (While in Majorca Georgie had had a story about a werewolf rejected by a Madrid newspaper.) Majorca, after all, was a cultural backwater, whereas Seville was a major city with a long tradition of producing writers of the first rank.

Borges arrived in Seville at a time when a group of young poets was in the process of discovering the European avant-garde. He first made contact with this group when he attended a lecture at the Theosophical Society (Centro de Estudios Teosóficos) given by a young man called Adriano del Valle. The Spaniard was immediately struck by this "family of artists," and recalled that first impression of the myopic Jorge Luis, wearing spectacles like "convex mirrors," and his sister, Norah, with her "pyramids of laughter."[11] Through Adriano, Borges was to meet Isaac del Vando Villar, the editor of a literary review called *Grecia* and a well-known figure in the Sevillian literary scene. These poets belonged to a movement known informally as "the Ultra." It had come into being about a year earlier, when a fellow Sevillian, the writer Rafael Cansinos-Asséns, who was based in Madrid, had called for young poets to be "Ultra-Romantic," by which he meant they should go beyond the worn-out rhetoric and themes of contemporary Spanish poetry. In effect the Ultra became the means by which some very young Spaniards got together to explore the poetic revolution that had been set in motion, largely in Italy and France, in the first decade of the century. When Borges arrived in Seville, the *Grecia* people formed a kind of outpost of the Ultra, whose center was in Madrid, but they did what they could to be *au fait* with current trends—on May 2, 1919, they had held a public reading of work by Apollinaire and Marinetti, and on November 20, *Grecia* published a selection of French avant-garde poems by Tristan Tzara, Francis Picabia, Pierre Reverdy, and Jean Cocteau, among others. In old age Borges chose to mock the *Grecia* poets for their provincialism:

> This group, who called themselves ultraists, had set out to renew literature, a branch of the arts of which they knew nothing whatever. One of them once told me his whole reading had been the Bible, Cervantes, Darío, and one or two of the books of the Master, Rafael Cansinos-Asséns. It baffled my Argentine mind to learn that they had no French and no inkling at all that such a thing as English literature existed. I was even introduced to a local worthy popularly known as "the Humanist" and was not long in discovering that his Latin was far smaller than mine. As for *Grecia* itself, the editor, Isaac del Vando Villar, had the whole corpus of his poetry written for him by one or another of his assistants. I remember one of them telling me one day, "I'm very busy—Isaac is writing a poem."[12]

Far from despising them at the time, however, the young Borges was eager to be accepted by the Sevillian ultraists, and he was warmly welcomed into the group. There he rediscovered the pleasures of male camaraderie, something he had scarcely known other than latterly in Geneva with Abramowicz and Jichlinski, and to a degree with Sureda in Majorca. Adriano del Valle became his closest friend, but Georgie was very keen, too, on Isaac del Vando Villar, whom he would refer to in letters as "the great Isaac." There may well have been a degree of self-interest in this professed admiration, for he was anxious to see his work in print and it was "the great Isaac" who would give him his first break when he accepted Georgie's "Hymn to the Sea," with a dedication to Adriano del Valle, for publication in *Grecia*.

Borges's knowledge of the avant-garde was really not much greater than that of the *ultraístas*. He wrote rather dismissively to Abramowicz, "The whole of this Spanish *ultraísta* movement is closely related to German Expressionism and Italian Futurism. As far as I am concerned, Whitman is still the Master."[13] Yet more than Whitman, it was his own father's poetry, such as it was, that exerted the greatest influence on his writing, though Georgie may not have fully realized this at the time. Father and son, at any rate, seem to have spent a good deal of time in each other's company. A small group of youths—Adriano, Isaac, Luis Mosquera, and one or two others—began meeting every night in the gloomy *salón* of the Borgeses' hotel, with its "Moorish tiles, potted aspidistras, carnations, and wicker chairs."[14] They would discuss literature and philosophy and also have their poems recited by the histrionic Adriano, who prided himself on his "sumptuous cathedral organ" of a voice. Dr. Borges would be present at these gatherings: Adriano remembered him "smoking his intellectual opium as he talked about Max Stirner, his translation of Omar Khayyám, and told us about his philosophical speculations on pragmatism and mathematical logic."[15]

As he had done with Abramowicz and Jichlinski in Geneva, Georgie resumed his habit of staying out most of the night, roaming the streets with his friends until the early hours of the morning. Occasionally they would all have themselves a feast of fruit and Andalusian sweetmeats that would go on until dawn; from time to time, Norah was allowed to accompany him, to the great delight of the *ultraístas* of Seville, who were quite bowled over by her. (After the Borgeses' departure, Isaac and Luis Mosquera wrote a play whose female protagonist, "Nancy," was based on Norah Borges.) For her part, Norah took to doing sketches of the boys—Adriano del Valle, who was doing his military service, reading his poems in his soldier's uniform, "with the expression," she told him, "of a Botticelli angel"; poor Mosquera was portrayed as a faun.[16]

Isaac del Vando Villar, who was some ten years older than Georgie, took the shy young Argentine under his wing. He introduced him to the gambling table, and they would go off at night with a group of friends to try their luck at baccarat or roulette. Of Isaac's various cronies, the most disreputable and fascinating was a Byronic figure from Málaga called Pedro-Luis de Gálvez. Borges was quite dazzled by this Gálvez, who was eighteen years older than he and seemed to have packed as many adventures into his life as any of the heroes Georgie might have come across in the books he had devoured as a boy. Expelled from a seminary in his youth, Gálvez had launched upon a picaresque career that had taken in four years in prison for insulting the king of Spain at an anarchist meeting, service in the Foreign Legion in Africa, countless wanderings across Europe, including combat as a mercenary in Albania, until finally he returned to Spain, an impoverished desperado, reduced to eking out a precarious existence in Seville and Madrid by sponging off his literary friends.

Gálvez embodied a marvelous combination of poet and adventurer that a timid youth like Georgie must have found irresistible. The young Borges thought there was a touch of genius in the man. Gálvez's work, which consisted of sonnets for the most part, was characterized by startling images and fierce passions, and it was this conjunction of violent emotion and formal constraint that may so have attracted Borges at this time. I believe that through Gálvez, as well as through Isaac, Adriano, and other *ultraístas*, Borges was able to get a renewed sense of the freedom he had dreamed of in Geneva. Certainly his thoughts turned to Geneva once again—not to his humiliating experience at the place du Bourg-de-Four but to his love for Emilie. He tried his hand at yet another Whitmanesque composition, although this time he would deal far more explicitly than in his "Hymn to the Sea" with his deep yearning to experience the fires of love.

Georgie was to publish in *Grecia* a prose text written in the first person about making passionate love to an unnamed sweetheart, who is referred to as "La Amada," the Beloved:

O Beloved, our kisses will light up the Night! (O Adamic phallus!). Throw open the Windows, for I want to invite the Universe to my Nuptials: I want the Air and the Sea and the Waters and the Trees, to enjoy your astral flesh, to partake of the febrile, brief feast of your beauty and my strength.[17]

But though written in Seville (there are references to Isaac and Adriano), the piece is set in Geneva. The Beloved's red hair, moreover, identifies her as Emilie, Georgie's first sweetheart. The poem is thus a fantasy about the sexual ecstasy he might have experienced with Emilie had Father not intervened to pollute his love for her virtually at its source. It is as if Georgie wished to redeem through the passion of his writing the failure that had been visited upon him by his father at the place du Bourg-de-Four:

Kiss me. Kiss me. All my doubts have already been extinguished. Already my woes have died, and with you by my side I feel strong as a God. I am a God. I can create life.

Despite such heady dreams of freedom, however, Borges was still very much under the influence of his father. The language and concepts he uses in his prose poem are virtually identical to those of his father's love poetry. He may have noticed as much when, on February 10, just three weeks after his "An Interlude of Passion" ("Paréntesis pasional") appeared in *Grecia,* Dr. Borges published excerpts of his translation of Omar Khayyám in the first issue of a new literary magazine called *Gran Guignol.* It had been founded by his friends the Romero Martínez brothers, one of whom, Miguel, was very probably the "Humanist" whom Borges recalled in his memoirs as possessing even less Latin than he did.[18] The following month Dr. Borges would also publish in *Gran Guignol* his own free adaptation of the Song of Songs.[19]

It was in Spain that Georgie would begin to get some sense of the effect upon his writing of this extraordinarily complex relationship with his father, a relationship compounded of very mixed emotions—love and admiration, but resentment also, and a growing horror as he came to realize the sheer strength of the ties that bound one to the other. In the same issue of *Gran Guignol* as Father's "Rubáiyát" appeared, Georgie published a strange little parable called "Liberation" ("Liberación"), which tells of a prisoner who has been chained to a hundred other men and condemned to seven years of penal servitude. One day the prisoner wonders, "Is this order of things so just after all? Perhaps my inheritance is life and all the victories of life." And yet, "He took fright at this idea, as if he had sinned through blasphemy and impiety." Finally he resolves to escape, but no sooner has he "reached this crucial decision than he saw that it was impossible to break free."[20]

Georgie's growing sense of being tied down by his family may explain why he turned to the avant-garde with such enthusiasm in Seville—he knew it was a territory his father would not, and could not, enter, for the Ultra was nothing if not a revolt of the young against the old, and Dr. Borges was irremediably wedded to the symbolist-derived poetics of his generation. By the end of January 1920, Georgie felt confident enough to write about "the true spirit of the Ultra" in what was probably the first theoretical statement of the movement.[21] He inveighed against the "inflexible norms" such as "clarity and harmony" in which traditionalists "seek to imprison all feeling and all beauty." The *ultraístas* are essentially individualists: they "want to discover life," "want to see with new eyes," and wish to capture the "unique," "virginal" qualities of the world around them. The "abrupt flowering of metaphors" in their poems represents the "effort to express the eternal youthfulness of life." Life is a "protean becoming" that, like the poet, "devours itself, rises up, and is reborn every second."

One of the earliest examples of Borges's attempts to express the "eternal youthfulness of life" was a very odd sonnet he would send his friend Abramowicz a few weeks after publishing his short essay on the poetics of the Ultra.[22] This "classical sonnet," he informed Abramowicz, had been "perpetrated by me—oh, unconfessable crime!—as a kind of exercise." Its subject was his hero, Pedro-Luis de Gálvez, "that drunken vagabond poet and worse," who had taken himself off to Switzerland for a few months. Borges imagined the Spanish ruffian bursting into the placid Swiss town of Martigny and shattering the peace of the Alpine landscape—"the mountains are wiped out, the sky caves in"—as Gálvez, "scoundrel and gentleman," appears "with forehead shining like mica / and hands full of poems of steel." Gálvez personified Borges's violent desire to break the chains of bourgeois conformity in order to "discover life" and "see with new eyes," as he had put it in his recent theoretical piece on *ultraísmo*.

These reflections on *ultraísta* poetics were dedicated to Isaac del Vando Villar, the leader of the Ultra in Seville. By this time, however, "the great Isaac" was minded to transfer *Grecia* to Madrid, where most of the *ultraístas* were now concentrated. As it happened, Borges, too, would shortly be visiting the Spanish capital with his family. They had originally intended to leave Seville by Christmas, but their departure was put off until March, when they resumed their planned itinerary and traveled to Madrid, visiting Córdoba on the way. Isaac would not arrive in Madrid until May, but he gave Borges the name of another young Sevillian poet, Pedro Garfias, who would effect his introduction to the *ultraísta* comrades in the capital.

Borges was fortunate to arrive in Madrid at the start of an exceptional period of ferment and renewal in Spanish letters that in due course would produce a number of first-rate writers, several of whom would eventually become figures of international renown. It was a time when a new generation was beginning to assimilate the literary and artistic trends that had emerged in Europe from around the turn of the century. Until 1918 the Spaniards knew very little about the avant-garde, despite the fact that in 1909 a young writer called Ramón Gómez de la Serna had published Marinetti's first futurist manifesto in a Madrid magazine only a few months after it had appeared in Italy. In 1916 the Chilean poet Vicente Huidobro, who was passing through Spain en route to Paris, tried to interest the writer Rafael Cansinos-Asséns in the new ideas of the avant-garde but, again, nothing came of that. Once in Paris, however, Huidobro befriended the Spanish painter Juan Gris and gravitated toward the circle of Gris's fellow Spaniard, Pablo Picasso, where he encountered Guillaume Apollinaire. Following Apollinaire's lead, Huidobro, a poet of extraordinary gifts, together with the Frenchman Pierre Reverdy, began to apply the tenets of cubism to poetry. In 1917 the two of them founded *Nord-Sud,* the magazine that launched "literary cubism." In the middle of the following year, Huidobro traveled to Madrid, where he tried to make converts to the cause of cubism, and this time he found a more receptive audience in Cansinos-Asséns and his young acolytes. The Spanish writers picked up from Huidobro the two cardinal principles of avant-garde poetics—the autonomy of the poem and the primacy of the image, but, to the chagrin of the mercurial Chilean, they resisted accepting cubism wholesale and remained open to other ideas that were coming into vogue in Paris and elsewhere.

It was Cansinos-Asséns, not Huidobro, who was to become the father figure of the new generation of poets in Spain. This happened virtually by accident, as the fortuitous result of an interview in which Cansinos talked of the need to be "Ultra-Romantic." The term "Ultra" was thereafter taken up as a kind of war cry by a small group of young poets, and by December 1918 there were plans to start up an avant-garde magazine to be called *Ultra.* This magazine, however, would take more than two years to see the light of day, but already the peculiar Spanish movement known as "the Ultra" or *ultraísmo* was born under the tutelage of the maestro Rafael Cansinos-Asséns.

Cansinos was to promote the Ultra both in Madrid and in his native Seville. When he took over the editorship of the literary review *Cervantes,* he steered it in an *ultraísta* direction, encouraging his disciple Isaac del Vando

Villar to do likewise with *Grecia* in Seville. It was, in fact, the *ultraístas* of the latter city who, on May 2, 1919, would hold the first public recital of the new avant-garde poetry in Spain at the Ateneo of Seville. Several of the young writers whom Borges would shortly befriend took part in this historic event— Isaac del Vando Villar, Adriano del Valle, Pedro Garfias, Gerardo Diego, Tomás Luque, Xavier Bóveda, and Pedro-Luis de Gálvez. As well as their own work, they read poems by Apollinaire, Marinetti, and, of course, by Cansinos-Asséns, who was by now reverentially called the "Apostle of the Ultra" or the "High Constable of the Ultra." The Ultra, nevertheless, was to remain a very eclectic movement, bonded by little more than a desire to explore new ideas in the arts and by a mischievous urge to annoy the Spanish literary establishment.

Upon their arrival in Madrid, the Borges family installed themselves in a *pensión* just off the Puerta del Sol, the bustling square at the very heart of the city. Shortly afterward Pedro Garfias, Borges's contact in the capital, took him to the favorite haunt of the Madrid *ultraístas,* a German alehouse on the Plaza de Santa Ana called El Oro del Rhin (The Rhine Gold), which was a short walk away from the Puerta del Sol. Of the many young writers Borges got to know in Madrid that spring—Pedro Garfias, the brothers Humberto Rivas and José Rivas Panedas, Gerardo Diego, Eugenio Montes, Xavier Bóveda, Tomás Luque—it was with Guillermo de Torre, a law student and aspiring poet, that he was to establish the most enduring connection. The two of them shared an interest in literary theory as well as in the new writing, but, additionally, Torre and Norah Borges, an accomplished artist whose faux-naïf style would be much admired by the *ultraístas,* would fall in love, and this would draw Torre closer to Borges.

As ever, literary life in Madrid revolved around that peculiarly Spanish institution known as the *tertulia*—an informal gathering of friends meeting regularly in a bar or coffeehouse to converse on topics of common interest. Rafael Cansinos-Asséns, the great panjandrum of the Ultra, held court once a week at the Café Colonial, a large, airy establishment furnished with red plush sofas and lit by globe lamps that reflected eerily off the tall mirrors lining the walls. The Colonial "was not a particularly literary place, it has to be said, for in the early hours of the morning it was a haven for journalists, theatrical types, pimps, and similar creatures, but it was there that the maestro Cansinos-Asséns had installed his 'lyrical divan.' "[23] Up to twenty or thirty young devotees of the Ultra would gather around the Master every Saturday to talk and argue about poetry from midnight until dawn. As Borges would recall, "Cansinos would propose a subject—The Metaphor, Free Verse, The Traditional Forms of Poetry, Narrative Poetry, The Adjective, The Verb. In his own quiet way he was a dictator, allowing no unfriendly allusions to contemporary writers and trying to keep the talk on a high plane"; the group "despised all Spanish local color" and "admired American jazz"; they "were more interested in being Europeans than Spaniards."[24]

Pedro Garfias took Borges along to one of these sessions, and at the end of it, as dawn was breaking, Cansinos-Asséns invited the young Argentine and a few other poets back to his house. On the way Borges did his best to engage the attention of the great man by declaring that in a couple of hundred years' time, when all those present had been forgotten, the name of Pedro-Luis de Gálvez would still live on, an opinion that, as Borges was to report to Adriano del Valle, did not immediately commend itself to the Apostle of the Ultra but served at least to stir up the kind of argument Borges always enjoyed.[25] Cansinos-Asséns, as Borges was to discover, lived "completely for literature, without regard for money or fame"; indeed, his whole house was a library: "It was like making your way through a woods. He was too poor to have shelves, and the books were piled one on top of the other from floor to ceiling, forcing you to thread your way among the vertical columns."[26]

All his life Borges would show a weakness for eccentrics, and Cansinos was a pretty rare bird for the Spain of the time. A tall, dark, handsome man—it was not for nothing he was a cousin of Rita Hayworth (née Cansinos)—he had a strange, melancholy air about him, accentuated by a languorous manner and a ponderous habit of speech. As a young man, he had studied for the priesthood in his native Seville, but "having found the name Cansinos in the archives of the Inquisition, he decided he was a Jew. This led him to the study of Hebrew, and later on he even had himself circumcised."[27] In 1915 had delivered himself of a book of erotic "psalms" called *El candelabro de los siete brazos* (*The Seven-Branched Candlestick*) but he mostly wrote essays and criticism, and, proficient as he was in several languages—he liked to boast that he could salute the stars in fourteen tongues—he became an indefatigable translator of, among others, Thomas de Quincey, Marcus Aurelius, Henri Barbusse, Marcel Schwob, Goethe, Dostoyevsky, and the *Thousand and One Nights*. The young Borges came to regard Cansinos as "something like the symbol of all culture, Western and Eastern," and he would imitate the prose style of the Master, who "wrote long and flowing sentences with an un-Spanish and strongly Hebrew flavor to them."[28]

Needless to say, Borges became an assiduous member of the *tertulia* at the Café Colonial. However, the literary scene in the capital was sharply divided at this time. There was another *tertulia* led by Ramón Gómez de la Serna (the man who had published Marinetti's futurist manifesto in Spanish as far back as 1909) that used to meet at the Café Pombo, also on Saturdays and also at midnight. The rivalry between the two groups was bitter—"*vehementísima*," according to Borges: "Both *tertulias* were mutually exclusive: whoever frequented

the one was religiously excluded from the other, and only Eugenio Montes succeeded, by some feat of intellectual dexterity that utterly amazed his comrades,
in alternating his argumentative presence between the two camps."[29]

Gómez de la Serna could hardly have been more different from Cansinos.
A writer of essays, novels, and plays, he was short and stocky, with thickset features and long sideburns that gave him the truculent appearance of a second-
rate matador. He was still very much taken with the futurists' delight in sheer
novelty, and his prestige in the Spanish avant-garde was due to his invention
of the *"grueguería,"* a term of his own coinage, which originally referred, he
would say, to the squeals piglets utter as they run after their mother. Ramón,
as he was known to his friends and acolytes, famously defined the *greguería* as
an equation—humor + metaphor = *greguería.* The result was a quirky, largely
visual, metaphor that was meant to jolt the reader out of his presumed complacency.

According to Guillermo de Torre, Borges did in fact attend the *tertulia* at
the Café Pombo from time to time, despite the "latent enmity" between
Ramón and Cansinos.[30] Such promiscuity was not at all surprising. Though he
may have felt a personal affinity with Cansinos, Borges was, after all, still finding his feet as a poet, and in any case the avant-garde was a very heterogeneous
affair at this time, even in Paris itself, where a number of different trends
would appear and just as quickly fade away in the period between the death of
Apollinaire in 1918 and about 1924, when surrealism established itself as the
dominant movement in the avant-garde. At this time, moreover, the literary
cubism of Reverdy and Huidobro was being steadily overshadowed by Dada,
following upon the arrival in Paris of its chief progenitor, Tristan Tzara.
Borges, in fact, was to flirt with Dada for a while in Madrid, attracted perhaps
by its playful iconoclasm. He wrote Tristan Tzara a letter from the Café Colonial, together with Guillermo de Torre and five others (including, curiously, a
young British Hispanist, L. Walton of Jesus College, Oxford, who a year later
would be appointed lecturer in Spanish at Edinburgh University), offering
him their "joyful adhesion to Dada" and sending him, "from this strident
cafe," a "collective poem" they had composed in the semiautomatic mode
practiced by the Dadaists.[31]

The letter and poem amounted to little more than a speculative attempt
by a group of young writers to catch the eye of a celebrity like Tristan Tzara.
More important for our understanding of Borges's development as a poet was
the rivalry between Cansinos-Asséns and Ramón Gómez de la Serna. It was a
rivalry, Borges came to realize, not just between two men but between two
sensibilities, two "spirits."[32] Of the two, Ramón had a better grasp of what the
avant-garde was about than did Cansinos, who never managed to shake off
the symbolist-derived aesthetics of Hispanic *modernismo.* But toward the end

of his stay in Madrid, Borges inclined decisively to Cansinos, believing that his work was imbued with emotion whereas Ramón's *greguerías* amounted to little more than whimsical conceits.

It was thanks to Cansinos that the young Borges was able to perceive more clearly the nature of his own sensibility. The "emotion" he discerned in Cansinos's work led him back to German expressionism, and it was while in Madrid that he wrote one of his first expressionist poems, called "Trench" ("Trinchera").[33] It was probably in Madrid, too, that he conceived of putting together a collection of maximalist or Bolshevik poems, which he thought of calling either *Ritmos rojos* (*Red Rhythms*), suggesting a Whitmanesque emphasis, or *Salmos rojos* (*Red Psalms*), an obvious allusion to Cansinos's own book of "psalms."

Toward the end of April, the Borges family decided to make their way back to Geneva, as they had planned to do all along. Leaving Madrid was a terrible wrench for Borges: in little under two months, he had met many of the leading Spanish poets of the new generation and absorbed in earnest the ideas of the European avant-garde. Just two days before the Borgeses' departure, Isaac del Vando Villar arrived from Seville in order to set up his magazine, *Grecia,* in the capital. On May 1 a dinner was held in his honor, to which all the *ultraístas* came—even the "great Pedro-Luis" (Gálvez) turned up, flush for a change, having won three thousand pesetas at the card table, and announcing to all and sundry his intention of leaving for Russia the very next day.[34] Little wonder that Borges, given his boundless admiration for the dynamic Gálvez, should have composed a prose poem called "Russia" ("Rusia") not too long afterward, which he stuffed full of images of revolutionary action.[35]

The entire Borges family, it seems, had thoroughly taken to life in Spain, but there was business to see to in Geneva—Georgie's military call-up for one thing, as well as the matter of his unfinished *baccalauréat.* There may well have been financial matters also, concerning the various properties they had rented out in Buenos Aires or the payment of Gran's pensions, which needed to be settled at the Argentine consulate in Geneva, through which they had conducted their official dealings with Buenos Aires over the previous five years. Finally there was the question of Dr. Borges's failing sight, for which he was hoping to seek further treatment in Geneva.

On May 3 they set off from Madrid but stopped for a time at Barcelona. Borges wrote to Abramowicz from that city with further reflections on the poetics of the Ultra. The aim of the movement was to "to destroy rhetoric" so that each line in a poem would count in its own right.

> We want to condense, to say only what is essential. To make the poem a living and organic whole where each line would be the achieved synthe-

sis of a sensation, of an impression of the world, external or spiritual, of a state of consciousness. . . .[36]

And he pours scorn on "manufacturers of sonnets who go so far as to construct 13 indifferent lines just to prepare for the entry upon the stage of the last, the raison d'être of their sonnet." In his view originality was the overriding aim of the Ultra; if the old rhetoric was to be destroyed it was in order to allow each individual artist "to create a universe made in his own image."

Once in Geneva, Borges underwent a medical examination to determine his fitness for military service, from which he was eventually exempted on the grounds of his myopia. (Records show that the authorities in Buenos Aires officially pronounced him unfit for military service on August 6, 1920.)[37] As for Dr. Borges, he had hoped to have his cataracts operated on in Geneva, but he was advised against this because of a heart condition he had developed. There was not much to keep them in Switzerland after all. Georgie appears to have lost interest altogether in his former sweetheart, Emilie, and he cannot have been too bothered about the *baccalauréat,* not least because he loathed and feared examinations. (He was never to finish his high school education, in fact.) Only his friendship with Maurice Abramowicz provided some relief in this rather cheerless period in Switzerland. He had some success in converting his Swiss friend to the Ultra and would continue to correspond with him for several years afterward, but otherwise, as he complained in a postcard to his Spanish friend in Madrid, Guillermo de Torre (postmarked June 5), Geneva was impervious to the Ultra, though lavishly supplied with prostitutes, alcohol, chocolate, formalities, and teenage girls.[38] The postcard is surprisingly risqué, foregrounding the naked white body of a voluptuous girl in the arms of an aging satyr: she is leaning back in abandon, her right breast cupped in his dark male hand, and turning her head to kiss her grizzled seducer on the mouth. Above this image, Georgie wrote in bold capitals an inscription in Latin to the effect that it represented everyday life in Geneva.

Why did Borges choose this pornographic image to epitomize Geneva? At first sight it seems no more than an adolescent attempt to impress his Spanish friend, but the picture may also have captured the smoldering resentment he must have felt toward his father for having sent him to visit the woman at the place du Bourg-de-Four several months earlier. And there was good reason for Georgie to feel resentment again at this point. By the beginning of June, the family would have been preparing to return to Spain. Both Georgie and Norah must have been keen to get back to Madrid: he to resume his activities in the Spanish avant-garde, Norah to see her boyfriend, Guillermo de Torre. Father, however, decided that they would all go to Majorca instead.

·   ·   ·

The Borges family arrived in Palma toward the middle of June, and at the beginning of July they went up to the mountains to spend the summer in the cooler air of Valldemosa, where they stayed at the Hotel de L'Artista, an establishment owned by a local doctor. There was nothing much to do there, as Borges told Abramowicz, but at least he could amuse himself with some female company—the doctor's mistress, Clarita, was staying at the hotel, as well as four "good-looking girls" accompanied by their mother, who was a friend of the mistress but seemingly "unaware of what was really going on."[39] He would also get to know another friend of the mistress, a girl called Ángela Márquez, who was twenty-three years old and "quite pretty"; and it was not long before Clarita conceived the idée fixe, as Borges put it, of marrying him off to her friend Ángela, who, for her part, would express a desire to visit Buenos Aires as well as her consternation at his lack of religious faith: "She urged me to abjure my blasphemies with regard to the Virgin, to go to mass with her, to make my confession, and take communion together."[40] However, in view of his "Stoical resistance," the two women would eventually transfer their attentions to another candidate for the fair Ángela's hand—a former sea captain who was pushing forty and weighed over 175 pounds.

At Valldemosa, too, Borges would see his friend Jacobo Sureda, whom he was to convert to the cause of the Ultra that summer, and a Swedish painter called Sven Westerman, who became Norah's art teacher. Even so, Borges would write to Guillermo de Torre complaining of terrible boredom—he was spending his time going for walks in the mountains, writing and reading (William James, Bernard Shaw, the German expressionists) and listening to an execrable phonograph; he was obviously frustrated at not being among the *ultraístas* in the capital and asked Torre for the latest news, and specifically about the sessions at the Oro del Rhin.[41]

Still, this second period in Majorca was to be of considerable importance in Borges's development as a writer. Shortly after leaving Madrid several months earlier, he had told Abramowicz that the Ultra was above all an attempt "to create new myths, to write in a way that would allow each artist to form a universe in his own image": "The ideal would be for each *ultraísta* in Spain to be absolutely different from his comrades."[42] And in Majorca that summer, far removed as he was from the literary hub of Madrid, he was to spend his time searching for originality, for whatever it was that would make him "absolutely different" from the others.

Not much has survived of Borges's writing in Majorca, but it appears to have consisted mostly of experiments in expressionist poetry and prose. He also started to translate a selection of German expressionist poems, which he would send to Guillermo de Torre in Madrid for publication in the Ultra-inclined review *Cervantes*. Indeed, he would immerse himself in German expressionism to such an extent that by the end of September, he would jokingly refer to himself in a letter to Torre as "Georg-Ludwig," so thoroughly Germanized would he claim to have become.[43] He said he was writing *ultraísta* prose pieces and spoke of stories described as *"gran-guiñolescos,"* which suggests he was trying his hand at texts along the lines of "Liberation," the brief expressionist piece he had published in *Gran Guignol* of Seville some months before going to Madrid.[44] He knew that Torre would not approve of writing prose at all; this was, he conceded, to commit a fundamental sin,[45] but he was clearly prepared to violate the principles of the Ultra itself if this led him to discover a unique voice as a writer.

For all that, he seemed unable to clinch the individuality of expression that he was after. He explained to Torre that the aesthetic problem of trying to be original was part of a larger problem—that of the individual before external reality: only when we came to know our own limits would the problem of originality be automatically resolved, too, as occurred in conversation with a friend.[46] In other words, his writing would express the uniqueness of his personality only when he had acquired a surer grasp of the difference between self and other.

Toward the end of August, he felt that he was getting nowhere. He had even begun to doubt his abilities as a poet: "I no longer believe in any Utopia, whether it be maximalist, Whitmanesque, or any other. . . . ," he would complain to Abramowicz. "I lack a goal or rather I have too many goals before me. I think I'm sunk, and won't be able to salvage more than two or three metaphors from the wreckage."[47] By September 3 he was telling Guillermo de Torre that he was tired of condensing stories into four or five handwritten pages; he had turned instead to writing poems of variable rhythm and crudely vivid imagery.[48] But even then he was not at all satisfied with the results, for no matter how hard he tried to make his words new and vibrant and fresh, he just could not get beyond his usual stock of images—lamps, flags, streets, waves, night, climax, collapse, airplanes, playing cards.

This crisis of confidence was aggravated by an unexpected turn in his relations with his father, which occurred, I believe, toward the end of the summer. Dr. Borges must have been nearing completion of his novel, *El Caudillo,* when he asked his son to read a draft. This request would have taken Georgie by surprise, since his occasional attempts to seek his father's advice about his own writing had always met with a refusal. Why, then, did Dr. Borges choose to submit *El Caudillo* to his son's critical scrutiny? He must surely have been acting upon some deep-seated doubt about his literary abilities; he was, in effect, appealing to Georgie to save him from failure.

This appeal, moreover, could not have come at a worse moment for the young Borges, who was himself doubting his talent as a poet that summer. At a time when he had been fighting a losing battle to achieve an original voice, Borges was asked to read his father's novel, where he would have discovered that his most exalted Whitmanesque aspirations were just another version of the older man's dreams, and that even his feelings of unworthiness were reflected back to him in *El Caudillo*—the self-doubting Carlos Dubois, the misgivings about Argentina, the fear of the patriarch, all were versions of Georgie's most intimate concerns. In my judgment it was at this point that Borges began to regard his father as a possible mirror image of himself, as an embodiment of the fate that might befall him were he to fail as a writer.

Georgie's quest for an original voice was now pursued with redoubled energy. In September he described his creative aims to Abramowicz: "I am striving to combine *ultraísta* techniques (plastic metaphors, concision, created images) with the expansive rhythms and the energy of my first Whitmanesque efforts—'Hymn to the Sea' and others."[49] On October 24 he told Jacobo Sureda that he had finished a poem called "Jewish Ghetto" ("Judería") "in the style of a biblical psalm" and also another called "Soviet Epic" ("Gesta soviética"), which was "very dynamic"; he was working, he said, on "a third *ultraísta* poem (a biblical one—inevitably) entitled 'Crucifixión.'"[50] And on November 6 he told Torre that the poems he was writing were of two sorts: dynamic and listless, an oddly contradictory description, but one that suggests that he had recognized a duality he could not resolve into a unified style.[51] A few weeks later, however, we find him writing a so-called Bolshevik piece called "Red Guard" ("Guardia roja"), which he described to Sureda as "very objective, dynamic and cold."[52] His writing thus tended now to alternate between dynamic poems (*dinámicos*), usually expressions of revolutionary struggle, and listless "psalms" (*desganados*), on themes of passive suffering and oppression. By the end of November, his quest for an individual voice had acquired a desperate urgency. He seems to have been writing in a kind of frenzy—more and more dynamic poems kept pouring out of his skull, he told Guillermo de Torre; the process was almost involuntary, automatic even, and as soon as he had finished writing, he would read the results with no little perplexity.[53] His poetry, in other words, was beginning to register the volatility of his inner life, characterized as this was by sharp swings from enthusiasm to despair as he surged up toward Whitmanesque visions of universal connectedness and then slumped into the solipsism that was his chronic condition.

At the end of August, the Borges family returned to Palma from Valldemosa. Georgie found the city irredeemably provincial; in Valldemosa he could at least count on the friendship of Sureda and the company of Sven Westerman, but in Palma there was no one he could call a friend, except for a young writer, Juan Alomar, the son of a prominent politican, who had shown some interest in *ultraísmo.* Borges took to frequenting the Círculo Mallorquín, the kind of men's social club found in most Spanish towns, where he made the acquaintance of a number of local intellectuals, mostly journalists and academics from the university. A half dozen of them would meet on Friday nights and pass the time in noisy discussions on sundry topics—"Nietzsche's Eternal Return, the Irish question, the 'I' and 'not-I,' Dada, social revolution, and—inevitably—the Ultra."[54] And he would also mention to Sureda "a series of binges, aesthetic discussions, infusions of alcohol, and a few attempts at the roulette table in the Círculo."[55] When the Círculo closed, Borges and his companions would repair to Casa Elena, Palma's best-known house of ill repute, where their discussions would continue through the night. He also befriended two young American painters who were staying on the island for about a month, and when they left at the end of November, their departure was marked by a massive alcoholic binge; after that, life returned to its usual monotonous routine.[56]

He was to find some respite from the general tedium when a local magazine named *L'Ignorancia* published a piece mocking *ultraísmo* on September 7. It was written by a journalist called Elviro Sanz, who wrote a regular column in the Majorcan dialect under the nom de plume "L'Aura de L'Illot." Borges seized on this article as an opportunity to liven up the dreariness of the literary scene in Palma. He got his friend Sureda to write in defense of the Ultra in the magazine *La Almudaina,* but when Borges tried to get his own reply published there, too, he was politely turned down because it was felt his piece was too aggressive. Borges was invited to submit a poem to the magazine *Baleares,* where his friend Alomar worked, but even then they managed to get his name irritatingly wrong—it appeared as "Jorge *Llinás* Borges." (Perhaps the typesetter got him mixed up with one of the regular contributors, a man called Josep *Llinás* Simó).[57] His reply to the article in *L'Ignorancia* came out instead on October 19 in the newspaper *Última Hora.* This flurry of literary polemic with Elviro Sanz provoked a further attack on *ultraísmo* later that month by a journalist, Agustín Palmer, who wrote under the pseudonym Pin in *Última Hora* itself. But just when Borges had got himself a nice controversy going, it fizzled out as unexpectedly as it had begun. The wretched Elviro Sanz went very quiet on them, and Borges could not figure out why—he jokingly suggested to Sureda that they might perhaps "goad our taciturn enemy" into action once more if they wrote an article themselves under a pseudonym, denouncing the Ultra and making suitably provocative references to Sanz.[58]

The frequency of Borges's correspondence with Guillermo de Torre in the autumn and early winter of 1920 is a gauge of the depth of his frustration at not being in Madrid. As far as he could tell, Torre was going from strength to strength and appeared to be on the point of assuming the leadership of the

Madrid avant-garde. On November 1, Torre produced what he called a "Manifiesto Vertical" outlining the aims of the Ultra, which caused quite a stir in the literary world. Later in the month, he seemed about to win full control of *Grecia* when its editor and proprietor, Isaac del Vando Villar, unexpectedly sold the magazine to a fellow *ultraísta*, José Ciria y Escalante, a wealthy youth who was only sixteen years old. Borges assumed it would be Guillermo de Torre who would actually run *Grecia* and, professing to welcome these developments, he did what he could to keep in with the ambitious Torre, placing himself at his friend's command, offering to distribute the "Manifiesto Vertical" in Majorca and even designating himself the ambassador of the Ultra in the Balearic Islands.[59]

Torre, according to Borges, had plans to turn *Grecia* into "a sumptuous international review publishing original work in foreign languages," but had decided to change its name to *Reflector* (*Headlight*), which sounded suitably twentieth century.[60] Borges viewed the transformation of *Grecia* with little enthusiasm, he told Sureda: if it meant anything, it meant the triumph of the kind of *ultraísmo* he disliked—"ingenious, fake and showy."[61] All the same he was anxious not to be left out, and when the first number of *Reflector* appeared in December, he wrote with congratulations both to young Ciria, the proprietor, and also to Torre, heaping praise on his friend and telling him that he had written to the editor of the German expressionist magazine *Die Sturm* asking for samples of expressionist works that might be used for the greater glory of *Reflector*.[62] But there was a considerable degree of envy of Guillermo de Torre all the same. He described him to Abramowicz as "the grand vizir, that's to say, the king's prime minister or absolute czar" of the new magazine,[63] and in an earlier letter to Sureda, he had already dismissed Torre as "our polysyllabic Lucifer of the avant-garde."[64]

Reflector, however, would not survive its first issue. It was eclipsed by the appearance on January 27, 1921, of the long-awaited *Ultra*, a magazine that, vitally, enjoyed the favor of the maestro Cansinos-Asséns.* *Ultra* was launched with a festival of avant-garde poetry held on January 28 at an establishment called La Parisiana in Madrid. This turned into a famously rowdy occasion when the *ultraístas*—to their great delight—were jeered and booed by the audience. As Borges reported to Abramowicz, "The cries and angry shouts of the public totally drowned the reading of two of my poems. The work of other *ultraísta* brothers suffered the same fate."[65] But the sad fact was, of course, that he was not at the event himself; he was stuck in Majorca with his family.

Seething with frustration, Borges complained to Torre about his exile

*Borges would contribute to almost every number of *Ultra* over the year of its existence, and so would Norah, whose woodcuts would frequently appear in the magazine.

from Madrid.[66] His frustration was no doubt compounded by the fact that, in the autumn of 1920, his father, having finished *El caudillo,* which he was currently having published at his own expense in Palma, had decided to quit Argentina for good and settle permanently in Spain, and specifically in the vicinity of Madrid; but first the family would have to return to Buenos Aires to sort out their affairs. The date of their departure had already been fixed: they would be leaving from Tarragona on March 4, 1921. As Borges explained to Guillermo de Torre in December, they would be staying in Buenos Aires for only five or six months before returning to Spain and settling in Valladolid, Aranjuez, Getafe, or someplace close to Madrid,[67] but this meant, of course, that he would not be in Madrid for about nine months and he would be forced to miss out on new developments in the avant-garde just when things had begun to look promising with the launch of Torre's magazine *Reflector,* and then *Ultra.* Dr. Borges, clearly, had not lost the knack of uprooting his family at precisely the wrong time for Georgie.

As he waited to go back to Buenos Aires, Borges did what he could to amuse himself in Majorca. He had managed by now to form a tiny circle of converts to the Ultra—Jacobo Sureda, Juan Alomar, and Jaime Moll, an opera singer whom he had got to know at the barber's. They used to meet at the Café de los Artistas on the Born, Palma's main thoroughfare, and would sometimes go up to Valldemosa to visit Sureda. Then, in January, the group found a good opportunity to make itself known to a wider public when the controversy over modern art flared up once more in Palma, as the result of an exhibition of painting by a young Castilian artist, Manuel Fernández Peña. The exhibition included a painting of a female nude that caused a huge scandal "in this priest-ridden and idiotic city," as Borges informed Abramowicz; even the canons of the cathedral "lined up two abreast to see it, to see *her,* rather"; no one bought a single painting, and the entire press attacked the artist; "I alone published an article praising him," he added proudly.[68] (It appeared in *Última Hora* on January 5.)[69]

Borges's defense of the nude painting goaded the egregious Pin to attack the avant-garde once more in *Última Hora* on January 28. Borges and two of his friends replied with an article signed by "Dagesmar" (a composite pseudonym: Sure*da*, Bor*ges*, Alo*mar*), which appeared in *Última Hora* on February 3.[70] Then on February 15 the magazine *Baleares* published a "Manifesto of the Ultra" written by Borges, together with a brief selection of the new poetry, to which Borges contributed the poem "Catedral," an *ultraísta* evocation of Palma cathedral.[71] In this "Manifesto of the Ultra," Borges made a distinction between "the passive aesthetics of the mirror" and "the active aesthetics of the prism": the aim of the Ultra was to achieve "a naked vision of the world," a vision "purified of ancestral stigmas," and "in order to conquer such a vision," it was necessary "to throw overboard the whole of the past"—classical aesthetics, Romanticism, naturalism, symbolism, "the whole of that vast absurd cage in which the ritualists wish to imprison the marvelous bird of beauty"; everything must be jettisoned until "we can each of us design our own subjective creation."

This aggressive manifesto provoked the desired reaction from his enemies, and Borges was beside himself with glee, reporting to Sureda in Valldemosa that they had caused a major scandal: "A pack of fossils—among them Elviro Sanz—is threatening to beat us to death with their walking sticks. . . . Did you see that pinprick by *Pin* in *U.H.* [*Última Hora*]? The *Correo de Mallorca* [a Catholic newspaper] is preparing a refutation of the Manifesto and an auto-da-fé of the poems."[72]

Borges could picture himself as a great rebel at last. Indeed, his appetite for rebellion was such that he was now prepared to assert a vision of the avant-garde that was quite different from that of the Madrid *ultraístas,* who were much taken with Dada at this time. Already, in a letter to Abramowicz written in October 1920, he had expressed his dissent from Dada: it was a mistake "to affirm that Dada constitutes the full realization of personality"; the Dadaists were too interested in "tangible reality" and failed to see that "an idea, a dream, even a theory, is no less real."[73] He went further, declaring that "the things that people are prepared to kill each other for are things that are spiritually real: honor, the *patria,* etc.," and that "it is precisely this interior reality that one must pursue." And so when Guillermo de Torre asked him early in 1921 to contribute a piece for publication in *Dadaglobe,* an international anthology of Dadaist work that Tristan Tzara was proposing to bring out (it never appeared in the end), Borges came up with a text in French called "Esquisse critique," a "critical sketch" in which he cockily dared to out-Dada Tzara himself by arguing for a kind of anarchism in art—every style, he declared, was "a cage," because there are "as many forms as there are individuals"; he looked forward to a situation in which each artist would be free to express his own unique style: "Oh, but what a radiant, popular, daily joy of a Dadaism without Dada!"[74]

Borges, certainly, had little time for Dada now; instead he wanted to reclaim the Ultra for expressionism, but he was frustrated by the fact that he could not directly influence his comrades on the Spanish mainland because he would have to absent himself in Buenos Aires for the next six months or so. However, in what was presumably an attempt to counter the current inclination toward Dada among the *ultraístas* of Madrid, he sent to Guillermo de Torre another manifesto called "Anatomy of My Ultra" ("Anatomía de mi Ultra"), where he asserted that the current movement of "literary renovation" was "essentially expressionist" and contended once again that the poet's experience of reality must be refracted through the "active prism" of feeling and imagination, so as to rise above contingent circumstances and "convey naked emotion, purged of the supplementary particulars that precede it."[75] And yet, on February 20, just five days after having exhorted his comrades in Majorca to throw the whole of the literary past overboard, and after having asserted his right to an uncaged poetic voice against Tristan Tzara no less, Georgie gamely took the ferry to Barcelona with his family and would embark two weeks later at Tarragona on a ship that would take him to the other side of the globe.

If we are to believe him, he spent much of his last weeks in Spain in an orgy of gambling and whoring. In February he reported to Guillermo de Torre that the *ultraísta* group he had formed in Majorca often met in a brothel, where, amid flourishes of sonorous verbiage, they would feel up the breasts and thighs of the smiling, uncomprehending girls; it was just like the gatherings at El Oro del Rhin, and rather Dadaist, too, did Torre not think?[76] And two days before departing for Buenos Aires at the beginning of March, he wrote to Abramowicz, posing as a kind of Baudelairean decadent, reeling from the sweet exhalations of his *fleurs du mal*:

> And then at roulette I enjoyed an unheard-of run of luck—at least for me—(60 pesetas with a capital of one peseta!) which allowed me to score three nights in a row at the brothel. A sumptuously filthy blonde, and a brunette we called "The Princess" on whose humanity I took off as if flying a plane or riding a horse. . . ."[77]

He was trying to cut a dash with his Swiss friend here, no doubt, but this compulsive fluttering about the lamps of harlotry suggests that he was straining desperately at the leash, testing how far he dared go in asserting his independence from his family. In letters and essays and manifestos, he kept insisting, with an almost hysterical vehemence, on the need to assert a unique, individual vision of the world. The irony was, of course, that he still had no idea of what was unique about his personality, for his own interior reality was a mass of contradictions—he craved freedom yet could not help but submit to his parent's wishes; he boasted about his exploits at the brothel yet was sunk in self-doubt after his botched initiation in Geneva.

Oddly enough, it was in the brothel that the young Borges was given a foretaste of a possible reconciliation of his inner conflicts. It seems that in the course of his visits to Casa Elena in Palma, he had established a curious friendship with a prostitute called Luz (which in Spanish means "light"), and this liaison had afforded the nervous, hypersensitive youth some inkling of what it might be like to enjoy a natural rapport with a woman, a rapport in which innocence and shame might finally be subsumed in a rare kind of tenderness. Borges would write wistfully to Abramowicz about his feelings for Luz:

That glory has now been extinguished. I feel "like a poor orphan without his older sister." I tell you, I really loved that Luz: she was so playful with me and behaved with such ingenuous indecency. She was like a cathedral and also like a bitch.[78]

Such a presentiment of love in the arms of a whore was the closest he had come to experiencing the passion he kept trying to articulate in pseudo-Whitmanesque poems like "Hymn to the Sea" and "An Interlude of Passion," but his actual experience of love was virtually nil, except for those few weeks with Emilie before his father's intervention destroyed that brief amour in Geneva.

In the absence of love, he had derived the greatest emotional satisfaction from friendship. And his hunger for friendship had grown ever keener. In Buenos Aires there had been Roberto Godel, Abramowicz in Geneva, Guillermo de Torre in Madrid, but most passionate of all were his feelings for poor, consumptive Sureda in Valldemosa. In the letter he sent Sureda on March 3, the day before he was to board ship at Tarragona, he begged his friend not to stop writing: "Don't let us break the scriptural [*sic*] cable that joins our two hearts across the Atlantic!"[79] And yet in his heart of hearts, he knew that such depth of emotion was impossible to sustain:

> I wanted more than anything to bare my soul frankly and entirely to my friend. I would have wished to divest myself of it and leave it throbbing there beside him. We went on talking and discussing, on the verge of saying farewell, until all of a sudden, with an unsuspected firmness of conviction, I understood that this "personality" which we tend to value with such inappropriate excess amounted to nothing. It occurred to me that my life would never justify a full, absolute moment that would contain all the others; they would all be provisional phases, each of them wiping out the past and looking to the future, and that outside of the episodic, the present, the circumstantial, we were no one.[80]

Borges, even so, would never relinquish his yearning for a "full, absolute moment"—for a plenitude of being that would rescue him from the solipsistic fog that had engulfed him as a child and filled him with despair.

PART TWO

A Poet in Love

(1921–1934)

CHAPTER 6

Buenos Aires

(1921–1923)

AFTER AN ABSENCE of seven years, the whole family was apprehensive about their forthcoming visit to Argentina. As Borges wrote to Adriano del Valle shortly before their departure, all of them were unhappy at the prospect of leaving Spain; to Guillermo de Torre he likened his own experience of Spain to a coat of many colors that he found hard to cast off; indeed, while still in Majorca he had confessed to Roberto Godel that he retained no more than twenty or thirty images of Buenos Aires in his memory.[1]

When finally they arrived in Buenos Aires on March 24, Georgie and his sister found their native city disappointingly modest and provincial. Since their house in Palermo and the other properties they owned were still rented out, they stayed at the Hotel du Helder on calle Esmeralda in the city center while they looked for more permanent accommodation. By the beginning of June, they had taken a lease on an apartment in calle Bulnes 2216 in a shabby area full of *conventillos* straddling the barrios of Palermo and Recoleta, popularly known as "Tierra del Fuego." This district had once been notorious for its delinquents and *compadritos,* and it was dominated still by the vast, cream-colored building of the Penitenciaría, the state prison, which stood, ringed by palm trees, in what is today the Parque Las Heras.

Buenos Aires now felt terribly alien to Georgie. He took to walking its streets, revisiting places he had known as a child. He went back to Palermo, to the house on calle Serrano where he had been confined for so many years as a boy, and was struck by how unfamiliar even this house seemed to him now— how many skies and sunsets and new moons there would have to be "before the house recognizes me again / and becomes once more a province of my soul!' "The Return" ("La vuelta").[2] He ventured into barrios he had never had a chance to see in his childhood: wandering about in the south side, once genteel but now extremely run down, left "a bitter taste in the soul" ("The South," "El Sur"); a highly imaged *ultraísta* poem on the dock area has "the foreseeable miracle" of dawn "dropping from the sky" and "rolling from soul to soul"

("Faded Dawn," "Alba desdibujada"); a suburb is described "as a motionless *via crucis* of suffering streets" ("Suburb," "Arrabal").

As he roamed like a stranger through the streets of his native city, "disheartened by the insolence of its false lights," his thoughts went back to a loved one, whose memory was "like a live coal / I never let go of / even though it burns my hands" ("City," "Ciudad"). That memory could have been of his former sweetheart, Emilie, in Geneva, or perhaps of some other girl he had fallen for in Spain, but certainly there was no one for him in Buenos Aires, for by June 21, on St. John's Night, when traditionally the promise of love is conjured up by bonfires blazing in the darkness, he describes his "loneliness reciting the whole night long / the dispersed rosary of scattered stars." ("La Noche de San Juan"). He had no male friends either, and he sorely missed Jacobo Sureda. In one of his letters, he sent him "many millions of calories from the dynamo of my heart," as he put it, only half in jest, for he signs off these early letters to Sureda with expressions of great ardor—"Your brother embraces you furiously" or "I embrace you with an unfurled heart"—and repeatedly begs his Spanish friend to write back straightaway: "Don't abandon me in this exile of mine, which is overrun by arrivistes, by correct youths lacking any mental equipment, and decorative young ladies."[3]

The Borges family had returned to Argentina at a time of political agitation and uncertainty. A sea change had occurred during the years they had spent in Europe, when in 1916 the Radicals had at last achieved power under their veteran leader Hipólito Irigoyen. Following this great victory, Irigoyen tried to meet the explosion of demands for change and reform by increasing state spending and creating a vast array of new jobs in government. This bonanza, however, produced high inflation and mounting industrial action by the anarchist unions, which came to a head in the infamous Semana Trágica in January 1919, a "tragic week" of riots and street battles that were bloodily repressed by the police. Irigoyen's expansionist policies and his attempts to nationalize the oil industry caused alarm in the *estanciero* oligarchy, who ran the vital export economy, and led to tensions within the Radical Party itself. The next presidential elections were due to be held in March 1922, but since the beleaguered Irigoyen was constitutionally barred from standing for a second consecutive term, the Radicals had chosen as their candidate Marcelo T. de Alvear, who, as a landowner himself, was far more palatable to the export interests.

By the time the Borgeses returned to Argentina in 1921, it was clear that Irigoyen had failed to break the grip of the oligarchy that had governed the country since 1880. A historic opportunity appeared to have come and gone for the likes of modest criollo families like the Borgeses. Little wonder, then, that Georgie found Buenos Aires a philistine place where, as he put it to

Sureda, there reigned "a disheartening incomprehension of and indifference to anything connected with art, because this pack of millionaires who now run the republic prefer to show off their wealth by spending it on motorcars and on clothes than on pictures or books."[4] It was the old family grievance—things were not what they used to be when the old criollo families were at the heart of society. He complained to Guillermo de Torre that he did not yet feel he fully beonged in his native Argentina, which was a much less joyful place than a Spaniard might imagine.[5]

Beyond his family's social displacement, however, Borges sensed that the Argentines suffered from a more general deracination. He attempted to articulate this in an essay he wrote on Buenos Aires, which he sent Guillermo de Torre in June for publication in a Spanish literary magazine called *Cosmópolis*.[6] In Buenos Aires "horizontal lines predominate over the vertical": it was a city of uniformly squat houses, "timid yet proud," which "translate into bricks and mortar" the "fatalism" of their inhabitants, a fatalism that was not "individualistic" or "anarchic" like that of the Spaniard but "the shamefaced fatalism of the criollo who these days tries to be a Westerner and cannot": "Poor criollos! In the depths of our soul we feel the wellsprings of our Spanishness, and yet they wish to turn us into yanquis, into counterfeit yanquis, and entice us with the baubles of democracy and the vote." The essay ends with a commemoration of Evaristo Carriego, who died in one of those modest houses of Buenos Aires, and it looks forward to the day when "our Messiah will be born" in another of those humble dwellings of the *orillas*.

To while away the time before his return to Spain, he began to frequent the *tertulia* of Macedonio Fernández, his father's old friend from school and university. Macedonio had become an eccentric, vagabond figure, living on the fringes of society. After the failure of the anarchist commune in Paraguay, he had worked for a time as a district attorney in Posadas near the Paraguayan border and then returned to Buenos Aires, where he set up a modest law practice on the avenida de Mayo. He remained a philosophical anarchist, encapsulating his basic beliefs in the formula "the maximum of the Individual, the minimum of the State," but after the crushing of the anarchist unions during the Semana Trágica he became disillusioned with politics. The death of his wife in 1920 was a devastating blow. He was left with four young children aged between three and eleven years, and, recognizing that he was too impractical to look after his family properly, he delivered them to the care of two married sisters of his, while he himself took to living in cheap boardinghouses or as the temporary guest of a succession of friends.

One of the few fixed points in Macedonio's erratic existence was his Saturday-night *tertulia* at the Café La Perla on the calle Jujuy, in a shabby area near the markets at Plaza del Once. There he had gathered about him a group of young men in their early twenties who spent their time talking mostly about literature and politics. Though lugubrious and taciturn, Macedonio was a charismatic figure with a whimsical sense of humor. His favorite ploy was to bring up a topic and let his young companions elaborate on it and then intervene either to give it an unexpected twist or deflate it altogether. Always an admirer of eccentrics, Borges was soon enough captivated by Macedonio. There was something about his marginal existence that appealed to Georgie, perhaps because it was so different from the buttoned-up respectability of his own family. But it was Macedonio's ideas that he would find especially engaging, since they enabled him to philosophize about his own inveterate tendency to solipsism.

Macedonio's rootless lifestyle grew out of a philosophical outlook characterized by the most extreme idealism. Macedonio denied the reality of space or time or even of the self, which he regarded as a transient bundle of mental states displaying no necessary connection between each other. His conviction that the world was unknowable and that individual personality was an illusion may have been influenced by two tragic events in his life, the death of his father when he was two or three years old and the more recent death of his wife. Macedonio did not accept the finality of death, professing to believe that the ultimate reality lay in an impersonal plane of psychic communication, a mental interconnectedness that transcended the limits of individual subjects and bodies. This belief in the "psyche without the body" led to a search for a "poetics of speculative thought," but since he rejected the continuity of time, space, or the self, he had difficulty achieving coherent form in his writing. Typically he handled this problem by digressing from an already proliferating story to engage his reader in discussions about his general reluctance to come to any conclusion.

Though he lived to think and write, Macedonio could not organize himself to get anything published. He was very little bothered with publication anyway, and tended to carry his papers about with him in shoe boxes or biscuit tins, sometimes leaving a trail of scribblings and half-finished notes behind him when he changed his place of residence. For years he had been writing a work of idealist metaphysics, and he even claimed to have entered into a correspondence with the American philosopher William James, whom he greatly admired, as did his friend Dr. Borges, but he was never to finish the book. His novels, too, remained incomplete, and it was only after Borges and some friends put together a collection of his writings in 1928 that he gradually got around to delivering his work to the printing press.

Macedonio's *tertulia* at the Café La Perla on Saturday nights became the highlight of the week in Borges's otherwise empty existence. The talk there, he was to recall, was largely about "the uses of metaphor or the inexistence of the self."[7] Borges joined in with tremendous enthusiasm. On June 22 he wrote to Sureda about the plot of a fantasy novel he had thought up and which he proposed to write with his fellow *tertulianos*. Its title was *El hombre que será presidente* (*The Man Who Will Be President*), an appropriately topical subject given the upcoming presidential elections in the following year. The plot involved a conspiracy to induce a collective nervous breakdown in the citizens of Buenos Aires so as to make Macedonio president of the republic and "open the way to bolshevism"; the revolutionaries would multiply little annoyances throughout the city so as to wear down everyone's nerves: "barrel organs wouldn't ever finish a melody, cutting it short halfway through; the whole city would be filled with useless objects, like barometers; the handrails on trams would be loosened, etc."; there was "no great danger" that they would ever write such a novel—"but it serves as a useful battleground for our verbal combat."[8]

In later years Borges came to regard Macedonio Fernández as a far better talker than he was a writer. Even so, the influence of Macedonio's ideas on Borges's writing was crucial, especially as regards two fundamental themes that would not come to maturity until the 1940s—the "unreality" of the material world and the nonexistence of the "I," or individual subject. Borges would elaborate this latter idea into one of his most striking themes—the arbitrariness of personal identity, the notion that an individual could, in principle, be any other, an idea he had already come across in Schopenhauer.

Apart from the weekly *tertulia*, Borges was lonely and depressed during his first few months in Buenos Aires: he looked forward to returning to "the Old Continent," which, as he told Sureda, "was newer than this one, this America, where everything seems lifeless and withered."[9] To all intents and purposes, he regarded himself as a Spanish poet, and he expected his "exile" in Argentina to last only five or six months at best. However, after about five months in Buenos Aires, his parents decided to postpone their return to Spain for a year. In August, Borges told Sureda that they would be going to Switzerland toward the middle of 1922, so that his father could have his eyes operated on in either Zurich or Geneva.[10] Whatever the reason may have been for his parents' postponement of their return to Europe, Georgie faced the dreary prospect of hanging around in Buenos Aires for another twelve months or so, followed by an indefinite period in Geneva, before the family could settle permanently near Madrid. It is no surprise that in the circumstances he should have been so taken with Macedonio's radical idealism. For the rest of 1921, he would pass the time toying with gloomy thoughts of his nonexistence as an individual and trying to work idealist fancies into the poems he was writing. In "Long Walk" ("Caminata") he wrote, "I am the only spectator of this street, / If I stopped looking it would die," a conceit that he expanded in "Daybreak" ("Amanecer"), where, following "the tremendous conjecture of Schopenhauer and Berkeley," he imagines that dawn is the hour when "it would be easy for God to kill off this deadening existence altogether."

By November, philosophy had begun to eclipse his interest in poetry, for Macedonio's theory of the nonself undermined Georgie's *ultraísta* poetics, based as this was on an extreme individualism in which each poet must strive to be absolutely different from all the others. In a letter to Sureda, he dismissed poetry as "something limited, shut in—a mere accident of literature," and summarized his "ideological position" thus: "The I does not exist, life is a mishmash of incomplete moments, Art (let's grant the poor thing a capital letter) must be without equal and possess a life of its own, the autobiographical must be drowned for the greater happiness of oneself and others, etc. . . ."; his confusion is evident in the proposal he put to Sureda that in Spain the following year they should collaborate on a book of "a joyful and definitive nihilism, where you would find all kinds of things—metaphysics, *ultraísmo, grueguerías,* and, at the end, a refutation of the book and its plan and its egoisms."[11]

Toward the end of the year, his interest in poetry had all but evaporated, and over the next few months, he would produce three essays on metaphysical topics inspired by his discussions with Macedonio. Quite rebarbative in tone and style, these pieces are of little interest in themselves, except to the extent that they reveal how this self-obsessed youth discovered in a few basic tenets of idealism the means of articulating his deepening introversion. In "The Nothingness of Personality" ("La nadería de la personalidad"), the phrase "The I does not exist" is the leitmotif that underpins his argument.[12] In January 1922, on holiday with his family in Patagonia, he whiled away the long hours in that wilderness of barren hills and windswept skies by writing another essay to which he gave the clumsy title "The Blue Sky Is Sky and Is Blue," ("El cielo azul, es cielo y es azul"), in which he contended that there was no point in looking beyond appearances, since there were no "things in themselves," no essences, for "reality," in a phrase of Macedonio's, "functions as an open mystery."[13] He followed this up with "The Crux in Berkeley" ("La encrucijada de Berkeley"), in which he argued that there is no center in consciousness to warrant an enduring sense of personal identity—not God, nor Schopenhauer's "Representation," nor the Energy of the materialists.[14] Neither self nor reality has any "essence," therefore. This is pure Macedonio, of course; so, too, is the wonderfully narcissistic figure he conjured up to describe the relation of self to world: "Reality is like that image of ours which appears in every mirror, a simulacrum that exists thanks to us, that accompanies us, gesticulates, and goes away, but which never fails to turn up as soon as we look for it."

Even though Borges was more interested in philosophy than he was in poetry by now, he was so bored with his life that, by October 1921 or thereabouts, he decided to amuse himself by starting up a branch of the Ultra in Buenos Aires, as he had done in Majorca. Probably his first recruit was his cousin Guillermo Juan Borges, the son of his uncle Frank, a highly strung youth known in the family as "Willie." Willie was a student at the Naval College in Buenos Aires and lodged with his widowed aunt, Berta Erfjord de Lange and her six children—five daughters and a son—in their large house in Villa Mazzini, a district that lay between Buenos Aires proper and what was then the separate town of Belgrano, several miles to the northwest. The Borgeses were related by marriage to the Lange family through Willie's mother, Estela Erfjord, who was Berta's sister. Both the Erfjords and the Langes, being of Norwegian extraction, were conspicuous for their fair-skinned, Scandinavian looks. What with their Nordic features and their relatively modern outlook, the five Lange sisters, though Argentine born, remained exotic creatures, who were rather frowned upon as being too "liberal" by the straitlaced ladies of Buenos Aires.

Indeed, Leonor Acevedo was none too keen for her daughter, Norah, or even Georgie, to associate with the Langes, but since Berta Erfjord was the sister of Frank Borges's wife, she could not really forbid them to see their Lange "cousins," and in any case her husband was himself a visitor to his sister-in-law's house. In fact, it was Dr. Borges who revealed the poetic talent of the young Norah Lange. Though she had started writing poems at an early age, she lacked the confidence to show her work to anyone until her "uncle," Jorge Guillermo Borges, challenged her to write a gloss on the phrase "the time is not yet ripe," and Norah rose to the occasion and obliged him with a poem. Thus did Norah Lange, who was only sixteen at the time, qualify for membership in the Ultra group that young Georgie was in the process of forming in Buenos Aires.

Borges's decision to set up a branch of the Ultra in Buenos Aires would in due course revolutionize the Argentine literary world. Up till then the European avant-garde had made no impact at all, and Argentine writing was still under the influence of *modernismo,* a movement based on French symbolism and Parnassianism, which had been founded by the great Nicaraguan poet Rubén Darío in the 1890s and had spread to all Spanish-speaking countries. Darío's disciple in Argentina, Leopoldo Lugones, was the country's preeminent poet, and his *Lunario sentimental* of 1909, a late *modernista* work, still enjoyed immense prestige. There had been the odd attempt to move beyond *modernismo,* however; notably by Ricardo Güiraldes, who tried writing in a plainer idiom on specifically Argentine themes but gave up after being totally neglected by the establishment. There was also a marginal group of young poets, led by a truculent Peruvian called Alberto Hidalgo, who were known as the *sencillistas* because they advocated writing in a more simple (*sencillo*) language than did the *modernistas.* There was not much else in Buenos Aires at the time; it was a complacent backwater in which the mighty Lugones remained the biggest fish.

Borges had no literary contacts to speak of in Argentina, so his problem was to find a way of announcing the arrival of the avant-garde. He came up with the idea of creating a "mural magazine," which would consist basically of a large poster on which he would print a sample of *ultraísta* poems and a manifesto of the Ultra's aesthetic principles. He decided to call it *Prisma*, in accordance with his idea that the poet's imagination must be an "active prism" in its processing of experience. He asked some of his Spanish friends—Jacobo Sureda, Adriano del Valle, Pedro Garfias, Isaac del Vando Villar, and José Rivas Panedas—to contribute an *ultraísta* poem each and encouraged his new comrades in Buenos Aires, namely his cousin Guillermo Juan and Eduardo González Lanuza, for a contribution. Alongside these brief poems was a woodcut by Norah Borges—a kind of stylized geometrical collage of typical features of Buenos Aires domestic architecture—and below it came a "Proclama" written by Borges himself but bearing the names also of Guillermo de Torre, Guillermo Juan (Borges), and Eduardo González Lanuza. Most of this "Proclamation" was taken up with a verbose rant against the stale rhetoric and "dessicated hearts" of the followers of Rubén Darío, and it concluded by asserting that the *ultraístas* wanted to "overcome the paralysis of art" by laying bare "unsuspected facets of the world" through the metaphor, the "primordial element" in poetry: "Each verse of our poems possesses its own individual life and represents an unprecedented vision. *Ultraísmo* thus tends toward the formation of an emotional and variable mythology."[15]

Thus—on the night of November 25, 1921, when Borges and four of his friends sallied forth with brushes and buckets of glue to stick up *Prisma* on the walls of Buenos Aires—was born the Argentine avant-garde (although five of the eight poets on display happened to be Spaniards). In the space of two nights, they put up about a thousand posters in the avenida Santa Fe and environs. But this strange "mural magazine" was greeted with resounding indifference by the middle-class citizens of the Barrio Norte, and the Argentine branch of the Ultra might well have died an instant death had it not been for the fact that a poster happened to catch the eye of Alfredo Bianchi, an editor at the prestigious literary journal *Nosotros,* who got in touch with Borges and invited him to write a piece explaining *ultraísmo* to his readers. In this article, which appeared in *Nosotros* in December 1921, Borges gave his standard expressionist version of the Ultra's aims, but a new element had entered his thinking: in the "Proclama" he had written for the mural *Prisma*, he had referred to the "superstition of the self," and now he elaborated on this concept by explaining that it was a "psychological error" to believe that the poet should express his "personality," because the "I" of the poet embraced "the plurality of all the states of consciousness," and it was "futile" to try to "fix in words a vagabond self which transforms itself at every moment"; *ultraísmo* aimed at transmuting "the palpable reality of the world into an interior and emotional reality."[16] Borges's expressionist version of the Ultra showed signs of succumbing to Macedonio's theory of the nullity of the self, but it was an influence that would not last very long, as we shall see.

After an unpromising start, the mural magazine *Prisma* attracted a good deal of attention—new friends, letters, many unsolicited contributions, and jibes from uncomprehending journalists, Borges informed Guillermo de Torre.[17] He could now count on about seven or eight members of the Ultra group, and another issue of *Prisma* was planned for the end of January. However, this second number was postponed in December because Georgie had to accompany his family on a visit to Patagonia to see his uncle Frank, who was commander of the naval base at Comodoro Rivadavia in Chubut. When he got back about a month later, the Argentine *ultraístas* resumed their campaign to promote the new poetry.

In February, Eduardo González Lanuza, one of the most zealous of the converts to the Ultra, gave a lecture and poetry reading at the Ateneo Universitario, where he launched a violent attack on the *sencillistas,* who made up the majority of the audience. The second number of *Prisma* was ready by the middle of March, but they thought it best to wait until after the elections because there seemed little point in putting it up on the walls of a city that was already covered in campaign posters. In the meantime Borges and his friends distributed the magazine in the literary cafés, and on March 27 he went with González Lanuza to see none other than Leopoldo Lugones, "the greatest literary godfather in these parts," as he described him to Sureda.[18] They presented the great man with copies of the two issues of *Prisma* and spent some three hours arguing with him, mostly about the relative merits of rhyme and free verse. Borges and Lanuza tried to outdo each other in their impertinence toward the older poet, each fearing he might appear too obsequious in the eyes of the other. With hindsight Borges realized that Lugones had been humoring them: "He could easily have crushed us. . . . But he didn't." Lugones simply "read our verses and said, 'Well, I see that I'm quite close to you.'"[19] It was his way of pointing out that these young upstarts were not doing anything particularly new, his own *Lunario sentimental* having already rung the changes on a plethora of innovative metaphors. At the time, however, Borges interpreted Lugones's polite praise as signifying a major triumph for *ultraísmo,* reporting to Sureda that the venerable poet had "declared himself to be a trampled lawn and a replete cemetery (though not in these words, of course)."[20] Much as he fancied himself a rebel against the establishment, it was only in private that this shy young man dared reveal the violent feelings he harbored toward his elders.

At last, in the first week of April, the second issue of *Prisma* was pasted up on the walls of Buenos Aires, and that month, too, Borges and some of his comrades—cousin Willie, Lanuza, and Francisco Piñero—traveled, at the invitation of an aunt of Piñero's, to the city of Rosario in the province of Santa Fe to give readings of *ultraísta* poetry at the University of El Litoral. Once again Lanuza gave a lecture on *ultraísmo,* this time to a capacity audience, which gave him an unexpectedly warm reception. Afterward some thirty students accompanied the *ultraístas* to a café and listened enthusiastically to the good news of the Buenos Aires avant-garde, deciding to form a branch of their own in Rosario.[21] Borges was pleased with progress so far: *ultraísmo* was making an impact, and despite continuing criticism and insults, he told Guillermo de Torre that he was receiving contributions and offers of support.[22]

Borges had managed to put together an Ultra group of about seven young poets, in addition to himself—his cousin Guillermo Juan, Eduardo González Lanuza, Francisco Piñero, Roberto Ortelli, Rolando Martel, the Chilean Salvador Reyes, and Norah Lange, the only girl. They had taken to meeting at the house of the Lange family on the calle Tronador, and there Borges was to find a relaxed, almost bohemian ambience, which he came to appreciate as a blessed refuge from his own stiff and awkward family. At the Lange house, what was more, he could enjoy the company of the opposite sex. In addition to the five Lange sisters, he got to know their school friends, the Soraggi sisters and the Guerrero sisters: Celia—Ruthy Lange's friend—and Concepción, the best friend of Norah Lange. And then, sometime in March, he found he had fallen in love with Concepción Guerrero. He described her to Sureda as "a very wonderful girl of sixteen, Andalusian blood, great black eyes, and an agreeably gentle serenity with deep reserves of tenderness."[23] She was the daughter of Spanish immigrants from Granada who lived, as he was to describe it to Sureda, "out there in one of the remoter suburbs, enduring the proud, difficult, monotonous and retiring existence of a decent but poor girl."[24] Her father was a primary-school teacher, and the family lived on calle Pampa, in one of those modest one-story dwellings that were so typical of the *orillas* of Buenos Aires, where immigrants tended to settle, and which contrasted so starkly with the large villa of the Lange family on the nearby corner of Pampa and Tronador.

The fact that his feelings were reciprocated by Concepción was something Georgie had not experienced since his ill-starred romance with Emilie in Geneva three years earlier. He was so taken with his new girlfriend that very soon his thoughts turned to the possibility of marriage, as he told Sureda in a letter toward the end of March.[25] But, for all that, he was extremely wary of his family's reaction to the girl and kept his relations with her a secret from his parents, fearing, no doubt, that they might interfere in his sentimental life once again. Concepción, after all, was a daughter of Spanish immigrants who tended to be despised by patrician criollos, and if the Lange girls were considered unsuitable by Mother, how much less acceptable would she find his new sweetheart?

After his recent sallies into metaphysics under the influence of Macedonio, he returned to poetry. However, the poems he now wrote were of a quite different tenor from those he had composed after his arrival in Argentina, when he was still seized with the bitterness of having been torn away from Spain. By the time the second *Prisma* appeared, in April 1922, he was beginning to find his native city strangely welcoming. He records his growing familiarity with its streets—the pleasure of discovering by chance that his dejection and listlessness are dispelled by hearing a snatch of *porteño* music, which he carries about inside him "like someone holding a banner" ("Discovery," "Hallazgo"). In "Music of the *Patria*" ("Música patria"), he celebrates the typical guitar music of the criollos, which has so penetrated the Argentine soul that if one hears it coming from a window at night, "the wanderer / feels as if a hand were caressing his heart." He writes of a street's entering his "yearning heart with the purity of a tear" and becoming so "intimate and enchanting" that he forgets for a while that he has never seen the place before ("Unknown Street," "Calle desconocida"). He finds a "secret amity" in "a porch, a gable, a water tank" ("Un Patio"). Even the great Plaza San Martín "opens wide like a generous bosom overflowing with reassurance" ("La Plaza San Martín").

There can be little doubt that it was his love for Concepción that renewed his appreciation of poetry. In April or thereabouts, he decided to collect his poems in a book that would form a record of his life in Buenos Aires, describing it to Sureda as "lyrical-metaphysical-magical-confessional" (*"lírico-metafísico-gualicheante-confesional"*).[26] At around this time, too, he decided to replace his mural magazine, *Prisma,* with a more permanent and substantial publication. He discussed a name for the proposed magazine with his friends, and they finally agreed on *Proa,* or "prow," a suitably vanguard title for this tiny cell of would-be revolutionaries. The members of the Ultra group contributed twenty pesos each toward the costs of production of what, in any case, was to be a pretty modest publication, consisting of a single sheet of paper folded twice to form a double-sided triptych with a total of six pages. The model Borges had in mind was the Spanish magazine *Ultra,* which, ironically, had ceased publication the previous month, its last number having appeared on March 15. The demise of *Ultra* was a sign that *ultraísmo* in Madrid was fading away and its members striking out on their own. But Borges nevertheless persevered with his Ultra project in Buenos Aires, which had brought him, after all, a certain notoriety in the literary world, an ever-widening circle of friends, and, not least, love.

When the first issue of *Proa* appeared in the early part of August, Borges's editorial hand was unmistakable—the cover was illustrated with a woodcut by his sister, Norah, and at the top of the front page he published a short piece by the founder of Ultra, Cansinos-Asséns, below which he placed the lengthiest item, his own metaphysical essay, "The Nothingness of Personality." The rest of the issue is devoted to poems by the Buenos Aires *ultraístas*—González Lanuza, cousin Willie, Norah Lange, and Roberto Ortelli—and by a few of his Spanish friends. Finally there were a couple of whimsical pieces by Borges's other maestro, Macedonio Fernández. *Proa*, in effect, was a halfway house between the avant-gardes in Madrid and Buenos Aires.

All the while that he was involved in his literary activities, a new problem was preying on Georgie's mind. His parents were still planning to leave Argentina sometime in the latter half of 1922—in late March he had told Sureda that they would depart in September[27]—but, having met Concepción Guerrero, Georgie was no longer keen to return to Spain. Virtually from the moment he fell in love with Concepción in March, he worried about what he would do when the time came to leave. Clearly it was a cause of concern to him that he lacked educational qualifications—he had asked Torre in March whether a Swiss or French *baccalauréat* was valid for admission to a Spanish university, claiming disingenuously to have completed five years of secondary education in Geneva.[28] Such a lack of qualifications would have made it all the harder for him to defy his parents, if necessary, and eventually marry Concepción. Still, he does seem to have made some attempt to remedy this lack. He decided to qualify as a teacher of English, and, in a letter to Sureda of July 25, he claimed to be studying, albeit halfheartedly, for examinations in English (very likely the Cambridge Proficiency Certificate), which he hoped to take that month; in the same letter, he confessed to being more in love with Concepción than ever but seemed very apprehensive about the future: "God knows how it will all end."[29]

His anxiety may perhaps have been aggravated by the fact that the timing of the family's return to Europe appears to have become somewhat fluid. In the letters he wrote to his Spanish friends between March and mid-August 1922, their departure is brought forward to August, then put back to September. I would guess that these fluctuations may have been caused by a difference of opinion between Dr. Borges and his wife, Leonor, about whether they should go back at all. It is very likely that Leonor, good criolla that she was, would have wished to abandon the idea of settling in Spain, while her husband must have wanted to resume his existence as an "invisible man" in Europe. By September a decision had been made—they would stay in Argentina. Georgie wrote informing Guillermo de Torre that they planned to move back to their old house on calle Serrano in Palermo by the end of the year.[30]

Georgie must have been mightily relieved that they were staying in Buenos Aires; he was free to pursue his love affair with Concepción and could put off the evil day when he might have to confront his parents over it. For Dr. Borges, however, that decision would have been a crushing disappointment, for it signaled the failure of all the objectives he had set himself when he decided to take the family to Europe in 1914. He had wanted to give his children a good education, but neither Georgie nor Norah had even graduated from high school; he had hoped to succeed as a writer, but his novel, *El Caudillo,* had made no impact at all in Buenos Aires, receiving only one or two polite reviews, and from Georgie's friends at that. It would appear, moreover, that Leonor, once back in her native environment, had reverted to type and become obsessed with the glory of her ancestors. From this point onward, Dr. Borges would fade into the background of family life, for the decision to stay in Buenos Aires had resulted in a decisive shift in power toward Leonor Acevedo, who, for all intents and purposes, had taken over as head of the family. The passivity that as a boy Georgie had sensed in his father had become a palpable reality. In his play about Bernardo del Carpio, young Georgie had fantasized about rescuing his father from the wicked king who held him captive, but rescuing Father from that passivity would now have entailed rebelling against Mother, for it was she who, more than anyone, upheld the sword of honor bequeathed by their ancestors.

Still, if there was anything from which Borges could draw strength, it was the love he bore Concepción Guerrero. At around this time, he wrote a number of poems in which he seems to have been girding his loins, as it were, for the inevitable confrontation with Mother over his relationship with Concepción. There are two poems, each entitled "Inscription on a Tomb" ("Inscripción sepulcral"), where he addresses his heroic ancestors, Colonel Suárez and Colonel Borges, respectively, with a kind of distant reverence—the glory of Suárez is compared to an island girt "by oblivion," and he piously "prays" that the other hero, Borges, will be accorded "immortality." But even though he pays his respects to these family heroes, he clearly wants to keep their memory at arm's length. In a further poem, tellingly called "Inscription on Any Tomb" ("Inscripción en cualquier sepulcro"), he denounces the attempt to seek "garrulous exceptions to the omnipotence of oblivion" by commemorating in funerary marble "the pomposities of name, reputation, feats and fatherland." Its central conceit is derived from Macedonio's metaphysics of the self—just as one person is equivalent to any person, so, too, is one tomb as worthy of note as any other tomb.

As Georgie's love for Concepción grows, so does his hostility toward Mother and his ancestors. In the poem "Rosas," he evokes the drawing room in the family home, calling it a "loveless ambit," "whose austere clock pours out a time lacking adventures or wonder by now"; and he recalls how the name of the tyrant Juan Manuel de Rosas, the man who dispossessed Colonel

Suárez and brought about the social decline of the family, cropped up in conversation in that drawing room and released a stream of hateful "memories and conjectures" that followed one upon the other "like a single blow is followed by a fight." One can be sure that this stream of vituperation came from Doña Leonor, for whom the old conflict between civilization and barbarism was still a vital preoccupation. Yet the paradox at the heart of the poem is that Rosas feels more alive to Borges than any of his ancestors. Suddenly "the image of the tyrant" is brought to life by "the alms of hatred" that his family dispenses to his ghost, and Rosas fills the room "like the shadow of a distant mountain."

In the affective economy of Borges's imagination, Mother's hatred of Rosas was so potent that to oppose her was to come alive, while to seek her approval was somehow to submit to oppression. Thus, "civilization" was associated with a deadening conformity; "barbarism" stood for passion, energy, fulfillment. The most arresting image in "Rosas" describes the "pitiful whiteness" of a tablecloth, which "shrouds the red passion of the mahogany." Here the color red is no mere cliché, for red was the color of Rosas's party, a color banned from the house by Mother for its associations with the *federales*, with gauchos, and so with infamy and barbarism.

In this scheme of things, Georgie's love for Concepción was unquestionably on the side of the tyrant Rosas and the *colorados*, the "reds." His love became politicized, so to speak, by the inflexibility of Mother's prejudices. And in contrast to Mother's fixation with her heroic forebears, he was to raise Concepción into a symbol of a more contemporary, more egalitarian Argentina that would permit him to escape the ancestral sword of honor. The most aggressive of these poems is "Empty Drawing Room" ("Sala vacía"), where he evokes the deathly ambience of the family home, with its mahogany furniture and old armchairs, with the portraits of the dead heroes as well as their silverware and their swords. He feels utterly oppressed by daguerreotypes that "lie" about the "closeness" of his forebears and are as "useless" as the "dates of hazy anniversaries." Even so, he cannot stifle "the anguished half-voice" of his ancestors, which seems to pursue him down the years. He puts up a resistance to it by imagining "the bustle of the street" outside the house, by throwing open the shutters to see how the light of day "punches a hole in the windows / and humiliates the senile armchairs, / and corners and strangles / the faded voice / of the ancestors."

The young Borges turned to the streets of Buenos Aires because they offered him a warmth and vitality that he felt he lacked at home. These streets, however, were not the cosmopolitan streets of the city center; he was drawn to the streets of the poor suburbs, "mellowed by trees and sunsets" ("Calles"). In the poem "Villa Urquiza," he wrote that the calle Pampa, the street where his sweetheart lived, was "as long as a kiss," and he declared that such a street, having "planted a tradition of love in the soul," needed no "vainglorious renown" to earn it "the praise of verse."

When Concepción spent a short period away from Buenos Aires, he found her absence quite unbearable. "I have been parted from my *novia*," he wrote to Sureda; "two eternal weeks will have to pass before I can see her again; I feel desolate and godforsaken" (*"dejado de la mano de Dios"*).[31] Concepción's absence was, indeed, a foretaste of death for him, "a terrible sun that never sets," binding "the soul like a cord around one's neck" ("Absence," "Ausencia"). His thoughts turned to God and death and the afterlife. "One must think about fundamental things," he rather pompously announced to Sureda, and explained that the night before, while listening to a mournful tango in a backstreet café, it occurred to him that "the total cessation of life would be more surprising perhaps, more inexplicable and senseless, than the idea of immortality. How can one conceive of an end to living, which is so intricate, so full of everything that God has created?"[32] And he copied for his friend some lines he found in a sonnet of Quevedo's, which he believed to be relevant to this insight of his:

> Médulas que han gloriosamente ardido,
> Venas que humor a tanto fuego han dado
> Serán ceniza, mas tendrá sentido,
> Polvo serán, mas polvo enamorado.

> [Marrow that has gloriously burned,
> Veins that have fueled so much fire,
> Ash they shall become, but ash that shall yet feel,
> Dust they may be, but dust that loves you still.]

Borges found these lines "almost pantheist," speaking as they did of the endurance of amorous passion beyond death itself.

The depth of his love for Concepción was such that it made him question Macedonio Fernández's notion of the nonexistence of the self (i.e., one person's being equivalent to any other). On the contrary, he began to marvel at the way personal identity appeared to endure through time. In "Year's End" ("Final de año") he wondered why at New Year—as 1922 turned into 1923—so much was made of "the numerical detail of substituting a three for a two," and he concluded that it was due to our sensing the "metaphysical possibilities of Time," to our "excitement at the miracle / that in spite of such infinite alternatives / something might persist within us / unchanging." Knowing that he could not bear his sweetheart's absence, he was overcome by the utter singularity of her delightful person. His love, indeed, acquired a religious intensity, and he praised "the incense of your presence / which I shall later burn in my memory" and regaled Concepción with extravagant devotional praise: "Your beauty lavishes its miracle upon time"; "As ever, your multifarious beauty / spreads brightly over my soul" ("Saturdays," "Sábados").

By the beginning of 1923, Borges felt a sense of belonging in his native Argentina that he had simply never known before. I reckon it would have been around this time that he wrote a poem in praise of the garden at the Lange house on calle Tronador, his trysting place with Concepción. The title he gave it, "Llaneza," can mean "frankness," "plainness," "simplicity," precisely the qualities that had been so conspicuously absent in his life so far. At the house on calle Tronador:

> I know the customs and the souls
> and that dialect of allusions and idioms
> which any human group contrives for itself.
> I need not claim or deny any privileges:
> I am well enough known by those around me,
> who know well enough my sorrows and my weaknesses.
> This is to attain the highest goal,
> what may perhaps await us in heaven:
> not admiration or victory
> but simply to be accepted
> as part of an undeniable Reality,
> like the stones and the trees.
> —*Fervor de Buenos Aires,* first edition, 1923, but revised
> in later editions

This is a poem that celebrates his emergence at last from the solipsism he had experienced since earliest childhood. Love has connected him to another human soul, and, thanks to Concepción, he has found a connection also to other people and to the reality of his native land. A measure of the difference that love has made to his outlook can be had by comparing this powerful sense of integration in the real world—"like the stones and the trees"—and that other image of reality as a mere narcissistic projection of the self upon a mirror that, under Macedonio Fernández's influence, he had offered only a year earlier in his essay on Berkeley.

He felt quite the Argentine by now, telling Guillermo de Torre that life in Buenos Aires was beautiful and expansive and dynamic, and he teased his Spanish friend about the risk he would run of becoming a criollo should Torre decide to visit them in Buenos Aires.[33] Borges seems actually to have been enjoying life, even portraying himself to Sureda as something of a young man about town:

> You ask if I get bored. I have to say, hardly ever. I'm rather taken—don't laugh—with society: I chat to young ladies, I play cards and chess, I comb my hair from time to time. If I were to say that I'm worried about my neckties I'd be telling a barefaced lie, but it might serve as a metaphor to define my present state of mind.[34]

Clearly he was very happy—happy with his friends, happy with Buenos Aires and, if his rather clumsy attempts at physical vanity are anything to go by, happy even with himself, which was no mean feat given his family history. And the source of such happiness was, of course, Concepción: "Happiness is in you like spring in the new leaf," he would write. "You, who were but the sum of beauty yesterday / are the sum of love today" ("Saturdays," "Sábados").

Through 1922 and into 1923, Borges's feelings for Concepción had been rising in a steady crescendo, and they reached a climax in "La Guitarra," the only poem of this period in which he captured something of the Whitmanesque passion he had always strived to express in his verse. Here passion wells up within him as he hears someone plucking the strings of a guitar in the little patio of a house on calle Sarandí in Buenos Aires. He fancies he can see the pampas—the quintessential landscape of the *patria*—"crouching in the depths of a guitar." And as the pampas unfold before his eyes, he repeats the verb "Vi. . . . Vi. . . . Vi. . . ." ("I saw. . . . I saw. . . . I saw. . . ."), a construction that will reappear in later texts by Borges, most notably in the final, ecstatic vision of his story "The Aleph," published in 1945. This, however, is the first instance of the topos in Borges's work, and, as in "The Aleph," the experience is vouchsafed by a woman's love: "I saw her too / whose memory awaits in all music." In "La Guitarra" the erotico-mystical aspirations he had first written about in "An Interlude of Passion" are reawakened. It was the memory of the Swiss girl, Emilie, that had aroused such ardent imaginings back in Seville in 1919, and now that he was in love again, and even planned to marry Concepción, he could look forward to the day when life would be transformed into one great "Hymn of Joy," as he had put it in an earlier poem, through the true nuptials of self and cosmos.

Toward the end of March 1923, however, all his plans were thrown into disarray. In a letter to Sureda, written (in French) probably in the first weeks of April, he said that he would be returning to Europe—"the happy-go-lucky, ironic, and very correct method or rather vision of life" which Sureda supposed he led, "risked collapse," he wrote, because in two or three months' time he would be back at the "Vieux Collège" in Geneva.[35] All the signs are that this decision to return to Europe was taken quite suddenly. Borges himself was certainly surprised and caught off balance by it. What were the reasons for the family's change of mind? The record is sparse and not wholly reliable at this point. The reason usually given is that Dr. Borges wished to consult a specialist about his eyesight. This may well be true, but why the haste? In the family of Concepción Guerrero, it was said that Borges's mother was opposed to her son's relationship with Concepción and that the trip to Europe was planned in order to break it up.[36] It may be that, even though Georgie had tried to keep his courtship of Concepción a secret from his parents, Leonor Acevedo had somehow got wind of the romance and was horrified at the prospect of her only son's marrying the daughter of some lowly Spanish immigrants. It is plausible to imagine the forceful Leonor deciding it would be best for the family to pack their bags and go to Europe for a year, where her husband could in any case consult an eye doctor in Geneva and Georgie would have time to get over his infatuation with the unsuitable Concepción. Whatever the reason for the family's sudden determination to visit Europe, the fact remained that Georgie did not want to leave Buenos Aires at this point—he wanted to be with Concepción, the girl who only a few months back he could not bear to be parted from. He was nearly twenty-four years old, so why did he not simply insist on staying in Buenos Aires—on his own, if necessary?

Georgie, in effect, was suddenly faced with the challenge of rebelling against his mother. This would have been a repetition of the battle of wills before the tiger's cage at the zoo, but if he was capable as a child of standing up to Mother, now he simply gave in; for all the strength he may have derived from his love for Concepción, it was not sufficient to enable him to defy the sword of honor. Instead he organized a secret resistance. He communicated his plans to Sureda: he would be returning to Geneva in two or three months' time (i.e., in June or July 1923) in order to finish his *baccalauréat,* possibly at the Collège de Genève, and would then return to Buenos Aires, enroll at the Faculty of Philosophy and Letters, complete the three-year degree course in two, and marry Concepción; in fact, they had already pledged to marry: "Despite the hostility of her family and the ignorance of mine, we became engaged out there in that modest suburb I have come to adore."[37] (I surmise from this that Borges was not yet aware that Mother had been apprised of his relationship with Concepción.) Borges gave his sweetheart a ring and a copy of the love poems of the Spanish Romantic Gustavo Adolfo Bécquer.[38] In the coming weeks, he and Concepción would arrange clandestine trysts in the garden or the drawing room at the Lange villa on calle Tronador: "We don't talk much," he tells Sureda in a letter he wrote in French; "we just sit there solemnly in a kind of trance, with a lump in our throats, feeling a sort of obscure anguish of happiness ["*à la gorge une sorte d'angoisse obscure de bonheur*"], until the darkness of the night comes upon us and Concepción's face next to mine seems somehow distant. When I kiss her, she trembles all over. . . ."[39] But as he signed off his letter to his Spanish friend, he was full of foreboding: "I am weary, troubled, almost drunk."

In a letter of June 26, he told Guillermo de Torre that on July 20 the family would embark on a journey that would take them to London, Paris, Geneva, and thence to Spain but added that it grieved him to leave Concepción, more than anything because the difficulties that had formerly separated them had been overcome and he was free to see her at her house, where he was made welcome by her family.[40] In the culture of the time, the privilege of being welcomed into the home of one's sweetheart was an indispensable step toward gaining parental consent for marriage, and yet in the same letter to Torre, Borges revealed that about a month earlier, in May, the Borges house in Palermo had been rented out again and the whole family had moved to a hotel (the Hotel du Helder on calle Esmeralda) to prepare for their departure in July.

In the intervening weeks, Borges threw himself into a whirl of activity in order to complete several literary projects. A second issue of *Proa* had appeared in December, and now he rushed to publish a third, which he was just able to bring out in July, within days of his departure. He intended to keep *Proa* going after his return from Europe, so in this third issue he gave "Florida 573," the address of the journal *Nosotros,* as a contact address for prospective readers.[41] He had also been planning to start a cultural journal called *Inicial* with two young intellectuals, Alfredo Brandán Caraffa, who had been active in the university reform movement, and Roberto Ortelli, one of his *ultraísta* comrades who worked as an editor at *Nosotros.* Their aim was to foster a renovation of ideas and values in Argentina by providing a forum for a new generation of writers. He had been discussing the plan since the beginning of 1923 but had to pull out now that he was leaving, though he would keep in touch with Brandán Caraffa and Ortelli while he was in Spain. In any event, the first issue of *Inicial* did not appear until October 1923, and Borges was to contribute an essay on expressionism to its third issue in December.

The most important project he wanted to complete was the publication of the book of poems he had been planning since about April of the previous year. Like most young poets in those days, he had to have it published at his own expense. He was given the 130 pesos he needed by his father and negotiated with the Imprenta Serantes a print run of three hundred copies for a book of sixty-four pages, though that turned out to be too long, and five poems had to be removed at the last minute. The printing was done in only six days, but, given the terrible rush, there was no time to correct proofs, and the first edition appeared with a number of typographical errors, no page numbers, no table of contents and no colophon. It was priced at 1 peso, and the cover was illustrated with a woodcut by Norah Borges showing the sun going down over a one-story house typical of the outlying barrios of Buenos Aires.

The title Borges chose for his first volume of poetry was *Fervor de Buenos Aires,* which encapsulated the deep attachment he had come to feel for his native city, but the fact was, the book was published only a matter of days before he was due to leave for Europe with his family on July 21. Indeed, time was so short that he gave his friends Brandán Caraffa and Roberto Ortelli sole rights to sell the book in Argentina through the magazine *Inicial,* which was due to be launched while he was abroad.[42] As for publicizing *Fervor,* all he could do in the little time he had left was to try to get it noticed by the people who mattered. He came up with an ingenious idea:

> Having noticed that many people who went to the offices of *Nosotros . . .* left their overcoats hanging in the cloakroom, I brought fifty or a hundered copies to Alfredo Bianchi, one of the editors. Bianchi stared at me in amazement and said, "Do you expect me to sell these books for you?" "No," I answered. "Although I've written them, I'm not altogether a lunatic. I thought I might ask you to slip some of these books into the pockets of those coats hanging out there." He generously did so. When I came back after a year's absence, I found that some of the inhabitants of the overcoats had read my poems, and a few had even written about them."[43]

He also sent copies to friends like Abramowicz, Sureda, and Guillermo de Torre and obtained from the well-connected Torre a list of names of relevant people to offer them to in Spain.

His book summed up his intellectual life and his experience of love in Argentina, he told Guillermo de Torre.[44] Most of the poems had been written in the two years he had spent in Buenos Aires, but he also included a number of poems written in Spain, such as "The Flame" (whose title was changed to "Llamarada"), which dated back to his first stay in Majorca in 1919. It was not chronology that mattered to him so much as consistency of tone and theme, and for this reason he rejected the strident, highly imagistic poems such as "Soviet Epic" and "Russia," inspired by German expressionism. He was by now fairly disenchanted with some of the early aims of *ultraísmo,* especially its relentless efforts to appear "modern" and its obsession with the metaphor as the primordial element in poetry. In a letter he sent Sureda in January or February 1923, he was cruelly dismissive of Guillermo de Torre's first book: "Did you know that the effervescent Torre has just squandered thousands of those polysyllables of his in a book of poems called *Hélices* (*Propellers*)? You can't imagine the sheer quantity of junk—planes, railways, trolleybuses, hydroplanes, rainbows, elevators, signs of the Zodiac, traffic lights. . . . I feel old, academic, moth-eaten, when pounced on by a book like that."[45]

Already, during his second sojourn in Majorca, while experimenting with expressionist themes and techniques, he had noticed a dichotomy in his work between "dynamic" poems and more "listless" compositions, but in Buenos Aires his love for Concepción led him to resolve these contrasting elements into a more integrated poetic voice that was better suited to his own more contemplative sensibility and to the tranquil ambience of the outskirts of the city. Earlier that year he had described to Sureda the kind of poetry he was writing under the influence of his love for Concepción: his poems were "long, not at all visual, with no great metaphorical displays, and with a metaphysical or religious background."[46] Nevertheless, even though his poetry no longer resembled either the raucous emotionalism of the German war poets or the imagism of Guillermo de Torre, he still regarded it as broadly expressionist, even *ultraísta*, as the title he gave his book, *Fervor de Buenos Aires,* indicates, "fervor" being a good expressionist word after all.

Within days of his departure, he presented a signed copy of *Fervor de Buenos Aires* to his fiancée, inscribing it, "To my sweet and loving Concepción," since it was she who had been its inspiration without a doubt.[47] But what is strange in a poet who so admired the ardor of Walt Whitman is that his imagination was rarely fired by passion for Concepción: his love poems never quite dispel a certain air of melancholy that hangs about them. In fact, the dominant figure in Borges's early poetry was the sunset, which would remain a key image for much of the 1920s and to some extent beyond. This topic originated in a very particular landscape that happened to impress itself upon a young man's heart. The northwestern barrios of Buenos Aires, such as Villa Ortúzar, Villa Urquiza, La Chacarita, are all crossed by long avenues reaching out toward the open horizons of the pampas. Even today the sunset on a clear evening can be spectacular, but in Borges's youth, when these areas directly bordered the great plains, the sun declining over the ragged extremities of the city must have been a breathtaking sight.

Sunset in the *arrabal* became a favorite image of nostalgia for Borges: it was as if the cobbled streets and low houses of the *orillas* were vestiges of an older Buenos Aires that had been cast aside by progress and clung, like his family, to bittersweet memories of days gone by. But, additionally, the figure of the sunset captured a certain fatalism in Borges, arising from a lack of faith in the possibility of his own happiness. Even at a time when one might have expected him to exult in the saving glory of his love for Concepción Guerrero, it was not of the sun at its noonday zenith that he sang but the moment when the huge, blazing fireball in the sky has mellowed to a lambent gold, its radiance progressively dimmed by shadows and hints of doom.

Borges dreaded the prospect of having to tear himself away from Concepción: "Between my love and I three hundred nights / will be raised like three hundred walls, / and the sea shall be a millennium between us" ("Leavetaking," "Despedida"). He knew that if the bond with his sweetheart were to be broken, he would lapse once more into solipsism, the numb unreality of the not-I. He was able to anticipate such a condition even as he wrote the prologue to *Fervor de Buenos Aires,* though he made light of it in a self-deprecating joke: "If the reader should find a successful line in the following pages he should forgive my temerity in having composed it before him. We are all one: . . . it is almost an accident that you are the reader and I the scribbler— the mistrustful and fervent scribbler—of my poems."[48] Indeed, as he prepared to leave Buenos Aires, he must have known that he faced the starkest of choices on his return—he would have to mount a rebellion against Mother, a rebellion more violent than anything he had managed so far, or else break the solemn promise he had made to his "sweet and loving" Concepción.

CHAPTER 7

Second Visit to Europe

(1923–1924)

ON JULY 21, 1923, the whole family, including Fanny Haslam, embarked at the port of La Plata on the *Highland Rover,* bound for Plymouth. Just under three weeks later, they arrived in England, a first visit for the Borges family but a homecoming for Fanny after living in Argentina for over fifty years. There were trips to Staffordshire to visit her birthplace at Hanley, and visits also to Oxford and Cambridge, but their time was spent mostly sightseeing in London. Surprisingly, Georgie was not much impressed by the city that had figured so prominently in his reading; instead, in a letter to Macedonio Fernández, he wrote about the confusion and anguish he felt at having left Concepción in Buenos Aires.[1] At the end of August, the family went to Paris, where they met Guillermo de Torre, who had traveled up from Spain to see his sweetheart, Norah. Torre had started to research a book on the avant-garde movements in Europe, and he and Borges agreed to collaborate on an anthology of contemporary European poetry, on which Borges would set to work in the coming months.

They finally reached Geneva in the middle of September and stayed at the Pension des Tranchées in the rue Malagnou, a short distance from the apartment they had rented during the war. Georgie took up again his friendship with Maurice Abramowicz and Simon Jichlinski and may well have seen old girlfriends like Emilie and Adrienne, but he missed Concepción very badly, and in a poem he wrote while in Geneva, he says that "the painful memory" of his sweetheart "has too often lent its glow to my darkness."[2] And yet the very fact that he missed his sweetheart so sorely must have raised the obvious question as to why he had left her at all, for it was his love of Concepción that had made him feel rooted in Buenos Aires, and this fuller sense of being a criollo had impelled him to seek more substantial forms of expression than provided for in the brief, discontinuous, image-centered poems characteristic of Spanish *ultraísmo.* This process had been interrupted by the family's sudden decision to visit Europe, and the longer he was separated from Concepción, the greater the risk of his becoming estranged once more from his native land, with the attendant risk that his self-belief as a poet might start to decline.

Not much else is known about the Borges family's sojourn in Geneva, except that Dr. Borges did not undergo an eye operation there after all. In late December they went to Barcelona, where they spent Christmas and the New Year. They also visited Majorca and stayed in Valldemosa at Dr. Giménez's *pensión*, where once again Georgie fell prey to the flirtatious attentions of Ángela Márquez, the girl with whom the doctor's mistress had tried to pair him off during his previous stay on the island. This time he seems to have been more receptive to her kittenish charms, and he may even have raised the girl's hopes of making a catch, for in the weeks following his departure from the island, she kept bombarding him with letters, to the point of becoming, as he told Guillermo de Torre, a thorn in his flesh.[3] This susceptibility to Angelita suggests a certain distancing from Concepción, which was not untouched, it seems, by feelings of guilt.

How long the family stayed in Majorca is difficult to say, possibly a month or so. Early in March they arrived in Madrid, and Borges set about promoting *Fervor de Buenos Aires* as best he could, sending copies to some of the most eminent writers and critics in Spain.[4] He also met up with Brandán Caraffa, who had arrived in the Spanish capital in January, and the two young Argentines together began to survey the literary scene. Borges was to discover that in the two years since his last visit to Madrid, Rafael Cansinos-Asséns had been eclipsed by Ramón Gómez de la Serna. Borges recorded his dismay at this development in a report he sent to *Inicial,* where he informed his readers in Buenos Aires that the *gruegería* had destroyed the "psalm," and young poets who had once uttered "austere lamentations" and "savored passionate images" in the "luminous shadow" of Cansinos were "today trying out jokes" in the Café Pombo, where Ramón held court.[5] Even so, he was not above going with Brandán Caraffa to the Café Pombo, nor above presenting Ramón with a copy of *Fervor de Buenos Aires,* which the Spanish writer was to review good-naturedly in Ortega y Gasset's *Revista de Occidente.* But Borges hated what he found at the Café Pombo, as he was to recall in his memoirs decades later:

> I went there once and didn't like the way they behaved. They had a buffoon who wore a bracelet with a rattle attached. He would be made to shake hands with people and the rattle would rattle and Gómez de la Serna would invariably say, "Where's the snake?" That was supposed to be funny. Once, he turned to me proudly and remarked, "You've never seen this kind of thing in Buenos Aires, have you?" I owned, thank God, that I hadn't.[6]

The defeat of Cansinos meant a defeat, too, for Borges's own expressionist belief in emotion as the core of poetry, but the triteness of Ramón and his circle, he believed, was part of a wider tendency in the European poetry he had been surveying for his proposed anthology: English poetry was dominated by "pitiful" visual imagery; in France, Cocteau was preferred to Mauriac; even in Germany, "suffering has stagnated in grandiosely empty words and simulacra of the Bible"; while the Spaniards, "contradicting their history," observed all of this and "judged it very good."[7]

This general neglect of emotion in Europe, moreover, precipitated Borges toward an embryonic cultural nationalism—what had been lost in the Old World must be preserved and developed in the New. The young poets of Argentina, he wrote, must accept the "grand and profligate gift" of the European classics and seek to create a poetic reality in their own idiom, in songs that would express the essence of their souls and of their native land: "I believe our poems should have the flavor of the *patria,* like a guitar that offers a taste of solitude and open country and a sunset beyond a field of clover."[8]

Still, his disappointment at Cansinos's decline was offset by a more heartening discovery toward the end of his stay in Madrid. Through his friend Guillermo de Torre, he came across the work of a young poet called Federico García Lorca, who had taken the Spanish avant-garde by storm since arriving in the capital from his native Granada a few years earlier. It is virtually certain that they met, very likely at one of Lorca's readings in the Residencia de Estudiantes, the Oxbridge-style college attached to the university. Borges was greatly impressed with Lorca's work, no doubt because he found a model in it of the kind of writing he had recently envisaged as appropriate for the young poets of Argentina, for Lorca's poems evoked the spirit of his native Andalusia by blending the forms and motifs of Spanish folk poetry with avant-garde techniques.

Borges's interest in Lorca remained keen even after he departed the Spanish capital in April. In the course of the two months the family spent in Portugal before returning to Argentina, he read the *romanceros* and *cancioneros*—the collections of traditional Spanish ballads and songs—from which Lorca had drawn much of his inspiration. Borges would even try his hand at writing a suite of "Soleares," brief poems in the style of the *cante jondo,* following the example of Lorca and other Andalusian poets at this time.[9] In June he wrote from Lisbon to Guillermo de Torre to ask if Lorca would be accompanying him on his forthcoming trip to see them in Portugal.[10] (It appears that he did not.) And his interest in Lorca would continue after his return to Buenos Aires, where he would publish two of the Spaniard's poems in a magazine he was to edit there.[11]

The success of Lorca's poetry stemmed from the sheer force of his creative personality, but the problem for Borges was precisely the fragility of his poetic self, his proclivity to self-doubt. Concepción had inspired in him a desire to rebel against his family's obsession with its glorious past, to stifle the voice of the ancestors and engage with the light and bustle and vitality of the streets of modern Buenos Aires, but this rebellious spirit had been quelled by his mother, since he had accepted her decision to return to Europe. Borges's attitude to Argentina, as a result, had become contaminated with feelings of unworthiness and self-reproach, as is evident in "The Plains" ("Los llanos"), a poem written in Spain, possibly during his time in Madrid from March to April.[12]

In "The Plains" he evoked life on the pampas in the days of the newly emancipated republic, and specifically the "nomadic empire" raised by the barbarous caudillo, Facundo Quiroga, when "a vigorous intensity" was to be found in "agile battles," in "cavalry charges," in "the license testifying to victory," in "unbridled pillaging," and, not least, "in the hot star traced by a man and a woman as they couple." And the barbarism of those gauchos was matched by the energy of nation builders like his own ancestors, to whom "the country was submissive as a woman to their desire." All that energy had passed away, however, "like the vehemence of a kiss passes without having enriched the lips that consented to it." The poem concludes with the dispiriting lines "It is sad that memory should include everything / And, all the more so, when it is a shameful memory."

The poet's reverence for the past exists in inverse relation to his self-esteem, as if the "shameful memory" of having abandoned the girl he loved were evidence of his moral inferiority to his ancestors. Borges's second visit to Europe had brought to the fore the unresolved question of his relation to Argentina—he was clearly torn between past and present, pampas and city, Mother and Concepción, and if his sense of national identity was so confused and unsettled, how could he hope to capture the spirit of the *patria* in the way Lorca had done for Andalusia?

As he prepared to return to Buenos Aires, Borges knew that a parting of the ways with the Spanish *ultraístas* was inevitable. His project was to develop a criollo version of the Ultra, drawing upon the emotionalism of Cansinos-Asséns and the German expressionists, in order to create something that, though new, would be unmistakably Argentine. And yet he was aware, too, that the success of this project depended on his clarifying the issue of the criollo identity, and this depended, in turn, on a resolution of his contrary loyalties to Mother and Concepción.

During Borges's absence abroad, the avant-garde in Buenos Aires had begun to lose momentum, and it would no doubt have dwindled away until his return had it not been for the fact that *Fervor de Buenos Aires* happened to catch the eye of a wealthy Argentine poet called Oliverio Girondo, who lived in Paris and had connections with some of the most important figures of the European avant-garde. Girondo was a friend of Jules Supervielle, and of the Chilean Vicente Huidobro; through the latter he had got to know Pierre Reverdy and made contact with Picasso and Apollinaire. During a period of residence in Rome, Girondo had also met Marinetti and other futurists, and in 1918–19, while touring Spain, he had befriended Ramón Gómez de la Serna, Cansinos-Asséns, and *ultraístas* like Isaac del Vando Villar. (He had even attended the first festival of the Ultra, which was held in Seville in May 1919, just a few months before Borges arrived in the city with his family later that year.) His first book, *Veinte poemas para ser leídos en el tranvía* (*Twenty Poems to Be Read on the Tram*), which was published in France in 1922, drew on various tendencies—its concentration on metaphor was inspired by Huidobro and the *greguerías* of Gómez de la Serna, its urban imagery came from the futurists by way of *ultraísmo,* and the outrageous sexual references betrayed a clear intent to shock derived from Dada.

Reading Borges's *Fervor,* however, raised Girondo's hopes of introducing the ideas of the European avant-garde into what he regarded as the backwater of the Argentine literary world. He got in touch with Ricardo Güiraldes, a writer from a similar social background, who also lived in Paris but spent long periods at his *estancia* in the province of Buenos Aires. The latter had become thoroughly disillusioned with the Argentine literary establishment after his book of poems, *El cencerro de cristal* (*The Glass Cowbell*), which exhibited some avant-garde techniques, had been ignored or mocked by reviewers. Girondo sought to persuade his friend that all was not lost, and to prove his point he produced a copy of *Fervor de Buenos Aires* and flung it down before Güiraldes.[13]

Girondo made contact with Brandán Caraffa at *Inicial,* the only literary magazine that displayed some awareness of the revolutionary developments in Europe, but its future was uncertain because of disagreements among members of the editorial committee. Casting around for alternatives, he came across *Martín Fierro,* a fairly conventional magazine of the arts that had been founded the month before under the editorship of the poet Évar Méndez. Méndez was soon won over to the cause of the avant-garde, and in the March 20 issue of *Martín Fierro* there appeared a selection of poems from Girondo's *Veinte poemas,* accompanied by a glowing profile of the author.[14] Then, in the May 15 issue, Girondo published a manifesto in which he inveighed against "the hippopotamic impermeability of the honorable public" and the "funereal solemnity of the historian and of the professor who mummifies all he touches," and appealed for support from readers who were capable of perceiving that "we are faced with a new sensibility and a new mode of understanding" that required "new methods and forms of expression."[15]

Girondo's manifesto caused a sensation among the young writers of Buenos Aires, and it remains a seminal document in the literary history of Argentina, but the call to rebel against tradition attracted the scorn of the literary establishment of the time. The "New Generation," as the young writers soon designated themselves, were mocked as *"los neo-sensibles"*—"the neo-sensitives"—because of the alleged existence of a "new sensibility" that they felt such an urge to express. This hostility prompted Girondo to join forces with Güiraldes and Méndez in forming a Frente Único, a "single front" of the young generation against the establishment. Furthermore, all three of them decided to set up a publishing house to disseminate the work of the nascent Argentine vanguard, and, very likely in recognition of Borges's pioneering role in bringing the Ultra to Buenos Aires, they decided to name it the "Sociedad Editorial Proa," after the little magazine Borges had founded in the months before his departure for Europe. Finally, in July, Girondo set off for Europe, but, an indefatigable traveler, he took a circuitous route through several Spanish-American countries in what *Martín Fierro* called an "intellectual mission" to establish links with avant-garde groups abroad. Over the next nine months, he would visit Chile, Peru, Mexico, Cuba, and New York before returning home to Paris.[16]

The Borges family arrived back in Buenos Aires on July 19 and stayed at the Garden Hotel while they looked for an apartment to rent. But shortly after his arrival, Borges was faced with a disastrous setback—Concepción's father had ordered his daughter to terminate the relationship, considering Borges an unsuitable prospect for her, partly because he believed that the patrician Doña Leonor did not approve of the socially inferior Concepción.[17] Borges was plunged into a state of dejection, as can be gathered from his poem "The Return to Buenos Aires" ("La vuelta a Buenos Aires"), where he complained that "kisses are strangers to my flesh and only the wind embraces my body / My shadow knows love no longer."[18] He enlisted the help of Norah Lange as a go-between, and the relationship with Concepción was eventually resumed—but in secret. He wrote to Guillermo de Torre that even though he had quarreled with Concepción's family, the two of them still saw each other regularly.[19] Their meetings took place at the Lange house, a short distance from where Concepción lived on calle Pampa, and so the villa on calle Tronador once again became a place of secret bliss where Borges felt sustained in the love of his sweetheart.

In addition to the problem over Concepción, however, Borges had another disappointment to contend with on his return to Buenos Aires. He happened to have arrived back in the same month as Oliverio Girondo departed on his "intellectual mission" to other avant-garde groups. The two men did not meet, but Borges would soon be apprised of the effects of Girondo's activities during his own absence in Europe. Only a year earlier, he had been the undisputed leader of the Argentine *ultraístas,* but on his return he found that this embryonic avant-garde had grown into a New Generation associated with *Martín Fierro* and had even acquired a publishing house, which had appropriated the name of his magazine, *Proa.* Borges had effectively been upstaged by Oliverio Girondo, and, what was worse, his rival was taking the avant-garde in a direction that was the opposite of where Borges proposed to go—Girondo had issued a powerful call in favor of revolt and innovation and was establishing international connections for the Argentine vanguard at precisely the time that Borges was reappraising his own attachment to the avant-garde and proposing to sever his links with Madrid in order to develop a distinctively Argentine version of the Ultra. He discovered, in short, that the dispute between Gómez de la Serna and Cansinos-Asséns had crossed the Atlantic, and the war between the *gruegería* and the "psalm" would have to be fought out in Buenos Aires itself.

Borges did not have to wait long to begin a counteroffensive. Indeed, even before he moved out of the Garden Hotel, he was approached by Brandán Caraffa with the proposal that they revive the dormant *Proa.* Caraffa had been in touch with Ricardo Güiraldes and another young writer, Pablo Rojas Paz, both of whom had fallen out with Évar Méndez at *Martín Fierro* and were interested in the new venture. The earlier *Proa* had been little more than a large sheet of paper folded into three sections, but what the four young writers had in mind was something far more ambitious: a monthly publication of around seventy pages printed on high-quality paper and bound in booklet form.

The first issue of the new *Proa* came out some three weeks after the Borges family's move in mid-August from the Garden Hotel to a rented apartment, and in a clear sign of Borges's proprietorial attitude to the magazine, the address given directly below the title was that of his new home, avenida Quintana 222. *Proa* got off to a promising start: Borges would tell Guillermo de Torre a couple of months later that it had about two hundred subscribers, received generous donations from high-society ladies of vaguely literary disposition, and collected 260 pesos in advertising revenue on each issue.[20] His own contributions to this first issue were carefully chosen: he translated an essay by Herwarth Walden, the editor of the German expressionist magazine *Der Sturm;* he wrote a critical evaluation of the Ultra's progress in Argentina in the guise of a review of a new book by his erstwhile *ultraísta* comrade, Eduardo González Lanuza, whose attachment to metaphor he now regarded with skepticism; and finally he published three new poems under the collective title "Psalms," a sign of the continuing influence of Cansinos-Asséns on his work.

The appearance of *Proa* threatened to split the Buenos Aires avant-garde, for the new magazine had been born in clear opposition to *Martín Fierro*—not only were Borges's poetics in conflict with Girondo's but also Güiraldes and Rojas Paz had joined *Proa* precisely because they had quarreled with Évar Méndez. Borges, what was more, omitted to send Méndez a complimentary copy of *Proa,* a discourtesy that was remarked upon in *Martín Fierro.*[21] However, the question most likely to cause an open breach between the two factions was the appropriation of the name "Proa" for the publishing house that Girondo, Méndez, and Güiraldes had been planning to set up, but for which Borges and González Lanuza claimed to hold the copyright. Clearly the Editorial Proa could not get started until this thorny issue was resolved.

The divisions that were appearing in the New Generation were a cause for dismay for Ricardo Güiraldes, who feared they would weaken the modernist movement in Argentina. And these concerns proved to be justified, for in October an exhibition by the cubist-inspired painter Emilio Pettoruti at the Galería Whitcomb caused a furor—his work was mocked and criticized in the press, and there were even demonstrations by opponents of the new art outside the gallery. The events at the Whitcomb persuaded the quarrelsome members of the New Generation of the need to consolidate the Frente Único as a bulwark against the forces of reaction. A compromise was worked out regarding the matter of the Editorial Proa—Évar Méndez agreed to launch the imprint with a book of essays by Borges and to publish his second book of poetry, *Moon Across the Way* (*Luna de enfrente*) later in the following year. Ironically, the Editorial Proa would become the one enduring hinge in the often fractious relations between the two wings of the Buenos Aires avant-garde, for Borges himself would always remain chary of the Frente Único, and even though he would write for *Martín Fierro,* his were minor pieces that tended to be out of line with the general views of the *martinfierristas.*

Although Borges had gone some way toward retrieving his position at the head of the Buenos Aires avant-garde, there remained difficulties with Concepción. In a note probably written in August, he complained to Norah Lange, "I spend my time playing solitaire with my memories of Villa Urquiza. I must speak to Concepción on Friday about a serious and unfortunate matter."[22] What this matter may have been is impossible to say, but the basic problem lay in the fact that he was at an impasse with Concepción, for on the one hand, her love gave him the self-belief he needed in order to write, but on the other, he would have to rebel against his mother and defy the girl's father if the relationship was to prosper. Obviously his failure to stand up to his mother a year earlier did not augur well for the future, so he was faced with the distinct possibility that he might eventually have to give up Concepción, in which case he would forfeit the very source of his inspiration.

Borges's pessimism and self-doubt are evident in an essay called "Complaint of Every Criollo" ("Queja de todo criollo"), where he tried to come to grips with the issue of the criollo identity. The character of the criollos had been defined in the early days of the republic, but economic progress had caused "the criollo tragedy": the advent of the railway, the replacement of ranching by "profit-seeking" agriculture, the "imprisonment" of the pampas by barbed wire, the subjugation of the gauchos, all had conspired to turn the criollo into a stranger in his native land and Buenos Aires into a veritable Babel; the criollos, however, must learn "to die with dignity," to die without complaining too much, to die "with a song" on their lips.[23]

This, of course, was a dead-end view of Argentine history, and Borges himself would write a swan song for the criollos, a poem he characterized as "the song of a *criollo final*," to which he gave the title, *"Dulcia linquimus arva,"* a quotation from the opening lines of the first eclogue of Virgil's *Bucolics*, in which the Latin poet regrets leaving his ancestral homelands, his "sweet fields," for the city of Rome.[24] Once again Borges praised the early nation builders, the "soldiers and ranchers" who had made the pampas "submit like a woman to their desire." He knew nothing of "those brilliant and noble days"; he was "a man of the city, the barrio, the street," whose sadness found a voice in the moaning of distant trams in the night. Patently he had not got much further than the sentiments already evinced in "The Plains" several months earlier, except to represent Buenos Aires itself as a spiritual wasteland, a place of alienation. The impasse over Concepción was beginning to produce a creative stagnation, as he revealed in a note he sent Norah Lange: "I received your poems, which are sorrow transformed into beauty, unlike other sorrows which, because they stagnate, only become wearing and exhausting, like my own."[25]

Around October, however, things began to change. Borges read James Joyce's *Ulysses*, which had been published in Paris the year before, and he wrote a review for *Proa*, exulting in being, as he put it, "the first Hispanic adventurer to have arrived at Joyce's book." Joyce was a kindred spirit who had done for the Irish what Borges had himself, as yet vaguely, envisaged doing for the Argentines. The Irishman had been able to render the specifics of time and place yet realize their universal qualities, and though the novel spanned just a single day in contemporary Dublin, it offered a variety of episodes comparable to the *Odyssey;* it was, moreover, lavish in vocabulary, rhetoric, and styles, and there was even in Joyce's Irishness a vindication of Borges's wish to create a criollo literature, for the Irish "have always been famous agitators of the literature of England," the implication being that they stood in relation to their "abhorred masters" as the Argentines to the Spanish.[26]

The influence of Joyce on his thinking is already evident in the essay "Beyond Images" ("Después de las imágenes"), in which he reiterated his belief that the Spanish and Argentine avant-gardes were too limited by their obsession with metaphor. He argued that the poet must do more than create metaphors, he must "hallucinate cities and spaces from a unified reality"; and the city Borges had in mind was Buenos Aires, which had not yet been immortalized in poetry: "In Buenos Aires nothing has yet happened, and its greatness is not accredited either by a symbol or a marvelous fable, not even by an individual destiny comparable to the *Martín Fierro.*"[27]

And yet to do for Buenos Aires what Joyce had done for Dublin required a sustained imaginative interpretation of the world. This was an idea that preoccupied Borges in the latter months of 1924. We find it in an essay on the baroque poet Francisco de Quevedo, whose brilliant conceits he had once admired but whom he now compared unfavorably with Cervantes: "Instead of the all-encompassing vision that Cervantes generates through the broad unfolding of an idea, Quevedo pluralizes insights in a sort of fusillade of partial glimpses."[28] It came up again in a review of Ramón Gómez de la Serna's memoirs, in which Borges observed that Ramón's "omnivorous enthusiasm" individuated each object instead of searching for "a total vision of life," "a concord," "a synthesis."[29] What Ramón lacked, Borges observed, was the sort of unifying principle that in the new mathematics was represented by the sign of "the Alef [sic]," "the infinite number which encompasses the others."[30]

In retrospect this reference to the Aleph is of enormous significance for an understanding of Borges as a writer. The Aleph would come to represent an abiding aspiration to achieve a unity of being in which the self could be fully realized yet integrated in the objective reality of the world. In due course this aspiration would be most fully articulated in one of his major stories, entitled, precisely, "The Aleph" (1945), where he sought to express the rapturous totality of self and world. At this early stage, however, the Aleph signified a unifying insight that would enable him to write a substantial work that, like Joyce's *Ulysses,* would identify the author with the particular world that had shaped him, while giving his experience a universal quality.

Running broadly in parallel to Borges's reflections on Joyce, we find a growing fascination with Norah Lange. On October 26 he told Guillermo de Torre that he was thinking of translating a passage from *Ulysses,* and in the same letter referred no fewer than three times to Norah, asking his Spanish friend what he thought of her poems.[31] A month or two earlier, he had undertaken to help Norah with the publication of her first book, *La calle de la tarde* (*Evening Street*). He negotiated a price with Samet, the publisher, and wrote a prologue for the volume.[32] He then got Brandán Caraffa to review it for *Proa* and arranged for a selection of the poems to be published in *Martín Fierro,* together with his pro-

logue, where he praised Norah in a high-flown lyrical style—she was "illustrious for the double brilliance of her hair and her haughty youth"; she was "light
and haughty and fervent, like a banner unfurling in the breeze."³³

Borges was not alone in his admiration for this extraordinary girl. In July
1924 there had appeared in *Martín Fierro* a melodramatic love poem by a
young man, Córdova Iturburu, portraying Norah as an "angel" with "sleep-
walker's eyes, tragic and sweet," an angel—nay, an "archangel"—capable of
conjuring up visions of the night "leaping at the blazing twilight" or of "Life
and Death going by like two sisters."³⁴ Another budding poet, Ulyses Petit de
Murat, also fell under the spell of what he, too, called this "angel" with "reddish hair and sharp profile," who possessed the "quasidivine aura" of some
"heavenly creature."³⁵ And she had caught the eye of older men, too, notably
the celebrated writer, Horacio Quiroga, "a great chaser of young girls," who
would come to her mother's literary soirées on a thundering motorcycle that
brought the little boys of the neighborhood running out into the street to
gawk at his splendid machine.³⁶

A good part of Norah's attraction lay in the exoticism of her family background. Her father, Gunnar Lange, was Norwegian, while her mother, Berta
Erfjord, though Argentine born, was herself the daughter of a Norwegian and
an Irishwoman. The Langes were to have five daughters and a son, and it was
to accommodate this growing brood that Gunnar Lange had bought a large,
detached house with an ample garden on the corner of calles Tronador and
Pampa in a barrio of the town of Belgrano known as Villa Mazzini (and later,
when Belgrano was absorbed by Buenos Aires, Villa Urquiza). Norah, the
fourth child, was born on October 23, 1906, and spent the first five years of her
life in the house at calle Tronador, but then her father, a civil engineer, was appointed to a post near the town of General Alvear in the province of Mendoza,
at the foot of the Andes. Four years after this move, however, Gunnar died
suddenly, and his widow (she was over twenty years younger than her husband) took the family back to the house in Buenos Aires. These were to be
years of increasing hardship, and Berta Erfjord would have to mortgage the
house and sell her assets to raise her children. But she was an intelligent, well-
educated woman, a friend of writers and artists, and the Lange children grew
up in a cultured, liberal, multilingual environment.

A particularly striking attribute of Norah Lange's was her mane of red
hair, an exotic attribute in a Latin country and one associated in the Hispanic
world with devilment and mischief. This sign of a fiery temperament was
borne out by her spirited behavior. She grew up the tomboy of the family, notorious for her escapades and practical jokes—her favorite turn in early ado-
lescence was to put on a poncho and a broad-brimmed hat and climb up on

the roof, from where she shocked the neighbors by shouting out a great, incomprehensible stream of words in various languages, punctuating it with insults and shrieks of laughter. Yet despite this apparently extroverted personality, Norah would remain something of an enigma to herself, and this inner mystery was to be the source of her creativity. She started to write when she was fourteen, and the first poems she published reveal a gentle sensibility possessed of a longing for some emotional anchoring, perhaps deriving from a sense of insecurity after the death of the father she idolized.

Gunnar Lange had indeed led a remarkable life as a soldier and explorer. After serving in the Norwegian army in his youth, he had made his way to America, and his adventures in the New World had included his taking part in the war between Honduras and El Salvador as commander of the Honduran artillery. In Argentina he distinguished himself as a cartographer, his greatest achievement being the charting of the Pilcomayo River, which flows from Bolivia across northern Argentina and Paraguay through the wilderness of the Chaco, a feat that earned him acclaim as "the Livingstone of the Pilcomayo."

Borges was, of course, extraordinarily susceptible to the romantic aura of men of action, and Norah's attachment to the memory of her father undoubtedly added to her mystique. In addition, the Langes were related to the distinguished Norwegian novelist and playwright Alexander Kielland, and this meant that Norah, like Borges, could boast writers as well as heroes among her forebears. To cap it all, the two families were related by marriage, Norah's aunt being the wife of Borges's uncle Frank, a connection that made Norah and Georgie *primos*, or cousins, in the Hispanic tradition.

Norah's, then, was a complex allure: her red hair spoke of passion, but her pale, Scandinavian looks called to mind the purity of an angel, and it was this tantalizing blend of innocence and fire that she captured in dreamy poems charged with erotic anticipation. Her poems, moreover, depicted a *paysage d'âme* not dissimilar to Borges's, a favorite topic being the sun setting over the barrios bordering the pampas. Small wonder that this sparkling, iridescent creature—poet, angel, temptress, and potential soul mate all in one—should have captivated the young Borges, with his all-too-small experience of the female sex.

In October, at around the time Norah published *La calle de la tarde*, she began to invite Borges and a select group of friends every Saturday evening to a party at her house. There they would recite their work, discuss literary and sundry other matters, and then dance to tangos played on the piano. These parties soon became the highlight of Norah's week: she would write that on Saturdays "the evening is suddenly lit up" by the presence of Georgie and his friends.[37] And so it was, too, for Borges, for these Saturday parties would convert the house on calle Tronador into the inner sanctum of his literary group, a place reserved for the *ultraístas* as distinct from the various other factions that made up the Buenos Aires avant-garde.

Still, the more he was drawn to Norah, all the more pressing became the problem of what to do about Concepción—should he marry her in defiance of their respective families, or should he leave her? Replying on November 27 to a rare letter from Sureda, he was guarded about the future: ". . . as for my getting married, it's rather premature, even though I am still engaged to Concepción."[38] Clearly he could not put off much longer the question of marriage, but this impending decision filled him with trepidation.

In the guilt-ridden poems Borges wrote as he agonized over his future, his dying love for Concepción is represented by the sunset, a trope of extinction expressing a melancholy that seeps into the poet's soul as he roams the empty streets on the edge of the pampas, taking stock of his life:

> The evening is like a Last Judgment.
> The street is an open wound in the sky.
> I cannot tell whether the light that blazed in the depths was an angel or
>   a sunset.
> Insistent like a nightmare, the distance bears down on me.
> The horizon is pierced by barbed wire.[39]

The future is barred, closed, threatening, and yet the figure of the sunset is ambiguous—it speaks of a fear that darkness will fall over his imagination, but it is reminiscent also of an angel, the attribute generally ascribed to Norah Lange by her admirers. This glimmer of hope is more evident in "Almost a Last Judgment" ("Casi Juicio Final"). Despite the burden of guilt he bore, the strophes had not denied him their grace:

> I can feel the terror of beauty: who would dare to condemn me when I
> have been absolved by this great moon of my solitude?[40]

That moon surely alluded to the mysterious Norah Lange, and its beauty, though still a distant promise, nevertheless quickened his faith in the powers of the imagination.

Borges, after all, was seeking a release from the creative stagnation that had afflicted him since his return from Europe and was in danger of thwarting his plans to create a criollo version of the Ultra. He had been at an impasse with Concepción: she had once represented the urge to revolt against the past in favor of the contemporary realities of Argentina, but he had failed to make good that revolt, and, far from stifling the voice of his ancestors, it was the ancestral voice that was threatening to stifle his own. What he needed was a point of balance, a synthesis, an Aleph, that would enable him to reconcile the traditional and the modern, the past and the present, the pampas and the city.

Finally, sometime toward the end of 1924, or possibly early in 1925, he decided to end his relationship with Concepción. This undoubtedly was a terrible betrayal of the poor girl, who had endured a whole year of Borges's absence and had been prepared, on his return, to defy her father for his sake. There was, understandably, great bitterness on her part—following her break with Borges, she broke, too, with her friend Norah Lange and never spoke to her again. However, it was precisely in Norah that Borges believed he might have found an alternative source of inspiration that might inject new energy into his writing. In January 1925 he published his own version of the last page of *Ulysses,* the first ever translation of James Joyce into Spanish.[41] The passage was the famous soliloquy in which Molly Bloom recalls the time when she had been ready to give herself to her lover. The fact that Borges chose one of the most erotic episodes in the entire novel—a lyrical stream of consciousness punctuated by the word "yes"—suggests that, in the New Year of 1925, he was peculiarly susceptible to Molly Bloom's powerful affirmation of desire.

Not long after giving up Concepción, Borges wrote an essay in which he expressed his wish for a synthesis of tradition and innovation. He would call it "Adventure and Order," since it was a discussion of a famous poem by Guillaume Apollinaire in which the great progenitor of the literary avant-garde in France made a partial recantation of his role in the revolt against tradition and advocated a reconciliation of the "adventure" of the avant-garde with the traditional "order" of literature.[42] This was an aim with which Borges could sympathize, but, unlike Apollinaire, he gave more weight to "order" than to "adventure"—there were few adventures to be found in the exercise of art, he asserted, not least because all adventure was "a future norm." Still, he professed to be content with either adventure or order, so long as there was "heroism" in whoever pursued them.

Oddly enough, Borges never once mentioned the title of Apollinaire's poem in his essay. Perhaps he felt it would have been too revealing to do so, for the original poem was called *"La jolie rousse"* ("The Pretty Redhead"), an allusion to Apollinaire's new lover, Madeleine Kolb, the girl whom the poet hoped might become the muse who would inspire him to resolve "the age-old quarrel between tradition and invention":

> Here comes the summer, the violent season
> And my youth is gone just like the spring.
> O Sun, this is the time of ardent Reason
> And I am waiting
> For her to assume the sweet and noble form

That will make me love her like no other.
And here she comes, drawing me like iron to a magnet,
She has the enchanting aspect
Of an adorable redhead.*

Borges, too, must have hoped that the red-haired Norah Lange might one day embody the "ardent Reason" of which Apollinaire had dreamed. He wanted to realize himself fully as a poet, he wanted to do for the Argentines what Joyce had done for the Irish, and he wanted his writing to blaze with the passionate splendor of a Walt Whitman, but he had yet to find the unifying insight, the Aleph, that would reveal the truth of the self and its vital connection to the reality of his native land.

*Voici que vient l'été la saison violente
Et ma jeunesse est morte ainsi que le printemps
O Soleil c'est le temps de la Raison ardente et j'attends
Pour la suivre toujours la forme noble et douce
Qu'elle prend afin que je l'aime seulement
Elle vient et m'attire ainsi qu'un fer l'aimant
    Elle a l'aspect charmant
    D'une adorable rousse
      —"La jolie rousse," ll. 31–39, Alcools et Calligrammes, ed. Claude Debon
       (Imprimerie Nationale: Paris, 1991)

CHAPTER 8

Adventures in the Avant-Garde

(1925)

By THE END OF 1924, the avant-garde in Buenos Aires had attracted a sizable number of recruits, mostly young men in their early twenties eager to join the cause of modern art against the old fogies of the establishment. The passport to acceptance in the New Generation was to have a poem or an article published in either *Martín Fierro* or *Proa*. Of the two magazines, *Martín Fierro* was the more accessible: it was an eclectic broadsheet open to a wide range of cultural trends, so long as they were deemed to be suitably vanguard. In addition to essays on art and literature, it published a variety of literary news, gossip, and humorous or satirical pieces. A much-loved feature was the burlesque "epitaph" in verse attacking older writers like Leopoldo Lugones or poking fun at other *martinfierristas*. *Proa* was more sober, more selective in its acceptance of contributions, and it reflected Borges's interests in the main—literature and ideas, but with a clear bias toward poetry.

A fairly boisterous social life evolved around the two magazines. In the early days, a *tertulia* was held at the bookshop of Manuel Gleizer, who also doubled as a publisher for these new poets. Another meeting place was Samet's bookshop, which occupied a basement on the avenida de Mayo under a theater specializing in flamenco shows, a proximity that caused the rickety shelves to shake visibly during the more vigorous *zapateados* of the dancers above. Other haunts of the New Generation were *confiterías* such as the Richmond on calle Florida and La Cosechera on the avenida de Mayo, as well as various cheap restaurants around the calle Corrientes, a particular favorite being a dingy eating house on calle Cangallo that they dubbed "El Puchero Misterioso" ("The Mysterious Stew"), since it was a complete mystery to them how they could be served a stew, with bread and wine thrown in, for only twenty cents. Nights were frittered away at some tavern or other in a suitably run-down *arrabal* or at a number of bars in the city center, and, when finances allowed, they would repair to the Cabaret Tabaris, where they danced with the girls and drank cheap champagne. On special occasions—for the launch of a book or in honor of a visitor from abroad—a "banquet" was held, usually at the Hotel Marconi on the Plaza del Once, and there, as often as not, they would one and all get terribly drunk. Indeed, much was made of wining and dining foreign writers—Marinetti, Pirandello, and Ortega y Gasset were among the celebrities who visited Buenos Aires in the mid-1920s—and after the customary banquet, the distinguished guest would be treated to a tango session at the Café Tortoni on the avenida de Mayo. It was there they took Luigi Pirandello, an occasion that was all the more memorable for the fact that Ricardo Güiraldes had brought Carlos Gardel, a singer as yet unknown to the wider world, to perform for their famous guest.[1]

However, the place that served as the informal headquarters of the New Generation was the Royal Keller, a basement dive on the corner of Corrientes and Esmeralda that catered after dark to ladies of the night and their solitary clients. This was the venue for the infamous *Revista Oral*, the brainchild of the Peruvian poet Alberto Hidalgo, not so long ago the originator of *sencillismo* but now a convert to the avant-garde. As the editor, Hidalgo would reserve tables on Saturdays for the weekly edition of the *Oral Review*, and at the appointed hour he would rise to his feet and announce the new issue, say, "*Revista Oral*, year one, number five" and, after declaiming his editorial, would orchestrate the recital of various articles, poems, and book reviews.[2]

Despite this broad spirit of camaraderie, certain ideological and financial disagreements would lead to frequent tensions and squabbles within the Frente Único. The most serious and persistent of these arose when a group of young writers decided to bring out a literary review called *Extrema Izquierda* (*Extreme Left*), advocating socialist realism and the engagement of literature in the cause of the people. The first issue was due to appear in August 1924, and, perhaps as a device to seek publicity, one of the socialists, Roberto Mariani, wrote an article in *Martín Fierro* criticizing the *martinfierristas* for the "scandalous respect" they accorded Leopoldo Lugones's writing and political beliefs.[3] He also questioned the appropriateness of *Martín Fierro*'s taking its title from Argentina's most famous poem, *The Gaucho Martín Fierro*, when its contributors tended to affect "a French elegance" while denying that the Argentine people possessed "any generic or common qualities."

Mariani's letter was to split the young writers of Buenos Aires into two camps: the socialists styled themselves the "Boedo group," after the street in a working-class quarter where *Extrema Izquierda* had its offices; their opponents became known as the "Florida group" because the "cosmopolitans" of *Martín Fierro* used to meet in the *confitería* Richmond on calle Florida in the city center. The Boedo writers accused the *Martín Fierro* people of aping foreigners, while the Florida group retorted that the socialists were actually on the "extreme right" in literary terms because they sought to revive Zola's naturalism "at its crudest and most sordid."[4]

The Boedo-Florida dispute would rumble on for many months, despite the fact that *Extrema Izquierda* ceased publication in December 1924, and, though it may appear petty now, this dispute was significant insofar as it reflected the wider crisis over the identity of the criollos. It was not for nothing that Mariani had challenged the *martinfierristas'* attitude to Lugones, for it had been Lugones who had extolled the gaucho as the symbol of Argentine identity and raised the poem *Martín Fierro* to its status as the epic of the criollos. Since delivering his famous lectures on the gauchos in 1913, Lugones had moved to the extreme right and espoused fascism. By 1924 he was calling on the armed forces to seize power in order to defend the established order and the traditional way of life against the hordes of immigrants, who, he feared, would destroy Argentina.

As for Borges, he was immensely irritated by the Boedo-Florida dispute and resented having been lumped in willy-nilly with the "cosmopolitans" of the Florida group. He had good friends in both camps, he protested, and all the young writers continued to fraternize anyway at the Royal Keller and their other haunts; the quarrel, he maintained, had been whipped up by Mariani and the *martinfierrista* Ernesto Palacio for no better reason than to imitate the factions of the Parisian literary world; the Florida people, in his view, were too elitist in their idea of art, preferring a bad sonnet to a good *milonga,* while the Boedo writers were too parochial in their evaluation of what was authentically Argentine and would favor an indifferent tango over a good sonnet, even though the latter might reflect a very Argentine stoicism.[5] But the question was—what did it actually mean to be an Argentine? Borges's own sense of national identity, as we have seen, was very unclear, if not contradictory, and so long as he regarded himself as a *criollo final* he was liable to be mistaken for a reactionary, with a nostalgic attitude to the past that was not intrinsically different from that of Lugones.

Precisely such a misunderstanding arose in March 1925, when *Proa* was criticized for disseminating fascist ideas by the author of an article in *Nosotros* concerning the threat posed by fascism to the democratic order in Argentina.[6] Borges was quick to rebut this charge in a letter to the editor of *Nosotros,* protesting that he had never been a victim of such "intellectual lapses" as fascism or imperialism.[7] His allegiances, he claimed, were more local, more specific: he felt more *porteño* than Argentine and identified with the barrio of Palermo, Evaristo Carriego's barrio, more than with any other place. Still, if Borges fought shy of any affiliation to the nation beyond the barrio of his birth, it was because he was torn over the issue of national identity—he felt alienated, on the one hand, from the great metropolis Buenos Aires had become, but humbled, on the other, by the hallowed memory of his nation-building ancestors.

The uncertainty surrounding Borges's political and cultural inclinations was not exactly dispelled by the fact that his essay on Apollinaire's poem, "La Jolie Rousse," was published in the same issue of *Nosotros* as the article accusing *Proa* of harboring fascist sympathies. Borges's essay raised suspicions among the *martinfierristas* that he was prepared to betray the principles of the avant-garde, and these suspicions were reinforced in April when he published a collection of critical essays called *Inquisiciones* (*Inquisitions*) that included several reviews of books on the gaucho and the pampas, as well as a hitherto unpublished essay, "Complaint of Every Criollo" ("Queja de todo criollo"), presenting Argentine history as a "tragedy" for the criollos. Borges's *Inquisiciones* had a mixed reception—"brickbats and praise," as he would report to Sureda—and it certainly did nothing to counteract the impression in avant-garde circles that its author might be ideologically unsound, a possible reactionary in both literature and politics.[8]

Thus, in March and April 1925, Borges found himself on the defensive, his position within the New Generation having been weakened by a general uncertainty about his attitude and ideas. After his second visit to Europe, he proposed to develop a criollo version of the Ultra, and he even entertained hopes of emulating James Joyce by finding a way of creating a substantial literary evocation of the life of his native city. But such projects inevitably raised the vexed issue of the Argentine identity, and Borges could not overcome his sense of being a *criollo final,* for whom present-day Argentina, let alone the Argentina of the future, was a source of disquiet and confusion.

And then, at precisely the time that Borges's bid to regain the leadership of the New Generation began to falter, Oliverio Girondo arrived back in Buenos Aires from his "intellectual mission" abroad. On April 22, the editor of *Martín Fierro,* Évar Méndez, wrote to Girondo giving an account of the troubles that had beset the magazine during the latter's nine-month absence. There had been countless difficulties—financial crises, apathy, envy, and indiscipline; at times, Méndez complained, he alone had shouldered the burden of running the magazine and the entire *martinfierrista* group, and he alone had coped with all the expenses and commitments.[9] The defection of Güiraldes and Rojas Paz to found *Proa* with Borges had almost sunk *Martín Fierro,* but he had been able to weather the storm and preserve the group, as well as the alliance with *Proa.* Subsequently, a more serious disagreement between the two magazines had threatened to wipe them both out, and there had been a danger that another publication of reactionary tendencies might be founded. However, he assured Girondo that he had planned a full program for the *martinfierristas*—a weekly work plan, lectures, meetings, *tertulias*, entertainment, monthly dinners, and a reorganization of the magazine itself. He asked Girondo for money: *Martín Fierro* had lots of debts.

The dynamic Girondo sprang into action. Two weeks after Méndez sent him the letter, a new issue of *Martín Fierro*—which had remained unpublished since January—appeared, on May 5. Significantly, it carried extracts from Girondo's new book, *Calcomanías* (*Transfers*), which would shortly be published by the Editorial Proa.[10] Girondo renewed appeals for solidarity among the New Generation. A joint meeting of the *Martín Fierro* and *Proa* groups was held at Évar Méndez's house in order to discuss ways of strengthening the Frente Único. Then Girondo and Méndez approached the editors of *Proa* and proposed a merger between the two magazines. Ricardo Güiraldes, keen as ever to preserve the Frente Único, was in favor of the merger, but Borges and Brandán Caraffa were strongly opposed.

Borges vented his frustrations to Guillermo de Torre in a letter of May 23.[11] He complained that the union between *Martín Fierro* and *Proa* proposed by Oliverio Girondo meant that *Martín Fierro* would bring a hundred pesos in debts, while *Proa* currently enjoyed a surplus of over a thousand pesos. To add insult to injury, he told Torre, the current issue of *Martín Fierro* carried a satirical epitaph by Enrique González Tuñón—with whom he claimed to have come to blows three months earlier—that had deeply irritated him because it linked his name with, as he put it, the notorious bugger Roberto Smith and implied that he was Smith's and Brandán Caraffa's bum-boy.[12] The whole situation had become grotesque, and after what had happened, no friendship was possible with the *martinfierristas*. In any case—and this was something Girondo himself acknowledged—*Martín Fierro* was getting more pathetic by the day; in fact, it was a load of rubbish, did Torre not agree?

Borges clearly feared that, on the pretext of preserving the Frente Único, Girondo was scheming to become the leader of the New Generation. As it happened, he had been given Girondo's new book to review for the June issue of *Martín Fierro,* and he took this opportunity to spike his rival's guns by neutralizing his claim to be a revolutionary. He professed to find the "efficacy" of Girondo's poems quite "frightening": "Girondo is a violent man. He stares at things for a long while, then lashes out, seizes them, and off he goes. There is no adventure in it since he never misses a blow."[13] In that snide reference to "adventure," Borges was recalling his recent essay on Apollinaire and implying that Girondo, for all his violent attacks on tradition, was not really capable of genuine invention.

Borges, in any case, was growing weary of the endless squabbling. As he wrote to Sureda:

I'm looking for a way of going beyond this semirenown in which I'm stuck, this semifame as a literary man who is read by other literary people but who doesn't reach the wider public. I'm going back to a criollo simplicity of expression and an austere vocabulary, shorn of ornaments.[14]

By the end of July, he had decided to quit *Proa* altogether: "So long Frente Único," he wrote in his letter of resignation. "Good-bye one and all . . . pass me my hat and my walking stick, I'm off."[15]

For over a year, Borges had been seeking to create a specifically criollo form of the Ultra that would allow him to express the soul of the *patria*. But he had been frustrated in this endeavor by his conception of himself as a *criollo final*, the last of a noble line who felt lost in the great Babel that Buenos Aires had become. He had looked to Norah Lange for inspiration to resolve this creative and ideological impasse, and there is reason to believe that, around the middle of 1925, he was given some inkling as to how he might reconcile his sense of the past with the reality of modern Buenos Aires.

In June he published an essay on the gauchesque classic *Fausto* (1866) by Estanislao del Campo, an odd dialogue in verse between two simple gauchos, one of whom recounts to the other his experience of seeing a performance of Gounod's *Faust* at the fashionable Teatro Colón in Buenos Aires.[16] Borges admired the author's success in capturing what he regarded as two distinctive attributes of the criollo spirit, namely "gaiety" (*alegría*) and "disbelief" (*descreimiento*), in the otherwise alien environment of the metropolis. By way of the two gauchos' irreverent appraisal of an imported European opera, Estanislao del Campo had conveyed the surviving presence of traditional criollo values in Buenos Aires and thereby established a continuity between past and present, the pampas and the city. It was in this continuity that Borges would find a key to breaking the deadlock of his *criollo final* complex.

Borges's essay exudes an uncommon sense of joy. "Happiness and beauty," he wrote, were to be found in the *Fausto,* "excellences that, outside of its pages, I have observed only in some perfect woman."[17] The gratuitous reference to the happiness inspired by a beautiful woman indicates, I believe, that his friendship with Norah Lange had taken a romantic turn at around this time. A firmer clue to the essay's hidden amorous source can be found in Borges's passing, and apparently superfluous, quotation from Christopher Marlowe's *Doctor Faustus:* "Make me immortal with a kiss," a quotation whose fuller context is revealing in the circumstances.

In Scene XIV of Marlowe's play, Faustus asks Mephistophilis:

One thing, good servant, let me crave of thee,
To glut the longing of my heart's desire,—
That I might have unto my paramour
That heavenly Helen, which I saw of late . . .

Faustus's wish is granted, and when Helen of Troy enters his study, he declares in wonderment:

Was this the face that launched a thousand ships
And burnt the topless towers of Ilium?
Sweet Helen, make me immortal with a kiss. (*Kisses her.*)
Her lips suck forth my soul; see where it flies!—
Come, Helen, come, give me my soul again.
Here will I dwell, for Heaven is in these lips,
And all is dross that is not Helena.

By means of this intertextual device, Borges, I would say, was alluding to the kisses he was receiving from his very own Helen of Troy, Norah Lange. (The name Norah, what is more, is an abbreviation of Leonora, which is a variant of Helen.) If the *Fausto* had served to dissolve Borges's sense of himself as a *criollo final,* then this was ultimately due, it would seem, to the inspiration of his Apollinairean *jolie rousse.*

The prospect of overcoming the *criollo final* impasse led Borges to conceive of writing a more extensive and substantial work about Argentina than allowed for by *ultraísta* poetics. Sometime in the last three or four months of 1925, he had a sense of this project—at least in outline. He was to describe it as "a history in verse of Argentina," with the title *San Martín Copybook* (*Cuaderno San Martín*). There are only two extant allusions to this project, so it is difficult to say when it first occurred to him, but he would tell Guillermo de Torre that the poems of this book would be in the style of "General Quiroga Rides to His Death in a Coach" ("El General Quiroga va en coche al muere"), a poem that was first published in *Moon Across the Way,* Borges's second book of poetry, which came out on November 4, 1925.[18] Six months later he published two poems in *Nosotros* and mentioned in a footnote that they might be included in *San Martín Copybook,* a book he was planning to write.[19]

Clearly we have very little to go on, but it is still possible to get some idea of the nature of Borges's project because, taken in sequence, the three poems Borges mentioned in connection with the history of Argentina in verse trace a line of continuity from the days of the early republic to the time of the poet's childhood. "General Quiroga Rides to His Death in a Coach" is a poem about the famous episode in which the caudillo Facundo Quiroga was assassinated

by agents of the tyrant Rosas. The second poem is an evocation of Villa Ortúzar, a poor northwestern suburb of Buenos Aires, where the countryside is
said to "weigh heavily" on the *arrabal*. The third is "The Mythological Foundation of Buenos Aires" ("La fundación mitológica de Buenos Aires"), which
turns on the conceit that the city was founded by the Spanish conquistadors in
the barrio of Palermo, and specifically in the very block in which Borges himself was raised as a boy. The Palermo depicted here represents a homage to
Evaristo Carriego: it is a place of pink-washed taverns, the music of the tango,
games of *truco,* moaning barrel organs, and a sweetheart's kisses. However, the
three poems are so different in form, tone, and subject matter that they indicate a lack of organic unity in the project as a whole: Borges still needed a unifying principle—an Aleph, as it were—that would make for a coherent vision
of Argentina and his own place within it.

Still, it was perhaps a newfound confidence arising from his new project
that led to his agreeing to relaunch the magazine *Proa* in November with his
friends Brandán Caraffa and Francisco Luis Bernárdez. He even consented to
a rapprochement—though not a merger—with his rivals in the Florida group,
for the advisory board of the new *Proa* included Oliverio Girondo and a number of *martinfierristas,* as well as Guillermo de Torre and Ramón Gómez de la
Serna. Borges had not, in fact, severed all ties with the Frente Único when he
resigned from *Proa;* there remained a connection through Évar Méndez, who
had committed himself several months earlier to publishing Borges's second
book of poetry. The new truce between *Proa* and *Martín Fierro* was cemented
with a dinner in December to launch the two books that the Editorial Proa
had recently brought out, Borges's *Moon Across the Way* and a volume of poems by Sergio Piñero, one of the cosmopolitan *martinfierristas.* The dinner
was described as "a happy and most cordial" occasion, to which Borges contributed a good-humored poem of thanks.[20]

Proa's revival, however, proved to be short-lived: there were to be only
three issues, that of January 1926 being the last. The cause of the magazine's
demise remains unknown: lack of funds maybe, or further infighting within
the New Generation, given that *Martín Fierro* suspended publication for a few
months shortly after the failure of *Proa.* Borges, at any rate, seems not to have
been greatly concerned about the fate of *Proa,* and this may have been due to
his having been invited to contribute on a regular basis to *La Prensa,* which, as
a national newspaper, would have given him access to a far wider public than
either *Proa* or *Martín Fierro* could ever have afforded him. But there was another, and more substantial, reason for his apparent indifference to the failure
of his magazine: by the end of the year, he believed he had at last found the basis for creating a mythology of the city and people of Buenos Aires.

The seeds of this enterprise can already be observed in his projected verse history of Argentina. The continuity of past and present had not yet been grasped as a realized concept because Borges had not properly shed the nostalgic mentality of a *criollo final*. His feelings of inferiority in relation to the heroes of the early republic are still evident in "General Quiroga Rides to His Death in a Coach"—he envies Quiroga's rootedness: the caudillo is "solidly planted in life like a stake firmly stuck in the soil of the pampas." In "*Arrabal on Which the Country Weighs Heavily*" ("Arrabal en que pesa el campo"), the poet's sadness finds a correlative in Villa Ortúzar's nostalgia for the life of the pampas. Only in the third poem, "The Mythological Foundation of Buenos Aires," does one find a celebration of the city in a tone comparable to the breezy insouciance of Estanislao del Campo's *Fausto*. The ending in particular has that carefree cynicism (*descreimiento*) that Borges so admired in the *Fausto*: "Don't ask me to believe there ever was a start to Buenos Aires: it's eternal, I tell you, like water and the wind." The "mythological foundation" of Buenos Aires, then, would come about by virtue of the poet's will—he would take the Palermo he had imagined while listening spellbound to Carriego's verses as a boy and transform that marginal barrio into the timeless essence of the city itself.[21]

CHAPTER 9

The Aleph

(1926)

DURING THE COURSE OF 1926, Borges would seek to develop his Joycean project of mythologizing Buenos Aires. In January he published an essay with the oddly melodramatic title "The Pampas and the Suburbs Are Gods" ("La pampa y el suburbio son dioses"), where he observed that it was natural that the pampas and the gaucho should be revered as "archetypes" or "totems" in a pastoral country like Argentina, but he went on to argue that the barrios of Buenos Aires had also acquired totemic status, for even though the great city was "Babel-like," a place that attracted immigrants "from the four corners of the world," the outlying districts were still permeated by the influence of the pampas, and while several poets had written about these poor suburbs, none had done so fully: the *arrabal* remained a "half-made symbol."[1]

The man Borges credited with having discovered the literary potential of the *arrabales* of Buenos Aires was Evaristo Carriego, and he cited one poem in particular, "El guapo," which was based on the life of Juan Muraña, a criminal renowned in Palermo for his courage and skill as a knife fighter.[2] Muraña had been the most famous *cuchillero* in the barrio, along with Suárez "El Chileno"; almost all the stories about *guapos* that were told in Palermo were attributed to Muraña, since he was felt to be worthy of any act of bravery.[3] Carriego had also made the connection between the *cuchilleros* and the gauchos of old: his poem on Muraña had been dedicated to the memory of "San Juan Moreira," a notorious gaucho who had lived on the pampas as a heroic Robin Hood figure. Carriego, Borges liked to say, had been so devoted to the cult of Juan Moreira that he had gone so far as to sanctify this *gaucho malo*.[4]

Borges acknowledged his debt to Carriego for the specific idea of portraying the *arrabal* as an intermediate, liminal zone between the pampas and the city. But Carriego had not appreciated the significance of his discovery: he had intuited the epic possibilities of the *arrabal* but had cultivated its sentimental aspects instead.[5] Indeed, Borges even blamed Carriego's mawkish poems for initiating the tendency to sentimentalize the tango. In his view the primitive tango, the tango of the Guardia Vieja, the "old guard," although born and bred in the brothels and tenements of Buenos Aires, preserved something of the qualities of the rustic *milonga* sung by the gauchos, but this primitive spirit of the *arrabal*—"impudence, utter shamelessness, the pure joy of courage"—was being devalued by a new wave of composers, mostly of Italian provenance, who were turning the tango into "a cowardly, sorrowful lamentation," "a catalog of failures."[6]

The epic potential of the *arrabal* provided Borges with the breakthrough he needed for his project to mythologize Buenos Aires. His aim was to compose an epic in which the *cuchilleros* of the *arrabales* would be elevated to the status of mythic heroes. This epic of Buenos Aires would be created from the popular culture of the barrios—the legends, anecdotes, songs, and sayings of the common people who inhabited the teeming *arrabales* of the great metropolis. He believed that modern Buenos Aires would remain "deserted and voiceless" so long as it was not "settled by some symbol," and just as José Hernández had made his character Martín Fierro into a symbol of the pampas, so, too, did Borges aspire to produce a work or a character that would come to represent the essence of his native city.[7] Only one example has survived of the kind of epic treatment of the *arrabal* that Borges had in mind in this period. This was a narrative sketch called "Legend of a Crime" ("Leyenda policial"), a brief account of a duel between two *compadritos,* published early the following year, in which he sought to endow a sordid knife fight between two *compadritos* with epic dignity and mythic resonance.[8]

His ideas were still in a state of flux, however. He had not yet decided whether the epic of Buenos Aires should be written in verse or in prose—in fact, he referred to it as a "novel" in either prose or verse—but he inclined toward verse because the guitars of the common people might then "offer it their fraternity."[9] Nor had he resolved the question of the language and style in which it would be written: should it be a form of *arrabalero,* the dialect based on the criminal slang known as *lunfardo?* He decided in favor of a Castilian Spanish inflected with an Argentine accent, because *arrabalero* was too limited a medium to cope with the range of feeling and ideas that an epic of Buenos Aires would require, unless a poet could be found who could do for the *compadritos* of the city what José Hernández had done for the gauchos with his *Martín Fierro.*[10]

The fullest exposition of Borges's new vision is to be found in "The Extent of My Hope" ("El tamaño de mi esperanza"), an essay that shows how completely he had overcome the *criollo final* impasse by the end of 1925.[11] In this essay Borges still adhered to the view that the process of modernization had threatened the traditional criollo identity. The character of the criollos had been established in the early days of the republic, and the greatest of these criollos was the tyrant Juan Manuel de Rosas. However, thanks to Rosas's liberal enemy, Domingo Sarmiento, a man who, Borges averred, hated and repudiated all things criollo, the process of economic development had got under way, but such "progressivism" amounted to "submitting to being almost–North Americans or almost-Europeans, always almost-others."[12] Even so, Borges no longer perceived progress as entailing a "tragedy" for the criollos; instead of the fear and loathing for the Babel-like metropolis that he had felt barely a year earlier, one finds a certain affectionate pride in his native city—its vastness and diversity posed a creative challenge to the writer, for, with the exception of the tango, no idea had been engendered that resembled Buenos Aires, "this innumerable Buenos Aires of mine."[13] Hence his Joycean project to mythologize the city: the bewildering metropolis must be tamed by the poet's imagination and turned into a familiar, lovable reality in which its inhabitants would feel rooted as the old criollos had once been rooted in the pampas.

Borges called his new endeavor *criollismo*, but the term had to be understood in a broad sense, he pointed out, for this was not a nostalgic cult of the gaucho and the pampas such as that of Lugones, it was a *criollismo* that would "converse with the world and with the self, with God and with death." His "hope" therefore extended well beyond an insular preoccupation with defining a criollo identity; it had a universal reach, too, because it meant developing a culture for the young nation that would bear comparison to the cultures of other countries. There were few legends, few original creations, in Argentina; the "living reality" of the country, of Buenos Aires itself, was far greater than "the reality of our thinking," and so this new *criollismo*, based as it would be in the urban realities of Buenos Aires, entailed a form of nation building:

> Already Buenos Aires, more than a city, is a country, and one must find the poetry and the music and the painting and the religion and the metaphysics that will do justice to its grandeur. That is the extent of my hope, which invites us all to be gods and to work toward its incarnation."[14]

Several young men would respond to Borges's call to strive for the "incarnation" of a new culture for Argentina, notably the poets Francisco Luis Bernárdez, Leopoldo Marechal, Carlos Mastronardi, Ulyses Petit de Murat, and Sixto Pondal Ríos. Unquestionably the most eccentric was the painter, poet, and mystic Xul Solar, the pseudonym of Alejandro Schulz Solari, a man of profuse imagination, who would count among his attainments the invention of *neocriollo*, a language for the Argentines from which the alleged defects of Spanish had been purged but whose sole inconvenience was that no Argentine had yet managed to understand it. Borges was their leader, and, having always been fond of taking long walks, he now urged his friends to walk the city with a purpose—to "feel Buenos Aires," to familiarize themselves with the different barrios and imbibe firsthand the stories, songs, and legends of the common people.[15] One can get some idea of these ambulatory explorations from a postcard Borges wrote to a friend: "Having exhausted Saavedra, that barrio of tin shacks, and the little pampas of La Paternal, I am infesting San Cristóbal Sur (you should see the idyllic *ombú* trees in Parque Patricios!) and also Barracas."[16]

All the while he sought by various means to develop his project to mythologize the city of Buenos Aires. Ulyses Petit de Murat would recall how he had once been buttonholed at the Royal Keller by Borges: "You live in Belgrano, don't you? Well, you could write a poem on your barrio. Pondal Ríos will do another. So will Mastronardi. It's for an anthology that Gleizer is bringing out, with a map on the cover by my sister Norah. Córdova Iturburu and Horacio Rega Molina will do the barrio of Flores."[17] Although nothing seems to have come of that particular venture, Borges and his friends persevered all the same in their quest for the true spirit of the criollos, seeking out typical scenes and fiestas of the common people. They relished going to *asados,* those gargantuan barbecues where huge quantities of meat, sausages, offal, and wine are consumed to the strains of festive guitars.[18] And in a letter to Guillermo de Torre, Borges mentioned a pilgrimage he was planning to make with Xul Solar and Paco Bernárdez to the shrine of Our Lady of Luján, the virgin of the criollos.[19] There were also battles to be fought against deviant tendencies that might traduce the pure spirit of the *arrabal,* and none more urgent than the defense of the tango against the new composers who were threatening to turn this spontaneous urban folk epic into the effeminate whinging of jilted pimps. From time to time, Borges and his followers would express their disgust at this perversion of the tango by issuing forth en masse from the Royal Keller to shout down the aficionados of the new genre at their weekly meetings in the Café Tortoni. They reserved a special loathing for the effusions of Juan de Dios Filiberto, a *gringo* from La Boca, whom they baited unmercifully for his tearjerking but hugely popular songs.[20]

At the very center of Borges's circle of *criollistas* was, of course, his Apollinairean muse, his Helen of Troy, Norah Lange. The Saturday-evening parties at the calle Tronador had become a sacred ritual by now, a ritual, as Francisco Luis Bernárdez would recall, in which the spirit of the criollos was celebrated with the utmost devotion. The young men would arrive at the house "like a whirlwind," and then the fiesta would begin:

> The piano started up. Partners were chosen. The first chords rang out. And the tango would open its great melancholy flower, whose languorous scent seemed to blend with the poems we had composed during the week. . . . In between dancing to "El Choclo" and "El Entrerriano,"

between "Don Juan" and "La Cumparsita," we would often slip out of the house with the goddesses of that Wagnerian paradise and take a short break at the fragrant bar on the corner, and the brandies we were served at the counter seemed to form part of some ritual ceremony which united us all with even greater conviction in a certain "fervor for Buenos Aires" which a young criollo, not long back from Geneva, used to disseminate with an almost religious zeal during his prodigious walks throughout the city. We would make our way back noisily to the villa and resume our boisterous merrymaking. And then Norah, she of the long flaming hair, would regain her throne and scepter, extend both hands to silence the uproar, and proceed to recite from *La calle de la tarde*, her poems never failing to calm the storm and induce a sunrise of the purest emotion.[21]

Toward the middle of 1926, Borges's relations with Norah Lange had reached an unprecedented intimacy. One of Norah's poems of this period suggests an encounter that was as much erotic as emotional—she describes herself going to her lover like dew to a freshly opened rose; her heart aches with bliss as she anticipates the feast that awaits her in his lips; she can imagine him within her, plain as the moon in the silence of the night.[22] This sense of communion in love was to exert a powerful influence on Borges's literary ideas. In June he published "A Profession of Literary Faith" ("Profesión de fe literaria"), the single most important essay of his youth, where he articulated the tenets of a literary credo that, except for one critical modification, as we shall see, would remain the basis of all his subsequent writing.[23]

Borges's ideas were rooted in the expressionism of his youth, but he had since elaborated an extreme form of confessional poetics. He likened the transaction between an author and a reader to "a confidence," and, like any confidence, its basis lay in "the trust of the listener and the veracity of the speaker." It followed that all literature was "autobiographical in the last instance." Writing was "the full confession of a self, of a character, of a human adventure," and, correspondingly, readers had "a lust for souls, for destinies, for idiosyncrasies," a lust so sure of what it sought that if fictional lives did not satisfy it, it would "lovingly probe the life of the author." He conceded that the "autobiographical substance" of a work might be hidden at times under the "accidents" that embodied it, but it was present all the same, "like a heart beating in the depths."

There was, nevertheless, an intrinsic problem in this ultraconfessional view of literary communication: "How can one insert into the breast of others the shameful truth about oneself?" The difficulty resided in the fact that the poet's very medium was an obstacle to sincerity—verse, rhyme, metaphor, language itself, tended to obscure rather than lay bare genuine feeling. His solution to this problem was that "words have to be conquered by actually living them." By this he meant that language, though generic and impersonal, had to be imbued with the writer's particular experience of the world so that the work should bear the stamp of its maker's unique personality:

> I have already identified, among thousands, the nine or ten words that go well with my soul; I have already written more than one book in order to be able to write, who knows, just one page perhaps—the page that will justify me, the page that will be the abbreviation of my destiny, the page that only the assessing angels will maybe listen to on the day of the Last Judgment.

This is Borges's first formulation of an idea that would remain with him to the end of his life—the idea of salvation by writing. A single page, a single poem, a single book—one genuine masterpiece—would suffice to justify the life of a writer, for the encapsulation of a unique destiny in aesthetic form amounted to the salvation of its maker, since it rescued him from the undifferentiated void of solipsism, from the "nothingness of personality."

A few months later, he would come across a realized example of salvation by writing. On September 3 he reviewed a book of gaucho poems by Pedro Leandro Ipuche and singled out for comment a poem about a gaucho killing a tiger.[24] This topic was a commonplace in gauchesque literature, he observed, but Ipuche had given it a truth that transcended the stereotype and "attained fully to his precious intimacy." Ipuche's poem thus offered a pattern for his own writing—he wished that one day he would be capable, like Ipuche, of seeing "definitively the things that are truly mine": "I make poems in order to feel that I belong more fully in Buenos Aires, in order to feel secure in my recovered intimacy with Buenos Aires." The creation of a poetic world amounted to the shaping of a personal destiny, and this distinctive configuration of meaning would constitute the final justification of a writer's existence. Writing, then, was both creation and discovery, for an author remained open to a mysterious power that would reveal to him in and through the process of writing itself the essence of the self and its relation to the world.

As far as Borges was concerned, the personification of that guiding power was Norah Lange: it was she who had enabled him to overcome his *criollo final* impasse, she who had inspired his ultraconfessional poetics of the heart, and she who, he hoped, would bring to a harmonious fruition all the various elements that existed in contradiction and disarray in his conception of himself. Norah Lange was uniquely qualified to be Borges's muse, because she could resolve the deep-seated conflict between sword and dagger in a way that

Concepción Guerrero could not. Concepción had represented the plebeian urban reality of modern Buenos Aires that had seemed to be at odds with the criollo identity he had inherited from his ancestors. His love for Concepción, therefore, had exacerbated the conflict rooted in his childhood between the ancestral sword, associated with Mother, which conferred honor, distinction, legitimacy, and the dagger, associated with Father, which symbolized the illicit energy of excluded desires. But his love for Norah allowed him to embrace those excluded desires, for, ironically, the woman who had inspired Borges's *criollismo* was not herself a criolla: Norah was Scandinavian, with an admixture of Irish, and this Nordic ancestry served to legitimize Borges's English heritage—the "foreign flaw" that his father believed made him unacceptable to pure criollos. Indeed, Borges, who spoke to Norah Lange mostly in English, entertained a fantasy of an ancient ethnic affinity with her, deriving from his paternal family's roots in the north of England. He would write in his memoirs, "It may be no more than a romantic superstition of mine, but the fact that the Haslams lived in Northumbria and Mercia . . . links me with a Saxon and perhaps a Danish past."[25] The fact that his blood was predominantly "Saxon" while Norah's was Scandinavian no doubt suggested an analogy between Norah's conquest of his affections and the Viking raids on Northumbria, with the resultant mingling of blood that produced the English race.

Norah's "Englishness" may be understood as a metaphor for the unrealized potential that Borges wished to incorporate into his understanding of himself and his relation to Argentina. Norah would allow him to forge a continuity between past and present, between the traditional and the modern, between his mother's criollo heritage and the immigrant side of his father's family. Not much of Borges's thinking in this regard has remained extant, except for a little-known speech he would make in 1928 outlining a surprisingly radical vision of a future for Argentina in which the criollos and the immigrants from the various nations of the world who had come to the country would "conspire" together "in order to disappear in a new man," a new kind of Argentine.[26] This idea clearly denied the criollos a privileged role in determining the national identity—even though it was the criollo who had created the nation, he must sacrifice his pride in this achievement for the sake of the greater honor of the country; the criollo must be one among many lineages in the Argentina of the future.

Borges would thus regale Norah with the three epithets that marked the road to salvation—she was "English, innumerable and an angel."[27] "English" because she would reconcile the foreign and criollo sides of his family heritage; "innumerable" because she represented the unifying Aleph, the "number which encompassed the other numbers"; and an "angel" because her fiery Nordic beauty would rouse him to that zenith of Whitmanesque ardor that would bind self and world in a passionate whole. Indeed, we find a mystical account of the Aleph in a curious little essay called "A History of the Angels"("Historia de los ángeles")—and we must recall that Norah Lange was widely hailed as an "angel" by the writers of the Buenos Aires avant-garde—that Borges published in March 1926. Here we learn that the Aleph was the sign used by the Kabbalists to denote the chief of the ten emanations of God: it was "the brain, the first commandment, the heaven of fire, the divine name 'I Am Who Am' and the seraphim called Sacred Beasts."[28] The Aleph, then, represented Borges's highest expectation of Norah Lange's role as his muse, for it was through her that he would fully realize himself in his writing and thereby gain access to the supreme emanation of Oneness in His heaven of fire.

By the middle of 1926, Borges had at last found what he had been looking for when he resigned from the Frente Único a year earlier—he had discovered the means of fashioning a new poetic order capable of reaching beyond the coteries of the avant-garde and speaking to his countrymen as a whole. His *criollismo*, however, was treated with great suspicion by the *martinfierristas*. In May the editorial offices of *Martín Fierro* moved to new premises on the third floor of a building at Tucumán 612, near the calle Florida in the city center, a location that confirmed the *martinfierristas'* designation as the Florida group, the cosmopolitan wing of the New Generation. Indeed, much was made of their dedication to modernity and cosmopolitanism in an editorial: "We are now where we should be, right in the very center, where the city is more abreast of what is going on, closer to what the future might hold."[29] A welcome was extended to all elements of the avant-garde, but the doors of the magazine would be "shut in the face" of people with "base motives" who indulged in "poisonous gossip." Whether these strictures were directed at Borges and the *criollistas* is hard to say, but the same editorial warned that becoming too attached to the *arrabales* could "impose limitations" on writers. Another item in the same issue took the *criollistas* to task for their suspicion of progress and their proclivity to nostalgia.[30] A few months later, the same writer would criticize "the Carriegos of yesterday and today" who went on endlessly about "the pampas and the suburbs and their sweethearts."[31]

Borges seems to have been unperturbed by this criticism. The fact was that the movement for modern art in Buenos Aires was running out of steam. Its original impetus had come from Europe—from futurism, cubism, Dada, and expressionism, but the Argentine avant-garde had remained an eclectic affair of half-assimilated revolutionary notions and a naïve obsession with metaphor as the key to poetic invention. By international standards it was not so much an avant-garde as a revolt against the tired symbolism of the generation of Lugones. The visit of Marinetti to Buenos Aires in June of that year showed the growing staleness of the movement. Futurism was so old hat by now that even the ultrarespectable ladies' journal *El Hogar* (*The Home*) saw fit to organize a dinner in honor of the famous Italian poet at which futurist pranks were conscientiously perpetrated—guests were required to sit astride their chairs and gallop three times around the table.[32] The fact was that the "cosmopolitans" at *Martín Fierro* were unsure quite where things were going. As ever, they looked to Paris for a lead. One of their best writers, Sergio Piñero, had left the previous December for an extended stay in the Ville Lumière and had been filing reports on the latest trends. Several other *martinfierristas*, including Oliverio Girondo, were planning to follow suit in the coming months.[33]

Borges's *criollismo*, by contrast, was increasing its influence among young writers—toward the end of the year, poems and stories set in the *arrabales* of Buenos Aires would begin to appear even in the pages of *Martín Fierro*. And such was the confidence Borges drew from this burgeoning *criollismo* that he took to bringing Norah Lange to the gatherings of the New Generation. The fact that Norah had yet to meet the leading *martinfierristas* was due in part to her mother's reluctance to let her stay out late at night, but also no doubt to Borges's wish to shield his muse from contact with his rivals. However, from about the middle of 1926, Norah was to accompany Georgie to some sessions of the *Revista Oral*, where she met Évar Méndez, who offered to publish her second book of poetry in the Editorial Proa. (It would come out in September with the title *Los días y las noches* [*Days and Nights*]). And on July 10 she went with Borges to a fiesta held to celebrate the relaunch of *Martín Fierro*.

This party rapidly degenerated into a famously drunken binge. Évar Méndez, Leopoldo Marechal, and a few others enthroned Norah Lange in a chair they pinched from a café and bore her on their shoulders to the basement of the Café Tortoni, where they proceeded to break up a meeting of tango enthusiasts. Paco Luis Bernárdez found his way to the *Revista Oral* at the Royal Keller and insisted on declaiming an "editorial" that ended in uproar when he started hurling insults at the audience. Girondo was seen to stagger across to the junction of Corrientes and Callao, one of the busiest in the city, and attempt to direct the traffic. And poor Raúl González Tuñón woke up the next morning in a strange house in the summer resort town of Adrogué, twenty-five miles from Buenos Aires, having been taken in by some kind soul who had come to his rescue the night before.[34] It had been a wild night even by the standards of the avant-garde, and when they tried to figure out how things could have got so badly out of hand, suspicion fell on Count Antonio Mordini, an eccentric Italian nobleman who had come to Argentina in the expectation of hunting elephants in the Chaco: this "fearsome alchemist," as he was described in *Martín Fierro*, appears to have spiked their drinks with an exotic drug.[35]

As Carlos Mastronardi was to recall, Borges was "still happy" in those days: he "enlivened conversation with witty jokes and great roars of laughter," and "had no desire 'to be an other,' either in this life or in imaginary lives to come."[36] On October 24, Borges published an essay called "Writing Happiness," in which he argued that happiness was incompatible with a belief in the nothingness of the self, for when we are happy, we cannot imagine "the negation of all consciousness, of all sensation, of all differentiation in time or space," since happiness entails "the satisfaction of the will, not its loss."[37] Many writers, he asserted, had attempted to portray the experience of happiness, but "the presentation of happiness, of a destiny that realizes itself in happiness," was perhaps the rarest art could offer.[38] Still, Borges's faith in himself had risen like a phoenix from the ashes of self-doubt, and he proposed to do now what he claimed few poets had ever done before—he would "write happiness," capture in words what it felt like actually to be happy: such were the ambitions of a young man in love.

On Saturday, November 6, Borges accompanied Norah Lange to a luncheon party at the restaurant by the Boating Lake in Palermo Park.[39] The party was being held in honor of Ricardo Güiraldes whose gaucho novel, *Don Segundo Sombra,* had been published by the Editorial Proa to huge acclaim earlier that year. This event was something of an emotional occasion, because Güiraldes had been struggling with cancer and would be leaving for Paris in a few months' time, a visit that was likely to be his last.[40] A photograph later published in *Martín Fierro* shows the guests gathered around Güiraldes.[41] Norah Lange appears fresh-faced and dreamy, gazing upward, head to one side, as if lost in a girlish reverie; next to her is Georgie, wearing a faintly wry smile that gives him an air of relaxed, proprietorial satisfaction. We have here a golden moment in Borges's life, a moment quite unique, a moment as precious and fragile and tremulous as a soap bubble about to burst. For, as luck would have it, an encounter was about to take place at this party by the lake in Palermo, and the happy self-belief—that sense of the Aleph—that Borges had attained through his love of Norah Lange was actually on the point of being smashed to pieces.

CHAPTER 10

Rejection
(1926–1927)

AT THE TIME of the party in honor of Ricardo Güiraldes, Norah Lange was known as a published poet and a literary protégée of Borges, but her contact with other members of the New Generation outside Borges's own circle had been very limited, and there was still a number of writers she had yet to meet. It was at the party by the Boating Lake in Palermo Park that Borges introduced Norah to Oliverio Girondo, and she was later to find herself sitting next to her new acquaintance over lunch. What struck her about Girondo was his voice—it was dark and resonant, "like mahogany" or something "underground"; at one point she knocked over a bottle of wine, whereupon Girondo leaned over toward her and said, "Blood will flow between us."[1] It was a remark that could scarcely have been better judged to impress a twenty-year-old girl like Norah, who was so susceptible to the advent of a man to whom she felt destined to give herself. After lunch they danced together, and then Girondo took her home. Norah had fallen head over heels for this stranger—"Oliverio was vital, passionate. I was in love with him from that day on."[2]

It was not that Girondo was handsome—he had protruding front teeth accentuated by a weak chin that he would mask in later years with a distinctive beard, but his pale complexion set off restless brown eyes, and his hair, which he kept long for the period, was swept back from a high forehead to fall in wavy locks around his neck. A not inconsiderable asset, too, was his grand cosmopolitan style, for he was very much a man of the world—privately educated in England and France, widely traveled, and currently resident in Paris. Oliverio liked to present himself as a rebel against the straitlaced mores of Argentine society, but he was, in fact, the scion of a powerful landowning family of Basque descent, and for all his bohemian airs, he was not averse to reminding people of his kinship with the Arenales and the Uriburus, two of the most illustrious of the great criollo dynasties. And so, what with that voice of his and the dramatic gestures he liked to affect, he possessed the kind of virile charm that a young woman like Norah Lange, who was fifteen years his junior, must have found hard to resist.

Norah had arrived at the party with Borges but left with Girondo, and that simple fact would bring a singular wretchedness to Borges's life. To lose Norah to another man would have been disaster enough, but to lose her to Girondo of all people was a desperate humiliation. His dislike of Girondo had arisen over a disagreement about the avant-garde, but there was also a marked difference in temperament—Borges was withdrawn, mild mannered, tentative; Girondo was a force of nature, brash and energetic, and a compulsive exhibitionist. Class resentment played a part, too. Though of patrician stock, Borges actually came from the urban middle class, whereas Girondo belonged to the ruling elite, the beneficiaries of the economic revolution in the pampas which the Acevedos and the Borgeses regarded as having caused their social decline. (This may have contributed to Girondo's being portrayed in Borges's fiction either as an overbearing aristocrat or a sinister megalomaniac.)

The consequences of that chance encounter between Norah and Girondo began to unfold with alarming speed. Girondo turned up at the Lange house the following Saturday, having been invited to the customary party by Norah. He was introduced to Señora Lange, and he later claimed to have got on so very well with her that they had ended up playing chess together under a table.[3] Girondo's appearance at the villa on calle Tronador was no doubt a very bitter pill for Borges to swallow, for he considered it a special domain of his own, a place where he was accepted by a circle of trusted friends and could find refuge from that inner solipsistic loneliness to which he was so prone. It now felt to Borges as if he had been expelled from paradise, like the first Adam cast out of Eden, a motif that would recur in his writing until well into old age.

Norah and Girondo began seeing each other almost every day. As she was to put it in a poem, her lover's voice promised to uncover life's possibilities for her, and as her feelings became more ardent, so did the insistent voice press her for something that she was too frightened to surrender in a society that placed such a premium on a woman's honor.[4] But then Girondo announced that he was leaving Buenos Aires—"He already had a ticket for Europe in his pocket," Norah was to tell an interviewer—and on December 4, barely a month after the party at Palermo Park, he embarked for Paris, leaving Norah in a state of the most acute distress.[5] She began writing to him almost daily, and as she struggled with the sudden void in her life, she decided to transform her letters into an epistolary novel through which she might come to terms with her predicament.

Norah Lange's *Voz de la vida* (*The Voice of Life*) has been all but forgotten today, and it is indeed so rare as to be virtually unobtainable in Argentina. It was published in October 1927, and, as Borges was to observe in a review, "the primacy of passion, the one and all-powerful reality of a deep love, provides the substance of the plot."[6] In actual fact, he said, it was not really a novel at all, it was "the third part of the one long poem which comprises all of this writer's books and days," a poem in which the only destiny that mattered was her own, and to which she had now added the theme of "two men who are in love."

Voz de la vida consists of a sequence of letters written by a young woman called Mila to her lover, Sergio, who has departed abroad. While Mila is unsure about Sergio's feelings for her, she is also being wooed by an old friend called Ivan. The narrative charts the vicissitudes of this triangular situation, in which Mila is clearly Norah herself, Sergio is Girondo, and the other man, Ivan, may be identified as Borges. As far as I have been able to ascertain from other sources, the dates of Mila's letters correspond very closely to Norah's experience, and real events appear to have been given the lightest veneer of fiction. For instance, Mila's first letter is dated November 6, the exact date of the luncheon party in honor of Güiraldes in Palermo Park at which Norah deserted Borges for Girondo; Mila is accompanied to a ball by Ivan, just as Borges had accompanied Norah to the party; the ball is held at a place called "Prince George's Hall," which is surely a veiled allusion to "Georgie," or Borges; Mila's encounter with Sergio is portrayed as a *coup de foudre* similar to Norah's own account of Girondo's impact on her; at the end of the evening, when Ivan comes to take his leave of Mila, we are told that his eyes could not help but reflect the pain he felt, which is likely to have been Borges's reaction to the unexpected turn of events at the luncheon party in Palermo; finally, after a few weeks, Sergio abandons Mila and departs for London, whereas Girondo left for Paris.[7]

Nothing, of course, could have been further removed from the decisive conquest of Norah Lange by Girondo than the protracted wooing to which she had been subjected by the nearsighted and stammering Jorge Luis Borges. However, as *Voz de la vida* makes plain, Borges was to embark on a very determined effort to win her back. The strategy he adopted initially was to present himself as a friend of Girondo's, while gradually disclosing the facts of the situation to Norah. On December 18, Mila writes that Ivan had informed her of the unlikelihood of Sergio's returning to Buenos Aires, and this made her doubt whether Sergio truly loved her. On December 23 she complains that Sergio has not written back, and she adds that Ivan meets her from work almost every day. She remarks on January 3 that she has never known Ivan to be more devoted to her. Four days later she writes again to say that Ivan had taken her to a café on the calle Corrientes, and as they sat sipping cocktails, he placed his hand on hers, leaving it there for a long while before telling her that she had been deceived by Sergio—the reason for his leaving Buenos Aires was that he had a woman in London. Mila had been struck dumb with amazement at this revelation, and she tells Sergio that she cannot bring herself to think of him in the arms of another woman. Does he live with her? Does he love her? Will he ever come back to Buenos Aires? But Mila was to receive no reply from Sergio; she had been abandoned to a hopeless passion.

Borges must have calculated that Norah would in due course get over Girondo and he might then be able to resume his relationship with her. However, it was not to be: Girondo's father died unexpectedly in January 1927, and Oliverio was back in Buenos Aires around the middle of February. As *Martín Fierro* reported, "The regrettable death of his father, which took him by surprise in Europe, made him change his plans to remain there for a long period, and he is now devoting himself to his personal affairs and to study, having withdrawn for the time being from artistic activities."[8]

Girondo stayed in Buenos Aires probably for about two months, but he was unwilling to revive the affair with Norah. In *Voz de la vida,* this development is represented in the receipt of a letter from Sergio on February 18 in which he offers Mila the hand of friendship. A furious Mila writes back the same day telling him that she cannot make do with friendship after having fallen so deeply in love; she will not renounce her feelings, and her anger is fueled by the very intensity of her passion for him. However, a month later, as is evident from Mila's letter of March 18, Sergio has confessed to having a wife in London whom he does not love but is not free to leave. (Girondo, it seems, was unmarried but had an established mistress in Paris.) Mila is hurt and offended at the thought that Sergio might have been toying with her affections, but she nevertheless reaffirms her uncontainable passion and declares her readiness to go to him.

Observing the conflict that was unfolding between Norah and Girondo, Borges continued to press his suit. In a postscript to her letter of March 18, Mila informs Sergio that Ivan comes to see her almost every day; she is touched by his loyalty and at times feels some affection toward him, but she nevertheless reassures Sergio that it is he whom she wants. Girondo, however, remained impervious to Norah's entreaties, and sometime toward the end of March, he left for Paris again. This second parting was utterly heartbreaking for Norah, since she had no idea if she would ever again see the man she was in love with. She poured forth her anguish in a poem—she felt weighed down by the absence of her beloved, unable to forget his voice, her lips branded by his kiss, as if he had sealed them with words of fire.[9]

Since Norah appeared to have been abandoned once more, Borges decided to make a bold move. In a letter dated March 28, Mila tells Sergio that Ivan has made a proposal of marriage and will not contemplate a refusal: he is prepared to wait until the pain of Sergio's absence has passed. At times she is tempted to accept Ivan's proposal, but the truth is that she does not want to stop loving Sergio, and the only impediment to their relationship is Sergio's reluctance to give up the woman he is married to, even though he says he loves Mila instead. She reproaches Sergio for his reluctance to disregard conventions, for not coming to her by reason simply of his being in a legal union with a woman he claims not to love. For her part, Mila would be prepared to forsake her mother's love and go to Sergio in order to find whatever happiness he might be prepared to offer her.

Once again Mila receives no reply to her letter. On May 2 she complains that a whole month has gone by without receiving a word from Sergio, and she confesses to being tempted to go to London anyway, although she is fearful of encountering an even greater void there than the one she is currently experiencing in Buenos Aires without him. She feels exhausted from the double pressure of wanting to be with Sergio, while resisting the temptation to give in to Ivan, who keeps pleading with her not to leave Buenos Aires, to wait a few weeks more.

On May 8, Mila presents Sergio with an ultimatum: he must reply to her letters within thirty days or she will marry Ivan and never write to him again. Four days later she notes that Ivan's eyes reveal his joy as the days come and go without a letter from Sergio. Only two days before the deadline, however, Mila writes to Sergio in despair, begging him for a letter, assuring him once more that she is willing to overcome any obstacle in order to be with him. Her despair is such that she feels like hurling herself out of the window to meet her end in the futile darkness of the night.

On June 12, the date of the deadline Mila had set, the longed-for letter from Sergio arrives—but only to reveal that his wife is pregnant. Mila feels she has suffered a double defeat: Sergio's wife has kept her man and would now bear his child. Mila therefore resolves to marry Ivan so that she can at least fulfill one of her deepest wishes, which is to have a child of her own. She informs Sergio that he should no longer expect any communication from her. But once again she falters in her resolve, and on July 15, which is the very eve of her wedding, she confides in a letter to Sergio that she is troubled by the prospect of marrying a man for whom she cannot feel the same degree of passion as she does for him. Even so, she is loath to break her promise to Ivan, because she knows that marriage would bring him great happiness and to deny him would condemn the two of them to desperate loneliness. She prays that she be given a child, but she feels uneasy all the same about the emotional deceit her wedding would entail.

Voz de la vida must not, of course, be taken as an exact record of what transpired between between Norah, Girondo, and Borges. I have not, for instance, been able to ascertain whether Girondo was actually married to the other woman, or whether indeed she became pregnant by him. The matter of the pregnancy was probably a fictional device used by Norah to indicate the strength of Girondo's attachment to his mistress in Paris, which would have explained his refusal to resume the affair, despite all her pleas. As for Borges, there is every reason to believe that he did in fact propose marriage to Norah, but it is more difficult to form a judgment about her response at this juncture. I would surmise that she accepted the proposal in principle but asked him to wait until the pain of Girondo's loss had subsided and she could bring her emotions under control.

I would say that Norah and Borges may have become informally engaged to each other around July 16, 1927, which is the date of Mila and Ivan's wedding in *Voz de la vida*. By this time Girondo had been absent for some four months and had turned a deaf ear to all of Norah's pleas. Borges must have hoped that Norah would put the whole sorry adventure with Girondo behind her and settle down with him. But again it was not to be, for around the middle of August, Girondo seems to have got in touch with Norah out of the blue—Mila receives an unexpected letter from Sergio telling her that the other woman has died and that he still loves Mila. The death of Sergio's "wife" in the novel may be taken as symbolizing Girondo's realization that he could not get over the young girl he had abandoned in Buenos Aires. He had tried to resist her for several months in order to remain loyal to the other woman, but he must have been more smitten with Norah than he had realized, and it may well have been jealousy of Norah's engagement to Borges that drove Girondo to acknowledge the strength of his feelings for her.

Girondo's sudden declaration of love brought fresh turmoil for Norah: having accepted Borges, she tried to resist Girondo. On August 19—barely a month after her marriage to Ivan—Mila writes back to Sergio expressing her anguish at the thought of being tied to Ivan when she knows that Sergio is now free of his marital bond. However, in another letter on September 4, she tells Sergio that she feels committed to her husband, so he must cease writing to her and put her out of his mind. And yet, knowing as she did now that Girondo was prepared to give up the other woman for her sake, Norah found it impossible to resign herself to a relationship with Borges. In *Voz de la vida*, Mila's marriage to Ivan is followed by a long interval of about nine months, and then, on May 27, Mila writes to Sergio again, telling him that she is tormented by the knowledge that he is waiting for her, by the memory of his voice, and by the prospect of discovering happiness in his arms. She finds her husband's kindness irritating, insufferable. Some time ago he had implored her to reciprocate his feelings, but she refused to do so, and he responded by being cruel to her, muttering Sergio's name in a threatening fashion. He then reverted to his usual obliging manner, which she found so annoying. Mila has resolved to leave her husband and go to Sergio. The only voice that could have restrained her would have been the voice of a child, but she has not been granted that happiness. She is fearful and anxious, but she is driven by the love she expects to find with Sergio. In her last letter, which is dated June 10, Mila writes that Ivan's response to her decision was not surprise but anguish. She will be leaving the very next day to be with Sergio, and she can scarcely contain her joy at the prospect of realizing the love she had dreamed of for so long in her tearful solitude.

The dates of the letters of *Voz de la vida* broadly correspond to the chronology of Norah's relations with Girondo and Borges, but the nine-month interval between the letters of September 4 and May 27 is clearly symbolic, indicating that Norah had come to the conclusion that she would not find personal fulfillment with Borges. Still, the denouement of *Voz de la vida*—Mila's decision to leave Ivan and join Sergio in London—may have reflected Norah's wishes, but the reality of the situation was rather different. Norah must have ended her relationship with Borges in the middle of September at the very latest, since *Voz de la vida* was published on October 12, but she did not go to Paris to seek out Girondo. It may be that Girondo had not in fact left his mistress, or perhaps Norah felt that she could not yet be sure of his intentions toward her. She was, in any case, only twenty-one, she was not well off, and it must have been hard to leave her widowed mother to go to an unknown city on the far side of the world with no reliable means of financial support.

Norah was still in the throes of indecision, however. The long months of suffering since her first parting from Girondo had taken their toll in sleeplessness and anxiety, but her agony now was so acute that she began to experience severe hair loss: "I suffered so badly my hair fell out," she was to recall. "For some time I had to wear a little bonnet to cover my head. After a while I grew back some lovely curls."[10] Her anguish was made worse by the fact that she had no one to confide in—she sorely missed Ruthy, the sister she had been closest to, who had married that year and had gone to live in Oslo with her Norwegian husband. "It was the most disconsolate period of my life," she confessed.[11] In the end she decided to go to Norway to spend a year with Ruthy, who was expecting her first child. On November 15, *Martín Fierro* announced a farewell party for Norah, whose novel had just been published and who would shortly be leaving for Europe.[12] Toward the end of November or early in December, she departed Buenos Aires on a Norwegian cargo ship bound for Oslo.

Borges's rejection by Norah Lange was to be one of the major reversals in his life. An early reaction to this personal catastrophe can be found in a short text called "Sentirse en muerte," an idiosyncratic title even in Spanish, whose meaning is perhaps best rendered literally as "Feeling in Death."[13] It is an account of an epiphany he experienced while walking the streets one night beyond the Maldonado River, somewhere between his native barrio of Palermo and Villa Mazzini, the district where Norah lived. He described how he came upon a street of low houses and saw a pink wall bathed in moonlight, and it struck him with great force that this scene had been untouched by time and that he, in turn, had been raised into a timeless condition, as if he were "an abstract perceiver of the world." The effect of this radical abstraction from time, as the title of the piece indicates, was to enter a condition akin to being dead: it was to be proof against change and loss and unhappiness and to eternalize a state of realized desire.

The fact was, however, that his hopes of realizing his desire for Norah Lange had collapsed. And as Norah became obsessed with her passion for Girondo, so did Borges's hopes fade away. In March, when Girondo was refusing to have anything to do with Norah, Borges had proposed marriage to her, but it seemed that the more Girondo made the girl suffer, all the more did she understand that she could not love Borges. Indeed, after having been abandoned a second time by Girondo at the end of March, Norah would repudiate Borges's love with unexpected cruelty. On April 28 she published in *Martín Fierro* a gratuitous review of *Fervor de Buenos Aires* and *Moon Across the Way* under the enigmatic title "Thinking of Jorge Luis Borges in Something That Does Not Quite Manage to Be a Poem." ("Jorge Luis Borges pensado en algo que no alcanza a ser poema").[14] With a few well-placed qualifications, she distanced herself from the poetry of the man whom she had been happy to acknowledge as her mentor for the past three years. Her one "reproach," as she put it, was that the Buenos Aires evoked in Borges's poems was too placid—it was always dressed in its Sunday best.

Norah's reproach must have hit home with all the precision of a bullet running through the heart of its victim—Borges was being repudiated by his Apollinairean *jolie rousse,* who was publicly spurning the poetic "order" he had envisaged and announcing her preference for the "adventure" of the avant-garde. And, as if to rub salt in the wound, in the very same issue of *Martín Fierro* where Norah had published her review, there appeared a further repudiation of his writing, this time in the form of a note about his failure to win the Municipal Prize for his book of essays, *El tamaño de mi esperanza.* One of the judges, a professor at the University of Buenos Aires called Nirenstein [*sic*], was reported to have denied Borges his vote "because he considered him an incomprehensible writer, an imitator of Carriego."[15]

Borges's response to Norah's critical review came just two weeks later, in the form of a brief essay on one of the greatest love poems in the Spanish language, the twenty-first of Francisco de Quevedo's "Sonnets to Lisi," in which the poet declares that his soul and veins and marrow have known the fires of love, and when he dies, they will lose their form but not their will:

Ash they shall become, but ash that shall yet feel,
Dust they may be, but dust that loves you still.

Serán ceniza, mas tendrá sentido,
Polvo serán, mas polvo enamorado.[16]

Quevedo's sonnet, according to Borges, was "a most original argument for immortality," an argument based on the proposition that "intensity is the promise of immortality," and not just any kind of intensity but the intensity of erotic desire or, more precisely, of the act itself: "Orgasmic joy, plenitude of being that it is, overflows its brief moment and affirms that someone who has lived so fully will never forget to go on living and can therefore never die."

Although Norah's rejection threatened to kill his very soul, he, like Quevedo, would move every fiber of his being to resist that death, for even in that agonizing will to survive, he might find some purchase on whatever residue of selfhood Norah might vouchsafe to leave him. Still, his confidence in salvation had been profoundly shaken by Norah's repudiation of his love, and his belief in the possibility of "immortality" would become ever more tenuous—in another essay written later that year, he would insist that even though the particular feelings or thoughts of a writer might fade with time, his "individuality" would cling "like a root" to the souls of his readers, allowing his literary personality to survive if only as "an echo," "a handful of shadows," "a mere wake in the absence of the word."[17]

Borges, nevertheless, began to slide into self-doubt, and by June he had revised the "Profession of Literary Faith" he had published only the year before. In an essay called "An Investigation of the Word" ("Indagación de la palabra"), he questioned the key tenet of his literary credo, namely, the belief that poetry entailed a full confesssion of the self based on the trust of the listener and the veracity of the speaker.[18] Such a transaction was impossible, he now argued, because language itself possessed a "hemisphere of lies and shadows" that betrayed the author or speaker's expressive intent; this opacity he called "the general tragedy of all writing"—linguistic meaning was "fickle and contingent," the sense of a sentence would differ according to the reader, and conversely, the structures of syntax were prone to misrepresent the intentions of an author; one had no choice, therefore, but to submit "to syntax, to its treacherous concatenation, to imprecision, to the maybes, to the excessive emphases, to the buts."[19]

Borges had made his profession of literary faith at the very zenith of his love for Norah Lange, when it had seemed to him that the highest goal of poetry was a transparency of communication comparable to that between lovers.[20] Yet now he realized that "only angels" could circumvent language and that even Norah, who had been revered as an angel by the young men of the Buenos Aires avant-garde, was no angel in this respect, for we mortals were the "never-angels," irredeemably "verbal," inescapably condemned to suffer the infidelities of the word.[21]

Borges nevertheless resumed his relations with Norah in July 1927 or thereabouts, as we have seen; they probably even became engaged for a while, but this state of affairs did not last for more than a couple of months, and by September, Norah had rejected him once more. This second disappointment was to bring forth another bitter denunciation by Borges of the "general tragedy of all writing." In a public lecture sponsored by *La Prensa* that he gave in September, Borges addressed the question of the language to be employed by Argentine writers, and he advocated the use of standard Spanish with an Argentine intonation, but in an extraordinary passage, he gave voice to a visceral mistrust of all language, declaring that it was the Devil—"that mocking serpent, that inventor of equivocation and adventure, that core of the fruits of chance, that eclipse of an angel"—who had baptized the things of this world.[22]

This outburst came only a few weeks after Norah had broken off their engagement—she had received a declaration of love from Girondo and could no longer deny her feelings for his rival. Yet, curiously, Borges's reaction to this latest rejection—beyond his anguish at Norah's decision—was a kind of admiration, even awe, at the extraordinary force of a passion that was sweeping this innnocent girl toward a fate no one could yet foresee. Shortly after the publication of Norah's *Voz de la vida* in mid-October, he wrote a poem called "To the Doctrine of Passion in Your Voice" ("A la doctrina de pasión de tu voz").[23] (The repeated use of *voz* and *vida* in the poem echoed the title of Norah's novel, and his sentiments fitted exactly those of a spurned suitor like Ivan.) The poem is addressed to an unnamed woman whose voice is "the sound of the passion of love." "Pity us," Borges writes, "who have heard it without having been found worthy." The beloved has declined to become the center of his world:

> but yours is the voice of passion in its power and glory
> and it floods the words you utter.
> How to forget what was not ours to hear?
> How to forget your voice of passion,
> when voices that once said "I love you" have been forgotten,
> and yours holds us in thrall?

And yet, despite this attitude of resignation, the poet looks toward a future in which it is conceivable that he might regain the woman's love, for the voice of passion holds out a promise that love is possible on this earth, and not only love but "the entire presence of bliss."

Borges evidently felt that all was not lost with regard to Norah: she had decided against going to Paris, and it was possible that, in the year she planned to spend with her sister in Oslo, she might get over her feelings for Girondo and he might then have a chance to win her back. Meanwhile, he had to face life in Buenos Aires without her, a bleak, comfortless prospect sure enough, and a period in which the whole of his inner world would remain in suspense, waiting for Norah to return, waiting to discover whether he might yet find salvation as a writer or be damned forever to the nothingness of the self.

CHAPTER 11

Revenge and Defeat

(1927–1930)

THE BREAK BETWEEN Norah Lange and Borges occurred at a time of renewed political ferment in Argentina as the president, Marcelo T. de Alvear, reached the end of his term of office. Alvear was barred by the constitution from standing for a second consecutive term of office, and, of the various contenders to succeed him, the most popular was Hipólito Irigoyen, the man who had been his immediate predecessor from 1916 to 1922. Irigoyen was a controversial and divisive figure. His election as president in 1916 had brought the Radical Party into government for the first time in its history, and during his term of office he had rewarded his followers by expanding jobs in the state sector and hugely increasing public spending. However, the consequences, in a world economy unsettled by the Great War, were high inflation and industrial unrest, culminating in the infamous Semana Trágica of January 1919, which saw confrontations between police and workers during a bitter general strike by the anarchist-led unions. Irigoyen's successor, Alvear, though a Radical, too, had tried to restore financial discipline, a policy that split the party in 1924 into a pro-Irigoyen party and a rump of "Anti-Personalist Radicals" loyal to Alvear. By 1928 the prospect of Irigoyen's reelection to the presidency alarmed the conservative ranchers who ran the vital export economy, but they were divided over how best to stop Irigoyen—whether to revive the system of controlled elections, if that were possible, or to dismantle the electoral system altogether and create an authoritarian, corporate state.

The approaching presidential elections exacerbated ideological conflicts among the New Generation of writers. Some *martinfierristas* veered to the left and, together with the writers of the Boedo group, gave their support to the socialists or to the fledgling Communist Party. The sharpest split, however, occurred between supporters and opponents of Irigoyen. Borges came out strongly in favor of Irigoyen, not just because he was a Radical by family tradition, his grandfather having been a friend of the party's founder, Leandro Alem, but also because the kind of urban, democratic *criollismo* he had developed found a natural representative in Irigoyen, the great champion of the popular classes.

The anti-Irigoyen group of writers within the New Generation regarded the Radical leader as a dangerous rabble-rouser who would destroy order and prosperity. These young reactionaries coalesced around a foursome comprising the *martinfierrista* Ernesto Palacio, the brothers Julio and Rodolfo Irazusta, and Juan E. Carulla. They espoused a right-wing nationalism that we shall henceforth term *nacionalismo*, to distinguish it from Borges's democratic *criollismo*, and which, though not strictly fascist, shared several common themes with the fascistic nationalism that Leopoldo Lugones had been advocating since Irigoyen's first term of office. Their basic contention was that the Argentine republic was threatened by the demagoguery fostered by party politics and mass immigration. In the short term, they wanted to restrict voting rights to native-born Argentines and to control immigration, but their aim was to institute a corporate society led by a supreme caudillo whose guiding principles would be derived from Catholic social doctrine and traditional criollo values. A key element in their strategy was to provoke a coup d'état, and even before the elections of 1928, the *nacionalistas* began to approach sympathetic army officers, urging them to seize power in order to forestall the reelection of Irigoyen.

In the latter half of 1927, the young *nacionalista* writers were preparing to launch a magazine called *La Nueva República*, whose first issue was planned for December 1. This would have been a cause for concern for Borges, because the *nacionalistas* were members of the New Generation and indeed friends of his—Ernesto Palacio was to marry a cousin of Borges's—and could well start to lure people away from his own moderate *criollismo*. It was, therefore, very likely in order to counteract the influence of the *nacionalistas* that Borges decided to become actively engaged in politics. Around October he founded the Committee of Young Intellectuals for Irigoyen (Comité de Jóvenes Intelectuales Irigoyenistas), which attracted a good number of writers. Borges himself served as chairman, Leopoldo Marechal as vice chairman, and Ulyses Petit de Murat as treasurer; other members of the committee were Macedonio Fernández, Francisco Luis Bernárdez, Pablo Rojas Paz, Carlos Mastronardi, Xul Solar, Roberto Arlt, Sixto Pondal Ríos, Raúl and Enrique González Tuñón, and Raúl Scalabrini Ortiz. Borges was the founder and moving spirit—the headquarters of the committee was established in his apartment at Quintana 222.

Although few records of the activities of this committee survive, Borges and his friends certainly played a very active part in Irigoyen's reelection campaign. They drew up a political manifesto, which they pasted up on walls all over the city. The manifesto, which was almost certainly written by Borges, identified "Three Phases" in the building of the Argentine nation: "1810–1816—Revolution [i.e., against Spain]; 1853–1860—Organization [i.e., of the republic]; 1916–1922—Argentine Consciousness [i.e., Irigoyen's first term as president]." The manifesto then looked forward to a new phase: "1928—We, the young writers, cherish the great hope of the *patria:* IRIGOYEN PRESIDENTE." It was signed by Borges and the members of his Committee of Young Intellectuals.[1] Ulyses Petit de Murat would recall attending meetings of the Central Committee of the Radical Party with Borges,[2] and on December 27, 1927, the mass-circulation daily newspaper *Crítica* published a letter, signed by Borges and the entire membership of the Committee of Young Intellectuals, denouncing ballot rigging at elections to posts in the Radical Party in the city of Córdoba. The style of the letter suggests that it was written by Borges himself: it accused Irigoyen's opponents of having deprived the people of their fundamental civil rights by cheating at these elections, and it appealed to members of the party to rally to the "true Radical doctrine," which "crowns the triumph of Argentine democracy," and which was at stake in the forthcoming presidential elections in April.[3]

In October or thereabouts, Borges and his friends put pressure on Évar Méndez, the editor of *Martín Fierro,* to have the magazine declare its support for the pro-Irigoyen campaign. Méndez refused, claiming that *Martín Fierro* had been politically neutral from its inception, and in the issue of November 15, he published a statement disassociating the magazine from any political or religious interests and disclaiming rumors that the magazine had founded a Committee of Young Intellectuals.[4] This disclaimer infuriated Borges, and in the course of December, the bad blood that had always existed between the *Proa* group and the *martinfierristas* burst into the open. Borges and his friends were accused by the "cosmopolitan" *martinfierristas* of having betrayed the ideals of the New Generation and of having formed the pro-Irigoyen committee for no better reason than to obtain jobs and patronage from the Radical Party, whose political committees were notorious for their corruption.[5] But Borges himself was indifferent to such attacks; if anything, they brought out an aggressive cynicism in him—Petit de Murat would recall how Borges whispered sarcastically to him during a meeting of the Radical Party, "I wonder when they're going to start handing out the meat pies," "meat pies" (*empanadas*) being slang for the rewards given to loyal supporters of the party.[6]

The dispute became so bitter that finally, on January 4, Borges, Marechal, and Bernárdez resigned from the editorial board of *Martín Fierro.* Évar Méndez then decided to close down the magazine altogether, possibly to forestall a subsequent maneuver by Borges to oust him and take over the editorship. The bad feeling between the two camps was further inflamed by Borges's extraordinary decision to maximize the publicity of *Martín Fierro*'s demise by releasing his letter of resignation to the newspaper *Crítica*, which published it in full on January 25, 1928:

Buenos Aires, 4 January 1928

Señor Évar Méndez, manager of *Martín Fierro*. We the undersigned have decided to forget about *Martín Fierro* for the following reasons:

a) On account of the prudent disclaimer—which was not entirely oblivious of the services you provide at the Casa Rosada—perpetrated by you in our magazine.

b) Because your gramophones, motorcars, electric razors, diving suits, roller skates and the rest of that junk seem to us as rhetorical as the dream palaces of old-fashioned versifiers.

c) Because we are not interested in having our work subjected to censorship and disclaimers.

d) Because we cannot understand by what right you claim to represent *Martín Fierro* against us, who are its true representatives.

e) Because our political activities are honest and well founded, and not the sort of fearful manipulation betrayed by your note.

f) Because religion and politics are serious matters and not a pretext for base self-interest.

Wishing you a long afterlife full of backbiting and misprints, we assure you once more of our lengthy and unwavering separation.

[Signed by]: Jorge Luis Borges, Leopoldo Marechal, Francisco Luis Fernández [*sic*]
Editors of the magazine *Proa*, which will reappear in March.

The letter was, of course, a vicious personal attack on Évar Méndez, for Borges would have known that Méndez was contractually barred, as a civil servant, from taking part in political activity. More particularly, Méndez worked in the library of President Alvear's private office and was personally acquainted with the president, so to have the magazine he edited declare its support for Alvear's great enemy, Irigoyen, would have damaged his career. But the letter also rejected the poetics and rhetorical style of the *martinfierristas*, as is evident in Borges's mockery of the hackneyed, machine-obsessed imagery of his opponents. And the questioning of Méndez's right to represent *Martín Fierro*, together with the self-important bluster about religion and politics, brought into the open the underlying power struggle that had troubled the Buenos Aires avant-garde since Borges's return from his second visit to Europe.

In fact, I believe that Borges may have contrived this quarrel in order to finish off *Martín Fierro* once and for all. It was not for nothing that he chose to describe himself and his two friends as the editors of the magazine *Proa*, "which will reappear in March." Indeed, this whole episode was very likely conceived by Borges, in the last instance, as his revenge on Oliverio Girondo, who had been the mainstay of *Martín Fierro* and who had effectively dealt *Proa* a mortal blow in 1925 with his proposal of a merger of the two magazines. And his revenge was fueled not only by literary resentment but also by emotional pain, for I suspect that Borges also forced *Martín Fierro* to close out of pique at his rejection by Norah Lange. It is strange that the quarrel should have flared up in the same month as Évar Méndez published Norah's *Voz de la vida* in the Editorial Proa; strange, too, that Méndez's disclaimer should have appeared in the same issue of *Martín Fierro* as the announcement of Norah's imminent departure for Norway.[7]

Borges's literary and political activities were very closely interwoven with his personal troubles. As if the humiliation of his rejection by Norah Lange in favor of his rival Girondo and her subsequent departure for Oslo were not enough, his activities were further affected by problems with his eyesight. He had suffered from acute myopia since early childhood, but over the last year or so, he had developed cataracts, an ailment that had afflicted his father and appeared to run in the family. Early in March 1928 he underwent an operation, the first of eight he would endure before going blind about twenty-five years later. Frustratingly, this operation took place just a few weeks before the Radical candidate for the presidential elections was due to be selected, on March 24, 1928. Borges and his friends had decided to publish a booklet in which each member of the Committee of Young Intellectuals for Irigoyen would set out his reasons for supporting their candidate, but Borges was still recovering from his eye operation, so he dictated to his mother a letter that is almost certainly his contribution to this booklet. We have here the fullest exposition of the young Borges's political views that has so far come to light:

> I have just been operated on and I have been inhabiting the darkness for some days now (days which certainly do not deserve the honor of being recalled) and which do not permit me any rhetorical elaboration or detailed exploration on paper. This is why I write to you by the hand of another and with the simplicity born of haste. . . .
>
> It is easy for me to give reasons for my conviction as an *irigoyenista*. It amounts to thinking before others what I have already thought for myself. Irigoyen represents Argentine continuity. He is the *porteño* gentleman who has experienced the vehemence of the Alsinistas [supporters

of the autonomy of the Province of Buenos Aires] and the great patriotic rising of El Parque [the Revolution of 1890, from which the Radical Party was born], and who continues to live in a modest house in the Southside (a district which exudes the ambience of the *patria* even for those of us who do not live there), but he is the man who best remembers our future with prophetic and hopeful memory. He is the caudillo who has decreed, with all the authority of a caudillo, the death without appeal to all forms of *caudillismo;* he represents the present, which, without forgetting the past and finding honor in it, turns itself into the future.

Irigoyen's heroic endeavor, his civic vocation, has been administered (I use the word advisedly) by a conduct which can rightly be said to be worthy of a man of genius. The facile and hereditary discovery of politicians was this: publicity, garrulity, frankness, outspokenness, arouse sympathy. Irigoyen's discovery was the inspired opposite of that, and can be expressed thus: the sober, prudent man, the circumspect man, the man of his word, the man who keeps his own counsel, can also be popular. That intuition was enough to save him from indulging in the obligatory public spectacles of politics. Irigoyen, that most noble conspirator for the Good, has not felt the need to offer us any spectacle other than his passionate existence, dedicated as it is to the *patria* with such jealous fidelity.[8]

The effusive style is similar to that of letters Borges tended to write to women he fell in love with, and this, in effect, is a love letter to Irigoyen composed as he lay blindfolded after the operation, in a pit of depression, and abandoned, as he saw it, by Norah Lange. In those black circumstances, he portrayed Argentina as an elusive mistress whom Irigoyen served with the "jealous fidelity" he had himself adopted toward Norah after her defection to Oliverio Girondo.

Borges's spirits failed to revive after the operation, even though Irigoyen was duly nominated the Radical candidate and went on to win a massive victory at the presidential elections on April 1. He was assailed instead by a preoccupation with death. On the eve of the elections, for instance, he went out with a friend "to feel Buenos Aires," and as they were walking near the Chacarita Cemetery, they heard the sounds of a guitar coming from the premises of a local branch of the Radical Party, where they found a young man singing a *milonga* that included the lines "Life is nothing more / than death's bright glow."[9] Borges was so struck by the song that he recalled it in a poem about the Chacarita Cemetery that he wrote in this period.[10] And then, just over a month later, he was shaken by the suicide of a close friend who blew his brains out in the basement lavatory of the Jockey Club in the city of La Plata.

Borges's depression was such that he appears to have done little to capitalize on Irigoyen's great victory—his Committee of Young Intellectuals disbanded after the election, and his plan to relaunch *Proa* in March came to nothing in the end. The reason for his lack of success with *Proa* may have been that Leopoldo Marechal and Francisco Luis Bernárdez, the other two associates on the editorial committee, had joined the Cursos de Cultura Católica (Courses in Catholic Culture), a program that brought together young intellectuals and priests in the study of the social doctrines of the Church. As it happened, the first issue of a new literary review called *Criterio,* sponsored by the Cursos de Cultura Católica, was published on March 8 of that year—the same month Borges had been hoping to relaunch *Proa*—and his friends Marechal and Bernárdez were to write for this new Catholic magazine.

Borges, it seems, allowed himself to go along with Marechal and Bernárdez for a time, even contributing a few reviews, articles, and poems to *Criterio.* It may be that he hoped to influence the members of the recently instituted Cursos de Cultura Católica in the direction of his own pro-Irigoyen *criollismo,* for in September he took the opportunity of stating his political vision at the opening of an exhibition of the works of the folklorist painter Pedro Figari organized by the Cursos. It was in this speech that he urged the criollos to forget their pride in their honorable lineage and become "confederates" (*conjurados*) with the immigrants in order to create a "new man" in a tolerant, hospitable Argentina where people from all over the world might find a home.[11] This was the boldest and most optimistic vision of Argentina that Borges was ever to propose in public, but his appeal to the young criollos fell on deaf ears, and not long afterward the Cursos became a fertile breeding ground for right-wing *nacionalistas* of the *Nueva República* variety.

Norah Lange's departure had left Borges in a state of utter despondency, and, in the absence of the beloved, his sense of the "nothingness of personality" threatened to engulf him once more. Although he resumed his habit of exploring the barrios of Buenos Aires after his eye operation, there was a desperate edge to these wanderings: he would venture in the dead of night into the most disreputable areas, places where delinquents went about armed with knives and guns and where fierce dogs were known to attack passersby. On one occasion he narrowly avoided grievous bodily harm while out walking with Ulyses Petit de Murat and Sixto Pondal Ríos in the Bajo at Belgrano, an unsavory district of stud farms and stables and a notorious haunt of petty criminals. The poor-sighted Borges was carrying a stick, which he used to feel his way in the dark along a metal fence, and the tapping noise caught the attention of a group of ruffians, who started hurling insults at the three friends. As the men drew near, Ulyses and Pondal Ríos decided to make a run for it, but Borges stood his ground and, to their horror, started whipping up the thugs into a fury by impugning their manhood: "What's that you're saying, Rosita?" he called out. "I can't hear you, Pelagia!"[12] In the end Ulysses and Pondal had to drag him bodily toward a nearby railway station and bundle him over a turnstile, from where they ran for their lives to the comparative safety of the town center at Belgrano.

Violence, however, drew Borges like a magnet. It was as if he could feel truly alive only by putting himself in the way of fighting and brawling and killing. A few months later, he would send a postcard to Ulysses describing an incident that had taken place in the calle Montenegro, off avenida Jorge Newbery, near the Chacarita Cemetery: "Some nights ago—taking advantage of our absence—a shoot-out between the police and some hoodlums flowered in that deep little street, and a mugger was shot; he was called, with an appropriate sense of local color, Antonio Rosendo."[13] Life, indeed, had a habit of taking advantage of Georgie's absence, for no matter how hard he tried to sense the thrill of being alive—the feel of the dagger, the power of the tiger—life was always somewhere else, always out of reach.

Still, he derived some solace from visiting the Lange family at the calle Tronador and was grateful in particular for the company of Norah's older sister, Haydée, although there was not, in truth, much comfort to be had there, because Haydée showed "no interest in me with marvelous affability and compassion," as he was to remark to a friend.[14] All the while he kept writing to Norah and had "frequent letters" back, but as her return from Norway drew closer, so did his anxieties increase.[15] Toward the end of 1928, he wrote his first essay on a topic that would come to fascinate him—the famous paradox of Achilles and the tortoise, in which the swift Achilles can never catch up with the slow-moving tortoise.[16] Zeno's paradox was a mirror of his fears—perhaps he, too, had been condemned to a fruitless pursuit of his own desires. And these fears can be seen again in the epigraph he chose for El idioma de los argentinos (The Language of the Argentines), a new book of essays he would publish that year. This was his own brief paraphrase of an idea he had come across in F. H. Bradley's Appearance and Reality: "For love unsatisfied the world is a mystery, a mystery which satisfied love appears to understand."[17] The return of Norah Lange would determine whether Borges's love would finally be satisfied or whether the entire universe would shrivel into an impenetrable mystery.

Borges had his answer, I reckon, in February 1929, for when Norah Lange arrived back in Buenos Aires, she declined to resume her relationship with him.* His reaction to Norah's rejection can be found in an essay he published

---

*In the story "The Aleph," the woman with whom the Borges character has been hopelessly in love dies in February 1929, and in "The Zahir" the unforgettable coin that the Borges character is given just after the death of the woman he loves is dated 1929.

in June devoted to the subject of hell. This was an inquiry into the nature of eternal torment—did it involve suffering without end or the mere extinction of the soul with no prospect of union with God? These theological speculations arose from personal experience, for in a postcript he described a dream in which he found himself in a room he failed to recognize:

> I asked myself anxiously: *where am I?* and I realized I didn't know. I thought: *who am I?* and I couldn't say. I was filled with fear. I thought: this disconsolate wakefulness already is hell, this pointless wakefulness will be my eternity. Then I woke up properly: I was shaking.[18]

Gone was the vision of the realized self, gone the ties that bound him to a particular world: the promise of the Aleph had vanished, and hell was a room in the middle of nowhere in which you had lost all sense of who you were.

The most telling sign of Borges's rejection by Norah Lange was the loss of his poetic voice. In February 1929 he published a poem in *Criterio* called "Paseo de Julio," after the notorious red-light district by the docks, and its theme is that prostitution is a "Heaven for those who live in hell."[19] This was the last poem he would publish for fourteen years. In August he brought out his third book of poetry called, *San Martín Copybook,* the title, ironically, he once had in mind for his "history of Argentina in verse," but such grand projects were beyond his powers now, as he acknowledged in an epigraph to the new book, a quotation from a letter by Edward Fitzgerald: "There are few men who have the leisure to read, and are possessed of any music in their souls, who are not capable of versifying on some ten or twelve occasions during their natural lives." Sadly, the music in Borges's soul had grown ever fainter since he broke with Concepción Guerrero: *Fervor de Buenos Aires* had contained forty-nine poems, *Moon Across the Way* twenty-seven, but when *San Martín Copybook* came out on August 7, 1929, it comprised twelve poems, and, of these, six were concerned with death.

San Martín Copybook was a valediction to Borges's life as a poet. He resigned himself to a career as an essayist and cultural commentator—in June 1929 he had told the magazine *Literatura Argentina* that he preferred prose to poetry and mentioned having started work on a biography of Evaristo Carriego.[20] His choice of Carriego as a subject suggests that, although he might have given up his ambition to be the bard of Buenos Aires, he was still attached to the idea of promoting the democratic *criollismo* he had derived from Carriego's songs of the barrio, very likely as a means of contesting the Catholic nationalists and the reactionaries of *La Nueva República*.

He found an influential ally for his residual cultural nationalism in a new friend, the writer Alfonso Reyes, one of the most famous Latin American men of letters, who had arrived in Buenos Aires the year before as Mexican ambassador to Argentina. Reyes took an active part in Argentine literary life and used to invite Borges and several other young writers to dinner every Sunday at the ambassador's residence. In 1929 he became the editor of a book series called "Cuadernos del Plata," which was associated with Évar Méndez's Editorial Proa, a reason perhaps that Borges was not a member of the editorial board, though his third book of poems would be published later that year in Reyes's series.

Reyes also planned to start a new literary magazine of a broadly nationalist orientation, called *Libra*, together with Borges, Marechal, and Bernárdez, but Marechal and Bernárdez were moving sharply to the right, and their ideological differences with Borges were becoming impossible to overlook. On May 27, 1929, Reyes wrote in his diary that Borges had resigned from the editorial board of *Libra* on account of "trivial clashes" with Marechal, and also with Bernárdez, who disapproved of Borges's friendship with writers whom he regarded as "impure" and unacceptable.[21] *Libra* appeared in August 1929, with only Marechal and Bernárdez as editors, but it did not survive its inaugural issue. By the beginning of 1930, Alfonso Reyes had tired of all the squabbling. On January 8 he confided to his diary, "No one cares about literature, only about the literary politics between the groups or *patotas;* individuals and groups betray each other constantly. They prefer fantasies based on gossip to reality. It's all very strange."[22] Not long afterward, he left for Rio de Janeiro to take up a new post as ambassador to Brazil.

If Borges fell out with Marechal and Bernárdez, it was because they turned against Irigoyen and defected to the *nacionalistas.* There would be a reconciliation with Bernárdez some years later, but not with Marechal, for whom Borges would continue to feel a great personal bitterness, a bitterness that was mutual, as is clear from Marechal's *Adán Buenosayres,* which would become one of the landmark novels of Argentine literature after it was published in 1949. Here Marechal looked back with scorn at his years as Borges's closest lieutenant in the cause of literary *criollismo.* He satirized the parties at the house of the Lange sisters on calle Tronador and ridiculed Borges in the character of the ungainly, pedantic Luis Pereda, a young writer who is mocked for cultivating a self-regarding mystique of the *arrabal.*

Not all was gloom for Borges in 1929, however. Things began to look up toward the middle of a year that had started so disastrously with the loss of Norah Lange. In May he received second prize for his book of essays, *El idioma de los argentinos,* in the competition for the 1928 Municipal Literary Prize, and then, a few months later, I reckon, he even managed to find himself a new girlfriend. This came about as a result of his visits to the city of La Plata to see Pedro Henríquez Ureña, a native of Santo Domingo and one of the best-known Latin American intellectuals, whom he had met through Alfonso Reyes and who was at the time a professor at the university there. Borges would often be accompanied to La Plata by a friend called Néstor Ibarra, a young Franco-Argentine who was writing a dissertation on the *ultraísta* movement at the University of Buenos Aires. Ibarra fell in love with one of the daughters of the landlady who ran the boardinghouse where they used to stay. The girl had to be chaperoned by her sister when she went out with Ibarra, so Borges was enlisted as the sister's escort, and eventually he became attracted to the twenty-year-old Elsa Astete, who appears to have been fairly receptive to his usual tentative wooing.[23]

In July, Borges moved with his mother and father and his English grandmother, Fanny Haslam, to a fifth-floor apartment at calle Pueyrredón 2190, where he would live for the next ten years. (His sister, Norah, who had married Guillermo de Torre in September 1928, had gone to an apartment in calle Paraguay.) The Borges family's new home was in the district popularly known as "La Tierra del Fuego," which was ideal territory for Borges's research on the biography of Evaristo Carriego. He met the local chief of police, who had been personally acquainted with the *cuchilleros* Juan Muraña and Suárez "El Chileno," but his richest source was a character called Don Nicolás Paredes, the former godfather of the Palermo underworld, who had been hero-worshipped by the young Carriego. Borges's first impressions of Paredes were disappointing: he was of medium height, strongly built and "excessively polite," but after several meetings Borges became fascinated by Paredes and started to call on him frequently.[24]

Paredes had started his criminal career as a simple knife for hire and then risen to be a *guapo*—a chieftain with bodyguards of his own—until finally he became the caudillo of the neighborhood, recruiting toughs to deliver the vote for the Conservative Party at elections and dispensing favors to clients. His wife's family was said to have once owned an *estancia,* which was why Paredes would refer to himself as *"el estanciero,"* even though he had fallen on hard times and was living in a small house, in considerable poverty, doing what he could to make ends meet as a cardsharp and nightclub bouncer.[25]

Paredes was puzzled by Borges's interest in Evaristo Carriego. It turned out that the old hoodlum had not been too impressed with the poetic talent of the anarchist bard of the barrio: he showed Borges a volume of poems Carriego had dedicated to him and said "in a tone of resignation," "As you can see for yourself, the lad wasn't up to much."[26] The reason for these misgivings,

Borges surmised, was that Paredes was used to the traditional octosyllabic verse of the Spanish folk tradition, which made Carriego's alexandrines and hendecasyllables sound clumsy to his uncultivated ear.

Still, Paredes seems to have been flattered by this timid young gentleman's interest in the life of old Palermo, and he did what he could to oblige. He once demonstrated his legendary prowess as a knife fighter by challenging one of Borges's more athletic friends to a duel, handing the youth a fearsome dagger but choosing for himself a wooden rod the size of a drumstick; try as he might, Borges's friend could get nowhere near the veteran *cuchillero,* who kept taunting his opponent while dodging his thrusts with effortless parries and feints.[27]

Through Paredes, Borges got to know one of the most celebrated ballad singers of the day, Luis García, a lisping midget of a man with impeccable manners who prided himself on being a native of "the barrio of the knife," as he called Palermo.[28] García and Paredes would spend hours playing old-style tangos and *milongas* on their guitars, and Borges was delighted to discover that they shared his contempt for the new style of tango. One night Borges was sitting with Paredes in a café when the band started playing a very popular new tango (now a classic) called "Caminito," by Juan de Dios Filiberto, the man whom Borges and his avant-garde friends used to bait at the Café Tortoni. Paredes scoffed at Filiberto's latest effort. "That stuff's too technical for me," he sneered, for, like many criollos of his generation, he believed that the Italian immigrants had spoiled the brave old tango with endless moaning about their faithless molls.[29] Indeed, a criollo of the old school did not have much time for women: "A man who thinks of a woman for more than five minutes is not a real man," observed Paredes, "he's a *marica.*"[30] (The memory of this callous remark would many years later give Borges the idea for his brutal tale "The Intruder," "La intrusa," in which two brothers fall for the same woman and end up killing her rather than let love come between them.)

Don Nicolás, in Borges's eyes, came to represent "the archetype of the criollo of the suburbs," but the truth was that the old fox was acting up terribly, trying to be "all the *guapos* he'd ever known rolled into one," so as not to disappoint his young admirer.[31] Still, he would occasionally try to bring the starry-eyed Borges down to earth with an anecdote that portrayed the *cuchilleros* in a less-than-flattering light. The great Juan Muraña, it seems, despite "owing many deaths," had not himself fallen victim to the knife: it was the drink that got him in the end—he rolled off his cart one night and cracked his head open on the cobblestones of the avenida Las Heras.[32]

Early in 1930, while Borges was spending the summer months as usual with his family at the Hotel Las Delicias in Adrogué, he heard that Paredes had died, and as a tribute to his departed friend, he decided "to record something of his voice, his anecdotes, and his particular way of telling them."[33] This led to a story about *cuchilleros*, "Men of the Outskirts" ("Hombres de las orillas"), that he worked on "in secret over a period of several months," slaving over every page, "sounding out each sentence and striving to phrase it in his exact tones."[34] Set in the saloon of a brothel, the story concerns a knife fighter, Rosendo Juárez, the pride of Palermo, who is challenged to a duel one night by a stranger from another barrio.[35] To the amazement of his followers, Rosendo ignores the challenge, and when his mistress, La Lujanera, hands him a dagger, he simply throws it out of the window and walks out. Rosendo's apparent cowardice so disgusts La Lujanera that she offers herself to the victorious challenger, and they leave the saloon together. The story is related to Borges by an unnamed *cuchillero* who claims to have been so ashamed at Rosendo's failure to respond to the challenge that he stole out of the saloon, only to catch sight of his former hero slipping out of the barrio on his own. Awhile later La Lujanera reappears in the saloon in a state of great distress and reports that a man has mortally wounded her new lover in a duel. The story ends with the narrator hinting that it was he who carried out the killing in order to redeem the pride of Palermo.

Apart from commemorating Nicolás Paredes, the tale of Rosendo Juárez's mysterious passivity suggests that Borges himself was at a loss to explain why Norah Lange had left him for his rival, Girondo. And in the narrator's shame at his hero's cowardice, one may see Borges's own disappointment in himself. The story may also reflect a further disappointment—his romance with Elsa Astete came to an abrupt end sometime during the various months it took him to compose the tale. It seems that Borges telephoned the girl's house and was informed by her mother that Elsa had become engaged to another man. Although Elsa would claim years later that Borges had given her a ring, it is difficult to determine how serious this romance actually was.[36] Certainly it pales into insignificance when compared to his attachment to Norah Lange and would scarcely be worth remarking on, save for the fact that four decades later the widowed Elsa Astete, by then middle-aged, would become Borges's first wife.

If the latter part of 1929 had held some promise of an improvement in Borges's fortunes, the following year saw that promise evaporate altogether. The death of Paredes and Borges's rejection by Elsa Astete occurred against a background of increasing difficulties for his political hero, President Irigoyen, in the course of 1930. Irigoyen's term of office had started well enough—high spending and a bonanza of jobs in the public services assured his popularity, but the Wall Street crash of October 1929 induced an economic depression that made it impossible to maintain such high levels of public expenditure. As inflation and unemployment soared, Irigoyen lost the support of the urban middle class and came under attack for failing to prevent corruption in government circles and for a general incompetence, which some attributed to senility. There was growing disorder in the streets—large demonstrations of students and workers, and fighting between *irigoyenistas* and various opposition groups. Irigoyen's fiercest critics were the right-wing *nacionalistas,* and following the Wall Street crash, for instance, the editors of *La Nueva República* suspended publication of the magazine and formed the Liga Republicana, a fascist-style paramilitary force of some three thousand youths who took to marching in the streets and calling on the army to rid the country of Irigoyen.

On September 6, 1930, Irigoyen was overthrown in the first Argentine coup d'état of the twentieth century. The insurgents, led by General José F. Uriburu, met with little opposition as they marched through Buenos Aires. The coup, in fact, was greeted with popular rejoicing and generally welcomed by the press as a liberation from the misrule that the Radical government had brought upon the country. But Borges remained unwavering in his loyalty to Irigoyen. In October he wrote to Alfonso Reyes in Rio de Janeiro:

> The revolution (or military rebellion with the backing of the public) is a victory of good sense over ineptitude, frequent dishonesty and muddle, but the bad things which have been overcome must be put into the context of a mythology, a loving spirit, a joy—as part of the whole bizarre myth of the Doctor [Irigoyen], conspiring silently on behalf of the people in the Casa Rosada itself. Now Buenos Aires has had to repudiate its homegrown mythology, and make do with a few scraps of enthusiasm, mixed with a few so-called acts of heroism in which no one believes, and the standard opinion that at least these soldiers aren't thieves. We have sacrificed Myth for the sake of realism, what do you think of that? No doubt Shaw would have approved. I don't know whether I'm expressing myself with sufficient clarity; before (as I say) things might have been fairly crazy, but there were rowdy opposition newspapers with their cries of *"Long live . . ."* and *"Death to . . .",* there was an easygoing idolatry that flourished on the walls of the city and in *milongas* and the lyrics of the tango; but now we have independence under martial law, a sycophantic press, the perpetual wrangling of the left-wingers, and the fiction that the former dotty administration was "cruel and tyrannical."
>
> Few spectacles of any note. A non-lethal exchange of rifle-fire on the Plaza Once, a machine gun half a block away on the calle Junín, two armories sacked by an insecure bunch of thugs in the calle Rivadavia: these are the visions I owe the revolution, and I am grateful for them.[37]

This letter reveals the extent of Borges's emotional investment in the cult of Irigoyen. Though he recognized the faults of the government, its overthrow spelled defeat for the heart and the imagination and, most tellingly of all, for "Myth."

The fall of Irigoyen proved to be the final nail in the coffin of Borges's *criollismo.* There was no getting away from the fact that his hero had been deserted by the people of Buenos Aires—Irigoyen's house had even been ransacked by a mob—and this collective betrayal made it impossible for Borges to feel his old enthusiasm for a Joycean mythologizing of his native city. The "homegrown mythology" of the *arrabales,* the "cult of courage" he had derived from Carriego, all of that, he now saw, belonged to "a mythical Palermo which existed in Carriego's memory and later in my memory of Carriego's memory, and which probably never did exist, and which I took, for the most part, from my many conversations with Don Nicolás Paredes, who was a great liar besides."[38]

In his disillusionment he wrote an essay that effectively destroyed the basis of his *criollismo.* In "Our Impossibilities" ("Nuestras imposibilidades") he abandoned any notion of a continuity between the past and the present, or between the pampas and the city.[39] The gaucho had been turned into a servile object of the crassest folklore, and the true criollo could be found only in the remotest areas, such as the northern provinces of Uruguay, where foreign immigration had not yet "stylized and falsified him." This latter assertion, moreover, contradicted his vision of the criollos and the immigrants' becoming "confederates" in the creation of a "new man" in Argentina. In Borges's jaundiced view, his compatriots suffered from two "distressing characteristics"— "imaginative poverty" and "rancor." The modern Argentine, Borges wrote, overvalued the place of Argentina in the world and showed little interest in other countries; he reveled in the failure of others and was given to expressing a general hatred of his fellow man through gratuitous insults or acts of aggression toward complete strangers. Such attitudes, according to Borges, "define our particular claim on death."

1. Colonel Francisco Borges Lafinur (1832–1874), paternal grandfather.

2. Fanny Haslam (1842–1935), paternal grandmother.

3. Isidoro Acevedo Laprida (1835–1905), maternal grandfather.

4. Leonor Suárez Haedo de Acevedo (1837–1918), maternal grandmother, with her daughter, Leonor (Borges's mother).

5. Jorge Guillermo Borges, Borges's father (fourth from the left), in 1895 with fellow graduates in law. Macedonio Fernández is second from the right.

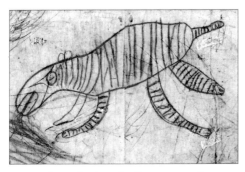

6. Drawing of a tiger by Borges, age four.

7. Borges and his sister, Norah, at the Palermo zoo in 1908.

8. The Borges family shortly after their arrival in Geneva in 1914.

9. Borges's father and mother in Geneva in 1923.

10. Borges in 1924.

11. Norah Lange in the 1920s.

12. Guests at the party in Palermo Park in honor of Ricardo Güiraldes, November 26, 1926. (*Middle row, standing*): Norah Lange (fifth from the left); Borges (sixth from the left). Güiraldes is seated fifth from the left. (*Martín Fierro*, December 12, 1926)

13. The editorial board of the journal *Sur* at its launch in 1930. (*Back row, standing*): Borges (second from the left), Victoria Ocampo (second from the right), Ramón Gómez de la Serna (first on the right); (*middle row, seated*): Pedro Henríquez Ureña (first on the left), Norah Borges (second from the left), Guillermo de Torre (first on the right, with a cigar); (*front row, seated on the floor*): Oliverio Girondo (on the left with a beard and a cigar).

14. Norah Lange dressed as a mermaid at a party to celebrate the publication of her novel *45 Days and 30 Sailors*, with guests dressed as sailors, November 1933. Oliverio Girondo (with a beard and tie) is standing in the center. Pablo Neruda is standing in the first row, second from the left. Évar Méndez is standing third from the right, with his arm across his chest.

15. Haydée and Norah Lange.

16. Haydée Lange and Borges on April 1, 1939, three months after his near-fatal accident on December 24, 1938.

17. Borges with Adolfo Bioy Casares at Mar del Plata, 1942.

18. Borges and Estela Canto in 1945.

19. Borges and his mother in London, 1963.

20. OPPOSITE: Borges and María Kodama in the late 1970s in Villa Palagonia, Bagheria, Sicily.

21. LEFT: Borges and María Kodama during a visit to the United States in the late 1970s.

22. BELOW: Borges and María Kodama in the 1980s in the Napa Valley, California.

23, 24. The front and back of Borges's gravestone in Geneva.

CHAPTER 12

Experiments in Fiction

(1930–1932)

BORGES'S BIOGRAPHY of Evaristo Carriego came out two weeks after General Uriburu's coup d'état, and it was received with little interest, not to say indifference. The problem, as Borges saw it, was that he had started out to do a straight biography but had become more interested in old-time Buenos Aires, with the result that "the book hardly lived up to its title, *Evaristo Carriego,* and so it fell flat."[1] But the book, in truth, was not so much a failure as an irrelevance, for by the time it appeared, Borges himself no longer believed in the *criollismo* that had inspired it. In any case, his attention had been engaged for some time in a different project—he was hoping to make up for the loss of his poetic voice by trying his hand at writing fiction.

Borges's early experiments in fiction are shrouded in mystery. He would intimate that "it was only after a long and roundabout series of timid experiments in narration" that he was to write "real stories," but he was vague about the exact chronology of this new phase in his writing: although he would state that "the real beginning" of his career as a story writer was "the series of sketches entitled *Historia universal de la infamia* [*A Universal History of Infamy*]," which he contributed to the literary supplement of the newspaper *Crítica* "in 1933 and 1934," he hinted at an earlier starting point with "Men Fought" ("Hombres pelearon"), the brief sketch of a knife duel, originally entitled "Legend of a Crime" ("Leyenda policial"), which he had first published in *Martín Fierro* in 1927: it had taken him six years, he claimed, to go from that early sketch to the story "Men of the Outskirts" ("Hombres de las orillas"), which he also published in *Crítica* in 1933.[2] In fact, "Men of the Outskirts" was written in 1930, not long after the death of Nicolás Paredes, so what did Borges write between 1930 and 1933? And why did he want generally to gloss over in his memoirs the six years between 1927 and 1933? It was no coincidence that this was precisely the period in which he was struggling to come to terms with the loss of Norah Lange. This personal disaster, as we have seen, caused a profound crisis in his writing, a crisis that undermined his ultraconfessional poetics and even made him abandon poetry altogether. When eventually—in

1930 or thereabouts—he turned to storytelling as a possible alternative to poetry, he was obliged to revise his literary ideas and work out all over again what it was he was writing for.

The earliest of Borges's reflections on fiction (as opposed to poetry) dates back to 1926, to a longish review entitled "Tales of Turkestan" ("Cuentos del Turquestán"), now entirely forgotten, of a German translation of a Russian version of these tales.[3] What struck him about these stories was the way in which "the marvelous and the everyday are entwined," with no distinction being drawn between fantasy and reality: "There are angels as there are trees: they are just another element in the reality of the world."* It occurred to him that magic in these tales was "an example of causality like so many others," for "primitive" people did not distinguish between subjectivity and objectivity; they lived in a world that was at times sweet, because desire and fulfillment seemed to be one, and at times frightening, because the mere expectation of danger might serve to attract it. And yet even though modern man had lost faith in magic and had placed his trust in so-called natural laws, fiction was capable of putting us in touch with something enduringly "primitive" about ourselves, because "we too live like that in our emotions" (*"así vivimos también nosotros en la emoción"*).

It followed that the modern reader was still susceptible to the marvels and wonders of traditional tales. Borges himself was charmed by the dragons, genii, demons, giants, and princesses that populated these tales of Turkestan. But above all he was taken with a "special character"—a magical, timeless bird with a human face and silver plumage called the Simurgh, "who saves the heroes in moments of greatest peril." This was a discovery of some moment, given that five years or so later, as we shall presently observe, the Simurgh would appear as a mystical symbol associated with Borges's very particular notions about his own salvation as a writer.

Borges had first encountered the magic of these Oriental tales when his love for Norah Lange was at its height. Indeed, "Tales of Turkestan" was published in August 1926, only a couple of months after he had written his ultraexpressionist "Profession of Literary Faith." But in 1930–31, as he was negotiating his uncertain passage from poetry to fiction, when his very survival as a writer was at stake, he would draw upon a number of seminal observations he had made in that early text to elaborate a series of reflections on the art of fiction written between 1930 and 1932.

*This review shows that in 1926 Borges had discovered the basic principle of what came to be known, some four decades later, as Latin American "magic realism," though he would never use the term as such, and his blending of fantasy and reality would be quite different from that of "magic realists" such as Alejo Carpentier, Gabriel García Márquez, or Isabel Allende.

In June 1931 he published "The Postulation of Reality" ("La postulación de la realidad"), in which he restated his belief that all art is essentially expressive.[4] However, he distinguished between the "romantic" writer, who "tries incessantly to express himself," and the "classical" writer, who "is not truly expressive: he limits himself to registering a reality, not to representing it." The facts we are given in a "classical" story may be laden with the author's experiences, but these can only be inferred from the story, they are not contained within it, for the "classical" author "presents us with an interplay of symbols, organized rigorously without a doubt, but whose eventual animation is left to us." A narrative is conceived, therefore, not as a mode of communication but as a screen between the author and the reader. Thus, if in "A Profession of Literary Faith" Borges had described the literary transaction as a "confidence" based on "the trust of the listener and the veracity of the speaker," now, after the loss of Norah Lange, he was proposing an aesthetics of radical mistrust, in which the author disappeared behind the screen of the text, leaving readers to determine their own interpretations and, in a sense, to create meaning for themselves.

Later that year he wrote "The Art of Narrative and Magic" ("El arte narrativo y la magia"), in which he questioned the premises of literary realism.[5] His basic contention was that fiction did not depend on the illusion of reality; what mattered ultimately was an author's ability to generate "poetic faith" in his reader. Naturalistic description, he argued, was not especially effective in making a reader suspend disbelief. A writer could employ techniques of indirection and suggestion to render fabulous creatures like centaurs and sirens aesthetically convincing. The fundamental problem of the novel, Borges asserted, was causality: the realist novel, "the slow-moving novel of character," presented "a concatenation of motives purporting to be no different from that which exists in the real world," but in novels of adventure, in short stories, "in the infinite, spectacular novel which is Hollywood," another order reigned—"the primitive clarity of magic." Indeed, magic, he contended, offered the best analogy for the way in which narrative actually worked. Magical causality operated by virtue of a general law of sympathy that postulated an inevitable link between distant objects, a necessary connection not just between a corpse and a bullet but between a corpse and a mutilated wax effigy, or a broken mirror, or spilled salt, or thirteen people at a dinner table. Narrative fashioned a comparable "teleology of words and episodes," "a precise interplay of observations, echoes and affinities," from the "Asiatic disorder of the real world." Fiction did not hold up a mirror to reality; rather it constituted "an autonomous sphere ("*un orbe autónomo*") of corroborations, omens and monuments" that was best illustrated by the "predestined *Ulysses* of Joyce":

I have distinguished between two causal processes: the natural, which is the unceasing result of uncontrollable and infinite operations; the magical, lucid and limited, in which details are prophetic. In the novel, I think the only possible honesty lies in the second. The first may be left to psychological simulation.

Still, if a writer was not necessarily constrained by verisimilitude in shaping the *orbe autónomo* of his narrative, would his fiction not become purely arbitrary or capricious? For an answer to this question, one must return to "Tales of Turkestan," to Borges's belief that the life of the emotions was more akin to the operations of magic than it was to reason. In the end it was the writer's emotions that determined the magical order of fiction. And so the art of narrative, as evinced in "The Postulation of Reality" and "The Art of Narrative and Magic," was analogous to a Chinese shadow play, for the screen of the Borgesian text would be illuminated by the author's imagination, and the cryptic figures that moved across its surface would follow the logic not of psychological realism but of their creator's hidden emotions.

By 1932 the basic tenet of the "literary faith" Borges had professed in 1926—that all poetry was "a confidence" based on trust—had quite dissolved. And yet if he was no longer concerned with communicating directly with the reader, for whom was he writing? Indeed, what was the point of writing at all? An indication of the new direction of his thinking can be found in his interest at this time in secret writing and secret knowledge. In "A Vindication of the Kabbalah" ("Una vindicación de la cábala"), he described the Kabbalistic belief that God had hidden a wealth of meanings in the Scriptures.[6] In a companion piece called "A Vindication of the Gnostics" ("Una vindicación de los gnósticos"), he described the unorthodox ideas of Basilides and some of his followers.[7] He was intrigued by their belief in the existence of a secret knowledge, a gnosis, that would bring release from this evil world and lead to a final union with God. What Borges found in both the Kabbalah and the Gnostics were analogues for a new cryptographical theory of writing that he was elaborating at this time, an idea of writing as the purification of experience, a process capable of yielding up a secret knowledge, a gnosis of the self, that would entail the author's salvation.

Borges had first articulated the idea of salvation by writing in his "Profession of Literary Faith" of 1926—his highest aim was to write a single page perhaps, but a page that would sum up his destiny and "justify" him at the Last Judgment. Inspired by his love of Norah Lange, that ambition had issued in the project of writing an epic novel about Buenos Aires in which his own destiny and that of his native city would be fully integrated in the one work. And yet, in 1931, after Norah was lost to him and his *criollismo* had collapsed, he still clung to his desire to find salvation in writing, but he discarded the notion of mythologizing Buenos Aires and decided instead to create a mythology of his own life—he would write an autobiographical novel through which he would strive to define the essence of what it meant to be Borges.

The only extant work of Borges's that approximates to this saving masterpiece is a novella called *The Congress* (*El Congreso*), which he was to publish in 1971. *The Congress,* in fact, was a project he had nurtured for several decades. He very rarely spoke about it, but in an interview of 1955, he referred to it as a "novel" and said that it "would sum up and would in addition be the resolution of everything I have written up until now."[8] In April 1971 he would express a hope that *The Congress* would be his "justification as a storyteller," in other words, that it might be the masterpiece that would save him as a writer, and he went on to explain that it was a story about "a mystical experience I never had," but "maybe before I die I'll be allowed to have it."[9]

The mystical experience he was referring to was a pantheist insight into the oneness of the universe thanks to the immanence of the divine in each creature. The first appearance of this theme in Borges's work occurred in 1936, in a very strange text called *The Approach to Al-Mu'tasim* (*"El acercamiento a Almotásim"*), which purported to be a review of a novel of that title allegedly published in Bombay "late in 1932."[10] Curiously, in 1971, the year *The Congress* was published, Borges would observe that the story had been "haunting" him "for the last thirty or forty years," which suggests that its roots went back to 1931 or thereabouts.[11] The fact that the basic story of *The Congress* occurred to Borges at around the time of the alleged publication of *The Approach to Al-Mu'tasim* persuades me that this so-called apocryphal novel in fact represents a very early attempt by Borges himself to write an autobiographical masterpiece, an enterprise that, after numerous revisions and reformulations, finally took shape as *The Congress* some forty years later.

In its quest structure and mystical climax *The Approach to Al-Mu'tasim* foreshadows *The Congress*. The Indian novel, we are informed, was modeled—in a manner reminiscent of the way James Joyce patterned *Ulysses* on the *Odyssey*—on a narrative poem called *The Conference of the Birds* by the Persian mystic Farid ud-din Attar.[12] This Sufi poem relates how the Simurgh, the king of all the birds, dropped one of his splendid feathers in China, whereupon the birds resolve to find it. They traverse seven valleys, each symbolizing a stage in a process of purification, until finally thirty birds arrive at a sacred mountain, only to discover that "they are the Simurgh and that the Simurgh is each one and all of them." The Simurgh, therefore, provides the climactic enlightenment regarding the pantheist idea of the interrelatedness of all creatures.

In Borges's version of the quest for the Simurgh the protagonist is an unnamed law student of Bombay who, despite having lost the Islamic faith of his family, is caught up in a riot and ends up killing a Hindu. The "freethinking" student is so bewildered by the strife between Muslims and idolators that he sets out on a quest for truth. He comes upon a round tower where he finds a corpse robber urinating in the moonlight. Hearing this wretch curse a woman of Palanpur, he reasons that the hatred of a man so vile "must imply a form of praise," so he goes in search of this woman. The object of the quest is not the woman as such (the implication is that the student will be disappointed in this respect) but the source of light in a world characterized by a general "infamy," for the student is convinced that somewhere on earth there must be a man from whom that light proceeds, a man known as Al-Mu'tasim. The student's odyssey takes place in seven different regions of India corresponding to the seven valleys of the birds' mystical quest for the Simurgh. In the final scene, the student arrives at a door through which he sees a light and hears the voice of Al-Mu'tasim: "The student draws back the curtain and enters. At that point the novel ends."

The autobiographical subtext of the novel can be discerned without much difficulty. The conflict between Muslims and Hindus was analogous to the conflict between the Argentine *unitarios* and *federales* in the nineteenth century. But, like the freethinking Indian student, Borges was seeking to transcend this historic conflict. At first a woman—Norah Lange—seemed to represent a higher truth, a unifying Aleph, as did the woman of Palanpur for the Indian, but she proved to be a disappointment, and as a result Borges was plunged into confusion, aggravated by the strife resulting from the overthrow of Irigoyen. Like the Indian student, he continued to search for salvation from the general infamy of the world, and the kind of salvation Borges envisaged was represented in the nature of the novel's ending, modeled on the resolution of *The Conference of the Birds:*

> In the twentieth chapter, certain words attributed by a Persian bookseller to Al-Mu'tasim are perhaps the amplification of others which the hero has uttered; that, and other ambiguous analogies, may signify the identity of the man sought and the seeker himself; they may also signify that the latter influences the former. Another chapter suggests that Al-Mu'tasim is the Hindu whom the student believes he has killed.[13]

The final revelation, in other words, is a form of self-discovery—"the identity of the man sought and the seeker himself." But just as the birds in the Persian poem discover that the Simurgh is each and every one of them, so are there clues in Borges's novel that point to the underlying unity between all the characters involved in the action. In addition, the fact that the protagonist remains nameless may imply that he may be the same person as the author, a Bombay lawyer called Mir Bahadur Ali, and since the novel's resolution depends so critically on the reader's picking up the various analogies, so does the reading experience itself come to parallel the protagonist's quest for enlightenment. The whole process, therefore, would culminate in an implicit unity, not just between the seeker and the sought but also between the author, the various characters, and, ultimately, the reader. In short, the novel would represent an Aleph in which the realization of the self would involve its final communion with a universal spirit that connected it to others.

The ending of *The Approach to Al-Mu'tasim* illustrates Borges's conception of salvation by writing. Although the "magical" order of fiction is shaped by the author's creative will, the process of composition itself entails a kind of purification, for in and through the activity of writing, the author may come to discover what is essential about himself, an enlightenment that would result in a sense of being integrated in the objective order of the world. Thus, the idea of writing a work that would sum up the author's destiny and justify his entire existence, an idea first adumbrated by Borges in "A Profession of Literary Faith," came to be elaborated, and indeed mythologized, in *The Approach to Al-Mu'tasim* as a mystical theory of writing leading to a kind of all-embracing Aleph symbolized in the pantheist Simurgh.

Borges had kept his distance from the Lange family since Norah's return to Buenos Aires. As he would have known, Norah was by no means over Girondo. While in Norway, and after her return home, she had written poems about her unquenchable passion, a passion that, if she gave in to it, might impel her beyond the limits of middle-class propriety, but one that, if she continued to resist it, would condemn her to her present state of unruly dissatisfaction. As before, Norah would pour her doubts and fears into her writing, and not long after her return, she started to write a novel based on her sea voyage to Norway.

The protagonist of Norah Lange's novel is an Argentine girl of Norwegian extraction called Ingrid, who is on a voyage aboard a cargo ship from Buenos Aires to visit her family in Oslo.[14] She is the only female on board, and, given her youth and innocence, she is by turns frightened, excited, repelled, and intrigued by the constant importuning of the sailors. The voyage thus becomes a metaphor for Ingrid's gradual discovery of her sexuality and her attractiveness to the opposite sex. One of the officers tries to embrace and kiss her on a number of occasions, but her most persistent admirer is the ship's captain, whose pursuit of Ingrid, fueled as it is by liberal drafts of alcohol, extends to his trying to force himself upon her one night. Ingrid does what she can to guard her honor, but she is flattered by so much male attention and is not above flirting with her admirers, even granting one or two of them the odd kiss as she becomes increasingly taken with the mystery of women's sexual power over men. In one scene the ship's steward shows her a photograph of his half-naked mistress, who he assumes is not always faithful to him during his long absences at sea, and yet he is not too concerned by her infidelities because he says that women who have had many men are best at making love—one must remember one's body, he tells Ingrid, for it is the best thing one posseses. Still, she remains wary of men's motives. In another scene she is told by the captain that he has just received a telegram informing him of his youngest son's death, but a suspicious Ingrid discovers that this is a well-tried ploy of the captain's to coax women into his bed.

In contrast to these predatory men, there is a passenger called Stevenson, a confirmed bachelor and a bookish, fastidious man who is very knowledge-able about Argentine literature and is obsessed with his ancestry. At Rotter-dam they come across another Norwegian vessel, the *Paris,* and Stevenson identifies a young officer on its crew as a cousin of Ingrid's. When he learns of the captain's harassment, Peter, her newfound cousin, advises Ingrid to trans-fer to the *Paris* with him. Ingrid, however, vacillates over this offer, and, curi-ously, she defends her lustful captain, claiming to understand his loneliness, his need for tenderness and solace in those long nights on the high seas. Still, after thinking it over, she decides to go with cousin Peter, who will deliver her safely to her family in Norway. One must not prolong a situation, she reckons, from which happiness has not naturally arisen, and only by leaving the ship of her own accord will she be able to enjoy happy memories of her days at sea. Even so, parting from her amorous captain is something of a wrench—he waves gloomily from the prow; she turns away with a tear in her eye.

Everything Norah Lange wrote, according to Borges, was a thinly veiled reflection of her own circumstances, and the ship's captain must have repre-sented the enduring temptation posed by Oliverio Girondo, while the concern to guard her honor is embodied both in the bookish Stevenson, a character no doubt partly modeled on Borges (who was a great admirer of Robert Louis Stevenson), and in Peter, who is a cousin of Ingrid's as Borges was of Norah's. Norah's dilemma on her return from Norway was thus the same as the one she faced when writing *Voz de la vida,* for just as Mila had to decide between her illicit passion for Sergio and marriage to Ivan, so, too, must Ingrid choose be-tween venturing into the uncharted waters of sexuality and remaining loyal to the honor of her family. If anything, there is a greater concern for her honor in this second novel, but even so, there is antipathy in her portrayal of the two characters modeled on Borges—Stevenson is evidently irritating to her, while cousin Peter is something of a prig.

Norah was chafing at the restraints imposed on a well-brought-up girl by the social conventions of the time. Clearly Girondo's allure remained as potent as ever, and even though she could still not bring herself to leave her mother and seek out her potential lover in Paris, Norah's capacity to contain her passion for him may have owed less to family honor than to his continuing absence from Buenos Aires. Still, toward the middle of 1930, she decided to collect her love poems to Girondo in a book, which she delivered to Évar Méndez for publication by the Editorial Proa. *El Rumbo de la Rosa* (*The Course of the Rose*) came out in August and was launched with a dinner in Norah's honor.

Shortly after the publication of *El Rumbo de la Rosa*, probably around September 1930, Oliverio Girondo was back in Buenos Aires. Why did he return? As may be inferred from *Voz de la vida*, Girondo had declared his love for Norah three years earlier, but she had decided to resist him and go to Norway instead. This measure had failed, and after a further year or so of resistance in Buenos Aires, Norah had brought out a book of poems that amounted to a public declaration of love for Girondo. Each of the lovers, therefore, had tried, in turn, to contain the mutual passion that was born at that fateful party in Palermo in November 1926, but by 1930 there could be no holding back.

If Borges saw little of Norah during this period, it goes without saying that he would have avoided any contact with Girondo. He found himself drawn nevertheless into the company of his rival when he accepted an invitation to become a member of the editorial board of a new literary journal called *Sur* that Victoria Ocampo, a woman of considerable intellectual and literary attainments and a member of one of the oldest and wealthiest dynasties in Argentina, was planning to bring out.

Sur would in due course become one of the most important literary magazines in Latin America, and Borges would become closely associated with it in the 1940s, but at this stage he showed scant interest in Victoria Ocampo's plans. He found her "easily dictatorial and excessively bossy" and resented the fact that she did not consult him about the contents of the first issue; *Sur*, in his view, lacked a coherent aim: it was not sufficient to have "illustrious contributors"; a literary magazine needed to be more "organic."[15] In any case, the first issue was "a veritable geography manual," illustrated as it was with pictures of the Iguazú Falls, Tierra del Fuego, the Andes, and the pampas: "Victoria had done this in order to show off Argentina to her friends in Europe," Borges would observe, "but it looked rather odd in Buenos Aires."

Beyond his irritation with Victoria's editorial judgment, there was another reason Borges may have been unsympathetic toward *Sur*, and this was the presence on the editorial board of Oliverio Girondo. And not only Girondo but

Guillermo de Torre and even Ramón Gómez de la Serna, who happened to be visiting Buenos Aires at this time. All three had, of course, been Borges's antagonists in the heyday of the avant-garde, and perhaps this may explain why he chose to make two such odd contributions to the first issue of *Sur*—one was an essay on gauchesque poetry, the other an eccentric little study of the hand-painted mottoes found on horse-drawn carts in Buenos Aires, hardly the sort of topics one would have expected in a journal of international scope such as *Sur* aspired to be, but there was, I suspect, a certain mischievous intent on Borges's part, for the two pieces harked back to his *criollismo,* which had been a bone of contention between himself and the likes of Girondo, Torre, and Ramón in the 1920s.

The launch of *Sur* in January 1931 was celebrated with a party for the editorial board at Victoria Ocampo's new modernist villa next to the Spanish embassy in the smart Recoleta district. Borges appears not to have relished the occasion. In a group photograph taken at the party, we find Oliverio Girondo at the center of the front row, relaxing with a big cigar, but Borges is standing on the left-hand corner at the back, and he is plainly ill at ease, looking askance at the camera, with eyes narrowed against the smoke of a scruffy cigarette stuck in his mouth.

At the time this photograph was taken, Borges would have known that Girondo had been conducting an affair with Norah Lange for several months. Virtually nothing has come to light about this phase in their relationship, except the fact that marriage and children would become a matter of conflict between them. According to an intimate friend of the couple's, Girondo would not contemplate marriage because he regarded himself as too set in his bachelor ways, and he did not in any case want to have children.[16] Norah, on the other hand, was passionate about becoming a mother, but, given the values of Argentine society, she could not find fulfillment outside of wedlock. Norah may have been frustrated also by a disagreement with Girondo over her novel about her voyage to Oslo. She appears to have shown Girondo the manuscript but he advised her not to publish it because, as Norah recalled, he thought it "too insubstantial."[17] It may be that Girondo's judgment was prudential as much as aesthetic—the subject of a young girl's awakening to her sexual attractiveness was still an extremely delicate topic for a woman to treat in public in Argentina, and Girondo may have wished to protect young Norah from her own excessive frankness. (Interestingly, in Norah's earlier novel, *Voz de la vida,* the heroine, Mila, rebukes her lover, Sergio, for being too concerned with social conventions.) The conflict over their possible future together proved insuperable, because sometime in the early months of 1931, Girondo decided to return to Paris. His departure would have reawakened memories in Norah of their first parting only four weeks after their original encounter in Palermo Park, and it must have caused her atrocious pain to accept that the suffering she had since undergone had all come to nothing in the end.

It was perhaps in desolation that she once more turned for support to her cousin Georgie. There is evidence to suggest that by June of 1931 some kind of rapprochement had taken place between Norah and Borges. The latter's essay "The Postulation of Reality" was published in a literary magazine called *Azul* in June 1931. The editor of this magazine was Pablo Rojas Paz, who had been Borges's coeditor on *Proa* in 1924, and I believe it is significant that the same issue of *Azul* should have carried an essay by Norah Lange describing the Eddas, the Nordic sagas recorded by the Icelandic bard Snorri Sturluson. This juxtaposition of essays in a magazine edited by a mutual friend from the old *ultraísta* days of *Proa* strongly suggests that Borges and Norah were seeing each other again by the middle of 1931. No doubt their relations were purely amicable, but it goes without saying that Borges would have been greatly heartened by this rapprochement with the woman whom he had once regarded as his Apollinairean muse.

Certainly toward the middle of 1931 we find in Borges a new spirit of optimism, indeed a new combativeness, for not only was there the prospect of a reprise in his love for Norah Lange, but also the possibility had arisen that his hero, Irigoyen, might yet return to power. The world depression had taken its toll on the popularity of General Uriburu's regime—on April 5, 1931, Uriburu had decided to allow a free election for the post of governor of the province of Buenos Aires in order to test the political strength of his government, but this had resulted in a massive victory for the candidate of the Radical Party. The relative weakness of the ruling junta led to growing unrest in the months that followed: opposition parties mobilized in protest against military rule, while the *nacionalistas* took to the streets in defense of General Uriburu. In addition to the Liga Republicana, there emerged a fascist group called the Legión Cívica, which recruited some ten thousand members within a few months and paraded them through the streets in gray shirts and jackboots, giving the fascist salute.

As a fervent *irigoyenista*, Borges could not resist taking part in the general agitation. The painter Xul Solar used to tell a story about how Borges got him into trouble with the Argentine fascists.[18] He was walking with Borges down the avenida Santa Fe when they saw a truck carrying a group of militants of the Legión Cívica. Suddenly Borges called out, "Long live Dr. Irigoyen!" at the top of his voice. The vehicle screeched to a halt, and out jumped the fascists. Insults were exchanged, fists flew, and Xul found himself involved in a brawl, but as they fought, he was astonished to see that Borges was shielding his good eye with one hand and hitting out wildly with the other. Afterward a rather battered Borges explained that he wanted to protect the one eye he could see properly out of rather than risk damaging both.

Borges's tentative optimism regarding his relations with Norah Lange is evident also in an essay that he must have written before March 1932, since it was published in the (southern) autumn issue of *Sur* magazine that year.[19] Its subject was the kenning, a figurative device found in Old Norse poetry in which a composite word is used as a metaphorical paraphrase of a common noun (e.g., "crowfood" for corpse, or "swordstorm" for battle). Borges argued that kennings were not valid metaphors, for they were employed in a largely formulaic manner and could not therefore have aroused surprise or wonder. This is reminiscent of the debates he engaged in during the 1920s when he had argued for his own brand of *ultraísmo,* based on his belief that an effective metaphor must be rooted in genuine feeling. Indeed, he concluded his essay on the kennings on a surprisingly personal note:

> The dead *ultraísta* whose ghost continues to inhabit me always, delights in these games. I dedicate them to a bright companion of those heroic days. To Norah Lange, whose blood might perhaps recognize them.[20]

It was no coincidence that one of the main sources for his essay on the kennings was Snorri Sturluson's *Prose Edda,* the work on which Norah Lange had published her essay in *Azul* a few months earlier. And the pointed reference to Norah's Scandinavian blood indicates a return to what I have called Borges's fantasy of Englishness: his romantic superstition about the Nordic roots he shared with Norah, a sign of their entwined destinies.

It was roughly at this time, in my judgment, that he wrote a poem—in English—to an unnamed woman.[21] The poem recalls his habit of wandering at night in the outskirts of Buenos Aires, and its basic conceit is that nights are like waves that bring "mysterious gifts and refusals." This poem, I believe, was addressed to Norah Lange, and it must be read in the context of their earlier, failed relationship. One such nocturnal "wave" had brought him his beloved Norah; this had been a "mysterious gift" but also a "refusal," for he had not been able fully to possess her—"we talked and you have forgotten the words." But another wave had delivered Norah to him once more, and this time he was determined to penetrate her "dark rich life"—"I must get at you, somehow," he tells her. "I want your hidden look, your real smile; that lonely, mocking smile your cool mirror knows." He wanted to discover the real Norah, the Norah who had remained hidden from him in the earlier phase of their relationship. In effect, this English poem was another version of the poem Borges had addressed to Norah as she was about to leave for Oslo toward the end of 1927, for once again he was expressing his desire to learn "the doctrine of passion" in her voice, the passion that had caught him unawares when it suddenly erupted in her feelings for Girondo.

By March 1932 Borges, it would seem, nurtured hopes he thought had been dashed forever—hopes of finding his way back into Norah's affections. At around this time, too, he would have been engaged in writing *The Approach to Al-Mu'tasim,* the autobiographical novel that he imagined might yet save him as a writer. But this reworking of the legend of the Simurgh had been conceived in the absence of Norah's love, and the final Aleph it envisaged, as we have seen, was a prosaic Aleph, not much more than a projected unity between the author, the reader, and the characters, which might be taken to represent a deeper pantheist unity. This was a far cry from that exalted, lyrical Aleph he had dreamed of in the mid-1920s, when he was at the zenith of his love affair with Norah Lange, but the renewal of his friendship with his former sweetheart must have given him grounds for hoping that he might one day raise her up to be his *jolie rousse* once more, the muse who might revive the music of poetry in his soul and bring him at last to experience the ecstatic Aleph of true being.

Borges's optimism would not last long, however. Already by the end of 1931, the likelihood of a return to power by Irigoyen had all but disappeared. Fearing that the great Radical leader might be swept back to office, the Argentine establishment engineered an election in November from which the Radical Party was excluded, and another general, Agustín P. Justo, formerly minister of war in Uriburu's junta, was elected president. The clouds that were gathering over the political scene by the turn of the year augured a similar darkening of Borges's prospects with regard to Norah Lange, for, toward the middle of 1932, his great rival, Oliverio Girondo, arrived in Buenos Aires, and this time he planned to stay for good.

There is no reason to believe that Norah started seeing Girondo again at this point. Their disagreement some eighteen months earlier would seem to have been pretty conclusive. Why, then, did Girondo decide to settle in Buenos Aires in 1932? Although I have been unable to ascertain the reasons, I would surmise that it was jealousy that drew him back to his homeland once again. After all, as a member of the editorial board of *Sur,* Girondo would have read the study of the kennings that Borges had published in *Sur* only a few months earlier. This was as recherché an essay as Borges had ever written, but it concluded, as we have noted, with a surprisingly emotional dedication to Norah Lange, his "bright companion" of the "heroic days" of *ultraísmo.* And Girondo would doubtless have understood what his old rival meant by invoking "the dead *ultraísta* whose ghost inhabits me always" and by his cryptic allusion to Norah's "blood," which he hoped might "recognize" the literary "games" he was playing in his essay on the Scandinavian kennings. Borges's essay, I believe, stung Girondo into realizing his own feelings for Norah—he could not stand losing her to his rival, and so he decided to return to Argentina in order to win her back. The old battle lines were being drawn once more, and the prize, as ever, was the love of Norah Lange.

The enduring conflict between Borges and Girondo was as much a war of literary ideas and sensibilities as it was a contest in love. Battle had first been joined in 1925, when Borges, invoking Apollinaire, repudiated the "adventure" of the avant-garde and called for a reconciliation with the "order" bequeathed by the literary tradition. The war between adventure and order had been prosecuted through *Martín Fierro* and *Proa,* respectively, and had led to the eventual demise of the two magazines. Now, in 1932, Borges chose to renew hostilities once more by collecting his recent piece on the Norse kennings in a book of essays called *Discusión.* These essays represented his various, more recent efforts to arrive at a new "classical" order of writing; they included his "vindications" of the Kabbalah and the Gnostics ("resigned exercises in anachronism," he called them), reflections on metaphysical issues concerning time and space, a study of the "theological difficulties" involved in the concept of hell, an essay comparing translations of the *Iliad* into English and French, a brief study of the "laconic" aspects of Whitman's rhetoric as opposed to his celebrated effusiveness, and two essays in which he developed further his appreciation of aesthetic restraint: "The Postulation of Reality" rejected "romantic" expressiveness and advocated a "classical" reticence masking experience from the reader, and "The Art of Narrative and Magic" likened the "order" of narrative to the logic of magical causality, thus disengaging fiction from any necessary connection with the real world.[22] Borges's collection of essays appeared to represent the driest, most esoteric pursuits of the literary mind, an impression that the author did little to dispel in the prologue to the book, where he seems to have done his best to banish the merest hint of literary adventure. Indeed, he affected a huge world-weariness, declaring that "life and death have been lacking in my life" and claiming to have derived from such existential "indigence" his "laborious love" of the literary "minutiae" he was offering the reader.

Discusión, in effect, was the complete antithesis of everything Oliverio Girondo believed literature should be. For his part, Girondo had brought from Paris the manuscript of a new book—his first in seven years—which consisted of a miscellany of twenty-four prose poems and seminarrative sketches. Strident in tone and imagery, and as ostentatiously erotic as ever, these texts already displayed elements of the surrealism toward which he would evolve in the coming years. Girondo's book, like Borges's *Discusión,* came out in 1932; it was published by his friend Évar Méndez's Editorial Proa with the title *Espantapájaros* (*Scarecrow*), a title indicating that the author was still very much a man who loved to shock the bourgeoisie: And, sure enough, in response to a wager that he could not sell the five thousand copies of his new book, Girondo devised a publicity stunt that has gone down in the literary history of Buenos Aires.[23] He rented a shop on the fashionable calle Florida, engaged several pretty girls as sales assistants, and piled up copies of *Espantapájaros* in the window. He then got a friend to make a huge papier-mâché effigy of a scarecrow, which he dressed up in a top hat, monocle, and pipe. This was meant to represent the "Academician," that is to say, the embodiment of everything Girondo believed to be pedantic and moribund in Argentine culture. He then hired from a funeral parlor an open carriage drawn by six horses and manned by coachmen dressed in the style of the French Revolution. The Academician was mounted on this funeral cortege and driven around the streets of the city center for an entire fortnight. Girondo's book sold out within a month.

To the literati of Buenos Aires, the parading of the Academician on a revolutionary tumbrel would have brought to mind the infamous avant-garde manifesto that Girondo had published in *Martín Fierro* in 1924, where he had railed against the "funereal solemnity" of the historian and against "the professor who mummifies all he touches." The funeral cortege conveyed a similar message—the bogey of conservatism would soon be laid to rest by the forces of the avant-garde. And who, in 1932, would have best represented the Academician whom Girondo proposed to send to the guillotine? Surely it was Jorge Luis Borges, the author of the dessicated literary essays recently collected in *Discusión*. It may be, then, that the strange pageant devised by Girondo was meant to convey a secret message to his rival—he was giving Borges notice that he would oppose the call to order represented by *Discusión* and conjure up instead the true spirit of the 1920s, the heady spirit of adventure that was proper to the avant-garde.

Girondo's presence in Buenos Aires was an obvious threat to Borges's renewed friendship with Norah Lange. By September 1932 we find signs of anxiety in Borges, as if he were afflicted by doubts about Norah. Asked in a questionnaire for a magazine, "Is jealousy a manifestation of love?" his reply was, "It is an embarrassing, genuine and inescapable manifestation of love."[24] In December he would reprint in a Spanish newspaper "The Perpetual Race Between Achilles and the Tortoise," the essay on infinite regress that he first published in 1929, a few weeks before he had been expecting Norah Lange to return from her year abroad in Norway.[25] Once again Zeno's paradox served to articulate the anxiety that Norah would always—tantalizingly—remain beyond his grasp.

It was in these troubled and uncertain months of late 1932 that he is likely to have abandoned his autobiographical novel, *The Approach to Al-Mu'tasim,* with its optimistic ending in the revelation of the Aleph-like Simurgh. Certainly by this stage he could no longer envisage the realization of the self. On the contrary, by January 1, 1933, he had reverted to his speculations about the "nothingness of personality," always a sign of depression in Borges. In a brief article, tellingly entitled "The Desire to Be an Other" ("El querer ser otro"), he wrote:

> All the lovers in this wide world who ever gave themselves to each other fully in an embrace, all the lovers who will embrace and do embrace, are the same bright couple: Adam and Eve. No one is substantially someone: anyone can be anyone else, at any moment in time. And with these speculations and games, I believe we have touched on mysticism.[26]

Racked by anxiety as he must have been at this point, he toyed with random permutations, shifting possibilities around, imagining that all lovers were the selfsame pair of lovers, just as one man was equivalent to any other man. But however much he might have wished to beguile his fears by persuading himself that space, time, and identity were relative and malleable—that it did not finally matter whether Norah ended up in Girondo's arms rather than his own—there was no getting away from the fact that in the New Year of 1933 he was in danger of losing his beloved forever.

CHAPTER 13

The Rivals

(1933–1934)

THE FRAUDULENT ELECTIONS of November 1931 delivered the presidency to Agustín P. Justo, who headed a coalition of conservative parties and anti-Irigoyen Radicals that became known as the Concordancia. After his official inauguration in February 1932, the new president tried to restore a measure of political freedom and even attempted to conciliate the Radicals by releasing Irigoyen from house arrest, but these measures were not sufficient to appease the parties and groups that had effectively been excluded from the system. Indeed, Justo's election was to mark the beginning of the "Década Infame," the "Infamous Decade," of Argentine history. It was infamous to the Radicals because they were to be robbed of power through ballot rigging, but it was infamous also to the *nacionalistas* because it would thwart their hopes of creating a fascist-style corporate state. The Radicals reverted to their historic attitude of "Intransigence"—a principled abstention from electoral politics and a recourse to armed rebellion. (There would be Radical uprisings in 1932 and 1933.) The *nacionalistas* protested against Justo's government in the way they knew best—by marching in the streets of the major cities and beating up their opponents.

A new element would enter Argentine politics at the start of the Década Infame. This was a strong anti-British sentiment based on the perception that Argentina was subservient to British economic interests. The immediate cause of this Anglophobia was the Roca-Runciman Treaty, a trade deal concluded in 1933 with Great Britain, Argentina's largest overseas market, whereby Britain agreed to maintain a certain level of imports of Argentine beef in return for concessions on British exports and privileges for British companies operating in Argentina. The Concordancia government argued that this agreement would ease the economic problems created by the world depression, but opposition parties denounced the Roca-Runciman Treaty as a sellout of national interests. The trade deal provoked public outrage over the British monopoly of transport in Buenos Aires and over alleged tax evasion by British and foreign meatpacking companies. Argentine politics thus became extraordinarily violent in the aftermath of Justo's accession to the presidency, but over the next few years, the Concordancia government would succeed in bringing a degree of political stability to the country, thanks, ironically, to the Roca-Runciman Treaty, which allowed Argentina to ride the world depression by maintaining a large part of its traditional exports to Britain.

The most enduring consequence of the great outburst of Anglophobia in 1933 was ideological—*nacionalista* intellectuals undertook a revision of Argentine history that would change the entire course of politics with the rise to power of Juan Perón at the end of the Década Infame. This revisionism began with the publication in 1933 of a book by the brothers Rodolfo and Julio Irazusta entitled *Argentina and the British Empire: The Links in the Chain,* in which they contended that Argentina had never been truly emancipated from the yoke of colonialism because Britain had constantly meddled in its affairs and won control over its economy in collusion with the export elite of *estancieros.* It was necessary, therefore, to break the links that bound Argentina to the British Empire in order to build a truly independent nation.

The year 1933 did not bode well for Borges. He remained a significant figure in the literary world, but his new book, *Discusión,* did not find favor with the critics, who were bemused on the whole by this very mixed bag of theological and metaphysical speculations, combined with strange reflections on magic and the art of narrative or on the reticence of the classical writer. Even his admirers professed a certain dismay. In August 1933 the literary magazine *Megáfono* canvassed the views of leading writers and critics on Borges's work, and, though favorable in the main, the survey registered the odd doubt. Tomás de Lara, for instance, noted the marked decline in creativity since *Fervor de Buenos Aires* and concluded by wondering, "Where is Borges going now; what does Borges want to do?"[1]

The fact was that Borges was at a crossroads once again. Since being rejected by Norah at the end of 1926, he had gradually lost his voice as a poet and had turned to essay writing to start with and then, very tentatively, to fiction, but his ideas had not yet cohered into a new aesthetic and his efforts to produce an autobiographical novel had not amounted to much. His future as a writer depended on his regaining the favor of Norah Lange, but he was facing a renewed challenge from his old rival, Oliverio Girondo, whose new book *Espantapájaros,* as we have seen, represented the antithesis of the abstruse essays collected in *Discusión.*

Shortly after returning to Buenos Aires, Girondo purchased a grand neocolonial house at the shabby end of calle Suipacha, an area of insalubrious tenements and decrepit mansions sloping toward the railway line that runs along El Bajo from the Retiro station. There he installed himself in bohemian splendor, amid the paintings, sculptures, and artworks acquired on his travels around the world. Girondo was said to own the largest private collection of pre-Columbian gold artifacts in the whole of South America, and of the many curiosities he had collected, the one that particularly amused his friends was a set of stuffed toads got up in human attire, which he put on display in the entrance hall of his new house. It was not long before he gathered about him a large circle of young writers and artists, and, given his scandalous reputation, he soon became the object of prurient curiosity in Buenos Aires. It was rumored that the former wild man of the avant-garde got up to all kinds of unmentionable things with his cronies at orgies that went on until dawn, although the truth—at least according to some of his friends—was that these fiestas were fairly innocuous affairs, amounting to little more than dancing and the consumption of huge amounts of alcohol.[2]

Borges must have feared that Norah's proven appetite for the social whirl would make her vulnerable to Girondo's charms once more. Perhaps an indication of his uncertainty about her was his curious decision to reissue his essay on the Norse kennings in the form of a pamphlet printed at his own expense in a limited edition.[3] He retained the postscript dedicating the essay to Norah Lange, where he reminded her of "the heroic days" of *ultraísmo* and of her Scandinavian blood, but the further dedication he wrote in the personal copy he presented to her is more effusive, crediting Norah with being the inspiration of his interest in Norse literature, while at the same time betraying a trace of self-doubt: "To Norah, this imperfect visit to a theme inaugurated by her. To Norah, with my usual admiration and long-standing affection. To Norah, in her splendor as always, Georgie."[4]

If Borges was unsure of how things stood with Norah, it was not because she was seeing Girondo again—she appears to have been keeping away from him—but rather because she was tempted to spread her wings as a "New Woman." In 1931 she had accepted Girondo's view that the novel based on her voyage to Norway was not suitable for publication, but by 1933, she was no longer disposed to heed her former lover's advice, and she offered it to José Torrendel of the Editorial Tor, one of the leading publishing houses in Argentina. As it happened, Torrendel was preparing to launch the first-ever paperback books on the Argentine market later that year, and he planned to celebrate this historic venture by the simultaneous publication of ten titles by different authors. A man with a sharp eye for publicity, Torrendel chose Norah Lange's risqué novel as one of the ten paperbacks. To increase its sensational effect no doubt, it was called *45 días y 30 marineros* (*45 Days and 30 Sailors*), an obviously provocative title for a book by a young woman in a conservative country like Argentina.

Norah's decision to publish *45 días y 30 marineros* amounted to a declaration of independence from Girondo and Borges, the two men who had dominated her life for the past five years and caused her such distress. As her novel showed, she was beginning to relish her allure, sensing the power she could exert over men, and in the course of 1933, she would be seen with increasing frequency at parties and literary dinners as an author in her own right and not as the protégée of either Borges or Girondo. This new independence of Norah Lange's found expression in her friendship with a third man, the Chilean poet Pablo Neruda, who arrived in Buenos Aires on August 28 to take up a post as consul at the Chilean embassy. The two of them hit it off so well that they liked to make jocular displays of their mutual affection in public places. At the fashionable restaurant Les Ambassadeurs, for instance, they once asked the orchestra to play "The Wedding March" while they paraded arm in arm around the room; after another bibulous dinner at a restaurant on calle Corrientes, the entire party spilled out onto the street, singing and shouting, and Norah was said to have called out, "Pablo, I'm going to sleep with you tonight!" To which Neruda replied, laughing wildly, "I'd be delighted!"[5]

In October the Buenos Aires literary world was dazzled by the arrival of the Spanish poet Federico García Lorca, who was to stay for about six months, until April 1934. Lorca soon became the talk of the town: he was feted everywhere he went, and his lectures, recitals, and plays received glowing reviews in the Argentine press. During his stay in Buenos Aires, the Spaniard struck up a great friendship with Pablo Neruda, and over the next few months they would see a great deal of each other. At a PEN Club dinner in the Plaza Hotel, the two poets delighted the Argentine literary world by giving a speech *al alimón*—by taking turns to deliver it from each end of the table. On another celebrated occasion, the newspaper magnate Natalio Botana laid on a great banquet in Lorca's honor at his country house—an entire roasted ox was conveyed ceremoniously to the table by ten waiters dressed up as gauchos—but the gossip afterward was of Lorca's having twisted his ankle when he fell down a flight of steps in mysterious circumstances. It appears that after dinner he accompanied Neruda and a lady poet on a walk in the grounds of Botana's house, and all three of them climbed a tower to take the night air. Neruda got carried away by the romance of the moment, however, and, as he was to write in his memoirs, "I took the golden girl in my arms and when I kissed her I could not help noticing that she was a woman of flesh and blood, firm and well built."[6] Emboldened by this discovery, Neruda asked Lorca to stand guard for him at the foot of the tower, but the Spaniard fell over as he raced down the stairs, bringing his friend's impromptu encounter to a sorry end. For the next fortnight, Lorca was laid up in his hotel room with a bandaged foot, and rumor had it that the girl who had caused all the excitement was none other than Norah Lange.[7]

Whatever the truth of such gossip, there can be little doubt that the story would have reached Borges, and he must have feared the worst—Norah was becoming a regular companion of Lorca and Neruda, and he knew that his rival, Girondo, was also a member of that glittering circle. Even so, this does not mean that Norah had resumed her relationship with Girondo, but she was certainly spending a good deal of time with him in the company of their mutual friend Neruda. She herself would recall a riotous night out with the two men when they hijacked a milk wagon in the early hours of the morning and drove it on to the avenida Leandro N. Alem, one of the busiest thoroughfares in the city. Norah ventured into the middle of the road, climbed into the traffic policeman's podium and brought the traffic to a halt. Then she saw the milk wagon speed past below her, Oliverio at the reins of the galloping horse and Neruda declaiming one of his most famous poems: "Sucede que me canso de ser hombre. . . ." ("It so happens that I am weary of being a man. . . .")[8]

In June or thereabouts of 1933, Borges had been invited to become a coeditor of the literary supplement of the daily newspaper *Crítica*, which had a massive circulation of around seven hundred thousand. He was offered the post through his friend Ulyses Petit de Murat, who was *Crítica*'s film critic at the time. The idea for the "Revista Multicolor de los Sábados," a Saturday color supplement devoted to literary and cultural topics, had come from *Crítica*'s proprietor, Natalio Botana, but he gave the coeditors, Petit de Murat and Borges, full responsibility for its production, as well as requiring them to contribute a piece of their own once every two weeks.[9]

Borges was to publish a great deal of his own work in *Crítica*'s Saturday supplement—articles, stories, historical and biographical sketches, reviews, and translations.[10] No doubt he drew on a good deal of material from his notebooks—he would, for instance, publish "Men of the Outskirts," the story he had written in 1930 in memory of Nicolás Paredes, as well as the fictionalized biographies that he would eventually collect in *A Universal History of Infamy* (1935). However, he tended to give his real name only to those pieces he was satisfied with, resorting to pseudonyms or even anonymity for those about which he felt less sure. From a biographical perspective, Borges's contributions to *Crítica* are of particular interest because, when considered against the chronology of other events in his life in this period, a good number of them yield up a cryptic record of his feelings and attitudes toward Norah Lange at a time when his relations with her were approaching a new crisis.

On September 23, Borges published the first of what he called "Ancient Germanic Myths" ("Antiguos mitos germánicos").[11] This one described a dragon who watches over hidden treasure night and day; he is a stranger to sleep, as are "the blazing guests of hell, whose cursed lids never drop over their miserable eyes," and all he can look forward to is the day when some hero might offer release by putting him to death. The sleepless dragon may well be taken to represent his own condition at this time, and the treasure an allusion to Norah Lange. Certainly a reminiscence of this Germanic myth would appear in Borges's "The Zahir" (1947), where a desperate lover tries to distract himself from the obsessive memory of the woman he has lost by writing a story based on the Norse myth of Fafnir, the serpent that guards a store of gold day and night until he is killed by the hero, Sigurd.

Two weeks later Borges published "The Witches" ("Las brujas"), another "Ancient Germanic Myth" regarding the belief that a witch could be identified by a sign in the shape of a toad that Beelzebub would imprint in her eyes.[12] Certain witches, however, were so "hypocritical and harmful" that they disguised even this telltale sign. Why the strange detail of the toad? It may be that Borges intended this as an allusion to the stuffed toads Girondo kept in the hallway of his house, so that this denunciation of women who hid the sign of the toad in their eyes could be read as signifying that Norah was socializing with Girondo again, and possibly even attending the so-called orgies at his house.

Borges's jealousy was further inflamed in October by the arrival in Buenos Aires of Federico García Lorca. Borges's hostility to Lorca has become notorious, but the truth is that he had once been a great admirer of the Spaniard's work: he had been keen to meet him through Guillermo de Torre during his second visit to Spain in 1924 and had even published two of Lorca's Gypsy poems in his magazine, Proa. In later life Borges chose to forget this early enthusiasm: he would, for instance, tell an interviewer that he had met Lorca for the first and only time during the Spaniard's visit to Buenos Aires and they had talked only for an hour or so, the implication being that they had very little in common—Lorca had struck him as being "a professional Andalusian," and he had been exasperated by Lorca's assertion that Mickey Mouse was a character "in whom you could see all the tragedy of American life."[13] But Borges's antipathy toward Lorca may well have had more personal roots, given that the Spanish poet made friends with Neruda, Girondo, and Norah Lange during his stay in Buenos Aires and was a frequent guest at their dinners and parties.

On November 4, Borges published "The Myth of the Elves" ("El mito de los elfos"), a third "Ancient Germanic Myth," which evinced an even greater degree of anguish than the earlier ones.[14] Bad elves were said to cause nightmares and insomnia, and the elves of Norway were particularly treacherous—they offered hospitality to the wayfarer, but no sooner did he accept their offer than the ground gave way and he fell into an abyss.

Borges did not have to wait long for the abyss to open up under him. Less than two weeks after the appearance of this third Germanic myth, Norah

Lange's novel was published by the Editorial Tor. On November 16, a grand dinner was held at the Hotel Marconi to celebrate the launch of the first ten Argentine paperbacks. Over two hundred guests were accommodated around one vast table, and it is small wonder, therefore, that La Fiesta de los Diez—the party for the ten authors—should have been such an "animated occasion," extremely "cordial and boisterous."[15]

While Norah was celebrating with her fellow authors, Borges was preparing to review 45 días y 30 marineros for Crítica.[16] The novel would have left him in no doubt about his chances of regaining Norah's affections. He would have noted the indifference, bordering on antipathy, that the heroine, Ingrid, shows toward the character called Stevenson, as well as her reluctance to follow her cousin Peter's advice to leave the ship where she is being harassed by the captain and other sailors. Borges would single out in his review the scene in which the ship's captain lies to Ingrid about the death of his infant son in order to arouse her pity "and get her to give herself to him." And, in what must have been coded advice to Norah, he quoted the reason Ingrid gives for finally deciding to quit the ship—one must not prolong a situation from which happiness has not naturally arisen.

Still, whatever moral influence Borges might have had upon Norah could scarcely have prevailed over the pleasure she derived from her literary success. There was a fun-loving, exhibitionistic side to her personality, and this, as Borges would have known, was what made her so vulnerable to the charms of Oliverio Girondo. Certainly it had not escaped Girondo that Norah loved being the center of attention. He was, of course, a past master at the spectacular coup de main, and on the occasion of the publication of 45 días y 30 marineros, he threw as extravagant a party in Norah's honor as any he had given. All the male guests had to dress up as sailors by way of illustrating the novel's central theme—the irresistible attraction felt by one and all for its beautiful protagonist, Ingrid. Photographs of the party were published in the society columns of the Buenos Aires newspapers, and many former martinfierristas can be identified in them, but the brilliance of the occasion was immeasurably enhanced by the presence of Federico García Lorca and Pablo Neruda, who also appeared in sailor's uniform in Norah's honor. This grand gesture of Girondo's would seem to have finally won Norah over, for one of the photographs of the party shows her in the guise of a mermaid, reclining on a platform bearing the title of her novel; she is surrounded by sailors, but standing over her is Oliverio himself, got up in the uniform of a sea captain, and the name of the ship of which he is master is none other than Norah, as can be seen on the painted backdrop.

Borges's reaction to Girondo's triumph may be gauged from a story he published on January 20, 1934, in Crítica.[17] A heretical Muslim prophet keeps his face covered from his followers because he claims that it radiates the dazzling light of God. The prophet's Gnostic doctrine is summed up thus:

> The earth we inhabit is an error, an incompetent parody. Mirrors and paternity are abominable because they multiply and affirm it. Disgust is the fundamental virtue. Two modes of conduct (the choice of which the prophet left open) may lead us to it: abstinence or license, the indulgence of the flesh or its chastisement.

However, when the prophet is defeated by the forces of a powerful caliph, he is exposed as a fraud—the veil is torn away to reveal a repulsive visage:

> The promised face of the Apostle, the face of he who had seen Heaven, was indeed white, but of a whiteness peculiar to leprosy. It was so bloated or unimaginable that it seemed more like a mask. It had no eyebrows; the lower lid of the right eye drooped over a wizened cheek; a heavy cluster of tubercles had eaten away at the lips; the nose, flattened and inhuman, was like that of a lion.

Borges's distress over Norah Lange was compounded by a general disillusionment with the state of Argentina. The signing of the Roca-Runciman Treaty in 1933 happened to coincide with the centenary of the seizure of the Malvinas (Falkland Islands) by the British, and public outrage over both Roca-Runciman and the Malvinas was skillfully exploited by the right-wing *nacionalistas,* who added their own virulent anti-Semitism to the general sense of grievance by claiming that British and Jewish financiers were ultimately responsible for Argentina's economic plight. In the latter months of 1933 and through 1934, the *nacionalistas* would attempt ever more aggressively to provoke another coup d'état. There were reports in the press of shoot-outs between fascists and socialists, and of arms caches being found by the police at fascist clubs.[18] In September 1933 some two thousand uniformed fascists of the Legión Cívica paraded in strict military formation through the center of Buenos Aires, a demonstration that required the largest deployment of police ever seen in the city.[19] The escalation of violence was such that, toward the end of that year, the leader of the Socialist Party would warn that the country was on the brink of civil war.[20]

Borges was to suffer personally at the hands of the *nacionalistas*. On January 30, 1934—just ten days after he published the self-hating story about the leprous prophet—he became the object of a gratuitous personal attack in the *nacionalista* magazine *Crisol* (*The Crucible*): an anonymous note appeared accusing him of "slyly" concealing his Jewish ancestry. Borges wrote a scathing reply with the title "I a Jew" ("Yo, judío"), claiming that he liked to think of himself as Jewish ever since he had come across his mother's surname, Acevedo, in a list of Judeo-Portuguese family names in Buenos Aires in the middle of the previous century.[21] He concluded with a paragraph mocking the absurdity of the *nacionalistas'* obsession with denouncing Jews.

Why did Borges become the object of this anti-Semitic attack? The reason must be sought in the considerable bitterness that existed in nationalist circles at Borges's desertion from the cause of *criollismo*, the cultural nationalism he had once professed with such ardor. To make things worse, at a time of acute political tension, when writers were expected to engage with political and social questions, Borges appeared to have immured himself in an ivory tower with his book *Discusión*. The critic Ramón Doll, who was a socialist with nationalist inclinations at this time, had censured *Discusión* for its "anti-Argentine" prose and for eschewing the natural idioms of the criollos in favor of a labored, bookish style.[22] A right-wing Catholic *nacionalista*, Ignacio B. Anzoátegui, had gone so far as to imply that Borges had prostituted himself by abandoning *criollismo*, thereby forsaking what he termed a "necessary literature" for the verbose and vacuous essays of *Discusión*.[23]

Borges had not, in fact, shut himself up in an ivory tower; it was simply that he had become alienated from the direction politics had taken—he despised the Anglophobia, the anti-Semitism, and, not least, the authoritarian tendencies that were threatening to turn Argentina into a fascist dictatorship. If he had chosen to reply in a sarcastic vein to the attack in *Crisol*, it was certainly not because he made light of Jew baiting, since he knew only too well what it might portend. Indeed, two weeks later he published in *Crítica* his own translation of a vivid report by Heinrich Mann on the political situation in Germany, describing the arbitrary arrests of Marxists and Jews by the Gestapo, the concentration camps, the disappearances of opponents, and Hitler's power play against Hindenberg. The article appeared under the title "Scenes of Nazi Cruelty" ("Escenas de la crueldad nazi"), and it was illustrated with a picture of a skull wearing a steel helmet and surrounded by swastikas.[24]

Borges's disgust may well have been aggravated by a sense of a general loosening of the moral climate in the country. We have already seen his dismay at Norah's going to parties and banquets with Neruda, Lorca, and Girondo, but this was symptomatic of a more general hedonism, for, in the latter months of 1933, the Buenos Aires press noted the popularity of a new social phenomenon— the French-style nightclubs, or "boîtes," which, in the opinion of *Noticias Gráficas*, were appearing "in response to the desire for social expansion," an expansion that appears also to have included the first nude shows in Argentina— advertisements in the press for the "Revista Prohibida" at the Casino boasted that "nudity has been incorporated this year in the repertoire of the cabaret."[25]

One can follow Borges's growing disenchantment with the condition of

Argentina in four historical sketches, written under the pseudonym José Tuntar, that were published in *Crítica* between September 1933 and March 1934—exactly the period during which he was witnessing Norah Lange's renewed fascination with Oliverio Girondo.[26] All four articles were based on Tacitus's account of the decadence of imperial Rome. (Tacitus had been one of Borges's favorite authors during his time in Geneva.) The first article relates the disillusionment of the brave Diocletian as he sees the constitution of the Roman republic being traduced by the corruption of his successors.[27] Diocletian decides to commit suicide as a "tragic gesture of defiance and despair." On October 7, another article alluded to the orgies of Augustus's daughter and granddaughter, both of whom were called Julia.[28] The third article, published on November 18—just two days after the great banquet given by the Editorial Tor to celebrate the launch of the first ten paperbacks in Argentina—has as its subject the prevalence of spies in imperial Rome, said to be a symptom of its moral degeneracy, and again there are references to the orgies sanctioned by Augustus's successors, Tiberius, Caligula, and Claudius.[29] The final article by José Tuntar, called "The Great Roman Orgies" ("Las grandes orgías romanas"), appeared on March 3, 1934, and offered a synthesis of the life of Petronius, describing the widespread corruption that had formed the background to the *Satyricon*.[30]

The four pieces by José Tuntar imply an analogy between Rome and Argentina: just as republican Rome was corrupted by the successors of the Emperor Augustus, so, too, was the early Argentine republic corrupted as a result of the oligarchic system created by the strongman General Roca in the 1880s. In this perspective one can more fully appreciate the historic and personal roots of Borges's enthusiasm for Irigoyen. The presidency of Irigoyen represented a historic opportunity to restore the civic virtues for which patrician criollos like Borges's ancestors had fought and died, but Irigoyen had been overthrown in 1930, and the nation had reverted to the fraudulent rule of a self-interested ruling class. To cap it all, the man who had overthrown Irigoyen, General José F. Uriburu, was, by some extraordinary irony, a family relation of Oliverio Girondo's, so the loss of Norah Lange to his rival and the corruption of the Argentine republic appear to have become fatefully entwined in Borges's imagination. Borges, then, felt himself to be doubly an outcast—expelled from the paradise he had once shared with Norah at the calle Tronador but estranged also from the *patria* itself after the downfall of Irigoyen. The persecuted outsider would thus become a recurrent figure in his work—in famous stories like "Death and the Compass" ("La muerte y la brújula"), "The Secret Miracle" ("El milagro secreto"), or "The Waiting" ("La espera"), an individual is hunted down by the agents of Rome, by the Nazis, or by nameless Argentine dictators.

Thoughts of suicide certainly preyed on Borges's mind in the months leading up to the final loss of Norah Lange. In the articles he wrote under the pseudonym José Tuntar, he alluded to brave military leaders who, in their revulsion at the pervasive corruption of Rome, chose to take their own lives. Suicide is presented as the highest form of the denial of the flesh, indeed as a noble act, for, in the words of Seneca, it is "the only way we have left to us to be free." [31]

Definitive as the loss of Norah Lange must have appeared to Borges, there was to be a strange coda to his long and tormented relationship with her. Sometime in the New Year of 1934, he received a short story from Norah for publication in the literary supplement of Crítica. Called "Un vacilante juego mortal" ("An Indecisive, Deadly Game"), it concerned a woman who plans to poison her unfaithful husband but keeps putting off the murder indefinitely.[32] Since Borges believed that everything Norah wrote was a reflection upon her own destiny, he must have inferred from this story that there remained certain matters yet to be resolved between Norah and Girondo. As a close friend of the Lange family, he must have known that a particular bone of contention between Norah and his rival was the question of marriage. Girondo still refused to marry Norah, because he felt he was too old for her,[33] but this refusal presented her with a dilemma: her passion for Girondo had proved to be irresistible, but to enter into a relationship with him outside of marriage would compromise her reputation. Allowing for the distortions and exaggerations of fiction, Norah's story very likely signified that she was toying with the idea of ending the relationship but could not bring herself to make the final break.

Under the circumstances Borges may have imagined that perhaps all was not lost with regard to Norah, so he may have decided to make one last appeal to her. Such was the context, in my judgment, that gave rise to a second "English Poem." It is clearly a sequel to the first "English Poem," in which he had expressed his resolve to possess Norah, to "get at you somehow." This second poem is designed as a series of "offerings" to her in response to the opening question, "What can I hold you with?" He offers her the poetic landscape they had once shared in the "heroic days" of ultraísmo—"lean streets, desperate sunsets, the moon of the jagged suburbs"; he offers her the memory of his glorious ancestors, his books, his loyalty; he offers her every last thing he has:

> . . . that kernel of myself that I have saved, somehow
> —the central heart that deals not in words, traffics not with dreams
>   and is
> untouched by time, by joy, by adversities.

But what could he really set against Girondo? Compared to his rival's wealth, his social status, his success in the literary world, Borges had very little to show for himself, having failed even to live up to his early promise as a writer. In the final analysis, all he could offer Norah was the sheer desperation of his longing for her:

> I can give you my loneliness, my darkness, the hunger of my heart; I am
> trying to bribe you with uncertainty, with danger, with defeat.

But the unfortunate truth was that he had misunderstood Norah: what he did not see, or could not bring himself to see, was that she simply did not love him. Norah may well have been vacillating over a final commitment to Oliverio Girondo, but, as both *Voz de la vida* and *45 días y 30 marineros* had already made abundantly clear, she did not regard her "cousin" Georgie as an alternative, and no amount of pleading would have persuaded her otherwise. Indeed, sometime in 1934—I reckon it must have been around April—the relationship between Norah and Girondo "became stable," in the words of a close friend of the couple.[34] For the sake of appearances, Norah would not actually move in with Girondo until she finally persuaded him to marry her nine years later, but from 1934 she was recognized in the Buenos Aires literary world as his permanent consort.

The end of Borges's long and complicated involvement with Norah Lange was marked by a fortuitously apposite symbol—the Lange family's decision to move out of their villa on the calle Tronador.[35] The Lange villa had, of course, acquired enormous personal significance for Borges—it was associated with love and all the promise love might hold for him, for it was there that he had first met and courted Concepción Guerrero and there that he had later courted Norah herself. But the villa had become too big for the Lange family's needs: the girls had taken jobs in downtown Buenos Aires, and their mother disliked being left for long periods on her own in a distant suburb like Villa Urquiza. In December 1933 they rented out the villa and moved to an apartment at calle San Martín 551 in the city center, and in November 1934 they would make a further move to an apartment on calle Arroyo 845, just around the corner from Girondo's house on calle Suipacha. The big house at calle Tronador would be rented out for the next ten years, until it was sold finally in 1945.[36]

It was the decision to sell the house on calle Tronador, probably toward the end of 1944, that seems to have triggered one of Borges's most famous stories, "The Aleph" (1945), whose autobiographical subtext alludes to his thwarted love for Norah Lange. Borges would cast himself as the protagonist, a writer who is unable to forget the death of his beloved Beatriz Viterbo. Her demise occurred in February 1929, which was about the time that Norah returned from her year in Oslo and informed Borges that she did not wish to resume their engagement. In retrospect Borges must have realized that this had been the true end—the death, as it were—of their relationship, but he had not been able to let go of the memory of Norah, as is hinted at in "The Aleph," where the Borges character takes to visiting the dead Beatriz Viterbo's house annually on her birthday, until he is informed one year that the house, "which alluded infinitely to Beatriz," was due to be demolished. He is then apprised of the existence of a magic orb called an "Aleph," which afforded the beholder an instantaneous vision of the entire universe; it is described as "a point in space which contains all the other points," and it is also likened to the Simurgh, "a bird who is in some way all birds."

Curiously, the magic orb that holds the Aleph is set into the nineteenth step of the narrow stairs leading down into a cellar under the dining room of Beatriz Viterbo's house. Here we have another veiled allusion to the Lange villa, which had two cellars under the dining and sitting rooms, respectively. These cellars held a special meaning for Norah Lange—as a child she had always regarded them as "a permanent and immutable place of safety."[37] So Borges placed the Aleph of his story in one such cellar, for since 1925 he had imagined that the "Aleph" vouchsafed by the love of Norah Lange would bring him an equally permanent and immutable sense of fulfillment. The protagonist of Borges's story, however, makes no attempt to prevent the demolition of Beatriz Viterbo's house, realizing, no doubt, that after her death he has no hope of making the Aleph vision truly his own.

PART THREE

A Season in Hell

(1934–1944)

CHAPTER 14

Failure

(1934–1935)

AFTER HIS DEFINITIVE REJECTION by Norah Lange, Borges was plagued by nightmares and insomnia and came to the brink of killing himself. He tried to cope with this suffering by throwing himself into his work at *Crítica*. Two stories he was to publish in *Crítica* give us some insight into the severity of this personal crisis. They were both written under the pseudonym "Alex Ander," and their crudely written, melodramatic style is hard to reconcile with the elegance of Borges's later writing, but it was consonant with the yellow-press populism of *Crítica* and must have owed not a little to their author's extreme anguish at the time.

The first story was called "30 Pesos Is the Price of Death" ("30 pesos vale la muerte"), and its unnamed protagonist is a part-time medical student who works as a journalist on a popular daily newspaper.[1] He suffers from feelings of inadequacy and an aggressive resentment toward other people. A psychiatrist has advised him to take a rest from his medical studies for a year, but "a month of loneliness, analysis and insomnia had decided him"—he would commit suicide, because "all possibilities of happiness had disappeared."[2] He goes to a shop to buy a revolver but happens to notice a record player and finally decides to order it instead of the gun. As he leaves the shop, he witnesses a road accident, to which he reacts as a true professional and calls his editor to send a photographer to the scene of the accident. Obviously more interested in music and in doing his job well, he forgets about the decision to end his life.

The second story, "She Wasn't Worth It!" ("¡No valía la pena!"), is barely more than a sketch about a young actor who kills himself because he is rejected by the actress he loves.[3] He woos her, but she blows hot and cold, until, out of the blue, she deliberately inflames his desire during a performance by giving him a long and passionate kiss on the mouth in full view of the audience. The actor "seemed to go out of his mind" and decided to confess his love openly to her:

She showed great surprise to see him come into her dressing room one night at the end of the show. And all the more so on hearing him blurt out a confused stream of impassioned words in which she believed she could make out an intemperate declaration of love, to which she responded simply with a forced laugh that brutally cut short his inspiration, like a cold shower, forcing him to rush out of her dressing room without another word and as red in the face as the rouge with which she was just about to make her wet lips even more tempting.[4]

After this final rejection, the actor kills himself.

These two stories, which were published on July 21 and September 8, 1934, respectively, suggest that Borges's suicidal crisis took place sometime between the publication of Norah Lange's short story, on April 7, and September 8. Yet there would appear to have been two distinct phases to this crisis, since the ending of the first story implies that the temptation to suicide was overcome by the protagonist's rediscovery of a measure of self-worth, arising from his interest in music and his pride in being a good reporter. I would deduce from this that Borges did in fact resist an initial temptation to kill himself in the belief that writing might offer a way out of his misery by giving some purpose to his life.

In Borges's text *The Approach to Al-Mu'tasim*, we are told that a second version of the novel of that title was published in 1934, and this leads me to believe that he began work not too long after April on a revised version of the autobiographical novel that he had abandoned two years earlier. The fundamental difference between the two versions of the novel, we are told, was that in 1932 the figure of Al-Mu'tasim, though symbolic, gave the impression of being a real person with idiosyncratic traits, whereas in 1934 the novel "lapsed into allegory"—Al-Mu'tasim became "an emblem of God," and the hero's travels symbolized the progress of the soul in its "mystical ascent."[5] In other words, the 1932 version described a process culminating in a specific resolution— the ultimate identity between the author, the characters, and the reader symbolized by the pantheist legend of the Aleph-like Simurgh, "the bird who is all birds." In the 1934 version, however, the fact that the sought-after God was called Al-Mu'tasim, meaning "seeker of refuge," implied an "extravagant theology" that Borges explained thus:

> . . . the Almighty is in search of Someone, and that Someone of Someone else who is superior (or simply indispensable and equal to Him), and so on until the End—or rather the Non-End—of Time, or until the cycle begins again.[6]

This ending, or nonending, clearly undermined the whole purpose of writing an autobiographical novel, for if Borges had originally intended the novel *The Approach to Al-Mu'tasim* to articulate what was essential to him, then he had come to the conclusion that there was no end, no purposeful destiny, in the life of a man. On the other hand, to abandon his autobiographical novel was to admit that there was no salvation to be found in writing after all, no possibility of writing a work that would justify the existence of the author. The loss of Norah Lange had destroyed his faith in the essential reality of the self—one man was, in principle, no different from any other man, because personal identity amounted to nothing more than a succession of discontinuous mental states in the endless process of time.

The temptation to commit suicide at this point must have become quite compelling, but even though he did not give in to total despair, the evidence points to a serious psychological breakdown. On September 15 he published a set of three short texts in *Crítica* under the collective title "Confessions," revealing fears of disintegration, madness, and death.[7] One text alludes to a desire to create an all-powerful tiger that results in the feeble image of a creature no bigger than a dog or as elusive as a bird; another relates the case of a mad girl who cannot bear the sight of mirrors because she can see only the reflection of Borges's face instead of her own; in a third he imagines his toenails growing relentlessly even after he has died, the only form of afterlife he can bring himself to believe in. By way of a final "confession," he reprinted the postscript to "The Duration of Hell," the essay he had published four months after Norah Lange had rejected him in February 1929 on her return from Norway, and in which he described his nightmare of waking up in a strange room bereft of a sense of self or place:

> I asked myself anxiously: *where am I?* and I realized I didn't know. I thought: *who am I?* and I couldn't say. I was filled with fear. I thought: this disconsolate wakefulness already is hell, this pointless wakefulness will be my eternity.[8]

In November 1934—the month in which Norah moved to an apartment close by the house of Oliverio Girondo—we find Borges in Uruguay as a guest of his cousin Esther Haedo and her husband, the novelist Enrique Amorim, at their summer villa in the hills above the riverside town of Salto. He sent his father a postcard on November 13 showing a picture of the Amorims' villa, and pointed out an effigy of a woman standing on the front lawn: "That phantom of a woman you can see . . . is the figurehead of a ship on a pedestal," a banal observation but one that resonates in the original Spanish with other allusions, for the term Borges uses is *mascarón de proa,* and *Proa* ("prow") was precisely the name of the two literary magazines he had edited in the 1920s.[9] If any woman could be said to have been the "figurehead" of *Proa* in those days it was, of course, Norah Lange. Evidently he could not get Norah out of his mind, and this may account for his listlessness while at Salto, for, in a postcard he wrote his mother on November 22, he reported that an essay on Nietzsche he was working on (its subject was infinite time and the Eternal Return) was proceeding "without inspiration but without interruptions," and that only the swimming pool "mitigates and domesticates the summer."[10]

He found a certain relief from this despondency in a visit he made to Amorim's *estancia* in the province of Tacuarembó near the border with Brazil. Driving along with Amorim in his friend's car, they suddenly came across a great multitude of horsemen. Borges cried out in amazement, "Good Lord! Three hundred gauchos!" but Amorim, who had grown up among cowboys on the *estancia,* scornfully replied, "Seeing three hundred gauchos out here is like seeing three hundred employees of Gath and Chaves [a department store] in Buenos Aires."[11] Still, for a *porteño* like Borges the plains of northern Uruguay were a revelation: "Everything I then witnessed—the stone fences, the longhorn cattle, the horses' silver trappings, the bearded gauchos, the hitching posts, the ostriches—was so primitive, and even barbarous, as to make it more a journey into the past than a journey through space."[12] It must have seemed that he was traveling back to a time when real gauchos roamed the pampas in the manner of the characters in *Martín Fierro* and rural life was as barbarous as Sarmiento had described it in his classic book, *Facundo.* And, as if to crown this sensation of having regressed to a time of barbarism, he happened to witness a murder.

The incident took place while they were visiting Rivera, a town separated by a single wide street from Santa Anna do Livramento, its counterpart in Brazil. These were lawless places, the cross-border haunts of smugglers and bandits. One morning Borges and Amorim happened to be sitting in a tavern next to a *capanga,* the bodyguard of some local bigwig, when a drunk came up to the *capanga's* table and began to pester him. The gunman lost patience with the drunk, drew his weapon, and shot him twice. Borges missed the actual killing because he had been too wrapped up in conversation to notice what was going on at the next table, and could only recall seeing the drunk approach the *capanga* and then hearing the shots. Yet what struck Borges was the nonchalance of the killer—the next morning they saw him again, sitting in the tavern having his customary drink.[13]

In retrospect Borges would realize that these wild borderlands had impressed him "far more than all the kingdoms of the world and the glory of them."[14] He had visited the Brazilian frontier at a time when the red-haired No-rah Lange still preyed on his mind, and the two experiences would become in-timately associated with each other. Even while he was still at Santa Anna do Livramento, he had the idea for a story based on the murder he had witnessed. It was published some years later as "The Dead Man" ("El muerto"), and its subject was the career of a city boy who becomes a gaucho and tries to usurp the power of the leader of a gang of smugglers.[15] His defiance of the bandit chieftain extends to sleeping with the man's red-haired mistress. In the end, however, the young man is shot dead by the chieftain's *capanga*.

"The Dead Man" is a story about a Nietzschean "will to power," as it were. It addresses Borges's long-standing desire to take up the dagger against the op-pressive authority of the ancestral sword of honor. This "will to power," more-over, is associated with sexual desire in the figure of the red-haired mistress, the prize of the youth's revolt against the chieftain. "The Dead Man" is signif-icant also because it projects the conflicts of Borges's inner world onto the canvas of Argentine history, for in this clear association of sexual desire with the lawlessness of the gauchos, he was creating a parallel between his inner conflict of sword and dagger and the quintessential Argentine conflict of "civ-ilization" and "barbarism." We see this analogy also in the symbolic value of the concubine's red hair, given that red was a color forbidden in the Borges household because of its association with the tyrant Rosas and the *federales*, the historic enemies of his family's *unitario* allegiance. By establishing this symbolic bridge between inner and outer realities, Borges was groping toward the connection between his ever-fragile sense of personal identity and his family's role in forging an Argentine national identity. Already a perception was taking shape that his reluctance to assert his will against Mother might stem from a fear of compromising his family's status as descendants of heroes who had won independence from Spain and had subsequently fought for civ-ilization against the barbarism of gauchos and caudillos.

Borges was at the very earliest stages of what would become a long and painful probing of his inner world through his writing. His visit to the bor-derlands of Uruguay and Brazil began to reveal the complexity of this interior reality, and in the story inspired by this visit, he had struck a rich seam, so rich, indeed, that it would become the source of other stories. In addition to "The Dead Man," he was to produce three stories set in or referring to these borderlands—"Tlön, Uqbar, Orbis Tertius," "The Other Death" ("La otra muerte"), and "The Gospel According to Mark" ("El Evangelico según Mar-cos").[16] (In this last story, as in "The Dead Man," the hero is punished for sleeping with a red-haired girl.) And in a number of other stories, he would explore themes cognate with those of "The Dead Man"—civilization and barbarism, rebellion, betrayal and punishment. He would (in due course) return to the idea of salvation by writing, but from 1934 he was to become increasingly absorbed in writing fiction as a means of self-exploration.

A few weeks after he got back from his holiday in Uruguay, Borges lost his job at *Crítica:* he and Petit de Murat were summarily informed by a new deputy editor that there were other plans for the paper and that the *Revista Multicolor* would be discontinued.[17] Editing the literary supplement had taken him out of himself at a time of great distress, so he was now thrown back on his own depleted resources, and he was still in a very bad way, tortured by insomnia and "atrocious nightmares."[18]

The summer months of January and February 1935 were spent as usual with his family at the Hotel Las Delicias in Adrogué. There he worked on an early draft of "The Dead Man" and on the preparation of a new book with the title *A Universal History of Infamy* (*Historia universal de la infamia*), a collection of fictionalized biographies and magic fables he had published in *Crítica.*[19] He would later describe himself as having been "exceedingly unhappy" ("*asaz desdichado*") at this time.[20] No doubt this unhappiness was due to his inability to get over Norah Lange, but it was aggravated by the long illness of Fanny Haslam, his English grandmother, who was now eighty-three and may have become unwell in the latter part of 1934. As Fanny's illness drew to its end, she summoned the family to her bedside and told them, "I am only an old woman dying very, very slowly. There is nothing remarkable or interesting about this."[21] Even so, they could not help but be upset: she had been their next-door neighbor in Palermo before they went to Europe in 1914 and had lived with them under the same roof ever since she later joined the family in Geneva.

Fanny's death on June 20, 1935, must have been a grievous loss to Georgie, who was so attached to his dear English Gran. But the loss was perhaps far worse for her son Jorge Guillermo, for she was the only parent he had ever known. At the time of his mother's death, Dr. Borges was a blind, ailing, self-absorbed figure, nursed with great constancy and devotion by his wife, Leonor Acevedo. He appears to have faded into the background of family life since the Borgeses decided to settle in Buenos Aires in 1922 instead of returning to Spain as originally planned, and even though an operation had partially restored his sight in the mid-1920s, it had begun to deteriorate once more after a few years and had all but gone by 1935. His health had been further weakened by heart trouble, very likely associated with an aneurysm that began to affect him at around this time.

The condition of his father induced Georgie to perceive a strange bond between them, a bond whose complexity he would strive to understand in the years following the death of Fanny Haslam. Something of the nature of this bond between father and son can be gleaned from Borges's presentation of the character of Herbert Ashe in "Tlön, Uqbar, Orbis Tertius." Ashe is said to have established with Borges's father "one of those English friendships which begin by excluding any confidences and very soon omit conversation altogether"; and Borges himself recalls a conversation about Brazil he once had with Ashe in which they spoke of "cattle-ranching, of *capangas,* of the Brazilian etymology of the word *gaucho.*"[22] The curious figure of Herbert Ashe—a man said to have suffered from "unreality"—thus obliquely connects father and son in a triadic relationship loosely associated with Borges's trip to the borderlands of Uruguay and Brazil. There Borges had encountered a primitive vitality epitomized in the bloody murder of a man by a *capanga,* but, on his return to Buenos Aires, he had continued to experience a progressive disconnection from the world—the loss of his job at *Crítica,* the loss of Fanny Haslam—and he succumbed to a fear of lapsing into a solipsism that would mirror the abstraction of the stricken Dr. Borges, a reflection of the father in the son that was somehow personified in the mysterious figure of the ghostly Ashe.

With Norah Lange gone, Borges had few defenses left against the threat of such "unreality." He clung desperately to the memory of his vanished sweetheart, as if memory itself might rescue him from that "nothingness of personality" he so dreaded. When *A Universal History of Infamy* was published in July 1935, only a few weeks after Fanny Haslam's death, it carried a dedication in English to a mysterious woman:

> I inscribe this book to I. J.: English, innumerable and an Angel. Also: I offer her that kernel of myself that I have saved, somehow—the central heart that deals not in words, traffics not with dreams and is untouched by time, by joy, by adversities.[23]

No one has identified the object of this impassioned dedication, but, given the circumstances, I have no doubt that she was Norah Lange. The initials I. J. remain something of a mystery, but they may stand for "Ingrid Julia." The heroine of Norah Lange's novel, *45 días y 30 marineros,* is called Ingrid, and in one of the articles by "José Tuntar" about the decadence of ancient Rome, which Borges published at a time when Norah was frequenting parties and so-called orgies with Neruda and Girondo, he referred to the Emperor Augustus's lascivious daughter and his equally dissolute granddaughter, both of whom were called Julia.[24] Additionally, in his story "The Secret Miracle" ("El milagro secreto," collected in *The Aleph*), the protagonist is writing a play about the rivalry between two men for the love of a girl called Julia. Both Ingrid and Julia, therefore, were names that Borges would have associated with his loss of Norah Lange.

The threefold characterization of the dedicatee as "English, innumerable and an Angel" points to Norah Lange and her association with the Aleph. She was "English" in the context of Borges's romantic superstition about their common Nordic ancestry; "innumerable" because she represented "the Aleph," the number that encompassed all other numbers; and an "Angel" because she was generally regarded as such by the young poets of the Buenos Aires avant-garde and because Borges had once believed that her love would lead him to experience the mystical oneness of all things.[25] Finally, the rest of the dedication, with its offer of "the kernel of myself" and the "central heart," is a direct quotation from the poem he had written in English in 1934, when he believed there was one final chance to wrest Norah back from Girondo.[26]

Borges was haunted by the memories of the happiness he had known when he thought Norah might love him. Sometime in 1935 he set to work on an essay called "A History of Eternity" ("Historia de le eternidad"), a reflection on the perennial human yearning to believe in a reality that might stand above and beyond the flow of time.[27] The notion of eternity, he asserted, was a human invention that appeared under various guises in different periods of history, but he reduced this "history of eternity" to three instances—the Platonic theory of forms, the Christian dogma of the Trinity, and, finally, to what he called his "personal history of eternity," which was contained in his text "Feeling in Death" ("Sentirse en muerte"), first published in 1928, and which he now reprinted verbatim with a brief additional commentary. "Feeling in Death" was one of the first texts he had written in response to Norah Lange's falling in love with Girondo in November 1926, and it described an epiphany he experienced one night when he came upon a humble street and was suddenly struck by the impression that it stood outside of time. At moments of great intensity, Borges now observed, the particular identity of things may appear to subsist beyond time, for even though the existence of time cannot be denied by the intellect, it can be refuted by the emotions.

The emotion Borges identified as the source of our strange yearning for "eternity" was nostalgia, and the example he gave to support this assertion could scarcely have been more eloquent about the distressing situation in which he found himself at the time of writing in 1935:

A rueful and abandoned man who recalls happy possibilities sees them *sub specie aeternitatis,* quite forgetting that to have realized any one of those possibilities would have excluded or put off the others. In a state of passion, our memory inclines to the intemporal. We blend various happy memories of the past into a single image; the sunsets of diverse shades of red which I look at every evening will become a single sunset in my memory.[28]

Eternity, he concluded, was the "style of desire," and the object of desire he had in mind was surely Norah Lange, for in the 1920s the sunset had been widely recognized as the emblematic image of Norah's poetry as well as of his own, and he had often used the image of the sunset to allude to Norah's flaming red hair.

Indeed, he was to remind Norah of this conceit in the copy of *A Universal History of Infamy* that he must have presented to her at precisely the time he was writing his essay on eternity. That book, as we have seen, already carried an emotional dedication to the cryptic I. J., but in the copy he gave Norah herself—Norah, who was now the consort of Girondo—he wrote a further dedication in his own hand, in which he permitted himself no emotion other than a guarded, hopeless nostalgia: "To Norah Lange, with the memory of so many sunsets, so much music, so much glowing hair, Georgie."[29]

I reckon that toward the end of 1935 or early in 1936, Borges began a new experiment to articulate in the form of a novel his "personal theory of eternity" as the "style of desire" rooted in nostalgia. A brief account of this experiment has come down to us in "An Examination of the Works of Herbert Quain" ("Examen de la obra de Herbert Quain").[30] The novel is said to have been published in 1936 with the title *April March*, which hints at an autobiographical aspect, reversing as it does the months of March and April 1934, when Borges wrote his final plea to Norah Lange and she conclusively rejected him.

The structure of *April March*, we learn, is "regressive and ramifying": the first of its thirteen chapters relates "an ambiguous dialogue between two strangers on a railway platform," the second the events of the previous day, the third recounts the events of another version of the previous day, and the fourth the events of yet another version of the same day; each of these three versions of the same day branches backward into three further alternate versions of earlier days to make up nine different narratives within the single work. The novel is a representation of a time labyrinth containing the various possible developments that existed at different moments in the past and had been excluded by the linear flow of time. And as with everything Borges wrote, there was an autobiographical subtext to *April March*, a grieving heart beating in the depths of the narrative, as it were, for this was a novel conceived by "a rueful and abandoned man" imagining all the possibilities of happiness that might once have existed had Norah Lange reciprocated his love, a novel born of nostalgia, which played with the notion that time might be reversible after all, or that it might branch out in multiple dimensions, allowing him to recover in one what might have been lost in another. But it was impossible to render this "eternity" of nostalgia in narrative form: the ramifying structure of *April March* would have generated infinite stories, branching to infinity, though Herbert Quain's "symmetrical fury," we are told, managed to reduce them to a mere nine.

Toward the end of 1935, Borges decided to put together a number of prose texts for publication in a new book with the title *A History of Eternity*. This was a very mixed bag indeed—in addition to the title essay, he included the essay on infinite time and the Eternal Return that he had partly written in Salto, a long three-part review of the translations of the *Thousand and One Nights*, the study of the Norse kennings that he had dedicated to Norah Lange and, strangest of all, two "Notes," one of which purported to be a review of a novel published in Bombay called *The Approach to Al-Mu'tasim*. Borges briefly outlined the plot and explained the basic difference between the 1932 and 1934 versions of the novel. However, the legend of the Simurgh—that symbol of pantheist enlightenment, that avatar of the Aleph—was reduced to the status of a mere footnote.[31]

What readership could Borges have had in mind for this miscellany of outlandish texts? Bereft of a key to their autobiographical context, no one could have grasped the vivid significance these pieces actually had for their author. Borges had withdrawn so far into his private world that he had effectively severed all communication with his readers. *A History of Eternity* was to mark the nadir of his fortunes as a writer. It was published on April 29, 1936, and by the end of the year, it had sold thirty-seven copies.

CHAPTER 15

Isolation
(1936–1937)

OF THE THIRTY-SEVEN READERS who purchased a copy of *A History of Eternity*, one was an aspiring writer called Adolfo Bioy Casares. Such was this young man's appetite for literary curiosities that he was taken in by Borges's hoax review of *The Approach to Al-Mu'tasim* and ordered the nonexistent novel from a bookseller in London. In due course Bioy Casares would become one of Borges's closest and most loyal companions, as well as the joint author with him of several collections of stories and a number of film scripts.

They first met early in 1932 at a luncheon party given by Victoria Ocampo in honor of some visiting French writer.[1] Despite a considerable difference in age—Bioy was only eighteen years old at the time and Borges thirty-two— they hit it off straightaway and sat on their own in a corner deep in conversation about writers they liked and those they detested. At one point Borges, clumsy as ever, knocked over a table lamp, attracting the attention of their hostess, Victoria, who glided over toward them and hissed, "Don't be such shits, come on over and talk to my guests."[2] They took no notice of her, however, and decided to leave instead, continuing their discussions in the car as Bioy drove his new friend home.

Despite their instant rapport, the friendship took several years to develop. The two men came from quite different backgrounds: Borges was a product of the urban middle class, whereas Bioy Casares's family was a pillar of the cattle-ranching oligarchy (his father was a cabinet minister in the conservative government at the time he first got to know Borges). Borges, in any case, was still very much caught up in his troubles over Norah Lange when they first met, and Bioy, who was a student of law at the University of Buenos Aires, became bored with his studies shortly afterward and went to live at Rincón Viejo, the family *estancia* in the province of Buenos Aires. He proposed to restore the estate, which had been rented out for the past twenty years and had suffered considerable neglect at the hands of the tenant. The young Bioy embarked on a tough apprenticeship as a countryman—buying and selling cattle, planting trees, renewing the wire fencing, and restoring the ranch buildings, all the while financing these activities by speculating in land sales. It was a time-consuming business, but he managed all the same to combine it with extensive reading and writing, since his real interest lay in pursuing his career as a writer.

The close friendship of Borges and Bioy Casares was cemented in the course of a week they spent together at Bioy's *estancia* sometime in the winter of 1935. Adolfito, as Bioy was known to family and friends, had been commissioned by an uncle to write a publicity brochure for a new brand of yogurt produced by the family firm, La Martona, one of the largest dairy concerns in Argentina. He thought it would be amusing to write the brochure with Borges, so he invited his friend to stay at Rincón Viejo. Borges was none too fond of the rural life, but when he arrived at the ranch, he chose to affect the airs of a countryman, even claiming he could ride, though when it came to mounting a horse, as Bioy recalled, he could not stop himself sliding off the other side.[3]

Outdoor pursuits were soon abandoned, however, and even the writing of the yogurt brochure took second place to what they really enjoyed, which was talking about books. Since they were both such aficionados of detective stories, Borges suggested they try their hand at writing one, and he even offered the outline of a plot concerning the headmaster of a boys' school, a huge Dutchman called Dr. Pretorius, who was given to killing his pupils "by hedonistic means" such as compulsory games and playing music at all hours.[4] The story of Dr. Pretorius was put aside after a few pages, but Bioy would claim that this first stab at writing together was the point of departure for all the spoofs that he and Borges would subsequently produce over many years under the common noms de plume of H. Bustos Domecq and B. Suárez Lynch.[5]

Bioy claimed to have been "a prolific writer of dreadful books."[6] He had made a precocious start at the age of fifteen, when his father paid for the publication of a collection of his stories; the next three years were spent struggling unsuccessfully to write a vast novel about a Spanish immigrant on the pampas; in 1933 he found a publisher for a book called *Diecisiete disparos contra el futuro* (*Seventeen Shots Against the Future*), which was meant as "a joke about the consequences to the author's reputation of the seventeen stories he was offering"; the following year there appeared a "copious volume of stories" called *Caos*, "abounding in transcriptions or paraphrases of dreams" that garnered invariably bad reviews; and in 1935 he published a novel influenced by Joyce, Apollinaire, and Cocteau among others, which he later characterized as "incomprehensible, tedious and willfully literary."[7] That same year he produced *La Estatua Casera* (*The Domestic Statue*), a collection of fantastic tales, poems, and reflections, which Borges was to review for *Sur* in March 1936. Borges pointed out that fantasy must be rooted in the author's experience: "I suspect that a general examination of the literature of fantasy would reveal very little of the fantastical about it"; indeed, what he found admirable about Bioy's book were the author's "occasional autobiographical confessions," and its "veracity, its music, its emotion, its meticulous despair."[8]

These observations may well have arisen from the discussions they had during the week Borges stayed at Bioy's ranch some months earlier. Bioy would recall one in particular that caused him to change his way of reading and writing. He never gave an account of that discussion other than to report his surprise at discovering that Borges argued in favor of a deliberate, conscious art: "He took the side of Horace and the professors against my heroes, the dazzling poets and painters of the avant-garde."[9] One may surmise that Borges talked about the ideas he had expounded several years earlier in his two seminal essays, "The Postulation of Reality" and "The Art of Narrative and Magic"—fiction was not a mirror of the world but an *orbe autónomo,* a play of symbols following rules that were more akin to the laws of magic than to the presumed laws of what was in any case an unknowable reality; writing was rooted in the author's experience, but this primary experience should not be expressed directly to the reader; expressive reticence was to be matched by a comparable stylistic restraint so as to counter what Borges had come to regard as a tendency to prolixity in the Spanish language. The effect of this discussion was that "the next day, perhaps that same night," Bioy "changed sides," and some time afterward he would begin to experiment with the new Borgesian principles in his own writing.[10]

In 1937 Bioy started work on a new novel, whose basic idea occurred to him after seeing his reflection repeated in the three panels of a Venetian mirror in his mother's dressing room. He thought of a machine capable of producing a perfect holographic image of a person. At first he considered writing "a hoax essay in the manner of Borges and commenting on the invention of that machine," but later "the novelistic possibilities of my idea brought a change of plan."[11] He would work on this project for the next three years, in the course of which he was to undergo "a complete metamorphosis" as a writer.[12] The result was *La invención de Morel* (*The Invention of Morel*), the chronicle of a castaway who comes across a group of people on a desert island and eventually discovers that they are holographic images projected by a machine invented by the eponymous Morel. This was the novel that made Bioy's reputation and would become a classic of Latin American literature.

Borges may have acted as a catalyst for Bioy's creative imagination, but what about his own writing in this period? He appears to have abandoned narrative at around this time and turned to drama. Bioy remembered him writing a play, although Borges did not discuss details of the plot with his friend.[13] Years later, however, Borges would refer to this play in outline: "I had thought out the idea of a drama in two acts, and in the first act you would have something very noble and rather pompous, and then in the second act you would find that the real thing was rather tawdry."[14] This description fits *The Secret Mirror,* a two-act play described in "An Examination of the Works of Herbert Quain," where in the first act "the characters are of vast fortune and ancient lineage; their feelings noble, though vehement," but in the second "everything is vaguely horrible, everything is put off or frustrated."[15]

The Secret Mirror opens in the country house of General Thrale, whose daughter, Ulrica, is adored by the playwright Wilfred Quarles, upon whom she has bestowed the odd distracted kiss. The first act consists of "a nightingale and a night," which is followed by "a secret duel on a terrace" after Ulrica jilts Quarles and announces her engagement to the Duke of Rutland.[16] The same characters appear under different names in the second act. Quarles has turned into the failed writer John William Quigley, who has never set eyes on Miss Thrale; instead he morbidly collects photographs of her that he finds in the *Tatler* or the *Sketch.* It turns out that the first act is entirely an invention of Quigley's and that General Thrale's country house is nothing other than the boardinghouse he lives in, which he has transfigured and magnified in his imagination.

In *The Secret Mirror,* we find a reflection of Borges's relations with Norah Lange and Oliverio Girondo. Ulrica, described as "haughty" and an "amazon," brings to mind Norah Lange, whose "haughtiness" Borges repeatedly praised; her father, General Thrale, recalls Norah's father, Gunnar Lange, who had been commander of the Honduran artillery in a war against El Salvador; the Duke of Rutland, Quarles's rival for the hand of the fair Ulrica, is reminiscent of Girondo in that he is rich, aristocratic, and, as the name Rutland suggests, a philanderer. And the wretched Quarles-Quigley is, patently, a picture of the lovelorn Borges himself.

In the drastic change that occurs between acts 1 and 2, Borges must have sought to convey the reversal he suffered when he lost Norah to Girondo, a reversal so devastating that it called into question the reality of his whole experience of love. He was clearly in thrall to the memory of Norah Lange, but his creative imagination was strangely blocked—he had lost his lyrical voice after Norah rejected him on her return from Norway in 1929, and since then he had remained incapable of exorcising this trauma by translating it into a satisfactory literary form.

To compound these personal and literary problems, the mid-1930s would rob Borges of any remaining hopes that his vision of a new Argentina—democratic, liberal, and hospitable to immigrants and foreigners—might be revived. Despite his tremendous disappointment at the overthrow in 1930 of his hero, President Irigoyen, he had continued to be identified with the militant, nationalist-inclined *irigoyenista* wing of the party, and he broadly sympathized with the Radical Party's often violent agitation against the Concordancia, the ruling coalition of General Justo. So much so, indeed, that in 1934 he agreed to write a preface for a gauchesque poem by Arturo Jauretche describing an armed rebellion by Radical militants who, in December 1933, succeeded in taking, and briefly holding, the town of El Paso de los Libres in the province of Corrientes. The poem was written while Jauretche was serving a prison sentence for his part in the rebellion, and in his prologue Borges praised the disinterested courage of Jauretche and his comrades, especially since the failure of the "patriotic uprising" was a foregone conclusion, given that the railway, the airplane, the telegraph, and the machine gun had virtually guaranteed the swift "vindication of Order."[17]

Borges's enthusiasm for *irigoyenismo* would shortly begin to wane, however. The following year, on June 29, 1935, Arturo Jauretche, together with Raúl Scalabrini Ortiz, who had been a member of Borges's Committee of Young Intellectuals for Irigoyen; the lyricist Homero Manzi, author of some of the most famous tangos of the period; and several other well-known writers, founded a new *irigoyenista* pressure group called FORJA (Fuerza de Orientación Radical de la Joven Argentina) whose motto was "We belong to a colonial Argentina; we want a free Argentina." Borges was invited to join FORJA, but he declined to be associated with it for reasons that remain unknown but must surely have been connected with the fact that the aim of FORJA was to put pressure on the leadership of the Radical Party to adopt policies that might deliver Argentina from its economic dependence on Britain.[18] The FORJA intellectuals had in effect adopted the historical revisionism of the right-wing Irazusta brothers, and in this ideological convergence of both right and left on the question of economic nationalism, and the concomitant hostility toward Britain, Borges may have seen the danger of a drift toward a fascist-style state in Argentina.

The key to the evolution of Borges's political thinking in the 1930s was his hatred of fascism and Nazism. His great fear was that the *nacionalistas,* in their zeal to pry Argentina from her economic dependence on Britain, might end up copying Mussolini, if not Hitler. As Europe appeared to slide inexorably toward war, he fell back for a while on the *americanismo* of his youth. In February 1936, as part of the celebrations to mark the four-hundredth anniversary of the foundation of Buenos Aires by Don Pedro de Mendoza, Borges made a radio broadcast in which he reviewed the history of the Argentine republic and the critical role Buenos Aires had played in that history.[19] He conceded that the people of Buenos Aires had a sentimental attachment to the figure of the gaucho, regarding him as a symbol of the country's past, despite the fact that the gaucho had been the historic enemy of the great city. But the gaucho, in his view, was a figure condemned to remain in the past; he was a nostalgic symbol, for the destiny of the *porteños* was more complex: the city they inhabited was "growing like a tree, or like a familiar face in a nightmare." He urged his fellow *porteños* to accept and embrace the future with hope in their hearts, and appended verbatim a passage from his 1928 address to young criollo nationalists:

> In this house which is America, my friends, men from various nations of the world have conspired together in order to disappear in a new man, who is not yet embodied in any one of us and whom we shall already call an "Argentine" so as to begin to raise our hopes. This is a confederacy without precedent: a generous adventure by men of different bloodlines whose aim is not to persevere in their lineages but to forget those lineages in the end; these are bloodlines that seek the night. The criollo is one of the confederates. The criollo, who was responsible for creating the nation as such, has now chosen to be one among many."[20]

He was reaffirming the forward-looking, democratic *criollismo* of his youth against the xenophobic nationalism fostered by the likes of Lugones, for whom the gaucho remained the preeminent symbol of the national identity, a brand of nationalism that had been recently taken up by the Irazusta brothers and now even by the Radical intellectuals of the FORJA group. Again, in April 1936, replying to a questionnaire by the magazine *Nosotros*, Borges urged his compatriots to trust in the material and spiritual capacity of the republics of the New World "to survive and develop their culture in the event of a European war"; he was convinced that the culture of the Americas was not inferior to Europe's—"for more than a century and a half French lyric poetry has been living off Whitman and Edgar Allan Poe."[21]

Nevertheless, this *americanista* idealism soon proved to be ineffectual, for not long after his reply to *Nosotros*, the ideological conflicts that were threatening to tear Europe apart flared up in Spain with General Franco's uprising against the Spanish republic in July. The Argentine intelligentsia divided bitterly over the Spanish Civil War, given the close kinship of the *nacionalistas* with the Spanish Falange and the Catholic integralists. The warring ideologies of Europe erupted again at an International Congress of the PEN Club held in Buenos Aires from September 5 to 15, whose proceedings were marred by political wrangles provoked largely by the aggressive interventions of fascist writers. Marinetti, notably, engaged in an angry row with the French novelist Jules Romains and with several Jewish writers and Italian communists. He also attacked Victoria Ocampo, "the richest and most beautiful woman in

Buenos Aires," as he called her, for describing herself as a "Common Reader," an expression she attributed, of course, to Virginia Woolf and Dr. Johnson, but which the volatile Italian chose to see as advocating the vulgarization of literature, and which led to his berating her for "snobbish bolshevism."[22]

In 1936 Borges's political outlook became distinctly bleaker, given the increasing strength of right-wing *nacionalismo* and its affinities with fascism. There is no record of his having attended the PEN Club congress, though he was certainly aware of the more scandalous clashes that had taken place (he would later make reference in a review for the popular weekly magazine *El Hogar* to Marinetti's altercation with Jules Romains).[23] And if he was absent, it was because he had already defined his own position with regard to the great ideological issues of the day. This position had been adumbrated in his reply to the *Nosotros* questionnaire in April, in which he asserted that the great achievements of European civilization would not be diminished in the event of a war in Europe. Culture, in other words, transcended politics, and the autonomy of culture—the right of the artist to create as and what he pleased without fear of dictation by ideologues of any party or regime—would become Borges's overriding political principle.

Borges had once again found a cause, and, like the other causes he had espoused in the past, there was more than a touch of perversity about it—he sought to advance the cause of anti-ideology at a time when ideological commitment had become all the rage in Argentina as in Europe. In October 1936 he would take a part-time job at *El Hogar* editing a fortnightly literary section called "Foreign Books and Authors," a title that in itself spoke of his commitment to the kind of "cosmopolitan" view of literature that was so frowned upon by Argentine nationalists of right and left. He would fill his book page with reviews, literary news, and capsule biographies of contemporary writers, a format that suited his eclectic tastes, embracing books in several languages and different genres, both high and low, from history, literary criticism, and works by writers like Joyce, Yeats, T. S. Eliot, or Evelyn Waugh, to thrillers and science fiction.

A more telling example of his anti-ideological stance was his attempt to found a literary magazine with Bioy Casares dedicated to the principle of creative freedom and cultural pluralism. They decided to call it *Destiempo,* an odd neologism that roughly translates as "out of time" or "untime," a title meant to indicate, in Bioy's words, "our wish to disassociate ourselves from the superstitions of the age."[24] By this he meant the belief that writing should be pressed into the service of nationalism or socialism or some such ideology: "We objected in particular to the tendency of some critics to overlook the intrinsic merits of works and dwell instead on aspects that were folkloric, telluric or connected with literary history or with sociological concerns and statistics."[25] *Destiempo* was ready for printing in the very month of the PEN Club meeting, and it was perhaps a mischievous satisfaction in swimming against the tide that prompted Borges to suggest to Bioy, as they left the printing works, that they mark the historic occasion of its birth by having their photograph taken at a cheap studio nearby.[26]

Certainly there could have been no greater contrast between the sound and fury of the PEN Club congress and the little magazine the two friends had just put to bed. *Destiempo* was an extremely modest publication, running to only six pages. Its first number, which appeared in October, had contributions from established writers like Alfonso Reyes and Pedro Henríquez Ureña, and from some of Borges's friends from the 1920s avant-garde, like Carlos Mastronardi, Horacio Rega Molina, and Xul Solar. But there were new names, too, like Manuel Peyrou, a journalist at *La Prensa* who wrote detective stories, and Silvina Ocampo, the sister of Victoria, who had trained as a painter but had turned her hand to poetry and fiction. Borges's contributions were four of the harrowing "Confessions" that he had published in *Crítica* in 1934, doubtless a sign of his continuing emotional turmoil. Bioy published a couple of magic fables and, with Borges, edited a section called "Museo" ("Museum"), which was a miscellany of literary quotations and commonplaces, an idea that Borges would resurrect a decade later when he came to edit *Los Anales de Buenos Aires.*

The second issue of *Destiempo* came out in November, and even though it carried no contribution from Borges himself, it reflected his tastes to the point of self-indulgence—the whole of the front page was devoted to a rather turgid piece on metaphysics by Macedonio Fernández; there was also an essay by the painter Xul Solar written in *neocriollo,* a language of his own invention that was intelligible mainly to himself; and a few poems by several lesser lights of the 1920s avant-garde. Bioy contributed a short story, as did Silvina Ocampo. Of some significance, too, was a fable by Franz Kafka, one of the first translations of a writer who was as yet unknown in the Spanish-speaking world, but one whom Borges had recently discovered and with whom, as we shall see, he would shortly feel a peculiar empathy.

However, the third issue of *Destiempo,* planned for December, failed to appear. Bioy, its financial mainstay, had been summoned urgently to his *estancia* to deal with an outbreak of disease that threatened to wipe out his flocks of sheep. This led to the indefinite suspension of the magazine when Bioy was further detained at the ranch in order to fight a proposal to build a road that would cut through the middle of his estates.[27] It would take Bioy a whole year to sort out the problems at his *estancia.*

Toward the end of 1937, Borges and Bioy made another attempt to launch *Destiempo.* In December a third issue appeared in the same format as the previous two, which included a poem by Bioy, a story by Silvina Ocampo, two "Inscriptions" by Borges, and an entire page of reflections on art and the Argentines by Macedonio Fernández. The rebirth of *Destiempo* was accompanied by an ambitious project to create a publishing house, a venture that represented an even more determined attempt by Borges and Bioy to exert influence in the Argentine literary world. The idea came originally from Ulyses Petit de Murat, who had been looking for a publisher for his latest book of poems when it occurred to him that the book might appear under a new imprint associated with *Destiempo*. The third issue of the magazine carried an advertisement for the "Editorial Destiempo," announcing the publication of Petit de Murat's book in December 1937 and five more titles planned for the year 1938: Alfonso Reyes on Mallarmé (February), new poems by Carlos Mastronardi (April), a book entitled *Buenos Aires* by Ezequiel Martínez Estrada (June), an *Anthology of Unreal Stories* (August), and *Fragments* by Novalis, translated with notes by Borges (October). On December 12, Bioy wrote to Macedonio Fernández asking him if he would contribute one of his books to the series and explaining that if the financial affairs of the Editorial Destiempo could be sorted out, he hoped to publish a collection of fantasy stories by Santiago Dabove, a book of detective stories by Manuel Peyrou, and some (unspecified) works in translation. These financial difficulties, however, were never resolved, and the Editorial Destiempo failed to prosper beyond the publication of Petit de Murat's book. The magazine, too, was forced to close after its third issue, December 1937, since it met with almost total indifference from the public and most of the print run had to be given away for lack of demand.[28]

The failure of *Destiempo* was a setback to Borges's efforts to regain his standing in the literary world. Where once he could command the attention of an entire generation of writers, now he could barely hold together a dwindling group of trusted friends. Worse still, while his capacity to exert influence diminished, the *nacionalistas* were becoming ever more aggressive in their antiliberal reinterpretation of history. In 1936 Julio Irazusta published a polemical essay on Rosas in the centenary of his assumption of power, which resurrected the old Argentine conflict between civilization and barbarism by rehabilitating the tyrant as a heroic defender of traditional criollo values against alien influences from Britain and liberal Europe. Borges had himself praised Rosas in his *criollista* days but, even in the 1920s, his appreciation of Rosas had been quite different from that of the right-wing *nacionalistas*—he had described Rosas as representing a very primitive and limited manifestation of criollo values, and his declared hope had been to elaborate a more fully realized criollo culture that, far from being nostalgic or xenophobic, would be conversant "with the world and the self, with God and with death."[29]

Still, the memory of Borges's praise of Rosas lingered among those former comrades of his who had since become *nacionalistas.* In 1938 he was approached by the writer Ernesto Palacio and invited to become an associate of the newly founded Instituto Juan Manuel de Rosas, a center for research into the history and politics of Argentina. But Borges would have nothing to do with the revisionist historiography represented by the Rosas Institute, which he saw as having purely ideological ends. There was little point in carrying out any research, he told Palacio, because the revisionists already knew that they would come to the conclusion that the liberal *unitarios* had been wrong and that Rosas was a patriot and a great man.[30]

Borges was alive to the dangers inherent in the revisionist project to establish the criollos as the true representatives of the nation. It smacked too much of the Nazi theory of Aryan superiority, and as Borges knew all too well, having himself been the object of the *nacionalistas'* anti-Semitism a few years earlier, both resulted in racism. In May 1937 he was to review in *Sur* a Nazi textbook designed to teach the children of the Third Reich to hate Jews.[31] This "pedagogy of hate" was, in his view, worse than the vilest pornography, and it represented a corruption of the German culture he otherwise so admired. He would return to this theme when he reviewed a history of German literature undertaken by a Nazi scholar who had contrived to omit the names of any Jewish or communist writers but seen fit to praise the speeches of Adolf Hitler and a long novel by Goebbels.[32] Borges lamented the Nazis' folly in sacrificing Germany's culture, its past and its probity, to a rancorous barbarism. It was this danger that the Argentine *nacionalistas* overlooked at their peril, and which vindicated his own defense of cultural freedom.

Nevertheless, he was too isolated to do much to counter the rising tide of ideology. Occasionally he would write a politically inclined review in his "Foreign Books and Authors" section for *El Hogar,* containing some criticism of the Nazis or even the totalitarianism of the Marxist left. On December 2, 1938, for instance, he reviewed in *El Hogar* a manifesto by André Breton and Diego Rivera denouncing the totalitarian regime in the USSR and calling for total freedom in art; he sympathized with this position in principle but criticized the authors for declaring that "the supreme task of contemporary art was to prepare for the revolution" and mocked their appeal for the foundation of an "International Federation of Independent Revolutionary Art" (IFIRA): "What a pitiful independent art they have in mind, subject to the pedantry of committees and to five capital letters."[33]

Borges would not countenance an art tied down by strings of Trotskyite committees any more than he would accept the proposition that to be a good Argentine one had to be confined to themes deemed to be authentically Argentine. His commitment to creative freedom drew on the very source that had made him a writer, for if he had taken up the pen as a boy, it was to rebel against the sword of honor of his ancestors. This was the true legacy of his father: an intellectual anarchism that drove him to assert the uniqueness of the self against any force that threatened to constrain or negate it. It was this will to freedom that made Borges so combative and polemical throughout his career—and so ambitious, for there was nothing he liked better, with the exception of writing and reading, than to be the leader of a literary faction involved in some embattled cause or other. But in the late 1930s he was an isolated, somewhat diminished figure, respected by many, admired even by a few, but a man generally regarded as having betrayed the high promise of his youth. His fate appeared to have been sealed by the dismal failure of *A History of Eternity;* and what a galling fate this was, too, for he was still the cleverest writer in Buenos Aires, but he had been reduced by failure to a waspish Lucifer, celebrated in the cafés for his acerbic wit yet feared in equal measure for his terrible put-downs.

The favorite object of his venom was, of course, Oliverio Girondo. They were often to be seen at the Jockey Club, a *confitería* on the corner of the calles Florida and Viamonte, sitting at different tables with their respective groups of friends. Girondo had by now set himself up as the mentor of a group of young surrealists who revered him as the embodiment of the iconoclastic spirit of the early avant-garde. Not that he needed much encouragement, for he was as keen as ever to scandalize the bourgeois and did his best to keep alive the memory of *Martín Fierro*—when he bought himself a sailing boat in 1936, he named it after the magazine, and on significant anniversaries of *Martín Fierro*'s founding he would host dinners for his old *martinfierrista* friends as well as for the many younger writers who formed his extensive circle of admirers.

The fact that Girondo seemed incapable of putting the 1920s behind him caused Borges no end of irritation. On February 26, 1937, he wrote an article in *El Hogar* arguing that there had been nothing revolutionary about the experiments of the Argentine avant-garde, since it had all been done before by Leopoldo Lugones.[34] But Girondo, tireless *vanguardista* that he was, would continue to take young poets under his wing, and even though he was himself going through a fallow period in the 1930s, his contact with new writers, and especially the surrealists, would rekindle the creative spark in him: in the 1940s he would publish several books of poetry, producing his masterpiece, *En la masmédula* (*In the Deepest Marrow*) in 1954, a book that remains a landmark in literary history as one of the most extreme and revolutionary experiments with poetic language ever undertaken by an Argentine poet.

Nothing would change Borges's opinion of Girondo's talents, however. He once dismissed him as "the Peter Pan of Argentine letters," a taunt that infuriated Girondo, who vowed to his friends that he would never forgive Borges that jibe.[35] In Borges's view Girondo's highly lauded experiments had not got him much further than the *grueguerías* of Gómez de la Serna; and he would tell an interviewer years later that Girondo was a "willfully extravagant man," "a labored imitator of Gómez de la Serna"; he had never liked anything Girondo had written, and he quoted a line of Girondo's on Venice—"Under the bridges, the gondoliers fornicate with the night," which he found "awful," "horrible": "If one admired verses like those, it would be hard to know what not to admire."[36] Every year Borges and his friends would take a vote on who was the stupidest writer in Argentina, and Borges's vote would always go to Oliverio Girondo.

At the bottom of this unyielding animosity lay, of course, the memory of Norah Lange. Borges thought Girondo had never truly appreciated Norah, and, according to Bioy, he regarded his rival as an "uncultivated brute" who had made his beloved Norah "harsh" and "insensitive."[37] Borges, after all, had nurtured Norah's poetic sensibility when she was still a very young girl and had encouraged her to publish her first books, so he must have regarded it as significant that she stopped writing poetry since taking up with Girondo. Instead, with Oliverio's encouragement, Norah had made something of a reputation for herself as an after-dinner speaker, though of the most unconventional kind: she would get up on a chair—when it was not the table itself—and deliver great, ranting orations, full of complicated conceits and rather labored humor.[38] And, thanks to Girondo's wealth and influence, she had become the reigning queen of literary bohemia, the cynosure of the fast set. At the parties the couple hosted at the house on calle Suipacha, Norah loved to do her star turn—halfway through the jollification, she would steal upstairs to her boudoir, change into a dazzling gown, and then make an appearance at the top of the staircase, her *bandoneón* (an Argentine accordion) at the ready, and with a toss of those famous red locks of hers, she would descend in all her majesty, singing a tango at the top of her voice.[39]

Borges, needless to say, never set foot in the house on calle Suipacha, nor did Bioy Casares, despite the fact that Girondo's parties drew the cream of the literary world. Bioy would explain that he refrained from doing so "out of loyalty to Borges," for even though his friend rarely spoke to him about Girondo, there was clearly a deep hurt there, a wound that had failed to heal.[40] But unforgiving as Borges was about Girondo, he would always have a tender word for Norah Lange. When she published *Cuadernos de infancia* (*Childhood Notebooks*) in 1937, a memoir of her growing up in Mendoza, he felt it was "a very beautiful book," although Girondo, he thought, "took that, too, as some sort of joke."[41] In the early 1940s, Norah began to probe her inner world in novels and stories that revealed a precarious sense of identity, tormented by anxieties about her estrangement from her true self and from other people. As far as Borges was concerned, Norah was a better writer than Girondo. He once told an interviewer, "He had the luck to marry Norah Lange. . . . She was much more talented than he, of course. Well, she had talent, he didn't."[42]

And yet things could have been so different. Bioy recalled Borges remarking wistfully to him after they happened to see Norah Lange in the street, "To think that I was so in love with her!"[43] And he would sometimes recite to his friend a passage from Apollinaire's "*La jolie rousse*," dwelling with particular fervor on these lines:[44]

> *Elle vient et m'attire ainsi qu'un fer l'aimant*
> *Elle a l'aspect charmant*
> *D'une adorable rousse**

He had looked to Norah as the muse who would take him beyond the adventure of the avant-garde to the high summer of mature achievement, and for a while, in that *annus mirabilis* that was 1926, it appeared that his courtship of Norah might yet raise him to a high plane of happiness where his pen would blaze in the Whitmanesque ecstasy of communing at last with the essence of the world. But the collapse of that dream had cast him into a void from which he had found it impossible to emerge. Time and again since 1929 he had tried, and failed, to give an account of his experience with Norah and Girondo in his writing. The truth was that for so long as he failed to understand why he had lost Norah, he would remain enslaved to her memory, trapped in a circle of nostalgia and frustration. It was only by burrowing down to the roots of his private suffering that he would discover the true subject matter of his writing, and in the last months of 1937, his life took such a wretched turn for the worse that, after a troubled gestation of nearly ten years, he would be born at last as a writer of fiction.

*"And here she comes, drawing me like iron to a magnet, / She has the enchanting aspect / Of an adorable redhead."

CHAPTER 16

The Death of Father
(1938–1939)

SOMETIME IN THE LATTER MONTHS of 1937, Borges's father suffered a stroke that left him paralyzed down the left side of his body. At the age of sixty-four, Dr. Borges was blind, debilitated by an aneurysm, and now immobilized. Borges would give us a glimpse of his father's condition in his story "The Other" ("El otro"): "His left hand resting on his right hand was like the hand of a child lying on the hand of a giant."[1] The stroke destroyed what remained of Dr. Borges's will to live: he wanted to die, he used to say, he wanted to die "completely," by which he meant dying in body and soul with no prospect of an afterlife.

It was very likely his father's plight that jolted Borges into seeking a full-time job for the first time in his life. He was thirty-eight and had no educational qualifications whatever, not even the Swiss *baccalauréat,* which he had never got around to completing. Having previously worked only as a part-time literary journalist at a number of short-lived, poorly paid jobs, he now found that the best he could manage by way of earning an independent living was a post as a library assistant in the Municipal Library Service. On January 8, 1938, he started work at the Miguel Cané Library in the working-class district of Almagro Sur on the south side of Buenos Aires, effectively at the other end of the city from where he lived. His salary was a measly 210 pesos a month, though sometime later, through the influence of friends, it was raised to 240 pesos, a miserable wage all the same.

On his first day at the library, he was surprised to find that "there were some fifty of us doing what fifteen could easily have done."[2] He was put to work as a cataloger and soon discovered that the library's holdings were so meager that cataloging was unnecessary. He set about doing an honest job of it anyway, but the following day he was taken aside by his colleagues and rebuked for working too hard—the cataloging job had been planned to give them some semblance of work, so he must ration the number of books he classified each day or they would all be out of a job.

If there was any advantage to be found in his post at the library, it was that he could finish his day's ration of cataloging in an hour and spend the rest of his time reading or writing either in the basement or up on the roof in the warm summer weather. Otherwise life at the Miguel Cané was pretty dire for a writer like Borges. None of his colleagues showed any interest in books; they spent their time talking about soccer and horse racing or telling each other smutty stories. He found their crude machismo repellent: one of them took off his shirt one day to show off the scars he had received in knife brawls, and when a woman reader was raped on her way to the lavatory, the male staff blamed her misfortune on the proximity of the women's facilities to the men's.[3] The depths to which he had sunk were brought home to him when a colleague came across a biographical note on a certain Jorge Luis Borges in an encyclopedia and pointed out the coincidence of their names to Borges, not realizing that they were one and the same person.[4]

A couple of upper-class lady friends once came to visit him at the library and were so horrified by what they saw that they rang him up and told him, "You may think it amusing to work in a place like that, but promise us you will find at least a nine-hundred-peso job before the month is out."[5] But working as a library assistant was not one of Georgie's more perverse jokes; it was the position he had attained by his own efforts as an independent adult in the world, and it caused him unutterable distress:

> Now and then during these years, we municipal workers were rewarded with gifts of a two-pound package of maté to take home. Sometimes in the evening, as I walked the ten blocks to the tramline, my eyes would be filled with tears. These small gifts from above always underlined my menial and dismal existence.[6]

Borges's anguish was compounded by his awareness of his father's disappointment in him. He would recall his father commenting on a well-known apothegm of the liberator General José de San Martín, in which the founding father of the nation extolled a man's overriding duty to fulfill his destiny: *"Serás lo que debes ser, y si no, no serás nada"*—"You must be what you ought to be, and if not, you will be nothing at all," which, in Dr. Borges's cynical gloss, became:

> *You must be what you ought to be*—you must be a gentleman, a Catholic, an Argentine, a member of the Jockey Club, an admirer of General Uriburu, an admirer of the extensive landscape paintings of Quirós, *or you will be nothing at all*—you will be a Jew, a good-for-nothing, a first assistant in a library; the Ministry of Culture shall ignore your books, and Dr. Rodríguez Larreta shall not send you any autographed copies of his own.[7]

The reference to a "first assistant" indicates that this conversation took place early in 1938, sometime after Georgie had started work at the Miguel Cané Library. It would have been painful enough for Borges to witness the depth of his father's disillusionment, but the pain must have been exacerbated by the knowledge that his father saw him as a failure, too. Neither had found much success in the world—the father had not fulfilled his aspirations as a writer and was now blind and paralyzed, while the son had squandered his early promise as a poet and risen to the giddy heights of "first assistant" at a municipal library in some godforsaken corner of Buenos Aires.

Still, as the reality of death drew closer, Dr. Borges could not reconcile himself to literary failure. He confessed to being dissatisfied with his novel, *El Caudillo,* and appears to have placed some of the blame on Georgie: he was unhappy with the expressionist metaphors his son had suggested to him in Majorca: "I put many metaphors in to please you," he told Georgie, "but they are very poor and you must get rid of them."[8] He then asked his son "to rewrite the novel in a straightforward way, with all the fine writing and purple patches left out," and the two of them would discuss ways of improving it.[9]

This strange request to rewrite *El Caudillo* was itself an index of Dr. Borges's sense of failure: when Georgie had first started writing poetry he was told by his father, "Each of us must save himself by his own efforts; you must never seek advice from anyone."[10] At the end of his life, however, the unfortunate Dr. Borges, having failed to save himself as a writer by his own efforts, turned to his son for help. But it was a request that put the son in a terrible predicament, for how could he "save" his father, when his own failure to write a self-justifying novel had pushed him to the brink of suicide four years earlier?

On the morning of February 24, Borges received a telephone call from his mother, who told him that the aneurysm had ruptured and his father would be dead in a matter of hours. He left the library and made his way across the city, arriving home in time to see his father pass away. Borges was profoundly moved by the stoic dignity with which his father met his end, but admiration was mixed also with a searing anguish, as is evident in a poem he wrote shortly afterward, an unpolished composition of thirty-two lines written on ruled paper taken from an exercise book and clearly dated 1938.[11] Next to the handwritten text is a rough drawing of a large tree, an image of strength and endurance that relates to the opening image of the poem:

> We have seen you die on your feet,
> bearing fruit like brave men die;
> we have seen you die with the steadfast
> spirit of your father amid the bullets . . .

Georgie praised his father's courage in meeting his death by likening it to the heroic death in battle of their ancestor, Colonel Borges. Twice he repeated the lines "We have seen you die on your feet, / bearing fruit, like brave men die." And yet, despite his brave spirit, Dr. Borges died wishing that his son might somehow bring to fruition the literary destiny that had eluded him. The grieving Georgie ended his valedictory poem with a desperate cri de coeur:

> Papa, don't leave me, take me with you wherever it is that you
> are going!

Borges's poem posited a connection between himself, his father, and the spirit of the latter's own father. As an adolescent he had already adumbrated such a triangle in his playlet about Bernardo del Carpio, where the young hero pays a ransom to release his captive father, only to discover that he has been tricked by the king, whereupon he avenges his father's murder by killing the king.[12] However, the self-belief displayed by the young Georgie had not survived in the grown man—Borges now felt himself to be a mere reflection of his father, since their respective attempts either to live up to the ideal of the ancestral hero or to rebel against his oppressive memory had ended equally in failure, and both father and son were mired in a paralyzing condition of "unreality" as a result.

The triangular relationship that bonded him to his father and both in turn to the figure of the patriarchal hero exerted a horrible fascination. Borges saw an emblem of this triad in the Christian notion of the Trinity. In his essay "A History of Eternity," he described the Trinity as a monstrosity that "only the horror of a nightmare could have engendered"; it was more terrifying even than the idea of hell, for "hell is mere physical violence, but the three inextricable Persons imply an intellectual horror, an infinity which is suffocating, specious, as of contrary mirrors."[13]

One of Borges's earliest attempts to analyze the dynamics of this trinity was "The Dead Man," the story that had first occurred to him after seeing a man shot dead in a tavern at Santa Anna do Livramento, the border town he visited with Enrique Amorim in 1934. It is impossible to say when the story reached its present form, but it is likely to have been in gestation in the course of the 1930s. In its final, published version, "The Dead Man" tells the story of Benjamín Otálora, a young *compadrito* from the poor suburbs of Buenos Aires who kills a rival and flees to Uruguay, where he falls in with a gang of drovers and smugglers led by a Brazilian called Azevedo Bandeira. Within a year this city boy has learned the skills of a gaucho. Emboldened by a newfound sense of freedom and power, he aspires to supplant Bandeira as leader of the gang.

To this end he befriends Bandeira's *capanga* or bodyguard, a man called Suárez, and confides his plan to him, receiving a promise of assistance with his rebellion against the old chieftain. Otálora then disobeys Bandeira's orders, gives the men counterorders of his own, and even sleeps with the boss's concubine, a woman with "resplendent" red hair. One night, however, Bandeira exposes Otálora's affair with the redhead, and his *capanga,* Suárez, pulls a gun on the usurper and shoots him in cold blood.

"The Dead Man" registers Borges's desire to rebel against the authority of patriarchal power, but its real interest lies in the protagonist's realization that he has been tricked by the old chieftain, who has encouraged his "will to power," only to expose it suddenly as a sham. The role of the *capanga* Suárez is critical here because he pretends to be a friend of Otálora's, while being secretly in collusion with Bandeira. Thus, if Bandeira could be said to embody the patriarchal spirit of the ancestors, then Suárez might represent Borges's father, who had, after all, fostered his son's "cult of courage," his "will to power," even to the extent of placing a dagger in his hand and urging him to show the school bullies that he was a man. "The Dead Man," in this respect, expressed Borges's resentment of his father for having, as it were, "tricked" him by encouraging him to rebel against the sword of honor while having at the same time preempted the desired outcome of that rebellion. And the principal instrument of the deception is the red-haired concubine, who is allowed to sleep with Otálora so as to provide an excuse for his murder. There is surely an allusion here to Dr. Borges's sending his son to a prostitute in Geneva. The fact that Bandeira's concubine is given red hair indicates, furthermore, some obscure recognition on Borges's part that the traumatic experience in Geneva had in some way prejudiced his relations with the red-haired Norah Lange and prevented him from attaining the freedom and self-determination he so desired.

Yet whatever resentment Borges may have felt was tempered by a sense of compassion as he witnessed his father's suffering and distress in the months preceding his death. Georgie could empathize with his father's condition— here was a man who had lost his own father at the age of nine months and who had consequently grown up under the shadow of a perfect dead hero whom he could neither measure up to nor reject. Dr. Borges, in consequence, had been torn between an "anarchist" urge to destroy the established order and a lingering wish to be accepted by the society of the criollos. Hence his restlessness—his disruption of the family's life in Buenos Aires in order to find happiness with Leonor in Europe. And Georgie, moreover, was conscious of the debt he owed his father—it was he who had introduced him to the world of books, to the world of philosophy, politics, ideas, and, above all, literature.

At the time of his father's final illness, Borges was engaged in translating a selection of Kafka's stories for the Editorial Losada, and it was Kafka who would provide him with the means of exploring further the ambivalent relations with his father and the ghost of their ancestral hero. In the prologue to his translations of Kafka, he would observe that the Czech writer had been secretly "despised" and "tyrannized" by his own father and that Kafka himself had declared that his entire work was derived "from that conflict and from his tenacious meditations on the mysterious favors and unlimited exigencies of patriarchal power."[14] Two "obsessions" governed Kafka's fiction—"subordination" and "the infinite," which is why none of the three novels he wrote was complete, for "the pathos of these 'inconclusive' novels stems precisely from the infinite number of obstacles that detain his identical heroes over and over again."[15]

Borges must have had in mind the "pathos" of his own "inconclusive" novels—the two attempts at the autobiographical *Approach to Al-Mu'tasim,* or *April March,* his equally inconclusive effort to render infinite time in narrative form. Thanks to Kafka he attributed this failure to a mysterious inhibition deriving from patriarchal power. In May, just a couple of months after his father's death, he published a translation of "Before the Law," Kafka's brief tale about a man who is prevented by an invisible obstacle from walking through an open door.[16] Kafka's protagonist asks to be admitted to the law but is refused entry by the doorkeeper who warns him that there are other halls inside with other doorkeepers who are even more powerful than he. The man waits for many years to receive permission to enter, and finally, when he is on the point of dying, he asks the doorkeeper why no one else has asked to enter the law, only to be informed that this entrance was reserved for him alone and now that he is about to die, it will be closed. In the curious inability of Kafka's character to defy the doorkeeper's prohibition, Borges must have recognized an identical inhibition in himself—and in his father too, no doubt—based on a fear of defying authority.

The period of his father's illness and death would constitute a decisive turning point in Borges's career as a writer. From the beginning he had conceived of writing as a means of expressing his true self, and, ultimately, of transcending the self in a rapturous fusion with the essential reality of the world. Even after losing his poetic voice in 1929, he had experimented with fiction in order to define his unique artistic personality by transmuting his unhappiness over Norah Lange into aesthetic form. But his repeated failure to rebel against the sword of honor and so dissolve the perverse, Borgesian trinity in which he was trapped had caused him to lose the love of a woman—first, Emilie in Geneva, then Concepción Guerrero, and, most disastrously of all, Norah

Lange. And without the love of a woman, he believed, there could be no hope of finding salvation by writing. In the aftermath of his father's death, therefore, Borges would abandon his quest for the essence of the self and would turn to writing as a means of exploring the nature of that abject failure.

Father's dying request that Borges rewrite *El Caudillo* epitomized the sheer impossibility of being saved by writing, for such an enterprise would entail the sacrifice of his own creative identity to his father's, while undermining his father's claim to be the novel's unique author, which would defeat the point of his having written it in the first place. Rewriting, in short, entailed the destruction of true authorship, of originality, of invention. By the middle of 1938, I reckon, Borges's reflections on the implications of rewriting another man's work had led him to the rudiments of a new story in which he would stand on its head the idea he had cherished for so long and portray its opposite instead—damnation by writing, or the death of the author.

We find elements of the new story that was taking shape in Borges's imagination in his review of Paul Valéry's *Introduction à la poétique,* which appeared in *El Hogar* on June 10, 1938, only two weeks after his translation of Kafka's "Before the Law" was published in the same magazine.[17] Valéry argued that the history of literature was not to be found in an account of the life and works of individual authors but in a transcendent "History of the Mind" ("Esprit") that was both producer and consumer of literature. And literary creation he regarded as the combination of the potentialities of a particular language according to forms established for all time. However, Borges found a contradiction between this view and a later assertion that works of art existed only in the act of being perceived by a reader or spectator, for the first assertion implied a large but finite number of possible works, while the second "admits that time and its incomprehensions and distractions collaborate with the dead poet." The same text, according to Borges, could mean different things to different readers in different periods, and he quoted a line from a poem by Cervantes to show that a reader in the twentieth century would derive a different sense from the very same words: "Time—a friend to Cervantes—has corrected the proofs for him."

Over the following months, Borges would work up this idea of time as a "corrector of proofs" into a story he would call "Pierre Menard, Author of *Don Quixote*" ("Pierre Menard, autor del *Quijote*"), a spoof review of the works of a fictional writer from Nîmes, recently deceased. In the character of Pierre Menard, we have a Paul Valéry who has woken up one morning to find himself transformed into Franz Kafka, for the nihilism of Menard was so absurdly perverse that it led him to "anticipate the vanity that awaits all human effort" by undertaking "an enterprise that was extremely complex and futile from the start"—he would rewrite Cervantes's *Don Quixote.* It was not a matter of copying the novel but of "repeating" the book—that is to say, writing his own text independently of Cervantes but with the aim of making it coincide "line by line and word for word" with the original. "Pierre Menard, Author of *Don Quixote*" thus presents us with an exact inversion of Borges's ideal of writing, for this is a kind of writing that results in the complete annihilation of personality. Had Menard succeeded in rewriting *Don Quixote*, he would have sacrificed his artistic individuality to the task, but, equally, he would have robbed Cervantes of his status as the unique author of the great classic. Menard's success would thus have amounted to the destruction of original creation, rendering authorship an arbitrary concept—one author would be equivalent to any other—so that over a sufficiently long period of time, any work could, in principle, be written by any author.

In addition to this death, so to speak, of the author, Borges elaborated the related idea of time as the "corrector of proofs" that he had briefly mentioned in his review of Valéry's book. If time changed the meaning of texts so that every reader derived a different meaning from the same set of words, then a reader, in a sense, could be said to invent the meaning of any given text. Accordingly, we learn that Pierre Menard had "enriched" the art of reading by opening up the possibility of attributing a given text to any author the reader might fancy, thereby filling "with adventure the most placid of books": "To attribute *The Imitation of Christ* to Louis-Ferdinand Céline or James Joyce, would this not be a sufficient renovation of those mild spiritual counsels?"

A bitter, self-mocking irony pervades "Pierre Menard," for in this story Borges had drained the act of writing of any vital purpose whatever. Menard's enterprise, in effect, converted the reader into an author and the author, in turn, into a glorified reader for whom writing had no connection with individual experience or feeling, and indeed was no more original than the work of a scribe "repeating" a preexisting text. Moreover, as Borges realized, such a conception of writing and reading led to the dissolution of objective meaning. He cited as an example of Pierre Menard's "enrichment" of reading *Don Quixote* Part I, chapter 9, in which history is called the "mother of truth." What was conventional rhetoric for a baroque writer like Cervantes becomes an "amazing" idea in a twentieth-century Frenchman—as "the mother of truth," history is regarded by Menard not "as an investigation of reality but as its origin": "Historical truth, for him, is not what happened; it is what we judge to have happened." And so one might infer that we invent the truths of history, we invent reality, in the way that readers might invent meanings for literary texts, with the result that reading, no less than writing, becomes an exercise in solipsism.

By one of those strange ironies that seemed to manifest themselves periodically in Borges's life, these reflections on the death of the author were interrupted by a sudden brush with the reality of his own physical death in a strange accident that occurred on Chrismas Eve, 1938. Borges had gone to fetch a girl at her apartment on calle Ayacucho, some five blocks from where he lived at avenida Pueyrredón, in order to accompany her home for dinner with his mother. The elevator was out of order, so he decided to run up the stairs, but in the poor light he knocked his head against a newly painted casement window that had been left open to dry. Despite his receiving first aid, the wound became poisoned, and for a week he lay in bed with a high fever and suffering from insomnia and hallucinations. One evening he lost his power of speech and had to be rushed to hospital for an emergency operation in the middle of the night. He had developed septicemia, and for a month he hovered between life and death. When he recovered, he feared he might have been left mentally impaired and might never write again. He decided to write something he had never done before so that he would not feel so bad if he failed, and this led him to write "Pierre Menard, Author of *Don Quixote*" while he was convalescing from his illness in the summer months between January and April 1939.[18]

"Pierre Menard" came out in *Sur* in May, and although it won plaudits from his friends, this was not sufficient to dispel his sense of failure.[19] He was still oppressed by the concerns that had preceded his accident on Christmas Eve, concerns that could only have been aggravated when, in July 1939, he lost his job as the editor of the fortnightly book page for *El Hogar*. He had nothing left but his dreary post at the Miguel Cané Library, and his depression can be gauged from an essay, which he published in August, called "The Total Library," where he imagined the entire universe in the form of a library.[20] The "total library" was based on the idea that, given a sufficiently extensive period of time, a limited number of letters or symbols would generate a finite number of combinations and, consequently, of books. This library, therefore, would contain all the books that could conceivably be written and would describe everything that existed or could possibly exist in the universe. In such a library, all writers would be reduced to the condition of Pierre Menard, for, as Lewis Carroll observed, they could ask themselves not "What book shall I write?" but only "Which book shall I write?" Dreadful as this idea was for Borges, he went further still, imagining a "total library" immersed in the appalling immensity of infinite time, where for every "intelligible line" of text there would be "millions of senseless cacophonies, verbal farragoes and incoherencies," where it was conceivable that "the generations of man might pass away altogether" without the shelves of the monstrous library yielding up "a single tolerable page."

The nightmare of the Total Library put him in mind of a kindred nightmare, the Trinity, and both nightmares he associated with the idea of hell:

One of the mind's habits is the invention of horrible imaginings. It has invented Hell, it has invented predestination to Hell, it has imagined the Platonic ideas, the chimera, the sphinx, the abnormal transfinite numbers (in which the part is no less copious than the whole), masks, mirrors, operas, the teratological Trinity: the Father, the Son and the insoluble Ghost, articulated in a single organism.[21]

The Library—the Platonic form of father's library in Palermo where he had been raised, or of the Miguel Cané Library in which he currently worked— would become the supreme metaphor of solipsism for Borges, an idealist counterworld, a prisonhouse of "unreality" so pervasive that it was as if the living universe itself had been transformed into a hell of endless books:

> I have endeavored to rescue from oblivion a subaltern horror: the vast, contradictory Library, whose vertical deserts of books run the unceasing risk of changing into others, affirming everything, denying everything, and then confounding it all like some deity gone raving mad.[22]

It was in this solipsistic frame of mind that he conceived a new story, "Tlön, Uqbar, Orbis Tertius," which would appear in *Sur* in May 1940.[23] This was a parody of Bishop Berkeley's philosophical idealism, in which the members of a secret society run by a millionaire called Ezra Buckley invent an imaginary planet called Tlön whose inhabitants lack any natural sense of there being a physical reality external to their own consciousness. In a series of brilliant comic maneuvers, Borges sketched the consequences of such congenital idealism for the languages, science, mathematics, literature, and religions of Tlön.

There are, however, a number of autobiographical allusions lurking in the farther reaches of the tale, among them the figure of Herbert Ashe, the taciturn English engineer afflicted by "unreality," who is a friend of Borges's father's and who dies of a ruptured aneurysm, like Dr. Borges himself. Finally a touch of paranoia creeps into the fable when Borges describes two incidents from his own experience that suggest that Ezra Buckley and his conspirators may be attempting to contaminate our world with the sinister idealism of the planet Tlön. The story, then, evinces Borges's fears of ending up as a reflection of his father—disengaged from the world around him and overwhelmed by a sense of unreality from which writing itself could no longer offer any salvation.

CHAPTER 17

The Example of Dante
(1939–1940)

By 1939 Bioy was growing weary of managing a cattle ranch and wanted to take a fuller part in the Buenos Aires literary world. He had become intimate friends with Silvina Ocampo since their involvement with *Destiempo,* and she had been coming out regularly to stay with Bioy at the *estancia,* where they indulged their passion for reading and writing. In the New Year, Bioy surprised his friends by announcing that he was to marry Silvina, and on January 15 they had a quiet wedding in the parish church of Las Flores near Bioy's *estancia,* at which Borges was one of the witnesses. Soon afterward the couple set up home in Buenos Aires, moving to a spacious two-story apartment occupying the seventh and eighth floors of a building on the corner of the avenida Santa Fe and calle Ecuador in the smart Barrio Norte. There were two large bedrooms on the lower floor and a spiral staircase leading up to an airy, semicircular living room on the floor above, with an upper gallery lined with bookcases and an adjoining reading area, which became the Bioys' library.[1]

This apartment was to become a congenial haven for Borges at a time when he was acutely unhappy. A kind of ritual came into being—Borges would drop by almost every evening, and after dinner he and Bioy would work on some literary project in Bioy's bedroom, which doubled as a study and afforded magnificent views over the rooftoops of the Barrio Norte down the avenida Santa Fe. (In 1940 he and Bioy, together with Silvina, worked on an *Anthology of Fantasy Literature* and shortly afterward they would compile an *Anthology of Argentine Poetry.*)[2] At times they would take a walk in one of Borges's favorite barrios or listen to music, although Borges never had much of an ear: he appreciated Brahms but otherwise tended to favor blues, gospel, and a little jazz.

Every Thursday, Silvina and Adolfito would hold a soirée for their literary friends, mostly writers who had been involved with *Destiempo* and had since gravitated toward *Sur.* Occasionally they would ask another guest or two to join them for dinner with Borges, which was not the most enticing of invitations from a culinary point of view, it seems—one had to be prepared to go hungry after dining at the Bioys', Borges liked to warn these occasional guests. Certainly the hosts were not distinguished by the splendor of their table: dinner might consist of a few strips of grilled meat accompanied by water (the Bioys were teetotalers) or else some improvised dish rustled up by Silvina from whatever she happened to have found in the refrigerator that evening. The real pleasure was to be had from seeing Borges drop his guard at these intimate gatherings and come into his own: he was genial, witty, full of malicious gossip, and endlessly inventive in the games he dreamed up to test the range and depth of his friends' reading.

Still, even though he became more fully engaged in the literary scene after Bioy and Silvina moved to Buenos Aires, Borges remained deeply troubled. He rarely exchanged confidences with Bioy, but at the very start of their friendship in the mid-1930s, he had confessed to his friend his ill-starred love for Norah Lange, and, in the early 1940s, when the two men started seeing each other almost every evening, he seemed to be "very sensitive" on the subject of Norah Lange; as Bioy recalled, it appeared "to cause him pain."[3] He would refer to Norah "obsessively," bringing her up in conversation only to say that he preferred not to go into the matter, though he would shortly afterward refer to her again, as if he were unable to take his mind off the woman; it was Bioy's impression that there was something that Borges kept "concealed" on the subject of the Lange sisters: there were "hidden depths" there, he surmised, "a mysterious element" that Borges reserved for his "secret life."

At around the time that Bioy became aware of what he called Borges's "obsession" with Norah Lange, he was also struck by his friend's concomitant "obsession" with Dante's *Divine Comedy*. Borges would later claim to have read the *Comedy* for the first time while traveling on the tram to and from his job at the Miguel Cané Library.[4] Since it is very likely that he was already acquainted with the general themes of Dante's poem, it may be that it was in the latter part of 1939 or early in 1940 that he first read the *Divine Comedy* from start to finish. At any rate, he was "dazzled by that book": it was "one of the most vivid literary experiences" he had ever been granted "in the course of a life dedicated to literature," and thenceforward he would regard it as "perhaps the highest work of literature, of all literatures."[5]

The *Divine Comedy* is, in essence, an account of the salvation of its author's soul. Dante describes an epic journey through Hell, Purgatory, and Paradise, culminating in a series of visions that reveal to him the final meaning of God's Creation. The Roman poet Virgil, author of the *Aeneid*, acts as Dante's guide through the nine circles of Hell and the seven terraces of Purgatory, but when the pair of them arrive at the Garden of Eden, which is situated at the summit of the mountain of Purgatory, Virgil departs and Dante is reunited with Beatrice, the deceased lady love whom he still adores, and it is she who leads him through the nine heavens of Paradise to the Empyrean, the plane of God's Absolute Presence beyond space and time. There, eventually, Dante is granted a vision of the Rose of the Just, formed by the souls of those who have won salvation. Suddenly Dante notices that Beatrice is no longer with him; he cries out in dismay but then sees her at her appointed place in one of the circles of the mystic Rose. Beatrice smiles at him one last time, before turning away to gaze in ecstasy at the fount of God's eternal love.

Beatrice is the character who plays a providential role in the initiation and unfolding of the entire *Comedy*. Thanks to her intercession, God permits Dante to undertake the journey in the first place, and it is she, too, who provides the inspiration for the composition of the poem that will reveal Dante's personal destiny and offer a final meaning for man's existence on earth. Who, then, was Beatrice? In an earlier work, the *Vita Nuova*, Dante gave an account of his love for a woman, generally thought to have been Bice Portinari, whom he claims to have seen for the first time when he was nine years old, and not again until nine years later, when she refused to acknowledge him. This rejection caused Dante to sublimate his love for Beatrice, a process that continued even after she married another man, Simone de' Bardi. With her death in 1290, at the age of twenty-four, Dante's love shed all earthly attributes and became entirely spiritual. At this point he was ready to undertake the composition of his great *poema sacro* in which Beatrice would figure as the the agent of his salvation.

Whether or not the *Vita Nuova* describes a genuine autobiographical experience is open to question, but what matters for our purposes is that Borges was convinced that it did. Indeed, he believed that it was the pain of thwarted love that had driven the immense narrative machine of the *Divine Comedy*:

> With Beatrice dead, Beatrice lost forever, Dante played with the fiction of meeting her again in order to mitigate his sorrow; I myself believe that he constructed the threefold architecture of his poem so as to insert that encounter within it.[6]

The truth was that Borges read the *Comedy* in a profoundly personal way, projecting onto it the heartbreak he had himself suffered as a result of his rejection by Norah Lange. So much so, in fact, that he would claim a unique personal insight into the emotional core of the poem. He located this in Canto XXXI of the *Paradiso*, where Beatrice smiles at Dante before turning away forever to face the majesty of God. These were "the most moving verses ever achieved in literature," but "even though famous, no one appears to have discerned the sorrow that is in them, no one has listened to them fully."[7] In Borges's view this scene was a splinter of Hell stuck in the heart of Paradise, for Dante was forced to relive his loss of Beatrice even as he saw her attain salvation in the divine scheme of things. These were "atrocious circumstances," and "all the more infernal, of course, for occurring in the Empyrean."[8] Conversely, he read the scene in Canto V of the *Inferno*, where Dante encounters Paolo and Francesca in the second circle of Hell, as an example of amorous fulfillment that the poet must have secretly admired and indeed envied, for Paolo and Francesca may have been damned to Hell for their excessive absorption in profane love, but since they were destined to be together forever more, they were the "obscure emblems" of the happiness that Dante could never hope to enjoy with Beatrice.[9]

Borges felt an extraordinary empathy with Dante over his unfulfilled love for Beatrice, but at the same time, the *Divine Comedy* was a great source of hope, for it was proof that a writer could transcend his sufferings and save himself through his art. Borges had discovered the *Comedy* at a very particular juncture in his life: his recent brush with death, following so closely upon the death of his father, had exacerbated his anguish over his apparent failure as a writer. But his reading of Dante confirmed a truth that had become obscured in recent years—it was the love of a woman that alone could deliver him from the hellish unreality he shared with his father and inspire him to write a masterpiece that would justify his life.

Dante's *Divine Comedy* served to relaunch Borges's project of salvation by writing. However, there was a difference between Dante and Borges. Dante was a Christian and could therefore draw inspiration from the belief that Beatrice could bring him to salvation. Borges was a skeptic, if not an atheist, so how could he compensate for the final loss, the "death," of his own Beatrice, Norah Lange? Around 1940, in my judgment, he came upon the idea of a "new Beatrice" who would give him what Norah had promised but never delivered— a love that would inspire him to write the autobiographical masterpiece that would justify his life as a man and as a writer. Reading the *Divine Comedy* thus led Borges to invent a poetic myth of his own salvation. The particular terms of this Dantean myth can be reconstructed from an array of allusions and symbols in Borges's writing. There is no space here to undertake their systematic elucidation, but I trust that some of these allusions and, especially, the central biographical significance of the myth itself, will become evident in the course of this book.

Borges's Dantean scheme took as its origin the Lange villa at calle Tronador, a place where his love of Concepción Guerrero and later Norah Lange had made him feel truly integrated in reality. This was his Garden of Eden, as it were, but Norah's rejection had driven him out of his earthly paradise, causing him to suffer the death of his imagination. He had since endured the hell of solipsism, symbolized by the "total library," but the advent of a new Beatrice would deliver him from that condition and allow him to regain the happiness he had once tasted at the calle Tronador. Fired by the love of this new Beatrice, a love figured in the symbol of the rose, he would write a book that would represent the realization of his true self. Thence he would proceed to "paradise"— an appreciation of the vital relation between self and world, a quasimystical synthesis represented in the vision of the Aleph or in the pantheist legend of the Simurgh.

This Dantean pattern of salvation would shape Borges's understanding of himself almost to the very end of his life, as we shall see in due course. Writing and experience would be bound up as inextricably as he imagined Dante's to have been in the composition of the *Divine Comedy*. His inner world, as a result, would be imbued with a sense of high drama, given that his entire fate appeared to hinge on the advent of a "new Beatrice" who might vouchsafe him the grace to write a book that would give some final purpose to his existence.

Bioy Casares was to describe the impact of Dante upon Borges as *"una ebullición,"* a ferment, and he noticed also a comparable ferment with regard to Borges's memories of the Lange family and the days of the avant-garde.[10] Borges would ask Bioy to drive him to certain outlying barrios that in the 1920s had been the *orillas,* the outskirts, of the great city. Bioy was never quite sure why his friend should want to return to such places, but it amused him to go along with his strange whims, so they would leave the motorcar and go for nocturnal walks together in drab, featureless streets in northwestern barrios like Palermo, Villa Urquiza, Villa Ortúzar, and Saavedra, which Borges seemed to find peculiarly evocative: these were his *patrias,* his homelands, he used to tell Bioy.[11] Borges's nostalgia for the happy days when he had been the leader of the avant-garde remained very powerful. From time to time, he would take his friend to the intersection of calles Tronador and Pampa, where the villa of the Lange family stood. It had been rented out since the beginning of 1934, but Borges, according to Bioy, liked to feel close to the Lange sisters—he wanted "to absorb their atmosphere"—and he would occasionally visit the apartment at calle Esmeralda 1394 where Señora Berta Erfjord de Lange now lived with her as yet unmarried daughters, Haydée, Chichina, and Norah (though the latter spent much of her time at Oliverio Girondo's).[12]

Borges had always enjoyed Haydée's company—she was intelligent, well read, and multilingual (they spoke mostly English to each other), but there was also an air of mystery about her that could not fail to intrigue a man of romantic inclinations like him. In Bioy's recollection, moreover, he had always greatly appreciated the "solace" Haydée had offered him with the "sorrows and troubles" he had suffered over her sister Norah.[13] She had also given him much-needed moral support after his near fatal accident on Christmas Eve of 1938. Since then they had taken to meeting after work and going to the cinema or to dinner at some restaurant in the city center. There is a well-known photograph taken at a park on April 1, 1939, in which Haydée appears smartly dressed in white, whereas an oddly bearded Georgie cuts an ungainly figure in a beret and a suit a size too small for his plump body.

Sometime in the early months of 1940, by my reckoning, Borges began to have other ideas about Haydée, taking it into his head that he had fallen in love with her. He even went so far as to propose marriage to her, but, predictably, she turned him down—as far as she was concerned, they were just good friends who had known each other since childhood, given that they were *primos*, "cousins" by marriage in the Hispanic sense.[14] He would not be deterred, however, and would turn up after work at the bank where Haydée was a bilingual secretary and continue to press his suit. This strange courtship eventually became something of a standing joke between them—Borges would signal a proposal of marriage from across the road, and Haydée would decline by wagging her finger in reply.

For the rest of his life, Borges would maintain to all and sundry that he had been deeply in love with Haydée Lange. Haydée, on the other hand, would tell her close friend, the poet Olga Orozco, that Borges, although he would hint at it, never actually declared his love for her. Why this curious emotional reticence in his wooing of Haydée? Perhaps her indifference suited him well, for so long as Haydée was content to play along with the ritual of his marriage proposals, his presumed love for her could remain in the realms of a poetic dream.

Borges's love for Haydée, in my view, owed more to aesthetic logic than to any compelling emotion: he had persuaded himself that he was in love with her so that he could cast her in the role of the "new Beatrice." She was, after all, his closest link to the lost paradise of the calle Tronador, and there would, moreover, have been a pleasing symmetry in the fact that she was Norah's sister—it was fitting that one sister should pave the way for the other in his Dantean myth of personal salvation.

By early 1940, I believe, he had derived sufficient inspiration from his romantic attachment to Haydée Lange to embark on the composition of his Dantean masterpiece. This he planned as a novel called *The Congress*. In 1971 he revealed to Fernando Sorrentino that he had conceived *The Congress* "more than thirty years ago," which would place its origins in 1940 or thereabouts; again, in April 1971, he would declare that *The Congress* had been "haunting" him for "the last thirty or forty years."[15] This suggests that the original idea for the story may have dated back to around 1930 but, as I have already argued, I am inclined to think that Borges saw *The Congress* as a reformulation of the autobiographical project he had been unsuccessfully pursuing in *The Ap-*

proach to Al-Mu'tasim, whose origins can be more certainly traced back to around 1930–31.

Despite its gestation over several decades, Borges rarely spoke about *The Congress.* The fullest account of the work that I have come across was in an interview of 1955, in which Borges outlined his general aims:

> It would be a book in which all my previous books would be implicated, a new book, but one which would sum up and would in addition be the resolution of everything I have written up until now. . . . It will be a novel of fantasy, not because it is about ghosts or science fiction, but in a psychological sense. . . . *The Congress*—an ideal Congress—would begin as a novel and end as a fairy tale.[16]

By the time of its publication in 1971, *The Congress* had been refined down to the dimensions of a novella (although it would still be the longest work of fiction Borges would ever produce).[17] Unfortunately, the absence of earlier drafts means that one can work only from the 1971 text, but this published version can still provide us with a good idea of how Borges drew inspiration from Dante to fashion a narrative that he hoped would clinch his destiny as a writer.

The Congress takes the form of a memoir written by Alejandro Ferri, a bachelor in his seventies, who lives modestly on his own in Buenos Aires. He gives an account of a defining experience that took place shortly after he had arrived in the capital from his native province a few years before the end of the nineteenth century. The story unfolds after Ferri is invited by his friend, a poet called José Fernández Irala, to join a secret society whose members are planning to organize a "Congress of the World" comprising delegates from all the nations of the globe. This is the brainchild of a wealthy rancher called Alejandro Glencoe, a man of Scottish extraction who divides his time between Buenos Aires and an *estancia* in Uruguay called La Caledonia. There are some fifteen to twenty members of the society, whose secretary and only female member is a beautiful Norwegian girl called Nora Erfjord. It soon becomes clear to Ferri that the power behind the throne is a sinister character called Twirl. Ferri observes how Twirl exploits Glencoe: first he recommends the creation of a reference library for the Congress, and then he advises that the library should be expanded to include the classics of each nation and in each language. The required volumes are supplied by one of Twirl's associates, a bookseller called Nierenstein, and they are paid for by Glencoe. Twirl next suggests that the Congress adopt a universal language and recommends that two delegates be sent, again at Glencoe's expense, to London and Paris respectively, in order to carry out research into the suitability of the various universal languages. Ferri is sent to London; the poet Eguren, another associate of Twirl's, to Paris.

In London, Ferri carries out research into Esperanto, Volapuk, Latin, and other languages in the Reading Room of the British Museum. There he meets an English girl called Beatriz Frost and falls in love with her. Ferri puts off his return to Argentina for a whole year, but Beatriz refuses to be tied down by getting married, so Ferri must return on his own to Buenos Aires, where he finds that Twirl has extended the library of the Congress to embrace practically any book in existence, given that no book, according to Twirl, is so bad that something good might not be found in it. Glencoe's house, in consequence, is being turned into a chaotic library of uncataloged books. His secretary, Nora Erfjord, has resigned in despair, only to be replaced by yet another of Twirl's friends. However, just as Ferri is about to deliver a report on his investigations at the British Museum, Glencoe appears at the house and orders all the books amassed at Twirl's instigation to be burned. It has been revealed to him that there is no point in continuing with his enterprise: "The Congress of the World began in the first instant of the world's being and will continue after we are dust. There is no place in which it cannot be found." He then takes them all for a ride around Buenos Aires in an open carriage so that they may "contemplate the Congress," and all those present are imbued with Glencoe's "resolution and faith":

> The mystics invoke a rose, a kiss, a bird which is all birds, a sun which is all the stars and the sun, a pitcher of wine, a garden or the sexual act. None of those metaphors are of any use to me for that long night of jubilation, which left us, tired and happy, on the brink of dawn.

During the mystical illumination, Nora Erfjord and Glencoe recite the Scottish "Ballad of Sir Patrick Spens." Even Twirl is moved to say, "I have wished to do evil and I am doing good." Ferri, the author of the memoir, tells us that he was never able to recapture that sublime experience, but as one of the last surviving members of Glencoe's society, he has decided to break the oath of secrecy and share the memory of it with his readers, so that they, too, may realize that they are unwitting participants in the congress of the world.

A wealth of autobiographical information is secreted in *The Congress*. The name Alejandro Ferri bears a dual association—his first name recalls Alexander of Macedon and the sword of the warrior, while the Italian surname Ferri translates into Spanish as *fierros,* which means "daggers" and also carries echoes of the gaucho poem *Martín Fierro,* written by José Hernández, whose name is echoed again in Ferri's friend, José Fernández Irala. Alejandro Ferri thus represents Borges's fundamental conflict between the sword of honor and the gaucho dagger, between civilization and barbarism, Mother and Father.

Nora Erfjord is clearly modeled on Norah Lange, who was herself of Norwegian descent on both sides of her family and whose mother's maiden name was Erfjord. The English girl, Beatriz Frost, is given attributes that are also reminiscent of Norah Lange: she is described as "tall, slim, with clean-cut features and a mane of red hair." What is more, an allusion to Borges's thwarted love for Norah Lange is embedded in the account of the final night of enlightenment in Buenos Aires. Here Nora Erfjord recites "The Ballad of Sir Patrick Spens," which tells the story of the eponymous knight who is sent to Norway to bring Margaret, the king of Norway's daughter, to Scotland, so that she may ascend the throne following the death of Alexander, king of Scots.

> To Noroway, to Noroway,
> To Noroway o'er the faem,
> The King's daughter of Noroway,
> 'Tis thou maun bring her hame.

The allusion to Norah Lange's sea voyages to Oslo and back in 1927–29 is inescapable, but additionally the ballad relates how Sir Patrick's ship is caught in "sic a deadly storm" that both he and the king's daughter are drowned at sea. The motif of drowning suggests not only the shipwreck of Borges's love for Norah but also Borges's belief that, in preferring Girondo to him, Norah had somehow forfeited her paternal birthright.

Oliverio Girondo is represented in Glencoe's chief adviser, who goes, we are told, by "the curious name of Twirl." When "twirl" is translated into Spanish as *girar,* the allusion to Girondo becomes more obvious. The verb *girar* had become associated with Girondo thanks to a celebrated burlesque *epigrama* that appeared in the "Satirical Parnassus" column in *Martín Fierro* on January 24, 1925: *"A veces rotundo / Y a veces muy blando / Se va por el mundo, Girondo girando."* We have here a seminonsensical rhyme playing on Girondo's name—associating *Girondo* with *girando* (turning or twirling) and relating it in turn to his penchant for traveling the world.[18] Some of Twirl's other attributes point obliquely to Oliverio Girondo. He is said to be vertiginously tall, but even though Girondo was of normal stature, Twirl's exceptional height would represent Borges's sense of Girondo's lofty social status, given his vast wealth and family pedigree. Girondo, famously, had a thick beard, Twirl has a "fulgent moustache"; Twirl's hair is red, although Girondo's was black, but the fact that its "violent color suggested fire" indicates that it could be taken as a symbol of Girondo's fiery personality, which Borges had once characterized as "violent" in his review of Girondo's second book of poems, *Calcomanías.*[19] Twirl's red hair serves also to associate him with Beatriz Frost ("whose red mane could have reminded me, and never did, of the oblique Twirl") and, through her, with the Norwegian Nora Erfjord. Borges thus slyly alludes to Girondo's links with Norah Lange, although in *The Congress* Twirl never actually has amorous relations with either girl.

In the name of Twirl's associate, Nierenstein, we come upon a secret door leading to the specific autobiographical subtext of *The Congress*. For the real Nierenstein was in fact a professor at the University of Buenos Aires and, more to the point, a member of the jury that refused to award the 1926 Municipal Prize to Borges for *El tamaño de mi esperanza,* the book that was meant to launch Borges's *criollismo.* According to a report in *Martín Fierro* in April 1927, Nierenstein had dismissed Borges as "an incomprehensible writer and an imitator of Carriego," and this same issue of *Martín Fierro* carried Norah Lange's public repudiation of Borges's poetic tutelage.[20] In the allusion to Nierenstein, therefore, Borges pinpointed the precise reasons for the bitter feud with Girondo that led to Borges's avenging the loss of Norah Lange by destroying the magazine *Martín Fierro* itself.[21] And even that act of vengeance is echoed in the incident in *The Congress* where the *compadrito* Nicolás Paredes challenges the poet Eguren, another of Twirl's associates, to a knife duel outside a brothel and makes him back down.

Alejandro Glencoe is the epitome of patriarchal authority and, as such, reflects Borges's own ambivalence toward father figures. The name Glencoe itself implies duality in as much as it alludes to the famous massacre of the Macdonalds by the Campbells at Glencoe, a duality noted by Ferri, who observes the "total change" that comes over the patriarch—he is an urbane gentleman in Buenos Aires but behaves like a primitive caudillo with the gauchos on his ranch. Tall, robust and with a reddish beard, he is reminiscent of Norah Lange's long-deceased father, Gunnar, and this points to a paternal association between Glencoe and his Norwegian secretary, Nora Erfjord, an association reinforced by their joint recital of "The Ballad of Sir Patrick Spens" on the night of their enlightenment. What is more, Glencoe's first name, Alejandro, and the fact that his estate is called La Caledonia make him an epigone of King Alexander of Scotland in that ballad.

There is also an implicit paternal link between Alejandro Glencoe and his namesake Alejandro Ferri, Borges's fictional alter ego. His ranch is on the Uruguayan border with Brazil, precisely the region Borges visited while in the throes of his suicidal crisis over the red-haired Norah Lange in 1934. An association is thus implied between Glencoe and the bandit chieftain of "The Dead Man," who has his young protégé Otálora killed for attempting to usurp him and for sleeping with his red-haired mistress, an intertextual connection suggesting that relations between Glencoe and Ferri are potentially destructive. (Indeed, Ferri is uneasy about his excessive absence from Buenos Aires, at Don Alejandro's expense, due to his affair with Beatriz Frost.)

However, the most profound and significant of all the patriarchal references are to be found in the parallels that exist between *The Congress* and *El Caudillo*, the novel written by Borges's father. The basic structure and plot of the two works are identical: there is a powerful chieftain poised between civilization and barbarism; Glencoe is advised by the sinister Twirl, much as the earlier Caudillo consulted the dubious Gringo; the secondary characters are divided according to their attitudes to a young hero—Carlos Dubois or Alejandro Ferri—whose love for a girl—Marisela or Beatriz—elicits a reaction from the chieftain that determines the outcome of the action; finally, the chieftains repudiate their advisers, the Gringo and Twirl, respectively.

Borges composed *The Congress* on the pattern of his father's novel, and this would suggest that he was seeking in part to fulfill his dying father's request that he rewrite *El Caudillo* on his behalf. That request amounted to a plea by the father that his son save him from literary failure, and the obligation to redeem his father, as we have seen, had resulted in the frustration of Borges's creative imagination, a frustration reflected in the literary enterprise of Pierre Menard, who, rather than invent on his own account, sought to rewrite *Don Quixote* and risked thereby annulling his own personality as well as that of Cervantes. However, if in *The Congress* Borges was rewriting *El Caudillo*, he did so, not just to mirror the earlier work but also to transcend it, and here one finds a further reason for his immense admiration for the *Divine Comedy*. The relationship between Dante and Virgil held a fascination for Borges second only to the relationship between Dante and Beatrice. He saw it as a filial relationship: "Dante is like a son to Virgil; but at the same time Dante is superior to Virgil because he believes himself to be saved."[22] And he would look to this father-son relationship between Virgil and Dante as a model to resolve the Kafkaesque relationship with his own father.

Dante's poem was, in a sense, a rewriting of Virgil's *Aeneid*, but this was not the type of rewriting undertaken by Pierre Menard, for Dante had not set out to eclipse Virgil in the way Menard threatened to do with Cervantes; on the contrary, he conceived of his poem as the fulfillment, under the Christian dispensation, of the spiritual truths that were latent in the epic of the great Roman poet. This accounts for Virgil's role as Dante's guide through Hell and Purgatory to the gates of Paradise, which Virgil, as a pagan, was forbidden to enter. Borges, likewise, sought to incorporate his father's destiny into his own myth of salvation. By analogy with Virgil, Dr. Borges had not actually found salvation by writing, but his creative aspirations would acquire some justification if his son were to succeed, like Dante, in writing a masterpiece that would secure his immortality as a writer.

In *The Congress*, therefore, Borges was to transfigure the sense of *El Caudillo* by exactly reversing the import of this father's denouement: the earlier novel ended in the destruction wreaked by the Caudillo, who could not tolerate his daughter's love for Dubois, but the amorous "congress" between Ferri and Beatriz Frost implicitly enlightens the patriarch Glencoe as to the interconnectedness of all things in the world. The difference is evident in the image of the river in both works. In *El Caudillo* the lovers' passion is symbolized by the river's breaking its banks and flooding the plain, but this transgressive passion angers the Caudillo, and the lovers are destroyed. Like his father, Borges chose the image of a river to depict the lovemaking between Ferri and Beatriz: "Oh nights, oh shared, warm darkness, oh the love that flows in the shadows like a secret river, oh that moment of bliss in which each one is both of us." The orgasmic union that provoked the Caudillo's wrath in the earlier novel is precisely what leads to the happy resolution of the latter, so that the shattered idyll portrayed by Dr. Borges is restored and vindicated in the story imagined by his son.

Borges therefore subsumed the structure of *El Caudillo* in his own projected novel and organized his narrative into a Dantean progression through hell and purgatory toward paradise. Indeed, the pattern of the *Divine Comedy* is not hard to discern in Borges's novella. Hell is represented in *The Congress* by the potentially infinite library recommended by Twirl to Glencoe: "It was like being in the center of a growing circle, expanding without end into the distance," an image that brings to mind the circles of Dante's Hell. Indeed, Twirl, "whose intelligence was lucid," is a latter-day Lucifer, plotting with his associates to effect the ruin of the patriarch Glencoe. However, the year Alejandro Ferri spends in London represents his passage through purgatory. Ferri's search for a universal language is conducted in a library, but this is the Reading Room of the British Museum, not Twirl's hellish library, and he will find his universal language not through bookish labors but in the love of Beatriz Frost. His idyll in London with the English Beatrice is thus equivalent to Dante's second meeting with Beatrice in the earthly paradise at the summit of Mount Purgatory, and it opens the way to a final release from Twirl's diabolical influence. Paradise is finally gained when Ferri returns to Buenos Aires, having been taught the language of love by Beatriz Frost. He finds that Glencoe has experienced a mysterious enlightenment that leads him to repudiate Twirl and order the burning of the books that are turning his house into a version of the "total library." From being a misguided caudillo, Glencoe emerges as a benevolent God the Father, who reveals to the members of the society the ultimate truth that all things partake of the same universal spirit. Good thus triumphs over evil, as even Twirl is obliged to recognize.

The unfolding of this tripartite, Dantean structure of Hell, Purgatory, and

Paradise is marvelously spare and elliptical in *The Congress,* for connections are made not by the causal links of a realist novel but by the kind of "sympathetic magic" that Borges had recommended in "The Art of Narrative and Magic," his essay of 1932. And in creating some of these magic links, what is more, Borges made vestigial use of the Dantean device of the *figura:* Ferri's meeting with Beatriz Frost "under the high cupola" of the British Museum's Reading Room foreshadows the overarching unity of the final revelation, while the "red labyrinth" of London, in which Ferri might have lost his way (as his rival Eguren does in Paris), prefigures the form of the Dantean "Rose of the Just" that the city of Buenos Aires will implicitly assume during the collective enlightenment at the end of the story.

The Congress, then, represents Borges's Dantean myth of salvation. The two constituent elements of this myth—the recovery of a woman's love and the writing of a book—are evident in the extant version of the novella, although in a considerably attenuated form, which may be the result of the process of condensation from novel to novella that *The Congress* underwent over the years. In the two women, Nora Erfjord and the red-haired Beatriz Frost, we have a *dédoublement* of Norah Lange. There is the merest suggestion that in a previous draft of *The Congress,* Ferri may have been in love with and rejected by Nora Erfjord—for in London, Beatriz Frost refuses Ferri's proposal of marriage because she, we are told, "like Nora Erfjord, was a devotee of the creed preached by Ibsen and did not want to be tied to anyone." And there is a hint also that, in an earlier draft, Ferri's episode of love with Beatriz Frost may have led to his regaining Nora Erfjord's affections, given that, on his return to Buenos Aires, he tells us that "Nora embraced me and kissed me, and that embrace and that kiss reminded me of others."

If the loss and recovery of a woman's love are hinted at in *The Congress,* so, too, is the theme of writing an autobiographical work that would represent the salvation of its author. We find that *The Congress,* which is Ferri's first-person memoir, is a long-delayed consequence of his final mystical enlightenment, and it reveals the author to be a man at ease with himself, serene and accepting of his place in the world, despite the fact that he never married. Additionally, his reason for writing the memoir is precisely to abandon the secrecy to which the members of the society had been sworn in order to communicate to his readers the nature of his enlightenment—an awareness of the omnipresent reality of the pantheistic "congress of the world."

It is impossible to say, on the evidence currently available, how far Borges had got with the composition of *The Congress* in 1940, but by September of that year, he had become profoundly troubled. A poem called "The Cyclical Night" ("La noche cíclica"), which he published in *La Nación* on October 6, reveals him to be in the throes of a personal crisis.[23] The poem describes a nightmarish vision where Buenos Aires, instead of being a pantheist version of Dante's Rose, as intimated at the end of *The Congress,* has become a labyrinth whose "unanimous streets" are "corridors of vague fears and dreams," a labyrinth in which the minotaur will moan in the infinite night of its "fetid palace," where "every night of insomnia will return: meticulously," where "an obscure Pythagorean rotation" takes Borges back to the *arrabales* he had roamed in the lovelorn nights of his youth and leaves him at "a remote street corner" in the north, south or west of the city, "but which always has a sky-blue wall, a shady fig tree and a broken pavement"—a scene evoking that other timeless scene that produced his strange, mystical experience of "Feeling in Death" ("Sentirse en muerte") shortly after he had been abandoned by Norah Lange in 1926–27:[24]

> There is Buenos Aires. Time, which brings men
> love or gold, leaves me scarcely more than
> this extinguished rose, this useless tangle
> of streets which repeat the bygone names
>
> of my blood: Laprida, Cabrera, Soler, Suárez . . .

The cause of this great surge of anguish was that Haydée Lange had fallen for another man, and as if fate wished to rub salt in Borges's wound, her new lover was a member of a group of poets, later known as the "Generation of 1940," who had been taken up by one of the most powerful literary patrons in Buenos Aires—Oliverio Girondo.[25] Borges's courtship of Haydée had thus ended in a cruel parody of her sister Norah's defection to Girondo. Far from being the "new Beatrice" who would allow him to regain the happiness he had once known at the calle Tronador, Haydée had brought him back full circle to the hell of solipsism. Borges found himself wandering once again in the "concave night," with nothing left but "the memory—the project?—of an unceasing poem," as he put it in "The Cyclical Night." In other words, he would have to abandon *The Congress,* his projected masterpiece, the great Dantean "poem" he had hoped might save both him and his father from oblivion.

The loss of Haydée provoked another suicidal crisis, at least in his imagination, for in the same notebook as he had composed "Tlön, Uqbar and Orbis Tertius," he sketched out the following scenario: after carrying out his duties as a second assistant at the library in the featureless suburb of Boedo, he bought a revolver in a gun shop on calle Entre Ríos, a mystery novel by Ellery Queen that he had already read, and a one-way ticket to Adrogué, where he booked into the Hotel Las Delicias, drank but failed to pay for two or three brandies and then shot himself in one of the rooms upstairs.[26]

Borges added that he had left behind a poem he had written in the Miguel

Cané Library that afternoon, the implication being that it was a kind of suicide note. The poem concerned was a very early draft of an unfinished composition that survives in a notebook also containing certain texts Borges published in 1940. In the extracts from this unfinished poem that have been translated into English and published by Donald Yates, we can see that the reason for wishing to commit suicide was literary failure, stemming ultimately from sexual self-doubt.[27]

The poem describes his dissatisfaction with the imperfect products of his pen and explains that he is taking up the revolver, not out of despair or boredom but in order to find out whether he really does exist. We have here further evidence that in 1940 Borges believed that his project of salvation by writing had been destroyed and that the only alternative was to kill himself. But the poem goes on to speculate on the possibility that he may be dead already anyway—as a result either of the accident in 1938, when he injured his head on the darkened stairway in the apartment building on calle Ayacucho, or of his experience in a mercenary bedroom in the middle of Europe twenty years earlier. The latter is doubtless a reference to his unsuccessful encounter with the woman in Geneva in 1919, an experience that he senses might have a connection with the overwhelming sense of unreality expressed in the poem, though it is a connection he does not yet seem properly to grasp.

The depth of Borges's disillusionment is evident also in three stories he wrote in these months. In "The Circular Ruins" ("Las ruinas circulares"), which he published in *Sur* in December 1940, he imagined a "gray man" arriving at a circular temple dedicated to the god of fire.[28] The man asks the deity for the power to dream a son and insert him in the real world. His wish is granted—he will dream a son whom everyone will take to be real, except that the god of fire and the dreamer himself will know that this creature is, in fact, a phantom, and immune to fire. The "gray man" feels a kind of ecstasy, since the purpose of his life appears to have been fulfilled. Shortly afterward, however, a fire ravages the temple, and the "gray man" discovers that he is unaffected by the flames. He then realizes that he, too, like the son of his dreams, is a phantom—someone else was dreaming him. Borges followed this up in January 1941 with "The Lottery in Babylon" ("La lotería en Babilonia"), in which he took the banal idea that life is like a lottery and contrived a situation in which it was impossible to say whether the lives of the Babylonians were ruled by chance or by the designs of a secret company.[29] Thirdly, in "The Library of Babel" ("La biblioteca de Babel"), another fable written in 1941, the universe is compared to a library where mankind searches in vain for an overall purpose to the vast, geometric edifice in which it is trapped.[30]

All three stories reflected the destruction of Borges's Dantean dream of salvation. Love had passed him by once more, and, untouched as he was by the god of fire, he was little better than a phantom who had himself been dreamed by that other phantom, the "gray man" who had been his father. He could, in consequence, find no end or purpose to his existence; his life might well be ruled by chance as by design. Indeed, the universe itself was like Twirl's library, though on a cosmic scale: it was a "total library," endlessly circular, in which "the same volumes are repeated in the same disorder."

CHAPTER 18

The Garden of Forking Paths
(1940–1944)

BORGES'S TROUBLES were compounded by his unhappiness at the turn of events in Europe. Hitler's invasion of Poland at the beginning of September 1939, and the resultant outbreak of hostilities, filled him with apprehension. He saw the war as an apocalyptic conflict between good and evil. In October 1939 he wrote in *Sur* that a German victory would result in "the ruin and degradation of the entire globe," and for that reason he hoped that the war would lead to the "fortunate annihilation of Adolf Hitler."[1] The war in Europe was to polarize the Argentine literary world: socialist and liberal writers, who supported the Allies against Hitler, took control of the SADE (Sociedad Argentina de Escritores), the Argentine Society of Writers; the pro-Axis *nacionalistas* responded with a writers' union of their own. Borges was to become closely identified with the SADE, and the war years would see his reemergence as a national figure in the cultural politics of Argentina after a long period of relative obscurity in the 1930s. This political involvement, however, would not directly impinge on his literary concerns, but his opposition to the growing power of the *nacionalistas,* and his concomitant fears at the extension of Nazi influence in Argentina, would add a particular urgency and intensity to his writing.

At the end of 1940, Adolfo Bioy Casares published *La invención de Morel,* the novel inspired by the principles advocated by Borges during the week the two friends had spent together at the *estancia* in 1935. Bioy's novel provided an object lesson in Borges's theory of fiction: it was set on an island that was itself a metaphor for the "autonomous sphere" of art, and the narrative rested on a fantasy—a machine capable of producing perfect holographic images of human beings—that was developed with extraordinary rigor to treat metaphysical issues of love and solipsism, time and eternity.

Bioy's admiration for Borges remained undimmed. In the prologue to an anthology of fantasy stories, *Antología de la literatura fantástica,* that Bioy, Silvina Ocampo, and Borges had put together over the previous year and which was published a month after *La invención de Morel*, Bioy lavished praise on Borges for having invented a new kind of fiction:

> With "The Approach to Al-Mu'tasim," with "Pierre Menard," with "Tlön, Uqbar, Orbis Tertius," Borges has created a new literary genre, which partakes of the essay and of fiction. These are examples of unceasing intelligence and ingenious imagination, devoid of weaknesses, of human elements, of sentimentality or pathos, and meant for intellectual readers, aficionados of philosophy, almost for literary specialists.[2]

Bioy asked his mentor to write a foreword to *La invención de Morel*, and Borges would take this as an opportunity to reiterate the core ideas of his 1932 essay "The Art of Narrative and Magic." He wrote that the realist or psychological novel is "formless"—the "total freedom" of the novelist results in "total disorder."[3] The realist novel, what is more, "prefers us to forget the fact that it is a verbal artifice," and he contrasted it with the "intrinsic rigor" of the novel of adventures, which "does not present itself as a transcription of reality: it is an artificial object which does not tolerate any element that cannot be justified." What is central is the plot, he argued, and against those who complained that the twentieth century was incapable of producing interesting plots, he affirmed that if the century was superior in anything to others, it was precisely in the excellence of its plots, and he cited the works of Chesterton, Kafka, and Henry James. As for *La invención de Morel*, "I have discussed with its author the details of its plot; I have reread it; I do not consider it an imprecision or a hyperbole to call it perfect."

Although Borges may have admired the plot of Bioy's novel, it could not have escaped him that he had effectively been upstaged by his own disciple, for if there was one thing that Borges himself had failed to produce after a decade of trying, it was precisely a story with a plot. His continuing sense of failure is evident in "An Examination of the Works of Herbert Quain," a spoof in the vein of "The Approach to Al-Mu'tasim" or "Pierre Menard, Author of *Don Quixote*," which was published in *Sur* in April 1941.[4] This purports to be a necrological memoir by Borges of an Irish writer who had just died and who was the author of a meager oeuvre consisting of four very disparate works, but the spoof may be taken to represent Borges's self-mocking parody of the products of his own unsuccessful pen. The first work by the wretched Quain was a detective novel called *The God of the Labyrinth*, which subverted the detective genre itself, given that the narrator hinted at an alternative possibility that undermined the solution to the crime that the detective believed he had found. The second was a novel called *April March* in which Quain tried to fashion a narrative capable of reflecting time as an infinitely ramifying labyrinth. The third was a two-act play, *The Secret Mirror,* about Wilfred Quarles's love of Ulrica Thrale and his duel with a rival, the Duke of Rutland, in which the reality of the action in the first act was called into question in the second. Quain's fourth work was a collection of eight stories called *Statements,* each of which "prefigured or promised a good plot, but was deliberately spoiled by the author" in a way that would lead readers to believe that they had invented the plots themselves. Quain used to argue that "readers were an extinct species": of all the kinds of happiness afforded by literature, "invention was the highest," but "since not all were capable of such happiness, many would have to make do with faking it." Quain had therefore written his stories to flatter the pseudocreative vanity of his readers, "those 'imperfect writers,' whose number is legion," and Borges, implicitly counting himself among the latter, claimed to have been "naïve" enough to have extracted his story "The Circular Ruins" from the third of Quain's stories, whose title, tellingly, was "The Rose of Yesterday."

However, in his continuing quest for the "happiness" of true invention, for the perfection of plot, Borges would look to the detective story. A longstanding devotee of crime fiction, he saw in the genre a potential for the kind of "classical" narrative order that the realist novel, he believed, had all but lost. As far back as 1933, he had published a brief essay called "Laws of the Detective Story" ("Leyes de la narración policial"), which he subsequently incorporated into an essay on G. K. Chesterton and what he called the "labyrinths of the detective genre."[5] Years later he would explain his interest thus:

> In this epoch of ours, which is so chaotic, there is something which, in its modest way, has maintained the classical virtues: the detective story. For a detective story cannot be understood without a beginning, a middle and an end.[6]

In the latter part of 1941, he and Bioy took up the idea of writing detective stories together, having tried their hand at the genre with the story of Dr. Pretorius during the week they spent at Bioy's *estancia* in 1935. They came up with a new character called Isidro Parodi, a convict in the Penitenciaría of Buenos Aires blessed with the gift of solving crimes without even having to set foot outside his prison cell. Neither writer regarded the Parodi stories as serious work, of course; they would get together in Bioy's study after dinner and spend hours inventing absurd problems for Parodi to solve. The stories were lighthearted parodies of detective fiction (the Italian surname Parodi is fairly common in Buenos Aires), and their simple structure permitted a good deal of social and political satire besides. The first was completed on December 27, 1941, and eventually collected with five more stories in *Six Problems for Don Isidro Parodi* (*Seis problemas para don Isidro Parodi*), published under the pseudonym H. Bustos Domecq, a nom de plume contrived from a family name of Borges and Bioy, respectively.[7]

Around the time he was amusing himself by writing the Parodi stories with Bioy, Borges also drew on detective fiction with more serious ends in mind, and his experiments bore fruit in "The Garden of Forking Paths" ("El jardín de senderos que se bifurcan"). Set in England during the First World War, it concerns Yu Tsun, a Chinese spy working for the Germans who is intent on conveying to his masters the information that the British artillery is preparing to bombard a town called Albert in France. Since he is being hunted by a British agent, Richard Madden, he must find a way of getting his message across before being tracked down and killed. He decides to pass on the name of the French town by killing a man who happens to be called Stephen Albert. The plot is highly teleological, inasmuch as both agent and spy are each pursuing specific goals, but as the action reaches a dizzying climax at Stephen Albert's house, a villa surrounded by a garden of forking paths, the alert reader will pick up clues that betray the fact that all three, ostensibly hostile, characters—Yu Tsun, Madden, and Albert—could, in principle, swap roles in different dimensions of time. The teleology of the detective-style plot is shown to be an illusion, since the forking paths of time branch into a maze of multiple directions, thereby nullifying the particular identity of each of the characters. In this story Borges had contrived to marry the self-aborting detective plot of Herbert Quain's *The God of the Labyrinth* with the time labyrinth of Quain's other novel, *April March,* and the result was what one might call a labyrinthine plot, displaying a mania for order on the surface, but ramifying endlessly in its metaphysical implications.

Shortly after the completion of "The Garden of Forking Paths," Borges decided to bring out a collection that would represent the new genre his young friend Bioy Casares professed to have identified. In addition to "The Approach to Al-Mu'tasim," which had appeared as a "Note" in *A History of Eternity,* he had published six "essay-fictions" since his near fatal accident in 1938: "Pierre Menard, Author of *Don Quixote,*" "Tlön, Uqbar, Orbis Tertius," "The Circular Ruins," "The Lottery in Babylon," and "The Library of Babel." But for the title story of the collection, he chose "The Garden of Forking Paths," his latest as-yet-unpublished tale, and this may well have been a mark of his satisfaction at having finally invented a story with a plot.[8]

The publication of *The Garden of Forking Paths* in December 1941 was considered a landmark event by the writers in the *Sur* group. Reviewing it in *Sur,* Bioy would repeat his claim that Borges had invented a new genre by discovering "the literary possibilities of metaphysics" and combining these with the pursuit of the "ideal" inherent in detective fiction, namely, "inventiveness," "rigor" and "elegance" in the structuring of a narrative.[9] The book was entered for the National Awards for Literature, a competition organized triennially by the Commission for Culture, but it failed to win any of the top three prizes. This must have represented a considerable disappointment for Borges, given that this was the first book he had published since the abject failure of *A History of Eternity* in 1936.

The lack of success of *The Garden of Forking Paths* was not due to any personal animosity toward Borges, however. The panel of judges included his cousin, Álvaro Melián Lafinur; Roberto Giusti, an editor of *Nosotros* who had known him since the days of the avant-garde; and the novelist Eduardo Mallea, a member of the *Sur* group. The truth was that the judges had simply not known what to make of Borges's weird "essay-fictions." In July 1942, Giusti published a note in *Nosotros* giving the judges' assessment of *The Garden of Forking Paths.* The panel had judged it inappropriate to recommend to the Argentine people "an exotic and decadent work" that followed "certain deviant tendencies of contemporary English literature," hovering as it did "between the tale of fantasy, a pretentious and recondite erudition, and detective fiction"; Borges's work amounted to a "dehumanized literature," "an obscure and arbitrary cerebral game."[10] In the end the judges played it safe and rewarded books (all since forgotten) on familiar Argentine subjects: the first prize went to a novel about gauchos, the second to a historical novel about the wars between caudillos, and the third to a collection of stories about the *arrabales* of Buenos Aires. So while the judges' decision may not in itself have been political, it had a political resonance in the climate of the time: it reflected a shift toward the kind of writing advocated by the *nacionalistas,* full of the "local color" that Borges and his friends were determined to avoid.

Indeed, in the course of 1941, the political tide had turned in favor of the *nacionalistas.* The Concordancia coalition, which had kept itself in power through ballot rigging for nearly a decade, had been weakened by a deep recession, and when ill health forced President Roberto M. Ortiz to relinquish office, his replacement, Ramón S. Castillo, tried to bolster his position by including military officers in his cabinet, a move that encouraged the *nacionalistas,* whose strategy had always been to goad the armed forces into seizing control of the state. Believing that their hour had come, the *nacionalistas* marched in the streets shouting slogans against the Allies and the Jews and urging support for the Nazis. In response to this right-wing agitation, the parties of the center and left—Radicals, Socialists, Communists, and others—formed the Unión Democrática and pressed Castillo to abandon the policy of Argentine neutrality and join with the Allies against Germany and Japan.

Borges's failure to win a National Award for Literature would thrust him into the public eye as one of the leading representatives of the anti-*nacionalista* and anti-Nazi intellectuals in Argentina. The judges' decision caused dismay, even outrage, among Borges's friends. As a way of "making amends" to Borges for the supposed injustice he had suffered, Pepe Bianco, the editor of *Sur*, reacted by publishing a homage to Borges in the magazine, in which twenty-one writers and critics wrote in praise of *The Garden of Forking Paths*.[11] Bianco would also organize a well-publicized dinner in Borges's honor on July 18, 1942, which was attended by some of the most distinguished and famous Argentine writers. Borges, in any case, had entered the ideological fray with his customary relish for polemic. In an article published in *Sur* in December 1941, he attacked the Argentine "Germanophiles" as a potential fifth column, since they could, in his view, provide the Nazis with a bridgehead in the event of an invasion by German forces in search of the precious lebensraum in which Argentina was so abundant.[12]

Despite his growing public role in the cultural politics of Argentina, however, Borges's writing continued to deal with profoundly personal concerns, and not least with the collapse of his Dantean myth of salvation after his loss of Haydée Lange. Early in 1942 he undertook a very ambitious story called "Death and the Compass" ("La muerte y la brújula"), in which he sought to represent the opposite of what he had hoped to achieve in *The Congress*—not a process of transfiguration and resolution but an articulation of the conflicts that had generated the condition of "unreality" or solipsism from which he continued to suffer. Once again he would resort to the detective story to organize the turmoil of his inner world into a semblance of order.

In "Death and the Compass," the detective Erik Lönnrot is investigating the murder of a Jewish scholar of the Kabbalah.[13] A strange hubris impels him to seek the killer by a process of pure reason. However, Lönnrot is in fact being manipulated by his archenemy, a Jewish criminal called Red Scharlach, who plans secretly to draw the detective to his death by trapping him in a labyrinth of misleading clues. Scharlach thus encourages Lönnrot to elaborate an intellectual hypothesis based on Kabbalistic ideas regarding the secret name of God. After three murders appear to have been committed, Lönnrot calculates that a fourth will take place at a villa called Triste-le-Roy. This villa, Lönnrot finds, is a nightmarish place, haunted by the "monstrous shadow" of a "two-faced Hermes":

Triste-le-Roy abounded in useles symmetries and maniacal repetitions: a glacial Diana in a gloomy niche was matched by a second niche with another Diana; a balcony was reflected in another balcony; a double staircase opened onto a double balustrade.

Expecting to surprise the murderer, Lönnrot is suddenly confronted by Scharlach, and it dawns on him that it is he who is to be the fourth victim.

The dualities of Triste-le-Roy reach their feverish apogee in this confrontation between the enemies, but at the very climax of the story, both men feel an identical sadness: the detective and the criminal seem to be mirror images of each other rather than polar opposites. The maddening dualities of Triste-le-Roy thus finally dissolve into a oneness, but this is not the mystical oneness of the realized self in communion with the cosmos; it is the vacuous oneness of solipsism, where everything turns out to be yet another version of the same. Triste-le-Roy—*le roi triste*—represents the abode of that sad king, the solipsistic subject, who may be sovereign in himself yet unable to connect with anything other than himself. Lönnrot and Scharlach, therefore, are two aspects of the same person, so that "Death and the Compass," as Borges himself would point out, is "in a symbolic way" a story about "a man committing suicide."[14]

There subsists, nevertheless, in this story the memory of a happier condition. All the windows Lönnrot opens at Triste-le-Roy reveal "the same desolate garden from various heights and various angles." This must surely be a degraded version of the garden of delights that was the Lange villa on calle Tronador, a place where love had made Borges feel as fully a part of reality as were "the stones and the trees." But love has withered and died in Triste-le-Roy—Lönnrot comes across "a single flower in a porcelain vase" in one of the bedrooms; at the first touch, "its old petals crumbled away." We can discern here a reference to Borges's Dantean myth, a reference that is encoded also in the title itself, for "Death and the Compass" is a demonstration that the intellect on its own leads to death, whereas love provides a compass (known to mariners as "the rose of the winds") that will lead us to salvation by taking us out of ourselves and engaging with another.

"Death and the Compass" was published in May of 1942, a year that, as the magazine *Leoplan* would report, was "not very propitious" for Borges as far as his health was concerned.[15] His problems were very likely caused by a serious deterioration in his congenitally poor eyesight. He had undergone an operation for cataracts in 1941, and possibly another the following year—there is a reference to blindness, "the visible darkness of John Milton"—in a poem written in this period, which may point to fears that he might lose his sight altogether.[16]

These recurrent bouts of ill health had brought him closer to his mother, Leonor Acevedo—she had nursed him at the time of his near fatal accident at the end of 1938, and he had relied on her assistance with everyday tasks for weeks at a time after his various eye operations. The illness and death of his father also played a part in bringing them together: Borges had much appreciated the devotion his mother had shown her ailing husband, and he admired her courage in coping with life as a widow. By this time, moreover, mother and son lived on their own under the same roof, and they would do so for the rest of Doña Leonor's long life. In 1941 they had moved from the family home at calle Anchorena 1672, which they had shared with Norah Borges and her husband since the latter's return from Spain during the Civil War, to an apartment at avenida Quintana 263, and thence they would move finally in 1947 to a small sixth-floor flat at calle Maipú 994.

As Borges found himself increasingly in his mother's debt, however, he became more conscious of the emotional ties that bound him to her, and this realization aroused certain anxieties in him. These are evident in "Death and the Compass," where the very name of the Jewish criminal, Red Scharlach, identifies him with the forbidden color of the tyrant Rosas, the historic enemy of Mother's family. Scharlach is motivated by a desire to take revenge on the Christian Lönnrot for an earlier attempt to compel him to convert to Catholicism. Even so, the Jewish criminal remains haunted by the fear that "all roads lead to Rome," that he may be absorbed into an all-embracing order that would wipe out his separate identity. Red Scharlach's final perception that he may be no more than a mirror image of Lönnrot fills him with sadness, because it suggests that his rebellion against "Rome," his efforts to be distinctive and free, like those of the would-be gaucho Otálora in "The Dead Man," may be self-deceiving fantasies after all. And Scharlach's fears were Borges's fears, of course, for there was a danger that his growing attachment to "Mother"— Madre, as he still called her—would compromise his already fragile sense of independence.

Still, this newfound closeness between mother and son served to bring into clearer focus the nature of the mysterious, Kafkaesque inhibition that had, time and again, neutralized his efforts to rebel against Mother. On July 26, 1942, just two months after the publication of "Death and the Compass," Borges published "The Shape of the Sword" ("La forma de la espada") in La Nación.[17] The narrator is an Irish rancher in Argentina, whose face bears a terrible scar shaped like a crescent moon. He tells Borges that he had been a rebel in the cause of Irish independence and that he had been betrayed to the British by a comrade called John Vincent Moon. It turns out that the narrator is himself the traitor Moon and that he has chosen to unburden himself of his guilt by confessing to Borges the tale of his own treachery in the persona of his victim. However, the scar on his face was inflicted by the sword of the man he betrayed, and it remains there as an indelible "mark of infamy."

The story is powered by Borges's own guilt feelings, and certain details hint at the nature of the concealed matter that may have caused such guilt.

The traitor Moon's ranch is called La Colorada, which literally means "The Red One." The color red was the forbidden color of Rosas, but the phrase *la colorada* is also used in Argentina to refer to a woman with red hair. One can discern in these associations a conflict in Borges's psyche that equates the freedom to associate with a redhead (a *colorada* like Norah Lange) with the betrayal of a hero (one, mutatis mutandis, like Colonel Suárez, his maternal ancestor, who fought in the wars of South American independence against the Spanish). And the price to be paid for such a betrayal of the hero figure is to be slashed across the face with the sword of honor.

Borges was reaching down to the roots of the mysterious inhibition that had prevented him from realizing his passion for a woman. In the "Dead Man" he had expressed his desire to rebel against the authority of his ancestors and had explained the failure of this rebellion in terms of a trick that had thwarted his "will to power." But "The Shape of the Sword" reveals the other side of the coin—his very real fear of betraying his ancestors and of being punished for bringing "infamy" upon the family. Between them the two stories illustrate the dilemma that had paralyzed Borges's creative imagination—on the one hand, he craved the freedom to assert his will as he pleased, but, on the other, he wished to uphold the good name of the family. Either way he ran the risk of being a traitor—if he opted for freedom, he risked "infamy," yet if submitted to the sword of honor, he would betray his true desires, which would spell his death as a writer.

In the latter half of 1942, it seemed impossible that he would ever resolve the dilemma and overcome his inhibition, but this meant that he would have to give up all hope of salvation by writing, since this hinged so critically on the inspiration of a woman's love. The sheer despair he felt at having to renounce the Dantean myth of salvation brought forth a new story called "The Secret Miracle" ("El milagro secreto").[18] The central character is a Jewish writer called Jaromir Hladík, who is arrested by the Nazis and sentenced to death by firing squad shortly after the German invasion of Czechoslovakia in March 1939. As the day of his execution approaches, Hladík cannot face dying without some justification of his existence. He reviews his literary career (which is not unlike that of Borges himself at the time) and wishes he could "redeem the whole of that dubious and unimpressive past" by completing his unfinished tragedy, *The Enemies*. Like Herbert Quain's *The Secret Mirror*, Hladík's play reflects Borges's involvement with Norah Lange and Oliverio Girondo. *The Enemies* concerns a tacit rivalry between Baron Roemerstadt and a certain Jaroslav Kubin over the love of Julia von Weidenau. In the final act, it becomes evident to the audience that the character of Roemerstadt is a projection of the thwarted Kubin and that the dramatic action is no more than the "circular delirium which Kubin endlessly lives and relives."

Hladík asks God to grant him the miracle of one year in which to finish the play, because this was a work in which he saw the "possibility of redeeming (in a symbolic manner) what was fundamental about his life." In Hladík's request for a miracle, we have the most explicit declaration of Borges's own desire for salvation by writing:

> If I could be said to exist in any way, if I am not one of Your repetitions and errors, I exist as the author of *The Enemies.* In order to bring the play to completion, this play which could justify me and justify You, I will need one more year. Grant me that span of time, You to whom the centuries and time belong.

Hladík's predicament reveals the depth of Borges's despair at the end of the very difficult year of 1942. Like Hladík, Borges could conceive of writing a saving masterpiece only by virtue of a God-given miracle. In "The Secret Miracle," time is suspended for a year, and this allows Hladík to finish his play before being executed by the Nazis, but such a miracle, in Borges's case, was a fantasy—the truth was that his emotional bond with his mother had sapped his will to rebel against the sword of honor, and the death he faced, as a result, was not by firing squad but by inanition.

Although Borges was under no immediate threat from his political enemies, "The Secret Miracle" articulated growing anxieties about the situation in Argentina, for in the latter months of 1942, rumors of a military plot to overthrow the Castillo government were circulating in Buenos Aires. The disaster Borges most dreaded appeared to be at hand—a coup d'état that would create a fascist state as a preliminary to a German invasion of the Americas. Three months after "The Secret Miracle" was published in *Sur* in February 1943, the rumored military uprising became a reality. On June 4 the Castillo government succumbed to a coup masterminded by a group of young army officers who were pro-Axis and strongly *nacionalista* in ideology. Up to seventy lives were lost in armed clashes between the rebels and units of the Argentine navy, but the success of the coup was greeted with violent rejoicing by *nacionalista* militants, who took to burning British-owned buses in the streets of Buenos Aires. And the new junta soon revealed its fascist inclinations, proclaiming its mission to preserve "the sacred interests of the nation" and to resist any attempts to subvert the foundations of "national identity." On June 18 a decree was issued condemning artists and intellectuals who showed insufficient interest in "historical themes," by which was meant Argentine history as interpreted by the *nacionalistas,* based as this was on the glorification of Rosas as the embodiment of authentic criollo values.[19]

It may have been this ominous development that prompted Borges to make a very public stand against the junta. On July 4, just two weeks after the June 18 decree, he published "Conjectural Poem" ("Poema conjetural") in the great liberal daily *La Nación.*[20] This was a dramatic monologue in which he assumed the voice of his ancestor, Francisco Laprida, who was murdered in 1829 by a band of gauchos acting on the orders of a traditionalist caudillo. The choice of Laprida was a telling one—he had been president of the Congress of Tucumán when it proclaimed the independence of the United Provinces of Río de la Plata in 1816. Borges was contesting the military junta by going back to the very source of the Argentine national identity and claiming it for liberals like Laprida who threw off the colonial yoke in order to build a free republic based on the values of the European Enlightenment.

"Conjectural Poem" could scarcely have been a more flagrant declaration of Borges's opposition to the military junta, but it was also a very intimate poem, imbued with a curious, almost suicidal, pessimism, as Laprida yields gratefully in the end to the sweet violence of death's embrace:

> At last the first blow.
> At last the hard blade ripping my chest,
> the intimate dagger at my throat.

Borges's attitude here was not so different from that of his character Hladík in "The Secret Miracle" as he faced execution by the Nazis. If there were no longer any chance—short of a miracle—of justifying himself as a writer, he might as well resolve his inner conflict by taking up the ancestral sword against the gaucho dagger and proving himself worthy of his heroic ancestors.

But fate, as it happened, chose to deny Borges such a resolution. On July 16, just two weeks after the appearance of "Conjectural Poem," Norah Lange married Oliverio Girondo after nearly a decade of fitful cohabitation. Girondo had given his consent on condition that the deed were done in private, and the wedding itself took place in such secrecy that even the Lange family was required to wait outside the fashionable Church of El Socorro, having tea and buns in a *confitería* across the road while Norah was getting Oliverio finally to tie the knot.[21] But as far as Borges was concerned, Norah's marriage to Girondo could not have failed to reopen the old emotional wounds, pointing up the contradiction between his public defense of "civilization" against the "barbarians" of the military junta, as expressed in "Conjectural Poem," and his unquenched desire to taste the "barbarism" of the passion he felt for the red-haired Norah Lange.

In the months following Norah Lange's wedding he composed a story called "Theme of the Traitor and the Hero" ("Tema del traidor y del héroe"), based on the conceit of a man who was publicly venerated as a national hero but who was secretly a traitor to the cause he had ostensibly championed.[22] It was as if Borges believed that by publishing "Conjectural Poem," he had betrayed the passion he had once felt for Norah and sacrificed the desire for freedom that had made him a writer. And it was a wish to expiate this private "treachery," I believe, that led him to pay homage to those memories of his youth in a volume of his collected poems—*Poemas (1922-1943)*—which the Editorial Losada was planning to bring out that year.

In this collection he secretly honored the memory of his love for Norah Lange by including the two poems he had written to her in English in the early 1930s. They appeared under the title "Prose Poems for I. J.," this being the same cryptic dedicatee as had appeared in *A Universal History of Infamy* of 1935.[23] The second of these poems, beginning with the line "What can I hold you with?," he now meaningfuly dated 1934, thus recalling the precise juncture that he had seen as offering a last chance to win her back from Girondo. Norah had been his Beatrice figure, but Borges also decided to honor the woman he had thought of as the "new Beatrice" who might have led him back to the paradise he had lost. Accordingly, he dedicated the poem "Llaneza" ("Frankness") from *Fervor de Buenos Aires* to Haydée Lange, for this was the poem in which he had celebrated the happiness afforded him by the Lange household on the calle Tronador.

No doubt Borges intended these dedications as signals to Norah and Haydée of his enduring appreciation. But their meaning was so private, so cryptic, that they resulted in a strange misunderstanding. When Borges's *Poemas (1922–1943)* came out on December 17, 1943, Haydée's boyfriend grew suspicious of Borges's dedication of the poem "Llaneza" to Haydée, and he persuaded himself, additionally, that the English "Prose Poems for I. J." must also have been secretly dedicated to her because, as he told his friends, Haydée's middle name was Julia, so he reckoned that Borges must have substituted the initial *H* of her first name with an *I*, the next letter in the alphabet, as a cryptographical device.[24]

Haydée's boyfriend appears to have been an emotionally unstable young man in the throes of a severe personal crisis at the time that Borges's collected poems were published. According to his close friend Olga Orozco, he became obsessively jealous of Borges, believing—quite wrongly—that the latter was conducting a clandestine affair with Haydée.[25] The young man's jealousy soon got out of hand, and his friends became concerned about his mental condition when they learned that he was staying up till the early hours of the morning watching the entrance to the apartment building where Haydée lived, in order to try to catch Borges visiting her in secret. Shortly afterward he seems to have become quite unhinged, and at the end of December 1943 he was found drowned in Buenos Aires Harbor. Haydée was devastated by her fiancé's death: she was never to marry and became even more enigmatic and reclusive than before.

Borges's involvement with the Lange sisters had brought him nothing but heartache, and the extent of his emotional disorientation at this point may be gauged from an episode that occurred very shortly after the death of Haydée's boyfriend. He met Elsa Astete, the woman whom he had briefly courted in 1930, when he used to stay at her mother's guesthouse while visiting Pedro Henríquez Ureña at La Plata. There survive two letters from this strange encounter with Elsa early in 1944.[26] One was dated "Friday 31st," which likely refers to the end of January 1944, and it shows that Borges had spent the previous morning and afternoon with Elsa. He characterizes their meeting as a miracle: she has become indispensable to him, and he begs her not to disappear from his life because she must save him from the pointlessness of his existence, from his loneliness. Everyone other than Elsa seems unreal; he would like to overwhelm her with a minute description of his bedroom so that his surroundings might thereby lose their phantom quality a little. He is overjoyed at the thought that he might perhaps see her again in a few days' time, yet how unbearable it was to think that in order to see her, he would have to wait those few days.

In the other letter, which is dated February 4, 1944, he tells Elsa that he thinks of her with unwavering intensity: the days and nights of loneliness he had to endure not only made him very unhappy, they were also unreal because he could not share them with her. He had just corrected the proofs of "Theme of the Traitor and the Hero" and would dedicate the story to her. In a postscript he mentions that in the early hours of the morning he tended to feel a desire that was infinite yet futile, and adds that he tried to take his mind off his troubles by burying himself in work.

What is one to make of this encounter, and the impassioned missives it produced? I suspect that, following Norah Lange's marriage and the tragic loss suffered by her sister Haydée, Borges was trying to relaunch his Dantean scheme of salvation at a time when he was under the most intense emotional stress. And in his despair he turned to Elsa Astete as a possible candidate for the role of the "new Beatrice" who might offer a miraculous deliverance from the knot of contradictions that was causing him so much pain. But he had lost touch with reality—Elsa had already spurned him once before, and, since she had married another man six years earlier, there was even less reason for her to respond to his desperate pleas at this juncture.

The Dantean scheme could not be revived: there was no hope of saving himself and no hope, therefore, of redeeming his father. The perverse trinity of father, son, and ancestral ghost seemed to be the inescapable condition of his existence. In a new story entitled "Three Versions of Judas" ("Tres versiones de Judas"), he reworked the paradox of the traitor and the hero, recasting it in terms of the Christian drama of perdition and redemption and pushing it to the extreme of conceiving the blasphemy of a "redeemer-traitor."[27] A Gnostic theologian, Nils Runeberg, believes that Judas was the true redeemer because Jesus could not have died on the cross had he not first been betrayed by Judas. This is God the Father's "guilty secret": He has condemned His son Judas to Hell in order that he redeem mankind. Runeberg believes, furthermore, that he has himself been punished for discovering God the Father's secret, and his punishment bears an uncannny resemblance to the afflictions visited upon Borges's own father—blindness and an aneurysm. Indeed, the subtext of the story is best understood from the imagined perspective of Borges's own father, for Dr. Borges had looked to Georgie to "betray" the ancestral sword of honor in order to redeem them both with his pen, but Georgie's rebellion had come to nothing, and he, too, had been condemned to hell by the unforgiving, patriarchal spirit of their ancestors. The story ends with Runeberg wandering the streets of Malmö, "intoxicated by insomnia and vertiginous dialectic" and crying out for the grace to share Hell with Judas the redeemer.

Borges had reached a dead end, and the temptation to suicide must have been as powerful now as in comparable situations in the past. He held on, no doubt, by burying himself in work, but even so, his suicidal tendencies were redirected toward politics. At the time "Three Versions of Judas" was published in *Sur* in August 1944, the military junta seemed to be paving the way for the creation of a fascist state in Argentina. Political parties had been driven underground; workers' leaders had been dismissed from the labor unions; Jewish property and organizations had come under attack. The appointment of Gustavo Martínez Zuviría as minister of justice and education bode ill for intellectual freedom. The author of bestselling novels under the pseudonym "Hugo Wast," Zuviría was a fervent *nacionalista* and a notorious anti-Semite, whose declared aim was "to make the country truly Christian" and "root out doctrines based on class hatred and atheism."[28] He proceeded to impose compulsory religious education in state schools and to weed out communists from the universities. Meanwhile, there was creeping censorship of the press, while *nacionalista* publications denounced "liberalism," "imperialism," and "cosmopolitanism." But, worst of all, a charismatic leader had emerged from among the cabal of young officers who had engineered the coup d'état of 1943. This was Colonel Juan Domingo Perón, who, as minister of labor, was building a huge base of support for himself by weaning the workers away from their traditional labor unions with a series of populist measures. Perón displayed the attributes of a Mussolini, and it could not be long before he orchestrated some sort of putsch that would give him the power to turn Argentina into a fascist dictatorship. It would be but a short step from there to a takeover of the country by the Nazis.

This, clearly, was a time of reckoning for Argentina, and Borges would rise to the occasion by challenging the growing totalitarianism of the regime in the cause of cultural freedom. In the latter part of 1944, he decided to publish a collection of the six new stories he had written since *The Garden of Forking Paths*. The title he chose for his new book was *Artificios*, which was in keeping with his belief that fiction constituted an artificial *orbe autónomo*, but it was also a title that asserted his right to be as politically disengaged and "cosmopolitan" as he pleased. The scandal over his failure to win a National Award for Literature two years earlier had made Borges one of the most prominent of the regime's intellectual opponents, and his friends in the *Sur* group and at SADE were alive to the possibility of exploiting *Artificios* for political ends. It was the Communist writer Enrique Amorim who came up with an idea that would maximize the political capital that could be made from the publication of Borges's stories: he proposed that SADE create a prize of its own and award it to Borges. The latter seems to have been quite happy to go along with this maneuver, and it may well have been Amorim's proposal that influenced his decision to reissue *The Garden of Forking Paths*, the object of the earlier controversy, under the same cover as *Artificios*, in order, as it were, to add fuel to the fire. This double collection was then called *Ficciones*, as unpolitical a title as *Artificios* and one that, under the circumstances, would make the likes of "Hugo Wast" see red. The book came out on December 4, 1944, and several months later it duly received the "Gran Premio de Honor" that had been specially created for it by SADE.[29]

The presentation of this "Grand Prize" was made at a dinner in July 1945, which, even more than the dinner held in Borges's honor when he failed to receive a National Award for *The Garden of Forking Paths*, became a political event, a rallying point for the writers who supported the Unión Democrática. In his speech of thanks, Borges was to reveal something of the raw suffering from which these *ficciones* had been distilled.[30] Having been criticized for the "dehumanized" quality of his work when he was denied a National Award in 1941, he spoke of the twenty years of "obscurity" that had preceded the receipt of the SADE award. He had been "nourished on dangerous poisons": he had fed on "darkness, bitterness, frustration, interminable useless evenings, and neglect." He rejoiced that the prize should have been given to a work of fantasy, because the literature of fantasy, far from being a "marginal genre," was in fact the most ancient of all: "Dreams, symbols and images traverse our lives; a welter of imaginary worlds flows unceasingly through the world." But he concluded on a political note, denouncing the *nacionalistas* and the Nazi ideology they so admired. Nazism, he said, posed a problem for the writer: it exalted the superiority of one's fatherland, language, religion, and race, and this conviction was one of the traditional themes of literature, but "a perverse sect" had so "contaminated those ancient and innocent inclinations" that to practice them today amounted to a form of "complicity." That was why, since 1939, he had not written a single line that might have led to any confusion on this issue. Although he was not "cut out for heroism" and his life as a man had been "an unpardonable succession of miserable experiences" (*mezquindades*), he hoped to achieve a greater dignity in his life as a writer.

Still, despite this cryptic allusion to the misery of his life, Borges's entire outlook had been transformed since the publication of *Ficciones* in December 1944. By the time he came to give his speech of thanks at the SADE dinner in July 1945, he had fallen for a young woman, and he had reason to believe that she might qualify as the "new Beatrice" who would release him from the hell described in his fictions and lead him to a paradise that only love could unlock.

PART FOUR

Of Hell and Heaven

(1944–1969)

CHAPTER 19

The "New Beatrice"

(1944–1946)

ONE NIGHT in August 1944, Borges was introduced to a young woman called Estela Canto at a party given by Bioy Casares and Silvina Ocampo. Slim, dark and pretty, Estela had searching eyes and a wry smile that gave her an appearance of fierce intelligence, which she would preserve into old age. At twenty-eight, she was eighteen years younger than Borges, and she had deviated from the conventional path of Argentine women by choosing not to marry and to follow instead a career in journalism and publishing. She was now making a name for herself as a writer, and two of her stories had recently been accepted by *Sur*. Her brother Patricio, a writer on the fringes of the *Sur* group, had introduced her to Silvina Ocampo, and Estela soon became a regular guest at the Bioys' literary soirées.

Her first encounter with Borges was unpromising: she had read his "Death and the Compass" in *Sur*, a story that had amazed her, but she was distinctly unimpressed by its author's appearance—although she had been told he was not very good-looking, he was even worse than expected: he was chubby, fairly tall, with a pale, fleshy face and remarkably small feet.[1] After absentmindedly shaking her hand, Borges took very little notice of her, a lack of attention that irritated Estela, because in those days she took it for granted that men would find her attractive. She was, in fact, a woman of wide sexual experience: she had had affairs with writers but preferred men of action, and when she met Borges, she was involved with an Englishman, "a British spy who constantly traveled all over Argentina and Brazil."[2]

After that first meeting, they hardly came across each other, but around the date that *Ficciones* was published, on December 4, Estela happened to be leaving the Bioys' apartment at the same time as Borges, and as they headed together toward the *subterráneo* (the Buenos Aires underground), she must have said something that caught Borges's attention, because when they reached the entrance, he suggested they walk on for a few blocks. It was past midnight, but a pleasant breeze was blowing up from the river and the jacarandas were still in blossom, a sign that spring had not yet given way to the stifling heat of the Buenos Aires summer.

They walked down the avenida Santa Fe until they reached the Plaza San Martín, but he offered to walk her home to the barrio of Barracas on the south side, a considerable distance away. They had been talking about the rise of Colonel Perón, the minister of labor, who had come to dominate the military junta and was creating a formidable power base in the trade-union movement. Estela, who was left wing, believed that a fascist takeover was a very real danger. Borges, too, regarded Perón's rise as a nightmare, but he believed that it would be over once the war ended in the expected victory for the Allies. At some point in their conversation, Estela mentioned George Bernard Shaw and quoted in English the ending of *Candida*. The fact that she knew English and could quote her favorite passages by heart pleased Borges enormously. When they stopped to have a drink at a bar, he looked at her closely, as if he were noticing her for the first time, and said in English, "The smile of the Mona Lisa and the movements of a knight on a chess board." Estela was flattered—and gratified that at last this man ("another man") had taken a fancy to her; and it was not just on account of her looks, for Borges then added, "It's the first time I've come across a woman who likes Bernard Shaw. How strange!"

They finally arrived at the apartment building where Estela lived, on the corner of calles Tacuarí and Chile, but Borges suggested they go to the Parque Lezama, since it was close, he said, though she knew it was actually twelve blocks away. The Parque Lezama is an oasis of refreshing greenery perched on the southeastern edge of the great city, just before the high ground slopes toward the docks and the old shantytown of La Boca. A traditional haunt of young lovers, it had once been very beautiful, but its discreetly romantic atmosphere had been diminished by years of neglect as the neighborhood declined from its former gentility.

Borges led Estela to an abandoned amphitheater in the park, across the way from the blue onion dome of the Orthodox church. Even in old age, Estela could visualize "the play of light and shadows as the leaves swayed in the breeze" that night; it was there she first began to appreciate "the nuances and the charm" of Borges's "quavering voice": everything he said had "a magical quality," and, like a conjuror, he seemed to produce "unexpected things from an inexhaustible hat"; this verbal magic "pointed to the man he really was, the man concealed behind the Georgie we all knew, a man who, in his shy way, was struggling to emerge, struggling to be acknowledged." It was well after three in the morning when Borges glanced at his watch and said it was time to go home. It had been an evening of mutual discovery and tantalizing promise: Estela had seen through Borges's unprepossessing exterior and sensed the exceptional spirit that was trapped within, while Borges had found himself intrigued by this mysterious young woman, whose smile hinted at a delightfully perverse nature, a woman who seemed to twist and feint like a knight in chess and who was likely, therefore, to take him by surprise.

That morning—just a few hours after they had parted—Borges called at Estela's apartment and left a book for her with the maid. It was a copy of Joseph Conrad's *Youth*. He did not ask to see her, though, and his negligence puzzled Estela. That evening he came around again, offering to accompany her to the soirée at the Bioys'. When she mentioned his earlier omission, he looked flustered, muttering something about not wanting to bother her. It seemed to Estela that he might have been embarrassed by the "poetic and innocent moments" they had shared in the park, but it was not embarrassment as such: he was flustered because he had fallen in love.

After their fortuitous tryst in the Parque Lezama, Borges made a habit of telephoning Estela from a public phone every morning before ten o'clock, and he would often turn up at her apartment bringing her the gift of a book. He had the awkward air of someone who feared he might be intruding, an apologetic attitude that soon began to irritate the down-to-earth Estela. They fell into the habit of meeting every evening at the entrance to the *subterráneo* at Constitución Station and going to the cinema or to eat at the Bioys'. They would take long walks in the barrios of Barracas or La Boca or in the warren of quiet roads around the huge railway terminus at Constitución. A favorite spot was the first footbridge across the tracks to the south of Constitución, a functional structure of crossed girders that nonetheless held considerable poetic associations for Borges, for it provides a vantage point from which one can see a maze of tracks splaying outward from the station, merging and crossing and dividing as they disappear eventually toward the south, toward the pampas, which, according to Estela, Borges always imagined as "something vast and free." On these walks together, they engaged in quite heated discussions, mostly about literature or politics, about which Estela held strong views of her own. She liked to plant an "insidious thorn" in his "fixed opinions." She could not abide Henry James, for instance, finding him convoluted, inhibited, fearful, but this view infuriated Borges, who would counter with sarcastic remarks about her literary tastes. The fact that Estela was not afraid to speak her mind must have made her even more desirable in his eyes, though he could not have anticipated at this stage quite where Estela's probing would eventually lead.

At the time Borges started seeing Estela regularly—in early December 1944—he began to work, or indeed may already have been working, on a new story, which he was to call "The Aleph." The stimulus for the story was very likely his learning toward the end of 1944 that the villa on calle Tronador was being put up for sale by the Lange family, who had been renting it out since they moved to the city center in 1934. The story would recapitulate his experience of amorous failure—he would describe the fruitless devotion of "Borges" to a beautiful woman called Beatriz Viterbo, a devotion so fruitless that the story would begin with the death of Beatriz and recount the protagonist's continuing obsession with this unreachable lady after her death, visiting her house every year on her birthday until he is informed that the house is due to be demolished, which is what prompts the final mystical vision of the Aleph—a quasidivine vision of the whole universe.

There are aspects of "The Aleph" that recall Norah Lange: the term "aleph" had first been used by Borges in late 1924, when he was becoming captivated with Norah, and then in mid-1926, at the height of his love affair with her; Beatriz Viterbo is said to have died in February 1929, and this was almost certainly the month and year of Norah's rejection of Borges shortly after her return from Norway.[3] But in this story Borges cast his experience with Norah in a Dantean mold. The name Beatriz Viterbo obviously recalls the Beatrice of the *Divine Comedy,* and Borges took from Dante the fundamental theme that a woman's love may lead to a vision of universal wholeness. However, the *Divine Comedy* was the result of Dante's rejection by the real Beatrice, whereas Borges suggests that his failure to win the love of a woman had deprived him of the ability to write a work embodying a sublime vision comparable to Dante's. "The Aleph," therefore, is not about the loss of love as such; it is a lament for the loss of what love might have afforded Borges. By way of emphasizing this point, Borges invented a comic character called Carlos Argentino Daneri, a cousin of Beatriz Viterbo's, who is laboring on the absurd enterprise of describing the entire world in a poem. Some have seen in the name Daneri a contraction of Dante Alighieri, and certainly this pedantic versifier is an anti-Dante, a man so obtuse that he cannnot see the impossibility of apprehending the world in language if one is lacking the demon of inspiration.

Borges had set himself a challenge in writing this story: he wanted to give the reader some sense of what the "Borges" character had lost through the death of Beatriz Viterbo, and he hoped to round it off with an example of the kind of ecstatic writing he had always aspired to but never been able to achieve. He proposed to do this by inventing the fantastic device of a magic orb—an "Aleph"—that would afford the "Borges" character an all-embracing vision of the universe. However, the creative difficulty lay in attempting to describe a mystical experience that was unknown to him precisely because he had never been granted its essential prerequisite—a woman's love.

Still, toward the end of 1944, we find Borges imbued with a certain optimism about his writing. In reply to a questionnaire to be published in a new literary review called *Latitud,* he said he planned in the immediate future to work on a number of fantastical and metaphysical stories, as well as a detective story in collaboration with Bioy Casares.[4] In the longer term, he proposed to write a long narrative or short novel entitled *The Congress,* which would reconcile "the habits of Whitman and those of Kafka." His "greatest literary ambition," however, was "to write a book, a chapter, a page, a paragraph, that would be all things to all men . . . that would dispense with my aversions, my preferences, my habits." This transcendental work should also be "unfathomable and eternal": it should "preserve (for me as for everyone else) a changing angle of shadow; it should correspond in some way to the past and even to the secret future; it should not be exhausted by analysis; it should be the rose without purpose, the Platonic, intemporal rose."

We may see in the mystical Aleph vision that Borges was proposing to compose as the climax of his new story a foretaste, as it were, of the impassioned, transcendental, roselike writing he enthused about in the questionnaire for *Latitud.* And now that he had fallen in love with Estela Canto, he would seek to enlist her assistance in firing his imagination for the rendering in language of that experience of rapture. Estela would recall that one night near the Plaza Constitución, Borges announced to her that he was writing a story about "a place that contained all the other places in the world" and that he would like her to help him with the enumeration of all the places he wanted to name. She declined the invitation to collaborate with him, suspecting that this might be a ploy he used to engage the attention of "budding poetesses." In the course of the next two months, however, Borges would repeat this request several times over. The truth may have been that he needed to feel close to the woman he was in love with in order to write the Aleph vision with an appropriate degree of conviction.

About a fortnight after they started going out together, Estela left Buenos Aires without bothering to tell Borges, even though she was seeing him practically every night. On December 18 he wrote to her home address, expressing puzzlement as to her whereabouts, since he did not know if she was still in Buenos Aires or in Uruguay. Her disappearance made him wonder about her feelings for him, but still he confessed that he had never felt closer to her; he thought of her constantly, but always with her back to him or in profile. And he added in a postscript that he had bought a lottery ticket for the two of them, which was, he pointed out, a curious way of multiplying uncertainty.

Estela had in fact gone to Uruguay for a time, very likely to be with her English lover, and although Borges seems to have been unaware of the existence of the Englishman, the uncertainty caused by her departure was to affect his ability to finish "The Aleph." In a letter sent in the latter part of January 1945, he says he is making progress with the story about the place that includes all the others, but he repeats that he would welcome her help with certain details, since the ending seems to subdivide infinitely, like the course of the tortoise in Zeno's paradox. He is missing her terribly and cannot figure out what is wrong with Buenos Aires, since it seems to allude to her infinitely—Corrientes, Lavalle, San Telmo, the entrance to the *subterráneo,* all of these places recall Estela with particular dedication.

After Estela returned to Buenos Aires, they continued to see each other, but then it was Borges's turn to leave on a summer holiday—he had been invited by his cousin Esther Haedo and her husband, Enrique Amorim, to spend most of the month of February at their summer villa outside Salto in Uruguay. He took "The Aleph" with him, but throughout his stay with the Amorims, he continued to experience difficulties in bringing the story to an appropriate end. In a postcard he told Estela (in English) that he was missing her, and he thanked her for the joy her letter had brought him. He was hoping to finish the draft of the story that he wanted to dedicate to her, the one about the place that encompassed all the other places in the world. And yet he was unable to arrive at a version he was happy with; he was missing Estela too much. He wrote to her again shortly before he was due to return to Buenos Aires, describing how he kept being overcome by memories of her smile, the inflection of her voice saying "Georgie," his watch lying on her purse, her fingers tearing up some paper. He felt terribly happy to think that in a week's time (maybe earlier), they would be seeing each other again, but the thought of having to wait so long was unbearable.

Indeed, he could barely contain his desire to be reunited with Estela. Three days later, on Wednesday, March 4, he wrote her another letter, confessing to a sense of unworthiness—he felt unworthy of the evenings and mornings, unworthy of the days he had spent with her, unworthy of the extremely beautiful places he had seen, and the reason for such feelings of unworthiness was that he was haunted by doubts about Estela's feelings for him. His days were consumed with anguish and uncertainty because he had not heard from her. He could not fathom the reasons for her silence, and all he asked for was a sign that he still existed for her. He expected to be in Buenos Aires on Friday, but he would tell her again that he loved her, and he assured her that they could both be very happy. He added a postcript, informing her that he had finished her story.

As soon as he was back in Buenos Aires, he wrote to Estela—in English— for no other reason, it would seem, than to make known his joy at the prospect of seeing her. He even apologized for the gushing, excessive sentiments he was expressing in his letter, and for carrying on in the vein of some horrible prose poet, as he put it. He also told her—contradicting his previous letter—that by the time she read the letter, he would have finished the story he had promised her, which he described as being the first in a long series.

Now that he was seeing Estela again, he became ever more excited—he would telephone every morning and send her notes and postcards reminding her, needlessly, that they would be meeting in the evening. Estela was bemused by these outpourings, but they may be explained by Borges's need to work himself up into an amorous frenzy in order to write the mystical vision in "The Aleph." Then one day he turned up at her apartment with a parcel containing, he said, an object that showed all the objects in the world. He called it an "Aleph," a word that meant nothing to Estela, and less so when it turned out that the parcel contained a kaleidoscope. Nevertheless, he was as happy as a child, and he gave an oddly mystical explanation for his interest in the toy—it was a magic object that could be one of the manifestations of God. The most likely explanation for Borges's strange exhilaration is that, after several attempts, he had finally got the Aleph vision right, and he was overjoyed that Estela should have inspired him to produce the most rapturous writing he had yet achieved. Even so, he continued to express himself in a private language to which he alone held the key—he kept telling Estela that he was Dante and she was Beatrice and that she was capable of releasing him from hell, even though she would not know the nature of that hell. "The Aleph," Borges told Estela, would constitute the beginning of a long series of stories, essays, and poems that would all be dedicated to her.

One night in March 1945, Borges invited Estela to visit Adrogué. He took her to dinner at the Hotel Las Delicias, where the Borges family had spent their summer vacations since their return from Europe. Estela believed he had chosen to take her there because Adrogué was a "terrifying" place for Borges, "sacred" to him. The Hotel Las Delicias had certainly seen better days:

> The passing of time was noticeable: the red and blue rhombuses of the windows had been partly replaced by clear glass; the ferns and potted palms were missing. The dining room, vast and badly lit, was almost empty. The food on the fixed-price menu was as bad as might be expected in a boardinghouse. But this was of no importance to him that night. The maître and two or three waiters came up to greet him. You could see that he was happy and excited in this old dining room, which had been robbed of its former splendor.[5]

Afterward they took a stroll in the grounds, which were as run-down as the building itself. He then suggested they go to the town of Mármol, which was the next stop on the railway line, and then walk back to Adrogué, a distance of some twenty blocks. As they made their way back to Adrogué, Borges evidently wanted to tell Estela something, and occasionally would take her by the arm and push her, as if he wanted to take her to a specific place. At times he would retrace his steps halfway along a block, and all the while he would be reciting verses from the *Divine Comedy:* Estela recalled a passage where Beatrice asks Virgil to accompany Dante in his journey through Hell. Borges would make mocking remarks about Beatrice, who flattered Virgil in order to achieve her objectives.

From Estela's account of that night, Borges would seem to have been imagining his life story in terms of the *Divine Comedy,* playing with the idea of Beatrice's asking Virgil to guide Dante through Hell and Purgatory toward Paradise, where he would be given a vision of the mystic Rose. And he must have brought Estela to the Hotel Las Delicias because it was there that he had himself experienced the torments of hell several times over—the hotel was associated with insomnia, with nightmares, and, indeed, with suicide, which he had contemplated on at least two occasions, and may perhaps even have attempted in one of its rooms. But Borges had chosen to revisit the hotel with Estela Canto on that "sacred" night in March 1945 in the hope that she would become his "new Beatrice," the woman who would finally release him from the emotional inferno he had experienced in the past.

At one point in their walk back to Adrogué, they decided to take a rest on a concrete bench, and it was then that Borges finally revealed to Estela what it was that had been preying on his mind. Sitting awkwardly astride the bench, he ventured in a trembling voice, "Estela, would you marry me?" She was taken aback: the declaration sounded to her like something out of a Victorian novel. For some reason it occurred to her to reply in English, the language Borges used in moments of great emotional intensity: "I'd be very happy to, Georgie. But don't forget that I'm a disciple of Bernard Shaw. We cannot get married without first going to bed with each other." Her reply elicited a poignant reaction—Borges took her at her word, and after that night he was to regard Estela as his fiancée.

His "engagement" to Estela now filled Borges with tremendous optimism. A month or so after their night in Adrogué, he took her to Palermo Zoo. He was wearing a plaid scarf that Estela had given him, and he had tied it around his neck in the jaunty style of a *compadrito.* After having their photograph taken outside the monkey house, they went to see the big cats, and as they stood watching the great Bengal tiger in its cage, he told Estela the plot of a new story he was working on, which he would eventually call "The God's Writing" ("La escritura del dios"). A man has been imprisoned in a dungeon, and every time a jailer lets in some light, he catches a glimpse of a tiger through an aperture in the wall. The man believes that one of the gods has somewhere inscribed a sacred formula that would bring deliverance from the woes of the world. One day the prisoner has a mystical illumination in which he sees an infinite wheel made of fire and water, a vision that gives him a sense of "the universe, and the intricate designs of the universe." He then realizes that the god's saving words are the stripes on the tiger's fur.

In this early version of "The God's Writing," as Estela recalled, the prisoner had not yet deciphered the divine formula inscribed on the tiger's fur, but in the process of his searching for it, the dungeon ceased being a dungeon, because the prisoner could sense the imminence of freedom. Even so, it is significant that the prisoner has not yet won his freedom, for Estela, after all, had set a precondition before she would consent to marriage, so Borges's newfound optimism, as expressed in this primitive version of "The God's Writing," was tempered by the knowledge that he had yet to clear one final hurdle before he could complete his Dantean passage from purgatory into the paradise of love.

The Allied victory in 1945 brought new hope that the end of the Second World War might see a restoration of democracy to Argentina. The parties of the Unión Democrática pressed for elections to be held, but the greatest obstacle to democracy was the power of Colonel Juan Perón, who had become vice president of the military government in addition to being minister of labor. On September 19 the Unión Democrática, encouraged by the outspoken support of the U.S. ambassador, organized a march in favor of "the constitution and liberty." The turnout was so massive that it looked as though the military junta could not survive much longer.

Borges had been unable to attend the march because he was ill in bed with chickenpox, but Estela was so pleased by the way things had gone that she made one of her rare telephone calls to Borges's home to tell him about it, and he asked her to tea at his apartment the following afternoon. She had been invited once before to have lunch with Borges and his mother, but it had become evident on that occasion that the old lady had not taken to her, and a mutual antipathy had since arisen between them.

When Estela came to tea, she was received by Doña Leonor and by Georgie, who was in his dressing gown. The conversation turned to family matters, and Doña Leonor launched into the story of her illustrious ancestors—she told Estela about the heroes who had fought in the independence wars and against the savage Indians on the frontier; about her own father, the commissioner of police, who had been the son and grandson of distinguished *unitarios,* opponents of the tyrant Rosas to a man; indeed, some of the portraits of these men, Estela should know, now hung on the walls of the National Historical Museum in the Parque Lezama. Estela was rather abashed by this display of family pride, and also rather embarrassed by what she regarded as bad taste in so patrician a lady as Doña Leonor, for she herself, had she wished, could have boasted of comparable glories in the past, since her own family, like the majority of the old families of Argentina and Uruguay, also preserved digni-fied memories of war heroes and of lands that had once been theirs. While Mother poured out this catalog of snobbish braggadoccio, Georgie said noth-ing, which surprised Estela, since he was normally so irritated by any sign of "vulgarity." After enduring this ordeal for about an hour, she decided to leave, but Borges asked her to come again for tea the following day.

The situation was repeated a second time—Mother was present through-out, and she again went on about her ancestors. When Estela was about to leave, Georgie once again invited her to come to tea, but Mother suddenly got to her feet, shaking her head and saying it would not be possible to meet the next day because she had to go out. It was only as she was leaving the building that Estela fully realized the import of Doña Leonor's words. She waited until Georgie telephoned her and then gave vent to her anger—she found it insult-ing that his mother should think her presence was required to prevent Estela jumping on Georgie. This exchange caused a rift between Estela and Borges, and they did not see each other for several days

After he had recovered from his chickenpox, Borges came to see Estela, and they had it out as they walked grimly along the streets around Constitu-ción Station. She told him she found his mother's attitude unacceptable. He replied that Doña Leonor was a very old-fashioned lady who believed she should be present at their meetings for the sake of Estela's honor—in her day a young woman was never left alone with a man even when that man was her fiancé. But Estela was in no mood to spare Georgie; she told him that his mother knew very well that they saw each other morning, noon, and night; there was nothing she could do to stop them going to a hotel if they so wished; his mother had meant what she said as a deliberate insult. Borges was "crushed" by Estela's reaction; he had wanted her, she felt, to accept his lie, to accept the fiction that his mother had simply wished to protect Estela's honor.

Estela was puzzled by the fact that, even though the Bioys were out of town, Borges seemed to want to retire early: they would go out at about seven o'clock and then, at around ten, he would become uneasy. She also noticed that when they were in a restaurant, he would get up to make a telephone call after giving his order to the waiter, returning shortly and looking very re-lieved, as if he had done his duty. One evening Estela happened to go to the ladies' lavatory while he was on the telephone, and as she walked past, she overheard him say, "Yes, yes, Mother. . . . Yes, . . . from here we'll be going to the Ambassador. . . . Yes, Mother, Estela Canto. . . . Yes, Mother." She realized that Doña Leonor required to be informed periodically of Georgie's where-abouts whenever he went out at night with a woman: it was standard proce-dure. And now she understood why he called her from a public telephone every morning before ten—she had already sensed that he would not have welcomed her calling him at home, and she avoided doing this as far as she could.

Doña Leonor's behavior, according to Estela, "destroyed any possibility" of her being able to get closer to Borges. She thought it ridiculous that a man who was over forty-five years old should have to account to his mother for all his movements, and she did not spare him the humiliation of telling him so. Borges, however, insisted that he was madly in love with Estela, that he wanted to start a family with her. He told her that in the days following their quarrel, he had been tempted to throw himself off the balcony of a friend's fifth-floor apartment. He knew he would go blind one day, he said, but it would not matter so long as she was with him: her love would bring redemption, and he once again referred to her as Dante's Beatrice, assuring her that they could be very happy together.

Estela was a combative spirit, a self-styled New Woman who was not prepared to brook any nonsense from a snobbish old lady and her timorous son. But she was nonetheless moved by Borges's desperate plea for love; she felt he was being absolutely sincere, and yet she believed that if she had agreed to marry him there and then, without preconditions of any sort, he would have enjoyed a moment of bliss but would soon enough have run to a public telephone to ask for his mother's permission, for he never would have dared stand up to Leonor Acevedo.

As Estela challenged Borges to assert his will against Mother's, his curious fate would have it that he should concurrently witness another assault on everything Doña Leonor stood for. By Estela's reckoning, her quarrel with Borges occurred about a week after their first taking tea together with his mother on September 20. Less than two weeks later, the political crisis that had been brewing in Argentina since the end of the war suddenly erupted. On October 9, 1945, the junta appeared to succumb to the pressure for a return to democracy. The vice president, Colonel Perón, was arrested and held prisoner on the island of Martín García. But Perón had grown too powerful to be summarily dismissed from the political scene. His suppporters began straightaway to agitate for his release. His mistress, the beautiful ex-actress Eva Duarte, an explosive orator, called upon the *descamisados,* the "shirtlesss" poor of the sprawling barrios of Buenos Aires, to rise up and free their leader. The military junta eventually relented and set Perón free after the labor unions organized a massive rally in Buenos Aires on October 17. Perón had clearly emerged as the most powerful man in Argentina, and when elections were held in February 1946, he was to gain the presidency by a landslide.

Borges believed that the whole business of Perón's imprisonment and release was no more than political theater, a charade designed as a pretext for Perón to seize power. The events of October 17 confirmed his fears that the movement headed by Perón would result in a populist dictatorship spawned by the xenophobic and anti-Semitic nationalism he had been denouncing since the late 1920s. At the end of October, he went to Montevideo to give a lecture at the university, after which his "Conjectural Poem" was read out to the audience by way of reaffirming the stance he had taken at the time of the military coup of 1943.

However, two years on, things were not quite so clear-cut. In opposing Perón he was raising the sword of honor his mother held dear, upholding the values for which his ancestors had fought and died; he believed he was defending civilization against Peronist barbarians who, if left unchecked, would surely destroy the country. But this public stand against Perón would produce a confusion of personal loyalties. Estela Canto's obvious hatred of Doña Leonor unnerved Borges, for he knew that he would lose his "new Beatrice" if he did not defy his mother, but in the context of the rise of Colonel Perón, such an emotional rebellion would become associated with infamy and betrayal. Borges was caught up once more in the old conflict between desire and loyalty, so that throughout the period of Juan Perón's assumption and consolidation of power, Borges, as we shall see, would be in a state of considerable psychological turmoil, which, though painful, would nevertheless prove to be extraordinarily fertile as far as his writing was concerned.

That spring, probably in early November 1945, a curious incident exposed the unresolved difficulties between these awkward lovers. Borges and Estela were sitting in the Parque Lezama one evening when a policeman asked to see their identity cards. Since neither of them was carrying any papers, the officer arrested them both for conducting themselves in an indecorous fashion and causing a public scandal. It was a ridiculous charge, especially where the fastidious Borges was concerned; at most, Estela reckoned, he would have had his arm around her shoulders while they sat on the park bench. But they were obliged to accompany the policeman to the station, where they waited for several hours for a superior officer to turn up. It occurred to Borges to mollify the officer by suggesting that they might have a common interest in criminology, since he was currently the editor of a series of detective novels for Emecé, a well-known publishing firm. Suitably impressed, the policeman let them off with a caution: they were told to behave themselves in the future, and when they protested that their conduct had been above reproach, the officer explained that things were rather topsy-turvy, given the political situation after the Peronist putsch of October 17.

This may have been a trivial incident in itself, but as far as Estela was concerned, it added to the malaise that had arisen between them after Doña

Leonor had effectively forbidden them to see each other alone in her house. In the days following their arrest, Estela noticed that Borges seemed deeply ashamed at having been detained by the police until three in the morning and upset at not having been able to telephone his mother. He regarded the whole episode, she believed, as demeaning—it was as if he had been punished for having done something that was out of order. She surmised that Georgie must have received a dressing-down from his mother, who probably told him that if he had been with a respectable lady, he would not have been arrested, and it annoyed Estela to think that he would not have dared stand up for her against Doña Leonor.

After this incident their nights out together became much abbreviated: they no longer went to a café after the cinema or for the long nocturnal walks they both enjoyed; instead, they would take the *subterráneo* right after the show, Borges would see her to her apartment, and he would then hurry off to catch the last train home. Estela became fed up with this situation, and at the end of November, she decided to spend the summer months in Uruguay.

By her own account, Estela saw her English lover in Uruguay: "I spent some of the most beautiful months of my entire life with him. I totally forgot about Georgie, whom in a way I treated badly."[6] Borges would write to her while she was away, but she could not remember whether she had bothered to write back at all. There were, indeed, plenty of other things on her mind, not all of them concerning the English spy, for she was to part from him, too: "I was inconstant. One fine day he left and I never saw him again. . . . By then I was in love with another man, a Spanish guerrilla."[7]

While Estela was falling in and out of love with other men during the three months or so she spent in Uruguay that summer, Borges found himself in the throes of a severe emotional crisis. Realizing that he was in danger of losing his "fiancée" yet again, he resolved to overcome his inveterate shyness with women. A friend recommended a psychologist, Dr. Miguel Kohan-Miller, and Borges began to attend twice-weekly sessions with him. However, unlike today, when psychotherapy is widely popular among the Argentines (there is even a district of Buenos Aires nicknamed "Freudsville"), psychoanalysis was little known or practiced at the time. Kohan-Miller was a forensic psychologist and not a psychoanalyst as such; his knowledge of Freudian theory was not very advanced, so Borges did not undergo psychoanalysis in the classic sense.[8] His sessions with Kohan-Miller seem to have been fairly casual, rambling affairs: the therapist would sometimes play the piano, and the conversation would often turn to literature—the doctor was a great admirer of Borges's work, and he was to receive an inscribed copy of *Ficciones*, which became one of his most prized possessions.

As far as the nature of the analysis can be reconstructed from information provided by Estela Canto in her memoirs and an interview that Dr. Kohan-Miller gave in old age, the sessions were devoted to discussing Borges's general anguish, focusing largely on his relations with his father.[9] Kohan-Miller considered Borges a man who suffered from a number of inhibitions, among which was his stammer and his fear of speaking in public. He believed that the root of Borges's difficulties lay in an acute sense of guilt, but he was confident that his inhibitions would be overcome in the context of a caring, trusting relationship with a woman, and especially in marriage.

These sessions with Kohan-Miller encouraged Borges to pursue his intention of marrying Estela, but judging from the surviving letters he wrote to her, he was beset by uncertainties. He would visit Estela's mother nearly every day to try to find out when her daughter might be returning from her very long summer holiday in Uruguay. In one of his surviving letters of this period, he could not hide his anxiety: he thanked Estela for her letters, which he had found very moving, and reiterated his desire to be with her, to feel her by his side, and before closing, he asked bluntly—when was she coming back?

Estela was in Buenos Aires by the first week in April. Borges suspected that she had been seeing someone else in Uruguay, but he was keen to maintain the engagement and still hoped to marry her. As soon as he heard that she was back, he telephoned to say that they had to see each other as soon as possible, because he had something very important to tell her. They arranged to meet that evening at the entrance to the *subterráneo* at Constitución, but he turned up at her apartment an hour earlier looking anxious and uneasy. As they walked aimlessly in the streets around her apartment building, he kept nervously reciting his favorite poems. Finally he said he wanted to ask a great favor of her: he had been seeing a psychologist for the past few months, and the analysis had reached a point where it would be helpful if Dr. Kohan-Miller could talk to her. Estela readily agreed, because she was curious and wanted to help him; there was something of Sherlock Holmes in her, she would write: she liked to delve into another person's deepest motives.

Estela's forthcoming meeting with his psychologist caused Borges a good deal of anxiety. In an undated letter he wrote to her, almost certainly before the interview with Kohan-Miller was due to take place, he tried to convey how badly he was missing her—he had almost wept as he walked by the Parque Lezama the day before—and then he poured out his heart. Before meeting Estela he had engendered ghosts: some of these—his stories—may have helped him endure his existence; others—his obsessions—had brought him nothing but death. Yet he was convinced he would conquer these obsessions if Estela were willing to help him; he was fighting for his honor, his life, and, above all, for the love of Estela Canto.

When Estela met Kohan-Miller, the psychologist explained that Borges was oppressed by an exceptional sensitivity in his relations with women. He related to her the young Borges's experience in Geneva, which he interpreted as a paternal command that the boy prove himself a man; on the other hand, in order to liberate himself from feelings of guilt, Borges needed the approbation of society. According to Kohan-Miller, marriage would provide a solution to the problem, and he asked Estela whether she would be prepared to get married immediately, setting aside the prior test she had set Borges. But Estela did not wish to get married, at least not for the time being, and Kohan-Miller did not press her any further, except to say that she should try to inspire confidence in Borges, she should be tender with him. He believed that with enough patience, all of Georgie's obsessions would disappear.

Estela Canto failed to record what happened between her and Borges after her interview with Kohan-Miller. They appear to have seen each other for several weeks, but it had become clear to them that the relationship was at an impasse. Estela tried to ease matters as far as she could by offering to have sexual relations with Borges, but this offer was rejected. She concluded from this refusal that Borges lacked the courage to cross the physical barrier in their relationship. But her proposed solution to the impasse betrayed a rather limited, not to say simplistic, view of liberation. Borges's difficulties with women were not physical, they were psychological, and, as Kohan-Miller perceived, he needed love and understanding if he was to find release from those feelings of unworthiness that had plagued him since childhood and had been so badly exacerbated by the ordeal he had undergone in Geneva.

Seeing that his engagement to Estela was doomed, Borges wrote her a letter, probably in the first week in June, in which he told her that there was no reason they should not remain friends. He confessed that he loved her very much—he owed her the best and possibly the worst moments of his life, and this had created a bond between them that could not be broken. Estela, he wrote, kept telling him that he could count on her and if this assurance were a token of her love, he would gladly accept it, but if she was offering to help him out of courtesy or pity, he could not accept the offer, because loving or saving a person was not something that could be done at odd moments. Still, what was the point of exchanging reproaches, which were the currency of Hell? He wanted to be with her, and he hoped she would not fail to meet him at Plaza Constitución later that day.

Clearly Estela's meeting with the psychologist had brought matters to a head. In Estela's view:

There was one flaw in Kohan-Miller's analysis of the situation: the fact that I had gone to see him made him believe that I was interested in normalizing my relations with Borges. That misunderstanding had been created by Borges himself, who had taken literally my frivolous words as we sat on that celebrated bench in the outskirts of Adrogué. I saw it as an adventure that I was prepared to see through to its ultimate consequences, but it did not touch me in the very least.[10]

And she came to accept that Borges's "inhibition" with regard to her proposal that they conduct a sexual friendship outside of marriage arose from the very same misunderstanding: "He wanted my *love* [her emphasis]. I could not give it to him. We were at a dead end, since he was not prepared to accept anything less."

The relationship's having foundered on this "misunderstanding," Estela returned to Uruguay, where another man, probably the Spanish guerrilla, was waiting for her, and for a period of about three years, she would distance herself from her friends in Buenos Aires. Many years later Estela would acknowledge in her memoirs the part she herself had played in creating the misunderstanding that had vitiated her relations with Borges. She had the courage to admit that her behavior cast "a certain shadow over my character," and she repented her lack of honesty, confessing that on the night he took her to Adrogué, she should have told him, "Georgie, I don't love you enough to marry you. We can be friends and something more if you like." In retrospect she was to observe of this strange, one-sided affair, "I behaved badly with Borges. I was moved by his despair, but I could do nothing about it: I was alienated. It was a very negative experience, which showed me that things in life were not as I had imagined them."

Even so, the affair was by no means a wholly negative experience for Borges. From the outset he had been drawn to Estela's unpredictability—she had reminded him of "a knight on a chessboard"—and in this he had not been mistaken, for she had blown away the clouds of mystification in which he wrapped his amorous feelings, forcing him to confront the awkward truth that if he was to find salvation in the love of a woman, he could not continue to gloss over the realities of sex. Estela may not have loved Borges, but thanks to her he would begin to probe the tangled roots of his psychological ambivalence to both Mother and Father. Estela was right to say that Borges "entered a terrain he had never visited before" and suffered deeply as a result, but what she may never have fully appreciated was the extent of that suffering, nor the many difficulties he would have to endure before, as she put it, he "emerged accepting himself."

CHAPTER 20

Humiliation and Anguish
(1946–1947)

THE BREAK WITH Estela Canto very likely occurred in early June 1946. We can get a good sense of Borges's reaction to his loss through some of his publications in this period. A few months before parting company with Estela, he took up the editorship of a new literary review called *Los Anales de Buenos Aires,* and he was so self-indulgent as an editor that his own contributions to the *Anales* obliquely registered his moods and preoccupations in the period leading up to and following the end of the affair.

The first issue of *Los Anales de Buenos Aires* under Borges's editorship came out in March, when Estela had not yet returned from Uruguay, and already there appeared a review by him of a book whose title, *The Road to Hell* (in English), sounded ominous enough. But it is in the May issue, after Estela had seen Kohan-Miller, that we find clear signs of distress. He published a brief pseudo-Oriental tale of a king who was forced to wander in the labyrinth that is the Arabian Desert and met his end from hunger and thirst; as well as a poem called "Limits" ("Límites"), which itemized a number of things he was fated never to experience again because "death consumes me, unceasingly."[1] In June, when it became clear that Estela did not love him, there appeared another poem entitled "The Poet Declares His Renown" ("El poeta declara su nombradía"), whose last lines are "The instruments of my labor are humiliation and anguish. How I wish I had been born dead."[2] By July, when it was all over between them, he imagined himself once more as a man condemned to hell. In a section called "Museo" ("Museum"), which he included in each issue, and which consisted of a miscellany of brief texts by other writers, some of them invented by himself or Bioy Casares, there are definitions of "A Hell of Fire" ("Un infierno de fuego"), and "A Mental Hell" ("Un infierno mental") as well as two texts on "The Abolition of the Past" ("La abolición del pasado"), and one entitled simply "Crucifixion."

The loss of Estela was calamity enough, but his perverse fate saw to it that this blow should coincide with the overwhelming victory at the polls of Juan Domingo Perón. In February 1946, Perón was elected president with 54 percent of the vote. Following his triumph he proceeded to purge public institutions of known opponents. This shake-out was nothing new in itself, since it was common practice in Argentina for a new government to dismiss a large number of state employees in order to reward its supporters with jobs. However, given the revolutionary aspirations of the Peronists, the traditional overhaul of personnel was more sweeping and ideologically motivated than in the past, and in the tense atmosphere of the time, it lent itself to the settling of scores and to acts of personal revenge. As a notorious anti-*nacionalista*, Borges would have known that he was likely to lose his job, but on July 15 he heard that instead of being dismissed from his post at the Miguel Cané Library, he was to be transferred on promotion to another department.

The exact nature of this promotion remains in dispute. In his "Autobiographical Essay," Borges gave the following account of the episode:

> In 1946, a president whose name I do not want to remember came to power. One day soon after, I was honored with the news that I had been "promoted" out of the library to the inspectorship of poultry and rabbits in the public markets. I went to the City Hall to find out what it was all about. "Look here," I said. "It's rather strange that among so many others at the library I should be singled out as worthy of this new position." "Well," the clerk answered, "you were on the side of the Allies—what do you expect?" His statement was unanswerable; the next day, I sent in my resignation.[3]

According to Estela Canto, Borges believed that his "promotion" had been instigated by a powerful individual in the municipal administration, a Peronist intellectual who was "one of Evita's men."[4] Certainly there were people at the Cultural Secretariat who fitted this description, and it may be that one of these men took it upon himself to "punish" Borges by placing his name on the dismissal list. Even so, one might question whether there really was any intention actually to punish Borges; there were, it seems, objective grounds for his dismissal. The official Peronist view was that Borges was put on the list because of his record of absenteeism at the library and his history of signing public declarations against Vice President Perón, which was an infringement of standard civil service rules against becoming involved in political activities.[5] And as for the possibility of Perón's having been personally involved in the matter, this was discounted by Raúl Salinas, who was secretary of state for culture for the city of Buenos Aires between 1946 and 1951, and who had meetings with Perón every morning. Salinas observed that Perón was completely oblivious to the fate of a library assistant like Borges and had in any case plenty of things to see to after being elected president.[6]

As the official responsible for deciding what changes of personnel would be made in the government's cultural services, Salinas recalled that Borges's name was on a list of about two thousand employees who were recommended for dismissal for a variety of reasons.[7] The only difference between Borges and the many others who were to lose their jobs was that he was one of the best-known writers in the country. And it was for precisely this reason that he gained the sympathy of certain writers who worked at the Secretariat for Culture. Indeed, it was Salinas's deputy, the Catholic poet Miguel Angel Etcheberrigaray, a friend of Francisco Luis Bernárdez, one of Borges's oldest friends, who requested that Borges be transferred to another department rather than be dismissed. A transfer, Salinas claimed, was the only way they could avoid sacking Borges, because the regulations stated that anyone whose name appeared on the list of those to be let go could not remain in post. In the end it was decided to promote Borges to a post as an inspector at the Dirección de Apicultura, the Department of Beekeeping. They chose the Dirección de Apicultura because beekeeping was deemed to be, as Salinas put it, "an appropriately sweet occupation for a poet."[8]

In the opinion of Salinas, it was Borges and his friends who saw this promotion as an opportunity to make a fuss: they distorted *apicultura* to *avicultura*, and spread the word that Borges was to be appointed an "inspector of chickens," thus making the promotion appear to be a calculated humiliation of a prominent writer by the new government. Salinas's version of events is similar to the one given by Arturo López Peña, another Peronist official at the time, in a little-known article published under a pseudonym in a nationalist magazine, *Pueblo Entero*, in May 1980. (López Peña pointed out that there was no such thing as a Dirección de Avicultura.)[9]

Although the account given by Salinas and López Peña may have been intended to exonerate the Peronist regime, it has to be said that Borges was certainly not above such a maneuver, for there was a prickly, aggressive side to his character, and he liked to give as good as he got. In fact, the two accounts may not be irreconcilable after all, because what might genuinely have been meant as a favor to Borges, or as the lesser of two evils, could well have been taken by Borges himself as a calculated insult. Borges knew he had enemies in the Secretariat for Culture, so when he learned of his transfer to Apicultura, he may have been predisposed to interpret this move as a punishment. Under these circumstances he and his friends in the Unión Democrática could have decided to milk the situation for all it was worth by trying to convert the incident into a notable instance of political persecution. And instead of beekeeping they may have hit on the idea of changing *apicultura* to *avicultura* and letting it be known in the Buenos Aires literary world that Perón was proposing to make Borges an inspector of chickens. (In his "Autobiographical Essay," Borges even added "rabbits" for good measure.)

Still, if Salinas's version is correct, then Borges and his cronies did a remarkably good job of convincing people that it was chickens and not bees whose welfare he was supposed to oversee. Within a very short time of the so-called promotion, the Peronist press itself was talking of Borges's having been made an inspector of chickens. On July 24, 1946, the Peronist newspaper *Democracia* published an anonymous piece under the headline JORGE LUIS BORGES, INSPECTOR OF POULTRY, regretting the "promotion" of the "illustrious writer."[10] The author appealed for "generosity" to the mayor of Buenos Aires, Dr. Emilio Siri, and asked, "Does Dr. Siri suppose that the *Patria* will progress very far if writers devote themselves to looking after chickens and poulterers to writing novels?"

On the whole, however, the news of Borges's strange promotion provoked undisguised gloating among the Peronists. On August 8 the hard-line party newspaper *Descamisada* published a scurrilous attack on Borges in its anonymously authored gossip column.[11] It dismissed him as "an Argentine writer who translates his stories from English and signs them as if they were his own." He is alleged to have "sponged off the Municipal payroll" at the Miguel Cané Library—"he read, he translated, and drew his wages." But when the Peronist revolution occurred, "he felt under the obligation to sign any manifesto which attacked Colonel Perón, as he then was, and the *descamisado* masses." The article then reveals the reason for Borges's promotion: "As a punishment, the mayor Dr. Siri sent him a short while ago to inspect chickens. The mayor did this because he wanted Borges to go back to his days as a *descamisado* and put himself in a position to understand this revolution, which he quite fails to do." The anonymous author twice alludes (anachronistically) to Borges's sympathy with the *descamisados*—Perón's working-class supporters—and this must surely be a reference to his days as the founder and leader of the Committee of Young Intellectuals for Irigoyen. Indeed, he alleges that Borges had himself been "something of a *descamisado* and a bohemian," in the 1920s. One might deduce from these allusions that Borges was being attacked for having failed to evolve from the populist cultural nationalism of his youth toward the kind of right-wing *nacionalismo* that eventually spawned Perón.

Whatever the truth about the nature of Borges's "promotion," Raúl Salinas was right to say that Borges and his friends chose to make political capital out of it. Lowly as his post at the municipal library had been, Borges's resignation was turned into a cause célèbre in the Buenos Aires literary world. Borges was a leading writer, after all, so the Argentine Society of Writers (SADE) sponsored a dinner for him at the Restaurante Marconi on the Plaza del Once. The president of the SADE at the time, the Communist Leónidas Barletta, praised Borges's courage and hailed him as an example of "the spirit of resistance" that "all Argentine intellectuals should follow."

On the occasion of the dinner, Borges wrote a violent attack on the Peronist regime that was read out by his friend Pedro Henríquez Ureña. Borges claimed to have resigned from the Miguel Cané Library because he had suddenly been "ordered to lend his services at the municipal administration" and had been informed that this was a "punishment" for having signed public declarations in favor of democracy. But this episode, he said, was of little significance in itself; more important was the fact that it had convinced him of the imperative need to fight dictatorship.

> Dictatorships breed oppression, dictatorships breed servility, dictatorships breed cruelty; more loathesome still is the fact that they breed idiocy. Bellboys babbling orders, portraits of caudillos, prearrranged cheers or insults, walls covered with names, unanimous ceremonies, mere discipline usurping the place of clear thinking. . . . Fighting these sad monotonies is one of the many duties of a writer. Need I remind readers of *Martín Fierro* or *Don Segundo* that individualism is an old Argentine virtue?[12]

The dinner in honor of Borges was a rallying point for intellectual opponents of Perón: there was hardly enough room in the restaurant to accommodate everyone who turned up, and there were people overflowing onto the street. Betina Edelberg, a prominent activist in the Unión Democrática, was present at the dinner, and she was to recall that Borges was already regarded by younger writers like herself "as a sort of Anti-Perón."[13] All the same, even though Borges had emerged as one of the intellectual leaders of the democratic opposition, his political commitment would become somewhat erratic in the following months and years. His "promotion" by the Peronists, it must be remembered, had occurred within weeks of his break with Estela Canto, and the bitter emotional legacy of that love affair would, as we shall see, periodically undermine his morale during the years of Perón's rule.

After resigning from the Miguel Cané Library, Borges was out of a job for several months. This situation caused him considerable distress, as there seemed to be few prospects of finding suitable employment. He applied for a position as a bank clerk and took an entrance examination together with a large number of other aspirants for the five available vacancies, but he was not in the end offered the position. Several months earlier, however, his friend Adela Grondona had taken him to see an old English lady who read tea leaves, and she had predicted that he would shortly undertake journeys, give lectures, and earn large sums of money.[14] When he told his mother, they both laughed, because public speaking was something he had never been able to face, but the clairvoyant's prediction was not too far off the mark: a friend found him a job as a teacher of English literature at the Asociación Argentina de Cultura Inglesa, and a short while later he was offered another job as a lecturer in American literature at the Colegio Libre de Estudios Superiores. He accepted these posts, since the courses were not due to start for another three months.

For the Colegio Libre, he planned a course of nine lectures and proposed to overcome his fear of public speaking by writing them out in full and committing each to memory. But he wrote the first one out at such enormous length that he left himself no time to write the second. As the time drew near to give his first lecture, which was to be on Nathaniel Hawthorne, he "became sicker and sicker."[15] He consulted his analyst, Kohan-Miller, who advised him to take a stiff drink beforehand. On the fateful day, he had lunch at the house of a lady friend, trying his best not to show how terrified he really was—his hostess assured him that he did not look at all nervous. When he turned up at the Colegio Libre, another lady friend, Ema Risso Platero, made him take a glass of peach brandy to steady his nerves. He then proceeded to deliver the lecture in a slow, hesitant voice, keeping his hands clasped tightly throughout. ("I was praying the roof would fall in," he was to comment afterward.)[16] His lecturing style thereafter would not change much: he always spoke hesitantly and in a rather monotonous voice, staring all the while into blank space. In time he would become a well-known and sought-after lecturer and would make something of a career of it.

> At forty-seven, I found a new and exciting life opening up for me. I traveled up and down Argentina and Uruguay, lecturing on Swedenborg, Blake, the Persian and Chinese mystics, Buddhism, gauchesco poetry, the Icelandic sagas, Heine, Dante, expressionism, and Cervantes. I went from town to town, staying in hotels I'd never see again. Sometimes my mother or a friend accompanied me. Not only did I end up making far more money than at the library but I enjoyed the work and felt that it justified me.[17]

The equable tone of the "Autobiographical Essay" should not deceive us into overlooking the pain he was feeling at this time. According to Bioy Casares, Borges "suffered grievously" over his rejection by Estela Canto,[18] for this most recent failure in love awakened the memory of earlier failures, adding a further vein of suffering to a many-layered distress; and so he turned in on himself and attacked those rich seams of anguish with redoubled fury, producing a succession of stories that he wrote up and published between August 1946 and July of the following year.

In November 1946 he published "The Dead Man" ("El muerto"), the story of a city boy who challenges the authority of an old gaucho chieftain, only to discover, before being shot dead, that his success was an illusion and that he was being duped all along.[19] Next came "The Immortal" ("El inmortal") (February 1947), a fictional exploration of Nietzsche's theory of the Eternal Return, in which infinite time has wiped out the identity of individuals, and even Homer can no longer recall that he had once been the author of the *Odyssey*.[20] "The Theologians" ("Los teólogos") appeared in April, and in this account of a murderous disputation between two divines, he reworked certain themes of the 1930s—the cycles of time, the rivals who are mere reflections of each other, and a number of Gnostic heresies about the cryptic relations between the world beyond and our own.[21] "The House of Asterion" ("La casa de Asterión") (May–June) retold the myth of the Minotaur, a lonely monster trapped in its labyrinth, according to this version, who longs to be put out of its misery by Theseus's sword.[22] "Averroes' Search" ("La busca de Averroes") (June) may have been a more recent story, although he had alluded to an earlier version of it in 1945.[23] The great Muslim philosopher attempts to discover what Aristotle might have understood by the words "tragedy" and "comedy," but since he has no inkling of what a theater might be, he is trapped in a labyrinth of preconceived ideas and can only define them erroneously in terms of established Arabic genres. And finally, in July 1947, Borges published "The Zahir," a story that brought to an end the flow of writing that had sprung from the pain of Estela's departure.[24]

"The Zahir," as Borges would observe, was "more or less 'The Aleph' once again."[25] As in the earlier story, the main character is "Borges," who has harbored an unrequited love for a beautiful socialite called Teodelina Villar. The loved one dies on June 6, and, after leaving the wake in the early hours of June 7, "Borges" stops at a bar to have a drink and receives a twenty-centavo coin in his change. That coin is the Zahir, and its peculiar virtue lies in its possessor's not being able to rid himself of its image. The fantasy of the Zahir is a metaphor for the love that Borges had just lost—the bar where his fictional alter ego receives the coin was on Chile and Tacuarí, the street corner where Estela Canto lived, and the date on the coin was 1929, the year of the death of Beatriz Viterbo in "The Aleph." The Zahir, we are told, can assume different forms in different places: in a region of India, "Borges" learns, the Zahir once took the form of a tiger, and among the victims it claimed was a Muslim fakir who died in captivity, leaving innumerable drawings of the fateful tiger all over the walls, ceiling, and floor of his prison cell. (We have here an ironic allusion to the story "The God's Writing," a primitive, optimistic version of which he had told Estela Canto when they visited the tiger at Palermo Zoo in 1945.)

The torments described by Borges in this story—the sleeplessness, the anguish, the maddening memories of the infernal coin—are, of course, displaced confessions of the extremity of his plight. Estela was to have been the "new Beatrice," inspiring him to create a work that would be "the rose without purpose, the Platonic, intemporal rose," but here he was again, sunk in the unreality of the labyrinthine self, with no prospect now of contemplating the mystic Rose of love. Even so, he tried to resist the void with the desperate thought that the Zahir might be "the shadow of the Rose and the rending of the Veil," hoping against hope that the sheer intensity of his pain might serve to tear apart the veil of solipsism and impel him toward some ultimate truth beyond the self. "Perhaps," the story concludes, "behind the coin one might find God."

CHAPTER 21

False Hopes

(1947–1950)

"THE ZAHIR" was the last substantial piece Borges would write for *Los Anales de Buenos Aires*. A few weeks after it appeared, in July 1947, he resigned the editorship of *Anales* following a disagreement with the proprietor, and his literary activity notably diminished thereafter—over the next nine months, he would publish the odd brief translation or prologue, and a handful of short reviews and literary "notes." No doubt he was exhausted after the many months of creative effort that had followed Estela's departure. Then again, there may have been a recurrence of his eye trouble, possibly even another of his operations. In 1947, too, he moved with his mother to a sixth-floor apartment at calle Maipú 994, only a stone's throw away from the Plaza San Martín. It was a tiny apartment—mother and son had a bedroom each, leading off the one large living room. Doña Leonor engaged a maid, Epifanía "Fani" Úveda de Robledo, a woman from the province of Corrientes who was to occupy the one room off the kitchen. This would be their home for the rest of their lives.

Borges continued to eke out a modest living by giving classes in private houses to the children of friends and delivering lectures at a variety of literary and educational societies in Buenos Aires and the provinces. One such was Pro-Arte, an informal association run by well-meaning society ladies whose aim was to offer financial support to writers and artists who were out of favor with the Peronist authorities. It was the brainchild of Sara "Pippina" Diehl de Moreno Hueyo, a Buenos Aires socialite renowned for her great beauty. She became a loyal friend of Borges's in these difficult years, and although she was a devout Catholic and married with several children, it was rumored that Borges had fallen in love with her. There is, however, no evidence to indicate that this attachment to Pippina Diehl was anything more than a close friendship.

Borges unquestionably enjoyed the company of women, especially if they were beautiful, well educated, and interested in literature. After his break with Estela Canto in particular, these friendships would multiply, as the dedications in the books and stories he published in the 1940s and 1950s attest. He would befriend a statuesque German blonde by the name of Ulrike von Kühlmann, a rich, much-traveled widow who settled in Buenos Aires in the late 1940s and lived there for several years. Borges would dedicate "Story of the Warrior and the Captive Maiden" to Ulrike, and she is mentioned by name in "The Other Miracle," both stories collected in *The Aleph* (1949). Several stories in that collection are dedicated to other women—the beautiful Uruguayan poet Ema Risso Platero ("The God's Writing"), Marta Mosquera Eastman ("The House of Asterion"), Cecilia Ingenieros ("The Immortal"), the poet and *recitadora* Wally Zenner, whom he had known since his days in the avant-garde ("The Zahir"). The dedication to *A Universal History of Infamy* was changed in the second edition (1954) from the cryptic "I. J." of the first edition (1935) to "S. D.," who was almost certainly Sara Diehl (de Moreno Hueyo). The "Two English Poems," which he had originally written in 1933–34, had again been dedicated to "I. J." in the first edition (1943) of his collected poems, *Poemas (1923–1943)*, but when an enlarged second edition was published in 1954, the first of these appeared with a dedication to a beautiful married lady friend, Beatriz Bibiloni Webster de Bullrich. He would ask other women to assist him in some of his literary projects—his *Ancient Germanic Literatures* (1951) was written with the collaboration of Delia Ingenieros, and in 1955 he would publish a short story, "Eloisa's Sister" ("La hermana de Eloísa"), written jointly with Luisa Mercedes Levinson. The following year he would dedicate the second edition of *Ficciones* to Esther Zemborain de Torres Duggan, a highly cultivated lady of patrician family who became a supportive friend for many years and would later collaborate with him on *An Introduction to North American Literature* (1967).

Such friendships amplified a reputation Borges had acquired since the early 1930s for a kind of adolescent naïveté in affairs of the heart. There was always a woman whom Borges was said to be wooing, and occasionally it appeared that he was paying court to several at a time. Yet no one seemed to take such liaisons seriously, not even, in most cases, the ladies in question, who were content to be flattered by the attentions of one of the leading writers in the country. Indeed, not a few of these ladies derived a certain amusement from the contrast between Borges's adolescent gushing over them and the satyric voracity of his friend, the handsome Bioy.

It was Bioy's wife, Silvina Ocampo, who memorably expressed the prevailing view of Borges's amorous inclinations: "Borges has an artichoke heart. He loves beautiful women, especially if they are ugly, because then he can invent their faces more freely."[1] Silvina was right about the fanciful quality of most of his infatuations, but wrong if by "artichoke heart" she meant that he was incapable of genuine feeling for a particular woman. Borges's literary dedications were tokens of friendship, sincerely meant without a doubt, but certainly no guide to the depth of his appreciation of the lady in question. Instead one should distinguish between the many women he admired and another set of women with whom he tried to conduct serious relationships, and who caused him a good deal of suffering on the whole.

In the first, rather numerous, category were women of the type whom his mother might well have chosen for him, mostly ladies of the criollo upper class. With these Borges would exhibit various degrees of attachment. There were some, like Susana Bombal or Esther Zemborain de Torres, with whom he enjoyed a genuine and abiding friendship without there being any romantic element to the relationship. Esther Zemborain, for instance, was separated from her husband when she first met Borges, but, as a practicing Catholic, she made it clear to him from the outset that she was not interested in an affair.[2] There were others, such as Pippina Diehl, Beatriz Bibiloni or Ema Risso Platero, whose company he relished either because of their decorous beauty or their witty conversation; yet others whom he respected for their literary or intellectual work, such as Silvina Bullrich, Delia Ingenieros, Alicia Jurado or Betina Edelberg; others still with whom he conducted amicable flirtations, very likely Ulrike von Kühlmann, for instance. There was indeed a certain self-mocking strain in Borges's character, and he liked to play up his reputation as an incompetent Lothario by indulging in mild parodies of courtly love service to an assortment of unreachable "goddesses" and "angels," and this was not because he had an "artichoke heart" but because in such platonic dalliances he could escape the raw truths of his emotional life and assuage for a while the very real pain that love had caused him to endure.

Far from being promiscuous in his affections, Borges was, if anything, too selective: he obeyed a single, involuntary criterion—he fell for women who would be unacceptable to Mother, either because they came from an inferior social class or because they did not meet the high standards of respectability required by Doña Leonor. Rebellion against Mother was the prerequisite of love, because love was the means to salvation, and salvation was predicated on freedom. Yet since love was inherently transgressive, sexual desire was laced with risk—he was attracted like a moth to the flame by women who would arouse the shame and guilt he associated with his encounter in Geneva. And so, to the thrill of rebellion was added the thrill of moral danger, and both converged in the figure of the *compadrito,* the delinquent knife fighter, who became the embodiment of virile passion in his writing.

Not much of substance is known about any serious relationship with a woman in the period immediately following the departure of Estela Canto. By my reckoning it must have been around 1947 that he entered into some kind of amorous friendship with Cecilia Ingenieros, the daughter of José Ingenieros, an influential writer of the generation of Lugones and Carriego whom

Borges's father had known in his youth. Cecilia was a professional ballet dancer, and although she came from a well-known family, she belonged to a relatively louche set of artists, dancers, and writers, and was a friend of Estela Canto's. An exceptionally striking young woman, possessed of sleek, dark good looks, she had trained as a dancer with Martha Graham in New York, but after sustaining an injury, she managed her own ballet company in Buenos Aires. The impression Borges gave his friends at the time was that Cecilia was one of the great loves of his life,[3] but virtually no information has survived that would permit us to get a fuller picture of this relationship. I believe that it could not have lasted more than a year, for by the middle of 1948, it was almost certainly over.

The end of his romance with Cecilia took Borges by surprise. He described it thus to an interviewer:

> She broke off the relationship in a very honorable way. She asked me to meet her at a tearoom that's on Maipú and Córdoba [the St. James]. I hadn't spoken to her for some time and thought, "How strange that she called me," and I was feeling very happy, and then she said to me, "I want to tell you something you're going to hear anyway, but I want you to hear it first from my lips: I've become engaged and I'm going to be married." So I congratulated her, and that was that.[4]

However, to Roberto Alifano he gave a different account:

> Together we planned a journey to Europe. We would get married there; that was the idea. But one afternoon we met in a *confitería,* and Cecilia told me, "I'm leaving for Europe in two weeks." "You mean, *we* are leaving," I corrected her. "No, I'm going on my own," she replied. "I've decided not to marry you." That's how our courtship came to an end.[5]

What comes across in both versions is the extent of Borges's ignorance of Cecilia's feelings. So much so, in fact, that one wonders just how much of this alleged love affair was simply a figment of his imagination. A mutual friend recalled Cecilia declaring that letters "came and went" between Borges and her, but that their relations amounted to little else.[6] This would bear out Silvina Ocampo's notion of Borges's "artichoke heart." Certainly his love must have been highly solipsistic, with very little sense of Cecilia as a person in her own right.

Early in 1948, at around the time that, by my calculations, he was involved with Cecilia, he began publishing a series of four articles on Dante's *Divine Comedy,* which appeared in *La Nación* at intervals of roughly two months between March and October. The first essay, "The Simurgh and the Eagle" ("El

Simurgh y el águila"), came out on the March 14, and here Borges argued that one of Dante's final visions in the *Paradiso* had an earlier analogue in the Persian legend of the Simurgh, which was the legend on which Borges had patterned the action of his failed autobiographical novel, *The Approach to Al-Mu'tasim,* and would also allude to in the pantheist vision that brings *The Congress* to an end. The last essay, called "The Meeting in a Dream" ("El encuentro en un sueñol"), appeared on October 3, and here Borges would argue that the whole of the *Divine Comedy* had been written by Dante in order to mitigate his sorrow at the death of Beatrice by imagining that he would meet her again in the afterlife.

In these essays on Dante, Borges was raking over the embers of an aspiration that had once fired him to attempt a work like *The Congress,* in which a woman would lead him to a "paradise" of self-realization. And since the essays ran in parallel with the latter stages of his relationship with Cecilia Ingenieros, it may be that he was hoping to revive those embers through his affair with her. However, by the time the last essay on Dante was published, his relationship with Cecilia must already have foundered: the vision of "paradise" had evaporated once more, and he was left with feelings of anger and resentment that are evident in a new story published in *Sur* in September 1948.

"Emma Zunz" was to be one of the key stories in his career.[7] He claimed he had been given the plot by Cecilia Ingenieros, and even though he professed not to like it much because it was based on revenge, which struck him as useless and cruel, he was to dedicate it to Cecilia all the same: "Or rather, I was not so much dedicating it to her as giving it her back."[8] The misogynist thrust of the story is unmistakable. Emma wants to avenge her father, who committed suicide after having been falsely accused of embezzlement. She hatches a plot to kill his former business partner, Loewenthal, the man responsible for his disgrace. She prostitutes herself with a sailor in a brothel and then shoots Loewenthal on the false pretext that he tried to rape her.

Borges drew attention to the name of the protagonist: "Emma with two *m*'s and Zunz with two *z*'s, I was trying to get an ugly and at the same time a colorless name. . . . [T]he name seems so meaningless, so insignificant."[9] And yet, as he would have known, the name is so heavily charged with meaning that it reverberates like a magic charm. Emma is an abbreviated female form of her father's name, Emmanuel, which in Hebrew signifies the "savior." Beginning and ending in vowels, Emma has an open, expansive quality, but Zunz is a thoroughly introverted word—the internal *u* and *n* are inverted mirror images of each other, and they are further boxed in by the two *z*'s, which themselves are shaped like capital *N*'s turned on their side. It is as if the fullness of Emmanuelle had been truncated to Emma by its juxtaposition with Zunz, and in that conjunction of *a* and *z* we again come across introversion—the *a,* which is the last letter of Emma, is also the first letter of the alphabet, but it is blocked by the *z*, which is the initial letter of Zunz, while being, of course, the final letter of the alphabet. The overall effect is of a confusion of beginnings and endings, of openings and closures, from which there is no issue other than in the blank space in the middle that divides one name from the other. In purely graphic terms, the name Emma Zunz functions as an ideogram of the kind of solipsistic labyrinth in which Borges imagined himself to be trapped, for all the elements end up turning in on themselves, pointing to nothing but reflections or distortions of each other, so that if there is a promise of salvation in the first name Emma, the second, Zunz, stops it dead.

In "Emma Zunz" we can see how Borges portrays a young woman (a potential savior) trapped in a labyrinth of sexual strife. Emma is nearly nineteen years old (the same age as Borges when he was sent by his father to the whore in Geneva), but "men still inspired an almost pathological fear in her," so that when she loses her virginity to the sailor, she experiences "a perplexing disorder of unconnected and atrocious sensations" that make her think of her father and the fact that he "had done to her mother the horrible thing they were doing to her now." In this extreme disjunction between sex and honor, we find a mirror image of Borges's own conflict. However, by projecting it onto a female character, he gave himself a critical distance from which to examine his fear of degrading himself by doing "the horrible thing" that his father had done to his mother.

The fact that "Emma Zunz" was published in September 1948, while the essay on Dante's last vision of Beatrice in Paradise came out on October 3, indicates, I believe, Borges's recognition that his whole Dantean project of being saved by a woman's love would remain an idle fancy so long as he failed to come to terms with the woman's sexual nature as well as with his own. Though dedicated to Cecilia Ingenieros, "Emma Zunz" could only have been written after his experience with Estela Canto. Estela had abused Borges's trust, but, by demanding sex of him, she had set him on the road to demystifying his tendency to regard women as angelic "saviors."

Meanwhile, the political situation continued to depress Borges. Perón had gone from strength to strength since his victory in 1946. His popularity was boosted by an economic boom based on Argentine food exports to a war-ravaged Europe, which allowed him to finance large wage boosts and massive increases in public spending. Perón rapidly expanded the role of the state, nationalizing the central bank, the telephone system, the railways, and the docks. The year 1947 was something of an *annus mirabilis*—the whole of the external debt was paid off, and with great fanfare Perón signed a "Declaration of Economic Independence" from foreign interests. He had, additionally, a priceless asset in Eva Duarte, whom he had married just before the election. "Evita" proved to be a populist of rare genius who knew how to play on the sympathies and grievances of the *descamisados,* the "shirtless" masses of the dispossessed. She embarked on "social welfare crusades" in the slums and shantytowns, and her methods were simple, direct, and vivid—she would amass huge quantities of food, clothes, medicine, and other goods in a garage at the presidential palace and oversee their distribution to the needy, often taking part herself in these handouts, kissing and embracing the poor and the sick. Evita soon became the object of intense devotion for the *descamisados,* the incarnate symbol of the aspiration to "social justice" that constituted the heart of Peronism. She would address huge crowds from the balcony of the Casa Rosada, making impassioned speeches attacking the "oligarchy" and appealing to the *descamisados* to offer their unconditional loyalty to her husband. She also advocated the vote for Argentine women, and when this measure was approved in 1947, Perón gained an enormous new source of electoral support.

Perón had come to power as a military caudillo, not as the head of a political organization as such. Once in office, he set about remedying this lack by founding a party of his own and providing it with an ideology called "justicialism," which was broadly corporatist in spirit, recalling aspects of fascism in its emphasis on the supremacy of the state over civil society, on social harmony between the classes, and in its authoritarian cult of the personality of a great leader. In 1948 a campaign got under way to modify the established constitution by introducing justicialist principles, such as a "decalogue" of workers' rights, and the rights of the state to intervene in the economy and nationalize property and natural resources. The reelection of the president for any number of six-year terms would also be permitted.

The proposed amendment of the great liberal constitution of 1853 was of enormous historical significance for Argentina—the survival of liberal democracy was at stake, since these amendments would effectively entrench Perón in power and enable him to create a corporate state. The opposition therefore rallied to defend the constitution, but Perón had already taken measures to intimidate and weaken his opponents. Following his election, he had limited the independence of the judiciary, purged the universities, and restricted public gatherings. There was also a concerted effort to manipulate the media: radio stations were instructed to refrain from all criticism of the government, a commission was set up to monitor "anti-Argentine activities" by editors and publishers, and supplies of paper to the press were selectively rationed—from October 1948, for example, liberal dailies like *La Prensa* and *La Nación* would be allowed only limited access to paper.

Opponents of Perón saw him as a reincarnation of the tyrant Rosas. According to *La Prensa*, for instance, numerous "official and unofficial" commemorations took place throughout the country on September 11, the sixtieth anniversary of the death of Domingo Sarmiento, the great liberal president and upholder of "civilization" against the "barbarism" of Rosas's tyranny.[10] This was the time of reckoning foreseen by Borges in his "Conjectural Poem," where he had evoked the memory of his own ancestor, Francisco de Laprida, the man of law who had been killed by gaucho "barbarians." Within days of the coup d'état of 1943, Borges had warned his countrymen that the barbarians were coming again. And yet now that the barbarians had arrived and were actually threatening the liberal constitution, Borges seemed incapable of bestirring himself, for it would seem that in the years since the 1943 coup, his troubles with Estela Canto and Cecilia Ingenieros had so deflated his spirits that he had no stomach for a fight.

Not so in the case of Mother, though. The Peronist threat to the consitution brought out a latent, ancestral heroism in this formidable woman. Doña Leonor Acevedo de Borges flung herself into the resistance to Perón, and her finest hour would come on the evening of September 8, 1948, when she joined a crowd of up to three hundred people in the calle Florida in order to demonstrate her commitment to the constitution of the Argentine republic. The demonstrators sang the national anthem, shouted "¡Vivas!" in favor of the 1853 constitution, and distributed flyers bearing the initials RUL for *Resistencia, Unidad y Libertad*. Their cries were countered by shouts of "¡Viva Perón!" from students at the balcony of the Centro Universitario Argentino in the building opposite. According to a statement released to the press by the authorities, an anonymous telephone call was received by the federal police at 7:10 P.M. informing them that an antigovernment demonstration would be taking place a few minutes later in the calle Florida, between calles Sarmiento and Corrientes.[11] After requesting the army to send a detachment of infantry "to forestall any eventuality," the police went to the scene, arriving just in time to prevent some thirty counterdemonstrators (probably Peronist students) from assaulting the protesters. Most of the original demonstrators dispersed at the behest of the police, but a few ladies stood their ground and continued to sing the national anthem. Detectives ushered them into a nearby shoe shop for their own safety, and a few moments later another group, shouting Peronist slogans, started to burn the flyers scattered about on the road. Passersby later reported that one of the demonstrators was set upon and punched by an unknown assailant.

The ladies arrested in this incident were Leonor Acevedo de Borges, Norah Borges de Torre, Adela and Mariana Grondona, Raquel Pueyrredón de Lastra, María González Acha de Tomkinson, and a Uruguayan lady and her daughter, who claimed to be innocent bystanders. They were charged with causing a breach of the peace and "with infractions of the edict relating to public gatherings," and three days later they were each sentenced to thirty days' imprisonment, the maximum penalty for these offenses. Leonor Acevedo, who had been escorted to the courtroom by three policemen, received the same sentence, but in consideration of her age—she was seventy-two years old—was permitted to serve the month's imprisonment under house arrest. The others were committed to the San Miguel Prison for women offenders. Norah Borges passed much of her time in prison writing reassuring letters home so as not to worry her family and producing sketches of the felons and common prostitutes who were her fellow inmates.

Borges would say that the imprisonment of his mother and sister was "distressing, but something honorable too."[12] Indeed, so oppressed was he by feelings of unworthiness that he felt obliged to articulate them in a story called "Redemption" ("La redención"), which he wrote toward the end of 1948.[13] The story concerns Pedro Damián, a man who has lived with the shame of having been a coward in battle forty years earlier. On his deathbed, however, he dreams that he had died a hero in that conflict. Curiously, Borges, the narrator, discovers that the memories of the other survivors of the battle have changed, and instead of recalling Damián's cowardice, as they had done earlier, they remember him as the hero he had hoped to be. Damián has thus found "redemption" in a dream that has miraculously altered the truths of the past.

In the context of Leonor Acevedo's clash with the Peronist authorities, this story addresses Borges's old anxieties about being a coward. He had been put to shame by Mother's courage and wished he could find redemption in her eyes by doing something worthy of the memory of his heroic ancestors. But equally he was aware that this wish to live up to Mother's expectations conflicted with his desire for fulfillment, which could come about only by rebelling against her authority. He was caught in his double bind once more, paralyzed by his instinctive reluctance to submit to his mother, yet bereft of any faith in his own capacity to rebel. This was a situation he would compare to that of a man imprisoned in a dungeon, who knew exactly what he must do to be released but who still could not effect his own liberation.

In February, a month after "Redemption" appeared, Borges published in *Sur* another story called "The God's Writing," a version of the story he had told Estela Canto four years earlier by the tiger's cage at Palermo Zoo.[14] The prisoner in the dungeon is now an Aztec priest who can see a jaguar on the other side of the wall. The priest has discovered the sacred formula that the god has written on the jaguar's fur. It consists of fourteen words, and if he utters these words, he will be released, drive the Spanish invaders from Mexico, reconstruct the empire, and inherit the throne of Montezuma. But the prisoner chooses not to utter the magic words, because "whoever has seen the universe and its brilliant designs cannot concern himself with one man, with his trivial fortunes or misfortunes, even if that man is himself."

The prisoner in the early version, according to Estela Canto, had not yet discovered the secret of the god's writing, but even as he searched for it, he felt sure he would one day be free; the character in the later version discovers the secret yet chooses not to say the words, and so he remains a captive in the dungeon. Estela took this as yet another sign of Borges's lack of courage, and in a sense she was right, but she took no account of the fact that when Borges told her the early version, she had recently agreed to marry him, whereas the second version registered an indifference to his fate after she, and then Cecilia Ingenieros, had turned him down.[15] From a story of liberation, "The God's Writing" had become one of resignation.

The fact was that Borges was torn between wishing to be redeemed in his mother's eyes and his desire for a woman's love. He could see no way of reconciling the conflict at this juncture. His dilemma is represented in a new story that appeared just three months after "The God's Writing." In "Story of the Warrior and the Captive Maiden," he contrasted civilization and barbarism.[16] On the one hand, we have Droctulft, a Visigothic barbarian, who is won over by the civilization of his Roman enemies when he contemplates the beauty and order of Ravenna; on the other, an Englishwoman who freely chooses to remain a captive of the pampas Indians on the Argentine frontier, even though Borges's grandmother, a fellow Englishwoman, offers to rescue her from that barbarism. Droctulf sees civilization as "a complex machinery whose purpose is unknown but in whose design one might divine an immortal intelligence"; the English captive has found a sensuous fulfillment in barbarism, and she conveys this in a single action—she throws herself off her horse and drinks the warm blood of a freshly slaughtered sheep as "a challenge or a sign" to Borges's Victorian grandmother. In Borges's eyes the motives of each character are equally mysterious: "the two of them were seized by a secret impulse, an impulse which was deeper than reason, and both submitted to that impulse, which neither would have been able to justify."

By the time "Story of the Warrior and the Captive Maiden" appeared in the May issue of *Sur,* he was putting together for publication a collection of the stories he had written since 1944. He decided to call the new book *The Aleph,* the title of the story he had written just after he had fallen in love with Estela Canto toward the end of 1944, and which he had dedicated to her. Why this choice of title? I believe it was because at around the time *The Aleph* was published on June 26, 1949, Estela Canto had entered his life once more, and Borges was again tempted to see her as the "new Beatrice," whose love would bring release from his woes.

Estela skates over this second phase of her relationship with Borges in her memoirs, but she includes the text of a postcard Borges sent her from Santiago del Estero on October 4, 1949, while he was on a lecture tour of northern Argentina.[17] We can deduce from his message that he was interested in resuming his romance with Estela but had so far met with uncertain results. This might explain the muted colors of the landscape he describes in the postcard. He tells Estela that Santiago has a peculiarly sad, wistful flavor of its own: the land has a yellowish hue, the soil is largely sand, and the green looks more like gray. He comments on some old houses, which he finds very beautiful and noble. And then he tells her that he misses her all the time.

When he went to Mar del Plata, probably in December, to work with Bioy on a screenplay, he left Buenos Aires without bothering to let Estela know. Estela, however, telephoned the Bioys' villa, but Borges had already retired for the night. The following morning he wrote to thank her, telling her that he had dreamed she had phoned him and was therefore delighted that she had indeed called.[18] He apologized for not having told her he was leaving Buenos Aires, but he had neglected to tell her out of courtesy or maybe fear, because he was convinced that, at bottom, he was nothing but a nuisance or an obligation to her. Still, Estela's telephone call had given him new heart: it encouraged him to think that there were forms of destiny that repeated themselves, for there he was in Mar del Plata once again, wanting her and looking forward to the night or the dawn that they would both fully possess. Shortly before his return to Buenos Aires, he wrote to Estela again to say that everything in Mar del Plata seemed to allude to her, this being the fate of any place in which he happened to find himself. He told her that he was working on the screenplay with Bioy Casares, but only with an external part of his soul, because something deep within him kept recalling her all the time.[19]

Borges's thoughts once more turned to marriage. Bioy Casares and Silvina Ocampo tried to help things along by inviting him and Estela to spend the summer month of February at their *estancia*. Meanwhile, Borges persuaded Estela to have another interview with Kohan-Miller, hoping no doubt that the psychologist would have more success in persuading her to marry him without preconditions. But neither Estela nor Kohan-Miller could summon up much enthusiasm for the subject, and Borges must have realized that there was little point in pursuing the matter.

By the time they were due to go to the Bioys' *estancia*, it was all over between them. The month they spent at the ranch turned out to be a rather glum experience. Borges and Bioy worked on their screenplay; Estela passed the time with Silvina. The closest the two of them came to any physical contact was when Estela helped Georgie shave off a rather absurd beard he had grown at the time. This was in deference to Bioy's mother, a grand lady of the old school, who was also staying at the *estancia* and had complained to her son Adolfito about his friend's unkempt appearance.

After they returned to Buenos Aires from Bioy's *estancia,* Estela severed her connection with Borges and shortly went off to live abroad. Some bond had been broken, Estela would observe in her memoirs, and Georgie no longer trusted her, not even as a friend, but she also suspected that in the three years of her absence from Buenos Aires, his mother had not been inactive.[20] Clearly Estela's hostility toward Doña Leonor was as unbending as ever, and this remained an impediment in her relations with Borges.

This was the second time Borges had failed to win the love of Estela Canto. It seemed as if fate kept wheeling him up to great peaks of hope only to drop him suddenly into a pit of despair. With Estela gone, there seemed nothing to live for. No matter that Perón was becoming ever more authoritarian: Borges was sick to death over his failure in love. At around the time of Estela's disappearance, he set to work on a new story called "The Waiting" ("La espera"), where he portrayed a man on the run from political assassins hiding out in a boardinghouse in some dingy suburb of Buenos Aires.[21] The fugitive discovers a copy of the *Divine Comedy* on a bookshelf in his room and, for want of anything better to do, begins to read a few cantos. When his killers finally track him down, he just rolls over meekly to face the wall and resigns himself to the inevitable.

CHAPTER 22

Borges Against Perón

(1950–1955)

THE PARANOIA that imbues "The Waiting" reflects the rising tension in Argentina at the time. A new Peronist constitution had been introduced in 1949, granting extensive powers to the state and permitting Perón, in effect, to rule for life. But the economic boom had come to an end as European countries recovered from the war and Argentine exports started to decline. By 1950 Perón found himself in difficulties. In order to keep up his spending bonanza, he had to resort to foreign borrowing, which contradicted his much-vaunted economic nationalism. More worrying still was the fact that both unemployment and inflation were rising sharply, and this encouraged the opposition to stir up popular discontent. It was imperative, therefore, that he tighten his grip on the country. In a drive to "Peronize" Argentina, universities and schools were purged, and government control was extended over professional bodies and employers' organizations. The repression of opponents intensified—an austerity package was foisted on the unions, and dissident labor leaders were thrown in jail. There were even reports of torture, including the use of the infamous *picana,* an electric prod applied to the genitals.

Eva Perón proved herself invaluable in the campaign to consolidate her husband's power. She enjoyed an almost hypnotic rapport with the *descamisados,* and in July 1949 she established the Eva Perón Foundation, which was financed by "contributions" from the trade unions and businesses and employed some fourteen thousand workers in administering a vast empire of social welfare, embracing housing for pensioners, the unemployed, and the homeless, as well as hospitals, schools, vacation camps, and even an entire "Children's City" in Buenos Aires. The foundation represented the positive aspect of Evita's influence, but there was a negative aspect, too. She was well aware of the power of the media, and from 1948 she had begun to acquire radio stations and newspapers through a consortium of sympathetic businessmen. A single company, Alea S.A., which she controlled, would buy up a range of established titles—*El Hogar, La Razón, Noticias Gráficas, Crítica, La Época.* Many other publications were simply got rid of—in 1950 some sixty provincial newspapers were closed down, as well as the socialist papers *Argentina Libre* and *La Vanguardia*.[1] Evita's followers were also instrumental in eliminating dissident trade-unionists and placing loyalists in key positions. In 1950 Perón would jail a leading Radical politician, Ricardo Balbín, for the crime of *desacato*, or "contempt" of authority, since he had suggested that Eva Perón might be enriching herself through her charitable foundation.

Perón's lurch toward totalitarianism caused alarm among writers and intellectuals. In 1950 Borges was approached by several of his friends and asked to run for the presidency of SADE, the Argentine Society of Writers. With his long-standing reputation as an antifascist, Borges had excellent credentials to lead SADE in these troubled times. But he could not rouse himself from his apathy since his second break with Estela Canto, even though his inaction gave him a bad conscience:

> I tried to think as little as possible about politics. All the same, just as a person who has toothache thinks about that toothache the moment he wakes up, or a man who has been left by a woman thinks about her as soon as he opens his eyes, I used to say to myself every morning: "That man is in the Casa Rosada," and I would feel upset, and in a way, guilty too, because I thought that the fact of not doing anything or of doing so little—but what could I do? I would make some joke or other about him in my lectures. There was precious little else I could do; I didn't feel capable of doing much else. All this used to make me very depressed.[2]

In the end he relented and accepted the nomination, but he revealed his mixed feelings in a letter to the artist Attilio Rossi.[3] He was not cut out for such a public role, he told Rossi, since he detested any kind of authority and felt out of place at meetings and social gatherings, but he believed it was his duty to repay the debt he owed SADE for the prize they had awarded *Ficciones* in 1945, especially since his book *The Garden of Forking Paths* had been refused a National Award for Literature a few years earlier. He added that his mother was right to point out that he had incurred a debt of honor to SADE. Indeed, Leonor Acevedo's values permeate her son's letter, with its references to honor, commitment, noblesse oblige, and repayment. This is especially evident when Borges declared to Rossi that they were living in a time of barbarism in which it was obligatory to praise Rosas, Hitler, and Mussolini, a time of ignorance that was detrimental to the *patria*. Yet he confessed to feeling as if he had been caught up in the nightmarish symmetries and repetitions of Triste-le-Roy. Perhaps he feared that if he assumed a public role such as the presidency of SADE, his enemies might lure him into a trap, much as the criminal Scharlach in "Death and the Compass" tricks the detective Lönnrot into actively seeking his own destruction. Still, this letter strongly suggests that Mother had shamed him into taking up the sword of honor in defense of "civilization" against the "barbarism" of Perón.

Borges expected to be given a rough ride by the Peronists. When he invited Betina Edelberg, who had been sacked from her post as a lecturer in the University of Buenos Aires, to become a member of the SADE committee, he warned her that she was being offered "a crown of thorns."[4] These anxieties turned out to be misplaced, however, because Perón's most effective weapon against SADE was not terror but neglect. Perón, after all, had little to fear from an association of writers when he already had the mass media effectively under his control. And the quality press would shortly be cowed into submission, too—within a few months of Borges's becoming president of SADE, the government closed down La Prensa and handed it over to the confederation of labor unions.

By this time, in any case, most of the members of SADE had taken fright. As Borges put it, "Many distinguished men of letters did not dare set foot inside its doors."[5] Only a hard core of committed anti-Peronists would turn up to do what they could to express their opposition to the regime, which did not really amount to very much. According to Luisa Mercedes Levinson, "We would gather every week to tell the latest jokes about the ruling couple and even dared to sing the songs of the French Resistance, as well as 'La Marseillaise.'"[6] To keep their spirits up, they would occasionally hold a dinner at the SADE headquarters next to the Biblioteca Nacional on calle México. It was a grand enough building, having once been the town house of Victoria Ocampo's family, but there were so few active members left in those days that a SADE dinner had dwindled to little more than a handful of diehards sitting out in the courtyard to share a pot of locro, a bean and meat stew. The one thing that could be said for such gatherings, as one of Borges's friends observed, was that they were "very cozy."[7]

Borges would persevere nonetheless in his attempts to criticize the regime. "In every lecture I gave, I would always express my views against the government."[8] On October 22, 1950, he published "The Wall and the Books" ("La muralla y los libros") in La Nación, a veiled attack on the xenophobic cultural policy of the Peronists. The essay purported to be an ironic reflection on the Chinese emperor who sought to keep out foreign influences by building the Great Wall and who attempted to abolish the past by ordering the destruction of all books written before his time. Borges remarked on the intrinsic futility of these aspirations, for the building of a wall acknowledged the fragility of what was being defended, while the burning of books attested to their power, since books teach what the whole universe or the human mind is capable of teaching.

These attacks, of course, were the merest pinpricks against Perón, who appeared to be ever more contemptuous of the opposition. By the end of 1950, the Peronist machine was gearing up to ensure a massive victory for "El Conductor" at the next presidential elections, due in November of 1951. Rallies, parades, and marches were organized; huge pictures of Perón and Evita were hung in public places; anthems poured from radios; slogans were raised on banners—PERÓN CUMPLE, EVITA DIGNIFICA, "Perón Delivers, Evita Dignifies." A feverish atmosphere was being whipped up among the populace, but a secret weakness had appeared in the very heart of the system, a secret known as yet only to Perón's inner circle—Evita had cancer, and the prognosis was uncertain.

Throughout the period of Perón's rule, Borges maintained his habit of dining most evenings with his old friends Bioy Casares and Silvina Ocampo. As ever, he and Bioy amused themselves by writing stories or working on translations together. To lighten their depression over the political situation, they liked to compose satirical sketches against Perón, such as the "The Monster's Fiesta" ("La fiesta del monstruo"), a burlesque account of a Peronist rally written in a Buenos Aires slang that is virtually impenetrable to outsiders.[9] Although such pieces may have allowed them to vent their frustration with the dictator, there was no hope of getting them published, so they were just circulated among their friends.

Borges also found relief from the oppressive political atmosphere in a friendship he struck up with a dancer called Margarita (Margot) Guerrero. A friend of Estela Canto's and Cecilia Ingenieros's, Margot was one of those unconventional beauties in whose company Borges found distraction from the genteel salons of upper-class ladies whom his mother valued as her friends. Borges was intrigued by Margot's interest in the occult, and he took to accompanying her to the Librería Kier, a bookshop on the avenida Santa Fe that specialized in such matters. There the two of them would pass the time browsing contentedly through manuals of astrology, numerology, palmistry, and the like.

It was Margot who suggested to Borges that he collaborate with their mutual friend Betina Edelberg on the script for a ballet. Borges agreed, and he would come regularly to the Edelbergs' apartment to work on the project. Betina found it enormous fun working with Borges and was amazed by his "vitality" and "enthusiasm."[10] He had a great appetite for verbal clowning and would roar with laughter as he tried out little parodies of the pompous language used by the Peronist officials he loathed. His "crazy" sense of humor, Betina thought, was very much in keeping with the spirit of old Buenos Aires, with the *sobrada criolla,* a teasing irony designed to keep one guessing about the speaker's real intentions.

The ballet was called *La imagen perdida* (*The Lost Image*), and it evolved from a standing joke Betina had with her husband about his seeming to become invisible every time he tried to hail a taxi. The central character was a man called Geist ("ghost" in German), who became invisible whenever he was absorbed in thought. There was surely an element of self-parody here on Borges's part, since Geist's predicament was his own in a nutshell, for he, too, was given to losing himself in a mental world that tended to cancel out the physical side of life. The script of the ballet has been lost, but the story seems to have ended happily enough: Borges was to tell Jean de Milleret that it closed with the appearance onstage of the nine Muses, who performed the final dance.[11]

This inspirational ending may well have reflected the fact that, while Borges was working with Betina on *La imagen perdida,* his friendship with Margot Guerrero had taken a romantic turn, and it is possible that, thanks to her, he was beginnning to feel more at ease with himself. In any case, Betina Edelberg recalled that while he was working with her on the ballet, he was visiting a psychoanalyst in Montevideo once a week.[12] It would seem that he was determined to persevere in the process of self-understanding on which he had embarked several years earlier during his relationship with Estela Canto.

Certainly the whole question of his inhibitions with regard to the opposite sex was very much on his mind at this time. He turned up one day at the Edelbergs' apartment and asked if either Betina or her husband, Gerardo, could think of a synonym for the word "mud." He needed it, he explained, for a new story he was writing. Betina came up with *légamo,* "slime," a word he liked and which subsequently appeared in the finished text. He would call this story "The Sect of the Phoenix" ("La secta del Fénix"), and it was a fable about a worldwide confraternity that performed an occult rite known as "the Secret."[13] Many devotees of the sect found the Secret "banal, embarrassing, vulgar and (what is even stranger) incredible," and they could not bring themselves to admit that "their parents had stooped to such manipulations." The Secret was associated with feelings of disgust—slime (*légamo*), we are told, was often employed in the execution of that hidden act. Years later Borges would tell Ronald Christ that he meant the Secret to refer to sexual intercourse.[14]

Still, Borges's relationship with Margot Guerrero undoubtedly boosted his self-esteem, and he was greatly encouraged also by a translation of *Ficciones* that Gallimard, the leading French publishing house, brought out in Paris that year. This was the first of Borges's books to be translated into a foreign language, and he was tremendously keen to see this French version by

Paul Verdevoye and Borges's friend Néstor Ibarra. This modest sign of recognition in France would have been especially gratifying at a time when the Peronist government was intent on closing the nation's doors to foreign influences. Betina Edelberg drove Borges out to Ezeiza Airport to pick up a copy a friend had sent him from Paris, and when he held the book in trembling hands, his joy was "impossible to describe."[15]

On December 17, 1951, Borges gave a lecture at the Colegio Libre de Estudios Superiores, entitled "The Argentine Writer and Tradition" ("El escritor argentino y la tradición"), in which he attacked the central aim of Peronist cultural policy—the fostering of a supposedly authentic national culture that would have the gaucho as its archetype and *Martín Fierro* as its folk epic.[16] While conceding that *Martín Fierro* was one of the most enduring works created in Argentina, it was not the Bible or the canonical book of the Argentines; gauchesque poetry was as artificial a literary genre as any other, and quite different from the kind of poetry actually written by gauchos. Even a novel about gauchos, like Ricardo Güiraldes's *Don Segundo Sombra,* which nationalists so admired, could not have been written without foreign influences such as French symbolism or Rudyard Kipling's *Kim.* Argentine tradition, he declared, encompassed the whole of Western culture. The American sociologist Thorstein Veblen had argued that the preeminence of Jews in Western culture was due not to innate superiority but to the fact that they could act within that culture while not feeling bound to it by any special devotion. Borges declared, "We Argentines, we South Americans in general, are in an analogous situation; we are capable of handling all the European themes, handling them without superstition, with an irreverence which may have, and already does have, fortunate consequences"; Argentine writers, therefore, should not limit themselves to purely Argentine subjects, "for either being Argentine is an unavoidable destiny, and in that case we shall be so whatever we do, or being Argentine is a mere affectation, a mask."

This lecture would become one of Borges's most influential texts, but at the time it was delivered, it scarcely impinged on the public consciousness, for in the course of 1951, the political atmosphere had become too highly charged for the words of a mere writer to have much resonance. In the run-up to the presidential elections in November, pressure had built from the labor unions for Evita to be nominated for the vice presidency. She was expected to announce her candidacy at a mass rally to be held on August 22 in the avenida 9 de Julio, the immense avenue that cuts a swath through the center of Buenos Aires. About 1 million Peronists turned up on the day to hail Evita, and yet when she appeared onstage, she gave an impassioned speech but made no mention of the candidacy. Perón also omitted any reference to it in his speech. The multitude cried out for Evita to declare herself, but Evita resisted: she needed time to think about it; she must be given a few more days. But still the masses implored her to stand. Evita looked pale and unwell, Perón distinctly uneasy. Nine days later she shocked her followers when she declared on the radio that she would "renounce" the vice presidency because her mission was no other than "to communicate the hopes of the people" to Perón.[17] On September 10, Perón awarded his wife a special medal for her heroic "renunciation." Evita's "sacrifice" provoked a volcanic outpouring of fervor from the masses, a fervor that reached a pitch of intense, religious adoration when it was announced that the great patroness of the poor was terminally ill with cancer. Thus was created the myth of "Santa Evita," the sacred martyr in the cause of the people.

On November 11, 1951, Perón won the presidential elections by a landslide, beating his main opponent, Ricardo Balbín of the Radical Party, by a margin of two to one. The opposition had been utterly crushed at the polls, their presence in Congress having been reduced to a rump of fourteen deputies. Perón was helped to victory by the votes of Argentine women, who were exercising their right to vote for the first time. (The Peronist media published photographs of an emaciated Evita casting her vote in a ballot box that had been brought to her sickbed.) By the end of the year, there seemed to be nothing that could stand in the way of Perón's ambition to turn Argentina into a state-controlled Comunidad Organizada under a single leader and a single party.

As her life ebbed away, Eva Perón became more strident and aggressive than ever. Over the radio, or from the balcony of the Casa Rosada, she would deliver violent speeches expressing her boundless love for the incomparable Perón and urging the masses to rise up in the event of any attempt to overthrow him. It was rumored that she had purchased thousands of guns to be distributed to her followers in case of a coup d'état.[18] On May 1, 1952, she addressed the workers from the balcony of the Casa Rosada, but she was so enfeebled that Perón himself had to hold her up by the waist. This was to be her last speech, and it was one of her most inflammatory, a virtual incitement to insurrection should "the oligarchy" counterattack.

For opponents of Perón, the future could not have looked bleaker: the country seemed to be facing the prospect of either a totalitarian dictatorship or a civil war. Bioy Casares, for one, imagined himself in a situation akin to that of the nineteenth-century liberals fighting for "civilization" against the "barbarism" of the tyrant Rosas. In March or April 1952, "in a moment of extreme desolation," he conceived a story, "Homage to Francisco Almeyra," about a young writer who longs to take up arms against Rosas and, despite being warned of the dangers, goes off to fight and gets his throat cut.[19]

Borges, too, began to work up an idea for a new story. The protagonist of "The South" ("El Sur") is Juan Dahlmann, a resident of Buenos Aires of mixed

German-Protestant and Argentine-Catholic ancestry, who nonetheless feels "profoundly Argentine" for being the grandson of a hero of the Wars of Independence.[20] Even though the family estates have long since gone and he works at a modest desk job in the city, Dahlmann has managed to retain possession of an old mansion in the pampas to the south of Buenos Aires, the empty remnant of the ancestral *estancia*. In the second part of the story, we find him setting off by train to visit the mansion, but the train unexpectedly comes to a halt somewhere in the middle of the pampas, and while he waits in a bar, Dahlmann is picked on by a group of ruffians. Unsure how to react, he suddenly resolves to rise to the challenge after an old gaucho throws him a dagger.

This story, like Bioy's, indulged the fantasy of taking up arms against Perón. But Borges's treatment of this theme was very different from his friend's, for Bioy, who came from a powerful *estanciero* family, could identify wholeheartedly with the struggle of the Buenos Aires liberals againt the tyrant Rosas, but Borges, who was wooing Margot Guerrero at this time, must have been especially conscious of his own more complicated loyalties. "Civilization," in his case, was identified with Mother's ancestral sword of honor, whereas he was drawn as much, if not more so, to a kind of "barbarism" associated with Father and symbolized by the dagger of the gaucho and the *compadrito*. "The South," in fact, registers a shift of allegiance from Mother to Father, for at its heart there is the curious interruption of Dahlmann's train journey, as a result of which he will never get to the mansion of his patrician ancestors but must instead prove his mettle by picking up the old gaucho's dagger and confronting the bullies in a duel.

Borges was changing the terms of his opposition to Perón. He had agreed to become president of SADE at Mother's instigation, and in so doing, he was, as it were, taking up the sword of honor to defend "civilization" against the dictator. But "The South" suggests a defiance of Perón on a quite different basis—it is presented as a return to the timeless spirit of the gaucho, to a tradition of the individual's resistance to the power of the state that Borges derived from the anarchist ideas of his father and Evaristo Carriego. The motif of the old gaucho's throwing Dahlmann a dagger recalls the episode when Dr. Borges handed young Georgie a knife, urging him to show the bullies at school that he was a man.

Indeed, while working on "The South," Borges was also writing a critical study of *The Gaucho Martín Fierro* with the assistance of Margot Guerrero (whom he was to credit as a collaborator when it came out as a book in 1953).[21] He was immersing himself once more in the world of gauchos, knives, and duels, the standard topics of Argentine "barbarism," which, as he knew, Mother thoroughly disliked. This was a sign, I would say, that his romance with Margot had put him in a mood to rebel against the sword of honor, and Dahlmann's taking up the dagger against the bullyboys in the tavern is a reflection, I believe, of the self-confidence Borges drew from his relationship with her.

He was, in fact, besotted with Margot, so besotted that he was prepared to overlook the fact that his girlfriend's interest in literature was not as consuming as his own. And yet it was impossible for Borges to conduct any kind of relationship that did not involve some sort of literary activity, so he came up with a project that was extravagant enough to compete with Margot's interest in the occult. He set about making a catalog of the weirdest animals the human mind had dreamed up, and he persuaded Margot to assist him in putting together this strange bestiary, which would eventually be published in 1957 as *Manual de zoología fantástica*.[22] Despite such diversions, life with Margot was fairly stormy—he was living through "a reign of terror," he would jokingly sigh to his friend Betina Edelberg.[23] But he was happy enough to comply with his girlfriend's wishes, and the only explanation Betina could find for such docility was that Borges was so terribly "anxious to find love."

And then disaster struck—Margot broke off the relationship, a decision that took Borges completely by surprise. Neither Betina nor her husband was able to work out quite what had caused the break, but Margot was a law unto herself, and the Edelbergs surmised that she may simply have wearied of Borges's relentless obsession with literature. Whatever the reasons for the break, Borges took it very badly: "It affected him terribly, terribly," Betina would recall. "He suffered hugely. He was devastated. I even saw him weep."[24]

On the evening Margot broke the news to him, Borges went out for a long walk on his own and eventually came to the first bridge over the railway tracks outside Constitución Station. Standing there, amid the roar of trains "weaving labyrinths of iron" as they departed for the south, for the pampas, he experienced "a sort of ecstasy," a "revelation," as if he were attending the Day of Judgment; the next day he tried to express in a poem this sense of "an infinite voice" rising from "the invisible horizon" and from "the center of my being," and revealing to him the great diversity of the world, a revelation that served only to oppress him with the thought that "you have wasted the years and they have wasted you, / and still you have not written the poem."[25] As he was to tell an interviewer, he reproached himself for having squandered his talents: "I have received the gift of unhappiness this evening, and even this has not been sufficient to make me a great poet."[26]

Like his various sweethearts before her, Margot Guerrero had been assigned the role of the "new Beatrice," whose love would inspire Borges to write a "poem," a masterpiece, that would define him in the way the *Divine Comedy* had defined Dante. But her loss had dashed his hopes of finding salvation by writing, and the title he would give the rueful poem that came to mind as he stood on the railway bridge at Constitución was a biblical reference, Matthew,

XXV:30: "And he shall be cast into the outer darkness, and there shall be weeping and gnashing of teeth."

Margot's rejection, I believe, occurred before Borges had finished writing his anti-Perón story, "The South," and the outcome of the story may have been influenced by the impact of her loss. In the published version, Dahlmann sustains an injury to his head that puts him in the hospital, an accident identical to the one Borges himself suffered in 1938, shortly after the death of his father. As a result the ending of "The South" may be read in two ways: either the train journey to the pampas and Dahlmann's confrontation with the bullies takes place in reality or it is just a dream of Dahlmann's as he lies dying in a Buenos Aires hospital. The simple act of seizing the dagger thus becomes ambiguous, doubtful, and possibly unreal.

On July 26, 1952, the Argentine media announced that Eva Perón had "entered immortality." A period of official mourning of one month's duration was decreed, the labor unions ordered all workers to wear a black tie or other sign of mourning for three days, and all Argentine organizations were expected to show an appropriate mark of respect. As president of the SADE, Borges received a visit from two policemen, who asked him to put up a portrait of Perón and another of Evita on the walls of the premises. Borges refused and told them it was a ridiculous demand. "Very well," came the reply, "you shall have to face the consequences."[27] He was put under surveillance by the authorities: a policeman sat in on his lectures, taking notes, and he noticed that he was being followed by a detective. Borges would claim in his "Autobiographical Essay" that he used to take the detective on long, aimless walks and eventually befriended the man, who "admitted that he too hated Perón, but said that he was obeying orders."[28] In September the Peronists delivered a final blow to SADE by forcing it to close, thereby obliging Borges to stand down as its president. "I remember the last lecture I was allowed to give there. The audience, quite a small one, included a very puzzled policeman who did his clumsy best to set down a few of my remarks on Persian sufism."[29]

Borges had agreed to stand for the presidency of the SADE in order fight for intellectual freedom, but he had also wanted to avenge the humiliation he believed he had suffered in 1946, when the Peronists proposed to make him an inspector of chickens. In his letter of 1950 to Attilio Rossi, he claimed that his infamous promotion had been a very clever way the Peronists had found of damaging him and diminishing his reputation. The closure of the SADE meant that the Peronists had damaged him a second time, as was borne out by the visit of the Spanish writer Julián Marías, who arrived in Buenos Aires shortly after the closure of SADE. It was impossible for Borges, as president, to hold the usual reception for the distinguished visitor; instead one of Borges's friends brought a lamb from his ranch, and they had it roasted at a tavern across the road from the SADE building on calle México.[30] After dinner a friendly janitor let them into the premises, and they showed Marías around by candlelight. That tiny group of writers leading a foreign guest through a dark building by the light of guttering candles was vivid proof of the extent to which the SADE had been diminished under the rule of Juan Perón.

The sense of defeat and humiliation experienced by Borges at the forced closure of SADE led him to fantasize about taking up the dagger, like Dahlmann in "The South," and confronting Perón in a duel man-to-man. However, his recent disappointment in love had undermined his belief in himself, and he felt divided between the need to make a stand against Perón and his own renewed feelings of unworthiness. This self-doubt was expressed in a very strange tale he wrote some time toward the end of 1952. In "The Challenge" ("El desafío") an aging *cuchillero* called Suárez (one of the surnames in his mother's family), receives a letter challenging him to a duel in a town in the province of Santa Fe.[31] Suárez writes back declining the invitation: "He explains that he dare not leave his mother on her own, since she is so advanced in years." His challenger nevertheless seeks him out on his home ground, and a duel ensues. Doubting his ability to defeat his opponent, Suárez allows himself to be cut on the left forearm and then, placing his boot over it on the ground, wrenches off the whole of his left hand. Impelled by the excruciating pain of this self-amputation, Suárez makes a desperate lunge at his opponent and delivers the fatal thrust. "The Challenge" reflects yet again the double bind with which Borges had to contend—Suárez is divided between loyalty to his mother and a desire to assert himself fully as a man, and the violence of the self-amputation suggests that the only way Borges could imagine coping with this conflict was by inflicting grievous damage upon himself.

Borges published "The Challenge" in *La Nación* on December 28, 1952; "The South" appeared in *Sur* eleven days later, on February 8, 1953. The two stories register a decline in Borges's self-confidence after his rejection by Margot Guerrero. A third text, "The Dagger" ("El puñal"), written probably early in 1953, reveals the autobiographical memory that underlay these two stories about daggers and duels.[32] It takes its title from the old Spanish dagger that Dr. Borges used to keep in the drawer of his writing desk, and which Evaristo Carriego once held in his hand. This was also very likely the dagger his father had allowed the thirteen-year-old Georgie to handle in order to encourage him to stand up to the bullies at school. The grown-up Borges recalls the magnetic pull the dagger used to exert on him as a boy and imagines it as possessing a will of its own:

It is more than a piece of metal: men conceived and formed it for a very specific end; it is in some way eternal: it is the dagger that last night killed a man in Tacuarembó and also the daggers that killed Caesar. It wants to kill, it wants to spill sudden blood. In one of the drawers of the writing desk, among drafts and letters, the dagger endlessly dreams a simple dream of killing its tiger, and the hand that holds it comes alive because the blade comes alive, the blade that can sense, as soon as it is held, the killer for whom it was fashioned by other men.

This is the dagger of Borges's earliest dreams, the dagger of the tiger man, and its magic is so powerful that the merest touch would make it spring into action. Borges would dearly wish to hold it in his hand but cannot bring himself to pick it up. And so he just gazes at the dagger as it lies there dreaming of "its tiger": "It moves me to pity at times. Such firmness, such faith, such impassive, innocent pride, and yet the years go by, and nothing happens."

At around the time I reckon Borges wrote "The Dagger," Perón was facing his gravest crisis yet. The economy was doing badly and the opposition growing more restive. There was, moreover, no Evita to distract the populace from their troubles. On the contrary, her hallowed memory was sullied by the mysterious fate of her brother, Juan Duarte, who was found dead on April 9, having allegedly committed suicide over his involvement in a financial scandal, though it was rumored that he had in fact been murdered. These signs of dissension and skulduggery within the inner circles of the regime made Perón himself appear vulnerable. On April 15 there was an attempt on his life when bombs went off at a rally, killing and maiming several people. Peronist militants responded by going on the rampage in Buenos Aires and destroying the headquarters of the Radical, Socialist, and Conservative parties. The Jockey Club, long regarded as the symbol of the cattle-ranching oligarchy, was put to the torch, and its priceless collection of books and paintings went up in flames.

Borges could not have failed to be encouraged by the cracks that were appearing in the Peronist regime. Twice, in his opinion, he had been humiliated by Perón, and for the best part of the previous year, he had fantasized about taking some kind of revenge, but his sense of powerlessness continued to trouble him, as is evident in an essay he wrote at this time. In "Dialogues Between the Ascete and the King" ("Diálogos del asceta y del rey"), Borges characterized the ascete as "a zero" or "nothing" by comparison with the king, who is "a plenitude," and he wondered whether there might exist some "magic" by which "the zero, the ascete, might in some way equal and overcome the infinite king."[33] In other words, how effective could a writer be in opposing a man of power? What, in truth, could he set against Perón?

Sometime between April and September of 1953, I believe, he made a final effort to conquer self-doubt by trying to act out the duel he had imagined in "The Challenge." Like Suárez, he would overcome his disabling connection with his mother, if not literally by self-mutilation at least by exposing himself to real danger. He took the text of "The Dagger" and offered it for publication to *La Nación*.[34] It was refused, of course, for at a time when there had been attempts on Perón's life, how could *La Nación* risk publishing a text by Borges, a notorious enemy of the dictator, invoking "the daggers that killed Caesar" and portraying a knife that "wants to kill, wants to spill sudden blood"?[35] It was clearly a mad and reckless thing to do, but it was a test of courage Borges had devised for himself in a bid to make his writing engage somehow with the real world. And the failure of this desperate attempt at self-assertion would bring forth yet another story about daggers and duels, called, fittingly, "The End" ("El fin").

In "The End," Borges was to rewrite the ending of *The Gaucho Martín Fierro*: it relates the final duel between Martín Fierro and El Moreno, the brother of a black gaucho whom Fierro had killed in a barroom brawl in Part One of the famous poem.[36] This time, however, it is Fierro who is killed, but the death of the protagonist does not in the end provide a clear-cut resolution to the action, for the victor, El Moreno, has to all intents and purposes taken on Fierro's identity:

> Having accomplished his mission of revenge, he was nobody now. Or rather, he was the other man: there was nowhere he could go in this world, and he had killed a man.

When El Moreno kills Fierro, he takes on his victim's destiny, and the seemingly contrary identities of killer and killed, avenger and victim, dissolve into one another, thereby opening the story up to a potentially infinite progression, for El Moreno will eventually meet a fate similar to Fierro's: perhaps one of Fierro's sons will seek to avenge his father's killing, just as El Moreno had sought revenge for the murder of his brother's. And the series could, in principle, be extended to infinity, in an endlessly recycled sequence of periodic duels.

The action is observed by a third character called Recabarren, but he, unlike Martín Fierro and El Moreno, is an invention of Borges's. Recabarren is a wholly passive witness to the duel, having been paralyzed by a stroke, but there are hints in the text that he may have conjured up the encounter in his imagination as he lies helplessly on his bed looking out through the window at the vast, empty plains. Indeed, the cycle of desire and frustration that characterizes this tale of pointless revenge is encapsulated in the bilingual pun latent in the name Recabarren. *Recabar* means "to ask for, to demand, to insist on," but in "Recabarren" the word *recabar* is fused with the English word "barren," so that the name itself suggests that all our efforts to assert a unique, authentic self are futile: we must be resigned to open-endedness and irresolution.

After "The End" appeared in *La Nación* on October 11, 1953, Borges would not publish another story until 1969. He had, in truth, nothing much left to write about: the successive losses of Estela and Cecilia and Margot had demonstrated his inability to realize his own desires, and, like Recabarren, he lay prostrated by his own despair, gazing out, as it were, at the emptiness of the pampas, waiting for a revelation that never seemed to come.

The following year, 1954, was a dismal, uneventful time. Borges's eyesight had been declining steadily: although he had all but lost the sight in one eye, the other was still sound enough to permit him to read and write, even though he now had to bring the text to within a few inches of his eyes in order to make out the letters. At the end of 1954, however, he suffered an accident while on holiday with the Bioys in Mar del Plata—he fell over on the seashore, and as he struggled to get back on his feet, he realized that he had lost the vision in his good eye.[37] Bioy and Silvina rushed him to a doctor, who advised them to take him to Buenos Aires as soon as possible for an emergency operation. The fall had caused the retina in his eye to become detached, and it was uncertain whether the damage could be repaired. To everyone's distress, the prognosis was not at all hopeful: the doctors warned that he might never recover his sight.

For several weeks into 1955, Borges remained in the clinic, convalescing after his operation. The outcome was not successful: he could still see well enough to get about on his own, but there was no question of his being able to read and write again. From now on, his sight would become rapidly weaker, and within a few years, both eyes would cloud over and he would make out only the rough outline of things and had no sense of color except for yellow and orange. The fact that he could no longer read or write was a cruel blow for a man whose entire life had been devoted to books. His friends rallied around and tried to help him continue with his literary activities. Esther Zemborain offered to buy him a tape recorder so that he could work on his own. She was surprised, however, by Doña Leonor's reaction to this proposal: "What am I here for?" she protested.[38] Leonor Acevedo had looked after her husband with exemplary dedication after he went blind, and now that her son had so tragically succumbed to the same affliction, she would care for him with an equally selfless and unswerving devotion.

Borges's reaction to his blindness was not anger—he was well beyond anger by now—but stupor, a kind of dazed incomprehension at the inscrutable fate that seemed to have destroyed all possibility of salvation by writing. On February 15, 1955, not long after leaving the clinic, he wrote a short text about Dante's last days at Ravenna.[39] The dying poet has a dream in which God reveals to him "the secret purpose of his life and work." "Filled with wonder," Dante "learned at last who he was and what he was, and blessed his woes," but upon waking he discovers that he can no longer recall that secret purpose. In other words, even Dante had not been saved in the end by writing the *Divine Comedy;* he had "been given and had lost a measureless thing, something he could not retrieve or even make out, for the workings of this world are far too complex for the simplicity of man."

CHAPTER 23

La Revolución Libertadora

(1955–1959)

As Borges was recovering from his eye operation in the early months of 1955, the Peronist regime was under severe pressure from its opponents. Perón had set out to challenge the power structure in Argentina, but he made a fatal error by antagonizing the Catholic Church with a series of measures, such as the introduction of secular education and the legalization of divorce and prostitution, which alienated vast numbers of Catholics and undermined the popular consensus he needed for the success of his revolution. The divisions that were opening up in Argentina became palpable on June 11, when the traditional Corpus Christi procession through the center of Buenos Aires turned into a massive demonstration of Catholic disaffection from the regime. Borges happened to be at the Plaza de Mayo watching the procession with his nephews, Luis and Miguel de Torre, when the police charged the crowds. In the ensuing melee, young Luis was arrested and taken off to prison at Villa Devoto, where he was detained for a week before being discharged.[1]

The Peronists responded to the Corpus Christi procession with a huge rally of their own in the Plaza de Mayo. But a number of military units rebelled against Perón during this rally, and when the Casa Rosada, the presidential palace on the Plaza de Mayo, was strafed by combat airplanes, several hundred Peronists were killed or injured in the process. Peronist mobs went on the rampage in Buenos Aires after this outrage, and civil war seemed inevitable, but at the eleventh hour Perón drew back from the brink and made conciliatory gestures to appease the opposition.

While these momentous events were taking place, Borges's personal life had taken an unexpected turn for the better. He had resumed, somewhat tentatively, his friendship with Estela Canto, who had returned to Buenos Aires to look after her sick mother, having lived in Europe for several years.[2] Their friendship became closer after the death of Estela's mother, and by the middle of 1955, they were discussing the possibility of a more intimate kind of relationship. Certainly the situation seemed more favorable than ten years earlier, when Estela had been involved with another man and had taken Borges's proposal of marriage too lightly; but now she was unattached and had turned forty, and after her mother's death, she appears to have been taking stock of things, and was more amenable to the idea of a permanent relationship, and perhaps even marriage.

In her memoirs Estela was quite reticent about this third phase of her relations with Borges, merely stating that the "old flame" revived for a while.[3] I reckon this may have occurred in June or July, for on July 11, *Noticias Gráficas* published an interview in which Borges talked about his project to write a novel called *The Congress,* "which would sum up and would also be the resolution of everything I have written up till now."[4] He explained that "*The Congress*—an ideal Congress—would begin as a novel and end as a fairy tale." From our subsequent knowledge of *The Congress,* we may deduce that by this "fairytale" ending he would have been alluding to that pantheist vision of personal and universal integration, which he saw as an analogue to Dante's last vision of Beatrice in Paradise. Indeed, Estela's reappearance must have seemed nothing short of miraculous to Borges, for she had reentered his life when he had given up all hope of personal salvation. It was as if he were being granted one last chance of finding love before going totally blind.

Borges's interview with *Noticias Gráficas* was published at a time of unprecedented crisis for the Peronist regime. The uneasy truce between the government and the opposition parties that had followed the attack on the Peronist rally in June was on the point of collapse. On August 31, Perón had appeared at the balcony of the Casa Rosada and made an inflammatory speech in defence of his revolution, exhorting his followers to kill anyone who got in their way and adding, famously, that for every Peronist that fell, five of their opponents should be killed. There followed three weeks of grave tension as the country awaited the reaction of the armed forces. On September 19, General Eduardo Lonardi led an uprising in the city of Córdoba that spread to units throughout Argentina. Yet even now Perón failed to counterattack, and for several days there was a standoff between the rebel forces and those remaining loyal to Perón.

Borges was greatly encouraged by these developments. On the night of September 22, he was advised by friends that the air force would bomb areas surrounding the Casa Rosada. Since his flat at calle Maipú was close to the danger zone, he decided to move his mother to his sister's apartment in the Barrio Norte. He was too restless to sleep that night, so he went out and roamed the city streets waiting for the bombing to start. However, nothing seemed to be happening, and eventually, finding himself outside the apartment building where his friend Susana Bombal lived, he went up to see her. When she opened the door, Susana threw her arms around him and cried out,

"My noble friend!" He was puzzled at first by this theatrical greeting, but then it dawned on him that Susana had been so carried away because Perón had been overthrown. As it turned out, the bombing never took place because Perón had fled the Casa Rosada and sought refuge in the Paraguayan embassy. That same night he was allowed to escape into exile.

Borges immediately phoned his sister to break the news to his family. Then he went out again: the entire population of the Barrio Norte seemed to have surged into the streets to celebrate the news of Perón's downfall. It was pouring rain, but no one minded—there were crowds everywhere, wandering about aimlessly, singing and shouting. Borges himself was deliriously happy and kept crying out "*¡Viva la patria!*" at the top of his voice. He ran into a girl he knew on calle Libertad, and by the time they had found their way back to the avenida Santa Fe, he was soaked to the skin and had lost his voice with all the shouting. "I remember the joy we felt; I remember that at that moment no one thought about themselves: their only thought was that the *patria* had been saved."[5]

The fall of Perón, in Borges's view, had opened up the best political prospects for Argentina since the coup d'état which had ousted Irigoyen in 1930. He could once again dream of a democratic Argentina, free from the scourge of caudillos. And the fact that this new dawn in the nation's history had virtually coincided with the rekindling of romance with Estela Canto would explain the extraordinary euphoria felt by Borges at the downfall of Perón—the *patria* had been saved just when he had himself been given a final chance to be saved. In this rare accord between the personal and the public spheres of his life, Borges would have had a presentiment of that happy state to which he had aspired throughout his life—the sublime realization of the self and its integration in the reality of the world.

Borges did not have long to wait before tasting the fruits of victory. Within weeks of Perón's defeat, he was appointed director of the National Library, no less. In his "Autobiographical Essay," he claimed that "two very dear friends," Esther Zemborain de Torres and Victoria Ocampo, had "dreamed up the possibility" of his appointment, and he even hinted at a certain modest reluctance on his part: "I thought the scheme a wild one, and hoped at most to be given the directorship of some small-town library, preferably to the south of the city."[6] Esther Zemborain, however, recalled that Borges had gone with his friend, Margarita Bunge, to see the new minister of education, Attilio Dell'Oro Maini, who told them that someone else was about to be appointed to the post.[7] They decided nevertheless to enlist the help of Victoria Ocampo and consult the well-connected Esther Zemborain, who advised that they must immediately put together a petition from various cultural organizations and present it to Dell'Oro Maini before eleven o'clock the following morning; otherwise it would be too late, and the other man's name would have to be announced. Reverting to Borges's version of events: "Within the space of a day, a petition was signed by the magazine *Sur* (read Victoria Ocampo), by the re-opened SADE (read Carlos Alberto Erro), by the Sociedad Argentina de Cultura Inglesa (read Carlos del Campillo), and by the Colegio Libre de Estudios Superiores (read Luis Reissig). This was placed on the desk of the Minister of Education, and eventually I was appointed to the directorship by General Eduardo Lonardi, who was Acting President."[8]

The most likely explanation for the inconsistency in these accounts is that the appointment was in fact "dreamed up" by Borges and his mother. At the time there was a general impression among Borges's friends that it was Doña Leonor who was working behind the scenes to promote her son's career, and this would have been entirely consistent with her strong personality and lofty social aspirations.[9] Leonor Acevedo was a sharp, intelligent woman, and she would have recognized that the overthrow of Perón presented her with a historic opportunity to restore her family's social standing by propelling her son to a position of appropriate eminence. The "Autobiographical Essay" hints at a degree of collusion in this matter between mother and son. Even before the appointment was confirmed, the pair of them could hardly contain their excitement: "A few days earlier, my mother and I had walked to the Library one night to take a look at the building, but, feeling superstitious, I refused to go in. 'Not until I get the job,' I said. That same week, I was called to come to the Library to take over. My family was present, and I made a speech to the employees, telling them I was actually the Director—the incredible Director."[10] Borges confessed to feeling "very important" when he got the job, and it was, of course, precisely this feeling of importance that Leonor Acevedo had craved since she was a little girl.

As Estela Canto noted in her memoir, Borges was "delighted" with his new post, but, as his girlfriend at the time, she looked upon this triumph with considerable misgivings, for she had always been wary of Doña Leonor's influence on Georgie, and it was her impression that in the past few years his eye trouble and a few "upsets" in his dealings with women had drawn him closer to his mother.[11] Doña Leonor, certainly, was not happy that Georgie was courting Estela Canto once again. Of all the women that he had taken it into his head to fall in love with, Estela was by far the most unsuitable in her eyes. She was already well known for her sexual freedom, but things had got worse—she had become a Communist and was said to be a heavy drinker. Bioy Casares remembered Leonor's telling him how worried she was about Georgie and Estela going out on their own at night; what with her son being virtually blind and the near-sighted Estela's love of the bottle, how could they be relied upon to survive those long walks of theirs around the city?[12] The old conflict between Leonor Acevedo and Estela Canto was set to flare up again, but this time it was not

Doña Leonor who would present the greatest obstacle to the success of Borges's love for Estela—it was to be the changing political fortunes of Argentina.

The coup d'état that ousted Perón became known as the Revolución Libertadora, the "Liberating Revolution," and its leader, General Lonardi, had declared that there would be "neither winners nor losers" after Perón's departure. It had been assumed that once Perón had been removed, the political divisions in the country could be healed and democracy restored, but within weeks it became clear that the realities on the ground were rather more complex than anticipated. Perón had succeeded in institutionalizing his power—he had founded his own party and also controlled the confederation of labor unions, which guaranteed him an enormous following among the working classes, but, additionally, he could draw on the quasireligious fervor that his supporters felt for his deceased wife, Evita. The real question, then, for the victorious military junta was how to govern the country when so much of the population was still in thrall to the man they had just overthrown.

The anti-Peronist coalition divided over the issue. There were those, like the Communists, Socialists, and left-leaning Radicals, who were conscious of Perón's extraordinary hold on the labor unions and therefore argued for an accommodation with Peronist leaders and Peronist organizations, though not with Perón himself. The Radicals and Conservatives, on the other hand, were opposed to any compromise, believing that a "democratic regeneration" could be achieved only by suppressing Peronism altogether and rebuilding the constitutional order of liberal Argentina.

In November 1955, General Lonardi, who had been in favor of striking a deal with the Peronists, was removed from the leadership by General Pedro E. Aramburu, an advocate of "democratic regeneration." Aramburu's provisional government proposed to secure the Revolución Libertadora by eradicating Peronism completely and overseeing thereafter a gradual restoration of liberal democracy. The first step in the process would be the election of a Constituent Assembly, whose task would be to formulate a new constitution. This would be followed by presidential and congressional elections as and when circumstances allowed.

Borges did what he could to assist the Revolución Libertadora. As director of the National Library, he sponsored several measures intended to overcome what he saw as the narrow-minded philistinism of the Peronist regime. He sought funding to expand the National Library's holdings so as to repair the damage done by the petty nationalism of the Peronist era; he would shortly revive *La Biblioteca,* the defunct journal of the National Library; and he instituted a program of lectures by distinguished speakers committed to the cause of intellectual freedom. Another important element in the cultural reconstruction of Argentina was the purging of the universities of Peronist placemen, and here, too, Borges played a role, albeit a minor one, when he was appointed to a post teaching English literature at the University of Buenos Aires.

As a Radical, Borges was a supporter of "democratic regeneration," and in the aftermath of the coup, he published a strong condemnation of Peronism in *Sur*. There were two aspects to Perón's regime, he wrote in "L'Illusion comique," a "criminal" record consisting of "imprisonments, torture, prostitution, robbery, murder and arson," and also a theatrical façade made up of "stories and myths suitable only for idiots."[13] Even its supporters did not believe in a political theater of such "gross sentimentality," and yet none of them rejected it, for the true purpose of these "duplicitous fictions"—the propaganda, slogans, and gestures—was to conceal "the atrocious and sordid realities" of Perón's rule. The public had entered into a "willing suspension of disbelief" because, Borges implied, no one had had the courage to denounce the corruption at the very core of the system.

However, Borges's support for Aramburu's "democratic regeneration" brought him into conflict with Estela Canto. She would write of her relations with Borges that the "Revolución Libertadora, which should have brought us closer, drove us apart."[14] As a Communist, Estela was in favor of reaching an accommodation with the Peronists. She argued against Borges that if democracy meant anything at all, it was a government for the people elected by the people, whereas Aramburu was trying to put the clock back to 1910, when the oligarchy ruled through manipulated elections. A return to such a system was no longer possible, in her view, so the only realistic alternative to free elections was military violence. Their political differences, moreover, became entangled in the old power struggle between Estela and Doña Leonor. Estela was inclined to attribute her disagreement with Borges to his fear of gainsaying Mother: "He clung to his mother's point of view."[15] She thought Georgie was being a coward, a mother's boy: he should rebel.

What she quite failed to see was that Borges had his own integrity to defend. Far from being in favor of oligarchy, Borges had, since the 1920s, held a democratic vision of a new Argentina, free from the rule of caudillos like Perón. But the fall of Perón created a fearsomely difficult problem for advocates of liberal democracy. Perón had been removed from power, but he had not been defeated politically: his influence was still enormous, and he was capable of winning a majority of votes in any election, even though he was patently no democrat himself. The Argentine situation was indeed more awkward even than that in postwar Italy or Germany, where the fascist regimes had been discredited by military defeat and the slate could be wiped clean to make way for a liberal society. So what was to be done? In Borges's view the Revolución Libertadora offered the best prospect of expunging pro-fascist tendencies in Argentina and putting the country back on the road to democracy.

Estela, however, was urging Borges to compromise this political vision. She was, in effect, pushing him to make the most painful of choices—he must either give up the possibility of saving the *patria,* as he saw it, or renounce the chance of finding love. The thought that love might yet again slip from his grasp must have been unbearable for Borges, but the kind of love Estela appeared to be offering him would be so deeply compromised that it would surely not bring him the fulfillment he hoped for. And so, rather than abandon his desire for "democratic regeneration," he chose instead to sacrifice Estela's love. He decided to end the relationship, even though he must have known that in doing so, he was condemning himself to a form of death.

When it came to it, Estela refused to accept that the relationship was over. She took to pursuing Borges in order to make him change his mind. She would wait at a bar across the street from the National Library, ready to pounce when he came out of the building; she was even said to have chased him along platforms in the *subterráneo.*[16] One day she turned up at the Bar Munich on Plaza Constitución, where Borges was having a drink with his friends, and made a terrible scene. Eventually she gave up, and they stopped seeing each other for many years.

Three times Borges had courted Estela, and three times he had lost her. The tortured saga of their relations, what was more, had been played out against the background of Perón's rule: it had started shortly before he was elected in 1945 and had ended soon after he was overthrown ten years later. This symmetry may in part explain the visceral, unyielding hatred Borges would always feel for Perón. For, however irrationally, he may have blamed Perón for coming between him and Estela Canto: Borges was a man in his mid-fifties, he knew that he was condemned to lose his sight, and yet he had been forced to sacrifice what was likely to be his last chance of love because of a disagreement with Estela over Perón's enduring influence in Argentina.

To mark the demise of his relationship with Estela Canto, Borges wrote "A Yellow Rose" ("Una rosa amarilla"), in which he portrayed the Italian baroque poet Giambattista Marino lying on his deathbed next to an open balcony, facing the sunset.[17] A woman places a yellow rose in a vase before him, and this moves Marino to recite some of his own verses on the beauty of the rose. But then he has a "revelation": "Marino suddenly *saw* the rose, as Adam might have seen it in paradise, and felt that it was in its eternity and not in his words" (Borges's emphasis). The many volumes of his writings were not "a mirror of the world"; they were "just one more thing added to the world." As he is about to die, Marino realizes that he has quite failed to capture the truth of the rose with his pen.

Bereft of Estela, Borges would embrace anti-Peronism with a vengeance. He had no qualms about becoming identified with Aramburu's junta, even as it became more repressive in its endeavor to expunge all traces of Peronism from the political system. On March 5, 1956, a law was passed proscribing the Peronist Party and prohibiting the display of any images of Perón or Peronist leaders, or the use of Peronist banners, symbols, or music. The names of Perón or of his relatives, or the expressions *peronismo, peronista, justicialismo* were banned on pain of imprisonment or fines. Efforts would also be made to discredit the myth of "Santa Evita" by providing evidence of Eva Perón's alleged corruption. Her personal possessions—enormous collections of jewels, furs, shoes, and dresses—were put on public display and later auctioned off. Additionally, the Unzué Palace, which had been Perón's official residence, was razed, and plans were drawn up in due course to erect a new building in its place to house the National Library (of which Borges happened to be the director).

Many writers and intellectuals balked at the ferocity of these measures to destroy the legacy of Perón. One of the most prominent of these was the cultural commentator, Ezequiel Martínez Estrada, who had long been associated with Victoria Ocampo's journal *Sur* and had been a well-known anti-Peronist. He now argued that intellectuals should seek to understand the roots of Perón's massive following among the poor. But such arguments cut no ice with Borges, who proceeded to combat these tendencies to sympathize with Peronism by organizing and publishing a manifesto, signed by over sixty writers, expressing support for Aramburu and forming a group of writers and intellectuals known as ASCUA (the acronym means "ember" in Spanish), with the aim of promoting freedom of thought and expression, which Perón's Comunidad Organizada had been on the point of stamping out. Indeed, he was content to become a semiofficial spokesman for the junta, and in June he accepted an invitation from the Argentine embassy in Uruguay to deliver several lectures in Montevideo. In an interview with a Uruguayan paper, he expressed his support for the Revolución Libertadora and criticized Martínez Estrada for having "indirectly" praised Perón in articles and speeches.[18]

Five days after Borges's criticism of Martínez Estrada in Uruguay, military officers sympathetic to Perón led an uprising against Aramburu. The rebels were demanding that the ban on Peronism be lifted and free elections called that year. The rebellion was put down, and its leaders were tried by courts-martial and given sentences of up to four years in prison. But on June 12, Aramburu's government, disregarding the sentences handed down by the military judges, executed thirty-two of the rebels by firing squad.

It was in this bitter atmosphere of violence and repression that Martínez

Estrada published a reply to Borges on July 10, accusing him of "the utmost vileness," of being "a paid lackey" of the government, and of "preaching the catechism of dishonor."[19] Borges responded to this intemperate attack with a terse note in *Sur,* asserting his integrity as a man who had always opposed Perón, even when the prospect of overthrowing him was but a distant hope: "I believe that the dictator was the embodiment of evil and it is a romantic superstition to suppose that his cause was not perverse merely because it is a lost cause today."[20]

Whether Peronism was in fact a lost cause was open to doubt. Aramburu had called elections in July for a Consitituent Assembly, but no Peronist candidates were allowed to stand. The Radicals, who were the largest party, split over the question of what to do about Perón: a faction led by Ricardo Balbín opposed any deals with Peronism; another led by Arturo Frondizi was more amenable to an accommodation. Perón ordered his supporters to return blank votes. The results were to show that the sum of these blank votes exceeded the votes gained by any party. Balbín's Radicals obtained 2.1 million votes, Frondizi's group 1.8 million, but the true victor at the polls was, of course, Perón.

The outcome of these elections increased the clamor for the lifting of the ban on Peronist organizations and for a return to free elections to the presidency and the Congress. Borges, however, was adamant in opposing any softening of the government's anti-Peronist stance. An interview he gave to *El Hogar* on November 2, 1956, gives us an insight into his reading of the political situation, as well as casting an interesting sidelight on his private feelings toward Estela Canto.[21] He claimed that before the Revolución Libertadora, almost all Argentine writers opposed Perón's dictatorship, "in some cases, actively, in others, through abstention." However, when he and Bioy Casares had recently drawn up a manifesto in support of the revolutionary government, they had been criticized by some writers. "And the curious thing is that those who reproached us for that declaration of support are the extremists of left and right, especially the Communists." (Estela Canto, one might recall, was a Communist.)

In Borges's view, therefore, the Communists were chiefly to blame for having divided the opposition to Perón, and this was because they had an affinity with the Peronists in their common adherence to totalitarian ideologies. Communists "are in favor of totalitarian regimes, and systematically combat freedom of thought, oblivious of the fact that the principal victims of dictatorships are, precisely, intelligence and culture":

Many people are in favor of dictatorships because they allow them to avoid thinking for themselves. Everything is presented to them ready-made. There are even agencies of the state that supply them with opinions, passwords, slogans and even idols to exalt or cast down according to the prevailing wind or in keeping with the directives of the thinking heads of the single party.

As for the argument that Communists or Peronists enjoyed the support of the people, he attributed this claim to a "double game" of "demagogic dictators" who both "deceive and flatter the popular classes, by getting them to believe that it is they who inspire and influence their leaders when it is the latter who manipulate them as they see fit in order to garner more power and profit for themselves."

He compared the condition of Argentina to that of a sick man who is "rapidly recovering his health": "But there still remain many recalcitrant patients who refuse to get better and who resist revolutionary therapy. We shall have to persist with the treatment, increasing the dose of democracy for the more rebellious to see if they can be cured once and for all." And in reply to the interviewer's question as to which road the country should follow in order to achieve "a full recovery of its institutional life," Borges further elaborated on the metaphor of illness: "As occurs with patients who have just overcome a grave illness, sudden shocks may occasion a relapse." There were people who were "too impatient"—"in the best of cases, they overlook the dangers that still threaten us, in the worst, . . . they foment, provoke and exploit" such dangers. What Argentina needed was "a suitable regimen": "I believe that the government is doing the right thing and that one should help it maintain and improve the process of recovery." Borges was adopting a very hard-line position: "democracy" must be applied in gradual doses because "sudden shocks"—a premature acceptance of free elections, presumably, or the legalization of the Peronist Party—might occasion a relapse into dictatorship. He was, in fact, slipping into a contradiction: he was advocating an indefinite suspension of democracy until such time as "the people" were deemed to be ready for democracy.

Borges's loyalty to Aramburu was to bring its rewards. In 1956 he received a National Award for Literature and was elected to the chair of English and American Literature at the University of Buenos Aires. He gave a benign account of this latter appointment in his "Autobiographical Essay":

> Other candidates had sent in painstaking lists of their translations, papers, lectures and other achievements. I limited myself to the following statement: "Quite unwittingly, I have been qualifying myself for this position throughout my life." My plain approach gained the day. I was hired and spent ten or twelve happy years at the university.[22]

As in the case of the directorship of the National Library, he implied that this was an unsought-for honor, but Betina Edelberg gave a different version of events.[23] She had returned to her post at the university after the fall of Perón, and one day she received a telephone call from Borges's mother, who told her that her son was interested in applying for the chair of English and asked whether she might be prepared to put in a good word for him. Betina went to see the dean of the faculty, the historian Alberto Salas, who as "Decano Interventor" had been charged by the Aramburu government with the task of getting rid of Peronist appointees and naming new professors. The fact that Borges lacked any academic qualifications whatever—he had not even graduated from high school—proved to be no obstacle to his appointment. In any case, this inconvenience was shortly put right when he received an honorary doctorate from the University of Cuyo in Mendoza, the first of the many honorary degrees he was to receive in his life. Very likely, then, it was string-pulling as much as his "plain approach" that led to his election to the chair.

By the end of 1956, Borges was one of the most controversial public figures in Argentina. In December he was attacked in an article by the novelist Ernesto Sábato, who sided with Martínez Estrada and accused Borges of not taking account of the "tragic dispossession" of the "risen people."[24] Sábato had been a staunch anti-Peronist and a member of Borges's ASCUA, but he had become increasingly perturbed by the repressiveness of the Aramburu junta and, as editor of the journal *Mundo Argentino,* had published allegations that Peronist militants were being tortured by the authorities. Sábato had then withdrawn from ASCUA[25] and published a booklet called *The Other Face of Peronism* (1956) in which he argued that Argentine intellectuals were guilty of having ignored the social injustices that had led the masses to give their support to Perón. Borges wrote a sharp riposte, accusing Sábato of wishing to ingratiate himself with Perón, "the multiple monster." "In any case, ethics are not a branch of statistics; something does not cease to be atrocious just because thousands of men might have acclaimed or practiced it."[26]

Borges was becoming conscious of the predicament that would plague him—as indeed it would Argentine politics—for the rest of his life. For how do you create a democracy when the largest sector of the electorate will elect a totalitarian leader who is ideologically hostile to liberal democracy? Must one accept the "will of the people" regardless of principles and values? Borges was being driven to a position whereby he wished to restore democracy but could only trust an unrepresentative elite to bring it about. It was a contradiction, of course, and there can be little doubt that he was conscious of its implications, both for the country and for himself. Perón was forcing him to question the wisdom of "the people," and this threatened to compromise, if not destroy, his dream of a democratic Argentina. He had given up Estela Canto for the sake of political principle, yet if saving the *patria* proved to be impossible, then he would have sacrificed love for nothing and would have squandered the last opportunity of making his life have any sense at all.

In the course of 1957, Borges would succumb to a growing alienation. An alienation, certainly, from political events that were beginning to elude him, but also a more profound alienation: an estrangement from his heart's desire. He gave voice to this curious disaffection in "Borges and I" ("Borges y yo"), which came out in March 1957 in the first issue of *La Biblioteca,* the revived journal of the National Library.[27] Here he makes a distinction between the "I"—his intimate, personal self—and an external self called "Borges," whose name appears "on a short list of professors or in some biographical dictionary" and who has "the perverse habit of falsifying and magnifying" the things the two of them have in common:

> It would be an exaggeration to say that our relations were hostile; I live, I allow myself to live, so that Borges may devise his literature, and that literature justifies me. I have no difficulty in admitting that I have achieved some worthwhile pages, but those pages cannot save me, perhaps because what is good no longer belongs to anybody, not even to the other, but to language or tradition.

"Borges and I" derives its force from the paranoia that underlies this account of self-alienation. "Borges," the public man, bears down upon his fugitive "I" like a ravenous beast closing on its prey:

> Years ago I tried to break free of him and went from the mythologies of the *arrabal* to playing games with time and the infinite, but those games belong to Borges now and I shall have to invent other things. And so, my life is a flight, and everything is lost to me and everything is claimed by oblivion, or by the other. I cannnot tell which of us is writing this page.

He had always kept moving on, searching for that truly creative part of himself that would make his writing come alive, but the tragedy of "Borges and I" was that, even as he wrote it, he knew there was no point in searching anymore—he no longer believed that writing gave one purchase on the real, and he appeared to have missed his last chance at love.

In January 1958 he published "The Maker" ("El hacedor") in *La Biblioteca,* in which he cast himself as the blind Homer remembering two key moments of his past life.[28] It opens with a vigorous rendering of the joy Homer experienced as a young warrior thanks to his immediate engagement in the world around him. Homer recalls the experience that had impelled him to take up arms: he had complained to his father about having been insulted by another boy, and his father had taken a bronze dagger, "beautiful and charged with power," and given it to him; "the father's voice was saying: *Let them know you are a man,* and there was an order in that voice." The young Homer felt the "magic force" of the dagger in his hands and became a warrior because he wished to recapture "the precise flavor of that moment," "nothing else mattered to him." The ecstasy of holding the dagger was connected with his later quest for love. "A woman, the first the gods had given him, had waited for him in the darkness of an underground chamber, and he had searched for her along galleries that were like nets of stone and down slopes that plunged into shadows." Homer's blindness, then, is a metaphor of his failure to find the woman, a failure that condemns him to reflect rather than to act, to remember rather than enjoy. And yet it is this failure that makes him a poet; he understands that he was not meant to be a warrior or a lover; his destiny is to sing of "love and risk," to sing "the Odysseys and Iliads" that will reverberate forever in the memory of man. Borges is here recanting his belief that the pen can capture the sublime joy of handling the dagger. Writing is a vicarious activity, born of an incapacity to satisfy one's true desire, and even though it may bring its consolations, it may be insufficient in the end to justify a life: we do not know what Homer "felt as he descended into the final darkness."

"Borges and I" and "The Maker" are texts written out of a growing sense of dread, for in the course of 1957, Borges must have realized that the prospects of creating a democratic Argentina—the one last hope he nurtured—depended critically on the outcome of the presidential elections that were scheduled to take place in July 1958. The fact that the elections had been called demonstrated the extent of the influence Perón still enjoyed despite living in exile abroad. Borges personally would have been in favor of a longer period of "convalescence" before the country returned to democracy, but General Aramburu had been pressured into calling an election by the rising clamor from the opposition for an end to undemocratic military rule.

Once again, however, Peronist candidates would be banned from these elections, but the front-runner in the campaign, the dissident Radical Arturo Frondizi, had secretly wooed Perón and had gained the tacit backing of the Peronist machine. On February 23, 1958, Frondizi won the presidency by a convincing margin, thanks largely to the votes of the Peronists, though 800,000 ballot papers, even so, were returned blank. Frondizi's pact had paid off—he had won the election—but the price he had paid was to open the door for Perón to make Argentina ungovernable.

The chief reason for Perón's continuing popularity in Argentina lay in the fact that he had ushered in a social and economic revolution, even though he had failed to carry it through. First and foremost he had materially improved the condition of the great mass of the people. He had also, in a sense, modernized Argentine politics, having granted workers their rights, extended the vote for women, secularized education, and legalized divorce. But these gains had been achieved on the basis of an authoritarian personality cult, and Perón's *caudillismo* would not grow any less virulent after his overthrow: he remained free to influence the course of events in Argentina from his villa in Madrid.

Perón would thus become an incubus on the Argentine body politic, his personal power preempting the development of democratic institutions. The resulting deadlock set the country on a downward spiral, for it became impossible to manage the economy without Perón's consent, and this in turn aggravated popular grievances. Unlike in postwar Italy or Germany, therefore, no consensus emerged in support of liberal democracy in the aftermath of Perón's downfall. In the coming decades, Argentina would experience periodic convulsions in an otherwise paralyzed system, convulsions that would become progressively more violent, as industrial unrest gave rise to guerrilla terror, which would in turn be met by military counterterror to the point where the nation would all but tear itself apart.

Frondizi's victory in the 1958 elections convinced Borges that the Revolución Libertadora had failed in its basic aim of "democratic regeneration." His dream of ridding Argentina of *caudillismo* had effectively collapsed, and so he resigned himself to embracing the contradiction that had haunted him since 1956—he might believe in democracy, but he found himself unable to trust "the people," since they were "chained to ideological myths" propagated by Perón.[29] The extent of his disillusionment is evident in "Ragnarök," which must have been written sometime following the victory of Frondizi.[30] In Norse mythology Ragnarök denotes the twilight of the gods, heralding the end of the world.

Borges's version of Ragnarök involved a dream about an invasion of the Faculty of Philosophy and Letters by a mob of strange creatures. "Human and animal cries" were heard rising from El Bajo, the low-lying fringe of slums around the docks of Buenos Aires. Someone announced that these creatures were "the gods," and everyone applauded their arrival. Then four or five of these gods detached themselves from "the mob" of deities and mounted the platform in the main hall of the university. One of them proceeded to emit a "victorious clucking noise," and it was then that Borges began to suspect that the gods had lost the power of speech, that "centuries of fugitive and feral life had atrophied what was human in them." He recoiled in disgust: "Very low foreheads, yellow teeth, sparse mustaches, like a mulatto's or a Chinaman's, bestial snouts, all advertised the degeneration of the Olympian race." And disgust turned to fear: "Suddenly we felt that this was their last gamble, that they were obstinate, ignorant and cruel, like aging beasts of prey, and that if we allowed ourselves to give in to fear or pity they would end up destroying us."

"Ragnarök" is imbued with a comprehensive disgust for "the Gods." Their clothes display "the flashy elegance of the gambling dens and brothels of El Bajo." More specifically: "A carnation bled at a buttonhole; a tight-fitting jacket betrayed the outline of a dagger." It transpires that "the gods" who are desecrating the university are precisely the *compadritos* who had embodied the "cult of courage" in his writing and whom he had envisaged as the heroes of the urban epic of Buenos Aires that he had hoped to write in his youth. But the *compadritos* have now turned into the henchmen and minions of Perón; and the dagger, which had been the master symbol of his heart's desire, is no longer the life-enhancing weapon of the tiger man but an infamous object of treachery and stealth.

In "Ragnarök," Borges was expressing his dismay at the Revolución Libertadora's failure to bring about "democratic regeneration": he had to accept that Perón had destroyed everything he had ever believed in or hoped for. And given that the people persisted in supporting Perón, they were now perceived as a threat; he had to destroy them before they destroyed the values he held dear. And so: "We took out our heavy revolvers (revolvers suddenly materialized in the dream) and we happily opened fire on the gods, putting them to death." Estela Canto had been proved right—the only alternative to making a deal with Perón was to accept military violence. Nevertheless, there is something perverse in this image of Borges "happily" firing on a horde of savages pouring out of strange, dark, forbidden places in the lower depths of El Bajo. If there was any joy in the massacre, it was a kind of mad, self-punishing glee, for in writing "Ragnarök," Borges, as Estela had predicted, was siding with Mother—he was grabbing the sword of honor but using it, finally, to cut out his heart.

On August 3, 1959, a few weeks before his sixtieth birthday, Borges was to write "The Other Tiger" ("El otro tigre"), one of his most poignant reflections on the failure of his fundamental creative endeavor.[31] "I was walking up and down the library," he would tell Richard Burgin, "and then I wrote that poem in a day or so."[32] The figure of the tiger had haunted his imagination ever since, as a small boy, he used to gaze at the great Bengal tiger in Palermo Zoo, and it was precisely his own confinement in the "penumbra" of the "vast laborious library" that had made him think of a tiger sparkling like a "fateful jewel" in the wild, a creature that was "strong, innocent, blood-soaked and new" and for whom there were "no names, neither past nor future, only a true instant." All the tigers he had ever written about, he mused, were nothing like a real tiger "fulfilling in Sumatra or Bengal / its routine of love, indolence and death";

they were but "literary tropes and memories of encyclopedias." And yet something imposed on him the "senseless and ancient" adventure of searching for "this other tiger, the one that is not in the verse," even though, as he would later observe to Antonio Carrizo, he knew that the quest was "infinite and vain," because "reality is unreachable through art."[33]

The fact was that he had come to the same conclusion six years earlier in his story "The End." Everything that had happened to him since had turned out to be a tantalizing distraction—the renewed promise of Estela's love, the fall of Perón, the prospect of writing *The Congress,* a glimpse of the Aleph, these were revealed now as so many baubles that fate had dangled before his failing eyes. All that was left was the library, the National Library, a gigantic avatar of that other library he had known as a boy in the family house at Palermo. But Father's library at least had afforded him the freedom of reading, which had spared him from an even worse fate—total subjection to the will of Mother under the shadow of the sword of honor. His appointment as director of the National Library could therefore have been a homecoming of sorts, a return to a time before he had pursued the chimeras of the tiger and the dagger. Yet even the freedom of reading had been denied him by his blindness:

> Little by little I grew to understand the strange irony of events. I had always imagined Paradise under the aspect of a library. . . . And there was I, in some way the center of 900,000 volumes in various languages. I discovered that I could hardly make out the title pages or the spines. I then wrote "Poem of the Gifts."[34]

Borges wanted the opening lines of the poem to sound "calm, like a prayer,"[35] the sort of prayer that might have come to his lips as he wandered around his "city of books" with unseeing eyes:

> Let no one debase with tears or reproach
> this declaration of the mastery
> of God, Who with magnificent irony,
> gave me both books and the night.

And he compared himself to the king of Greek legend who died of hunger and thirst "among fountains and gardens."

CHAPTER 24

The Rule of Mother
(1958–1963)

BORGES'S LIFE SETTLED into a quiet routine. He saw to his duties at the National Library, taught his courses at the university, gave public lectures in Buenos Aires, and, from time to time, would undertake lecture tours of the provinces, more often than not accompanied by his mother. By the late 1950s, Esther Zemborain recalled, this odd couple—the patrician lady and her blind son—had achieved a kind of "mythical status" in the Buenos Aires literary world.[1] Doña Leonor had become her son's secretary and business manager, his general guide and protector, and she had gathered about her a circle of well-bred ladies who fussed over Georgie and acted as an admiring chorus to his every success and distinction.

Borges's growing blindness had thrown mother and son together as never before, and there can be no doubt that Leonor Acevedo blossomed through this association: reading aloud to Georgie stimulated her into developing her hitherto rudimentary English, and she would assist him in his translations, to the point where she was capable of undertaking translations in her own right. Her innate intelligence was thus allowed much freer rein than would ordinarily have been the case with a woman of her class and generation, and by her own efforts she was able to overcome what Borges described as the "inconceivable" ignorance of the Acevedos.[2] As far as Borges himself was concerned, however, Mother had taken him over. The critic Emir Rodríguez Monegal recalled having lunch with the two of them at the their apartment, and after the housekeeper poured out some wine for him, she turned to Doña Leonor to ask whether she should serve Borges wine, too.[3] The reply was quite firm: "*El niño no toma vino*" ("The boy doesn't have wine"). Doña Leonor might have become Georgie's amanuensis, taking dictation and reading aloud to him, but, as Monegal observed, "it all was done the way a mother helps her child with his homework."

Borges's interest in epic and myth reawakened in a curiously attenuated form in this period. In his youth he had read epic poems because he aspired to mythologize the criollos in a verse history of Argentina, but at this stage in his life, his interest revived as an exercise in amateur scholarship. He decided to teach himself Anglo-Saxon in order to read Old English texts in the original, and it occurred to him to ask his students at the university whether they might be interested in learning the language with him. From about 1958, four or five students, mostly girls, would come to the National Library on Saturday mornings to accompany Borges in the deciphering of Old English texts with the help of Sweet's *Anglo-Saxon Reader,* his knowledge of German and a large dictionary given him by a Scots friend in Buenos Aires. The group would painstakingly negotiate their way through *Beowulf, The Dream of the Rood,* and passages from the *Anglo-Saxon Chronicle.* His first encounter with the language produced a strange exhilaration—he sallied forth into the street with his students declaiming a passage they had succeeded in deciphering that morning. Learning Anglo-Saxon afforded him "the pure contemplation of a language at its dawn,"[4] and in this recondite pastime he was able to escape to another time and another place, far from Buenos Aires, where everything otherwise was exasperation and gloom.

Borges would publish very little in these years, and he wrote no fiction—storytelling had always served as an arena for the articulation of inner conflicts, so there was not much point in undertaking such explorations any more. His output was confined to poems or brief prose reflections. In 1960 his editor at Emecé, Carlos Frías, suggested that he put together a new collection of his work, but Borges did not feel he had a great deal to offer. Since the mid-1950s, he had composed about a dozen short prose pieces and some two dozen poems. One dull Sunday afternoon, he rummaged around among his papers and came up with a number of other items for the new book, consisting mostly of texts he had contributed to *Crítica* and *Destiempo* as far back as the 1930s.

All the texts that were to go into the new collection had been produced during periods of despair at his failure to become a poet like Walt Whitman. No doubt in recognition of this common factor, he made his prose text, "The Maker," the title piece of the 1960 collection, for it was here that he had described both the transcendent episode when he first sensed the magic power of his father's dagger and his subsequent failure to realize that power in his writing. As he intimated in "The Maker," he now saw the function of the poet as entirely traditional—he must keep alive the memory of brave men's deeds and lament the passing of time. The poems he wrote in this period thus tended to the elegiac: they were disabused, buttoned-up compositions—sonnets more often than not—about time and loss and the enigmas of destiny. The object of poetry, he declared in "Arte Poética," is "to convert the outrage of the years / into a music, a murmur and a symbol," for poetry "returns like the dawn and the sunset," and, like a mirror, it may reveal our own face to us or give us a sight of home, like Ulysses' Ithaca, but since all in the end is transience and dreaming, poetry, like time, like ourselves, is what passes and remains, the same and yet other, "like the endless river" itself.[5]

He stood aloof, for the most part, from political developments in the country. Needless to say, these were deeply uncongenial to him. In the late 1950s, a new generation of intellectuals was undertaking a reevaluation of Peronism. Although socialists or Marxists, these young men and women chose to gloss over Perón's authoritarianism, his ideological roots in Italian fascism, his affinities with General Franco in Spain, hailing him instead as an emancipator of the working class and a defender of the *patria* against neoimperialism. Borges, inevitably, came under fire as a cosmopolitan writer with little feeling for "*lo nacional.*" This had become a familiar charge by now—he had been hearing it from a chorus of assorted *nacionalistas* and "Germanophiles" since the early 1930s. In those days Argentine nationalism had been largely associated with the right, and Borges's own kind of nationalism, his *criollismo,* with its hospitable ideal of creating a "new man" in Argentina, was correspondingly perceived as belonging to the left. But in the 1960s, Borges would come to be regarded as a "reactionary" by the new generation of intellectuals: his record as a democratic, pro-Irigoyen nationalist and as a defender of intellectual freedom against Argentine sympathizers of the Nazis and fascists was overlooked and eventually erased from memory.

Borges's whole understanding of Argentine history was by now in disarray. When *La Nación* asked him to write a poem to mark the 150th anniversary of the criollos' first revolt against Spain in May 1810, he was at a loss—"I thought I could do nothing with such a theme," he was to tell Carrizo—but then he came up with a poem called simply "To the *Patria* in 1960" ("A la patria en 1960"), which he said was more like an elegy than an ode, for it was "an intimate poem, the least official of poems."[6] He compared his relationship with Argentina to an "intimate dialogue" between "the drop" and "the river," and he enumerated memories and sensations that added up to his very personal appreciation of his native land. Beyond that, he could not say what the *patria* might truly be, and yet "we live and we die and we yearn" for that barely glimpsed face, "O inseparable and mysterious *patria.*"

The Cuban Revolution served to alienate Borges even further from the young generation. Borges's view of Fidel Castro was conditioned by his hatred of Perón: he saw the new regime in Cuba as yet another manifestation of authoritarian nationalism, with a tendency to totalitarianism. He was to speak disparagingly of Castro and the Argentine-born guerrilla hero Che Guevara, criticism that earned him more obloquy from the left, for whom the Cuban Revolution, which was still in its euphoric phase, heralded the eventual liberation of Latin America as a whole from what was perceived to be its neocolonial dependency on the developed countries.

Still, as might be expected from a man of his skeptical temper, Borges would not allow mere politics to come between him and his friends. When Pepe Bianco, the editor of *Sur,* accepted an invitation to go to Havana in 1961 as a member of the jury for the *Casa de las Américas* literary awards, he incurred the wrath of his boss, Victoria Ocampo, the proprietor of the journal. Victoria insisted on publishing a statement in the March–April issue of *Sur* disassociating her journal from its editor's political sympathies. On his return from Cuba, Bianco had little option but to resign. He felt "deeply hurt" by this quarrel with Victoria Ocampo, and he was out of a job to boot.[7] Borges, however, took him out to dinner and, as Bianco noted in his memoirs, "had the tact to drive away my sadness by leading the conversation toward light, impersonal subjects." In the course of the meal, Borges mentioned a couple of jobs Bianco might wish to consider. This understated concern for his friend was much appreciated: "His attitude moved me more than he could have foreseen."

Borges's life would have continued on this grim, uneventful course had it not been for a stroke of luck that came like a bolt from the blue in May 1961. He was having lunch one Sunday at the house of Bioy Casares when he received a telephone call informing him that he had won an international literary prize he had never heard of before. At first he thought it was a joke, but in fact it was a prize that was being awarded for the first time that year. Six publishing houses—Gallimard of France, Einaudi of Italy, Rowohlt of Germany, the Spanish firm of Seix Barral, Weidenfeld and Nicolson of London, and Grove Press of New York—had created the International Publishers' Prize, which would be awarded to an author "of any nationality whose existing body of work will, in the view of the jury, have a lasting influence on the development of modern literature."[8] The winner would receive ten thousand dollars and have a book translated and published in each of the countries represented by the sponsoring publishers. Six committees were set up, comprising writers, critics, and academics from each of the language areas (among them were eminent writers such as Alberto Moravia, Iris Murdoch, and Hans Magnus Enzensberger).[9] In May the members of the various committees convened at the Hotel Formentor in Majorca. Two names eventually emerged—Samuel Beckett and Jorge Luis Borges. The French, Hispanic, and Italian committees argued in favor of Borges, but the British, Americans, and Germans preferred Beckett. The organizers had planned to call on a seventh, Scandinavian committee, which would have broken the deadlock, very likely by voting for Beckett with the "northern" block, but there had not been time to put it together for that year. The Americans at one point tried to break the deadlock by introducing the candidacy of Henry Miller, but this late proposal was thrown out. Eventually it was resolved to bring the matter to an end by splitting the prize equally between Beckett and Borges.

"As a consequence of that prize," Borges was to write, "my books mushroomed overnight throughout the Western world."[10] His international reputation, in fact, would take several years to become established, but he received swift official recognition from France and Italy, where his name had been known for some years in small but influential circles. He was given the title of "Gran Commendatore" from the president of Italy, during an official visit to Argentina in 1961, and in November of the following year the French government made him "Commandeur de L'Ordre des Arts et des Lettres," on the recommendation of André Malraux, the minister of culture under Charles de Gaulle.

The critic Roger Caillois, a member of the French committee for the International Publishers' Prize, had been one of Borges's most passionate advocates during the debates at the Hotel Formentor. Caillois had first come across Borges's work while exiled in Buenos Aires during the war and, on his return to Paris, had commissioned the first foreign translation of *Ficciones* for La Croix du Sud, a series of Latin American works he edited for Gallimard. This French translation of 1951 can be taken as the true origin of the immense reputation Borges would eventually gain abroad. The following year Caillois brought out his own translation of an anthology of stories with the title *Labyrinthes,* and Borges swiftly came to the attention of top French writers and critics. In September 1952 two essays on Borges's work appeared in prestigious literary journals: *Critique* published an introductory study of his work by Paul Bénichou, one of his translators, and the renowned critic, Étiemble, wrote a substantial review of *Ficciones* in Sartre's journal *Les Temps Modernes.*[11] In 1955 *Les Temps Modernes* published eight essays by Borges and two years later, it would also publish "The Aleph."[12] In 1957 Gallimard brought out Paul and Sylvia Bénichou's translation of the critical essays *Other Inquisitions* (*Otras inquisiciones*) under the title *Enquêtes,* and the following year Caillois published his own translations of *A Universal History of Infamy* and *A History of Eternity.* By the late 1950s, therefore, the French literary world had access to three collections of Borges's stories as well as to a major anthology of his critical essays and a selection of his metaphysical speculations.

Thanks to these early translations into French, his work was to be translated also into Italian and German. In Germany an anthology with the title *Labyrinthe* was published by Hanser Verlag in 1959, though it passed largely unremarked at that stage. In Italy, by contrast, Borges came as a revelation. The French version of *Ficciones* was noticed by Elio Vittorini at the publishing house of Einaudi, which led to the appearance in 1955 of an Italian anthology translated by Franco Lucentini with the title *La Biblioteca di Babele.* According to Italo Calvino, Borges soon began to exert a wide influence in Italy "on creative writing, on literary taste and on the idea of literature itself."[13]

Borges first reached Spain via Italy, largely on the initiative of the poet and publisher Carlos Barral, a partner at Seix Barral, who had connections with the Italian publishing house Einaudi. A leading light on the Spanish left, Barral decided to introduce into Spain a number of Latin American authors whose experimentalism he saw as conducive to widening the cultural horizons of a country that had been dominated for so long by the monolithic Catholic-nationalist policies of Franco's dictatorship. Indeed, it was Barral who had proposed Borges for the International Publishers' Prize. He had chosen Borges because of his seminal influence on the up-and-coming generation of Latin American writers who would shortly be published by Seix Barral and would shoot to worldwide fame. Younger writers, such as Gabriel García Márquez, Julio Cortázar, Carlos Fuentes, and Mario Vargas Llosa, the future stars of the so-called Latin American boom, admired Borges for his ironic, understated prose style, which was seen as quite revolutionary in Spanish at the time, as well as for his essays advocating the fabulous and fantastic in narrative fiction, which had prepared the theoretical ground since the early 1930s for the eventual emergence of "magic realism."

Borges's reputation would take somewhat longer to become established in the English-speaking world. Even so, in 1961 he was invited by the Edward Larocque Tinker Foundation to spend a semester as a visiting professor at the University of Texas at Austin, where he would give readings and teach a course on Argentine literature. When he left Buenos Aires on September 10, accompanied by his mother, it was the first time that either of them had set foot outside the region of the River Plate since 1924. They made a rather odd impression as a couple when they arrived in the United States. James E. Irby, a Latin American specialist at Princeton, who interviewed Borges in December, thought they could have been mistaken for man and wife—Borges, with his large head and silvery hair, looked distinguished, rather like an American senator, while the diminutive Doña Leonor was surprisingly youthful and good-looking.[14] Borges, though bilingual, had never spent any length of time in an English-speaking country other than a couple of weeks in England in his early youth, so it came as a mild surprise to hear English spoken by everyone around him—even by "ditchdiggers" on campus; English to him had been very much a literary medium, "a language I had until then always thought of as being denied that class of people."[15]

He was to stay in the United States for nearly six months, returning to Buenos Aires on February 25, 1962. He visited New Mexico and California and gave lectures at Harvard, Yale, Columbia, and at the Library of Congress and the Organization of American States in Washington, D.C. What he particularly relished about his sojourn in the United States was the opportunity it gave him to indulge in a sentimental journey to places connected with authors he admired. For this reason he especially enjoyed his visit to Harvard, where he was the guest of Raimundo Lida, the distinguished Argentine philologist. Professor Lida's wife, Denah, took him to the Georgian mansion on Brattle Street in Cambridge where Longfellow had lived for decades, and in the car Borges kept reciting from memory long passages of Longfellow's writings.[16] He then wanted to see Emerson's house at Concord, and Denah recalled driving him through the snowbound countryside and Borges's spending an unconscionably long time gazing at the house (while Denah worried that her sight-impaired guest might at any moment slip on the icy ground), before remarking finally that it was not as grand as Longfellow's. But beyond its purely literary amenities, what America afforded him was a sense of its Puritan heritage, the fact that "people in the United States approach things ethically": "This—amateur Protestant that I am—I admired above all. It even helped me overlook skyscrapers, paper bags, televisions, plastics, and the unholy jungle of gadgets."[17] This "Protestant" ethical approach was to be an important influence on him as his own country declined further into political disorder in the coming years.

In 1963 Dr. Neil MacKay, the director of the British Council in Buenos Aires and a good friend of Borges's during the hard years of the Perón regime, arranged a lecture tour of Britain for him, and again he would be accompanied by his mother. For sentimental reasons they would make brief visits also to Madrid and Geneva. They set off on January 30, at the height of the Buenos Aires summer, to encounter a severe winter in Europe. First they went to Madrid, where they were to spend only one full day, but Borges had been eager to arrange a meeting with Rafael Cansinos-Asséns, who was eighty-one years old and a very sick man. (He would die the following year.) They had one morning together in Cansinos's house, reminiscing about the days of the Ultra and the Madrid avant-garde. Throughout their conversation Borges held his old maestro's hand, and when the time came for him to leave, he was weeping silently as he whispered a farewell in Cansinos's ear.[18] His visit, however, passed largely unremarked by the Spanish media: the lecture he gave at the Instituto de Cultura Hispánica that afternoon failed to attract much of an audience, but La Razón of Buenos Aires reported that his talk on metaphor at the Ateneo de Madrid was warmly applauded by an audience comprising "the most prominent intellectual and academic figures" in Spain.[19]

After Madrid came a few days in Geneva, where he revisited old haunts with Mother and had another brief, emotional reunion with the two best friends of his years in Switzerland, Maurice Abramowicz and Simon Jichlinski. Neither had pursued a literary career, but they had both retained their left-wing affiliations: Abramowicz had become a lawyer and had served as a member of the city council for the Communist Party, while Jichlinski was a doctor, with a practice in a poor district of the city. There followed a week in Paris as the guest of an organization called Congrès pour la Liberté de la Culture. Finally they arrived in London, where on February 19 he gave a lecture to the Hispanic and Luso-Brazilian Council at Canning House in Belgrave Square on the Argentine classic *The Gaucho Martín Fierro,* a lecture he was to deliver at various universities and similar venues, and which he had given the somewhat august title "The Spanish Language in South America: A Literary Problem."

Still, this lecture tour of Britain was little more than a pretext for visits to places he associated with the literature he loved above all others. From London he was taken down to Henry James's house at Rye in Sussex and to H. G. Wells's in Sandgate. His talk at Bristol led to visits to Bath and to Glastonbury, the latter for its Arthurian associations. He spoke at Oxford and Birmingham, from where he visited Shakespeare's birthplace in Stratford-upon-Avon and Hanley in Staffordshire, one of Arnold Bennett's towns in the Potteries, where Borges's grandmother Fanny Haslam was born, as well as Lichfield, where he paid homage to Dr. Johnson. While at Manchester he was driven by a trio of young Hispanists from the university to The Downs in Bowdon, Cheshire, to visit a private house that had once belonged to Thomas de Quincey, one of his favorite writers. Then came the Lake District, with its reminiscences of Wordsworth and Coleridge, and finally Scotland, where he spoke at Glasgow and Edinburgh. Borges had been hoping to visit the Highlands, but the weather in Scotland was so severe that Doña Leonor caught a chill, and it was thought best to cut short their tour and return to London, from where they returned to Buenos Aires on March 11.

Nobody in Britain had heard of him, of course. The poet Philip Larkin's reaction to this South American probably summed up the general attitude—affecting a superior insularity of mind, Larkin enquired derisively of a journalist, "Who is Jorge Luis Borges?" In London, other than Stephen Spender, who had met him the year before at a PEN Club meeting in Buenos Aires and who had published three of his stories in *Encounter,* Borges saw few people of any significance—the poet George MacBeth, V. S. Pritchett, and the exiled Spanish historian Salvador de Madariaga. In Edinburgh, which Borges was to call one of his favorite cities—no doubt because it was the birthplace of Robert Louis Stevenson, a writer he loved with a passion—the British Council tried to raise an audience by persuading the Spanish Circle to hold a special meeting, and on March 7, in the dreary premises of the old Mackenzie-Robinson Hotel at Drumsheugh Gardens, Borges addressed the membership on the literary problem of the Spanish language in South America. The honorary secretary dutifully recorded afterwards, "Prof. Borges, himself no mean literary writer, was obviously carried away by his subject and spoke at some length without any notes, as he is almost blind."[20] It was only after the publication of several English translations in the 1960s—*Ficciones* and *Labyrinths* (1962), *Dreamtigers* and *Other Inquisitions* (1964), and *A Personal Anthology* (1967)—that his reputation would take off in the English-speaking world, especially in the United States. In the latter half of the decade, there would appear a number of reviews and essays by established writers and critics—John Updike, John Barth, John Ashbery, William Gass, Alfred Kazin, Paul de Man, George Steiner—and Borges would come to be recognized as a figure of major stature.

Back home in Argentina, the political situation was once again in turmoil. Perón's destabilizing influence on the internal politics of the country was demonstrated by the removal of President Arturo Frondizi by a military coup d'état in March 1962. Frondizi had led an increasingly embattled administration since 1958 and eventually tried to appease the labor unions by legalizing the Peronist Party, which went on to win a majority in congressional elections. This victory proved unacceptable to the armed forces, who promptly ousted Frondizi and, after a hiatus under a caretaker presidency, tried once more to establish a semblance of democratic government that would be able to govern the country without doing deals with the Peronists. New presidential elections were called for July 1963, from which the Peronists were banned, though Frondizi was allowed to stand. However, the military decided to back Arturo Illia, a politician from a rival faction of the Radical Party, whom they hoped to impose over Frondizi.

Borges had begun to lose faith altogether in the Radical Party, which he had supported since the 1920s. He certainly had no illusions about Frondizi, who was contesting the election with the declared support of the Peronists. But Borges was not convinced that Illia would not in due course try also to reach an understanding with Perón. And defeating Perón remained for Borges the cornerstone of any democratic reconstruction in Argentina. He was still convinced that Perón was a corrupt tyrant who would install a populist dictatorship if given the chance, but equally he knew all too well that a clear majority of the electorate would not hesitate to elect Perón if allowed a free vote.

The logic of this position, of course, called into question the wisdom of the democratic process itself. Yet despite the bitter, repressive anger he had displayed in "Ragnarök," Borges could still not quite bring himself to accept that position with an easy conscience, and he had retained his membership in the Radical Party. As the elections approached, however, he found himself discussing the political situation with Elba de Loizaga, one of his patrician lady friends. "You are a Conservative," she told him. He bristled at being so described—no, he was a Radical, he protested, but she insisted and "proved" to him that he was "the very image of a Conservative."[21] "I thought about it, saw that she was right, and decided to join the party." He had come to the view that Argentina had known "periods of real prosperity" only under Conservative governments. What was more, despite having been a passionate supporter of Irigoyen in his youth, he now believed that when the Radicals had actually been in power, "they had been a calamity," so it was "absurd" to call himself a Radical for no better reason than "out of reverence for my ancestors" or "just because my maternal grandfather Isidoro Acevedo had been a close friend of Alem," the founder of the party.[22] The Conservatives, moreover, belonged to a coalition of anti-Peronist forces whose candidate was none other than General Pedro E. Aramburu, who had been the leader of the Revolución Libertadora, and since Borges was still wedded to the idea of "democratic regeneration," he felt able to give his support to Aramburu as a matter of principle.

A few days before the elections, Borges was enrolled as member No. 12013 of the Democratic Conservative Party. On July 1 the Conservatives held a reception at their headquarters to publicize their recruitment of the famous writer. Borges gave a speech in which he recalled Leopoldo Lugones, who had been criticized for his "inconstancy"—Lugones had been an anarchist in his youth and then successively a socialist, a fascist, and a conservative.[23] "But that apparent inconsistency," argued Borges, "signified the essential constancy of Lugones, his sincerity." He then made a rousing call to action: "We are all committed to saving the *patria*. This *patria* of ours, which can appear to be so obstinate at times, as if it were reluctant to be saved. And yet, against the will of the many, against the will of the majority, our vocation is to save what will always in the end be saved: the *patria*."

Despite this very public show of support for the Conservatives, Borges's enthusiasm for the party was never very great. He revealed his misgivings soon enough after Illia won the election in July. He confessed to his friend Silvina Bullrich in September that he had been very pleased that the Radicals had won, and he explained that he had joined the Conservative Party because it was "the only party that had not sought to make a deal with the Peronists. All the others had tried to do so."[24] His lukewarm support for the Conservatives suggests a continuing unease about his undemocratic stance—if he was prepared to gainsay the will of the electorate, it was only as a temporary expedient, because he believed that the mass of the people had been misled by Perón. It was a contradictory position certainly, but it stemmed from the fundamental incoherence of Argentine politics at the time: liberal democracy could not work in Argentina because in a free vote a majority would elect Perón, a man who felt no commitment to the principles of liberal democracy. Borges's inconsistencies must be seen in the context of this insoluble contradiction, which was continuing to paralyze the entire political system.

What concerned Borges above all was the imperative to remain loyal to a set of political values, and not necessarily to a specific party or ideology. As he was to tell Jean de Milleret a few years later, he felt "indifference, not to say contempt," for politicians; "skepticism about politics is the essential thing for me": "If you are a conservative, you cannot be a fanatic, because one can't feel any enthusiasm about conservatism, any more than you can conceive of a fanatical conservative."[25] What mattered was conscience, rather than ideology. Hence his praise of Lugones's "essential constancy," his "sincerity," for Borges believed that he was keeping faith with a vision of the *patria* that, broadly speaking, he had adhered to since his youth—an Argentina based on a progessive, open form of nationalism, in which democratic institutions would supersede the *caudillismo* of demagogic leaders like Perón.

Still, if Borges had certain misgivings about joining the Conservative Party, there had been none at all where his mother and sister were concerned: they were "very pleased" he had become a Conservative, he would tell Milleret.[26] For Leonor Acevedo this was a kind of vindication, after all. As a young girl, she had entertained dreams of grandeur as she lay back and gazed up at the little brass crown on the canopy above her bed, and now her son, Georgie, had revived the social importance of the family—he was director of the National Library, holder of a chair at the premier university in the country, a member of the Argentine Academy, and the recipient of honors from the presidents of Italy and France. Georgie had surely delivered to Mother everything she could have wished for in this regard, short of leading a cavalry charge on the field of battle against the tyrant Rosas.

In himself, however, he was not happy. There is a photograph of Victoria Ocampo with Borges and his mother, probably taken in November 1962 when both Victoria and Georgie had been decorated by the French ambassador, in which, as the wickedly perceptive Estela Canto was to observe, Borges looks "fed up and distant," whereas Doña Leonor leans over her son, eyes gleaming with satisfaction, as she stands next to the regal Ocampo.[27] The cause of Borges's apparent misery, despite such distinction and acclaim, is hinted at in a poem of this period in which he sees himself as an Adam "cast forth" from a garden, a "bright paradise."[28] He looks back upon that garden wondering whether it might not have been a dream, but he knows that "it exists and endures, / though not for me":

> Still, it is a boon to have loved,
> to have been happy, to have touched
> the living Garden, if only for a day.

What garden could he have been referring to? Perhaps it was the garden of the Lange villa at calle Tronador, his trysting place with Concepción Guerrero and later with Norah Lange, a place he had once compared to a "heaven" where he felt as securely a part of "an undeniable Reality" as "the stones and the trees."[29]

The fact that he had allowed himself to write a poem about past happiness would suggest that he was beginning to chafe under the rule of Mother. Perhaps his burgeoning fame abroad was bringing him a new confidence, tempting him, if only sporadically, to give vent to feelings he would normally have kept in check. There were times, it seems, when he could not help but feel the odd stirrings of desire. He let slip to a journalist that when he had received the invitation to teach at the University of Texas, he had hoped there would be more girls than boys in his classes, but "straightaway I felt ashamed of these thoughts; it was as though I had imagined something sinful"; and yet "the magic of the female was so potent," he observed, as he launched into gushing praise of the opposite sex: "How enchanting women are! How agreeable it is to listen to them speak! What a mysterious power they must possess to make everything around them seem so interesting!"[30] And at Austin, Texas, while visiting the house of a university colleague, he was surprised by another involuntary reaction. His host put on a record for him, and Borges found himself listening in horror to the kind of mawkish tangos he had always loathed. "And while I was judging them intellectually," he told Carrizo, "I felt tears: they were mine, I was crying with emotion. I mean, there I was condemning them intellectually, but at the same time they had got to me. And I was crying."[31]

A third episode occurred at the University of Buenos Aires, when four young men walked into a class he was giving on Coleridge and asked him to stop lecturing because a student assembly had voted to suspend all classes as a gesture of solidarity with a workers' strike in the port.

> And then I was taken aback, and suddenly I found that without knowing it I had walked from this side of the room to the other, that I was facing these four young men, telling them that a man may make a decision for himself but not for other people, and that they were crazy to think that I would stand for that kind of nonsense. And they stared at me because they were astounded at my taking it in that way. Of course I realized I was an elderly man, half blind, and they were four hefty young men. But I was so angry that I said to them. "Well, as there are many ladies here, if you have anything more to say to me, let's go out on the street and have it out."[32]

He was embarrassed by the violence of his reaction; he felt "rather ashamed of having shouted and of having felt so angry," but he could not allow himself to be bullied before his students, he told himself, because if he did, "they would not respect me and I won't respect myself."[33] The situation had clearly brought out atavistic feelings in him—it was as if he had been responding to his father's handing him a dagger and urging him to stand up to the bullies at school. In effect, he had challenged the young men to a duel, for all the world as if he had been Juan Dahlmann in "The South" or one of those knife-wielding *compadritos* he had repeatedly fantasized about in his writing. This involuntary surge of feeling—on this occasion as on the other two cited earlier—was a sign that, somewhere beneath the glacial lucidity with which he had submitted to the rule of Mother, there survived a few embers of that old desire of his to assert his right to freedom.

CHAPTER 25

Deconstructions
(1963–1967)

IN ABOUT 1963, Borges became friendly with a young woman in her twenties called María Esther Vázquez. He had first come across her in 1957 when she had worked at the National Library. Her love life at that time had been complicated and unhappy, there having been more than a touch of melodrama about it, which was perhaps what brought her initially to Borges's attention. She had been the girlfriend of a young writer and critic whom Borges knew as the author of one of the first critical studies of his work, but this deeply troubled young man became so intensely jealous of a rival for María Esther's affections that one day he shot himself in the presence of his beloved.[1] Vázquez left her job at the National Library after becoming seriously ill and, when she recovered, went to live in Europe for a time. On her return to Buenos Aires in 1961, she worked as a journalist and eventually renewed her acquaintance with Borges.

In March 1964, Borges was due to attend an international writers'conference in Berlin at the invitation of the Congrès pour la Liberté de la Culture; this was to be followed by a tour of Germany and Britain, as well as shorter visits to Paris, Stockholm, and Copenhagen. As always, he required a traveling companion on account of his blindness, and he asked María Esther to accompany him on this long trip abroad. Accounts vary regarding Doña Leonor's reaction to this invitation. Vázquez herself has written that Doña Leonor decided not to accompany her son because she was nearly eighty-eight years old and the trip to Britain the previous year had tired her too much.[2] However, in the version provided by a close friend of Doña Leonor's, the old lady had been making preparations to travel with her son and was deeply upset when Borges broke the news to her that he would be going with María Esther instead.[3] If the latter account is correct, then Borges's invitation to María Esther amounted to a form of rebellion against Mother, another attempt to assert his independence of her.

The Berlin conference was not the type of event that Borges much relished; he preferred touring a number of German cities, where, as in the United

States and Britain, he could visit places with strong literary associations for him. He was especially keen to visit the Baltic coast at Schleswig, where he asked be taken to the beach and, falling to his knees, dipped his hand in the sea, reciting out loud a number of Anglo-Saxon poems about the Vikings.[4] He persuaded María Esther that they should make a brief visit to Denmark for no better reason than to visit the castle at Elsinore where *Hamlet* is set. The next stop was Paris, where he had been invited by UNESCO, together with the Italian poet Giuseppe Ungaretti, to speak at a celebration of the fourth centenary of Shakespeare's birth. From Paris he flew directly to London, where he spent several days before going to Yorkshire as a guest of the art historian Sir Herbert Read at his house on the moors. Once again he was very much taken by the Vikings when he visited the city of York, and would write a poem on a Viking sword at York Minster. Next he traveled to Scotland, visiting St. Andrews and Edinburgh, and also the Highlands, which he had been prevented from doing the year before because of the bad weather. Afterward they went to Sweden, where he had been invited by his publishers, and from Sweden to Spain, visiting Madrid, Santiago de Compostela—which he would call one of his favorite cities—and then Alcalá de Henares, Cervantes's birthplace, where he wished to pay homage to the Spanish writer he most admired and loved.

When he returned to Buenos Aires, his friendship with María Esther appeared to become closer. Borges invited her to collaborate with him on a couple of literary projects. They worked together on a short *Introduction to English Literature* (1965) and also on a revised version of *Medieval Germanic Literatures* (1966), which he had first brought out in 1951 with the cooperation of Delia Ingenieros. And his friendship with María Esther rekindled his fascination with gauchos and *compadritos*. On April 27, 1964, the newspaper *La Razón* reported him as saying, "In spite of myself I am writing a lot of poetry—lyrics for tangos and *milongas*."

Friends noticed that relations between Borges and Doña Leonor had become very tense. The old lady was afraid that he might take it into his head to propose to María Esther, but she thought the girl far too young for Georgie: he should look for someone older. "But apparently he could not be persuaded, was terribly stubborn and resented what he saw as Mother's interference."[5] Doña Leonor would telephone her confidantes and pour out her worries;[6] she feared, allegedly, that María Esther might take advantage of Georgie;[7] and when the book *Medieval Germanic Literatures* was eventually published in 1966, Leonor was reportedly "furious to see a certain name tagged on to that of her son."[8] Certainly Borges and María Esther had formed a close friendship, and there very likely was a romantic element to it, but it is not clear all the same whether he ever had it in mind to marry her. Some of Doña Leonor's friends were under the impression that marriage was in the cards,[9] but

Vázquez herself would later write that, after accompanying him on the trip to Europe in 1964, she already knew that marriage was out of the question: as far as she was concerned, she did not love him enough to risk making them both unhappy.[10]

Borges introduced María Esther to his circle of friends. In the summer of 1964–65, for instance, he took her to stay with Bioy Casares and Silvina at their villa in Mar del Plata. There she met the grande dame of Argentine culture, Victoria Ocampo, who had just returned from Europe gushing with admiration for the Beatles and "swinging" London. María Esther would recall an embarrassing confrontation that took place between Victoria Ocampo and Borges that summer.[11] After dinner one evening, it occurred to Victoria to get Borges to try on a longhaired Beatles wig that she had brought back from London. Borges refused, but Victoria kept insisting; the exchange became louder and angrier, until a furious Victoria lashed out, "Look here, my friend. You're such a stuffed shirt you'll get absolutely nowhere in this life."

Stuffed shirt or not, Borges was not prepared to be made to look a fool in front of other people; he was, after all, a man in his sixties with a considerable international standing as a writer. Perhaps his touchiness over the Beatles wig was a sign that he harbored certain doubts regarding the appropriateness of a man of his years consorting with a woman who was his junior by several decades. He might, indeed, have already been apprised of María Esther's doubts about the future of their relationship, and this may also account for his defensiveness. At any rate, by the time he went to Peru with María Esther early in 1965, their friendship appears to have come under strain, and the difficulties must have got worse over the next few months, because María Esther did not come with him on his trip to Colombia and Chile in July; he was accompanied instead by Esther Zemborain de Torres.

Whatever the true nature of his feelings for María Esther, Borges's friendship with her certainly stretched his emotional loyalty to his mother, reviving yet again within him all the old tensions between the sword and the dagger. More honors and prizes came his way that year. On August 9, 1965, he was invested with an honorary knighthood at the British embassy in Buenos Aires. In September or thereabouts, he received an invitation from Harvard University to spend the academic year 1967–68 as Charles Eliot Norton Professor of Poetry, one of the most prestigious appointments offered by that university to creative artists of the first rank. On November 20 the Italian ambassador presented him with the City of Florence Prize for Poetry, awarded by the Dante Alighieri Society of Italy. But despite the fact that his international reputation was reaching such lofty peaks, Borges's attention was engaged at precisely this time with very local Argentine themes—the *compadritos*, the primitive tango, Carriego's "cult of courage." On August 23 he gave a lecture entitled "The History of the Tango" to a full house at the Teatro San Martín. In the month of October, *La Nación* announced that he would be giving a series of four public lectures on the following topics: "Origins and Virtues of the Tango," "The *Compadrito*," "The Rio de la Plata at the Beginning of the Century," and "The Tango and its Derivations"; these lectures would be based on Borges's personal knowledge of the "seedy" Palermo of *compadritos* and *orilleros,* on "many reminiscences and anecdotes" and on "documents and firsthand experience."[12] On November 24 he published *Para las seis cuerdas* (*For the Six Strings*), a collection of tangos and *milongas* he had composed the year before.[13] Its publication was accompanied by the release of a record of Borges's tangos set to music by the celebrated composer Astor Piazzola and sung by Edmundo Rivero, one of the most popular tango singers of the day.[14]

As Borges was to acknowedge, Mother was "pretty cross" with him for having published *Para las seis cuerdas;* she was "ashamed" of it and told him he should never have written on such "inferior" subjects.[15] But he was clearly deriving some perverse enjoyment from annoying her—he just would have to keep rehearsing in public his intimate knowledge of all those unsavory topics associated with that wretched man Carriego, and this at a time when he was being showered with honors at home and abroad. Indeed, only two days after the publication of *Para las seis cuerdas,* he was due to receive an award that probably meant more to Leonor Acevedo than all the other honors her son had received so far. The government of Peru was to invest him with the Orden del Sol, the "Order of the Sun," which had been created in 1821 by the Argentine liberator San Martín no less, when he was in Peru preparing the final destruction of Spain's power in America. The Order of the Sun was redolent of the glory that Colonel Suárez had won at the battles of Junín and Ayacucho in Peru during the Wars of Independence, and thus it symbolized the origins of Leonor Acevedo's claim to patrician status.

On November 26, 1965, Borges's family and friends attended a ceremony at the embassy of Peru, where he was to be invested with the Order of the Sun. At the reception afterward, he was told that María Esther Vázquez had decided to get married to the poet Horacio Armani in just under three weeks' time.[16] Borges's close friend Esther Zemborain recalled that he was devastated by the news—he suffered a sort of emotional "collapse."[17] Yet why should this information have affected him so deeply, when he must have known for several months that María Esther was not in love with him? It must surely have been due to the symbolic significance of the occasion. When María Esther's wedding plans were revealed to Borges at the Peruvian embassy he must have been struck by the hollowness of the distinction he had just received, for the Order of the Sun might well have signified that he had proved himself worthy of the ancestral sword of honor, thereby fulfilling the highest expectations of his family—but at what cost had this distinction been won? At the cost of having repeatedly sacrificed his chance of happiness with a woman.

The history of his doomed relations with women had kept repeating itself, if not as farce then as ever more cruel mockeries of earlier manifestations. But the axis around which these perverse cycles turned had worn increasingly thin, and the shock of María Esther's news caused it to snap altogether. There had been so many failed rebellions against Mother's authority, so many attempts to grab the dagger of desire, that the dagger as a symbol of his opposition to the sword of honor had all but lost its value by now. This latest upset jolted him into seeing that the problem lay not in either the sword or the dagger but in the nature of the fatal dialectic by which he kept swinging back and forth between his rival loyalties to Mother and Father. The force of this realization would launch him into a process of demystification of both sword and dagger, and, in a remarkable series of stories, he was to dismantle the interlocking family myths that had brought such wretchedness to his life.

We can follow this process of liberation fairly closely. It would have started in December 1965, just a few weeks after the reception at the Peruvian embassy and around the time that María Esther married Armani on December 14, 1965. The process, I believe, was triggered by Borges's anger against his mother. Earlier that year he had been asked by the bibliophile Gustavo Fillol Day for a short story to be published by him in a limited edition. "A few months later I was ready to get down to work, and at the beginning of 1966 I dictated 'The Intruder' to my mother."[18] This was the story of two inseparable brothers, notorious knife fighters in the *orillas* of Buenos Aires, who, despite themselves, fall in love with the same woman.[19] They share her, and then try to get rid of her by selling her to a brothel. However, they discover that they cannot do without her, but rather than have her come between them, the elder brother decides to do away with her altogether. After the murder, the brothers are united by a new bond—the woman they have "sacrificed" and "the obligation to forget her."

According to Estela Canto, Borges had told her a version of this story in the 1950s, at a time when he was involved in a struggle to reconcile his love for Estela with his loyalty to Mother.[20] She saw it as the subconscious expression of his relationship with his mother, which resembled a "blood pact" between two men involving the destruction of anyone else that threatened to come between them.[21] While there is something to be said for Estela Canto's interpretation, I believe it is too crude and self-serving. "The Intruder" ("La intrusa"), in my view, captures Borges's experience of being split—torn between honor and desire—whenever he fell in love with a woman. And it is also about the pain involved in having to sacrifice the woman so as to regain a measure of integrity. (The brothers prefer to stay together rather than allow the woman to drive them apart.)

Still, Estela was basically right to see the story as directed against his mother, for when asked by interviewers about "The Intruder," Borges rarely failed to associate it with his mother, crediting her with supplying a suitable ending. He would claim to have been "stuck at the end of the story, unsure of the words the elder brother would say," when Mother, "who from the outset thoroughly disliked the tale, gave me the words I needed without a moment's hesitation."[22] And horribly brutal words they were, too: "Let's get to work, brother. The vultures will do the rest later. I killed her today. Let's leave her here with all her trinkets. She'll do us no more damage." This heartless tale—which Mother had instinctively known how to round off—was delivered to Fillol Day to be privately printed as a collector's item in a luxury edition of only fifty-two copies. It came out in April 1966, a month before Doña Leonor's ninetieth birthday.

Borges saw "The Intruder" as "the first of my new ventures into straight-forward storytelling. From this beginning I went on to write many others, ultimately collecting them under the title El Informe de Brodie."[23] Indeed, these tales of the mid-1960s record a profound sea change in Borges's inner world. At first glance there is little that is new here—the stories appear to return to the familiar topics associated with the cult of courage, with civilization and barbarism, with the quest for identity, and so on; but he was to turn these themes inside out, as it were, in order to lay bare their underlying premises. The chronology of the process of composition cannnot be charted with certainty, but even though the stories that went on to form the collection entitled Brodie's Report were not actually dictated until 1969, many of them would already have taken shape in his imagination before the end of 1966, for, as we shall see, by the end of that year, Borges had completed the process of deconstructing the sword and the dagger and, in doing so, had freed himself from the psychological fetters of a lifetime.

The theme of sacrifice one finds in "The Intruder" is central to another violent tale, "The Gospel According to Mark" ("El Evangelio según Marcos").[24] This relates the strange case of a medical student, Baltasar Espinosa, who is stranded by floods in a remote ranch on the pampas. He is put up by the Gutres, a family of rustics so devoid of civilization that they have completely forgotten the language and religion of their Scottish ancestors, the Guthries. In the evenings Espinosa reads the Gospel of St. Mark to his hosts from an old English Bible he finds in the ranch. Espinosa is an unbeliever, and his readings are "an exercise in translation," but the story closes with the degenerate yokels seeking to avoid the fires of Hell by crucifying Espinosa in a barbarous parody of Christ's passion.

At the core of the tale lies the notion of a family's sacrificing a man of intelligence and culture in order to gain redemption. Borges may have had in mind his mother's family, the Acevedos. (It was in 1966 that he would tell Jean de Milleret that "the ignorance of the Acevedos, who are on my mother's side of the family, is inconceivable.")[25] But certain allusions to Fanny Haslam may also be detected in the story. Borges associated Bible reading with his English grandmother, and the Gutres, who are of Scottish Presbyterian descent, have an instinctive respect for the Bible that seems to "run in the blood," despite the fact that they cannot read. The ranch is located near the town of Junín, which is where Fanny lived with her husband when it was on the frontier of Indian territory. Although they have red hair, the Gutres have intermarried with Indians, and this suggests that they may be of similar stock to the offspring of that captive Englishwoman whom Fanny had once met on the frontier at Junín, an encounter that formed the basis of the "Story of the Warrior and the Captive Maiden." In this latter story, Borges had shown how throughly Fanny had absorbed Argentine fears about barbarism. And now in "The Gospel According to Mark," Borges adopted the viewpoint of Fanny Haslam as she might have contemplated the "degenerate," halfbreed descendants of the English captive girl who had refused her invitation to return to "civilization" and had chosen a life of "barbarism" instead.

A new story, "Brodie's Report," delved further into his English grandmother's preoccupation with "civilization and barbarism," but from an overtly imperialist British perspective.[26] Dr. Brodie is a Scots missionary who writes a report about a people he has come across that for convenience he chooses to call the Yahoos. "They are not a primitive nation but a degenerate one." The bulk of the tale is taken up with a description of their customs. Dr. Brodie concludes by observing that the "essential horror" of the Yahoos is that they may be "the most barbarous race on earth," but they have certain redeeming qualities, and it is "the duty" of Her Majesty's government to "save" them.

In both of these stories, Borges has conflated the situation of the two women in his family who had inspired in him a reverence for the ancestral sword of honor. There was his mother, Leonor Acevedo, resenting her family's decline and hating the gauchos and immigrants who had ruined the republic their ancestors had struggled to transform into a civilized nation. But there was Fanny Haslam, too, stranded in what she regarded as barbarous Argentina and idealizing the far-off civilization of Victorian Britain.

What lay behind these women's ostensible horror of barbarism? Borges began to analyze this fear in "The Old Lady" ("La señora mayor"), a portrait of Señora de Jáuregui, who is modeled on Leonor Suárez, Borges's maternal grandmother and the true source of his mother's obsession with Colonel Suárez and the sword of honor:

> The Jáureguis lived in a somewhat false situation. They thought of themselves as belonging to the aristocracy, but the people who mattered hardly knew of their existence, they were descendants of a hero, but the history books tended to overlook his name.[27]

Señora de Jáuregui lived entirely in the past—"She still continued to detest Artigas, Rosas and Urquiza"; the First World War had been less real to her than the Revolution of 1890 or the cavalry charge that her father had led in Peru. She lived "modestly" in Palermo with her daughter and a grandson, and since she never went out of the house, "maybe she wasn't aware of the fact that Buenos Aires had been changing and growing." On the occasion of her hundredth birthday, however, she was subjected to intense publicity on account of her being the sole surviving offspring of the generation of criollos who had fought for independence. The minister of war and scores of people turned up to celebrate her birthday, but a few days after the party, the old lady died. Perhaps the invasion of this "rabble" had hastened her demise, we are told. The story ends with a reflection by the narrator: "I think about the forgotten men of America and of Spain who perished under the hooves of the cavalry, and I would say that the last victim of that riot of lances in Peru was to be, over a hundred years later, an old lady in Buenos Aires." The narrative is imbued with compassion for the snobbish, beleaguered old woman, and its tone is far removed from the ice-cold anger one senses in "The Intruder." Señora de Jáuregui is portrayed as a victim of the sword, having clung to it in the belief that it alone would guarantee her a place in the world, while failing to appreciate that she had in fact sacrificed her entire will and freedom in the process.

Borges had come to understand that the women in his family were as much victims of the sword as he or his father had been. And this perception also explained the ambivalence of his bond with his mother. Leonor Acevedo's veneration of the sword of honor, her unyielding attachment to the memory of Colonel Suárez, was in fact a product of her own imagination—it was she who had invented the ghost of her ancestors, and it was this self-projected ghost that had compelled her to live up to a preconceived standard of honor. But this imaginary standard was a reflection of her own fears of losing what status and identity she and her family might have possessed by virtue of their being descended from the Hero of Junín.

Ironically, it was the sheer force of her personality that had enslaved Leonor Acevedo to the past. She had ambition, intelligence, and will, but it was precisely her condition as a woman in a deeply patriarchal society like Argentina that had prevented her from fulfilling herself as she might otherwise have done. Unlike her husband and son, who would attempt to fulfill themselves by rebelling against the constraints of family and tradition, Leonor chose to assert herself by conforming to that tradition. And she was to respond to this paradox in two ways. First, she invested her considerable energies in an excessive, fanatical promotion of her family's importance. Second, she would look to her son, Georgie, to fulfill vicariously her own dreams of grandeur. However, by urging her son to realize the ambitions she had defined for herself, she unwittingly induced a sense of unworthiness in him that became the chief obstacle to his self-assertion. And so the more fully she devoted herself to his welfare, the more she constrained his freedom to determine his own life.

Leonor Acevedo (and, in her way, his grandmother Fanny Haslam) had fixed upon young Georgie as the instrument of the family's redemption: they burdened him with tales of heroic ancestors, challenging him to make good the family's fall from grace. And this insidious pressure is reflected in the theme of the sacrifice of a young man for the sake of the redemption of a family or social group. This theme is most evident in the crucifixion of Baltasar Espinosa in "The Gospel According to Mark," but it appears also in "Brodie's Report." Here the Yahoos examine every male child after birth, and if certain stigmas are found, he is raised to be their king, in which case "he is gelded," his eyes are burned out, and his hands and feet cut off "so that the world should not distract him from the path of wisdom"; finally he is "confined to living in a cave." It is not fanciful to see Borges alluding here to the circumstances of his own upbringing: his confinement in the home, his isolation from other children, and his inability to engage freely with the world around him. The theme of sacrifice is taken up again when Dr. Brodie describes how poets, too, are treated with awe by the Yahoos—they shy away "under a holy dread," no one speaks to or looks at the poet, "not even his mother." "He is no longer a man but a god and anyone is free to kill him."

A further story, "Guayaquil," shows Borges's appreciation of the fact that if the whole family had lived in bondage to the sword—father, mother, and grandmothers, as much as himself—it was because all of them in their various ways had been victims of the condition of Argentina as a postcolonial nation.[28] The narrator of the story is one of the most distinguished historians of Argentina, a patrician criollo, whose ancestor, Suárez, had fought in the Battle of Junín and who therefore "carries history in his blood." The story involves the (fictitious) discovery of letters written by Simón Bolívar that promise to shed light on his secret conference with San Martín at Guayaquil, just before the final defeat of the Spaniards in South America. It is a matter of record that as a result of this meeting, General San Martín surrendered his command of the patriot armies and, renouncing "mere ambition," "left the destiny of America in the hands of Bolívar."

The criollo historian expects to be chosen by the Argentine government to take a copy of these historic letters. But he is faced with a rival, a foreign-born German Jew, a naturalized Argentine citizen, of much lesser academic reputation, who challenges the assumption that the criollo historian has some preordained right to be chosen for the mission. When it comes to it, however, the criollo historian concedes the privilege to the newcomer in a mysterious act of renunciation that mirrors that of San Martín himelf. Yet no act is involuntary, we are told, and if the criollo yielded to his immigrant rival, it was because "deep down he chose to do so." In this strange tale, Borges abandoned his family's special claims on the nation's history. The only way to avoid becoming a victim of the sword of honor was to renounce the sword, renounce the illusion of possessing a historic "birthright" that would guarantee a fixed identity. Instead he accepted that present-day Argentina was different but no less authentic than it was at the time of independence. The Jew had as much right to be regarded as an Argentine as did the old patrician criollo. Borges had finally understood that the family's obsession with the sword stemmed from a fear of forfeiting a status that they imagined their ancestors had conferred upon them. But at the same time, he came to perceive that this veneration of the sword was the mirror image of his own fascination with the dagger. Both were a response to the same fear—a fear of being despised, of losing a sense of identity, of being no one.

The analogy between sword and dagger is explicitly articulated in "Juan Muraña," a story named after the legendary *cuchillero* of Palermo, but which is in fact about his widow and her obsession with her dead husband's dagger: "The dagger was Muraña, it was the dead man whom she continued to adore."[29] The old lady has fallen on hard times and cannot afford to pay the rent she owes her Italian landlord. Facing eviction, the poor widow is driven to using her husband's dagger to murder the landlord. But she has so totally identified the dagger with Muraña himself that she credits her dead husband with the deed. "It was Juan who saved us," she tells her nephew.

The origin of the tale is to be found in Mother's anecdote about her relative Micaela Soler, daughter of the illustrious General Soler, who kept her father's sword in her wardrobe and used it to threaten her Italian landlord whenever he came to collect the rent.[30] But in his reworking of this family memory, Borges has degraded the sword of a hero of the Wars of Independence to the level of the dagger of a mere *compadrito* of the Palermo underworld. "In the story of that woman who found herself alone in the world and who confused her man, her tiger, with that cruel object he had bequeathed to her, the instrument of his exploits, I believe one may glimpse a symbol or several symbols." One could identify it as a symbol of the obsession of both Leonor Suárez and her daughter, Leonor Acevedo, with the sword of Colonel Suárez, and it could equally well symbolize Fanny Haslam's memory of her dead husband, Colonel Borges. But it could be a symbol, too, of Borges's own obsession with the dagger. His admiration for gauchos and *compadritos* was not intrinsically different from the matriarchal worship of the sword. And so the seemingly contrary obsessions with dagger and sword sprang from the selfsame fear of being "evicted," of not having anywhere to call your own, of becoming a nonentity.

Having deconstructed the family's complex attachment to the sword, and having unmasked its hidden symmetry with the dagger, Borges set about exploring further the psychological roots of his attachement to the "cult of courage." The story "Unworthy" ("El indigno"), relates the case of a young Jewish boy, Santiago Fischbein, who grew up in Palermo and became friends with a *compadrito* called Francisco Ferrari.[31] Fischbein's mother disapproved of her son's mixing with such "riffraff," but in that neighborhood "it was important to be brave," and young Santiago believed that people looked down on him for being Jewish: "I felt that people despised me and I despised myself, too." In his friendship with the delinquent Ferrari, therefore, he sees the possibility of gaining respect as a man.

Borges has pinpointed the motive for his fascination with the dagger in Fischbein's wish to rebel against his mother's snobbery. But he also shows how this desire to rebel is rooted in a wish to compensate for feelings of "unworthiness" (Jewishness in this case). Rebellion tempts young Fischbein into joining the Palermo underworld, but when Ferrari invites him to take part in a robbery, Fischbein informs the police. Paradoxically, however, it is in this betrayal that Fischbein finds salvation, for he has resisted being drawn into lawlessness and has decided to follow his own conscience rather than continue to seek the approbation of the *compadritos*. In time Fischbein becomes a man at ease with himself: a mild bibliophile, a married man with children, proud of being "a good Argentine and a good Jew." Not so Borges, of course, who had remained enthralled by the dagger of the *compadrito* until he was in his mid-sixties.

The most thoroughgoing deconstruction of Borges's obsession with the illicit dagger is to be found in "Rosendo Juárez's Story" ("Historia de Rosendo Juárez").[32] He was to describe it as "a sequel and an antidote" to the first story he had ever published, "The Man at the Rose-Colored Streetcorner" ("El hombre de la esquina rosada"), which was written in 1930 following the death of Juan Muraña's boss, Don Nicolás Paredes.[33] "The Man at the Rose-Colored Streetcorner" had shown how the *compadritos* of Palermo had been put to shame by the apparent cowardice of their champion, Rosendo Juárez, who had been challenged to a duel by a knife fighter from another barrio but had refused to be provoked. In "Rosendo Juárez's Story," the eponymous *cuchillero* explains to "Borges," the narrator, why he had refused to fight his challenger: "In that jeering blockhead I saw myself reflected in a mirror and I felt ashamed." After that flash of insight, Rosendo had cast aside the dagger and walked out of the saloon. "I wasn't scared," he tells Borges; "maybe if I'd been scared I'd have fought with him." What Rosendo had lost was nothing more than his fear of being judged by others; he had suddenly understood that genuine selfhood could be attained only by taking the simple expedient of exercising one's own free will. As Borges himself was to put it, the "seeming coward" of the first version turned out to be "a Shavian character who sees through the romantic nonsense and childish vanity of duelling, and finally attains manhood and sanity."[34]

Like Rosendo, Borges had come to perceive that his obsession with the dagger masked a fear of being despised by others. That fear had its origins in the primal scene of his childhood when his father had handed him a dagger and urged him to *let them know you are a man*. His feelings of "unworthiness," therefore, stemmed as much from his father as from his mother. The illicit dagger, in short, was the mirror opposite of the sword of honor; what had appeared to be an opposition was in fact a symmetry, an identity, for in fleeing the expectations of Mother, he had succumbed to the expectations of Father, the means of escape merely reproducing the predicament from which he was trying to escape. This vicious circle had generated some of Borges's most insistent themes—the rival who is a mirror image of oneself, the criminal who is a version of the detective, the creator who is a creature of another creator, the hero who is also a traitor, the traitor who is equally a savior, the monstrous nightmare of the internecine trinity in which the son cannot break free of the father because they have both been made in the shadowy image of some ancestral ghost. Little wonder, then, that Zeno's fable of Achilles and the tortoise had struck such a chord with Borges, for he had launched himself on a quest for his real self by means that drove him ever further from the man he could have been.

It is in a story ancillary to Rosendo's tale, however, that we discover the reason Rosendo was able to see through the nonsense and vanity of dueling. Rosendo had a friend called Luis Irala, whose mistress left him for another man. Though he admitted he no longer loved the woman, Irala was concerned that people might think him a coward if he failed to challenge his rival to a duel. Rosendo warned him of his folly: "Nobody takes anything away from anybody. If Casilda left you it's because she wants Rufino and you mean nothing to her." But Irala insisted on fighting the duel and ended up being killed.

Borges, likewise, had pursued his rivalry with Oliverio Girondo, not primarily because he was in love with Norah Lange but because of a fear of losing face. His enmity with Girondo had acquired a momentum of its own, for as long as he remained psychologically enslaved to the dagger as a symbol of virility, he would not be able put the loss of Norah Lange behind him.

Borges was to deconstruct his obsessive rivalry, his "duel," with Girondo in a number of stories. In "The Encounter" ("El encuentro"), he was to characterize the rivalry as an impersonal force that had swept both contenders along as its helpless victims.[35] Two young men quarrel over a game of poker and challenge each other to a duel; they take a couple of daggers displayed in a cabinet and fight like veterans, even though they have never handled knives before. As Borges was to observe, "the two knives have a will of their own, ruling the hapless young men who are supposed to be wielding them."[36] The fight transpires "as in a dream," with the killer finally asking forgiveness and sobbing openly as his victim expires. In "The Other Duel" ("El otro duelo"), the topic is reduced to absurdity when two criminal gauchos, who have hated each other for years and are about to be executed at the same time, agree to a grotesque race to see who can crawl farthest after a simultaneous beheading.[37]

In "The Duel" ("El duelo"), Borges went as far as he could toward unmasking the autobiographical origins of the theme without actually giving away the true identities of the rivals.[38] The story describes the secret enmity between Clara Glencairn, an abstract painter, and Marta Pizarro, "who started painting portraits of Argentine heroes and then went on to specialize in old houses of Buenos Aires." Borges was, of course, alluding to his old feud with Girondo but disguised it by making the rivals women and their medium painting instead of poetry. Like Norah Lange, Clara Glencairn was "haughty and tall and had fiery red hair"; her first exhibition was held at an avant-garde gallery on calle Suipacha (the street where Girondo lived). Marta Pizarro's nativist painting calls to mind Borges's *criollismo* of the 1920s. On the surface their relations were amicable, even generous: when Clara won a prize, Marta organized a dinner in her honor, and in her speech of thanks, Clara "observed that there existed no opposition between tradition and innovation, between order and adventure." This last phrase, once again, reveals the subtext of the story: it is a covert reference to the essay Borges published in March 1925 calling for the reconciliation of "adventure and order," in which he cited Apollinaire's poem *"La jolie rousse,"* an allusion also to his newfound love for the red-haired Norah Lange.[39] That essay was to spark the feud between the *criollistas* and the cosmopolitans in the Buenos Aires avant-garde, a feud that acquired a very bitter personal dimension when Norah Lange eventually deserted Borges for Girondo. In the closing lines of the story, there is no resentment, just wry amusement:

In that delicate duel, whose existence was suspected only by a few of us who were close friends, there were no defeats and no victories, not even an encounter, nor any visible particulars other than those I have endeavored to record with my respectful pen. Only God (whose aesthetic preferences are unknown to us) can award the final palm. The story that unfolded in darkness ends in darkness.

Still, the end of Borges's personal feud with Girondo came too late, it seems, for him to effect a proper reconciliation with his rival. Oliverio had been in poor health since 1961, when he was knocked down by a motorcar as he was leaving a cinema in Buenos Aires. The injuries he sustained had left him mentally impaired and requiring constant attention from Norah and a nurse. In 1966 his condition had declined markedly, and he died on January 24, 1967. The customary wake at his house on calle Suipacha was attended by family and friends. Two close friends of the Girondos', the poet Olga Orozco and Lila Mora y Araujo, would recall an unexpected visit on that occasion—the appearance of Jorge Luis Borges on the arm of his mother.[40] Borges went up to where Oliverio lay and kissed him lightly on the forehead, then departed without addressing a word to anyone. It was an astonishing gesture in its way, rendered more dramatic by the fact that it was performed before people who knew well enough of the antagonism between Borges and Girondo, but not the secret reason for their implacable hostility.

What did Borges wish to express by that kiss? At around this time, he wrote a brief parable about Cain and Abel meeting again after Abel's death. Cain asked Abel to forgive him. Abel replied, "Did you kill me or did I kill you? I can no longer remember; here we are together again as before." "Now I know that you have truly forgiven me," said Cain, "because to forget is to forgive. I shall also try to forget." Abel said quietly, "That's right. One is guilty for as long as one feels remorse."[41]

CHAPTER 26

Marriage
(1967–1968)

BORGES LOOKED to distract himself from his recent emotional troubles and his conflict with Mother by resorting to his usual remedy—writing. Since the end of 1965, he had been absorbed in composing the stories discussed in the previous chapter. But from the latter part of 1965, he turned also to his old friend Bioy Casares, and they resurrected their joint literary persona, H. Bustos Domecq, the apocryphal author of the burlesque Don Isidro Parodi detective stories, although they used him now to poke fun at modernist writers and artists. (When the *Chronicles of Bustos Domecq* appeared in 1967, it carried a dedication: "To those forgotten masters, Picasso, Joyce, Le Corbusier.") The *Chronicles* were finished by the beginning of July 1966, and Borges then invited another good friend, Esther Zemborain de Torres, to collaborate with him on an *Introduction to North American Literature,* which they undertook in occasional sessions at Esther's apartment for the rest of that year.[1]

In addition to composing stories and collaborating on writing projects with friends, he had his Anglo-Saxon classes on Saturday mornings at the National Library, which still attracted a faithful group of students. The previous year Borges had invited a young girl called María Kodama to join the group.[2] María had admired Borges ever since she had been taken by her Japanese father to one of Borges's lectures. She was only twelve at the time, but a family friend had introduced her to the writer afterward, and they had chatted about her favorite book, *Alice in Wonderland.* Borges had forgotten that first encounter, but some years later, when María was a student at the University of Buenos Aires, she enrolled in Borges's class on the epic, a subject that had fascinated her since her father talked to her about the tales of the samurai. After some time, however, María felt she was out of her depth and falling behind in class. She thought of giving up the course, but her classmates urged her to tell the professor about her difficulties. Borges encouraged her to persevere and invited her to come to see him at his apartment in the afternoons. They took to meeting occasionally in *confiterías* to talk about literature, and eventually he asked her to join his weekly Anglo-Saxon classes.

Borges was rather struck by this half-Japanese girl, whose frail beauty made her look even younger than she was. She had, moreover, a gentle, respectful, self-effacing manner. At a time of such secret emotional turbulence for him, she must have been a soothing presence, and he could pass the time doing what he loved best—expatiating endlessly on literary subjects while María hung on his every word, scarcely believing that she had been accorded the privilege of listening to the wisdom of her admired master. Predictably, it was not too long before his budding friendship with the girl turned into something more intense, though it was hard to define as yet what it was he actually felt for her. He would give her books as gifts and telephone her at home with increasing frequency. There was no reason María should have recognized these characteristic signs of infatuation, nor did she find it odd that she should be attracting so much attention from a man in his mid-sixties; it was her mother who, after a while, became somewhat concerned by the attention that her teenage daughter was receiving from her professor.

In the first half of 1966, Borges had been thinking about the invitation to Harvard and putting together some ideas for the six public lectures that he was required to give as the incumbent Charles Eliot Norton Professor of Poetry. The whole business of his visit to Harvard for two semesters in 1967–68 was a cause for concern. Clearly he needed a companion while he was in the United States, but his mother had turned ninety in May 1966, and though she was still remarkably fit and alert, her age had begun to tell on her during the journeys they had undertaken together a few years earlier. However, there was no one else who was prepared to spend a period of up to six months with him in a foreign country, so it was a matter of either taking Mother with him or turning Harvard down. The question took on some urgency when Harvard wrote offering him a one-bedroom suite in Leverett House, an undergraduate residence. This was clearly not suitable, so Borges wrote back to Professor W. J. Bate of the Charles Eliot Norton Committee, giving him the list of his public lectures and offering to teach a course or two in South American literature but also explaining that he needed accommodation that would also be suitable for his mother. Borges's letter is apparently missing from the Harvard archives, but a letter from Professor Bate to the dean indicates the nature of the problem. Bate explained that this was an especially awkward case, because Borges was nearly blind and was also his aged mother's only support, so it was unavoidable that she accompany him. Borges hoped that an apartment with two bedrooms could be found for them, since he was understandably reluctant to share a room with his mother.[3]

The practical problems Borges faced at Harvard foreshadowed a much graver predicament—who would look after him when his mother, who was in her tenth decade, passed away? According to Emir Rodríguez Monegal, mother and son "used to discuss the matter openly with friends."[4] Borges's sister, Norah, and her family were not suitable, because she and Georgie had drifted apart since her marriage to Guillermo de Torre, to whom Borges had taken a hearty dislike. Bioy Casares and Silvina Ocampo could not be expected to take him on, because, even though they had seen each other almost daily for so many years, the Bioys led largely separate lives in the pursuit of their respective affairs. As even Doña Leonor was able to appreciate, the only solution was marriage, but who would make a suitable partner? This, precisely, was the question that had divided mother and son since Georgie had fallen for his first girl in Geneva.

Borges was seeing María Kodama regularly by now and had become infatuated with the girl, but what chance did he stand with her? Time was surely against him, since he could scarcely expect, even on the most optimistic calculation, to marry the girl in time to take her to Harvard with him the following year. In any case, he had introduced María to a friend of his who had recently been separated from his wife and who appeared to be seeing a good deal of her, so he assumed—erroneously, as it eventually transpired—that María was becoming involved with this other man.

So who else would make a suitable marriage partner? In the latter half of 1966, Borges had resumed his friendship with Margarita Guerrero and had persuaded her to collaborate with him in producing a second, enlarged edition of the *Manual de zoología fantástica,* the bestiary of imaginary creatures they had produced during their brief amorous friendship in the early 1950s.[5] Borges, it appears, entertained the possibility of reviving his relationship with Margot, but would such a union last? Unlikely, on past evidence.

Mother, in any case, had other ideas. According to Bioy Casares, Doña Leonor heard that Elsa Astete Millán, the girl Borges had courted in the late 1920s, had been widowed a couple of years earlier after twenty-seven years of marriage to Ricardo Albarracín, by whom she had one son.[6] Leonor persuaded Georgie to contact her again through Elsa's sister Alicia, who had been married to his friend Néstor Ibarra. A meeting was arranged at Alicia's house, and the two of them spent the whole afternoon in conversation, then went out to dinner the following day.[7] On the face of it, Elsa Astete was a highly promising candidate. There had, after all, once been a certain tendresse between them. Elsa, in fact, would claim that they had become engaged: "I had been his fiancée when I was twenty years old. We had even exchanged rings. We were properly engaged."[8] And even after her marriage to another man, there had been a strange episode in the early 1940s when Borges had written her some passionate letters. As the possibility of taking the friendship further was being mooted, it appears that the old flame began to revive. Elsa showed Borges a ring he had given her, and the fact that she had kept it for so many years moved him deeply.[9] For his part, Borges produced a photograph of Elsa that she had given him some forty years earlier, and Doña Leonor told her that he used to look at her picture every night before going to bed.[10]

Even so, Borges was unable to make up his mind. Fani, the housekeeper, claimed to have overheard Mother ask Georgie at lunch one day, "Who are you going to marry, Margarita Guerrero or Elsa Astete?"[11] Borges did not reply. For a period in January 1967, he went to ground—Esther Zemborain, who was eager to complete the manuscript of the *Introduction to North American Literature,* found it impossible to track Borges down for several weeks.[12] In the end he chose the middle-aged widow, but it must have been an agonizing decision, for by January 1967, as we have seen, he had completed the cycle of stories narrating his liberation from the conflict of sword and dagger, and no sooner had he tasted this unprecedented psychological freedom than he was faced with the practical necessity of finding a companion in life. Elsa Astete accepted Borges's proposal, and they agreed on a civil marriage in a register office, but, as Elsa would recall, it was Doña Leonor who "encouraged" the idea of a church wedding,[13] for it would have been considered a scandal in the social circles to which Leonor Acevedo belonged to have anything other than a religious ceremony. It was decided that the civil marriage would take place in August and the church wedding several weeks later.

The news of the engagement was received with a certain incredulity by Borges's friends. No one had ever heard of Elsa Astete, since she did not belong to the Buenos Aires literary world nor to the circle of upper-class ladies who frequented the Borgeses'. When Georgie brought Elsa to lunch with some of his lady friends, they thought her frumpish, provincial, and rather plain; and when she first came to the Bioys' house for dinner, even the maid could not help sniggering when she opened the door to the woman everyone was talking about as Señor Borges's fiancée.[14] All the same, Leonor Acevedo was delighted with Elsa, who was appropriately respectful and deferential—to the point of yielding a place to her future mother-in-law next to Georgie on the sofa, as she was once observed to do when visiting Susana Bombal's house.[15]

María Kodama's impression was that Borges was ill at ease with the engagement. One afternoon, when she went for tea at his apartment in Maipú, Borges was wearing an engagement ring, but once Doña Leonor had left the room, he disappeared for a short while, and when he returned, María noticed that he had taken it off. On another occasion Doña Leonor told her about her son's forthcoming marriage and suggested to María that she congratulate him. María offered Borges her felicitations while he accompanied her downstairs in the elevator and was struck by how uncomfortable he looked at her mentioning his engagement.

In fact, he was in despair. As he put it in a poem called "The Labyrinth" ("El laberinto"), which he published in *La Nación* on June 11, 1967:

> Zeus himself could not undo the nets of stone that enclose me. I have
>   forgotten
> the men I have been; I just keep on down the hateful
> path flanked by monotonous walls
> which is my destiny. Straight galleries
> that curve into secret circles
> after all these years.

He portrayed himself as Theseus, who has lost Ariadne's thread and hears a "desolate roar" as he staggers about in the endless labyrinth:

> I know there is an Other lurking in the shadows, whose fate it is to
>   exhaust the lonely byways
> from which this Hades is woven,
> and to crave my blood and devour my death.
> We seek each other, the two of us. If only this
> were the last day of our waiting.

But that release seemed never to come, and, judging by another poem called "Labyrinth" ("Laberinto") he published that same year, there seemed no way out of his predicament—"there will never be a door"—not even by way of death itself:

> No use waiting for the charge
> of the bull which is a man, and whose strange,
> plural form imparts horror to the tangle of endless interwoven stone.
> Nothing exists. Nothing to hope for. Not even,
> in this crepuscular blackness, the beast.[16]

On August 4, Borges finally tied the knot: he and Elsa became man and wife at a ceremony in a register office, but although they had purchased an apartment at avenida Belgrano 1377, just a few blocks from the National Library, they decided to avoid the merest breath of scandal, so Georgie stayed on at the flat with Mother for the several weeks until the union could be sanctified in church. And during that strange hiatus between celibacy and marriage, he published a poem he called "Rubáiyát," after the famous poem by Omar

Khayyám, which his own father had translated. Borges took the hedonistic *carpe diem* theme and twisted it into a meditation on the vanity of all things, spinning it finally into a most violent formulation: "Today is yesterday. You are the others, / whose face is dust. You are the dead."[17]

Doña Leonor had assured her friends that, as befitted a middle-aged couple, the church wedding would be a quiet, discreet affair, but Borges was the most famous man in Argentina and his marriage was bound to attract the attention of the media. The date chosen, moreover, was September 21, the first day of spring in the Southern Hemisphere, and the equivalent in Argentina to St. Valentine's Day, when men present their sweethearts with a red rose to celebrate their romance. Esther Zemborain was late for the wedding, having been held up in a traffic jam caused by the annual spring pageant wending its way down the avenida Santa Fe, and when she arrived at the fashionable Church of Nuestra Señora de las Victorias, she found it overflowing with people, none of whom she recognized.[18] Bioy Casares was nowhere to be seen, but she spotted his wife, Silvina Ocampo, who had turned up after all, as had a handful of Borges's literary friends. Then she caught sight of the bride and groom standing in the middle of a jostling crowd, with paparazzi falling over each other to take pictures for the Buenos Aires press.

Clarín reported that the wedding had been a simple ceremony, attended by some fifty guests, and conducted by Monsignor Ernesto Segura, the auxiliary bishop of the Archdiocese of Buenos Aires.[19] Borges came to the church with his mother; the bride arrived five minutes later, on the arm of her brother, who was giving her away. Wearing a black dress and coat, she proceeded up the aisle to the strains of Mendelssohn's "Wedding March," and after the ceremony friends and relatives gathered around the couple to offer their congratulations.

Still, even before they left for the United States a week later, clouds had appeared on the horizon. A farewell party was organized for them by friends of Doña Leonor. So many people had been invited that Esther Zemborain had to borrow her mother's mansion on calle Schiaffino in the smart Recoleta district in order to accommodate them all.[20] All the guests were looking forward to the arrival of the new "Señora de Borges," as Elsa Astete was now known, but she showed no sign of turning up, so an anxious Doña Leonor finally asked Esther Zemborain to telephone her daughter-in-law at the marital home. Elsa, it transpired, had been very tied up with the preparations for the couple's imminent journey to the United States, and was, in any case, indisposed that evening.[21] Georgie, therefore, attended the party on his own.

When Borges and Elsa arrived in Boston on September 29, they were met by Raimundo Lida, a professor in the Department of Romance Languages at

Harvard. Borges, Lida would note in his journal, looked much older and worn since his last visit to Harvard in 1962.[22] Elsa immediately felt out of place in Cambridge. To begin with, she was unhappy with the apartment that the university had provided for them, and she soon found another in a building on the corner of Craigie Street and Concord Avenue, a stone's throw away from Cambridge Common. Then, having very little English, she showed scant interest in leading the life of a dutiful faculty wife and would rarely accompany her husband to functions, nor would the Borgeses entertain at their apartment. Elsa preferred the company of a cousin of hers who happened to be employed at the time as a language instructor in Spanish at Harvard. For much of the time her husband was entrusted to the care of a young Anglo-Argentine graduate student called John Murchison, whom the university had engaged to look after their blind Norton lecturer. Murchison would take Borges to the library at the Radcliffe College campus nearby, where he would read to him and sometimes take dictation.

The incumbent of the Norton Professorship of Poetry was expected to give six lectures, and by convention three would be delivered in the first semester, the remainder in the second. The *Harvard Gazette* of October 14 announced that Borges's series of public lectures, entitled "This Craft of Verse," would be given in the Charles Eliot Norton Lecture Hall at the Fogg Art Museum.[23] The individual topics were "The Riddle of Poetry" (October 25), "The Metaphor" (November 15), "The Telling of a Tale" (December 6), "Word-Music and Translation" (February 28), "Thought and Poetry" (March 20), and "A Poet's Creed" (April 10).[24] The audience for the inaugural lecture turned out to be so large that it had to be accommodated in the Sanders Theatre in Memorial Hall, a short distance from the Fogg Museum. As she walked through Harvard Yard to the new venue, Raimundo Lida's wife, Denah, overheard a group of radical students of the SDS (Students for a Democratic Society), discussing what sounded like a plan to disrupt Borges's lecture.[25]

Like so many other American universities, Harvard was no longer the tranquil place it had been when Borges first visited in 1962. The student opposition to the Vietnam War was now at its peak, and in the weeks preceding Borges's lecture, the *Harvard Crimson,* the students' daily newspaper, had been full of reports of demonstrations and protests. On the previous Saturday, October 21, for instance, a massive "March on the Pentagon" had resulted in serious clashes between the National Guard and protesting students; that same week there had been demonstrations against Harvard's alleged complicity with the Dow Chemical Company, the manufacturers of napalm; on the very evening of Borges's first lecture, Edward Kennedy spoke to an overflow audience at Harvard Medical School on the need for a reappraisal of the war.

It is hard to say to what extent this political unrest actually engaged Borges's attention. It is unlikely, in any case, that he would have been much interested, even supposing that he had not been blind. But his very lack of interest in politics was already earning him a reputation for conservatism even in the United States, where the rise of the New Left on American campuses had led to the expectation that Latin American writers show solidarity with the revolutionary struggles taking place in the continent. Only two weeks earlier, the front page of the student newspaper had carried a photograph of the murdered Che Guevara's body being put on display by the army in Bolivia,[26] and on November 17, two days after Borges's second lecture at Harvard, it carried a full-page report on a speech that Stokeley Carmichael, the leader of the Black Panthers, had given in Havana praising Che Guevara's "apocalyptic vision" and Fidel Castro's "great ideological victory."[27]

As it turned out, Borges's inaugural lecture at Harvard passed without incident, but in the threat of disruption by members of the revolutionary SDS, we find the beginnings of the dual reputation he would acquire abroad in the coming years—admired for his literary genius on the one hand but execrated as a political reactionary on the other. On this occasion, as on so many others, the blind old Argentine writer, with his blank, uplifted look and tremulous delivery, exuded an otherworldly aura that seemed to elicit a kind of reverence even from people who might otherwise have violently disagreed with his politics.

A good part of Borges's charm lay in the distracted insouciance with which he approached the whole business of public performance. He brought his first lecture in the Norton series to an abrupt end and then remained motionless at his seat for a good while after the vote of thanks. When Raimundo Lida, who had chaired the occasion, ventured to ask him if anything was amiss, Borges replied that his leg had "gone to sleep"—"like most of the audience, I expect." Still, according to Richard Burgin, who was a young student at neighboring Brandeis University at the time, Borges created "a genuine excitement in the Cambridge intellectual community," and his lectures "were very well attended and very well received."[28] Early in the following year, Robert Lowell would introduce Borges at a poetry reading by saying, "It would be impertinent of me to praise him. For many years, I've thought he should have won the Nobel Prize."[29]

Although Borges had entered into marriage with trepidation, not to say foreboding, he had genuinely nurtured the hope that the union might lead to some kind of fulfillment for the two of them. In those early days at Harvard, he was to compose a poem called "Elsa," in which he called to mind the many long, hard years during which he had been deprived of a woman's love; nevertheless, he professed to regard these years as necessary steps on the way toward "the pure heights of blue that persist in the blue of the evening of this day and of my days."[30] The poem ended on a tender note: "Elsa, your hand is in my hand. We see / the snow in the air, and cherish it."

Unfortunately, the marriage showed signs of being in difficulties soon after their arrival at Harvard. One evening Raimundo Lida came home with the news that Borges had quarreled with Elsa and had booked himself into the nearby Continental Hotel.[31] Although Borges was eventually persuaded to go back to his wife, it was becoming evident by now that they were not getting on. Borges's attendance at classes became erratic, and rumor had it that he was spending too much of his time giving talks at other universities and colleges. This may have been the reason Juan Marichal, the chairman of the department, had become "so very irritated" (*irritadísimo*) with him, as Lida noted in his journal. The gossip and speculation about the couple's alleged disagreements were getting back to Doña Leonor in Argentina, principally through the widow of a Spanish professor at Harvard whom Borges had known in Buenos Aires in the 1930s.

Borges's unhappiness while at Harvard would inspire a new story called "The Other" ("El otro"), in which he depicted himself sitting alone by the Charles River when a young man unexpectedly sits next to him on the bench.[32] This turns out to be an apparition of himself as an adolescent in Geneva. The sexagenarian Borges then embarks on a dialogue with his youthful self, ruefully probing the aspirations of the young man in the implicit knowledge of his current despair. Only the most acute estrangement from his own past could have inspired such a story, but as his marriage to Elsa began to fail, it seemed that even his past life was more real than the present, which was so empty, so insubstantial, so unbearable. In the poem "Cambridge," he pushed this idea to the extreme of asserting that the past—the things that have disappeared—lives on within us: "We are our memory, / we are the chimerical museum of inconstant forms, / that pile of broken mirrors."[33] And in "The Unending Gift," he pushed the idea further still, reflecting on the power exerted by absent things.[34] On learning of the death of his friend, the painter Jorge Larco, he thought of a picture that Larco had once promised him, and it occurred to him that if he had actually received the picture, it would have become one among the many, barely noticed things about the house. Its absence, however, made it "limitless, unceasing, capable of assuming any form and any color and tied to none." As a result, "it will live and grow like a piece of music, and shall be with me to the end." He had stumbled on a new theme—what is past or absent is more vivid than the actuality of our experience. This belief in the virtual power of the imagination would assume a critical importance some ten years later, though in very different circumstances from the hopeless situation in which he now found himself.

There came a certain relief from this terrible gloom thanks to a chance meeting with Norman Thomas di Giovanni, a writer and translator who lived not far from Boston. The thirty-four-year-old American had come across Borges's work while engaged in producing an anthology of Latin American poetry, and when he heard that Borges happened to be at Harvard, he wrote offering to undertake a translation of a selection of his poems, as he had done two years earlier for the Spanish poet Jorge Guillén, who was currently living near Cambridge, having retired from Wellesley College. Di Giovanni met Borges on December 3, 1967, and this first, tentative encounter was to lead to a remarkable collaboration over a period of several years. For despite a glaring difference in temperament, the go-getting American and the world-weary Argentine managed to work well together, and for much of the rest of his time at Cambridge, Borges helped di Giovanni with the preliminaries for the projected anthology of his poetry. He gave the young American a free hand to deal with English-language publishers on his behalf and agreed to equal shares of the royalties from any English translations undertaken together.

The six months Borges spent in the United States led to his being recognized in the English-speaking world as a writer of major stature. Richard Burgin was to write, "By the time of his last lecture at Harvard, Borges was the literary hero of Cambridge. I understand that wherever he went in the country, giving his lectures and his poetry readings, his reception was equally enthusiastic. In Cambridge, writers like Robert Lowell, Robert Fitzgerald, Yves Bonnefoy, John Updike and Bernard Malamud attended his lectures and lined up to meet him. John Barth said Borges was the man 'who had succeeded Joyce and Kafka.'"[35]

In April, Borges and his wife returned to Buenos Aires. Outwardly they settled down to a life of placid domesticity at their apartment on avenida Belgrano. Borges would spend a few hours at the National Library in the morning, return home for lunch at one, and then take a nap before returning to the library for a few hours in the afternoon. Most evenings he and Elsa would dine with the Bioys and later spend some time reading at home before retiring to bed. But not long after their return from Harvard, it became obvious to close friends that the marriage was under strain. Borges himself could not adjust to a marital relationship, while Elsa had not, after all, turned out to be an appropriate substitute for Mother.

Elsa soon felt out of place among the cosmopolitan writers who were Borges's friends. And, needless to say, having spent much of her life as a provincial housewife in La Plata, she became the subject of vicious gossip among the aristocratic ladies in her mother-in-law's social circle. This gossip was accompanied by a subtle persecution. Elsa, for instance, would be reminded over tea how fortunate she was to be married to such a famous writer, whom women found so very attractive.[36] Elsa's discomfiture led her in the end to ban all women from setting foot in her apartment, and as her social opportunities in Buenos Aires declined, she took to visiting her family and friends in La Plata.

During Elsa's absences it was to María Kodama that a somewhat disoriented Borges would turn for company. María was the only female whom Elsa would countenance in the house; this neat, self-effacing youngster, with her white blouses and plaid skirts, would quietly help her blind husband pass the time by reading to him and assisting him in deciphering his Anglo-Saxon texts. Borges's loneliness was plain to see, but María could only imagine the extent of his inner anguish, for their relations were characterized by an extreme reticence—they continued to address each other in the formal vocative *usted*—and even though she found herself becoming attached to her revered teacher, she could not put a name to whatever it was she felt about him.[37]

As for Borges, the feelings he had harbored for María before his marriage began to revive, but he appears to have been loath to acknowledge them, for the last thing he could have wanted was to reopen the old wounds that love had inflicted on him over the years. Better perhaps the bleak, steady unhappiness of marriage than the torments of unrequited passion. But it was no use, he could not deny his feelings; love had taken possession of him once more, and in a poem called "A Man Under Threat" ("El amenazado"), he compared it to being pursued by an enemy or finding himself in a prison from which there was no escape:

> This is love. I shall have to hide or flee.
> The walls of its prison grow, as in a terrible dream.
> The beautiful mask has changed, but as ever it is the only one that
>   matters.
> . . . Being with you, or not with you, is the measure of my time.[38]

And he brought the poem to a close by expressing the fear, but also the unbearable need, aroused by his love for María Kodama:

> There is a street corner I dare not walk by,
> The armies have now surrounded me, the hordes.
> (This room is unreal; she has not set eyes on it.)
> The name of a woman gives the game away.
> A woman aches through the whole of my body.

Di Giovanni, meanwhile, had been setting up several publishing deals in the United States for translations of Borges's work into English. His first success was a contract with the publisher Seymour Lawrence for an anthology of Borges's poetry, which would appear as *Selected Poems (1923–1967)* under the Delacorte Press imprint in 1972. This was a complex enterprise that would require di Giovanni to commission and coordinate the work of several translators, including John Updike, John Hollander, Richard Wilbur, Alastair Reid, and di Giovanni himself. He had also been approached by Jack Macrae of E. P. Dutton in New York, who was interested in publishing English translations of Borges's entire output, but it proved impossible to obtain the rights for most of the stories that had already been translated into English, and Macrae eventually signed a letter of agreement with di Giovanni for a translation of *El libro de los seres imaginarios* (*The Book of Imaginary Beings*), which had come out the previous year in Spanish. He also came to an informal understanding with di Giovanni that he would publish whichever books by Borges remained free of copyright problems. Finally di Giovannni negotiated a deal with the *New Yorker* to submit poems and stories by Borges on an occasional basis, a potentially lucrative agreement, given the handsome fees paid by the magazine.

In view of these various deals, di Giovanni believed it was essential that he reinforce his personal ties with Borges, so he applied to the Ingram Merrill Foundation for a grant to help him live for a few months in Buenos Aires and work alongside Borges. And so, toward the middle of November 1968, Borges's forlorn domestic existence was enlivened by the arrival in Buenos Aires of the ebullient American, Norman Thomas di Giovanni. He was met at the airport by Borges and Elsa, who took him to a modest hotel they had found on the avenida de Mayo, not far from their apartment.

Little time was lost before getting down to the business of translating poems for the Delacorte anthology, and the very next morning they commenced their collaboration on "Heraclitus" ("Heráclito"). In the seven months since Borges had departed the United States, di Giovanni had been sent around seventeen uncollected poems for translation and publication in the *New Yorker* and elsewhere. Were these recent compositions, di Giovanni now asked Borges, or work found in a bottom drawer?[39] Borges said they were new, but when di Giovanni suggested that he collect them in a book, Borges flew into a rage and refused to entertain the idea. However, the following evening, while dining with Bioy, Borges raised the matter again: "Di Giovanni has a crazy idea. He wants me to publish a new book of poems." Bioy thought it a splendid idea, and a few days later Borges went to see Carlos Frías, his editor at Emecé, and told him that he wished to bring out a collection of new poems.

Di Giovanni also set about finding out which of Borges's books were free from copyright in English and discovered that there were eight, but the problem was that these were mostly works of less obvious interest to an Anglo-

American readership, such as the biographical study *Evaristo Carriego,* about which even Borges had his doubts, or *Discusión,* the miscellany of essays from the early 1930s, or the eccentric *A History of Eternity,* which had attracted a mere thirty-seven readers when it was first published in 1936. Still, these would have to form the basis of the multibook contract di Giovanni hoped to negotiate with Jack Macrae of E. P. Dutton, but there was clearly a need for a book that would be more commercially viable in the U.S. market, so it was agreed to put together an anthology of stories and prose pieces, which would be published in due course under the title *The Aleph and Other Stories.*

While di Giovanni was proceeding with these deals, Borges remained mired in his emotional difficulties over his unhappy marriage and his feelings for María Kodama. And as had occurred while he was at Harvard, he was prone to dwell on the vividness of the past as compared to the hopeless present. On the morning after di Giovanni's arrival in Buenos Aires, Borges showed his American friend around the National Library and "a few spots nearby on the old south side of the city that he both worshipped and had turned into myth."[40] Di Giovanni found it touching that the old writer should want to apologize for the run-down streets and the dusty park of the neighborhood, but he could sense the pride that lay beneath such courtesy. "After all," Borges explained, "these places mean a great deal to me; they're my past."[41]

On December 4, less than three weeks later, di Giovanni accompanied Borges to the barrio of Palermo. He had not visited Palermo for thirty years, he told di Giovanni. They went to an *almacén,* a traditional street corner tavern, where they ordered *cañas quemadas,* a kind of rum, and as they sipped their drinks, they noticed two men playing cards at a wooden table. This could have been a scene out of Borges's youthful poem "El Truco" from *Fervor de Buenos Aires,* in which he had imagined a group of card players repeating the words and actions of countless predecessors, thereby nullifying the reality of the present and bringing the past back to life. Later, "like an eager schoolboy," Borges showed the American a cobbled alleyway that he said was uncharacteristic because it ran in a diagonal rather than forming the side of a square.[42] And on that spot, which may well have been especially redolent of the far-off days of his youth, Borges came out with the plot of a story that he had already worked out in his head. It was "Juan Muraña," the tale about the old widow who used her husband's dagger to kill the landlord who threatened her with eviction. No sooner had he finished telling this story than he informed di Giovannni that he would never manage to write fiction again. But the truth was that Borges had privately composed a series of new stories some three years earlier, so he may have been probing di Giovanni, obliquely tempting him to press further, perhaps hoping that the decisive American might help him enter a territory into which he had not yet found the spirit to venture on his own.

PART FIVE

Love Regained

(1969–1986)

CHAPTER 27

Iceland

(1969–1971)

SINCE DI GIOVANNI'S ARRIVAL in Buenos Aires, Borges was engaged in two projects. In the mornings he would dictate new poems in Spanish to a secretary in the National Library, with a view to collecting these and the poems he had written since about 1966 in a new volume to be called *In Praise of Darkness* (*Elogio de la sombra*). Then, in the afternoons, di Giovanni would pick him up at his apartment at four o'clock and take him back to the National Library, where they would collaborate on the translations of his work into English for the American publishers. This routine was interrupted for about two weeks while Borges visited Israel with Elsa in the early days of the New Year, but he got back to work as soon as he returned. The poems he was jointly translating with di Giovanni for the *Selected Poems* commissioned by Delacorte Press were finished in February 1969, and they would go on to translate *The Book of Imaginary Beings* for E. P. Dutton, adding some new entries along the way.

Borges was also seeing María Kodama throughout this period, of course. They continued to conduct themselves with their usual reserve and propriety, still employing the formal mode of address to each other, as they discussed and translated Anglo-Saxon texts. But Borges's feelings for the girl may be gauged from a poem he wrote at this time. He called it "The Rose" ("La rosa"), and it evoked the rose of love in its various manifestations—"the young platonic rose," indicating the innocence of his early loves, and also that other flower, the rose of passion, "ardent and blind," whose praise he did not yet feel truly qualified to sing. He was to include "The Rose" in a new edition of his first book, *Fervor de Buenos Aires*, which Emecé was bringing out that year.[1] On the face of it, this was a curious decision, but the tenor of this new poem was quite different from that of the poems he was collecting for *In Praise of Darkness*, which reflected his unhappiness at his disastrous marriage; "The Rose" was a paean to love, celebrating its capacity to revive anew "from tenuous ashes," so he must have deemed it more appropriate to include it in *Fervor de Buenos Aires*, the book that had been inspired by his love of Concepción Guerrero.

The loss of that early love may well have been weighing on his mind again, for even though the rose of love might have blossomed once more in his feelings for María Kodama, he was also trapped in marriage to Elsa. How could he find a way out of this predicament? Would he lose the rose again? The hopes and anxieties that his love for María Kodama aroused in him were expressed in a sequence of tankas (tanka is a Japanese verse form related to the haiku), which he probably composed around the time of his seventieth birthday.[2] First of all, there is the aching desire: "High on its summit / the whole garden is a moon, / a moon of gold. / More precious still is the brush of your mouth in the dark."* But then an awareness of lack: "The voice of the bird / the shadows hide / is mute now. You stroll in your garden. / Something, I know, is missing." Next he is gripped by a fear that passion will devour him to no purpose: "Under the moon / the tiger of gold and shadow / observes its claws. / Little does it know that in the dawn / they destroyed a man." And, finally, he is oppressed by the sadness of "being earth," of "not being the days / of man, the dream, the dawn," for his entire life has been void so far, and even his writing has brought no true fulfillment: "Not to have fallen, like others of my blood, in battle. / To be in the vanity of the night / the one who counts the syllables." This sense of life's having passed him by must have been more intolerable than ever—he knew full well what had to be done, he had the key to freedom, but it remained to be seen whether he could find the courage to unlock the door that would release him from the labyrinth of despair.

Since his nostalgic visit to Palermo with di Giovanni, Borges would from time to time tell his American friend the plots of other stories he had in mind. Di Giovanni began to keep a tally of these stories and eventually drew up a list of eight. Clearly there was a basis for a new collection, so di Giovanni initiated what he called "a subtle campaign of egging him on" to publish these stories, a campaign that started to bear fruit by the middle of April 1969, when it became known that Borges was dictating a story to a secretary at the National Library.[3] When he received the typescript some three weeks later, di Giovanni was delighted to find a polished tale of two young men who engage in a duel after being mysteriously drawn to a couple of knives they find in a cabinet. This was "The Encounter," which di Giovanni translated over the next few weeks and sent to the *New Yorker*.

Meanwhile, Borges's output had been steadily increasing: by the end of May, the translation of *The Book of Imaginary Beings* had been completed, and toward the middle of June, the bulk of the poems for *In Praise of Darkness*

---

*I have not observed the syllable count of the tanka form in my translation of Borges's tankas.

were delivered to Emecé. (This collection of new poems in Spanish would be published on August 22 to great acclaim.) Borges and di Giovanni now started on their next project for Dutton: the anthology of prose fiction, *The Aleph and Other Stories.* However, after dictating "The Encounter" in May, Borges appears to have dragged his feet about proceeding any further with the dictation of new stories. At the end of June, they heard from the *New Yorker* that "The Encounter" had been accepted, and this news sent Borges's "confidence soaring," according to di Giovanni, but still he would not get around to dictating any of the other stories.[4] It may be that this reluctance was due to his awareness that the sequence of stories he had composed in 1966–67 described the psychological liberation that had preceded his marriage to Elsa and that the process of committing them to paper would make his current unhappy situation even more painful to bear.

Still, in September—at around the time he was composing the tankas about his love for María Kodama—he broke through his inhibitions and began to dictate "Rosendo Juárez's Story," the tale where the knife fighter refuses to fight a duel because he realizes that there is no point in doing something simply in order to conform with other people's expectations. This was followed in October by "Unworthy," where the Jewish boy, Fischbein, finds his true self by doing what he thinks is right rather than trying to impress the *compadrito,* Ferrari. Both stories show that the will is the key to selfhood, and the fact that Borges chose to dictate these two stories at this juncture suggests that he was bracing himself to take the necessary steps to recover his freedom at last.

In December he went with Elsa and di Giovanni to the United States, where he had been invited to preside at a conference on his work organized by the University of Oklahoma. Borges would later recall this trip as one of the unhappiest in his life, because of his disagreements with Elsa.[5] After Oklahoma he went to Washington to give a lecture at Georgetown University and thence to New York to meet his American publisher, Jack Macrae, who had organized a reading of his work at the Poetry Center in the YM-YWHA on Ninety-second Street in order to publicize *The Book of Imaginary Beings,* Borges's first book for E. P. Dutton. Macrae lent Borges and Elsa an apartment at Seventy-fourth Street on the Upper East Side between Park and Lexington Avenues, but he noticed that they were not happy together—there was "an awkwardness" between them,[6] and the truth was that Elsa, who could barely speak English, was feeling out of her depth among all the publishers and editors and journalists who were making such a fuss over her famous husband. Having committed Dutton to a multibook deal, Macrae was keen to promote Borges in New York, and after the reading at the Ninety-second Street Y, he gave a party in his honor at a brownstone on Seventy-eighth Street, which Elsa chose not to attend. However, María Kodama, who happened to be visiting a friend in New York at the time, did go to the party, and Borges, appearing tremendously relieved to see her, asked if she would do him the favor of looking after Elsa, since she was finding it all too much.[7]

It was finding Borges in such obvious distress that made María understand the nature of her feelings for him—she finally acknowledged to herself that she loved him. It was a "marvelous" feeling, but a "terrible realization" nonetheless, for it was bad enough that he was several decades older than she, worse that he was married to someone else, but worst of all was the fact that he was so wretchedly unhappy and there was nothing she could do to remedy the situation.[8] On the flight home, she told herself that if God existed, she would pray that Borges find happiness in his life, even if it meant that she herself was denied it.

After returning from the United States, Borges and di Giovanni continued working on the English translations for *The Aleph and Other Stories*. Di Giovanni then had the idea of including a brief autobiographical account of Borges's life in the anthology, but Borges would not hear of it, perhaps because it would have been too painful to review his life at a time when he was feeling so unhappy in his marriage. Still, the visit to Oklahoma and New York seems to have stiffened Borges's resolve, and the pace at which he revised and dictated the new stories accelerated prodigiously. By mid-January he had finished "Juan Muraña," and this was followed in quick succession by "The Duel" and "The End of the Duel." By late February he was finishing a draft of "Guayaquil." On March 5 he began work on "Brodie's Report," and on the day he finished "Brodie," he started work on "The Gospel According to Mark." By about April 13, he had completed the last story. The rate at which he produced these stories—seven in three months—indicates that all of them had already existed more or less fully formed in his imagination before he dictated them to a secretary at the National Library. Getting these stories down in writing must have had a cathartic effect, since they constituted a deconstruction of the basic conflict between sword and dagger that had been the source of so much anguish and inhibition, especially in his relations with women, and the quickening pace of dictation suggests a growing urgency to regain his freedom. On April 20 he presented his editor at Emecé with the typescript for the new collection, which would be published later that year under the title *Brodie's Report*. The next day he finally agreed to write "An Autobiographical Essay" for the Dutton anthology.

Even so, only three days after starting on the essay with di Giovanni, work ground to a halt. Borges's schedule had apparently become very busy: there was a constant stream of visitors to attend to, and he had received several invitations to lecture. Di Giovanni began to despair of getting the "Autobiographical Essay" ready for Dutton to publish *The Aleph and Other Stories* on time. What he did not know was that Borges had reached a crisis in his private life—he could no longer bear to be married and had decided to leave Elsa. The only problem was that he did not know quite how to go about the separation. He approached his old friend Alicia Jurado, who was herself separated, and asked her advice. If he left the marital home, could he come and stay for a while at her country house while things were sorted out? Alicia pointed out that it would not look good from a legal standpoint if he left his wife to go live in the house of an unmarried lady friend.[9] Had he told Elsa about his intentions? He had not. Alicia suggested that it would be only fair to do so; Borges protested that he could not bear scenes.[10] He must have known that there was little point in entering into discussions with Elsa—he must cut his losses and recover the freedom he had taken so long to conquer and had come so close to throwing away.

On May 16, some three weeks after work had been suspended, Borges returned to the writing of his memoir, but di Giovanni noticed that he could not settle down; there was something on his mind. Then Borges blurted out his troubles. The American lost no time in getting down to business—he arranged a meeting that same Saturday afternoon with a lawyer, and two days later proceedings were set in motion to obtain a legal separation. (There was no provision for divorce in Argentine law at that time.) Borges could not bear to confront Elsa with his plans, so the entire operation had to be conducted in secret over the next six weeks.

It was at around this time that Borges began to see Haydée Lange again. Haydée, who had never married, lived with her sister Chichina at the apartment on calle Talcahuano that they had shared with their late mother since the early 1940s. According to Bioy Casares, Borges had always been fond of visiting the Lange family; "he liked their aura, he wanted to be close to them,"[11] but he may well not have had much contact with them during his marriage to Elsa. And it is virtually certain, moreover, that through Haydée, he would have had news of her widowed sister, Norah, and may even have started seeing the latter socially from time to time, since she now lived close by in an apartment on the same street as her sisters.

Norah Lange remained a legendary figure in the Buenos Aires literary world. Despite her age, she cut a dash at parties, dressing entirely in black, smoking from a cigarette holder, and displaying still the sensational red mane of her youth. Even so, she was much subdued since the days when the poets of Buenos Aires were enthralled by the speeches she delivered from the tabletops of countless literary banquets. She had stayed on at calle Suipacha after the death of Oliverio Girondo, but she came to feel that the old house was too big for her and too full of memories. In any case, it was slowly crumbling away—

one day the ceiling of her bedroom fell in, and the same would happen shortly afterward in the room that had been Oliverio's study. Gradually she scaled down her social activities and devoted herself to editing her husband's works and to writing a new novel; in 1970 she decided to move closer to her sisters. Most of her husband's possessions—the paintings, the African artifacts, the erotic Inca figurines—she sold off or gave away. The celebrated effigy of the "Academician" that Oliverio had paraded around the streets of Buenos Aires in 1932 was given to his friend, the poet Enrique Molina, as well as the set of stuffed toads. But rather than see the house demolished by property developers, she offered it, together with Oliverio's collection of books, to the adjacent Museo Fernández Blanco. Some things, however, Norah could not bear to part with, and among these prized possessions was the original street plaque that bore the name "calle Tronador."[12]

The fact that Borges was in touch again with Haydée and Norah Lange when he was in love with María Kodama and had decided to leave Elsa was of enormous significance for him. In the personal mythology he had devised over the years, Norah Lange represented the original Beatrice to his Dante; it was she who in 1925–26 had been his embodiment of the Aleph, the supreme unifying principle, the number that encompassed all the others. And it was then he had conceived the idea of salvation by writing—the creation of a masterpiece which would distill the essence of his life and so justify his existence. After Norah had rejected him for Oliverio Girondo, he experienced the agonies of a personal hell, but in 1940 he had fallen in love with Haydée Lange, the "new Beatrice" who would offer him the salvation that Norah had denied. This was the period when, under the influence of Dante, he had begun to compose *The Congress*, the masterpiece he hoped might save him as a writer.

Haydée Lange, however, had also rejected Borges, so he had tried to find other women who would play the saving role of his "new Beatrice." He had sought to fill this role with Estela Canto, Cecilia Ingenieros, Margarita Guerrero, and no doubt others, too, but he had failed with them all; his life, in consequence, had closed in on him, and even his late marriage to Elsa Astete had ended in failure. However, the impending separation from Elsa opened up the prospect once more of realizing the Dantean pattern of salvation, even though he had yet to discover whether his new love, María Kodama, would consent to become the "new Beatrice" in his life. A sign of this burgeoning optimism was that around May, while he was waiting to be legally parted from Elsa, he chose to undertake once more the composition of his Dantean masterpiece, *The Congress*.

While Borges was working simultaneously on the "Autobiographical Essay" and *The Congress*, news came that the preparations for his separation from

Elsa were complete. The plan was for Borges, accompanied by di Giovanni, to take a flight to the city of Córdoba, where they would stay for a while until the matter was settled. Poor Elsa had been kept completely in the dark, and indeed, when Borges left home for work as usual on the morning of July 7, he neglected to tell his wife that he would not be coming back for lunch. He and di Giovanni took a taxi to the airport, where a couple of fellow conspirators were waiting at the flight counter with tickets for them. Borges was "a trembling leaf and utterly exhausted after a sleepless night."[13] The flight was delayed by poor weather, which added to Borges's anxiety, but finally the pair set off and absented themselves for a week from Buenos Aires. Elsa first heard about her husband's intentions when a lawyer turned up at her front door and served her notice of Borges's application for a legal separation. She did not oppose it, and later that year they parted company. Elsa kept the apartment as part of the settlement; Borges went back to live with Mother at calle Maipú.

Work on the "Autobiographical Essay" and *The Congress* resumed when Borges returned to Buenos Aires. On July 29 he finished composing the "Autobiographical Essay" with di Giovanni, and it was sent off to the *New Yorker*. The closing words of the essay indicate a surge of optimism in Borges after his separation from Elsa: "I no longer regard happiness as unattainable; once, long ago, I did. Now I know that it may occur at any moment but that it should never be sought after. . . . What I'm out for now is peace, the enjoyment of thinking and of friendship, and, though it may be too ambitious, a sense of loving and of being loved."[14] His separation from Elsa had left him free at last to pursue his love for María Kodama, but he could not yet be sure whether she would reciprocate his feelings—perhaps it was "too ambitious" to feel himself worthy of being loved by a woman.

On August 12, two weeks after finishing the essay, he completed *The Congress*. Di Giovanni had been puzzled by Borges's habit of referring to it as a "novel" when they were working on it together, even though the piece did not in the end run to more than forty pages or so in typescript; he was puzzled, too, by Borges's inscribing "Buenos Aires, 1955" by way of an epigraph to the text when it came to preparing it for publication by a small publishing firm, El Archibrazo.[15] (*The Congress* would come out on March 17, 1971.) These, however, were signs that Borges was, privately, all too conscious of the long prehistory of this autobiographical story, for he had last attempted it in 1955, when the third phase of his relationship with Estela Canto had coincided with the Revolución Libertadora, and at that stage he still conceived of it as a novel. Indeed, as he would tell an audience at New York University a few months later, the project that was to result in *The Congress* went back some "thirty or forty years."[16] (In my view its origins probably lay in the autobiographical novel *The Approach to Al-Mu'tasim*.) By 1970, however, the complex tangle of experiences on which the projected novel was based had been pared down and synthesized in a marvel of allusive storytelling, a brilliant example of narrative minimalism, which possessed the oneiric resonance of so much modern art while retaining the luminous simplicity of a parable.

In August, the same month that *The Congress* was completed, Emecé brought out *Brodie's Report,* his collection of new stories. In September his "Autobiographical Essay" appeared in the *New Yorker,* and it was included also in *The Aleph and Other Stories,* which E. P. Dutton published in October. Borges had every reason to feel optimistic: he was free of his marriage to Elsa, he was publishing new work again, and his international reputation was soaring to unimagined heights. Indeed, in March 1971 he was due to travel to Oxford to be invested with an honorary doctorate that had been conferred on him the year before, and he had also been invited to Israel to receive the Jerusalem Prize. The resourceful di Giovanni would secure a grant from the British Council and arrange for a number of poetry readings and speaking engagements in the United States and London in order to cover the expenses of the entire trip. At the same time, di Giovanni prepared a surprise. Having noted that Borges had expressed a wish in the "Autobiographical Essay" that he might one day make "a pilgrimage to Iceland," it occurred to him to try to fulfill this wish, and through a friend who was a travel agent in Buenos Aires, he booked a flight from New York to Tel Aviv that allowed for a brief stopover in Iceland.

When Borges heard about the visit to Iceland, he was amazed. Anything that could be construed as disclosing the hand of destiny—coincidences, repetitions, auguries—held a peculiar fascination for him, and the surprise arranged for him by di Giovanni would have had an especially powerful resonance, for Iceland had acquired a kind of sacred aura in his imagination: through poems on the battles of Saxon and Viking in ancient Britain, through a whole range of allusions to topics enshrined in the Eddas, he had raised Iceland into a complex imaginative terrain in which he had figured his troubled relations with Norah Lange and the associated theme of his failure in love. And it was very likely this unexpected opportunity to visit Iceland that sowed in his mind the idea of inviting María Kodama to accompany him there. For it must have appealed to his poetic sense of destiny to declare his love for María in a place that was so redolent of Norah Lange, the original Beatrice in his private mythology.

The correspondence between myth and reality was reinforced by his renewed contact with the Lange sisters in 1970. His friendship with Haydée had developed into a weekly ritual—they would meet for tea every Friday at five o'clock and then go to the cinema or have dinner together, and whenever they were unable to meet, they would make sure to speak on the telephone at noon, again on Fridays.[17] When his new book, *Brodie's Report,* was published in August he presented Haydée with a copy that he inscribed (in English), "To that shining Northern goddess Haydée—Yours as ever, Georgie."[18] He was reminding her of what she had once meant to him, for Haydée had been the first in a succession of "new Beatrices," each one in turn a hoped-for surrogate for the irrecoverable Norah Lange. And perhaps he saw fit to recall this unremitting desire for love because he had arrived at yet another crossroads in his life. On November 1 he published "Browning Resolves to Be a Poet" ("Browning resuelve ser poeta"), in which he contemplated a stark alternative: "If a woman shares my love / my verse will brush the tenth sphere of the concentric heavens; / if a woman spurns my love / I will turn my sadness into music, / into a high river that will continue to resound throughout the course of time."[19]

As he stood at this fateful crossroads once more, he called to mind the woman who had been the original Beatrice to his Dante, the woman who years ago had refused him the gift of love. That initial rejection had remained fixed in his memory as an eternal instant, clear as a diamond in its pitiless definition. In a poem he dated November 3, 1970, he invoked a nameless woman standing "tall in the evening, haughty and adored"; she crosses the "chaste garden" and places herself "in the exact / light of the irreversible, pure instant/ granted us by this garden and the noble, silent / image."* He can see her "here and now" but also in different times and places—in some "ancient twilight," descending the steps of a temple that has since turned to dust, or "inhaling the fragrance of a rose in England"; she is to be found "wherever there is music," "in the hexameters of the Greek," "in our solitudes that seek her out," "in the serenity of a balcony / looking out over sunsets and gardens." And the poem ends with a melancholy envoi, recalling its author to an inescapable truth—that "behind the myths and the masks, / is the soul, which is alone."

Still, however stark the memory of loss might have been, whatever fears might have been stirred up by his decision to take a further gamble on love, he resolved all the same to invite María Kodama to Iceland. What he did not

---

*The poem was first published in July 1971 in the *Revista de Occidente* and later collected in *The Gold of the Tigers* (*El oro de los tigres*), 1972. See *OC* II, p. 470. He gave it the title "Susana Bombal," but according to María Kodama, Borges was never in love with Susana, and certainly not in this period. I regard the title as one of those dedications to certain female friends by which Borges sought to mask the real subject of the poem, who, in this case, I believe, was Norah Lange. Its first line, *"Alta en la tarde, altiva y alabada"* ("Tall in the evening, haughty and adored") contains two key words—*tarde* and *altiva*—which echo Borges's prologue to Norah's first book of poems, *La calle de la tarde*. There he described the villa on calle Tronador as standing in "the very depths of the evening" (*"la tarde"*) and praised Norah for the "double brilliance of her hair and her haughty youth" (*"altiva juventud"*), characterizing her "soul" as "light and haughty and fervent, like a banner unfurling in the breeze" (*"Leve y altiva y fervorosa como bandera que se realiza en el viento"*), see my Chapter 7, pp. 124–25.)

know at the time was that María had been secretly planning to travel to England anyway, in order to surprise him in Oxford by turning up at the ceremony for the award of his doctorate.[20] Borges's invitation forced her to reveal these plans to him. He was delighted to learn that she cared enough for him to travel to England for his sake, but there was to be an additional surprise, for when María rearranged her flights to include Iceland in her itinerary, she was required to make a stopover in Oslo for a couple of days before taking an onward flight to Reykjavik.[21] That chance detour of María's must have been laden with secret meanings for Borges, for Oslo, of course, was the city where Norah Lange had lived for a year, and it was on her return from Oslo that she had turned him down. But was this coincidence an augury of good fortune or of bad? He was poised yet again between bliss and disaster: the "pilgrimage" to Iceland would reveal whether the failures of the past would be repeated one more time or finally redeemed in the person of María Kodama.

At the end of March 1971 Borges set off with di Giovanni and the latter's new wife to the United States. His literary reputation was at its peak, and the visit became a round of award ceremonies, talks, and readings in halls packed to overflowing with enthusiastic audiences. He went to Brigham Young University in Utah; he was made an honorary member of the Institute of Arts and Letters; he presided at a recital of his poems at the Poetry Center at the YM-YWHA in New York; Columbia University awarded him an honorary doctorate, and held a colloquium on his work; Yale organized "An Evening with Borges," which attracted such a large audience that the venue had to be changed at the last minute. Then, at last, after these spectacular public appearances, he flew to Iceland on April 13 with di Giovanni and his wife, a visit he was to describe as "the greatest revelation of my life."[22]

When he arrived in Iceland, where María was waiting for him, he felt "a kind of ecstasy"; it was "a kind of dream come true."[23] He was struck by the desolate landscape of snowbound volcanoes and steaming geysers. There were visits to the Althing, where he saw the remains of the medieval parliament of tribal chieftains, and to Snorri Sturluson's house at Borgafjord, as well as to other historic sites, and as he went from place to place, reciting his favorite passages from the great Norse sagas, he was moved to tears by the emotion of it all, for in Iceland, he would explain to Carrizo, "you have the sagas and the Eddas, and I have always felt deeply about all of that."[24] It seemed to him that the past was coming to life again: "I often thought I could hear the voices of those illustrious Scandinavians intoning their beautiful songs."[25] And it was in this state of heightened emotion that he summoned up the courage to declare his feelings to María, and she in turn responded by admitting that theirs was far more than a friendship, it was love. Borges then confessed to María that it felt as if he had been waiting for her all his life, and it was in the context of a long-standing dream come true that he conceived the idea for a story that, as he told María in Iceland at the time, he proposed one day to dedicate to her.[26] The germ of this story was an encounter between an elderly man and a young woman who reminds him of a girl who had rejected him in his youth; as he makes love to the woman, he feels that the memory of that earlier, unrequited love is finally wiped away.

After their brief stay in Iceland, Borges and María parted company once more: she flew to London, while he went to Israel to receive the Jerusalem Prize. In the recollection of his New York publisher, Jack Macrae, Borges was in exceptionally high spirits during the four days he spent in Israel, so much so that when they visited the Dead Sea together, Borges took off his shoes and socks and waded right in up to his waist.[27] Back at the King David Hotel in Jerusalem that night, Borges asked Macrae to help him get ready for bed, and as the latter was leaving Borges's suite, he heard a faint murmur behind him and, looking back, saw that it was Borges, who was humming to himself with tears rolling down his cheeks; the song was a tango, the kind of music Borges associated with rebellion, with virility, with passion.[28]

Borges and María were reunited once more in London and then traveled up with di Giovanni and his wife to Scotland to stay for a few days with Alastair Reid, the poet and translator, who was living at the time in an old house outside the university town of St. Andrews. Reid recalled Borges reciting Scottish Border ballads as they sat by the fire in that freezing early spring on the coast of Fife, and at one point he asked an odd favor—he wanted to be taken to the sea front so that he could spend some time on his own.[29] His host obliged by taking him down to the promenade at St. Andrews and leading him to a spot by the ruins of the cathedral, but as Reid walked off, he happened to glance over his shoulder and saw that Borges had somehow ended up facing inland, so he had to go back and gently point his blind friend in the direction of the sea.[30]

Why should Borges have wished to commune on his own with that stretch of water between Scotland and Norway? An answer may be found in the fact that he had published *The Congress*—his Dantean story of salvation through the love of a woman—on March 17, just two weeks before leaving Buenos Aires on his current journey abroad. And at its climax Alejandro Glencoe's Norwegian secretary, Nora Erfjord, is moved to recite the Scottish Border ballad of Sir Patrick Spens. In Sir Walter Scott's version, Patrick Spens crosses the water to Norway in order to bring back Margaret, the king of Norway's daughter, so that she may succeed to the throne of Scotland after the death of King Alexander III:

To Noroway, to Noroway,
To Noroway o'er the faem,
The King's daughter of Noroway
'Tis thou maun bring her hame.

But the knight's voyage ended in disaster when his ship was lost at sea, and this was analogous to that other disaster—the shipwreck of Borges's hopes of love after Norah Lange returned from Norway by sea at the beginning of 1929. Bearing in mind that only a week earlier he had been granted the love of María Kodama in Iceland, Borges's wish to commune with the North Sea at St. Andrews was not so strange, for he had, as it were, brought the king of Norway's daughter home at last—the broken promise of his youth had been fulfilled, and, like the characters at the climactic resolution of *The Congress,* he was ready to experience that Simurgh-like feeling of oneness with the world in a place that would otherwise have reminded him of his many long years of frustration and despair.

After this sojourn with María in Scotland, he traveled down to Oxford for the awarding of his honorary doctorate on April 29. Then he went to London, where he was due to give a series of four lectures at the Institute of Contemporary Arts, between May 3 and 13. The ICA lectures were a triumph: he spoke to a capacity audience on May 3, and for the second lecture three days later, the organizers had to move the event to Central Hall at Westminster to cope with the demand for seats. The Argentine press reveled in the extraordinary acclaim Borges was receiving in London—he had been given a standing ovation, it was reported, by "an audience of London hippies," "hairy, disheveled, wildly enthusiastic young people."[31]

Borges's work had reached a peak of popular acclaim by this time. The anthology of his stories and essays that Penguin brought out in Britain in 1970 under the title *Labyrinths* had achieved cult status. Borges's name, moreover, had already become associated with the New Wave in European cinema after several famous French directors—Jacques Rivette, Jean-Luc Godard, Alain Resnais—had cited his work in a number of films in the 1960s. But in 1970 this association of Borges with the movies had reached unexpected heights with the release of two films that were to become international box-office hits. *The Spider's Stratagem,* by the Italian director Bernardo Bertolucci, was a version of Borges's story "Theme of the Traitor and the Hero," and the film won critical acclaim at the Venice and New York film festivals of that year. Another film, *Performance,* directed by Nicolas Roeg and Donald Cammell and starring Mick Jagger of the Rolling Stones, was to turn Borges, rather improbably, into something of an icon for the cultural vanguard of "swinging London." The film paid homage to Borges in several ways—Mick Jagger is heard quoting from "Tlön, Uqbar, Orbis Tertius" and "The South," twice Borges's photograph appears on the jacket of his *Personal Anthology,* and at the very end, when Jagger is shot by the gangster played by James Fox, an image of Borges flashes on screen for a split second. *Performance,* moreover, owed its convoluted plot to some of Borges's most compelling themes, such as the labyrinth, the double, and the enigma of personal identity, albeit weirdly transposed to a world of sex, drugs, and rock and roll.* The film, it must be said, was not to everyone's taste: the critic of the *New York Times,* for one, attacked its "mindless pretension" and complained that "even that great writer, Jorge Luis Borges, is dragged into the cesspool."[32]

Beyond these relatively ephemeral associations, Borges had already gained recognition as an international literary figure of the first rank, and in the coming years he would be widely regarded as a leading candidate for the Nobel Prize for Literature. Still, there was a certain irony in the fact that he was receiving this trememdous acclaim largely for the stories collected in *Ficciones* and *The Aleph,* which played on the basic theme of "the nothingness of personality," because only a few weeks earlier he had undergone a sea change in his personal life, thanks to his momentous experience of mutual love in Iceland. After his return to Buenos Aires following these triumphs in the United States, Britain, and Israel, Borges would ponder the implications of Iceland, and his reflections would bear fruit in two stories, "Ulrica" and "The Night of the Gifts" ("La noche de los dones").

"Ulrica" was the story that had occurred to him in Iceland, the one he had told María Kodama he would dedicate to her.[33] The plot, as such, is negligible. An aging South American professor falls for a Norwegian girl called Ulrica, whom he meets on a visit to York, and she, unexpectedly, offers him a night of love, "a gift no longer hoped for" by an unmarried man of his years; this "miracle" reminds him of his youth and of "a girl from Texas, fair and slim like Ulrica, who had denied me her love."

The story, however, is sown with secret autobiographical allusions. The mysterious girl who affords access to the paradise of love at Thorgate is called Ulrica, and the only other girl of that name in Borges's fiction is Miss Ulrica Thrale, a character in "An Examination of the Works of Herbert Quain" (1941). She is the "haughty Amazon" who spurns the love of the writer Wilfred Quarles and becomes engaged to the Duke of Rutland in Herbert Quain's play *The Secret Mirror.* These details suffice to identify this Ulrica Thrale as an alter

---

*Some other well-known films by Nicolas Roeg, such as *Don't Look Now* (1973) and *The Man Who Fell to Earth* (1976), which starred another rock musician, David Bowie, also bore traces of Borges's ideas.

ego of Norah Lange, but it follows that the Ulrica of the new story cannot represent Norah, precisely because she does not deny her love to the Borges figure. Who, then, is the new Ulrica? According to María Kodama, Borges told her that Ulrica was meant to represent her, but if so, why is she Norwegian?[34]

In my judgment Borges made the girl Norwegian for the purposes of this story, so as to symbolize the fact that the experience of mutual love with María Kodama in Iceland had fulfilled and transcended the hopes denied him in his youth by Norah Lange. In other words, Borges meant to signify that he had found his "new Beatrice" in María Kodama, whom he envisaged as playing the saving role in his life that the Beatriz Frost character played in *The Congress.* Accordingly, he fashioned a female character in "Ulrica" who would be reminiscent of the two interrelated characters in *The Congress:* Beatriz Frost and Nora Erfjord. The red-haired Beatriz Frost came from the north of England, so he set "Ulrica" in York, and he made the eponymous girl Norwegian because Nora Erfjord, Glencoe's secretary, was Norwegian.

"Ulrica," after all, is a story about the unexpected fulfillment of the desires of Borges's youth, but it is also about being released from his enslavement to the memory of those desires. The girl tells the professor, "I will be yours in the inn at Thorgate." "Gate" is derived from an Anglo-Saxon word for "street," so Thorgate means "the street of Thor" or "the street of the Thunderer," which translates into Spanish as "calle Tronador," a reference, therefore, to the house of the five Lange sisters, whom the narrator also cryptically invokes in a passing reference to the windows in the cathedral at York known as "The Five Sisters." The house at calle Tronador was the "garden," the "heaven," which the young Borges had lost when Norah Lange left him for Girondo. The calle Tronador is secretly recalled in "Thorgate" in order to exorcise Borges's nostalgia for what it represented. Similarly, when the old professor makes love to Ulrica, he is said to have possessed the "image" of Ulrica for "the first" but also for the "last time." In other words, Borges would no longer be haunted by the "image" of Norah Lange; he would no longer be enthralled by the crystalline memory of the tall, arrogant woman in the chaste garden, that unchanging image of eternal rejection he had evoked in the poem he wrote not long before inviting María Kodama to Iceland. So the fact that in "Ulrica" the night of love takes place in "Thorgate" signifies the fulfillment of the Dantean pattern whereby a woman's love leads finally to the paradise Borges had sought in his youth.

The theme of transcending the past is embedded also in the name of the old professor, Javier Otárola, which recalls the protagonist of "The Dead Man"—Benjamín Otálora. "The Dead Man" was conceived by Borges after he had witnessed a murder in the Brazilian border town of Santa Anna do Livramento during his vacation in Uruguay in 1934, a few months after being finally rejected by Norah Lange.[35] Young Otálora was killed on the orders of the old bandit chieftain for daring to usurp his position, including sleeping with his red-haired mistress. So the name Otárola, like the girl Ulrica herself, is also reminiscent of a time in Borges's youth when he was denied love by Norah Lange. But the names of the two characters are not quite identical—the *l* and the *r* of Otálora, the "dead man," have been metathesized in Otárola, the old professor. The story "Ulrica," then, secretly evokes "The Dead Man" so as to indicate that the aspirations of the young Otálora have been "resurrected" and fulfilled in the love Ulrica offers his near namesake, Javier Otárola.

By way of an epigraph to "Ulrica," Borges used a quotation from the *Völsunga Saga* in the original Icelandic—*"Hann tekr sverthit Gram ok legger i methal theira bert"*—which translates as "He takes the sword Gram and lays it between them." The topos of the sword refers to the tragic love affair between Sigurd and Brynhild in the *Völsunga Saga*. The lovers are forced apart as a result of a magic draft administered to Sigurd by the queen Grimhild. Later in the narrative, however, Sigurd finds himself wooing Brynhild once more—but on behalf of his brother Gunnar. In a crucial scene, Sigurd, who is impersonating Gunnar, lies next to Brynhild but places his sword, Gram, between them. The sword thus represents a self-imposed obstacle to congress between the former lovers.

This motif is taken up by Ulrica and the professor as they make their way to Thorgate:

> "I shall call you Sigurd," she declared with a smile.
>
> "If I am Sigurd," I replied, "you shall be Brynhild."
>
> She slowed down.
>
> "Do you know the saga?" I asked.
>
> "Of course," she told me. "The tragic story the Germans spoiled with their later Nibelungs."
>
> I did not want to argue, and replied:
>
> "Brynhild, you are walking as if you wished there to be a sword between us in the bed."

The textual references to Sigurd and Brynhild have a very precise autobiographical import—like the magic draft given to Sigurd by the queen Grimhild, it was through the influence of his mother, Leonor Acevedo, that Borges's will had become so confused that he kept placing the sword of honor, as it were, between himself and other women. However, when the Norwegian girl makes love to the old professor at Thorgate, that impediment is overcome at last: "There was no sword between the two of us."

If "Ulrica" was about Borges's liberation from the sword, then "The Night of the Gifts" was about his liberation from the dagger. The story concerned the sexual initiation of a thirteen-year-old boy with a young prostitute known as "The Captive" ("La Cautiva"). The initiation comes about unexpectedly when the brothel is invaded by a group of drunken knife fighters. One of them, Juan Moreira, picks a fight with another man. The young boy takes fright at the impending violence and flees upstairs, and there he encounters "The Captive," who offers herself as a reward for his being a man of peace. Afterward she shows the boy a way out of the brothel, and as he makes good his escape, he happens to see Juan Moreira being bayoneted to death in the street by a policeman.

This, we are told, is a story about "first occasions that can't be forgotten," and it is inconceivable that Borges could have written on such a subject without having in mind his own unsatisfactory initiation with a prostitute in Geneva. It was this experience, more than any other, that had assigned sexual desire to the realm of the illicit, thereby creating a conflict between honor and desire, between the sword upheld by Mother and the dagger associated with Father. But "The Night of the Gifts" narrates a release from this conflict. The young prostitute's nickname, "The Captive," indicates that she is the prisoner of the male desire for illicit sex, so her voluntary initiation of the boy is an act of rebellion against a patriarchal system that has degraded the love of a man and a woman and consigned it to a brothel. Additionally, she offers herself to him as a reward for his "cowardice" in fleeing from the violence of the men who storm into the brothel.

The story may well have been rooted in the memory of that unexpected tenderness that Borges had confessed to feeling for Luz, the young prostitute at the brothel he used to frequent in Majorca.[36] His experience with Luz had given him the merest foretaste of love, for it had been stifled by the conflict between honor and desire that had bedeviled his relations with women. However, in "The Night of the Gifts," the young prostitute symbolically frees the boy from servitude to forbidden sexuality by literally showing him the way out of the brothel; she also breaks the connection between virility and transgression—as he leaves the brothel, the boy witnesses the killing of Juan Moreira by the police, and Moreira, of course, was the name of the legendary gaucho outlaw who had been revered by Evaristo Carriego as "San Juan Moreira," the patron saint, as it were, of the macho "cult of courage." The girl's offer of love, then, amounts to a radical subversion of the machismo that underpinned the "cult of courage" that had so fascinated Borges since childhood.

"The Night of the Gifts," furthermore, is associated with Borges's father. First, it arises in the context of a discussion between a group of men, which includes both Borges and his father; and second, the story is set in 1874, the year of Dr. Borges's birth. The unnamed protagonist's liberation from the brothel could, therefore, apply to Dr. Borges as much as to his son, an ambiguity that implies a recognition on Borges's part that his father's philandering, his interest in the dagger, and the "cult of courage" had been self-defeating attempts to rebel against the sword of honor.

"The Night of the Gifts" was published in *La Prensa* on December 19, 1971, eight months after the visit to Iceland.[37] Yet its companion "Ulrica" would not be published for another two and a half years. Borges was still too wary of publishing a story that was so patently autobiographical. Its subject matter, in any case, was too challenging for some of his friends, who thought it an "indecent story," as he would later confess to an interviewer, even though he himself believed "there was something pure to be found in that story."[38] But "Ulrica" and "The Night of the Gifts" are obviously complementary inasmuch as they explore the pychosexual underpinnings of sword and dagger, respectively. Just as in "Ulrica" Borges showed how the sword was a self-imposed obstacle to love, so, too, did he show in "The Night of the Gifts" how the dagger constituted a similar impediment in his relations with women. With the rejection of both sword and dagger, however, came a redemptive openness to the love of a woman. In "Ulrica" she is portrayed as a golden, Nordic goddess; in "The Night of the Gifts," she is a dark prostitute with half-Indian features, but the distinction between goddess (so pure that he feels unworthy of her) and whore (too shameless to be worthy of him) is erased by the girl who in each case freely offers herself to the man, a gift that is gratefully accepted and consummated in a spirit of wonderment and awe.

This motif of lovemaking as a liberating force, which is common to both stories, has its source in a third text—*The Congress,* and specifically in the episode in which Beatriz Frost and Alejandro Ferri make love in London. Both Ulrica and "The Captive" are, effectively, avatars of Beatriz Frost. All three texts, moreover, employ the same metaphor—a river flowing in the darkness—to allude to the saving experience of love. The lovemaking in "Ulrica" is described thus: "Old as the centuries, love flowed in the darkness." At the end of "The Night of the Gifts," the anonymous narrator observes that he had felt "dazed by the powerful flow of events," and it is Dr. Borges who interjects— "in the great river of that night." And when Beatriz Frost makes love with Ferri in *The Congress,* the narrator exclaims, "Oh nights, oh shared, warm darkness, oh the love that flows in the shadows like a secret river."

The metaphor of the river, moreover, has its origin in a fourth text—*El Caudillo,* the novel written by Borges's father in Majorca. At the climax of this novel, the river that flows through the Caudillo's land bursts its banks, isolating the lovers Marisela and Dubois in the latter's house. Marisela then urges Dubois to make love to her, and during the one night they spend together, they experience a mystical union with the spirit of the universe. When the flood subsides, however, the Caudillo disowns his daughter and has Dubois killed. The river of love that flowed in the darkness of that single night ended in the destruction of the lovers at the hands of a vengeful patriarch.

The intertextual connection between *El Caudillo* and the three stories by Borges adds a further dimension of meaning to the redemptive value Borges ascribed to his experience in Iceland. The love of María Kodama had exorcised the memory of Norah Lange, it had released Borges from the legacy of his initiation at Geneva, but it had also fulfilled vicariously the thwarted dream of passion represented in *El Caudillo*. It was no coincidence, therefore, that the exclamations that accompanied the lovemaking of Beatriz Frost and Alejandro Ferri in *The Congress*: "Oh nights, oh shared, warm darkness, oh the love that flows in the shadows like a secret river," should have echoed the joyous cries of Dr. Borges's poem "The Song of Songs," written in sunlit Majorca, where he and Leonor Acevedo recaptured their youthful ardor "in siestas swollen with passion," while their son, Georgie, dejected still by the encounter in Geneva, was writing "The Flame," a poem in which passion is described as "an ember of a fire that went out centuries ago."[39] But after Iceland, the river of love, Borges imagined, would sweep away such unhappiness, and the bewildering maze of loyalties to father, mother, and ancestors would yield at last to a sense of the mystic Rose, the Aleph, or the Simurgh—to that ineffable oneness that secretly sustained the great diversity of things in the world.

CHAPTER 28

Between Sunset and Dawn

(1971–1975)

BORGES HAD INTERPRETED his experience in Iceland in terms of the ideal pattern of meaning laid down in *The Congress*. As we have seen, this was the poetic design he had in mind when he composed "Ulrica" and "The Night of the Gifts" in the months between his return to Buenos Aires in May and the end of 1971. In this Dantean scheme, María Kodama had been assigned the role of the "new Beatrice" who would make up for Norah Lange's rejection and guide Borges from the hell of solipsism to the longed-for paradise where the rose of love would bring fulfillment and inspire a book that would ensure his immortality. Yet who, in fact, was this "new Beatrice"?

María Kodama was the daughter of a Japanese chemist, Yosaburo Kodama, and María Antonia Schweitzer, the Argentine-born daughter of a German father and a Spanish mother.[1] A boy and a girl were born of the marriage, but husband and wife separated three years after María's birth, and the children were raised by their mother and their Spanish grandmother. The family's circumstances were unusual in the socially conservative, Catholic Argentina of the time—separated parents and the fact that the absent father was a foreigner, and an Asian at that. Perhaps these circumstances contributed to María's having had few friends as a child, and in any case she was not allowed out of the house much. In María's recollection, the dominant influence in the home was that of her Spanish grandmother, whom she depicted as a quite formidable woman, an unbendingly devout Catholic who would have wanted to be a nun and for whom the Catholic faith was the only possible one. Her grandmother would take her to mass, make her say the rosary, and generally try to draw her into the world of intense Catholic piety.

On weekends, however, the girl was allowed to see her father, who would take her for walks and to visit museums. María found these outings a welcome respite from the enclosed, suffocating atmosphere of the family home, and, naturally enough, she was drawn to her father's Japanese heritage—he taught her the rudiments of his native tongue and told her stories about his country's turbulent history. She especially enjoyed the tales of the samurai and became fascinated by their code of honor and deeds of valor. Elements of the Japanese love of etiquette and of the values of the samurai survived in her father's approach to her: he treated her with a curious formality, always addressing her in Spanish as *usted*, rather than the familiar *tú*, and he instilled in her a sense of honor, stressing the importance of individual responsibility. As a Shintoist, he had an approach to life that was undogmatic—he would never actually forbid her to do anything but simply explained to her the likely consequences of her actions. If she wanted to climb a tree, for instance, he would spell out the dangers of doing so and then tell her that if she went ahead and hurt herself, it was no use her coming crying to him.

Japanese father and Spanish grandmother did not see eye to eye. When her grandmother talked to her about God, Heaven, and Hell, she would ask her father what all of that meant, and he would tell her that when she grew up, she would be free to find out about such things for herself and choose whether or not to believe. As a little girl, she had dreamed of becoming a sailor and setting off to seek adventure on the high seas, but Grandmother pronounced this impossible, because women were not meant to be sailors. María also became conscious of how her own mother's aspirations had been thwarted, for she had wanted to be a concert pianist but had been unable to fulfill that ambition. Instead she had allowed herself to be molded by the traditional expectations of Hispanic women—her mother would buy María dolls and tell her that when she grew up, she would have children of her own. Young María used to find such a prospect rather frightening and asked her father if one was obliged to get married, but he replied that no one could force her to do anything she did not want to do. He treated her no differently from a male child, and she responded to him accordingly; he used to tell her that she was a human being with the same obligations and rights as any other.

Divided between the traditional values of her Spanish grandmother and the ethical individualism of her Japanese father, she felt *descolocada*, "out of place" in relation to other people—she had few friends, never had a boyfriend, and spent her time in solitary pursuits such as swimming, horse riding, and reading. No doubt the fact that she was half Japanese was a barrier to her being fully accepted in the Argentina of that period, but thanks to her father's counterbalancing influence, her Japanese identity was a source of strength also: it enabled her to resist attempts to mold her, to pin her down to a set of values that she felt might not suit her, for she had grown up with a great wariness of being dominated by her grandmother, who kept threatening to absorb her into a world of fanatical Catholicism or to coerce her into accepting a very narrow definition of a woman's place in society.

María was to become an intensely private and self-sufficient person: having been a rather solitary child from an early age and spent a lot of her time reading, she felt enveloped in a special world of her own, a world that opened up a great number of possibilities but also closed off many others. And she was prepared to defend this inner world above all else, for it constituted the core of who she felt herself to be in the somewhat inhospitable environment in which she had been raised. Indeed, Borges was able to observe firsthand María's independence of character early on in his friendship with her. While she was still a student at the university, he asked her to accompany him on a trip outside Buenos Aires, but she declined the invitation because she was preparing to take an examination. He was irritated by her refusal and continued to press her, but María would not relent, because she felt that if she were to miss the exam, she might never get around to taking it again. They argued a good deal over this; Borges got very cross indeed but eventually came to understand her point of view.[2] It was this unyielding quality of María's that must have intrigued Borges, for, unlike so many other sycophantic young women who had exploited his fame to advance their literary careers, María was capable of standing up to him. Additionally, her quiet self-possession stood in salutary contrast to the tortuous equivocations Borges had experienced in his life on account of his contrary allegiances to Mother and Father. And her independence of spirit must have been all the more attractive because Borges knew by now that the essence of his predicament lay in his attempts to escape his mother's expectations by striving to live up to his father's: he had never successfully asserted his own will against theirs.

For her part, María had initially been drawn to Borges because she found in him a spirit that reminded her of her father's: she could share with him the aesthetic values and ethical principles that her father had upheld. However, as she got to know Borges's work, she became intrigued by the unhappiness implicit in his writing. One of her favorite poems was the second of the "Two English Poems," written in 1934, which ended with a plea to an unnamed woman: "I can give you my loneliness, my darkness, the hunger of my heart; I am trying to bribe you with uncertainty, with danger, with defeat." As she got to know him better, she was able to appreciate the reality of this emotional "hunger" concealed behind the mask of civility; Borges's character, she came to realize, was compounded of "passion and reserve," *"pasión y pudor,"*[3] and as she read to him during some of the bleakest periods of his unhappy marriage, she must have sensed the depths of inarticulate passion dammed up inside that blind, hopeless man. A tacit affection had grown up between them as a result, an affection that had to remain undeclared until such time as Borges decided to leave Elsa and di Giovanni provided the practical assistance to effect the separation.

· · ·

After his return to Buenos Aires in 1971, Borges resolved to learn Old Icelandic with María as a way of keeping alive the flame that had been ignited in Iceland. He acknowledged that at his age he could not hope to get very far with the language, but this hardly mattered, because, as he put it in a poem, his "quest" of that ancient tongue had been inspired by nothing less than "love, ignorant love, Iceland."[4]

Still, the love he had found in Iceland had to be translated to the realities of everyday life in Buenos Aires, and even as he was composing "Ulrica" and "The Night of the Gifts" in the latter part of 1971, he became troubled by the lack of opportunities to develop his relationship with María. Quite apart from the restrictions imposed by his blindness, he had gone back to live in the tiny apartment he shared with his mother and the housekeeper. Doña Leonor was ninety-five years old and, though frail, was still active and alert, so he could not be sure how she would react to his love affair with a woman as young as María Kodama. On top of these restrictions, there was the further impediment represented by Norman Thomas di Giovanni, who was keen to press on with the translations: E. P. Dutton was to bring out the English version of *Brodie's Report* that year, the *Selected Poems* for Delacorte Press was nearing completion and due to come out in 1972, the translation of *A Universal History of Infamy* was under way, and there was also the new book of poems, *In Praise of Darkness,* waiting to be put into English.

Borges, however, was becoming irritated by publishers' deadlines and the like and could no longer be bothered with translating. His mind was on other things: on September 19, 1971, he published a poem in *La Nación* in which he declared, "A woman is all that matters to you / one who is no different from the others, except that it is she."[5] In early 1972 he decided to part from di Giovanni. They would not see each other again for another ten years, and even though there would be a few brief meetings after that, their friendship would never be fully restored. Still, the American had been instrumental in making Borges known in the English-speaking world; he had also enabled the wholly impractical Borges to make some money from his writing, and, not least, he had helped to deliver Borges from his miserable marriage. Di Giovanni would henceforth work on his own on the translations contracted to E. P. Dutton.

At around the time of his break with di Giovanni, we find Borges preoccupied with the anxiety that he might squander love yet again—he felt that his life was in suspense, hanging in the balance between his unhappy past and an uncertain future. In a poem written on March 9, 1972, he described his "days and nights" as being "interwoven with memory and fear," fear being "a form of hope."[6] His life had ever been "a two-fronted Janus, looking at the sunset and the dawn," and though he had made a resolution to "celebrate" the immediate future, he could not banish "the unbearable memory of places in Buenos Aires / in which I have not been happy / and in which I shall never be able to be happy."

Ten days after writing this poem, he traveled to Michigan, accompanied by Mariana Grondona, an old family friend. He was to receive an honorary doctorate from Michigan State University, where his friend and translator Donald Yates was a professor of Spanish. In the United States, he wrote another poem elaborating on the idea of being suspended between the past and the future. In "The Gold of the Tigers" ("El oro de los tigres"), he reached back to his childhood memories of watching the tiger at the zoo in Palermo "until the hour of the yellow sunset" and then called up visions of other tigers and their coats of gold, and yet further images of gold—Zeus and his shower of "amorous metal," the gold ring in the Eddas that every ninth night engenders nine rings, and each of these rings nine rings more, multiplying themselves to infinity.[7]

These were not memories of real experiences—they were golden tigers of desire, long-held aspirations that had never come to fruition, that had eluded him in the way the tortoise had forever eluded Achilles. And yet Borges's cries of desire for what had remained beyond his reach were superseded in the end by an even keener burst of fresh desire:

> Oh sunsets, oh tigers, oh splendors
> of myth and epic,
> oh, for a gold more precious still, your hair,
> which these hands crave.

His desire for María Kodama was strong enough to overcome the burden of unhappy memories and lost illusions. But after he got back to Buenos Aires, he fell prey once more to regret for those missed opportunites in the past. On June 18, 1972, he published a sonnet called "What Has Been Lost" ("Lo perdido"), in which he asked, "Where can my life have gone, the one that could have been and never was . . . ?" and concluded by invoking "that companion who once waited for me, and may perhaps be waiting still."[8] That "perhaps" suggests an uncertainty, a doubt, about the survival of his love of María Kodama in such unpropitious circumstances.

It was a doubt that must surely have been aggravated by the news of the sudden death of Norah Lange. Although she had been in good health, Norah woke on the morning of August 6 with a severe headache and lost consciousness; an ambulance was summoned, but she died from a brain hemorrhage before reaching the hospital.[9] A few months later, his mother's health began to falter. Her sudden decline appears to have been the result of an accident in which a chickpea became lodged in her throat, causing her acute discomfort for quite some time until it was surgically removed.[10] Already ninety-six, she was laid low by the physical shock of this experience and lost her legendary zest for life: she stayed indoors and gradually grew thinner and weaker, until by 1973 she would spend most of her days in bed.

These two women—Norah Lange and Leonor Acevedo—personified the basic conflict that had destroyed the hopes of his youth. On June 3, 1973, he published in *La Nación* a poem called "I" ("Yo"), in which the attributes of selfhood are "the memory of a sword / and of a solitary, setting sun."[11] In the sword is figured his mother's obsession with her family's former glory, while the sunset had been a seminal image he had shared with Norah Lange in the days of *ultraísmo,* though it was characterized now as having been "dispersed in gold, in shadows, in nothing." Another allusion in the poem harks back to those unrealized passions of his youth: "I am the one who sees the prows from the port." The word "prow" must surely be taken as an allusion to his review *Proa,* and it is redolent of the revolutionary impulses of his early career as an avant-garde poet. But he had renounced the "adventure" of the avant-garde in favor of "order," and as a result he had not set sail upon the high seas of life but had stayed safely behind in port, only to find himself now as "the one who envies those who have already died," a man "stitching / words together in the room of a house." By 1973, then, Borges was poised between the sunset and the dawn, between memories of the past and the uncertainties of the future—and he was starting to doubt the capacity of even his "new Beatrice" to rescue him from an ever deepening sense of having wasted his life.

Borges's fears that his love for María might be crushed by the sheer weight of his unhappy past were exacerbated by developments on the political front. By the early months of 1973, it appeared likely that Juan Perón would find his way back to power in Argentina, for the Peronists had succeeded in making Argentina ungovernable since the overthrow of their leader nearly twenty years earlier. The Radical Frondizi had been succeeded in the presidency by another Radical, Arturo Illia, but neither had been able to survive without making secret deals with Perón. In 1966 a military coup had brought to power a junta led by General Juan Carlos Onganía, and it succeeded in suppressing the Peronists until May 1969, when an extraordinary uprising took place in the industrial city of Córdoba, led by students and car workers protesting against cuts in government spending. Onganía's authority swiftly crumbled after this episode— the Peronist trade unions revived their agitation, and the junta found itself continually assailed by strikes and riots.

A legacy of the Córdoba riots of 1969 was the belief among radical students that the capitalist state could be overthrown by direct revolutionary violence. Young Peronist revolutionaries formed a guerrilla army with the aim of launching a war of "national liberation" against the "oligarchy" of ranchers and multinational companies that ran Argentina's export economy. Calling themselves "Montoneros," after the irregular gaucho forces who fought the liberals of Buenos Aires in the nineteenth century, the guerrillas initiated their armed struggle against the state in 1970, and they also began to compete with the old-guard Peronist bosses for control of the trade unions. In March 1970 the Montoneros kidnapped one of the architects of Perón's downfall, General Pedro Aramburu, the leader of the Revolución Libertadora of 1955. Their aim was to discover the whereabouts of Evita's body, which had been secreted away by the military in 1955. Since Aramburu was unable to provide this information, he was killed in cold blood. His remains, it was announced, would not be returned to the family until Evita's whereabouts were made known to the people.

Aramburu's murder threw the military high command into disarray, and there followed a period of infighting that resulted a year later in a takeover by General Alejandro Lanusse, who sought a compromise with Perón that would allow the armed forces to bow out of politics without losing face. As rumors circulated about secret negotiations between the junta and the Peronists, Borges felt compelled to warn his compatriots against taking what he regarded as the disastrous course of inviting Perón back from exile. Shortly after his return from London in May 1971, he became associated with a committee, the Comisión Promotora de Concentración Cívica en pro de la República, whose aim was to rally citizens "in support of the Republic," and, banking on the immense prestige he enjoyed in Argentina, he issued a personal statement to the news media denouncing Perón for having betrayed his responsibilities as a leader:

> Given that he was virtually omnipotent, he could have instigated a revolt of the masses by revealing to them through his own example a new set of ideals; but all he did was to imitate in a crass and grotesque manner the least admirable traits of the enlightened oligarchy he was pretending to attack.[12]

He called Perón's regime "our vernacular imitation of fascism" and asserted that Perón had corrupted the people's soul by dint of theft, euphemistically called "business deals," by the torture of opponents, by the confiscation of property, by filling the jails with political prisoners, by indiscriminate censorship, by the burning of archives and churches, by the execution of workers, and by the abolition of liberty. And he expressed his disgust at the general disinclination to resist the dictator: "So many dreadful smiling portraits and not a single caricature; so many self-interested panegyrics and not a single satire!"

Borges chose to publish this statement, called "Legend and Reality" ("Leyenda y Realidad"), on May 25, 1971, the National Day of Argentina, but his warning went unheeded. A few months later, the Montoneros pulled off a sensational coup when they traced the remains of Eva Perón to a cemetery in Milan, where she had been interred under a false identity. In September the body was taken to Perón's home in Madrid, where it was kept as a sacred relic of the movement in the attic of his villa. Reports that Evita's body had been disfigured by the military inflamed her followers, but Borges and his associates were undeterred by the rising political tension in Argentina, and in December 1971 a ceremony was organized by the Agrupación Democrática Argentina at the grave of General Aramburu to honor his memory and reaffirm the principles of the anti-Peronist Revolución Libertadora. Borges was one of several public figures who addressed the gathering, and he explained to journalists that he had done so "in order to render just homage" to Aramburu.[13] He declared that the history of Argentina had been "characterized by atrocities and heroic actions," and he reiterated his earlier condemnation of the abuses perpetrated by the Peronist regime.

Nevertheless, General Lanusse, the leader of the military junta, persevered in his secret negotiations with the Peronist leadership and eventually struck a face-saving deal that permitted Peronist candidates, though not Perón himself, to stand at elections to be held in March 1973. The train of events that would lead to Perón's return had been set in motion—Hector Cámpora, a stalking horse for Perón, won the presidency in March and promptly changed the law to allow Perón himself to stand at a future election.

Borges remained unyielding in his opposition to the Peronists. When Cámpora won the election in March, Borges told an Italian newspaper that the people who had voted for him were "six million idiots": he would go into exile if he could, but this was impossible: "My mother is ninety-six years old and gravely ill. . . . And, in any case, what would a blind man of seventy-four do in London or Paris?"[14] He was convinced that the Peronists would be out for revenge against known enemies like him, but the truth was that his international fame made him politically untouchable. Even Perón was wary of criticizing him in public: when asked by a journalist about his attitude toward Borges, Perón replied, "If we put up with him for ten years when we were in government, there is all the more reason to do so now that he is an old man."[15] And when it became known around June 1973 that Borges was thinking of resigning as director of the National Library, Peronist officials, concerned about the negative publicity that would inevitably result, gave him assurances that he could remain in the post without interference.[16] But Borges felt that his position as director, which he owed after all to the Revolución Libertadora, would become untenable if Perón were to return to Argentina, as expected, so he remained determined to quit and would resign in due course, with effect from October 1973.

Cámpora's victory, as it turned out, served to widen rather than heal the divisions within the Peronist movement itself. Following the election, left-wing Peronists took to occupying public buildings, as if preparing for a frontal assault on the bourgeois state. Perón, however, was not in the business of installing the dictatorship of the proletariat. His stooge, Cámpora, concluded a "social pact" between employers and labor unions in an attempt to stabilize the economy. The urban guerrillas would have none of it, though, and persisted with their campaign of bombings and assassinations. Perón decided to return to Argentina before things got out of hand; Cámpora resigned, and elections were called for September 1973, which Perón won with 62 percent of the popular vote. Once back in office, he pursued a set of surprisingly moderate, social democratic policies. He maintained the social pact and succeeded in bringing down inflation and increasing the real value of wages. Once he had consolidated his hold on power, he began to tackle the guerrilla problem, repudiating the Montoneros and passing harsh laws against subversion. He also turned a blind eye to the activities of a sinister organization calling itself the Argentine Anti-Communist Alliance—known as the "Triple A"—that commenced operations against the revolutionary left at the beginning of 1974, abducting and killing known militants.

Borges, nevertheless, continued to denounce Perón, and his influence was not inconsiderable. On December 10, 1973, *Newsweek* carried an interview with him that touched upon the political situation in his country; he was quite free in his criticism of Perón, calling him a "second-rater." That edition of *Newsweek* was banned in Argentina. And yet the truth was that Borges was stuck in a time warp: he entertained fantasies about having it out man-to-man with the "tyrant" and even composed a story, "Avelino Arredondo," about the eponymous youth who in 1897 assassinated the president of Uruguay in cold blood.[17] But having indulged in similar fantasies such as "The South," "The Challenge," and "The Dagger," he must have known how ineffectual these were other than as a means of airing his frustration at the perversity of politics.

Perón would not last more than nine months in power. He was an ailing seventy-eight-year old, and on July 1, 1974, he died in office. As set out in the constitution, he was succeeded by the vice president, who was none other than his third wife, María Estela, known as "Isabelita," a former nightclub dancer whom he had met in Panama, and a woman of no political experience whatsoever. The political situation soon spun out of Isabelita's control: the social pact collapsed, and no further stabilizing measures could be made to prevail against the huge strikes organized by the labor unions against their own Peronist government. Seeking to exploit the vacuum at the heart of government, the guerrillas redoubled their efforts to produce a revolutionary crisis that would bring down the capitalist system.

After the death of Perón, Borges, too, lost his bearings. As long as Perón was president, he knew whom to blame for the deteriorating situation, but with Perón now gone, it became far more difficult to figure out what was going on in the country. Borges simply could not understand what the Montoneros were trying to achieve. Their claim to be the heirs of the "barbarous" gauchos in their wars against the oligarchy seemed to him to reverse, if not defeat, the whole purpose of Argentina's history as a postcolonial nation. As he told a journalist,

> I believe that to belong to a country means above all to make an act of faith: one must "feel" part of that country. When in 1816 the decision was taken to stop being Spaniards in order to become Argentines, the word "Argentine" meant nothing at all, but I don't think that Laprida and the other members of the Congress of Tucumán wished to become gauchos or Indians; such a vision would have horrified them.[18]

The Montoneros, in other words, were breaking faith with the founding fathers, threatening the consensus that had led to the birth of the nation itself.

So confused was Borges by the turn of events, however, that he no longer held to any particular view of the *patria*—for all he knew, the Montoneros' vision of Argentina's future might be as valid as any other. In a sonnet addressed to a friend, the writer Manuel Mujica Láinez, which was written sometime in 1974, he observed that just as Scripture may have as many meanings as it has readers, so, too, are there many possible versions of the *patria*.[19] His own version of the *patria* was merely a "nostalgia" for "ignorant knives and antique courage," a nostalgia that made him regret the passing of the Argentina he had once known. The sonnet closed with the rueful lines "Manuel Mujica Láinez, there was a time when we possessed / a *patria*—do you remember?—and the two of us have lost it."

Borges had come to the view that the true cause of the country's problems lay not in a particular ideology or political vision but in a general loss of values. He believed that it was necessary for an individual to act according to his conscience, for a man "knows by virtue of an ethical instinct when he must do good"; this "ethical instinct" was the only remedy against the malaise afflicting Argentina:[20]

Our country is going through a moral crisis. We have taken to worshipping luxury, money and other myths and dogmas. I think ours is a venal country. I don't have any recipe for salvation, any panacea. All I can do is try to carry out my duties honestly from one day to the next. All I can recommend is sincerity, honesty.[21]

This insistence on the need for an "ethical instinct," however, implied a continuing mistrust of the will of the people. Despite his acceptance of several possible versions of the *patria,* he remained caught in the contradiction into which he had been led by Perón—he had always wanted to see the creation of a genuine democratic order in Argentina, but he still doubted whether the people were ready for democracy. Perón's second coming only confirmed his doubts of 1955, and he still clung, albeit reluctantly, to an elitist view of the political situation: "I used to be a liberal," he told an interviewer, "but no longer. I think I would support an enlightened dictatorship, so long as it were not demagogic."[22] Yet if he believed in ethics as a solution to the nation's troubles, who would provide the moral example? An ethical elite seemed to be the only answer, ruling through an "enlightened dictatorship" that would keep in check the base instincts of the people.

In November 1974 the government of Isabelita Perón declared a state of emergency, which gave the army a virtually free hand to go on the offensive against the guerrillas. The military repression was aided by the operations of the death squads of the Triple A, which were said to be controlled by José López Rega, minister of social welfare and the real power behind the throne. Meanwhile, Isabelita made pathetic attempts to bolster her popularity by associating herself with Eva Perón: she took to dressing her hair in a chignon like her predecessor and even authorized the repatriation of Evita's remains, which she installed in the presidential residence at Olivos. But it was all to no avail, for there was nothing that could be done to mend the stricken economy in the teeth of a ferocious guerrilla insurgency. Indeed, an extraordinary situation had come about in which the two extreme wings of the Peronist movement had turned on each other, threatening to bring down the entire country with them.

Toward the end of 1974, Borges's distress at seeing the *patria* spiraling into an abyss was compounded by personal woes. His mother was by now largely bedridden—this most sociable of women had lost interest in seeing people, and her mind, once so sharp, was becoming increasingy erratic. Borges, whose room was only a few feet away, could not avoid being reminded constantly of her sufferings. And then, in November, the family was struck by a tragedy that affected him deeply—his great-niece Angélica, the four-year-old daughter of Luis de Torre, was accidentally drowned in a swimming pool. Lamenting in a poem the cruel extinction of this little girl, he wondered how many lives must have vanished "in this poor, diminutive death"—"an entire future" had been extinguished "with this flower," while "over us—atrociously—looms the shadow of History."[23]

The death of Angélica epitomized the fears that had plagued him since his return from Europe three years earlier, fears that the past, the "shadow of History," might engulf his hopes for the future and kill off the seeds of new life that had been sown in Iceland. Yet it was perhaps also the shock of Angélica's death that strengthened his determination not to allow the forces of darkness to prevail. At the time of the tragic accident, he was preparing a new collection of stories—to be called *The Book of Sand* (*El libro de arena*)—for publication the following year. Emecé had asked him for eight new stories, but he had delivered eleven. In December 1974 he added a twelfth—"Ulrica," the story that had been inspired by his experience in Iceland.

On December 13, Borges undertook a final revision of "Ulrica" before delivering it to his publishers. A journalist, Carlos Burone, gave an eyewitness account of that session.[24] He accompanied Borges, his editor Carlos Frías, and a secretary, to an eighth-floor apartment on the calle Juncal. Since it was a balmy summer night, the windows were thrown wide open, Borges took off his jacket, sat in an armchair, and brought out a manuscript written in a tiny female hand. Frías proceeded to read out passages for the secretary to type, and as he did so, Burone observed with astonishment that Borges would analyze every sentence word for word, "because all of them, absolutely all of them, together with full stops, commas, capital letters, dashes, the spelling of foreign words and everything else one could imagine, were recorded in Borges's memory as in the negative of a photograph." While revising the text, Borges "would move his head and smile, as if he were spying on his two characters. He was like a little boy playing on his own with his toys or fascinated by the illustrations in some old book." As he observed Borges at work, Burone "felt happy to see him so happy."

The journalist was able to appreciate that "Ulrica" was an exception to the rule in Borges's fiction, and his excitement is evident in the opening line of his report for *La Opinión:* "In a book to be published in April 1975, Borges deals for the first time with the fires of passion" (*"En un libro que publicará en abril de 1975, Borges se ocupa por primera vez de los ardores de la pasión"*). Borges himself was to confirm Burone's impression in his epilogue to *The Book of Sand,* which he wrote on February 3, 1975: "The theme of love is quite common in my poems; not so in my fiction, of which there is no other example than 'Ulrica.'"[25] His decision to publish "Ulrica," the most directly autobiographical, if not confessional, of all his stories, testified to his belief in the possibility of redeeming the tribulations of the past through the power of love.

The Book of Sand was published in March 1975; later that year Borges would bring out a new volume of poetry comprising the poems he had written since 1972. These poems captured the vicissitudes he had endured since his return from Iceland—joys and desires, but also anxiety, sadness, even despair. He called it *La rosa profunda* (*The Profound Rose*), and he gave the last poem of the collection an English title, "The Unending Rose," which echoed the title of the book itself.[26] Here Borges cast himself as the Persian mystic, Attar of Nishapur, author of *The Conference of the Birds,* the source of the legend of the Simurgh. The poet Attar is blind, but he is conscious of the presence of a rose, "the unceasing high tide" of whose fragrance rises toward his aged face. The rose, Attar believes, will endure beyond adversity:

> Each thing
> is an infinity of things. You are music,
> firmaments, palaces, rivers, angels:
> profound rose, limitless yet intimate,
> which the Lord shall reveal to my dead eyes.

CHAPTER 29

A New Dawn in Iceland

(1975–1976)

BY 1975 IT WAS CLEAR that Doña Leonor had not long to live. Virtually bedridden for the best part of two years, she had gradually faded into an emaciated little ghost of a woman and, on July 8, she died at the age of ninety-nine. The next day she was laid to rest with her ancestors in the family mausoleum at the Recoleta Cemetery. Borges was accompanied at the funeral by family and close friends, but even this most private moment did not remain untouched by his extraordinary fame, and the following morning the front pages of the Buenos Aires press displayed photographs of Borges fighting back his tears.

The tie that bound mother and son was preternaturally strong—except for the brief interval of his marriage, this was the woman with whom he had lived his life. A few days after Doña Leonor's death, he wrote a sonnet called "Remorse" ("El remordimiento"), which opened with a self-punishing declaration: "I have committed the worst sin a man can commit. I have not been happy."[1] He asked to be "dragged away by the glaciers of oblivion" and "ruthlessly destroyed." His parents had engendered him "for the risky and beautiful game of life," but their "youthful will" had not been done: he had not been happy. Instead he had applied himself to "the symmetrical challenges of art, which weaves mere nothingness," and he was haunted still by "the specter of having been a hapless wretch."

The poem sprang from a grieving consciousness of the passion that had brought him into being. Leonor and Jorge had fallen in love at first sight and married within the year, but, as may be inferred from Jorge's novel, this early passion had fallen under the shadow of the patriarch, the fantasy of the perfect dead hero, who filled his descendants with a sense of unworthiness. Leonor had tried to live up to this impossible ideal by striving to be an impeccable criolla; Jorge reverted to being the disaffected anarchist, who never felt reconciled to Argentina. Even so, that early bond would be proof against later adversities. Leonor had uprooted herself from Buenos Aires to accompany Jorge to Europe, where he had hoped to recover their first happiness together;

she had nursed him in his physical decline and had remained devoted to his memory in the long years of widowhood, continually invoking him in conversation with her friends. This unbending will had been her glory—a magnificent testimony to her passionate nature, which was what had first drawn Jorge to her; but her indomitable character had also bred an unshakable loyalty to the memory of the family's heroic ancestors.

Still, in her last years, Leonor Acevedo appears to have seen this cult of the ancestors under a different aspect. She once told Bioy Casares that she had spent her life with "two madmen"—"*dos locos*"—her husband and her son, and that she sometimes wondered "whether those two *locos* might not have been right all along."[2] Perhaps she had come to appreciate the possibility that, like the unnamed protagonist of her son's story "The Old Lady," she had herself been a victim of the sword of honor, and that it had been the sword, as it were, that had lain between her and Jorge. Indeed, in old age she would tell friends that she had "fallen in love all over again," having come across a box containing the very beautiful letters Jorge had written to her in their youth.[3] And as her life drew to a close, it would appear also that she perceived what it was her son required of her. On one occasion, when Borges asked María Kodama to read to his bedridden mother, Doña Leonor took Georgie's hand and then reached out for María's, and since by that stage she lacked the strength to speak, she could do no more than bring their hands together over her ailing body.[4]

In the aftermath of Doña Leonor's death, Borges wrote a poem called "The Iron Coin" ("La moneda de hierro"), in which he laid bare the root cause of that sense of unworthiness that had plagued him throughout his life.[5] The poem revolves around the question "Why does a man need a woman to love him?" and he examines the two aspects of the question as displayed on each side of the "iron coin." One face depicts an ordered cosmos—"Adam, the youthful father, and the youthful Paradise. Evening and dawn. God in each creature"; the reverse shows the void—"no one and nothing and shadows and blindness," and "that is what you are." The two sides of the iron coin symbolized the extreme polarization that had characterized his attitude to a woman's love. His fate had appeared to turn on a judgment of his worth—to be accepted by the beloved was to enter paradise, to be found wanting was to be cast into the void. And yet, as he now realized, the ultimate cause of his sense of unworthiness was his fear of being subjected to another's judgment—the judgment of his ancestors, his mother, his father, the judgment of the women with whom he fell in love. To place himself before each or any of these imagined judges was in some way to "echo" the Last Judgment of God Himself. And yet, Borges now asked himself in "The Iron Coin," what if God simply forgot to judge? Why should a woman not love him, "soiled by infamy" though he might be?

Love did not require one to judge or be judged, for the beloved need be no better or worse than oneself: "In the shadow of the other we seek our own shadow; / in the mirror of the other, our reciprocal mirror."

Having finally quashed the verdict of the imaginary judge who had condemned him as unworthy of another's love, he was free to embark on "the risky and beautiful game of life," free to love, free to redeem the passion that had gone into his making, for in María Kodama he had found a "new Beatrice" whose love might not only justify his own existence but also vindicate the dream of passion that had been crushed in *El Caudillo*. And so, after his mother's death, his thoughts turned to his father, and he went back to the clumsy poem he had written immediately after his father's death and transformed that raw cry of grief into a limpid sonnet. His father had expected "to see nothing on the other side" of death, but his "shadow" may well have "made out" "the ultimate archetypes dreamed by the Greek," for "no one knows to what dawn the marble holds the key."[6] Despite the sadness of his mother's passing, therefore, he could see the glimmer of a new dawn, a dawn that would enable him to play Dante to his father's Virgil and shape his life into the saving pattern envisaged in *The Congress*.

In September 1975, Borges received a visit from his American friend Donald Yates, who had come to Buenos Aires to persuade him to attend a symposium on his work that the English department at Michigan State University had organized for the first week of October. It was short notice, but Borges accepted the invitation, even though he already had a number of speaking engagements in Buenos Aires at that time. As ever, he required a companion, so he invited María to accompany him to Michigan, but he suggested that they should first get married in order to avoid causing scandal when they traveled together: he was something of "a Victorian gentleman," he told her, and being married to the woman he loved was of great importance to him.[7]

Borges's proposal put María in a difficult position, since she had resolved never to marry. Her parents' separation when she was only three years old had been extremely traumatic for her; her difficult relationship with her grandmother, moreover, had inspired a horror in her of being taken over by someone else. What she prized above all else was her autonomy, and it was vital to her that she preserve this by remaining financially self-sufficient, having earned her living from a very early age by teaching Spanish to Japanese businessmen in Buenos Aires.[8] Marriage would clearly put this independence in jeopardy. If, as a girl, she had feared being co-opted by her grandmother into a rigid Catholicism, there was all the more reason to fear being absorbed, if not devoured, by Borges's monstrous fame.

Still, the fact remained that she was in love with Borges. She had found herself drawn over the years to the "hunger of his heart" and had gradually come to know the private man behind the mask of fame. Marriage, in any case, was likely to compromise that intimate bond by exposing it to the public gaze. Indeed, María had seen firsthand how Borges's marriage to Elsa Astete had been undermined by the patrician ladies in Doña Leonor's circle and by the insatiable curiosity of the Argentine media. Like Elsa, she was a social outsider, but additionally she was half Japanese and decades younger than Borges. María therefore reminded Borges that years ago she had told him about her decision never to marry; it was sufficient in her view that they pledge their love for each other; love, as she understood it, must be founded on unconditional trust, on absolute respect for the other's freedom.[9]

Borges understood only too well how human relations can be deformed by coercive expectations, so he consented to María's principle of free mutuality as the basis of their relationship. He indicated his acceptance of this special bond in a prose poem in which he cited the passage in Book 23 of the *Odyssey*, where Penelope refrains from acknowledging Ulysses as her husband until she has tested him by referring to a secret they shared, the secret of "their common marriage bed, which no other mortal could shift because the olive-wood it was made from bound it to the earth."[10] The fable of the marriage bed, Borges wrote, was a kind of "metaphor or myth," for Penelope knew that the stranger was truly her husband "when she recognized herself in his eyes, when she felt in her love that she was being met by the love of Ulysses." As a token of their mutual bond, Borges made María a gift of a turquoise necklace that he had been given by a native American on one of his previous visits to the United States.[11]

About a year later, Borges would write "Endymion on Latmos" (Endimión en Latmos"), a poem that described a night of bliss.[12] Portraying himself as the eponymous shepherd boy of the myth, he imagined that his body, "which the years have spent, was beautiful":

> Diana, the goddess, who is also the moon,
> found me sleeping on the mountain
> and slowly lowered into my arms
> gold and love in the flaming night.
> I pressed my mortal eyelids shut,
> not wishing to see the lovely face
> profaned by these lips of dust.
> I breathed in the fragrance of the moon,
> and heard her infinite voice utter my name.
> Oh, the pure cheeks meeting each other,
> oh, rivers of love and of the night,
> oh, the human kiss and the tension of the bow.

The "rivers of love and of the night" connect this poem with "Ulrica" and "The Night of the Gifts," but its paradigm, as we have seen, was the Beatriz Frost episode in *The Congress*. As had occurred after his visit to Iceland with María, Borges was once again interpreting his life according to the Dantean pattern of salvation laid down in *The Congress*—María would free him from the trammels of the past; passion would lead to the blossoming of the self, and this realized self would attain at last to the longed-for integration in the universal spirit as figured in the legend of the Simurgh.

At East Lansing, the town where the Michigan State campus was located, Borges and María were put up in Donald Yates's house. María was given a bedroom upstairs, Borges a book-lined room in the basement, but the following morning Borges asked Yates if he might find him alternative accommodation, because he had suffered a disturbing nightmare that first night and felt there was "something terrifying about the basement with all those books."[13] Yates found him a hotel close to the campus and left him in the company of María for the duration of their stay.

Borges's new happiness in this period shows through in a number of poems. In "The Ingénu" ("El ingenuo"), he expressed surprise that "the rose should smell like the rose," and in another poem he professed himself incapable of finding the words to convey the passion aroused in him by the music of Brahms.[14] Secure in the love of María, he overcame his fear of time, and even death appeared to have lost its sting. "The last drop of time," he wrote, would consist "not of water, but of honey," and even though this golden drop might "sink into the dark," it would contain "the blessings" that "Someone or Something" had once bestowed upon Adam—"mutual love and your fragance, the act of understanding the universe."[15]

This exultant mood would continue well into the New Year, for such was the success of the symposium that Borges was invited to return to Michigan State in January 1976 for a semester as visiting professor. During this second visit to East Lansing, Borges and María were accommodated in a two-bedroom apartment on campus, so he was able to spend an extended period living in relative privacy with the woman he loved. Even so, he had a busy schedule: he was required by the university to teach two courses and to deliver five public lectures in the course of the semester, and when it became generally known that he was in the United States for several months, he was showered with invitations to speak at other institutions. Yates himself would accompany Borges and María to colleges in Michigan, Ohio, Indiana, Iowa, and California. There were visits also to Emory University in Atlanta and to the University of Texas. He was invited to New York to receive an Edgar Award from the Mystery Writers' Guild and was asked by the director of the Folger

Library in Washington, D.C., to give the keynote address at the annual Shake-speare conference in April. Donald Yates recalled that, despite these numerous engagements, Borges seemed tireless and "open to everything."[16]

Happy as he was living with María in East Lansing, he could not help but reflect from time to time on the condition of Argentina. The news from home could scarcely have been more discouraging: there were reports of kidnap-pings, killings, and bombings by the guerrillas and the Triple A; the economy was in dire straits, with inflation topping 100 percent; several massive strikes virtually paralyzed the country in February and March. Borges was moved to write another "Elegy for the *Patria*" ("Elegía de la patria"), in which he praised the valor of the great men who had forged the nation, but lamented their de-scendants with their "parliaments, centenaries and sesquicentenaries," which were "merely the ashes, the afterglow" of that "ancient flame."[17] On March 24, however, the government of Isabelita Perón was overthrown by the armed forces. Borges was in California at the time, and someone broke the news of the coup d'état while he was attending a cocktail party. Donald Yates, who was present at this party, remembered that Borges could not disguise his joy—there were tears in his eyes as he threw his arms around an Argentine col-league.[18] The fall of Isabelita Perón, after all, held the promise of a final defeat of Peronism.

Borges's relief at the turn of events in Argentina ran in parallel with his joy at having found love with María Kodama: everything was falling into place at last—he was free of the conflict of sword and dagger, he had paid the debt of happiness he owed his parents, and his long alienation from the political real-ities of his native land showed signs of drawing to an end. It must have seemed to him that the Dantean pattern of salvation was closer to being realized in his own life than ever before. The extent of Borges's euphoria at this juncture is evident in his decision to spend a fortnight with María in Iceland before re-turning to Buenos Aires. Donald Yates, who saw them off at the airport, had the impression that they had "dreamt up" this visit to Iceland "at the last minute," and he surmised that they must have had "some common bond in the sagas and in the study of the Icelandic language together."[19] Certainly Borges's sojourn in the United States had renewed his bond with María, and he once more looked to Iceland as a symbol of new beginnings. The dawn in Iceland, he would write in a poem, was somehow eternal: it was like "a great hanging wall," and "time does not touch it."[20]

So he went back to Iceland, seeking a brief interval of private bliss with María after the pressures of his recent speaking engagements in the United States and before the further pressures he would doubtless face when he re-turned to his troubled country. But he was too famous to escape recognition, even in Iceland. While dining at a restaurant in Reykjavik he was approached by a group of very tall men, one of whom fell to his knees and, rather alarmingly, started covering Borge's hand with kisses.[21] Borges had been spotted at the restaurant by a local poet, who had promptly summoned several of his friends to come and pay their respects to the Argentine master. Afterward Borges and María were taken on a round of the houses of the Icelandic poets. Huge quantities of aquavit were consumed that night, but Borges himself was careful to stick to mineral water as he listened in rapture to those boisterous Norsemen reciting from the sagas into the early hours of the morning.

Borges kept quizzing his hosts as to the grammar and pronunciation of Old Icelandic and about the customs of the island. He was curious to know whether the old pagan culture of the sagas had survived into modern times. The Icelandic poets assured him that it had, but several days later, while visiting a Lutheran church, he learned from the pastor that there was in fact only one pagan priest to be found on the island. The latter turned out to be a tall man in his fifties, with bright blue eyes and a long white beard, who lived on his own out in the country in a house full of black cats and shelves displaying assorted animal bones. He claimed that there was a revival of interest in the old religion, and a great many people came to him to be married. When Borges inquired whether he and María might be wed according to the ancient rite of the god Odin, the priest was only too pleased to oblige.

However tenuous its actual connection with pagan culture, contemporary Iceland seemed to be vitally informed by the spirit of the past. And it was this capacity to defy time that Borges took as inspirational and exemplary. In his poem "Iceland" ("Islandia"), he celebrated the island, declaring that it was "a boon for all men" that it should exist.[22] Iceland was an "icy rose" that had salvaged the "buried mythology" of the Germanic races. He compared its tranquil present to the heroic past—the strong men who today are "sailors, boatmen and pastors" once "discovered a continent." And he concluded with the enigmatic assertion that Iceland possessed a "great concave memory" that was not "merely nostalgia," by which he may have meant that Iceland resounded with the echoes of history but was not in thrall to the memories of the past. His idyll with María on this remote island created an impression of timelessness, as if past, present, and future had been subsumed in an eternal moment of "unsated hope."

When he returned to Buenos Aires in late April, there was a certain aggressive triumphalism in his declarations of support for the military junta. He accepted an invitation to lunch with its leader, General Jorge Videla, and thanked the general "for what he had done for the *patria*, having saved it from chaos, from the abject state we were in, and, above all, from idiocy."[23] He had no qualms whatever about identifying himself with the military enemies of the Peronists, for in statements to the media he would compare the situation to the Revolución Libertadora of 1955, when he had been a hard-line advocate of "democratic regeneration," that is to say, the total suppression of Peronism and the gradual application of appropriate "revolutionary therapy" to restore Argentina to political health.

It was not long, however, before Borges's euphoria began to be dissipated by the realities of everyday life. He knew that if the truth about his relationship with María Kodama were to become known, it would cause resentment, if not scandal, so he maintained the fiction that she was just another friend among friends, or his "literary secretary" at best. As had occurred after his return from Iceland in 1971, he found considerable difficulties in conducting his relationship with María. To begin with, he chose to hide its true nature from his immediate family—his sister, Norah, and her two sons. Owing to his blindness, he depended on his nephew Luis de Torre, a lawyer, to manage his finances. Luis was responsible for his royalties, fee income, pensions, and bank accounts. He had to contend also with his redoubtable housekeeper, Fani Úveda, who occupied the maid's room off the kitchen, as well as with her daughter, Stella Maris, and her grandson, José Manuel. After the death of Doña Leonor, Fani ran his domestic affairs, and he developed a system of interleaving banknotes of various denominations in certain of his books at home for Fani to pay the bills. According to Stella Maris, the housekeeper and her family made their presence felt in Borges's day-to-day life: "Señor Borges was always very kind to us. When I was at school he would help me with my homework, and with my lessons. He did the same with José Manuel. . . . He would let us share his things, but only up to a point."[24]

Beyond this domestic circle, there was his circle of friends. The Bioys still invited him to dinner several times a week, and there were upper-class lady friends he had inherited from his deceased mother. Then there was an outer circle formed by innumerable associates and acquaintances, ranging from journalists and academics to younger writers who were avid for his company. Beyond that there was another circle still, for he seemed to possess a magic aura that drew total strangers to him—he was regularly stopped in the street by admirers who wanted to shake his hand or ask for his autograph. And finally there was the Argentine media, with its seemingly insatiable desire to record his every word and movement.

Enclosed as he was within these circles, Borges was forced to lead a divided life. Outwardly he lived up to his image as the venerable, sightless bard, the impractical yet delightfully perverse "Borges," an image that had been fashioned for him several years earlier, at least in the English-speaking world, but he found this public role increasingly hard to bear, for what the myth of the unworldly "Borges" quite failed to encompass were the intense emotional realities of the inner man. In a sonnet called "A Man in Love" ("El enamorado"), he complained of the need to hide his feelings for María: "I must pretend that there are others. It's a lie. / Only you exist. You, my misfortune / and my fortune, inexhaustible and pure."[25]

The gulf between his public and private lives accentuated his isolation. Much of his time was spent in the living room of his tiny apartment.[26] He would rise at around nine o'clock in the morning and after breakfast would receive visitors or work on some poem or article until about noon. Lunch was followed by a siesta, and later in the afternoon one of his many acquaintances might come around to read to him or to take dictation of a poem or a story he had composed earlier in the day. He rarely went out, on account of his blindness, and disliked parties because he felt uneasy in large gatherings, much preferring small groups where he could talk to a single person at a time. When he did go out, it was mostly to visit bookshops, because he enjoyed being among books and talking to people about them. (He was often to be found at La Ciudad, a bookshop in a shopping arcade across the street from his apartment building.) At night he would retire to his spartan room, which resembled a monk's cell with its narrow iron bed, single chair, and two small bookcases where he kept his collection of Anglo-Saxon and Scandinavian books. The other bedroom in the apartment had been Mother's, but even though she suggested he turn it into a study after her death, he had refused to change anything, because he did not wish to "profane" her room in any way.

Under the collective gaze of family and friends, not to mention the ravenous Argentine media, it was difficult for Borges and María to have time to themselves. She would come to be with him several times a week, and after their precious hours together, they would go out to eat in a restaurant, usually at the Hotel Dorá across the street or at the Cantina del Norte round the corner on calle Charcas. Then she would accompany him back to the apartment and, for the sake of appearances, had to leave him there on his own, prey once more to the ghosts that beckoned from the past.

Borges's enthusiastic support for the Argentine military junta was noted by the regime of General Pinochet in neighboring Chile, which had come to power in 1973 when the armed forces ousted the government of President Salvador Allende. Between 1970 and 1973, Allende had led a coalition of Socialists and Communists in an attempt to create a Marxist state by peaceful, parliamentary means. The repression of Allende's supporters had been so brutal, however, that General Pinochet's junta had incurred worldwide odium, and it was for this reason that the pariah regime in Chile saw a distinct political advantage in associating itself in some way with Borges, a man of immense international renown.

Within a few weeks of Borges's lunch with General Videla, the Chilean junta honored him with the Grand Cross of the Order of Merit, which he received at the embassy of Chile in Buenos Aires on July 21, 1976, together with Dr. Luis Federico Leloir, a winner of the Nobel Prize for Chemistry. He also received an honorary doctorate from the University of Chile and was invited to the Chilean capital, Santiago, for the ceremony in September. Borges's friends counseled against the visit, warning him that he would risk forfeiting the Nobel Prize for Literature, which, it was rumored, he stood an excellent chance of winning that year. But Borges thought it disgraceful to conceal one's political beliefs for the sake of winning a prize. If anything, such warnings made him more determined to assert his principles—"*ahora me obligan a ir,*" he reportedly told his friends: he felt "obliged to go."[27] Accordingly, he scheduled a weeklong trip to Chile, following a visit to Spain in August.

During these visits to Spain and Chile in 1976, Borges was in an extraordinarily combative frame of mind, and he took a perverse delight in smashing the idols of the international left. His political declarations to the media would cause irreparable damage to his reputation at home and abroad. While in Spain he trumpeted his support for the military regimes of South America, dismissing democracy as a "superstition." The situation in Argentina was "chaotic," but the regime of General Videla was slowly overcoming this chaos; Videla's was "a government of soldiers, of gentlemen, of decent people."[28] Such opinions were guaranteed to cause outrage in Spain, since the country was attempting to reestablish a parliamentary democracy after forty years of military dictatorship under General Franco, who had died less than a year earlier. But there was worse to come: Borges declared his admiration for the *Generalísimo,* adding that he had supported the Spanish republic during the civil war but now realized the value of what Franco had achieved.

To add insult to injury, he chose to make a gratuitous attack on Federico García Lorca, who had been murdered by fascists at the outbreak of the Spanish Civil War and whose memory was venerated by the Left and by liberals in Spain. Borges, however, showed no regard for these sensitivities: "I saw García Lorca only once in my life," he declared, "but neither he nor his poetry have ever interested me. I think he's a minor poet, a picturesque poet, a sort of professional Andalusian."[29] And, for good measure, he added: "The circumstances of his death were rather favorable to him; it's convenient for a poet to die in that fashion and, what's more, his death provided Antonio Machado with the opportunity to write a marvelous poem." Influential people on the left could not forgive him such remarks. The forthcoming publication of the respected Madrid-based journal *Cuadernos Hispanoamericanos,* which was to have been dedicated to studies of Borges's work, was cancelled at the last minute "for technical reasons." (This homage to Borges would not appear for another sixteen years.)

Borges was unrepentant even so, and, as if impelled by a reckless desire to bait his left-wing enemies, he continued to express scandalous opinions while in Chile. He arrived in Santiago on September 15, and during the week he spent there he was profusely acclaimed and feted by the authorities. On the day he received his doctorate from the rector of the University of Chile (who was a general in the armed forces), he was lavish in his praise of the military as men of honor. At the Chilean Academy, he chose to echo the poet Leopoldo Lugones—in his fascist period, no less—by calling upon the armed forces to create a "*patria fuerte,*" a strong fatherland that would guarantee civilized order in a barbarous continent.[30] To cap it all, he accepted an invitation to a private dinner with the president of the military junta, General Augusto Pinochet, who awarded him the Grand Cross of the Order of Bernardo O'Higgins, the liberator of Chile. Afterward Borges told journalists that he had discussed with Pinochet the necessity of rescuing "liberty and order" in Chile, Argentina, and Uruguay from the anarchy stirred up by the communists.[31]

The visit to Chile finished off Borges's chances of ever winning the Nobel Prize. That year, and for the remaining years of his life, his candidacy was opposed by a veteran member of the Nobel Prize committee, the socialist writer Arthur Lundkvist, a long-standing friend of the Chilean Communist poet Pablo Neruda, who had received the Nobel Prize in 1971. Lundkvist would subsequently explain to Volodia Teitelboim, one of Borges's biographers and a onetime chairman of the Chilean Communist Party, that he would never forgive Borges his public endorsement of General Pinochet's regime.[32]

In Chile, Borges seemed to embrace with a vengeance the contradiction into which he had been forced by Perón after the Revolución Libertadora—he was a democrat who was in favor of an "enlightened dictatorship" by an ethical elite for the sake of the long-term good of democracy. That perverse contradictoriness is best exemplified in his insistent recourse to the image of the "sword of honor" in the various speeches he gave in Chile. At the University of Chile, he declared that it was the sword that had inspired his ancestors to come to Chile to fight for the independence of South America, and it was the sword that had brought him to Chile, too, for the sword was "drawing the Argentine Republic out of the quagmire," just as it had done a few years earlier in Chile itself.[33] In his speech at the Chilean Academy, he even compared Chile's elongated shape to "an honorable sword" and declared his preference for "the sword, the bright sword" over the "furtive dynamite" of the enemy.[34]

Ostensibly Borges was attempting to save a certain vision of the *patria* from the threat represented by the guerrillas, but the excessive emotion invested in that defense betrays a deeper anxiety. He was cleaving to the sword of honor because he was trying to preserve not a patrician status as had his mother and grandmothers before him but a very hard-won interpretation of the meaning of his life. For if the likes of Generals Videla and Pinochet were not the ethical elite he had envisaged, if the "enlightened dictatorship" were not made to work, if Peronism were not defeated, he might remain forever alienated from the political reality of Argentina, and then the whole poetic design of his life might start to come apart: there would be no prospect of experiencing the Simurgh—that marvelous sense of oneness of self and world—and if no Simurgh, then perhaps the perennial dawn of Iceland might turn out to have been an illusion after all. Borges's invocation of the sword was, in truth, a sign of despair, for he had perceived long ago that the sword of honor was really no defense, the cause was as good as lost, and his raising of the sword in Chile was little more than a last, quixotic stand against the rising tide of darkness that threatened to engulf the beautiful order of meaning he had somehow contrived from the hopes and dreams that had dominated his life.

CHAPTER 30

Blue Tigers

(1976–1979)

BORGES'S HOPES of preserving the ideal pattern of his life's meaning did not long survive the visit to Chile. After his return to Buenos Aires, the turmoil of politics showed no signs of abating as the armed forces conducted a ruthless counterinsurgency operation against two well-armed guerrilla forces, the Montoneros and another group, the Trotskyite People's Revolutionary Army (ERP, Ejército Revolucionario del Pueblo). The guerrillas resorted to terrorist atrocities on a regular basis, but the military responded with methods that were as illegal as they were inhuman, although these were not reliably known to the general public at the time.

The guerrilla war was fueled by economic failure: the junta was having trouble conquering rampant inflation and controlling the public deficit. Attempts to roll back the vast state sector created by Perón were producing massive unemployment, a sharp drop in living standards, and general misery. Largely as a means to distract the populace from its discontents, the ruling generals decided to play the nationalist card by stirring up nationalist feeling in the country over a claim to three islands in the Beagle Channel in the Straits of Magellan, which were currently under Chilean jurisdiction. It had been agreed in 1971 to refer the matter to the International Court of Justice, but the Argentine junta seemed ill disposed to accept an unfavorable verdict. This quarrel over the Beagle Channel islands would spell the end of Borges's illusions about an ethical elite and an "enlightened dictatorship." He could make no sense of Argentine history, for the "men of honor" who had rid the country of Peronism were now displaying the same kind of aggressive nationalism that had been one of the chief reasons for his hatred of Perón.

Life at home, moreover, was becoming increasingly fraught with misunderstandings: his housekeeper, Fani, disliked María's frequent visits to the apartment, perhaps seeing these as encroachments into her domain by Borges's "literary secretary." These tensions came to a head when Fani intervened in a private discussion between Borges and María, then took umbrage when she was rebuffed.[1] Fani decided to give her notice, but Bioy Casares and

Silvina persuaded her not to leave. So she relented and stayed on, though, by her own admission, she remained a watchful presence in the tiny apartment.[2] Borges's friendship with Bioy and Silvina came under strain, too. Their relations had cooled somewhat at the time of his marriage to Elsa Astete, of whom Bioy rather disapproved. For all their unconventional lifestyles, Bioy and Silvina belonged to the grandest families in Argentina and were not comfortable with people outside their social circle who were not writers or artists. Bioy had come to dislike María, as he had Elsa before her, and this made it increasingly awkward for Borges to continue to see him. He went less often to dinner at the Bioys', and eventually they would stop seeing each other altogether.

By the latter months of 1976, Borges's Dantean dream had all but evaporated. On November 7 he published "Endymion on Latmos" in *La Nación,* the poem in which he portrayed himself as the shepherd boy to whom the moon had deigned to make love.[3] Recalling that sublime episode, he wondered whether "that tumult of gold on the mountain" had been real "or just a dream." Another poem, "Alexandria, 641 A.D.," took as its subject the burning of the great Hellenistic library at Alexandria by the forces of Caliph Omar.[4] In an accompanying note, Borges would point out that Omar was a "projection of the author" and that the burning of the library had occurred in 1976, not "in the first century of the Hegira."[5] In other words, the subject of the poem was himself and the library a symbol of his solipsism. But the destruction of the Alexandrian Library, wrote Borges, had not been definitive, for even if all the books in the world were to be destroyed, human beings would contrive to "engender once again each page and each line, / each labor and each love of Hercules." And so we may interpret the poem as indicating that he thought his solipsism—as symbolized by the Library—had been destroyed by the flames of love in 1976, but he now feared that it was in the process of being engendered all over again. He repeated this idea in the epilogue to *A History of Night* (*Historia de la noche*), which was dated October 7, 1977: "Might I be permitted to repeat that my father's library has been the chief event in my life? The truth is that I have never emerged from it."[6]

A brief tale called "The Leaves of the Cypress" ("Las hojas del ciprés") evinces the depth of Borges's despair following the collapse of his faith in the Dantean pattern of salvation. It purports to be the transcript of a nightmare that took place on April 14, 1977.[7] Borges is awakened in the middle of the night by his "one enemy," who orders him to get dressed and follow him to the place where his execution has been ordained. There follows a ride in a coach through the deserted streets of Buenos Aires; there is a full moon and the face of a clock showing no hands or numerals. When they reach the south side, he is led to a cypress tree whose leaves seem eerily artificial—they are stiff and lifeless, and each one is marked with a monogram. Borges is ordered to lie on his back and extend his arms to form a cross. A political dimension to the nightmare is hinted at when we are told that Borges catches sight of a she-wolf as he lies on the ground. This historic symbol of Rome may be an allusion to the fascism Borges had strenuously opposed when it first raised its head in the late 1920s and when it later threatened to establish itself in Argentina under Perón.

What we have here is a demonic inversion of Borges's Dantean dream. The coach ride in the middle of the night recalls that other nocturnal coach ride through Buenos Aires at the climax of *The Congress,* when the members of Alejandro Glencoe's secret society experience a blissful sense of true pantheist being. But in this latter tale, Buenos Aires has become a city of blank clocks and trees that "cannot grow"; it is not so much timeless as stagnant, for it is a city that will not allow him to escape the past, a city whose spirit is embodied in the mysterious enemy—the specter of Perón perhaps, or of Oliverio Girondo, or the ghost of his ancestors?—who revels in punishing Borges with a kind of "black joy." And so, far from offering him the healing oneness of the Simurgh as envisaged in *The Congress,* Buenos Aires condemns him to recurrent crucifixions. At the end Borges finds himself a victim of the sword—or the dagger—once more. Lying outstretched on his back and clutching a tuft of grass in each hand, he sees the flash of a blade—and then wakes up in his bedroom on the calle Maipú.

As had occurred several times in the past when he could find no point to life, his thoughts turned to suicide. Probably in the first months of 1977, he composed a story about this recurrent temptation to kill himself. "25 August 1983" is a "prophetic dialogue" between two instances of himself in "two times and two places."[8] It opens in the year 1960 with Borges arriving at the Hotel Las Delicias in Adrogué, on the day after his birthday, and booking into Room 19 with the intention of committing suicide. When he enters the hotel room, however, he encounters a much older version of himself calmly waiting to die after consuming a bottle of pills. This older Borges claims not to be in the Hotel Las Delicias at all but in Mother's room in the apartment on calle Maipú, and the year is 1983, not 1960. Each version of Borges believes he is dreaming the other, and they talk of an earlier attempt—"the draft of the story of this suicide"—when a still-younger version of Borges had bought a gun and gone to the Hotel Las Delicias to shoot himself.

The story moves gently back and forth between various times, places, and selves, but what actually binds the two versions of Borges into the semblance of a single identity is the persistence through time of a pattern of hope and disillusion featuring a woman, whom neither could bear to name, and the writing of "a masterpiece." The older Borges observes to his younger self that their "supposed oeuvre is nothing but a series of drafts, miscellaneous drafts," and that he will succumb to "the vain and superstitious temptation" to write "a great book," the kind of superstition that "had inflicted Goethe's *Faust, Salammbô* or *Ulysses* upon us." And yet this masterpiece, when published, would turn out to be nothing more than a "museum" of their customary themes. "That book was one of the roads that led me to this night," says the older Borges; unjustified by love or by writing, each version of Borges is driven to suicide for the same reason—the failure of the Dantean pattern of meaning whereby a woman's love would inspire him to write a "masterpiece" that would save him from the absurdity of his pointless existence.

With the disintegration of his Dantean dream, Borges's inner world was thrown into confusion. The extravagant poetic and metaphysical meanings he had ascribed to the advent of love in his life—the vision of the mystical Rose, of the Aleph, or of the Simurgh—had quite dissolved by now, leaving him with nothing but the bare reality of his emotional attachment to María Kodama. In "The Waiting" ("La espera") he expressed the dreadful anxiety caused by his needing her so much:

> Before the hurried bell rings
> and the door is opened, and you enter, Oh you
> whom my anxiety awaits, the universe must have
> executed an infinite series of concrete acts. No one
> could compute that vertigo.
> . . . .
> Grains of sand would not suffice to count them.
> (In my breast, a clock of blood measures out
> the fearful time of my waiting.)[9]

Sometime in 1977 he wrote a poem called "A History of Night," a poem that was significant enough to become the title poem of the collection he would publish in November of that year.[10] Here Borges reviewed the myths and imaginings that human beings had devised to characterize the night. The various concepts of night, he observed, are creations of the human mind, but none would have been possible without "those delicate instruments: our eyes," for night—"that interval of darkness between the two twilights"—could acquire meaning only in relation to our perception of light. Given that he was blind, the poem had a symbolic sense: the love he bore María represented the eyes of his spirit, and the writing of "A History of Night" implied a hope that the light of her love might steer him through his current darkness toward the recovery of that other twilight—the dawn.

In May 1977, Borges went to Italy with María to give lectures in Milan, Parma, Venice, and Rome. He was challenged by journalists about his endorsement of General Pinochet and was branded a fascist in some newspapers, even though his unqualified support for the military juntas in Argentina and Chile had lasted barely six months after his visit to Santiago. He tried to distance himself from his notorious declarations of the previous year. In Rome, for instance, he observed that the current military regimes in South America were "necessary evils" and made it clear that his support for the likes of General Pinochet was relative: "I would approve of this regime for Chile, but not for the rest of the world."[11]

From Italy he went to Geneva, which he had last visited with his mother in 1963. María was not too keen on going to Switzerland: she had always found mountains and lakes oppressive; they caused her "anguish" because she felt "imprisoned" in that kind of landscape.[12] Borges, however, assured her that she had nothing to fear; the Alps were not as high as the Andes, and Lake Leman was so big that it was like a sea. On their first morning in Geneva, Borges announced to María, "Let's go back to my past," and he took her on a tour of the Old Town, showing her the apartment building where the family had lived, the Collège Calvin, "La Jonction" where the Arve River joins up with the Rhône, and various other places he had frequented in his youth, which he recalled with amazing precision. He also introduced her to his old friends Maurice Abramowicz and Simon Jichlinski, with whom he reminisced about the old days—the old tavern Le Crocodil where they used to get drunk, the girls they had known, the snowball fights, swimming in the Rhône, their rock-climbing expeditions to Mont Salève.

It was not long before he returned to the city. In October 1977 he had occasion to go to Paris, Crete, and Madrid. In Paris he spoke at the Sorbonne, inaugurated a conference on Ricardo Güiraldes's work, and opened an exhibition of Xul Solar's paintings; he was in Madrid for the launch of a new book, comprising two new stories, "Paracelsus' Rose" ("La rosa de Paracelso") and "Blue Tigers" ("Tigres azules"), which a Spanish publishing house, Sedmay, was bringing out under the title of *Borges: Rosa y Azul;* and he accepted an invitation to Crete to visit the labyrinth at Knossos. During this trip to Europe, he took time off with María in Geneva, where they stayed at the Hôtel Touring Balance, an establishment with venerable literary associations—Mary Shelley was said to have written parts of *Frankenstein* there, and other famous guests had included Byron, Keats, and Wagner.[13] They went to Geneva again early in 1978, following another visit to Paris to receive an honorary doctorate from the Sorbonne on February 4. On this occasion they stayed at the Hôtel L'Arbalète on the edge of the Old Town, which was greatly to Borges's liking because he fancied there was something Calvinist about it—it was comfortable yet austere, and even though it was by no means luxurious, the furnishings, china, and bed linens were of excellent quality.[14] Thenceforward he and María would stay at L'Arbalète whenever they came to the city.

Borges's visits to Geneva could have become mere exercises in nostalgia, but Geneva did not belong to a dead past: he had put down roots there many years ago, and when he returned to it in old age, it was pregnant with new possibilities. To begin with, he was to resume his friendship with Maurice Abramowicz, who had been one of the dearest friends of his early youth. Borges and María would be invited to dine at Abramowicz's house, or they would go to a restaurant as a foursome with Maurice's wife, Isabelle Monnet. María would often leave the two elderly men conversing together for several hours about the books they had discovered together, the poetry they had written, what they had done with their lives since they had parted in their youth. This revived friendship with Abramowicz must have been especially rewarding at a time when Borges was feeling increasingly estranged from Buenos Aires, but there was a more intimate significance to his rediscovery of Geneva, for this was the city in which he had first known love and also the place where the innocence of that first love had been sullied by his untimely initiation.

Nevertheless, the fact that he had returned to Geneva with María Kodama amounted to an exorcism of his unhappy memories of the encounter at the place du Bourg-de-Four. And given his distaste for the Argentine military junta, his rediscovery of Geneva at this time assumed a political significance, too. He had come to admire the tolerance of the Swiss; even as a boy, he had appreciated their respect for the freedom of the individual. As he had observed in a letter he wrote to his Argentine friend Roberto Godel shortly after departing Geneva in 1919, lovers in Switzerland could embrace and kiss freely in parks, and no one complained; people just minded their own business.[15] He now echoed these views in his observation to María that Switzerland "functioned without curtailing individuality," and in his commending the Swiss for their hospitality during the First World War, when they accepted refugees from other countries, and in his praise for their political "modesty," which was evident from the fact that no one outside Switzerland could name the president of the country.[16]

Around 1978, therefore, Geneva emerged from Borges's distant past as a city of rebirth and new beginnings. Indeed, he was so taken with Geneva that he began to regard it as an alternative home city to Buenos Aires, and he kept suggesting to María that they settle there permanently.[17] María, however, would not agree to this proposal. She had earned her own living from the age of sixteen, so she was not prepared to become financially dependent on him and compromise this hard-won personal freedom. "You are a prisoner of freedom," Borges would protest. "You don't want to be tied down, and in order to be free you are prepared to break with everything, but that too can be a kind of prison."[18] But María would counter this reproach by insisting that if freedom were a prison, then "that prison is fine by me," because "psychologically" that was the only kind of prison she could put up with. Borges was to accept this determination of María's, albeit with some reluctance. Instead he proposed to visit Geneva with her as often as he could, and he resolved that it should remain a haven of privacy for them both by never accepting any public engagements there. Geneva, he told María, would be "their refuge, their paradise." Several years later he would confess to an interviewer, "Every time I go to Europe, I make it a point to visit Switzerland."[19]

In refusing to settle in Geneva, María was reaffirming the principle of free mutuality on which their relations were based. Borges might have wished to settle in Geneva in order to recover his past, his youth, his memories—but what of María herself? Was she to become a mere vehicle for yet another of Borges's self-projected interpretations of his destiny? Borges had accepted a mutual bond when they pledged their love for each other after the death of his mother, but he had not fully realized its implications—he was still too caught up in his Dantean dream of love as the key to his personal salvation. Yet now that his poetic dream had disintegrated, María's very strong sense of autonomy was to produce a revolutionary transformation in his understanding of the nature of love.

The elements of this transformation are already to be found in "Blue Tigers" ("Tigres azules"), a story he would have completed by the middle of 1977.[20] The central character is a Scotsman, Alexander Craigie, who is professor of "Eastern and Western Logic" at the University of Lahore. Like Borges, Craigie has been fascinated by tigers since childhood, so when he learns about a rare species of blue tiger, he resolves to find one. In due course he arrives in a remote village whose inhabitants claim to have knowledge of the strange beast, although they regard it with a peculiar dread. Craigie is warned against venturing into a plateau above the village, because any human who does so would be "in danger of seeing the deity, and of going blind or mad." Craigie presses on regardless and climbs up to the plateau, eventually discovering a number of little blue stones shaped like disks in a crack in the ground. These stones are the "blue tigers," and he soon realizes why they instill such terror— the disks multiply or diminish without rhyme or reason in a species of "dreadful miracle" that "destroyed mathematics" and "undermined human science." The discovery that "disorder is admissible in the universe" threatens to drive Craigie out of his mind, for "if three plus one can make two or make fourteen, then reason is madness."

What do the blue tigers represent? Borges's preoccupation with tigers, like Alexander Craigie's, went back to the very earliest days of his childhood. Its origins lay in his desire to escape both the sense of unworthiness inflicted by his mother's sword of honor and the solipsism fostered by his father's library. The tiger appeared to embody a state of realized being, and Borges, in consequence, had sought to connect with the tiger by various successive means. But in "Blue Tigers," Borges acknowledged that his quest for the tiger was intrinsically impossible to fulfill, for the ideal tigers of his imagination were of a "blue that we are permitted to see only in our dreams." He had magnified and dramatized his childhood fascination with tigers into a quest for union with the Absolute, employing various poetic figures—the Simurgh, the Rose, or the Aleph—to represent that sublime experience. However, to seek such a goal was to aspire to a form of being that was proper only to God, for knowledge of the true order of the universe was beyond the reach of man and to seek to possess it was to commit a kind of sacrilege, hence the baffling nature of the "blue tigers" and the fear of blindness or madness associated with their discovery.

The story, nevertheless, ends with a sense of hope, or at least of new insight. Craigie comes to a mosque and prays to be relieved of the crazy stones. A blind beggar suddenly appears and asks for alms; Craigie gives him one of the stones, but the mysterious beggar asks for them all. "He who has not given everything has given nothing," he declares. The Scotsman pours all the "blue tigers" into the palm of the beggar's hand. The beggar then tells Craigie that his gift to him will be no less "awesome": "You will keep your days and your nights, sanity, habits, the world." Craigie, in short, can regain his sanity only by shedding all desire to attain to the Absolute, but in the blind beggar's injunction ("He who has not given everything has given nothing"), there is an indication that in the act of surrendering to another, one may discover the means of being reconciled to "sanity, habits, the world."

"Blue Tigers" expressed once more Borges's disillusionment with his Dantean scheme of salvation, but the meaning of the story was not wholly negative, for in the very failure of the quest for union with the Absolute, there lay the seeds of a more modest form of personal salvation. Indeed, the enigmatic title of the story contained an allusion to the ceramic figure of a blue tiger that he had been given by María Kodama, which he had hung on the wall next to his bed.[21] The significance Borges attached to this particular blue tiger can be found in *The Book of Imaginary Beings* of 1967, where, under "The Tigers of Annam" ("Los tigres del Annam"), it is noted that the four points of the compass are characterized by tigers of different colors: "The Blue Tiger presides over the East; it is associated with spring and plants."[22] María's gift thus represented the exotic "other" of the East and its associations with vernal rebirth and natural growth.

The notion of María's intriguing "otherness" was elaborated in the poem "Music Box" ("Caja de música"), where he evoked the "music of Japan," whose notes are compared to "drops of slow honey or invisible gold" that "repeat a pattern" at once "eternal and fragile, mysterious and clear," as they are "grudgingly" released by "the clepsydra."[23] The poem suggests that the moments he shared with María played over the course of time like the notes of a melody carrying intimations of an order beyond words. Yet where was the source of this music to be found? "I shall never know. It doesn't matter. In that music / I am. I wish to be. I bleed away." In the exotic music of love, in other words, he would find new life by a kind of transfusion, by allowing the self to "bleed away" into the self of the other.

In March 1978 the journalist Rodolfo Braceli became an accidental witness to Borges's newfound joie de vivre. He arrived at the flat on calle Maipú to conduct an interview with Borges and found his interviewee "radiant" with happiness.[24] Borges asked him to help with the revision of a poem he had recently composed. Its working title was "Timelessness" (in English), though it was later changed to "La dicha" or "Bliss."[25] In this poem Borges celebrated the miraculous irrelevance of time in the garden of love: "Whoever embraces a woman is Adam. The woman is Eve." And the source of such bliss was to be found in the giving of oneself to another: "Praise be the love in which there is no possessor and no possessed, just mutual surrender." The poem concluded with the assertion that in love's garden "everything happens for the first time"—"Everything happens for the first time, but in a way that is eternal."

The episodes of bliss vouchsafed him in the love of María could not, however, altogether distract Borges from the misery of life in Buenos Aires. In his personal life, he had still to keep up the charade that María was just a friend among others; and as for politics, the military junta was proving to be more dangerously nationalistic than Perón had ever been. The International Court of Justice had ruled in favor of Chile in the dispute over the sovereignty of the islands in the Beagle Channel, but it was rumored that the Argentine generals were preparing to go to war with Chile if current negotiations on this vexed issue were to fail, as expected. Borges was appalled at the prospect of a war over a few barren islands at the very ends of the earth, and he was not loath to make his dissent known to the press. On August 30 a Chilean newspaper, *Últimas Noticias,* published an interview in which Borges criticized the Argentine junta for rejecting the verdict of the International Court of Justice. "If you accept the judge, you must accept his verdict," he declared. "A war would be folly and a crime; only demagogues are in favor of it."

Such views went down very badly in Argentina. The mass-circulation daily *Crónica* reported Borges's interview in *Últimas Noticias* under the headline A TRAITOR TO BOOT: BORGES BACKS CHILE![26] The following day Borges sent a press release to the news agency EFE stating that he "did not feel a traitor to the *patria* or to anyone." But *Crónica* was unconvinced and published a vitriolic article denouncing "Georgy" Luis Borges, among other things, for his alleged sympathy "with Her Britannic Majesty," the "usurper of the Malvinas." It appeared under another screaming headline: BORGES AGAINST THE GOVERNMENT, AGAINST THE STATE, AGAINST THE LAW, AGAINST ARGENTINA![27]

Little wonder that, by the end of 1978, he should have felt so divorced from his native land—the country seemed to be on the brink of a lunatic military adventure, and he had been branded a traitor in the press. He was overcome at this point by a general sense of hopelessness. On December 31, 1978, he published an "Elegy" in *La Nación*, in which he alluded to a sorrow so private that he wanted no one to know about it, "not even the mirror":

> On the other side of the door, a man,
> compounded of solitude, of love, of time,
> has just wept in Buenos Aires
> over the way things are.[28]

Despite the oppressive circumstances of life in Buenos Aires, he continued to place his faith in the love he bore María Kodama. At around the time he was being vilified in the Argentine press, he was offered the possibility of visiting Japan. An official at the Japanese embassy in Buenos Aires, a student of María's, undertook to arrange a tour of Japan under the auspices of the Japan Foundation. The prospect of going to Japan intrigued Borges. On September 9, 1978, he composed a poem about the Japanese game of Go, a kind of Oriental chess, as he called it, "in which men can lose themselves / as in love or in the day."[29] As with his learning Anglo-Saxon or Old Icelandic, he accepted that he might never master the culture of Japan, but he resolved nonetheless to embark on that adventure, for he was still capable of reaching sublime moments of personal happiness with María. In the first months of 1979, for instance, he composed a poem called "Hymn" ("Himno"), whose title harked back to the Whitmaneque "Hymn to the Sea" that he had written as a young man in Majorca.[30] But if that youthful poem was merely aspirational, this poem of old age was replete with images signifying the ecstatic joys of love.

> This morning
> the air brings an incredible fragrance
> of the roses of Paradise.
> On the banks of the Euphrates
> Adam discovers the freshness of water.
> A shower of gold falls from the sky:
> it is the love of Zeus. . . .

And after itemizing a series of unique acts, a climax is reached in the following lines:

> Whitman sings in Manhattan.
> Homer is born in seven cities.
> A maiden has just caught
> the white unicorn.
> The whole of the past returns like a wave
> and these ancient things recur
> because a woman has kissed you.

All the same, there seemed to be no end to the disappointments he had to endure in Buenos Aires. In April, the same month that "Hymn" was published, there occurred a very damaging quarrel in the bosom of his own family over a joint account he held with his sister at the Banco de Galicia.[31] Family relations never fully recovered from this disagreement. Borges was furious with Norah's side of the family—he even asked his sister never to visit him again. Bioy Casares and his wife tried to intercede, as did other friends, but Borges would not relent. After some time he would patch up his differences with Norah, though not with other members of the family.

Given these difficulties with relatives and friends, and alienated as he was from a political situation he could no longer understand, only María's love meant anything to him. On May 20, 1979, just a few weeks after the quarrel about the bank account, he published a poem, "*Inferno, V, 129,*" implicitly comparing himself and María to the two lovers in Dante's *Inferno*, Paolo and Francesca, who are so absorbed in each other that they are oblivious to everything around them.[32] Dante's verse 129 reads, "We were alone and deemed no danger nigh,"[33] and in Borges's elaboration of this line, the lovers feel happy because they have discovered "the only treasure there is; they have found the other." And so they "gaze upon each other with incredulous wonder"; "they alone exist in the world," for they are "all the lovers who have ever been / since Adam and his Eve / walked upon the meadows of Paradise."

Borges still regarded love, vestigially, in Dantean terms, as a saving grace in the hellish circumstances through which he was forced to live. However, toward the middle of 1979, he had cause to believe that he would shortly contend with the ultimate of life's hazards—he was in pain, an acute pain at times, and thought he might be dying. The shadow of death, in any case, seemed to be closing in on him. His dear friend Haydée Lange had been unwell since the previous year, and their habit of meeting every Friday had had to be discontinued, although they endeavored to keep in touch by speaking to each other on the telephone.[34] Haydée died on July 10, and her passing severed his one remaining link with the happy days of his youth at the calle Tronador, for Haydée's sister Norah had passed away in 1972, as had his former sweetheart, Concepción Guerrero, in the same year.

How long would he survive himself? Two days after the death of Haydée Lange, he published a brace of poems—"The Desert" ("El desierto") and "Blake"—in the newspaper *Clarín*.[35] "The Desert" is an arcane, riddling poem that articulated his fear that the rose of love might be snatched away by death at any moment. He imagined being tortured in "the dark kingdom" of Hades by memories of the rose he had been offered so late in his long life. If he were to die at this point, nothing would have made sense. And the possibility of his dying only deepened the mystery of his love for María. What did love signify? What was its cause, its end, what its true nature?

Instead of accepting the rose in all its innocence, Borges was tempted to continue to regard love as the key to some absolute truth about himself and the world. Still, he realized that this infernal metaphysical curiosity constituted a threat to his enjoyment of love itself. This was the theme of the second poem, "Blake," a gloss on the English poet's "A Sick Rose," in which "the invisible worm that flies in the night" threatens love's "bed of crimson joy." Borges gave Blake's "invisible worm" a philosophical connotation: he was thankful for the "intimate gifts" the rose of love had lavished upon him, but even though it had been given him to know the contingent attributes of the rose—its color, fragrance, weight—what was its Platonic form? It was precisely this wish to arrive at some final, metaphysical understanding of the mystery of love that threatened to destroy his "bed of crimson joy."

Borges's sense of life's futility was heightened by the fact that he would reach his eightieth birthday on August 24, 1979. He was regaled with honors at home and abroad in the course of the year: he would receive the Order of Merit from the Federal Republic of Germany, an honor from the Republic of Iceland, a Gold Medal from the Académie Française, and telegrams of felicitation from the president of Argentina and the heads of state of several Latin American republics on the day of his anniversary. However, on the eve of his birthday, he published a poem in *Clarín* in which he reviewed a number of modest things he had experienced in his lifetime, concluding with the wry observation that "none of these things is rare, and taken as a whole they have brought me a fame I cannot altogether comprehend."[36]

Three days after his birthday, he was interviewed on the telephone by a journalist from the Montevideo newspaper *La Mañana*. When asked about his health, Borges replied that it was "very bad": "I am in great pain and I don't have the courage to bear it." He referred to what he regarded as his "imminent death" and "bade farewell to his friends in Uruguay."[37] Tests had revealed a tumor in his prostate, and he was shortly to go into the hospital to have it surgically removed. On August 28 he made a will naming María Kodama the sole heir to all his goods, monies, assets and investments, royalties, and whatever else constituted his property.[38] On September 3 he underwent an operation under local anaesthetic. He had sufficiently mastered his anxieties by now to entertain the surgeon and his colleagues with a discussion of the etymology of the word *quirófano* ("operating theater").[39] Fortunately, he was not at death's door: the tumor was benign, but he was detained in the hospital for a few days, where he had occasion to be puzzled yet again by his extraordinary renown when nurses discovered a press photographer hiding in one of the lavatories in hopes of catching their famous patient unawares.[40]

While convalescing from the operation at home, he lapsed into a state of extreme dejection and alarmed María by claiming that he could not get out of bed because he was unable to walk.[41] Even though his doctor could find nothing wrong with him, Borges insisted he was paralyzed. Evidently the strain of the last few months had taken its toll: he had become disenchanted with family, friends, and country; he was blind and weary; and even as he entered his ninth decade, he still had no idea what to make of his life.

He was due to travel to Japan in the first week of November as a guest of the Japan Foundation. María asked him if he wished to go ahead with the tour. Yes, he was as keen as ever, he assured her, but still he claimed that his legs were paralyzed. In the end he agreed to an experiment—if he managed to walk to the restaurant opposite his apartment building, he would accept that he was fit to travel. With some difficulty at the outset, he hobbled across the street on María's arm, and when he got to the restaurant, he was greeted by the waiters with a round of applause. "Well, María," he remarked, "we've made it to Japan."[42]

CHAPTER 31

The Music of Japan

(1979–1981)

BORGES AND MARÍA arrived in Tokyo on November 5. His first days in Japan were taken up mostly with official engagements—luncheons, dinners, a press conference, and several interviews with writers and academics. His curiosity for things Japanese had been awakened in boyhood by his reading of A. B. Mitford's *Tales of Old Japan* and by the writings of Lafcadio Hearn, which he had come across in Geneva; in Switzerland, too, Schopenhauer had led him to learn about Buddhism, which had become a lifelong interest, but he was looking forward, he said, to his encounter with the "enigma," "the beautiful labyrinth" that was Japan.[1]

His hosts at the Japan Foundation had organized a program designed to give him an impression of the history and culture of the country. His first visit, on November 7, was to the Meiji Temple, the greatest Shinto center in Tokyo, where he was shown around by the *gushi,* the chief priest, who explained through an interpreter the nature of the Shinto religion, the most ancient faith in Japan. At its most basic level, Shintoism is a synthesis of old animistic beliefs, but as the closest thing in Japan to a national religion, it had been politicized by traditionalists in the early twentieth century and converted into a fundamental element in Japanese nationalism. This aspect of Shintoism is unlikely to have interested Borges, given his aversion to nationalism in general; what he found peculiarly inspiring was the attitude of openness and tolerance with which he was received by the chief priest at the temple, and he would come to regard this spirit as encapsulating the essence of what he learned in Japan.

María Kodama noted in her account of their visit that Borges had approached his encounter with Japan as "an intellectual adventure," but "as the days pass his spirit begins to grow lighter."[2] On November 14 they arrived in Kyoto, the old imperial city, where they spent eight days. It was here that Borges underwent a series of spiritual experiences that would mark him deeply. That first afternoon he was taken to a traditional tea ceremony and was gratified to be invited to participate in the proceedings. He was enchanted by the soft bubbling of the boiling water and, taking the tea bowl in his hands, began to stroke it, "trying to feel the delicacy of its form"; he remarked afterward to María that he had been impressed by the fact that the ceremony was not at all "remote or hieratic," rather that it was "integrated in the nature of man and his surroundings." He began "to absorb everything that was offered to him, trying to anticipate what was coming next, and asking repeatedly what was on the program." At the Hokoji Temple, he asked to hear the sound of the great bell; later he enjoyed a recital of *gidayu* and *kouta*, traditional Japanese songs, and despite never having had much of an ear for music, he was intrigued by sounds that were so alien to the Western tradition.

"This is marvelous," he kept repeating to María. "Each day brings a new gift." He was eager to savor the exoticism of Japan, its rhythms, forms, and textures, and, yielding to the utter strangeness of it all, he now instructed his guide not to tell him in advance what was on the agenda, because he wished to wake up each morning and allow the day to unfold as a series of surprises. Shortly afterward it was announced that they would be spending one night in the holy city of Nara. There they visited the Daibutsu-den, a vast wooden temple housing an enormous statue of the Buddha, said to be the largest in the world. Although he could not see the image, he was nevertheless curious to know whether there was not "something terrible in that face," and as he was led up to a platform at the base of the giant Buddha, he was amazed to hear laughter and clapping coming from a wing of the temple where some young students were squeezing through a hole in one of the wooden pillars, a feat said to bring long life. Such lack of solemnity added to his impression that the sacred and the natural were intricately conjoined in Japan, and this brought him an intimation of the pantheism that had always appealed to him, a sense of the interconnectedness of things, which was further reinforced by the delight he felt at discovering that the deer grazing in the vast grounds surrounding the temple were trusting enough to let him approach and stroke them—"those deer were benevolent and tolerant with me." That night they were accommodated at a *ryokan*, a traditional Japanese inn. He was given a kimono to wear and green tea to drink, and, with what struck María as an almost childish enthusiasm, he asked whether he might be allowed to sleep on the floor in the traditional Japanese manner. The following morning he remarked to María, "I can now say that I have truly entered into the spirit of Japanese life."

They had to return to Kyoto after only one night in Nara because they had arranged to attend a performance of Noh plays with a Japanese academic, Professor Kishi, whom Borges had first met in Washington when he gave his talk on Shakepeare at the Folger Library some years back. Borges had once been to a performance of Noh drama in Buenos Aires, but he was quite unprepared for what awaited him in Kyoto. The program consisted of a series of plays, starting at eight in the morning and lasting some nine hours. The atmosphere was quite unlike that in a Western theater—when the chorus began to intone the introduction to the first play, the audience fell silent and a kind of religious devotion enveloped the auditorium as the spectators followed the words in their textbooks, reminding María of a congregation reading their missals at a Catholic mass. One play succeeded another at a preternaturally slow pace, and even Professor Kishi eventually showed signs of becoming bored, but Borges was caught up in the spell of the Noh from the start, and although his blindness prevented him from actually seeing the spectacle, he was enthralled by the voices of the actors and the chorus, and he kept murmuring in wonder to María, "Their voices are extraordinary; they are like the wind!"

Borges was "overwhelmed by the atmosphere" at the Noh theater, and as María noted, this experience seemed to "predispose him to talk about religion." The next day they had tea with a Buddhist nun at the Rinkyu-ji Temple, and Borges proceeded to quiz her about her way of life, his curiosity driving him to ask questions of a quite personal nature: Was she happy? Had she ever regretted becoming a nun? During a visit to the Rioan-ji Temple, a center of Zen Buddhism, he met a monk, Morinaga Yushoku, with whom he had the most searching conversation of his entire visit to Japan. As with the nun, Borges wished to learn something of Yushoku's commitment to the contemplative life, but above all he wanted to know whether the monk had ever experienced a mystical enlightenment. María recalled that Borges kept pressing this point, and Yushoku replied that he had twice experienced nirvana but that it was impossible to convey such an experience to someone who had not himself found enlightenment.[3]

All the same, Borges described to the monk an experience he had undergone one night in the 1920s while roaming the outskirts of Buenos Aires, when the sight of a particular moonlit street had induced a preternatural sense that time was an illusion.[4] (This was the episode recounted in "Sentirse en muerte" or "Feeling in Death," first published in 1928.) Might such an episode qualify as a mystical illumination? That was possible, came the reply, since an illumination could be prompted by any number of things, such as the ringing of a bell or the sound of water flowing over a stone, but true enlightenment would entail a complete transformation of the soul and would change everything in a man's life. The monk explained that one must dispel the illusion of selfhood in order to experience enlightenment: our sense of personal identity was the product of our conditioning, but otherwise there was nothing within us, no basis for the existence of the self, and so one must shed all notions of individuality and start again from zero before one could reach nirvana.[5]

The dialogue with the Buddhist monk led to further discussion with María. She acknowledged that the quest for enlightenment had been a constant in his writing—in *The Congress*, "The Aleph," "The Zahir," "The God's Writing," and a good number of other texts and poems, but she pointed out that he was seeking the sort of enlightenment that only religion could offer, while being unable to quell rational doubt. "There can be no illumination without faith," she told him. "And faith is like love: either you feel it or you don't."[6] María was right, of course: Borges desired the ends of faith yet could not possess faith as such. However, the dialogue with the monk had brought home to him that the kind of mystical illumination he desired could not involve the annihilation of the individual personality: he could not easily "cease being Borges," he told María.[7]

Borges had not been persuaded of the Buddhist way, for the idea of the vanity of the self that lay at the heart of Buddhism was too similar to the notion of the arbitrariness of personal identity—one man could be any man—that he had inherited from Macedonio Fernández in his youth. And if this notion had become such a prominent theme in his writing, it was because it filled him with horror and revulsion. What Borges desired was the fulfillment of the self in union with the Absolute, a kind of salvation that was more consonant with the thinking of Christianity than with Buddhism. This was the type of union represented by Dante's mystic Rose in the *Divine Comedy*, where the souls of the elect are accorded their due place in the divine scheme of things. Borges had been ravished by the beauty of Dante's intricate eschatological design, but he could not believe in the Christian God, even though he coveted the form of salvation that sprang from faith in God. Christianity enjoined belief in a set of doctrines that resulted in the submission of the individual will to the Will of the One True God under pain of eternal suffering in Hell. Borges, however, could not accept such belief—the salvation he sought would somehow entail a concordance of the individual with the higher spirit of the cosmos. Hence his attraction to pantheism, where the divine might subsist in every creature without this detracting from their singularity. More than Dante's Catholic vision, therefore, it was the Persian legend of the Simurgh, which he regarded as a form of pantheist allegory, that appealed to him.

After Kyoto, Borges and María went to the city of Toba, from where he made an excursion to the ancient Shinto temple at Ise, a place of pilgrimage for the Japanese. There he submitted to a ceremony of purification and observed a group of nuns perform a ritual dance to the slow, monotonous music of flutes and drums in honor of one of the Shinto gods. He was profoundly moved, and as he left the temple, he told María that he had felt the presence of the divine "in a way that had never occurred to him in churches or cathedrals." He told María that he wished he could return to Japan one day to spend several months in a Shinto monastery.[8]

Borges's discovery of Shintoism acted as a catalyst for the spiritual awakening he underwent in Japan. In retrospect it was his meeting with the chief priest at the Meiji Temple, just a few days after his arrival in Tokyo, that would assume the greatest spiritual significance for Borges. On November 27, about a week before he was due to depart Japan, he gave an interview to the journalist Mie Uchida in which he spoke of the "plot," as he put it, of a poem that had occurred to him as he was conversing with the Shintoist priest; he had been moved by everything the priest was saying, not so much on account of the man's words but because Borges felt that he was "being penetrated by his voice, the spaciousness of the gardens, the calm of the temple precinct," and at that moment it had occurred to him to write a poem.[9]

The poem that eventually resulted from his encounter with the Shinto priest was called "The Stranger" ("El forastero").[10] Here Borges adopted the persona of the *gushi*, who receives "an aged poet from Peru" at the temple with a serene yet bemused forbearance. The priest explains his faith through an interpreter, yet he cannot tell whether the foreigner has understood him. The old poet, who is blind, says he will recall their dialogue in a poem. The priest does not know if he ever will, or if they will see each other again, but even though priest and poet are strangers to each other, their meeting has created a bond between them and, through them, with the world itself—the two men share "the garden air and the smell of the damp earth and the song of birds or of gods." The poem thus represents the immaterial bond between the two men, for it enacts in language a free exchange between self and other based on trust. And just as the priest had placed his trust in the good faith of the blind old South American poet, so, too, did Shintoism itself appear to be founded on trust. The Shinto is "the lightest of cults. / The lightest and the most ancient"—its writings are "so archaic they are now almost blank." We must do good, it tells us, but it "has not laid down a code of ethics"; it does not declare that "a man must weave his karma" nor does it wish "to intimidate with punishments or bribe with rewards"; "its followers may accept the doctrine of Buddha or of Jesus." Shintoism proposed no absolute order, no final truth, no dogma, not even a code of ethics; it simply trusted its followers to interpret its values and principles without fear or guilt.

Shintoism thus taught Borges not to look for explanations: the way to salvation was not to know but to trust—to trust in the benevolence of the Spirit or spirits who might rule the universe. In the eight million deities worshipped by Shintoists, he saw a metaphor for the ultimate mystery of the numinous. Even so, these myriad gods could offer solace in times of fear or desolation by the revelation of their contingent presence at unexpected moments. In a poem called "Shinto," Borges observed that when we are "annihilated by misfortune," we can be saved, if only for a second, "by tiny adventures of attention or memory," for "eight million are the deities of the Shinto, / and they travel the earth in secret. / Those modest deities touch us, / they touch us and then depart."[11] He would endeavor to capture these fleeting touches of the Shinto gods in a series of haikus, for the object of a haiku, Borges was to state in a subsequent lecture on his experience of Japan, was "to appreciate a precious instant."[12] There were no metaphors in a haiku, no comparisons of one thing with another; it was "as if the Japanese felt that every single thing was unique."

Borges would characterize Shinto as "a sort of pantheism,"[13] for the respect it accorded the unique nature of each and every thing allowed him to be uniquely Borges—which Buddhism did not—while putting him in touch with something beyond the self. On the other hand, by persuading him to accept the fragmentary, heterogeneous, plural quality of his experience, Shintoism released him from the coercive anxiety to strive for that miraculous vision of the Absolute—that saving insight into the essence of the self within the final unity of things—which Christianity appeared to offer but in which he could not ultimately believe. Even so, Shintoism did not suffice in itself to meet Borges's spiritual needs. The vagueness of Shinto theology, especially with regard to the last things—death and the destiny of the individual soul—could not fully satisfy his hunger for personal salvation. The visit to Japan, therefore, did not resolve Borges's spiritual yearnings, but what it did was to awaken him to a new consciousness of a numinous reality beyond the self, and Shintoism, specifically, acted as a catalyst for the elaboration of what we might call an "agnostic mysticism" of his own, for its accommodating mysteries allowed for a reconciliation of metaphysical perplexity with a kind of religious awe.

Borges and María flew back to Buenos Aires on December 3, and in the course of the following year, he would develop the "agnostic mysticism" whose seeds were planted during this first visit to Japan: a number of poems he published in 1980 reveal a new attitude to the questions of time, identity, and destiny that had preoccupied him from the outset of his career. Already the new spirit of trust absorbed in Japan may be observed in a poem he must have written a few weeks after his return. In "The Web" ("La trama"), he wondered about his final destiny.[14] He was still preoccupied with old age and death, still a wanderer in the labyrinth of existence, with no end, no goal, no purpose, but even though he had found no remedy for the collapse of his Dantean dream, the poem evinces a new equanimity. In which of his cities would he die—Geneva, Montevideo, Nara, Buenos Aires, or Austin, Texas? In what language would he meet his end—the Spanish of his ancestors or the English of that Bible his grandmother used to read from on the edge of the pampas? At what hour would death arrive? Borges accepts that we may never discover the reason we came to be, but the old anxieties to divine answers to questions about his destiny have dissolved, and he is willing to surrender to the openness of his fate and even looks forward to his death "with impatient hope."

In April he went to Spain, where, on the twenty-third of that month, he received from King Juan Carlos I the Cervantes Prize, the premier literary award in the Spanish-speaking world, at a ceremony in Alcalá de Henares, the birthplace of Cervantes.* This visit was to be something of a journey into his own past. With María he would go to Madrid, Seville, Granada, Barcelona, and Majorca, all of them places he had lived in or first visited as a young man with his family.

In Majorca he and María called on Robert Graves, a long-term resident of the island, at his house in the mountain village of Deya. Blind and deaf, Graves had plainly not long to live, and Borges was not even sure that the English poet had actually registered their presence, since he uttered not a word during the entire visit. But when they took their leave, Graves shook Borges's hand and kissed Maria's. At the garden gate, his wife called out, "You must come back! This is heaven!"[15]

It was indeed a kind of heaven: Borges would write of Robert Graves that there was "nothing further from the struggle and closer to ecstasy than that seated old man surrounded in his immobility by his wife, children and grandchildren, the youngest sitting on his knee."[16] This was the kind of patriarchal serenity that he might have wished for himself, but he knew that he could not be Robert Graves any more than he could be Whitman or Dante or Shakespeare; he could not opt out of "the struggle," could not cease being Borges.

Yet what did it mean to be Borges? If anything, his visit to Japan had deepened the enigma of selfhood. In "To Flow or to Be" ("Correr o ser") he would ask whether the self was just "a series of blank days and dark nights" or whether there might exist some "secret I," some personal being beyond the reach of time? "Perhaps on the other side of death / I shall learn whether I have been a word or someone."[17] In another poem, called "Yesterdays," a key poem at this juncture, he presented the self as a motley of diverse things—this "I" of his comprised not only his "lineage of Protestant pastors and South American soldiers" but also his father's voice, the books he had read, his memories, every single moment of his long life.[18] The poem ended with the chilling possibility that the self was nothing but "a mirror, an echo," or, worse still, "the epitaph," of memories, of experiences or even of other lives that had been swept away by the river of time.

Pessimistic though it may be, "Yesterdays" is significant also for the elements it contains of a notion that would blossom into the most powerful and

*The fact that he was to share this prize with the Spanish poet Gerardo Diego, a member of the extraordinary "Generation of 1927," of whom Lorca remains the best-known figure outside Spain, was regarded by some as implying a snub to Borges by a section of the Spanish literary establishment on account of his declared support for the military juntas in Argentina and Chile, which had apparently cost him the Nobel Prize in 1976.

liberating of all the ideas Borges was to conceive in the final phase of his life. We may call this "virtuality" because it postulated the belief that certain mental or emotional events may be more real to us than the immediate objects of perception in the material world.[19] In addition to the land of one's birth, Borges suggested in "Yesterdays," there were certain places to which one could become profoundly attached:

> Chance or destiny, those two names
> of a secret thing we do not know,
> lavished *patrias* on me: Buenos Aires,
> Nara, where I spent a single night,
> Geneva, the two Córdobas, Iceland.

It was depth of emotional significance that created a virtual bond with a place that could be just as strong as a "real" or material association. Geneva was so thoroughly woven into the fabric of his youth that it was as much a *patria* as Buenos Aires. But so, too, was Iceland, where he had first discovered mutual love with María. And Nara was a *patria,* even though he had spent just one night there, because it enshrined the experience of his spiritual awakening in Japan. However, the origin of these *patrias*—the fount, indeed, of virtuality—had to be that "secret thing we do not know" which might lie concealed behind the vagaries of chance or destiny. And on the existence of this "secret thing" would depend, in turn, the possibility of there being a "secret I" that could stand above the flow of time. Otherwise, as the poem concludes, the self would be nothing more substantial than the "epitaph" of other bygone, transient selves.

At the end of October, Borges traveled with María to the United States, where he had been invited to spend a month as a visiting professor at Indiana University. But first he went to New York as a guest of the PEN Club, and on October 29 he visited The Cloisters, a branch of the Metropolitan Museum in Fort Tryon Park at the northwestern tip of Manhattan. The museum owed its name to a set of medieval cloisters reconstructed from authentic remains shipped over from Europe. Borges was inspired by these medieval relics to write a poem remarking that "time knows no order in this place," for "the cloisters" were not "apocryphal"; they had been built and inhabited in medieval France, and when transplanted to Manhattan, they conveyed to him the sounds and voices that once were heard in Aquitaine when the forces of Islam were pressing at the frontiers of Christendom.[20] The Cloisters thus took one back to a past that predated the discovery of the continent in which they were housed: "The laurels I am touching will blossom / when Lief Ericsson descries the shores of America." The sensation produced in him a kind of "vertigo," since he was not "accustomed to eternity."

The relativities of time and space induced by this foretaste of "eternity" at The Cloisters would prove to be extraordinarily liberating for Borges. The accelerating frequency of his comings and goings between Buenos Aires and numerous countries attests to a newfound zest for life. He gladly accepted invitations to lecture around the world, becoming a habitué of airports and night flights, traversing oceans and continents and time zones, but the very intensity of these displacements would allow him to float above it all in a kind of timeless capsule of happiness with María. She would describe it as being enclosed in a "magic circle," each absorbed in the presence of the other and oblivious to everything around them.[21] Between public engagements they would repair to one or other of their favorite havens, their virtual *patrias*—Geneva, Iceland, Venice, Marrakesh—so that the dizzying round of lectures, readings, press conferences, and award ceremonies would be interspersed with secret interludes of mutual bliss.[22]

All his life Borges had felt himself to be a victim of solipsism, a nebulous entity floating over a sea of illusions, but, paradoxically, it was the experience of mutual love—that giving of oneself to another—that allowed him to perceive the objective limits of the subject, and even suggested the existence of a virtual self that might constitute the abiding center of one's being. Virtuality, then, was intrinsically different from solipsism, since it was underwritten, as it were, by the reciprocity of love, and it was from this firmer sense of self that Borges would develop his faith in the virtual powers of the mind.

By the end of 1980, Borges had further elaborated the notion of virtuality by associating it with the creative imagination. On December 7 he published a poem about a Chinese lacquer walking stick that "was discovered by María Kodama."[23] It occurred to him that the stick was once shaped to fit its owner's hand by an artisan about whom he knew absolutely nothing. And yet the fact that he was wondering about that untraceable stranger created a link with him: "It is not impossible that Someone has premeditated that link. It is not impossible that the universe might need that link." Here we find a distinct advance in Borges's "agnostic mysticism"—the creative imagination was capable of putting one in touch with a transcendent Other, a Someone who might be secretly governing the universe. He returned to the idea of a creative collaboration with this mysterious cosmic spirit in "The Third Man" ("El tercer hombre"), where he wondered about the third man whom he chanced to have passed in a crowded street the previous Saturday.[24] To write a poem about this total stranger was "to execute an irreparable act"—"I have forged a link."

Both "The Lacquer Walking Stick" and "The Third Man," according to Borges, were "fundamentally the same" because they referred to "the secret bonds that unite all the beings of the universe."[25] This was a reformulation of the pantheism he had always been drawn to, but with the difference that it was now the creative will of an individual that had actively helped to establish those secret, pantheist bonds. The two poems adumbrated the idea of a "magic act" by which the virtual powers of the creative imagination might be purposefully applied to generate order and meaning in an otherwise mysterious universe. In a further poem, called "The Just" ("Los justos"), he suggested the possibility of salvation through "magic acts"—he listed an arbitrary collection of individuals, among them a gardener, a music lover, two chess players, a typesetter, and a devotee of Stevenson, and concluded that "those people, who are unknown to each other, are saving the world."[26] Borges was developing the idea that the links created by the "magic acts" of the imagination corresponded to the dispositions of the "secret thing we do not know." Virtuality could save us, in other words, because it represented not a world of illusions but the coincidence of our individual wills with the Will of that Someone who might well exist beyond time.

Nevertheless, this tentative elaboration of a faith in virtuality was not without its stumblings and reversals: Borges was still prey to doubt and to weariness, and at times he would regard death—extinction even—as a welcome release from the existential struggle. Toward the end of December, he was traveling again with María, to Madrid once more, having been invited to join the panel of judges for the next Cervantes Prize. They spent New Year's in Geneva, where, as usual, he sought out Maurice Abramowicz. This was to be the last time the two old friends would see each other—Maurice died a few months later. And it may have been a premonition that his friend had not long to live that reminded Borges of his own longevity. In "Two Forms of Insomnia" ("Dos formas del insomnio"), he compared a long life to the curse of sleeplessness, to the "horror of being and of continuing to be."[27] Again in "Eclesiastes, 1, 9" (the biblical reference is to the theme "And there is no new thing under the sun"), he looked forward to the peace of oblivion, to receiving the "gift" of possessing that "virginal maiden: death."[28] These dispiriting poems would seem to indicate that in the early months of 1981, Borges's "agnostic mysticism" was in crisis: Abramowicz's death, and the probable imminence of his own, may have concentrated his mind on the fundamental issue that Shintoism had not been able to answer for him—what happened to the individual soul after death? Could virtuality compensate ultimately for the eventual extinction of the self?

Toward the middle of 1981, however, he was looking to love once more to restore his faith in the virtual powers of the imagination. In "That Man" ("Aquél") he lamented his condition—his blindness, his childlessness, "the fame no one deserves," "that bad habit, Buenos Aires"—but he reckoned also with the moon, "which always surprises us."[29] He associated the moon with María Kodama, and it was this faith in the replenishing virtues of the moon that led him to choose "The Cipher" ("La cifra") as the title poem of a new collection of poems he was putting together in 1981.[30] "The Cipher" was a wistful variation on the *carpe diem* topic: the time will come when he shall see the moon no more, but since one's destiny is a cipher, the only recourse is to cherish the "silent friendship of the moon":

> We keep discovering and forgetting that sweet habit of the night.
> One must gaze upon her truly. It may be the last.

On May 17, 1981, he dedicated his new collection of poems to María Kodama, stating that to dedicate a book is "a magic act," "as are all the acts of the universe."[31] In this dedication he was renewing his faith in the related mysteries of love and virtuality. A true gift, he wrote, is "reciprocal": "To give and to receive are the same thing." And it was thanks to this paradox that he had found not the Dantean Rose of final meaning, still less the godlike vision of the Aleph or of the all-embracing Simurgh but an intimation that the twists and turns of everyday life might trace the whorls of a mysterious flower, a flower capable of inspiring a pristine wonder at the great, multifarious beauty of the world, a wonder that shines through in his dedication to María—"how many mornings, how many seas, how many gardens of East and West, how much Virgil."

CHAPTER 32

Deconstructing the Nation
(1980–1983)

SINCE 1976, when he declared his support for General Videla and made his notorious visit to Chile, Borges had largely turned away from politics and become increasingly preoccupied with personal matters—his search for a new understanding of love, and the anxieties about illness and death that preceded his visit to Japan. This self-absorption, however, coincided with the worst years of the conflict between the armed forces and the powerful guerrilla armies of the Montoneros and the ERP.

The war had been under way since before the return of Perón to Argentina in 1973. Perón had tried to suppress the guerrillas and had even turned a blind eye to the work of death squads, who snatched suspects and caused them to "disappear." Under his successor, Isabelita Perón, the armed forces were given the powers to prosecute an all-out campaign of repression against the guerrillas, who, for their part, carried out terrorist bomb attacks against presumed military targets with little concern for the maiming and killing of innocent civilians. It was after the military coup of 1976 that the activities of the death squads became ever more indiscriminate—people were kidnapped from city streets in broad daylight and spirited away to secret detention centers where they were subjected to the most horrendous torture and often killed.

The anti-inflationary economic policies of the military government added fuel to the fire: massive cutbacks in public spending, including social welfare, caused a sharp rise in unemployment and widespread poverty. There followed an explosion of industrial unrest, and in response the military death squads extended their reach to include labor activists. This vicious internal war—which came to be generally known as the "Dirty War"—reached its height during 1977 and 1978, but even though the campaign against the guerrillas had succeeded by 1979, the economy was still in dire straits, with continuing hyperinflation, huge numbers out of work, and rapidly mounting public deficits.

Even as early as 1977, Borges had become disillusioned with the military rulers whom he had initially hailed as the potential saviors of the nation, but while he publicly dissented from their aggressive foreign policy toward Chile and been branded a traitor for his pains, he remained silent about the alleged activities of the death squads. He would later say that he was not fully aware of what was going on, since, owing to his blindness, he had largely to rely on what other people told him about current affairs. There is some plausibility in this claim, especially since the Argentine press was curiously reluctant to run stories about the "disappearances" after the editor of La Opinión, Jacobo Timerman, who had called into question some aspects of the conduct of the antiguerrilla campaign, had himself disappeared in 1976. The only paper that had not been cowed into silence was the English-language Buenos Aires Herald. Its editor, the Englishman Robert Cox, had once been prominent in his condemnaton of the terrorism of the guerrillas and had even supported the coup by General Videla, believing that it would put an end to the mayhem under Isabelita Perón and to the activities of the death squads her government had condoned. But Cox was also the first to write about the possibility that people were being made to disappear under Videla, and this earned him the displeasure of the military government. Arrested in April 1977, he was released under pressure from the foreign news media, but in December 1979, after persistent threats, he decided to flee the country in the interests of his own and his family's safety.

The silence surrounding the fate of the desaparecidos gave rise to a protest movement of mothers whose sons and daughters had vanished without trace. Their first protest took place on April 30, 1977, exactly a week after Cox's arrest, when fifteen women gathered in the Plaza de Mayo, the square outside the president's palace, to bear silent witness to the fact of these disappearances. The gatherings of these "Mothers of the Plaza de Mayo," held on one Thursday of each month, grew in size and influence, attracting the interest of foreign journalists, which afforded the women a measure of protection. Even so, they quite failed to elicit any information about the desaparecidos from the authorities.

When Borges started to criticize the junta's aggressive stance toward Chile over the issue of the Beagle Channel in 1977 and 1978, some Mothers of the Plaza de Mayo visited him to enlist his support for their cause. He declined to do so, suspecting that he might be manipulated into publicly endorsing the guerrillas. It was perhaps understandable that he should have been wary of being exploited for unforeseeable political ends, given the likelihood of disinformation emanating from one or other of the contending sides. However, his reluctance to give his support to the Mothers of the Plaza de Mayo was symptomatic of a deeper reservation—although he may have privately questioned whether the military junta was an ethical elite capable of running the kind of "enlightened dictatorship" that he had envisaged for Argentina, he continued to believe that they were preferable to the Cuban-inspired Marxist nationalism of the Peronist guerrillas. He was still laboring under the contradiction into which Perón had led him nearly two decades earlier—he favored a liberal democratic system in principle but feared that the people would persist in voting for Perón or his heirs. And so, seeing no alternative to their rule, he clung to the military junta as the lesser of two evils.

Still, it was during his visit to Spain in April 1980 in order to receive the Cervantes Prize that he began to change his mind. He attributed this change to the fact that he was put under intense pressure by the Spanish press to give his views on the Dirty War and the *desaparecidos* in particular. "They interrogated me a good deal," and "they also taught me a lot," he would later confess.[1] The Argentine public had its first indication of Borges's change of heart in an interview he gave while in Spain to the respected Argentine journalist Manfred Schonfeld, which was published in *La Prensa* on May 6. Borges openly called for an investigation into the fate of the *desaparecidos*. All the same, he was careful to criticize the guerrillas as well as the military: "It is impossible for me to ignore either the serious problems existing in connection with terrorism or those connected with the repression. Nothing can make me be silent about these deaths and disappearances."

Shortly after his return to Buenos Aires, he received a visit from an old acquaintance, Agustina Paz Anchorena, a woman of impeccable patrician lineage, who worked as a public relations executive but was also an active Mother of the Plaza de Mayo. She informed him that her daughter had disappeared on April 21, 1976, and she had been unable to find out what had happened to her or the reasons for her abduction. "Borges listened to me very carefully and with great respect," Agustina recalled, "and he was able to get a sense of the full extent of a mother's grief."[2] He then explained to her that "he lived a very insulated life because he was blind and could not read the newspapers, and was dependent on whatever information other people chose to give him," but he was persuaded by her story and believed that she was not acting from political motives. Sometime later Agustina came to see Borges with another Mother of the Plaza de Mayo, the journalist Vera Jarash, whose daughter had also disappeared in mid-1976, and they asked him to sign a petition calling upon the government to provide information on the fate of the disappeared. He agreed to sign without hesitation and was also instrumental in persuading Adolfo Bioy Casares to add his signature. This was the first of several public declarations in support of the *desaparecidos* to which Borges would lend his name. It was published on August 12, 1980, in *Clarín*, and was signed also by the writer Ernesto Sábato, the man with whom Borges had publicly quarreled in 1956 over their divergent attitudes to Peronism.

Borges's decision to support the campaign for human rights in Argentina represented a very significant shift in his attitude to the military government, but it did not mean that he had withdrawn his support for the military's war against the guerrillas. His concern was with the ethics of the situation, with the need to uphold the rule of law. He was opposed to the "secret justice" that the military was alleged to have carried out against the subversives, and he appealed for a proper judicial investigation of the allegations of torture and murder: "If you're accused you should be allowed a lawyer and a judge also. But in this case all these things are done on the sly and that is wrong."[3]

All the same, he was now regarded as a public enemy by the military. The international edition of *Newsweek* of January 12, 1981, was banned in Argentina because it carried an interview with Borges that was deemed to be too critical of the political situation.[4] And to add to his repeated appeals for an investigation into the *desaparecidos*, Borges again criticized the government's nationalistic policy toward Chile over the sovereignty of the islands in the Beagle Channel. The Argentine junta had refused to accept the verdict of the International Court of Justice in favor of Chile in 1977, and the question had been referred to the Vatican, but by the end of 1980, the Vatican, too, had found in favor of Chile. Borges once more urged the government to accept the official verdict, but his critical stance earned him the vicious hostility of the nationalist press. For instance, the newspaper *El Sol* of Catamarca, under the headline: BORGES, GROTESQUE TRAITOR TO THE NATION, accused him of "discrediting the armed forces," and declared it "unacceptable" that an Argentine citizen like Borges should urge the nation to renounce its "sovereign rights" over its own territory.[5] But the Vatican's judgment had put the Argentine military in a quandary—they could neither accept nor reject the verdict of the Holy See—and this frustration over the Beagle Channel would shortly find a different outlet in another, more hazardous form of aggression.

Borges's international standing was so high that the violent attacks on him by extreme nationalists caused unease in government circles, doubtless because there was a danger that they might backfire. In July 1981, the military censors banned a television program called *Operación Ja-Ja* because it included a comic sketch in which the actor Mario Sapag impersonated Borges. The sketch was deemed to constitute "an attack on the cultural patrimony of Argentina," for, as the general who headed the Comité Federal de Radiofusión, the board of censors, explained, Borges was "a most worthy ambassador of our culture throughout the world," and the censors wished "to ensure respect for those personalities who enhance the honor of the nation."[6]

Borges himself was abroad at the time of this incident. He had been conferred an honorary degree by Harvard on June 4 and another by the University of Puerto Rico shortly afterward, and when he heard from journalists about the banned TV sketch, he was in Milan speaking at a symposium organized by Franco Maria Ricci. Clearly exasperated by this act of censorhip, he defended the comedian's right of expression: "Really, this ban shows just how far the state has degenerated," he declared to the press. "The state interferes in everything. We have a country full of public functionaries who want to have a finger in every pie, have views on everything, make decisions about everything. And all the while there is less and less freedom."[7]

Borges's repeated attacks on nationalism, on the state, on populism, were all symptomatic of his hatred of any institution or movement that threatened the freedom of the responsible individual, for the one enduring ideal that had underlain his changing political allegiances was fundamentally a libertarian and democratic one, based on an "anarchist" vision of the ethical individual living in a community of free individuals, which he had learned in his youth from his father and Macedonio Fernández. Since the previous year he had been describing himself as "an inoffensive anarchist," even "a revolutionary," who was "against the idea of the state and against the frontiers between states."[8] And he was more specific about his "anarchism" to Uki Goñi of the *Buenos Aires Herald*: "Nationalism is the greatest evil of all. And of course the unequal distribution of material goods, that is wrong also, and the division of land in different countries. It makes for war, arbitrary distinctions. You see I'm really a student of [Herbert] Spencer, an old anarchist."[9]

There can be no doubt that, by the end of 1981, he was thoroughly disenchanted with the military government. And yet, he could find no alternative for Argentina. He would maintain that the country was not yet "ripe for democracy": "I think this government is a necessary evil because democracy would give us another Frondizi or at worst another Perón."[10] He was still caught in the old contradiction, so he clung for as long as he could to the idea that the generals were fundamentally well meaning. He told Uki Goñi, "I suppose this government means well but what it has done cannot be justified."[11] And he also told the writer Victoria Slavuski, "It might be that this government is made up of some well-meaning but incompetent people."[12]

The signs of that incompetence were everywhere to be seen. Even though the guerrillas had been defeated by 1980, the military junta seemed incapable of arresting the country's economic decline. General Videla and other moderates within the junta, alarmed at the extent of the misery caused by attempts to privatize the gigantic state sector, slowed down the process, but economic growth faltered as hyperinflation took off again and exports fell sharply. A series of major financial crashes was followed by a run on the peso after a sudden devaluation in February 1981. The financial outlook was dire—the foreign debt had climbed to over $35 billion, and over one-third of export earnings went in interest payments alone.

In March 1981, General Videla handed over the presidency to another moderate, General Roberto Viola, but there was evidence of serious infighting among the generals, and in December 1981, Viola was ousted by the hard-line General Leopoldo Galtieri, who introduced an economic austerity plan designed to bring hyperinflation down. This further round of belt tightening served only to produce even more industrial turmoil, and the junta found itself assailed by massive strikes, lockouts, and demonstrations. Fearing that he might lose control of the situation, Galtieri decided to play the nationalist card once more, only this time he decided to gamble on the most inflammatory issue of all—the Argentine claim to the Malvinas (Falkland Islands), a small archipelago in the South Atlantic that had been a British possession since 1833. On April 2, 1982, the armed forces launched an invasion of the Falkland Islands, and within hours the streets were filled with delirious crowds chanting nationalist slogans. The junta's troubles seemed to melt away: Galtieri was the hero of the hour.

The Argentine military had calculated that Britain would not bother to recover distant territories that were of no apparent value to her, but the British prime minister, Margaret Thatcher, dispatched a powerful naval task force to recover the islands. When the British fleet arrived in the South Atlantic it engaged Argentine forces in a conflict that began to take a heavy toll of lives on both sides. The islands were steadily reconquered by British troops, and on June 11 the commander of the Argentine forces occupying the Falklands formally surrendered to the British.

Within days of the Argentine surrender, General Galtieri's junta collapsed, and a new government was formed under a retired general, Reynaldo Bignone, who inherited a truly chaotic situation—an economy in ruins and a frenzied populace that could not comprehend the disaster, since they had been duped by the junta's propaganda machine into believing that they were heading for a glorious victory over the British imperialists. In the months that followed, General Bignone was to negotiate with the leaders of the political parties the terms of the military's withdrawal from politics and the restoration of electoral democracy.

Borges was in New York when he first heard news of the invasion of the Malvinas. He was appalled as much by the huge outpouring of nationalist fervor among the populace as by the prospect of a war against a foreign power. Three days after the war ended, he was in Dublin as a guest speaker at the annual celebration of "Bloomsday," June 16, the date on which James Joyce chose to set the events of his novel *Ulysses*. Asked about the Malvinas war at a press conference, he described it, notoriously, as "two bald men fighting over a comb," by which he meant to convey the futility of the conflict, but the remark came across as flippant and dismissive, and this added to his reputation abroad as a distrait old bibliophile with no understanding of contemporary affairs.

The truth was that the war caused him untold distress. In the weeks following the end of the war he wrote a poem that encapsulated the "anarchist" values he had publicly endorsed for several years past. "Juan López and John Ward" are the names, respectively, of a young Argentine who had a love of Conrad and a young Englishman who had learned Spanish in order to read *Don Quixote*.[13] They had been fated to live "in a strange epoch," in which the planet had been divided into different countries, a division that "fostered wars." "They could have been friends, but they only once met face to face, in some all too famous islands, and each of the two was Cain, and each, Abel." They were buried side by side. "The episode I have described took place in a time which we cannot understand." After its publication in *Clarín* on August 26, 1982, Borges's poem was taken up by the anticonscription movement which had been formed in the aftermath of the Malvinas war, and it was displayed on posters on the walls of Buenos Aires.

Borges was to learn from veterans of the war that many of the Argentine soldiers had been mere conscripts with minimal training and poor equipment, and yet they had been sent to the Malvinas to face the enemy's professional troops. A large number of these conscripts, moreover, were poor Indians or mestizos from the interior provinces who were unaccustomed to the cold, windblown climate of the South Atlantic. Borges's outrage and pity brought forth another antiwar poem, "*Milonga* for a Soldier" ("Milonga de un soldado"), which was published in *Clarín* on December 30, 1982.[14] He praised the courage of the soldiers killed in the war, but rather than a glorification of battle, the poem was a lament for those young men who had been wickedly sacrificed by their leaders in the interests of the state.

By September he was telling a journalist that he had "changed," he was "decidedly a pacifist."[15] The war had been "a nightmare" in which thousands of "honorable men," Argentine and British, had been sent "not just to be killed but to kill," and all on account of a hasty decision made "without weighing up the consequences."[16] He felt that the Argentine invasion had been unethical— the juridical case in favor of the Argentine claim to the Malvinas was one thing, but the actual invasion was quite another. He added his voice to the demands for the indictment of the leaders of the military juntas. He believed there should be a rendering of accounts by the generals who had run the country: "There should be an investigation into the economic ruin, the disappearances, the war."[17]

Far worse than the war over the Malvinas were the atrocities committed by the armed forces during the so-called Dirty War against the guerrillas. After the installation of Bignone as caretaker president, the Argentine media felt more at liberty to investigate the allegations of torture and murder, and by the last months of 1982, it was becoming clear that the most terrible violations of human rights had occurred under successive military juntas. No longer could Borges entertain any illusions that the military leaders were men of honor, or even "well meaning." The knowledge of these atrocities changed his whole approach to the Argentine political situation, finally dissolving the contradiction in which he had been caught since the late 1950s, when Perón had contrived to frustrate the aims of the Revolución Libertadora that had overthrown him. He believed the leaders of the military governments, far from being an ethical elite, were corrupt and evil men who were quite unfit to provide the kind of enlightened dictatorship he had thought necessary until such time as the Argentine people were mature enough for democracy. "It is true that we have had dictators," he observed to Victoria Slavuski, "but they had popular support. These [i.e., the military] are gangsters. This is a country of madmen. No, this is a country of wise but desperate people in the hands of madmen."[18]

The only remedy was to find a way of delivering the people from the madmen: "I believe our only hope is democracy. Our only way out is an election."[19] On the other hand, he feared the outcome of an election: "If elections are held, the Peronists will win, and there will be acts of revenge because they have been persecuted; and if they aren't held we shall continue to be governed by people who are equally discredited."[20] The enormity of the political catastrophe had left him confused and disoriented, at times advocating democracy as the only hope, at others fearing that democracy would lead nowhere but to a further cycle of violence. He simply could not explain what had happened to Argentina: "We had all the advantages: a large influx of foreign immigrants, no racial problems, a strong middle class, the most influential class of all, but which is in the process of disintegrating. Now the factories are closing and there are huge numbers of people out of work, people going hungry just outside Buenos Aires, and even in Buenos Aires itself."[21] He was at a loss to offer any solution to the country's ills: "What might await us? I don't know. Anarchy perhaps. Or incompetent governments, or coups d'état."[22]

Meanwhile, his literary reputation was reaching ever greater heights. In January 1983 he was invited to Paris to receive the Légion d'Honneur from the president of France, François Mitterrand. On January 11 he gave a lecture at the Collège de France, called "La Création Poétique," which was attended by Michel Foucault and Raymond Aron, two of the most famous intellectuals in France. He also signed a contract with Gallimard for an edition of his collected works in the prestigious Pléiade series, a high honor indeed, since it indicated that he had been deemed worthy by the French cultural establishment of taking his place as a classic writer alongside the great writers of France.

Yet, curiously, while his literary reputation could scarcely have been higher, many of the people who admired him for his work detested him for his allegedly reactionary politics. He was still being dogged by his pro-Videla and pro-Pinochet declarations of 1976. Even at the Collège de France, he was unable to escape this reputation as a reactionary, or at least as a man culpably indifferent to political issues. A member of the audience rose to say that Borges was not qualified to comment on the Argentine situation "because he lived in an ivory tower." Irritated at being taken to task over Argentine politics, Borges replied,

> Ivory towers are found only in the game of chess. I am very aware of what is happening in my country and in the world. And I have proved it—I criticized Perón in his time and now the generals and their government. I know that there are people in Argentina who do not have enough to eat. And that situation is unacceptable. I don't know what future awaits us, but I imagine it will be a sorry one because I can see no solution.[23]

On his return to Buenos Aires, he would become even more despairing of the nation's prospects. Superficially there were positive developments, for, at the end of February 1983, General Bignone announced that free elections would be held the following October. Borges, however, remained pessimistic, since he still expected elections to result in a victory for the Peronists. Far more worrying, however, were the nature and scale of the atrocities committed during the Dirty War. Borges was appalled by the depths of cynicism displayed by the military rulers who had condoned such crimes. In the very month that elections were called, a member of the junta saw fit to declare to the media that some seven thousand people had been made to "disappear," but that there was no point in looking for them because they were all dead and buried. Borges observed to a journalist that in the time of the tyrant Rosas, his liberal opponents published "Tables of Blood" listing the people who had been exterminated, but now it was the government itself that published its own tables of blood.[24] The malaise ran very deep: "I believe the military defeat [i.e., in the Malvinas] is the least of our ills. Far more grave is the economic defeat of our country. And much graver still than the economic decline is the ethical impoverishment of the Argentine people." He viewed the nation's future with profound apprehension: "They say we are touching bottom, and indeed all we have done so far is to sink ever lower. But I believe space is infinite, and there is no bottom, so we may continue to fall indefinitely."

The extremity of the situation was such that it plunged Borges into a crisis of faith in the viability of Argentina as a nation. This crisis, I believe, started in the aftermath of the Malvinas War and was to last until the middle of 1983.

The process was already under way in December 1982, when he was approached by members of his family to sign a petition to erect an equestrian statue of their ancestor General Miguel Estanislao Soler, a hero of the War of Independence. Borges was clearly exasperated by this proposal to honor a military ancestor just after the Malvinas debacle and when evidence of abuses of human rights by the military was pouring out through the media. He told Victoria Slavuski at this time that he had refused: "I said no. The last thing we need is another equestrian statue."[25] In this refusal to glorify General Soler, I detect an implicit association of the heroes of the independence wars with the latter-day generals who had prosecuted the Dirty War against the guerrillas and the war over the Malvinas. For what concerned Borges, above all, was to get at the roots of the catastrophe that had befallen the nation.

Just four months later, he published a strange little text to which he gave the modest title "A Storyline" ("Un argumento").[26] It is presented as the outline of a plot for a novel that Borges claimed he could not be bothered to write. On closer examination, however, it is one of the most horrifying pieces he ever produced. In essence it proposes a "conspiracy of the old against the young, of fathers against sons," a story of "weak and evil men getting together to kill strong young men." The motives of these evil men are diverse:

Some, being crippled, impotent or infirm, envy the normal health of the young; others, in their avarice, are loath to let their sons inherit the wealth they have worked so hard to amass; another feels frustrated, and cannot resign himself to his son's good fortune; yet another, in a sober and lucid fashion, sincerely believes that the young are prey to fanatical ideas and are incapable of seeing sense.

Given that the text was conceived and written in the aftermath of the Malvinas War, it is hard not to see it, in the first instance, as an indictment of the aging generals who conspired to send young men to die in a senseless conflict. But the fact that it is framed in such general terms suggests that Borges saw it as representing a more profound and far-reaching phenomenon. What he was doing in "A Storyline" was attempting to uncover and define the psychological dynamic that had driven the nation to the brink of self-destruction.

This dynamic Borges identified as a complex resentment of one generation against the other—the old envy the vigor of the young, while the young "may well be accomplices of the old men who have resolved to destroy them." In the last paragraph, this dynamic is pared down even further:

It might perhaps be as well to renounce the concept of a conspiracy and reduce to two the number of protagonists. One, the old man who realizes that he hates his son; the other, the son who knows he is hated and feels guilty.

Borges was drawing an analogy between nation and self—fathers attempted to compel their sons to remain loyal to their own values and allegiances, and while the young might resent these constraints upon their freedom, they were nevertheless complicit in this conspiracy of the old against them, because they were themselves reluctant to break completely with the past. In a sense, each generation invented the ghost of its forefathers and passed on a burden of guilt to the next, constraining the freedom of the young ("On the verge of suicide, a young man accepts with relief the sentence of his elders"). Even to rebel against the ancestral ghost was a perverse, self-defeating attempt to shape the past in order to define one's identity in the present.

"A Storyline" represented Argentina's violent history as stemming from a guilt-ridden fixation with the past. Indeed, so compulsive was this fixation that in the very year in which the armed forces were being accused of horrendous crimes, Borges's own family was proposing to erect a public monument to the greater glory of their ancestor General Soler. It was as if the ghosts of the heroic founders of the nation were presiding over the generations of their descendants, brandishing the sword of honor, and challenging them to remain true to their memory. But how could these cycles of internecine conflict be broken? Borges's projected novel remained open-ended—the "storyline" of the nation's history, as much as that of his own relations with his father, awaited a proper resolution: "The novel concludes when the end has not yet arrived. Both of them [i.e. father and son] are still waiting for it." (In Spanish the verb *esperar* can mean "to wait," but also "to hope.")

Just three days after "A Storyline" appeared, he published a poem called "The Possession of Yesterday" ("Posesión del ayer"), a meditation on the theme that "we possess only what we have lost": we possess the past by virtue of our yearning for it, and not because we know it as it actually was.[27] Thus, "Ilion once was, but Ilion endures in the hexameter that laments it." Our possession of yesterday would seem inescapably to be a form of solipsism, the projection of our present desires and fears onto imaginary versions of the past. The poem concludes that "there are no paradises other than lost paradises."

Borges's crisis of faith in the nation put his notion of virtuality to the test. If our minds can shape virtual meaning, it would appear to be impossible to distinguish good meanings from bad. How, then, could one distinguish between different views of the nation? Was a democratic or liberal view no different from a fascist view? Were all forms of apprehending the past merely attempts to recover an imaginary "lost paradise"? Perhaps the Argentine fixation with the past was rooted in that unresolved conflict between fathers and sons, between the old and the young, which Borges saw as the basic driving force of the nation's "storyline." "My father has died and is always by my side," he wrote in "The Possession of Yesterday." But how to free Argentina from the ghosts of fathers and forefathers, from its obsession with the "lost paradises" of yesterday?

In another poem, called "All Our Yesterdays, a Dream" ("Todos los ayeres, un sueño), Borges reflected on the possibility that all the various myths of the nation's identity were equally illusory.[28] And he did not spare his own image of Argentina from this radical critique. He confessed to having once "erected a mythology" about daggers and guitars, Muraña and duels, but that "bloody mythology," too, was part of "yesterday" and just as fruitless as "the sage history of the schoolrooms," for, as he knew from his own experience, to oppose the sword of honor with the dagger of rebellion served only to reinforce the opposition between adulation of the hero and guilt-ridden attempts to dethrone him. There was no one true vision of the past: "The past is clay which the present shapes as it pleases. Interminably." But if all the "yesterdays" of the nation were nothing but a dream, what did Argentina amount to?

In a beautifully laconic and allusive poem published on April 23—the same month as "A Storyline" and "The Possession of Yesterday" appeared—Borges questioned the very basis on which the nation had been founded. In "*Milonga* of the Infidel" ("Milonga del infiel"), he addressed the most potent of all the founding myths of the nation—the belief that Argentina was built by civilized men who tamed the barbarism of the American wilderness.[29] He imagined an Indian of the pampas coming into contact with the society of the white man for the first time. The infidel is puzzled by doors, sees his own image in a mirror and fails to recognize himself. By empathizing with the bemused innocence of the Indian, Borges implicitly subverts the pretensions of the criollos who had fought to make the land safe for Christian settlement by exterminating the "savages" of the pampas. The final verses are barbed with condemnation:

> Nor would it surprise him to know
> that he would be defeated and done to death;
> his story we call the Conquest of the Desert.

The last line shocks by its very unexpectedness, for the reader is obliged to weigh up the significance of the historic term the "Conquest of the Desert." Was the fate of the Native Americans so different from the fate of the "*desaparecidos*," or of the raw conscripts who were dispatched to their deaths in the attempted conquest of the Malvinas?

Borges would seem to be implying that the founding of the nation might have initiated a tradition of violent exclusion as the means of creating and preserving a national identity: the sword had won the criollos independence from Spain and had subsequently been used to define an identity for the inchoate polity that had come into existence. Hence the bloody dichotomies of Argentine history—Christians against infidels, *unitarios* against *federales,* criollos against immigrants, Peronists against liberals, Montoneros against the military, each side fighting the other in order to defend a particular vision of the nation.

At the beginning of April 1983, Borges went with María to the United States to attend a conference at Dickinson College in Pennsylvania. They spent some time in New York, María's favorite city, and on his return to Buenos Aires, he took up once more the question of possessing the past, but now, doubtless replenished by his trip abroad with the woman he loved, he approached it in a quite different spirit. On June 8, 1983, he published a poem called "What Is Ours" ("Lo nuestro"), in which he articulated once more the paradox that "we possess only what we have lost," but the formulation of this paradox was crucially different—"We love what we do not know, what is already lost to us."[30] While he acknowledges the power of the past to define who we are and what is ours, the accent here is not so much on possession as on love. Love transforms our apprehension of the past—we love "the ancients who can no longer disappoint because they are myth and splendor," we love our ancestors "with whom we could not converse for more than a quarter of an hour," we love our "friends who have died." Once we relinquish our desire to take possession of the past in order to shape it for our own ends, the past becomes a benign myth, for we no longer strive to recover what we think we have lost, and we are free to love the past for its own sake, love it in the way we might love "what we do not know" or what is other than ourselves, such as "languages we can scarcely decipher" or "the woman who is at our side and who is so different from us." As Borges had discovered through his love of the half-Japanese María Kodama, only in surrender do we perceive what was not already part of us before.

Love was the antidote to solipsism. Just as it had freed Borges from self-obsession, so did it hold the key to freedom from the larger solipsism that was nationalism. Like the self, national identity was best defined in relation to others, rather than by the projection of present concerns onto the past. And so the solution to the perverse conspiracies of fathers against sons that had characterized the "storyline" of Argentina was to enshrine the value of trust at the heart of the political culture. Borges was drawing on his personal experience in order to analyze the ills of the nation, and since the basis of his relationship with María Kodama was the principle of free mutuality, so now was he to accept this principle as the means of resolving the intergenerational conflict he regarded as having blighted the country's history. Fathers had to accept the freedom of their sons, the old had to trust the young; this alone would bring to an end the nefarious role the sword had played in the "storyline" of the nation.

The fruit of Borges's intricate reflections on "the possession of yesterday" was "The Confederates" ("Los conjurados"), a poem he would come to regard as his political testament.[31] Written sometime in 1982 or 1983, it has as its basic conceit the idea that since 1291, the year in which several cantons came together to form the Swiss Confederation, there has been a "conspiracy" afoot to build a "tower of reason and firm, solid faith" in the heart of Europe. (*Conjuración* can mean either a "conspiracy" or a "pact" in Spanish, and Borges drew on the connotations of both terms in the title "Los conjurados.") The "confederates" or "conspirators" are "men of diverse races, who profess different religions and speak diverse tongues" and who have "taken the odd decision to be reasonable," "to forget their differences and accentuate their affinities." There are twenty-two cantons at present (and the canton of Geneva, Borges says, "is one of my *patrias*"), but tomorrow the entire planet will be composed of such cantons. "It may be that what I say is not true; let us hope that it is prophetic."

The word *conjurados* creates a link with "A Storyline," with its wholly negative "conspiracy" of the old against the young, but it also harks back to the positive "conspiracy" he invoked in his 1928 speech to young criollo nationalists, in which he urged them to become *conjurados* in the creation of a "new man"—a fusion of criollo and immigrant—in Argentina. That vision had been destroyed by the sword of right-wing *nacionalismo*: initially by General Uriburu's coup d'état and latterly by Perón. The *nacionalistas* had sought to impose a particular interpretation of the past upon the whole nation, and the eventual results, in Borges's view, had been economic collapse and the twin disasters of the Dirty War and the war over the Malvinas. The poem "Los conjurados," in this respect, was a vindication of Borges's youthful *criollismo*, but it incorporated the essence of subsequent insights in order to transcend nationalism altogether, by drawing on the principle of free mutuality he had learned from his love of María Kodama and by embracing a utopian, "anarchist" ideal of universal brotherhood such as his father had once envisaged, a confederation of free individuals coming together on the basis of rational cooperation and dispensing with the paraphernalia of states, armies, churches, and flags.

By the middle of 1983, Borges's crisis of faith in Argentina as a nation had been overcome. As the presidential elections in October approached, he was to offer certain unmistakable signs of his hopes for the future of the country. In August he embarked on another round of lectures and courses in Europe and the United States. He went to Spain to receive the Grand Cross of Alfonso the Wise from the recently elected Socialist government. The success of the Spanish Socialists at the polls in 1982 marked the consolidation of Spain's transition to democracy after the death of Franco. Borges spoke at a university summer school in Santander, where he was presented with his award, and in Madrid he was invited to a private lunch with the new prime minister, Felipe González, a meeting that had a particular resonance back home since it signaled Borges's hopes that, like Spain, Argentina might make an orderly transition to democracy. On October 5 he was in London, at the invitation of the Anglo-Argentine Society, to inaugurate an annual series of lectures named in his honor. The first "Jorge Luis Borges Lecture," held at the Royal Society of Arts, took the form of a question-and-answer session that was entirely confined to literary topics, but in agreeing to attend such a gathering only fifteen months after the Malvinas/Falklands War, Borges was indicating his wish for a reconciliation between the two countries, as he had implied in his poem "Juan López and John Ward."

Later that month he traveled to the University of Wisconsin at Madison to receive an honorary degree. On the evening of October 30, which was the day of the presidential elections in Argentina, he was invited to a Halloween party and surprised himself by purchasing a wolf mask, despite always having had a terror of masks. When he arrived at the party, he started howling like a wolf and calling out, "*Homo homini lupus*" ("A man is a wolf to another man").[32] He had not taken leave of his senses, he was merely citing Plautus, and the full quotation sheds an interesting light on what might have been running through his mind: "Man is not a man but a wolf to another man, when he hasn't yet found out what he's like." ("*Lupus est homo homini, non homo, quom qualis sit non novit*," Plautus, *Asinaria*, line 495.) The fact that he could bring himself to wear a mask at all was a sign of a new self-possession. And then, as if his wearing a mask were not amazing enough, someone tugged at his sleeve and broke the news that Raúl Alfonsín, the Radical candidate, had been elected president of Argentina. "It was a double miracle," Borges would recall. "That victory and the fact that I'd worn a mask."[33] It was a miracle because this was the first time the Peronists had ever been defeated in a free election, and it must have seemed to Borges that the kind of vision he had outlined in "Los conjurados," a Swiss-style "confederacy" in favor of reason and good faith, might in due course be possible in Argentina after all: "I felt very good then because we had emerged from a nightmare, and that collective act of faith was what could save us all."[34]

A few weeks after returning to Buenos Aires, he was invited to a reception by Raúl Alfonsín, and in an address to this gathering of Argentine writers, intellectuals, and politicians, he confessed to a newfound optimism: "I had lost faith in democracy, believing it would result in chaos. But what happened on October 30, a historic date, gives us the right, the duty, to be hopeful."[35] He counseled patience all the same, "because democracy may need many years to develop," but he believed that after the "agony" the country had been through, there would be "a resurrection." At the end of his speech, "with a tremulous voice," "almost stammering," he cried out: "*¡Viva la patria!*"

CHAPTER 33

The Weaver of Dreams
(1984–1985)

ON JANUARY 14, 1984, Borges wrote an "Elegy" for his friend Maurice Abramowicz, who had died three years earlier.[1] Since he was himself eighty-four years old, he believed he was unlikely to live much longer, and thoughts of dying, as ever, brought to mind the issue of personal salvation and, in particular, that most compelling preoccupation of his, the continuing debate between self and nonself. Abramowicz, he reflected, would know for certain what lay beyond the veil of time: whether everything we experience on this earth is wiped away or whether our every action "projects an infinite shadow." The elegy for Abramowicz closes with a poignant attempt by Borges to engage the absent Maurice in a dialogue across the gulf of death: "I cannot tell whether you are still someone, I cannot tell whether you are hearing me."

In April of that year, he planned to spend a month in Japan with María, having been invited to speak at a conference in Tokyo on the theme of the decline of the West and the possibility of a "second renaissance" in the East.[2] After the conference, which took place from April 4 to 6, he and María went to Kyoto. It was there that Borges, during his first visit to Japan, had engaged the Buddhist monk in conversation about the reality of the self and the quest for enlightenment. On this second visit, however, he was moved to write a poem, not about the Buddhist nirvana but about the crucifixion of Christ. In "Christ on the Cross" ("Cristo en la cruz"), he struggled to grasp the central mystery of Christian salvation, but despite this hunger for faith, he could not bring himself to accept the truth of redemption: "What help could it be to me that this man suffered, if I happen to be suffering now?"[3] Even so, he felt unable to resign himself to unbelief; he would continue to search for Christ's true face "until the last day I walk upon this earth."

As before, he was to find solace in the tolerant spirit of Shintoism. A visit to a Shinto temple at Izumo on April 27 would inspire a parable called "On Salvation by Deeds" ("De la salvación por las obras"), describing a meeting of the Shinto deities to consider the future of humanity in view of the invention of "an invisible weapon which could put an end to history"—the atomic bomb.[4] The Shinto gods are in favor of permitting the human race to be destroyed as a punishment for its folly, but one of them recalls another invention, "something quite different, which fits in the space encompassed by seventeen syllables." After the dissenting god utters these seventeen syllables, it is decided to forgo punishment—and thus, "because of a haiku, the human race was saved." This tenuous sense that the world, ultimately, was ruled by benevolent spirits was as much as Borges could do to overcome skepticism. So he persevered in his "agnostic mysticism," clinging to his faith in virtuality and, more specifically, in writing as a "magic act" capable of bringing "salvation by deeds"—the act of creation was a means by which man might cooperate with those secret spirits who made the world proof against the forces of evil.

All the while he continued to travel, enclosed in that hermetic sphere of happiness he had found with María. He went to Crete in May to receive a doctorate from the University of Heraklion. In July he was in Paris to address the Académie des Sciences et des Lettres on the centenary of Kafka. This was followed by a brief visit to England to be invested with an honorary doctorate by the University of Cambridge. At the end of July, he flew to Washington, D.C., to attend an extraordinary function in his honor: his friend, the Italian publisher Franco Maria Ricci, who was about to launch his cultural magazine *FMR* in the U.S. market, had conceived the idea of celebrating Borges's eighty-fifth birthday with a banquet at the Library of Congress no less. (The location may be explained by the fact that Ricci had published the Italian edition of *The Congress* and had contracted Borges to write prologues for "La Biblioteca di Babele," a series of classic stories.) Four hundred fifty guests had been invited to this glittering social event, at which Ricci presented Borges with a case containing eighty-five gold sovereigns, the number corresponding to his age.

Travel kept renewing Borges's wonder at the riches of the world. But despite this openness to change and diversity, he still could not quell his desire for some unifying experience that would reveal to him some final destiny beyond death. In a prose poem called "Someone Is Dreaming" ("Alguien sueña"), he posed the question "What has time dreamed of so far . . . ?" and named all kinds of things, interspersing personal memories with great historical events, concrete objects with abstract ideas in a random enumeration that recalled the visionary outpouring with which he had concluded his story "The Aleph."[5] Unlike in "The Aleph," however, there was no magic device here to pull that mighty chaos together. Time was dreaming "that Someone is dreaming it," but that Someone refused to show His face. In another prose poem, "The Long Search" ("La larga busca"), Borges imagined this Someone as "an invisible animal" existing "before time or outside of time," which "we men seek and which seeks us," yet which "eludes us from one second to the next."[6]

At the end of September, he and María embarked on a varied journey that would take them to Madrid, Seville, Rome, Amman, Cairo, Marrakesh, Lisbon, Geneva, Milan, and, finally, New York. It was during his visit to Geneva in early October that this faith in virtuality was confirmed in an extraordinary epiphany that occurred while he was dining with Abramowicz's widow and María at a Greek restaurant near the summit of the Colline Saint-Pierre in the Old Town. A Greek song was playing in the background, and its lyrics suddenly acquired a peculiar resonance, for the song declared that while the music played one would deserve the love of Helen of Troy; while the music played Ulysses would return to Ithaca. Listening to this song, Borges succumbed to a powerful intuition that the life of his dear friend Abramowicz had not been extinguished, that he was present with them that night. Deeply moved by this realization, he asked María and Isabelle to raise their glasses and drink to the memory of Maurice.

That same night Borges composed an account of his epiphany:

> Tonight I can weep like a man. I can feel the tears roll down my cheeks, because I know that there is not a single thing on this earth which is mortal and which does not project its shadow. Tonight you have told me without words, Abramowicz, that we should enter death as we might enter a fiesta.[7]

For the whole of 1984, he had been seeking an answer to the appeal he had addressed to Abramowicz in the "Elegy" written the previous January: "I cannot tell whether you are still someone, I cannot tell whether you are hearing me." And on that night in Geneva, the dead Maurice had conveyed his reply through the Greek music—he had not died, he was indeed "someone," death was "more unbelievable than life," and "the soul therefore endures when its body is chaos."

The force of the epiphany was such that it clinched Borges's belief that what we have lost can be more fully real to us than the things that actually surround us. Indeed, death itself might be overcome by the mystery of virtuality, and this conviction led to a great burst of enthusiasm for his "agnostic mysticism." In the prose poem "Someone Shall Dream" ("Alguien soñará"), he wrote a visionary paean to the virtual powers of the human mind.[8] He envisaged "the indecipherable future" dreaming a world where those powers have reached a preternatural intensity:

> It [the future] shall dream dreams more vivid than our waking life today. It shall dream that we can work miracles, and that we won't carry them out because it will be more real to imagine them. It shall dream worlds so intense that the voice of a single bird could kill us.

Here the notion of the "magic act" has evolved into the utopian fantasy that the creative imagination might one day be capable of changing the face of reality. And the process by which the virtual is made actual is likened to dreaming: the poem concludes by citing Novalis: "Life is not a dream, but it may come to be a dream."

After returning to Buenos Aires from this long journey overseas, Borges would buy an apartment in calle Rodríguez Peña in the Barrio Norte. The reasons for this purchase in November 1984 have not come to light, but it may be that he wished to get away in due course from the apartment at Maipú 994 that he had shared with his mother for over thirty years and which, partly as a consequence of that, had become a place of persistent tensions with his housekeeper over his relationship with María Kodama. It may be that in his new, optimistic frame of mind, he was proposing to make a clean break with the past.

Something of Borges's novel sense of freedom can be found in a book called *Atlas* that he and María published the following month. Here they recorded the impressions of their travels together in photograhs taken by María and words written by Borges. "María Kodama and I," he wrote in the prologue, "have shared the joy and wonder of finding sounds, languages, twilights, cities, gardens and people, all of them distinctly different and unique. These pages would wish to be monuments to that long adventure which still goes on."[9]

They traveled again to Europe at the year's end. Borges was to receive the Etruria Literary Prize at Volterra, near Pisa, and, as he had done several times in the recent past, he planned to see in the New Year with María in Geneva, where he proposed to write the prologue for a new collection of poems. He had moved from Emecé, his publishers in Buenos Aires, to Alianza Editorial, based in Madrid, and publication of the new book had been scheduled for the middle of 1985. In the prologue he wrote in Geneva on January 9, he referred to the "beautiful fate," "the bliss," of writing. Writing was a kind of dreaming:

> There are many dreams in this book. I should explain that they were gifts
> of the night or, more exactly, of the dawn, and not deliberate fictions. I
> have hardly dared to add one or two circumstantial details, of the sort
> our age requires ever since Defoe.[10]

At first glance, the passive role Borges assigned here to the writer as a mere vehicle for the transmission of dreams would seem to be inconsistent with his belief in virtuality, in writing as a "magic act," but this inconsistency is reconciled in a maxim: "Each work entrusts to its writer the form that it is seeking."

The writer's creative will realizes a form that was already virtual in the subject matter itself.

Certainly, in the early months of 1985, Borges conceived of writing in an almost mystical light, for the epiphany at Geneva had given him cause to believe that he might find a kind of salvation in the virtual powers of the imagination. On April 11 he published in *Clarín* a poem called "Greek Music" ("Música griega") in which he glossed the words of the song he had heard in the taverna.[11] The phrase "While this music lasts . . ." becomes an incantation on every other line of the poem. As long as he could hear the music that had brought him the surviving presence of his departed friend Abramowicz, he could believe that he would find salvation from nothingness, for the Greek music created a virtual reality of its own in which dreams of fulfillment could prosper—he could dream that all his troubles would finally be assuaged, that all his fears of being unworthy of love, of being crushed by the sword, of being mocked by mirrors and masks, of being cheated as a poet by words falling lifeless from his pen, all would be swept away, for as long as he was held in the spell of that music, he would feel himself "worthy of the love of Helen of Troy," he would "believe in free will," he would "be the word and the sword," he would "be worthy of the mirror and the mahogany," he would deserve "your great voice, Walt Whitman," he could even believe that his life might have a specific end, like "the arrow in the air"; the Greek music, in sum, gave him the creative faith to believe that from the crest of that hill in Geneva, he had been granted a glimpse of "the Promised Land."

In the same month as "Greek Music" appeared in *Clarín*, he went to the United States with María, where he lectured at the University of California at Santa Barbara and then at New York University and Columbia. The Argentine novelist Luisa Valenzuela came across them by chance in an Italian restaurant in Greenwich Village. It had been several years since she had last seen Borges, and what struck her about him was his extraordinary vitality: "He gives the impression of frailty, and his strength comes as a surprise."[12] Borges recounted to Valenzuela several of his recent journeys with María, dwelling on a trip they had taken in a hot-air balloon over the Napa Valley in California. "Our joy was infinite," he declared. "As in dreams, you get the true sensation of flying, billowed by the winds." Valenzuela imagined a soft wind transporting the couple across the world—"the venerable old man and the woman who has pulled the venerable old man out of his encapsulation and brought him into contact with life."[13]

Even though Borges had attained an unprecedented happiness in his personal life, his hopes for the future of Argentina would prove difficult to keep alive. The new Radical president, Raúl Alfonsín, had made a good start in dealing with the legacy of the Dirty War. On December 15, 1983, five days after assuming office, he had created a commission of inquiry into the *desaparecidos* under the chairmanship of the writer Ernesto Sábato. CONADEP (Comisión Nacional Sobre la Desaparición de Personas), had no judicial powers as such; its purpose was to receive information about the disappeared, and in November 1984, the commission published its findings in a volume entitled *Nunca Más* (*Never Again*), together with an appendix listing all the missing persons, which ran to over twenty thousand. The CONADEP report increased the growing clamor from the public that those responsible for the abductions and torture be punished. Alfonsín duly acknowledged this public pressure and authorized the arrest of the leaders of the various military juntas, from Videla to Galtieri, and other military officers.

Borges was of the view that a true regeneration of the *patria* would come about only when the evil of the Dirty War was fully expunged, and since the fall of Galtieri, he had been calling for the matter of the *desaparecidos* to be investigated and those responsible punished—with death sentences if necessary. At about the time the trials of the military officers started, Borges was due to bring out a new book of poems in Madrid in June 1985. This was a miscellaneous collection, comprising the work he had produced since 1981, but he decided to give it a political slant by calling it *The Confederates* (*Los conjurados*), after the poem in which he had held up the Swiss Confederation as an example of rational cooperation and good faith among men of different races, languages, and religions.[14] This political message was reinforced by placing poems such as the pacifist "Juan López and John Ward," together with the antiwar "Milongas," at the end of the book.

However, by the time *The Confederates* came out in June, Borges had good reason to entertain doubts about the future. The armed forces were seething with resentment at the trial of their former leaders, and the specter of a coup d'état was to hang over the entire process of bringing the military officers to book. The economic outlook was also unpromising. Alfonsín's victory in October 1983 epitomized a general desire in Argentina to make a clean break with the past and restore a stable democratic system. Evidence of this desire was the emergence of a consensus between the Radicals and the Peronists regarding the need to bring to justice those responsible for violating human rights and also to stabilize the economy, which had been wrecked by the military governments—the foreign debt stood at $45 billion and consumed 50 percent of export earnings in interest payments alone, while inflation had reached an annual rate of 1,000 percent. But in June 1985, Alfonsín introduced austerity measures designed to bring this chaotic situation under control, and it remained to be seen whether the consensus between Radicals and Peronists would hold good as the trade unions came under pressure to defend the interests of the workers.

In addition to these hazards, what caused Borges to question the likelihood of "democratic regeneration" was his profound dismay at the extent of the moral depravity that had taken root in Argentine politics during the period of military rule. On July 22 he attended a session of the trial of the leaders of the military juntas and heard the testimony of Víctor Melchor Basterra, a man who had been imprisoned by the military from August 10, 1979, until December 3, 1983, and subjected daily to physical punishments and humiliations. Borges was so upset at what he heard that he told journalists as he left the courtroom, "This is too much for me. I'm leaving because I'm horrified by what I've heard. And if you tell me that this was one of the milder testimonies, I can't imagine what the others must have been like."[15]

Four days later he sent an open letter to *Clarín* expressing horror at what he had learned.[16] He referred to Basterra's account of a grotesque episode that had occurred one Christmas Eve, when the prisoners were ushered into a room and served Christmas dinner at a long table set with a linen tablecloth, cutlery, and a porcelain service, by the very men who routinely tortured them and would torture them again the following day. What Borges found so shocking about this incident was that it had been well meant, it was not a macabre joke, and for that reason it was evidence of "a kind of innocence of evil." This terrible moral blindness, he believed, might yet impede the process of coming to terms with the Dirty War, for the soldiers who had destroyed the rule of law were now seeking refuge in the law and engaging skilled advocates to defend them in the courts. The government, he wrote, must pursue justice with appropriate vigor, because if one failed "to judge and condemn" a crime, one became "its accomplice."

Borges doubted whether the government of Alfonsín had the will to see justice done. He feared that Alfonsín would eventually succumb to military pressure and either declare an amnesty for all military officers or allow some face-saving convictions of the main culprits and then commute their sentences sometime later. Given the gravity of the situation, the decision to call his new book *The Confederates* had clearly been insufficient, and he would have to find some other means of using his personal authority to influence the moral regeneration of the *patria*. But, what could he do? He was blind and well into his eighties, and, in any case, he began to feel unwell a few weeks after attending the trial. His regular doctor tried to reassure him, but the physical discomfort persisted, and after further fruitless consultations, he asked María to find him another doctor for a second opinion.[17] A friend of María's recommended Dr. Jorge Patricio Fellner, who referred him to the Instituto Diagnóstico for a series of tests, which were to reveal a tumor in his liver. Finally, on September 13, a biopsy performed at the Hospital Alemán confirmed that he was suffering from cancer.

Borges received the news in a stoical spirit. He refused chemotherapy, preferring to carry on as normal and let nature take its course. What exercised him most of all was the certainty that if it became known that he was terminally ill, he would become the victim of a huge media circus. "They'll try to record my last breath," he told María, "and offer it for sale."[18] He was, of course, well used to the intrusions of journalists in his private life. There had been a gross abuse of his goodwill at the time of his mother's final illness, when pictures of the bedridden Doña Leonor had been published in the press. But he cited to María the more recent case of the veteran Radical politician Ricardo Balbín, pictures of whom had appeared on billboards all over Buenos Aires after paparazzi had bribed nurses to let them take photographs of the dying man in the intensive-care ward. The last thing he wanted was for María to have to endure the agony of seeing his final illness being turned into a national spectacle, with photographs splashed across magazine covers and billboards the length and breadth of the country.[19]

He did not have to wait long for his fears to be confirmed. On September 13, the very day he had received the result of his biopsy, an evening paper in Buenos Aires reported that he was "gravely ill" as the result of a "gastrointestinal infection," and that his condition was reported to be "worrying," but when a journalist rang the Maipú apartment, this report was "categorically denied"; Borges was said to be "recovering from fatigue."[20] The fact that reports about his state of health had reached the press so quickly suggested that he could not fully trust people around him. Under the circumstances Borges decided that only María, his lawyer, and Dr. Fellner should know the truth about his condition; others were told that he was suffering from hepatitis. On September 18, *La Nación* informed its readers that Borges had been confined to bed the previous week with flu.

By the middle of September 1985, Borges was aware that he would die in the near future, even though he was unsure precisely how long he had to live. And his death, as he realized, would occur at a crucial juncture in Argentina's history, for the nation seemed poised between a faltering hope of "democratic regeneration" and a return to the downward spiral of destruction. He felt a need to support what he had called "the collective act of faith" that had brought about the resurgence of democracy, but he doubted that the country would truly come to terms with the enormity of the Dirty War and achieve a true national reconciliation. His gloom over the condition of Argentina is evident in an interview he gave to a French journalist, Patrick Séry.[21] He painted a bleak picture of the situation—he was "ashamed" of what had gone on under the military juntas: "ethically," the country "did not exist"; "politically," it did not "count for much"; the military had "looted, bankrupted and sacked it." As for Alfonsín, he was "honest and well meaning," but that was not sufficient for effective government. Borges feared there might be "uprisings, exoduses." "I love my country very deeply," he said, "but it leaves me with little hope."[22]

On October 16 he gave another interview at his apartment in Buenos Aires to Jacques Secretan of the *Tribune de Genève*.[23] He informed the Swiss journalist that he was due to go to Italy at the end of the following month and would subsequently visit Geneva, "as I do whenever I come to Europe." Then he took Secretan to see his mother's bedroom and showed him a wooden plaque with the insignia of all the Swiss cantons, doubtless a souvenir of the family's years in Geneva that Leonor Acevedo had brought back with her. He would very much like to become a Swiss citizen and end his days in that country, he told Secretan, but he imagined it was very difficult to do so. Secretan promised that when he got back to Geneva, he would find out what was required to obtain Swiss nationality.

What is one to make of Borges's rather odd wish to become a Swiss citizen when he already knew he was dying? I believe he may have been toying with the idea, not of renouncing his Argentine citizenship altogether but of holding dual Swiss-Argentine nationality. Certainly the news that Jorge Luis Borges, Argentina's most famous son, had become a citizen of Switzerland would have created a sensation in his native land, and this would have driven home the political message of his poem "The Confederates" far more powerfully than his choosing it as the title poem of his last book. However, on November 18, Secretan telephoned Borges and informed him that twelve years' residency was required for an adult to qualify for Swiss nationality, but only six for a minor; in Secretan's view, Borges would be able to count the four years he had lived in Geneva in his youth, and the Swiss authorities might conceivably waive any further residency requirements in consideration of his advanced age and literary fame.[24] It was obviously too late for Borges, given the state of his health, to acquire dual nationality, so he would have to find some other means of creating an exemplary link between his two most significant *patrias*—Buenos Aires and Geneva.

If Borges had come to believe in anything in the last years of his life it was in the virtual powers of the mind, and it was to this faith in the mind's capacity to fashion a form of truth in its own right that he would turn in order to find what salvation he could as he approached the end of his earthly existence. In an interview he gave in November 1985 to Amelia Barili, an editor at *La Prensa*, he offered some insights into the tenor of his thinking at this juncture.[25] He started by explaining his love of Geneva, declaring that "in a certain manner, I am Swiss." Then he recalled Abramowicz and that "beautiful night" when the Greek music in the taverna had made him feel "that Maurice was not dead, that he was there with us, that nobody really dies, for they all still project their shadow." He professed a continuing skepticism about the existence of God; he had tried to believe in a personal God, but "I do not think I try anymore": the "intellectual instinct" made us search while knowing we were never going to find the answer. Twice in the course of the interview, he quoted an "admirable expression" of Bernard Shaw's—"God is in the making," implying that what the intellect denied might become accessible by other means. Indeed, doubt was "the most precious gift": "I am almost sure to be blotted out by death, but sometimes I think it is not impossible that I may continue to live in some other manner after my physical death." Still, he was not a thinker, he told Barili; he had never "arrived at anything," he was just a "man of letters," "a weaver of dreams."

His characterization of the writer as "a weaver of dreams" was, in effect, a statement of his belief in the virtual powers of the imagination. Borges could not attain to a belief in God, but since "God was in the making," he might arrive at God, or whatever it was he wanted from God, by the "magic act" of dreaming. As he had observed in his prologue to *The Confederates*, "each work entrusts to its writer the form that it is seeking," and so, analogously in my view, he would make, or "write," his own salvation by revealing the form his life was seeking—he would arrive at the fullness of his days in this world by orchestrating his end in such a way as to generate the greatest possible significance from it. By the time he gave his interview to Amelia Barili in November 1985, Borges, in my judgment, had already invented the "magic act" that would weave his dreams of salvation into a pattern of hope for himself and for Argentina.

The rebirth of hope can be observed in a poem he composed that same month, very likely the last thing he ever wrote in his native land. Called simply "1985," it was an act of faith in Argentina's capacity to regenerate itself.[26] The *patria* was not to be found in some "famous date" or in the "short-lived fury or fervor of the fickle masses"; he felt it in more intimate things, in the odor of jasmines, in a daguerreotype, a garden at dusk, maybe in "a sword that has served in the desert" or "a history annotated by a dead man." What, then, was the *patria*?

> Something in my breast and in your breast,
> Something dreamed of yet never made,
> Something blown away by the wind, yet not mislaid.

On November 22, Borges made a new will. This was in fact a revision of the will he had made on August 28, 1979, a few days before he was due to have the tumor in his prostate removed. In the will of 1985 he named María Kodama his sole heir on exactly the same terms as in that of 1979. The principal difference between the two wills lay in a substantial change to the legacy to Epifanía Úveda de Robledo, his housekeeper.[27] In 1979 he had left her half the money in cash or held in bank accounts in Argentina or abroad, which were his property at the time of his death, but in 1985 she was left twenty-five hundred australes (approximately sixteen hundred dollars at the time). This reduction suggests that Fani's evident dislike of Borges's relationship with María Kodama had not diminished since she had threatened to resign some years earlier and may indeed have got worse.

In neither will did Borges leave anything to his relatives by blood, other than two legacies: one, the several volumes of Burton's *One Thousand and One Nights* to his nephew, Miguel de Torre; the other, his share in the family mausoleum at La Recoleta, which he ceded to his sister. This legacy may be an indication of his continuing estrangement from Norah and her family since they had fallen out in 1979 over their joint bank account. Indeed, the surrender of his share in the family tomb may indicate his repudiation of the whole cult of ancestor worship that the patrician cemetery of La Recoleta represented in Argentine society. If Borges had consented to be laid to rest in La Recoleta, he would have effectively given himself over to a veritable orgy of criollo triumphalism, for he, the most famous writer in Argentine history, would have been installed in glory beside the remains of Colonel Suárez and the other illustrious forebears. But such an end would have contradicted the whole of his personal evolution over the previous two decades, for he had come to believe that the veneration of the sword of honor was at the root of Argentina's ills, and after the Malvinas and Dirty War in particular, he had vaunted publicly his espousal of "anarchism" and "pacifism."

There was, additionally, the question of María Kodama. If he were to join his ancestors at La Recoleta, María would effectively be relegated to the position of a parvenue, a discredited outsider, and her vital contribution to his late-flowering happiness would be nullified, the whole of that lifesaving experience of mutual love traduced by a resurgence of ancestral pride.

Borges's will, therefore, represented his final and decisive rebellion against the sword of honor. And with the 1985 will in particular, he placed María Kodama squarely, unequivocally, at the very center of his life. No doubt he was conscious of the outrage such dispositions were likely to provoke after his death, but his commitment to the half-Japanese woman he loved manifested the principle that had saved him from himself and which he believed would save the *patria*—an acceptance of the other, the full inclusion in the nation of all its sons and daughters so that a new Argentina might be born.

Borges, what was more, did not propose to wait until after his death for the true nature of his relationship with María to become publicly known. For fifteen years they had kept up the fiction that they were merely friends and, latterly, that she was no more than his literary secretary and traveling companion, but now he wished to correct this misconception by asking her to marry him. He had still to contend with María's aversion to marriage, of course, but given that he was so close to death, there was a reasonable expectation that she would accept his proposal. Borges instructed his lawyer, Osvaldo Vidaurre, to see to the necessary arrangements for him to marry María. There existed a legal complication in this regard, owing to his previous marriage to Elsa Astete. The dissolution of that union counted only as a legal separation, since there were no provisions for divorce in Argentine law at this time, but it was common practice in such cases to seek a marriage licence in Paraguay, and there were well-established procedures by which Argentine lawyers could arrange a proxy marriage in Paraguay for their clients.

Having decided to continue with his normal schedule for as long as possible, Borges proposed to honor his engagements in Italy in December. He and María booked a flight to Milan on November 28. He told her that he wished to spend some time in Geneva after their visits to Milan and Venice, and it appears that he still had hopes of making a third visit to Japan. On the afternoon of November 27, the day before he was due to depart, he attended an exhibition of first editions of all his books, which had been organized at the bookshop of Alberto Casares. Borges was in an affable mood, chatting and joking as he signed copies of his books for his admirers.[28] He also met Adolfo Bioy Casares, with whom he had not been in touch for several years.

It appears that Borges was curiously evasive about his forthcoming trip to Europe. He made no mention of it to Estela Canto when they lunched together at the Hotel Dorá shortly before his departure.[29] Another friend, Viviana Aguilar, claimed he had promised to tell her about a visit to Japan he was hoping to make after his trip to Italy and Geneva.[30] Vilma Colina of the magazine *Somos*, who was at the exhibition at Casares's bookshop, reported having heard him say that he would be returning to Buenos Aires at the end of January, but other guests remember him calling out as he left, "I won't be coming back!"[31] And Roberto Alifano, who spent the morning of November 28 helping him revise the poem "1985," would later claim that they had agreed to meet again the next day to finish the task, and that Borges gave him not the slightest hint that he was booked on a flight to Europe that same evening.[32] Why was Borges playing his cards so close to his chest? There was a practical reason—as with his cancer, he must have feared that the media would get wind of his plans. But there was, I believe, a further reason for his reticence: since he was planning to give the story of his life a particular form, he would not have wished to reduce its dramatic impact by revealing it in advance to other people.

At midday on November 28, Borges had lunch with his sister, Norah, at the Hotel Dorá across the road from his apartment. It was a farewell of sorts, even though he made no mention of his departure for Europe that evening. Afterward he took his customary siesta. At around 5:00 P.M., he was called by the housekeeper, and then he left for the airport in a taxi with María. The "weaver of dreams" was about to embark on the "magic act" that would bring his life to a fitting end.

CHAPTER 34

Creating an End

(1985–1986)

No one heard from Borges or María for several weeks after they left Buenos Aires. They flew directly to Milan, where he gave several lectures in little over a week. Next he went to Venice and signed a contract there to write a screenplay for the benefit of the Venice in Peril Fund. While in Italy he proposed marriage to María, but she could not bring herself to consent, fearing the reactions such a marriage would provoke in Argentina. Borges, however, told her that marriage would provide him with the kind of personal fulfillment that he had been seeking all his life. She consulted their friend Franco Maria Ricci, who recommended that she accept the proposal, but even now she could not make up her mind.[1]

By the middle of December, they were in Geneva, where they booked into their usual suite at the Hôtel L'Arbalète. María had assumed that Borges wished simply to make a last visit to the city where he had lived in his early youth and which he had rediscovered in old age, so she was taken aback when he informed her that he did not propose to return to Buenos Aires:

> He had told me that we would be going to Italy and then we would stop over in Switzerland. I thought it was logical that he should wish to say his farewells, but when we arrived in Geneva, he said, "We're not going back, we're staying." It was clear to me that he had decided this beforehand, when he learned that he was going to die.[2]

Borges would have known that such a decision, when it came out, would be controversial, not to say scandalous, in Argentina, but he had made it in full consciousness of its political import. As he explained to María, he hoped to bring about "an awakening from the great dogmatic slumber" that had come over his native land:

> You see, I've become a kind of myth, and whenever the issue arises of my being buried over here, people may recall the book I have written, *The*

Confederates, and they'll think about it: people will come here and ask themselves: why?—that will be my small contribution to changing the world.[3]

During the last decades of his life, Borges had seen Argentina rent apart as brutally as it had ever been since its birth as a nation. In his poem "The Confederates," which he had written in the aftermath of the Malvinas War and the war against the guerrillas, he had extolled Switzerland as a model of tolerance and civic harmony for his strife-torn *patria:* the Swiss confederation was "a tower of reason and firm faith," where men of different races, religions, and languages had "resolved to forget their differences and accentuate their affinities."

This public stance, furthermore, had a deep personal significance for Borges. He had first been brought to Switzerland by his father, who had himself left Argentina in order to fulfill a dream of love with his wife, Leonor, that he had thought impossible to realize in his native land. It was in Geneva that Georgie had first fallen in love, but also in Geneva where his confidence in love had been unwittingly undermined by his father. Borges had come to perceive a certain paradigmatic quality about that division between father and son— he had characterized Argentina's violent history in "A Storyline" as a recurrent conflict between old and young, fathers and sons. However, by returning to die in Geneva, he wished to point to a resolution of that historic conflict by effecting a symbolic reconciliation with his father in the city where they had been driven apart.

Geneva, then, was the place above all others in which Borges could shape his life into the form it had been seeking—he would convert his death into the "magic act" that would forge a link between Buenos Aires, his native city, and Geneva, the most precious of his virtual *patrias.* And he would set the seal on this symbolic meaning by creating a last idyll of happiness with María Kodama, the woman who had offered him the redeeming love he had always looked for and had repeatedly been denied. Borges, the "weaver of dreams," had come back to Geneva in order to reenter the womb of time and breathe new life into all the dreams that might have been, before passing through the gateway of death into whatever lay beyond—nothingness perhaps, or God, or else some further dimension of being in the unfolding design of the cosmos.

Borges and María planned to spend their time in Geneva working on several projects. María wanted to get on with writing short stories, and Borges, in addition to several prologues for a series of classic works to be published by Alianza Editorial, had the Venice screenplay to work on, as well as the supervision of his collected works for Gallimard's Pléiade series. On January 4 he began work on the selection and annotation of appropriate material for the

Pléiade edition with the editor, Jean Pierre Bernès, a professor at the Sorbonne, who would travel from Paris on several weekends in the coming months.

It seems also that he had not given up the idea of making a third visit to Japan, but toward the end of January, his health took a turn for the worse, and he suffered from stomach pains, which turned out to be due to internal bleeding caused by the cancer of the liver. On January 26 he was admitted to the Cantonal University Hospital in Geneva, where he was treated by Dr. Patrick Ambrosetti. In view of this downturn in his condition, María urged Borges to return to Buenos Aires. Her concern was to make sure that if he stayed in Geneva, it would be as a result of a clear choice and not because he might have feared to undertake the journey home.[4] Dr. Ambrosetti himself also asked Borges if he wished to go back home, assuring him that an air ambulance could be arranged, but Borges insisted that he wanted to stay in Geneva. Over the next three weeks, his condition was stabilized at the hospital, and he was fit enough to return to the Hôtel L'Arbalète on February 16.

Once back at the hotel, he was kept under daily observation by Dr. Jean-François Balavoine, a physician recommended by Dr. Ambrosetti, and María engaged the services of nursing staff to look after him in the mornings and evenings. At the time of his leaving the hospital, however, his state of health did not give any immediate cause for concern. In the weeks following his discharge from the hospital, Borges again asked María to marry him, and once again she hesitated, but this time, after talking it over with Jean Pierre Bernès, she at last gave her consent. On March 18, Borges's lawyer in Buenos Aires, Osvaldo Vidaurre, was instructed to set in motion the process to obtain a marriage license in Paraguay. Vidaurre was also asked to effect the sale of the apartment at calle Maipú, after transferring Borges's furniture and possessions to the apartment at calle Rodríguez Peña, and to send certain items and books to Geneva. Borges was particularly keen to rent an apartment in the Old Town, where he could move to with María, but for this he needed a temporary resident's permit, and toward the end of March, he engaged a Swiss lawyer, Daniel Meyer, to apply for a permit on his behalf. Borges was to tell one of his nurses, Florence Bergeron, that he needed to sort out some "papers" so that he could buy an apartment and live in Geneva, where he was "unknown" and could enjoy "real peace."[5] These dispositions—the concern to rent an apartment in the Old Town of Geneva, the application for a resident's permit, the proposal of marriage—all point to the fact that Borges's intention was to create a final haven of peace and happiness in Switzerland with María Kodama.

However, even though he had made provisions before leaving Buenos Aires, both for a possible marriage to María and the sale of his apartment at calle Maipú, there arose a difficulty with these arrangements that the ever-impractical Borges had not foreseen. When his lawyer attempted to effect the transfer of his possessions from one apartment to the other, one of Borges's nephews, Luis de Torre, turned up at the flat on calle Maipú and, according to Vidaurre's account of the matter, objected to the removal of certain items on the grounds that they were held in common ownership with his mother, Norah Borges.[6] De Torre permitted Vidaurre to remove a number of items that indisputably belonged to Borges—his books, walking sticks, honors and decorations, and bedroom furniture, but he allegedly argued that the apartment was part-owned by his mother Norah and that she had a valid claim on the furniture and effects that had belonged to Leonor Acevedo or were family heirlooms. The disagreement over the latter centered on the silverware that had once belonged to Colonel Suárez and on a chiffonier that Borges claimed to have been left by his grandmother Fanny Haslam and to which he was sentimentally attached.[7] However, Borges refused to discuss the matter with his nephew, and he insisted on dealing directly with his sister. Luis de Torre then initiated proceedings to determine the rights of ownership of the apartment and the disputed items of property. This recourse to law meant that it became necessary to obtain a legal inventory of the contents of the apartment at calle Maipú.

The drawing up of this inventory on April 22, however, led to another dispute, this time with Borges's housekeeper, Fani Úveda. On that day, too, Vidaurre gave her three weeks' notice to leave the flat. Fani was, of course, not aware at this point that Borges had no intention of returning to Buenos Aires, nor that he was planning to marry María Kodama, so she must have been puzzled when she was told by Vidaurre to find alternative accommodation by May 15, and aggrieved that she was being offered a gratuity that she regarded as insufficient for her years of service with the Borges family. She was further put out when she found that, given the legal status of the inventory of the disputed contents, the main apartment was to be sealed off by a locksmith and she would be confined to her own room, which she could reach only through the service entrance.

Borges was also under increasing pressure from journalists. His long absence from Buenos Aires had led to rumors that he was seriously ill in Geneva. On several occasions María Kodama tried to defuse this pressure from the media by reassuring the representative of EFE, the Spanish news agency in Geneva, that the rumors were unfounded and that Borges simply wished to be left in peace so that he could get on with his work.

On April 26, four days after the inventory was taken at the Maipú apartment, Borges received the news from Vidaurre that the Paraguayan marriage license had come through, and that he and María had become man and wife.

The occasion was marked by a small celebration at the hotel, attended by the general manager and his wife, and the French professor, Jean Pierre Bernès. The newlyweds were toasted with champagne, although Borges, for medical reasons, took a glass of sparkling mineral water instead, remarking that "bubbles are a metaphor for champagne."[8] Bernès read Borges's poem "The Possession of Yesterday," which expressed the paradox of virtuality: we possess more fully what we have lost, but as Bernès would recall, when he came to the last line—"There are no paradises other than lost paradises"—Borges interrupted him to say that this line should be suppressed because he had found paradise at last, having married María.[9]

At around the time of the modest wedding celebration, however, Borges's condition deteriorated once more. Dr. Balavoine decided that he required closer medical supervision and referred him to the Clinique d'Arve, where he was to remain for approximately twelve days. Sooner or later, Borges realized, he would have to make public his marriage to María Kodama, but he wanted to enjoy a period of tranquillity with her before having to brave the storm that would surely be raised when news of it got out.[10] As his health improved, he decided to make a direct plea to the news media for his privacy to be respected, and on May 6, he wrote a letter to the Spanish news agency, EFE, explaining that he wished to settle in Geneva and asking that he be left alone to pursue his work: "I am a free man. I have decided to stay in Geneva, because I associate Geneva with the happiest days of my life."[11] This decision did not affect his "essential love of the *patria*," but the Buenos Aires he had known no longer existed. In any case, he felt "mysteriously happy" in Geneva. "I think it strange that someone should not understand and respect this decision by a man who, like a certain character of Wells's, has resolved to be an invisible man."

It was significant that Borges employed the term "invisible man," the term his father had used to express his desire to live anonymously in Europe in 1914, in order to describe his own decision to settle in Geneva. There can be little doubt that he identified strongly with his father during these last months: Jean Pierre Bernès remembered that Borges often used to make reference to his father during their various work sessions in Geneva.[12] And Dr. Balavoine, the physician who was treating him, came to the view that Borges was seeking to fulfill some private wish by coming to Geneva.[13] After Borges left the Clinique d'Arve, Balavoine would visit him every evening at the Hôtel L'Arbalète, and they would engage in long conversations, usually starting with a discussion of his current state of health and more often than not passing on to whatever it was Borges happened to be reading at that time. Never once did the writer explicitly mention death to his doctor, and Balavoine's impression was that Borges was determined to confront his demise with dignity and good grace.

Perhaps he had no wish to go back to Buenos Aires, even though he was still capable of undertaking the journey because, Balavoine surmised, "he might have had some important experience in Geneva, probably some kind of initiation in life, perhaps a revelation, an argument or a love affair, which led him to want to die there" and "complete a cycle which encompassed his whole life."[14]

Once again, however, Borges's plans to become an "invisible man" in Geneva would be upset by events in Buenos Aires. On May 12, the news of his marriage to María Kodama was leaked to a journalist. On learning about this unauthorized release of information, Vidaurre decided that it would be best to provide official confirmation of the news as soon as possible, so as to avoid having the press harass the sick man in Geneva. He invited journalists from the three main daily newspapers in Buenos Aires to a meeting on the evening of May 13 at the office of one of the lawyers Vidaurre had engaged to handle the proxy marriage in Paraguay. At this press conference, Vidaurre stated that Borges was "upset and anxious" because the news of his marriage had been made public without his permission, whereas he had hoped to make the announcement himself. The marriage had taken place, said Vidaurre, "in accordance with a long-standing wish of the writer's," and Borges "now requested that his privacy be respected."[15]

All the same, news of Borges's marriage to his "literary secretary," a woman younger than him by several decades, made front-page headlines in Argentina and throughout the Spanish-speaking world. There was wild speculation in the press about the reasons for the marriage, as well as rumors of disputes within the family. And despite Borges's earlier pleas for his privacy to be respected, reporters were immediately dispatched to Geneva to seek interviews with the couple. A media sensation was clearly under way, so much so that, on the evening of May 14, Vidaurre thought it wise to call another press conference in an attempt to set the record straight. He confirmed rumors of a serious rift in the family and mentioned the unresolved dispute with his housekeeper over her severance pay.[16] Vidaurre explained to the journalists that the question of the marriage was quite separate and distinct from the question of the inheritance. Borges's reasons for marrying María Kodama had nothing to do with the inheritance, declared Vidaurre; the author simply wished to leave a public testimony of the true nature of their relationship. In any case, it was not necessary for María Kodama to be married to Borges in order to be a beneficiary of his will, since in Argentine law a person who was named in a will had a right of inheritance that overrode the claims of any relatives of the deceased who had not been specifically named. This point was endorsed in *La Semana* the following day by Dr. Attilio Aníbal Alterini, a specialist in family law consulted by the magazine.[17] Even so, the disputes over

Borges's will would drag on for about ten years after his death in a series of lawsuits brought against María Kodama by Borges's nephews and the housekeeper. Kodama's opponents would also call into question the validity of the Paraguayan marriage documents, though without success. It seems incontestable that it was Borges's clear wish to be married to María Kodama before he died, and since remarriage was legally impossible in Argentina at the time, the only way he could satisfy this wish was to accept a proxy marriage in Paraguay. Vidaurre's account of the matter would be entirely vindicated in the end—the validity of the will and María Kodama's absolute right of inheritance were upheld in every case that was brought to court.

These acrimonious wrangles, and the media sensation that accompanied them, unsettled the tranquil haven Borges had hoped to create in Geneva. On May 14, precisely the day that the media storm was breaking in Buenos Aires, he was visited in Geneva by his friend Jaime Alazraki, a professor of Latin American literature, who had last seen the writer exactly three years earlier at the symposium at Dickinson College in the United States, when, as Alazraki recalled, Borges had been "lively and energetic, vigorous and tireless."[18] Now Alazraki found him "a physical ruin," with his head "deformed, as if the frontal bone had grown beyond proportion and was threatening to tear the skin through." Alazraki was so shocked by Borges's appearance because, like everyone else, he was unaware that his friend was being ravaged by cancer. In his patchy recollection of their conversation, Alazraki remembered Borges lamenting the political situation in Argentina, saying that the military had turned the country into their own lucrative business and that the official version of Argentine history was "a work of fiction." He told Alazraki about "his refusal to return to Argentina," and also complained about the problems he was facing in Buenos Aires, adding some details about his break with Adolfo Bioy Casares.

That afternoon, while Borges had his customary siesta, María showed Alazraki round the Old Town. She told him that "Borges was adamant about not returning to Argentina," even though "friends and relatives were pressing for his return." She then pointed out a beautiful building, saying that "she was about to sign a lease on one of the apartments in that building"; they had lived comfortably for the past six months at the Hôtel L'Arbalète, but they both wished to move to "a homier place." María had found a second-floor apartment at 28 Grand'-Rue in the heart of the Old Town, and they were hoping to move in within a matter of weeks. Borges, however, had still not received his resident's permit, and the nurse, Florence Bergeron, recalled that he used to fret over the length of time it was taking to obtain this permit.[19]

All the while, journalists kept pestering the couple for interviews. Rumors that Borges was terminally ill had begun to appear in the newspapers, and the possibility that Argentina's most famous writer might be close to death inflamed the situation even further. Borges's private life—insofar as this was known—was being subjected to intense scrutiny in the press, and it was an article that appeared in a Buenos Aires newspaper, *La Gaceta de Hoy,* impugning María's motives in consenting to the marriage that finally convinced Borges he must speak out in order to put the record straight. He asked Vidaurre to issue a press release in the form of a letter to the editor of *La Gaceta de Hoy,* dated May 21, in which he expressed "indignant amazement" at the "inexplicable" article by a journalist who was "an almost total stranger." "The decision I have taken to marry now is the result of a very private matter that has matured over a long period of time, and which should be of no interest to anyone other than my friends." He went on to reject any insinuations regarding his wife's motives. "María Kodama is the most irreproachable person, ethically and morally, that I have known in my entire life. With her I have finally found happiness. That article can only be explained by the resentment of a person who is without morals or principles or who is at the service of persons without morals or principles."

Nevertheless, despite all his troubles, Borges was happy to be in Geneva, or so it appeared to his friend Alicia Jurado when he telephoned her in Buenos Aires on May 21: "He had lots of plans, he seemed very happy. He didn't come across as a man who felt doomed. He was full of life. Maybe he thought he had more time than he actually did."[20] On May 25 he attended a reception at the Argentine embassy to celebrate the National Day of Argentina. Although he was in a wheelchair by this stage, the ambassador, Leopoldo Tettamanti, reported that Borges looked "happy."[21] With the other guests, he listened to Argentine music, including *milongas* set to his own lyrics, and he reminisced about his life in Buenos Aires.

Borges was to reveal some of his unfinished projects to Jean Pierre Bernès, his French translator and editor, who had been coming to Geneva from time to time to consult him about the Pléiade edition and who saw him for the last time on June 4. It seems he still regretted not having written a self-justifying masterpiece: "We spend our lives waiting for our book and it never comes," he told Bernès, with a certain resignation.[22] He had plans for a story called "The Friends," set in the period before the Revolución Libertadora of September 1955, which he had been talking about for years but had never got around to writing. There were two further stories he had in mind: one entailed a rewriting of the last chapter of the *Quixote* focusing on the death of Alonso Quijano, the old hidalgo who went mad from too much reading and turned himself into Don Quixote; the other, set in Venice, imagined Dante discovering the plot of a sequel to the *Divine Comedy.* He also spoke of a collection of more "realistic" stories, similar to those of *Brodie's Report* but, according to Bernès, "much bolder, because they would provide a pretext for certain clarifications and unexpected disclosures, for confessions which would have given us an image of his face, stripped of its mask at last."

Borges was still keen to move to the apartment at 28 Grand'-Rue, but the matter of the resident's permit had not been resolved, and arrangements had to be made to rent the apartment on Borges's behalf through a joint agreement with his French and Spanish publishers, Gallimard and Alianza Editorial. By the time they were able to move from the Hôtel L'Arbalète on June 10, he had grown much weaker. Clearly the end was drawing very near, and the move to the apartment was closely supervised by both Dr. Ambrosetti and Dr. Balavoine, because Borges had developed a heart condition, compounded by pneumonia.[23]

In these final days, Borges had been brooding over the question of personal salvation. He liked to talk at length with María about the possible existence of a life beyond the grave. Though he was composed and self-possessed regarding his own imminent death, he kept probing her: Did she believe that one died completely? Was reincarnation not a more logical possibility? Did she incline toward a Catholic idea of an afterlife or a Shintoist? Which did she prefer?[24] María had always regarded Borges as an agnostic, as she was herself, but given the insistence with which he spoke about a possible afterlife, she suggested that he might perhaps wish to talk to someone who might be more "qualified" to answer his questions. "You are asking me if I want a priest," he replied. He then proposed that they call two clergymen, a Catholic priest, in memory of his mother, and a Protestant minister, for the sake of his English grandmother. Accordingly, he was to receive visits successively from Father Pierre Jacquet and Pastor Edouard de Montmollin.

On June 13, María called their friend, the Franco-Argentine writer Hector Bianciotti, Borges's editor at Gallimard, who traveled to Geneva from Paris the same day. That evening he sat in vigil at Borges's bedside while María took some rest. Borges had drifted into a coma, and in the early hours of the morning, Bianciotti noticed that his breathing, which had been quite regular for the last ten hours or more, seemed to be fading. He decided to call María, but, as if guided by some intuition, she was already at the door.[25] She took her place next to Borges as, finally, he slipped away, his hand in hers, toward the dawn of Saturday, June 14.

Epilogue

THE DEATH OF BORGES AT 7:47 A.M. was announced to the news media later that morning. At the request of the two Swiss physicians who had treated him in his last illness, Dr. Jean-François Balavoine and Dr. Patrick Ambrosetti, the Conseil Administratif of the City of Geneva decided to confer upon Borges the honor of being laid to rest at the Cimetière de Plainpalais, a burial ground reserved for notable personalities, where the remains of John Calvin are interred.

María decided that it would be more appropriate for the funeral to be preceded by a religious ceremony rather than a secular commemoration, and as a mark of respect for Borges's mother and grandmother, she arranged for an interdominational service to be conducted jointly by the Catholic and Protestant clergymen who had come to see Borges shortly before his death. The funeral took place on Wednesday, June 18, after a service held at the Protestant Cathédrale de Saint Pierre, which was attended by about a hundred friends and associates, as well as a number of Argentine and Swiss dignitaries. Pastor Montmollin read the opening verses of St. John's Gospel—"In the beginning was the Word . . . ,"—and gave an address in which he observed that "Borges was a man who had unceasingly searched for the right word, the term that would sum up the whole, the final meaning of things," but man can never reach that word by his own efforts; he is lost in a labyrinth. As St. John taught, "it is not man who discovers the word, it is the word that comes to him."[1] For his part, the Catholic priest, Father Pierre Jacquet, revealed to the congregation that when he saw Borges before he died, he had found "a man full of love, who received from the Church the forgiveness of his sins."[2]

An official Argentine delegation, headed by the minister of culture and the ambassadors to Switzerland and the international organizations at Geneva, was present at the funeral. The president of Argentina, Raúl Alfonsín, declared national mourning as a mark of respect for the death of a great Argentine writer. Nevertheless, even in death Borges could not escape political controversy. Although it had been announced that a representative of the Peronist Party would join the Argentine delegation at the funeral, he failed to turn up. A spokesman for the party informed the press that this was not on account of Borges's well-known hostility to Peronism but "because of certain declarations he had made about the country."[3] Two days later, on June 20, a storm was raised at a meeting of the Concejo Deliberante, the City Council of Buenos Aires, when the Peronist members qualified their support for a motion of condolence on Borges's death. The leader of the Peronist group declared that her party was content "to praise Borges as a writer, but not as an Argentine, since he chose to die abroad."[4] This statement provoked a furious response from other members of the council. A Radical councilor called the Peronist declaration "almost fascist." In the heated debate that followed, another Peronist councilor was more forthright—Borges had made remarks about Eva Perón which were "unacceptable."

Another controversy flared up over Borges's alleged return to the fold of the Catholic Church. Father Pierre Jacquet's reference in his address at the funeral in Geneva to his visit to the dying man and to the latter's having received the Church's "forgiveness for his sins" led to rumors in Argentina, and to claims by elements within the Catholic Church there, that the famously agnostic writer had undergone a deathbed conversion. In order to clarify the matter, Monsignor Daniel José Keegan, rector of Buenos Aires Cathedral, wrote to Father Jacquet in Geneva, who replied on August 9 with an account of his visit to the dying Borges.[5] This visit had taken place "at the request of the family"; Borges was already very weak, and it was impossible to hold a conversation with him, although Jacquet's clear impression was that Borges "understood what I was saying"; he felt, moreover, that the dying man wished "to associate himself with the prayers and the sacrament of reconciliation" but added, "I believe it is not possible to derive from that meeting any interpretation regarding Borges's attitudes to the Catholic Church." The funeral had been held in the Protestant cathedral, according to Jacquet, because "Borges had, apparently, always been a man with an open mind about confessional boundaries," and, given that the City Council of Geneva had decided to honor him, it would have been normal practice for him to be buried in the official cemetery, where, in fact, he had been laid to rest not far from John Calvin's grave.

At the time of Borges's death, Argentina was a country racked by bitter ideological divisions. Borges himself had been caught up in all sorts of political quarrels and conflicts in the course of his life; he was remembered especially, and bitterly resented, as an implacable enemy of Perón, as the debate in the Concejo Deliberante amply demonstrated. However, in the last years of his life, he had undergone a profound change of heart. He had come to believe that the sword that had so blighted his personal life had also blighted the history of the nation, and that, just as he had struggled to overcome the inner conflicts caused by the sword, so, too, must the *patria* strive to transcend the divisions that kept threatening to tear it apart. It was Switzerland, with its diverse cantons and languages and races, that could offer Argentina an example of concord, a fruitful "confederacy" of reason and good faith.

Borges's grave at the Cimetière de Plainpalais in Geneva attests to his repudiation of the sword. The grave is marked by a rough-hewn headstone bearing his name, JORGE LUIS BORGES, and his dates of birth and death, 1899–1986. On the front of the stone is engraved an image found on a shield at the Anglo-Saxon burial ground at Sutton Hoo and reproduced on the cover of a book of Anglo-Saxon poems that Borges gave to María Kodama after they had finished translating "The Battle of Maldon," one of his favorite texts.[6] The image shows seven warriors, three of whom are holding aloft their swords, which are broken. Below this image is a quotation from "The Battle of Maldon": ". . . *and ne forhtedon ná*," ". . . and be not afraid" (line 21).

On the back of the gravestone is portrayed an image of a Viking longship. Above it is the legend "*Hann tekr sverthit Gram ok leggr i methal theira bert*," "He takes the sword Gram and places it between them," a quotation from the Icelandic *Völsunga Saga*, alluding to the hero Sigurd's placing his sword, Gram, between himself and his former lover, Brynhild, as they lie together. This is the text Borges had chosen as the epigraph for "Ulrica," the story that had been inspired by his brief meeting with María Kodama in Iceland in 1971, which tells of an encounter in York between an aging professor, Javier Otárola, and the eponymous Norwegian girl. Below the image of the longship, there is another reference to this story in the legend: "*De Ulrica a Javier Otárola*," "From Ulrica to Javier Otárola." This inscription recalls the gift that Ulrica offered Otárola at the end of the story—she accompanied him to Thorgate (the "street of Thor" or "calle Tronador"), and in an upper room at an inn whose "deep red" walls depicted "intertwined fruits and birds," love flowed in the darkness, and "there was no sword between the two of us."

Glossary of Argentine Terms

almacén   A corner store–cum–bar.

arrabal   A poor urban district or barrio.

arrabalero   Street slang used by the inhabitants of the *arrabales*.

caña   An alcholic drink distilled from sugarcane.

caudillo   (1) A general Spanish-American term denoting the political boss of a country, province, region, city or party, ruling through a combination of patronage and coercion; (2) in old Buenos Aires, the boss of a barrio charged with organizing and delivering the local vote for a political party at elections; (3) the leader of a gang of *compadritos* and *cuchilleros*.

compadrito   A dandified knife fighter who was often also a pimp and hired bodyguard.

confitería   A café or teahouse in Buenos Aires.

conventillo   A tenement building or dilapidated mansion subdivided into small dwellings and rented out to poor families.

criollo   An Argentine of Spanish descent.

criollismo   A movement with the aim of conserving and promoting the folkore and culture of the criollos.

cuchillero   A knife fighter.

esquina   A bar on a street corner.

estancia   A large rural estate devoted to cattle ranching and arable farming; its proprietor is an *estanciero*.

gaucho   A cowboy on the Argentine plains famed for his equestrian and cattle-raising skills.

gringo   A pejorative term used of a foreign immigrant, usually an Italian, in the nineteenth and early twentieth centuries.

guapo   Similar to *compadrito,* but a term of admiration reserved for *compadritos* of particular bravery or skill.

lunfardo   The slang of the Buenos Aires underworld.

malevo   A delinquent, often also a *cuchillero*.

mate   A tealike infusion made from a plant native to the region of the River Plate and Paraguay, which is served in a handheld gourd and consumed through a narrow tube.

milonga   A traditional rustic song; also a dance.

montoneros   (1) Irregular gaucho cavalry in the Wars of Independence and nineteenth-century civil wars; (2) name adopted by Peronist urban guerrillas in the 1970s.

ombú   A tree native to the River Plate area.

orillas   The poor barrios of the outskirts, literally the "shores," of Buenos Aires in the nineteenth and early twentieth centuries.

pampa   The vast plains to the west and south of Buenos Aires and in Patagonia.

payada   A song, often improvised, performed by a *payador* accompanying himself on the guitar. Also, a song contest between two *payadores*.

porteño   A native of the port city, as opposed to the province, of Buenos Aires.

suburbio   A poor urban district or barrio, synonymous with *arrabal*.

truco   A pokerlike game of cards peculiar to the River Plate area.

Notes

Preface

1. Interview with Ronald Christ in *Paris Review* 40 (1967), p. 155; quoted in Alazraki, *Borges and the Kabbalah,* Cambridge University Press: Cambridge, 1988, p. 52, n. 28.

Chapter 1: **Family and Nation**

1. Jean de Milleret, *Entretiens avec Jorge Luis Borges,* Pierre Belfond: Paris, 1967, p. 203.
2. See Miguel de Torre, *Borges: fotografías y manuscritos,* Renglón: Buenos Aires, 1987, p. 41.
3. See "Notes" in Jorge Luis Borges, *Selected Poems, 1923–1967,* Delacorte Press: New York, 1972, p. 299.
4. "América y el destino de la civilización occidental," *Nosotros,* segunda época, no. 1, April 1936, pp. 60–61. Reprinted in *Jorge Luis Borges: textos recobrados, 1931–1955,* Emecé: Buenos Aires, 2001, pp. 350–51.
5. Fernando Sorrentino, *Siete conversaciones con Jorge Luis Borges,* Casa Pardo: Buenos Aires, pp. 107–8.
6. Antonio Carrizo, *Borges el memorioso,* Fondo de Cultura Económica: Mexico, 1983, p. 127.
7. Leonor Acevedo de Borges, "Recuerdos," unpublished memoir, p. 22.
8. Ibid., pp. 12–13.
9. "Página relativa a Figari," *Criterio* 30, September 27, 1928, p. 406. Reprinted in *Jorge Luis Borges: textos recobrados, 1919–1929,* Emecé: Buenos Aires, 1997, p. 362.

Chapter 2: **Mother and Father**

1. Leonor Acevedo, "Recuerdos," p. 5. My account of Leonor Acevedo's family background is based largely on these memoirs.
2. See "Notes" in *Selected Poems,* p. 303.
3. "An Autobiographical Essay" in Jorge Luis Borges, *The Aleph and Other Stories (1933–1969),* Jonathan Cape: London, 1971, p. 205.
4. "An Autobiographical Essay," p. 210.
5. See Daniel Balderston, *Out of Context: Historical Reference and the Representation of Reality in Borges,* Duke University Press: Durham, N.C., and London, 1993, p. 91 and note 15.

6. See Ana María Barrenechea, "Jorge Luis Borges y la ambivalente mitificación de su abuelo paterno," *Nueva Revista de Filología Hispánica,* 40 (1992), 1005–24, (p. 1005, note 2).

7. *The Southern Cross,* October 4, 1878. See photographic reproduction of the obituary in Alejandro Vaccaro, *Georgie (1899–1930): una vida de Jorge Luis Borges,* Proa/Alberto Casares: Buenos Aires, 1996, and also p. 22.

8. See "Notes" in *Selected Poems,* p. 304.

9. See Barrenechea, *NRFH* above, and Vaccaro, *Georgie,* p. 32.

10. Jorge Guillermo Borges, *El Caudillo,* Academia Argentina de Letras, Buenos Aires, 1989 (originally published in Palma de Majorca, 1921), p. 45.

11. Alicia Jurado, "Prólogo" to *El Caudillo,* p. 15.

12. "An Autobiographical Essay," p. 211.

13. Interview with Elsie Rivero Haedo, Buenos Aires, March 30, 1994.

14. "El remordimiento" in *La moneda de hierro* 1976, in Jorge Luis Borges, *Obras completas.* Emecé: Buenos Aires, 1996, vol. III, p. 143. In subsequent endnotes the *Obras completas* (four volumes) will be referred to by the abbreviation *OC,* with the particular volume given in Roman numerals.

Chapter 3: **Childhood (1899–1914)**

1. See interview with Norah Borges in Vaccaro, *Georgie,* p. 55.

2. "An Autobiographical Essay," pp. 203–4.

3. Roberto Alifano, *Borges: biografía verbal,* Plaza y Janés: Barcelona, 1988, p. 27.

4. "An Autobiographical Essay," p. 208.

5. Sorrentino, p. 13.

6. Carrizo, p. 151.

7. Ibid., 152.

8. Victoria Ocampo, *Diálogo con Borges,* Sur: Buenos Aires, 1969, p. 11.

9. However, Ana María Barrenechea has shown that Borges takes a progressively more critical distance from his heroic ancestor in these poems. See Barrenechea, *Nueva Revista de Filología Hispánica,* 40 (1992), pp. 1006–24.

10. See "Notes" in *Selected Poems,* p. 304.

11. Milleret, p. 172.

12. "An Autobiograpical Essay," p. 208.

13. Ibid., pp. 208–9.

14. Ibid., p. 209.

15. Alifano, *Biografía verbal,* p. 31.

16. "El espejo" in *Historia de la noche,* 1977, *OC* III, p. 193.

17. "Al espejo" in *La rosa profunda,* 1975, *OC* III, p. 109.

18. "El espejo" in *Historia de la noche,* 1977, *OC* III, p. 193.

19. The quotations are, respectively, from the following texts: "Dreamtigers," in *El hacedor, OC* II, p. 161; "El tigre" in *Historia de la noche,* 1977, *OC* III, p. 173; and "Dreamtigers," as above.

20. Milleret, p. 20.

21. "Tigres azules" in *La memoria de Shakespeare, OC* III, p. 379.

22. See M. de Torre, *Borges: fotografías y manuscritos,* pp. 25–27.

23. "Propos de Mme. Leonor Acevedo de Borges," *Cahiers de L'Herne,* Paris, 1964, p. 10.

24. Alicia Jurado, *Genio y figura de Jorge Luis Borges,* Editorial Universitaria de Buenos Aires: Buenos Aires, 1964, p. 25.
25. "Propos de Mme. Leonor Acevedo de Borges," *Cahiers de L'Herne,* p. 10.
26. See "Simón Carbajal" in *La rosa profunda,* 1975, *OC* III, p. 93.
27. Richard Burgin, *Conversations with Jorge Luis Borges,* Holt, Rinehart and Winston: New York, 1969, p. 86.
28. "El puñal" in *El otro, el mismo,* 1969, *OC* II, p. 327.
29. Burgin, *Conversations,* 1969, p. 21.
30. Milleret, p. 24.
31. Carrizo, p. 182; Milleret, p. 22.
32. "An Autobiographical Essay," p. 209.
33. Roberto Alifano, *Conversaciones con Borges,* Torre Agüero: Buenos Aires, 1994, pp. 34–35.
34. "Propos de Mme. Leonor Acevedo de Borges," *Cahiers de L'Herne,* p. 10.
35. Alifano, *Conversaciones,* p. 32.
36. Ibid., p. 33.
37. Ocampo, *Diálogo,* p. 50.
38. Carrizo, p. 152.
39. "An Autobiographical Essay," p. 213.
40. Sorrentino, p. 33.
41. Alifano, *Conversaciones,* p. 34.
42. "An Autobiographical Essay," pp. 211–12.
43. Vaccaro, *Georgie,* p. 63, f.n.
44. Ibid., p. 56.
45. Ibid., p. 64.
46. "An Autobiographical Essay," p. 212.
47. Alifano, *Biografía verbal,* p. 26.
48. Vaccaro, *Georgie,* p. 64.
49. "An Autobiographical Essay," p. 212.
50. Carrizo, p. 256.
51. Alejandro Vaccaro, unpublished introduction to the letters of Borges to Roberto Godel.
52. Carrizo, p. 257.
53. "El hacedor" in the collection of the same title, *OC* II, pp. 159–60.
54. Burgin, *Conversations,* 1969, p. 46.
55. Vaccaro, *Georgie,* pp. 64–65.
56. See "Los sueños y la poesía" in *Borges en la Escuela Freudiana de Buenos Aires,* Agalma: Buenos Aires, 1993, p. 37.
57. "El hacedor," *OC* II, p. 160.
58. "An Autobiographical Essay," p. 206.
59. Burgin, *Conversations,* 1969, p. 24.
60. Ibid., p. 34.
61. Ibid., pp. 28–29.
62. I have consulted a typewritten transcript of this play. The manuscript is held in a private collection in Buenos Aires. This was possibly the first literary piece Borges ever wrote. He claimed to have first started writing "when I was six or seven," his first piece being "a kind of handbook on Greek mythology" written "in quite bad

English" ("An Autobiographical Essay," p. 211). When he was nine, he produced a Spanish translation of Oscar Wilde's *The Happy Prince* that was thought good enough to merit publication in the Buenos Aires newspaper *El País* on June 25, 1910. His first story "was a rather nonsensical piece after the manner of Cervantes, an old-fashioned romance called 'La visera fatal' ('The Fatal Helmet')" ("An Autobiographical Essay," p. 211). Alejandro Vaccaro has suggested that Borges may have been referring to this play about Bernardo del Carpio, which is untitled in the manuscript and was written in pseudoarchaic Spanish. (See Vaccaro, *Georgie*, p. 57.)

63. See *Evaristo Carriego, OC* I, p. 118.
64. Vaccaro, *Georgie*, p. 67.
65. See a photographic reproduction of the original publication of "El rey de la selva" in Vaccaro, *Georgie*, p. 163.
66. See Vaccaro, *Georgie*, p. 67.
67. See María Esther Vázquez, *Borges: esplendor y derrota*, Tusquets: Barcelona, 1996, p. 34. Leonor Acevedo also referred to this accident in *Cahiers de L'Herne*, p. 11.
68. "Momentos" in *Nosotros* 47, March 1913, pp. 147–148. Reprinted in Vaccaro, *Georgie*, pp. 45–46.
69. "An Autobiographical Essay," p. 214.
70. Ibid., p. 212.
71. Carrizo, p. 21.
72. Ibid, p. 22.
73. Interview with Miguel de Torre, Buenos Aires, November 13, 1995.
74. Ibid.
75. Carrizo, p. 257.
76. "An Autobiographical Essay," p. 206.
77. Carrizo, p. 257.

Chapter 4: **Geneva (1914–1919)**

1. Carlos Alberto Andreola, "Borges Helvético," *Conectándonos*, 18 (1994), p. 19.
2. Carrizo, p. 90.
3. Letter to Godel 1, undated but possibly written in March 1915. I have consulted typewritten transcripts of Borges's extant letters to Roberto Godel, which are held in the collection of Alejandro Vaccaro in Buenos Aires. Henceforward I shall identify them by date, where given, and by the number accorded them in the Vaccaro collection.
4. Milleret, p. 20.
5. "An Autobiographical Essay," p. 215.
6. Andreola, "Borges Helvético," p. 19.
7. See his story "El otro" in *El libro de arena*, 1975, *OC* III, p. 12.
8. Andreola, "Borges Helvético," p. 18.
9. See his story "El otro" in *El libro de arena*, 1975, *OC* III, p. 12.
10. "An Autobiographical Essay," pp. 216–17.
11. "Entretiens avec Napoléon Murat," *Cahiers de L'Herne*, p. 383.
12. "Entretiens avec James E. Irby," *Cahiers de L'Herne*, p. 400.
13. Vaccaro, *Georgie*, p. 99.
14. Carrizo, p. 90.

15. Interview with Donald Yates, St. Helena, California, March 27, 1999.

16. Alifano, *Biografía verbal,* p. 36, and also, interview with Donald Yates, St. Helena, California, March 27, 1999.

17. See, respectively, Carrizo, p. 155, and Milleret, p. 25.

18. "An Autobiographical Essay," p. 218.

19. Alifano, *Conversaciones,* p. 124.

20. "An Autobiographical Essay," p. 218.

21. As reported by Simon Jichlinski to Emir Rodríguez Monegal, *Jorge Luis Borges: A Literary Biography,* Dutton: New York, 1978, p. 115.

22. *El Hogar,* July 25, 1937, p. 30, quoted in Rodríguez Monegal, Jose Luis Borges, *A Literary Biography,* p. 120.

23. Letter to Godel 3, December 4, 1917.

24. Anthology of expressionists published in *Cervantes* (Madrid), October 1920. Reprinted in *Textos recobrados, 1919–1929,* pp. 62–63.

25. Letter to Godel 3, December 4, 1917.

26. Letter to Godel 4, May 23, 1918.

27. Ibid.

28. Letter to Godel 3, December 4, 1917.

29. Ibid.

30. Letter to Godel 4, May 23, 1918.

31. Ibid.

32. Vázquez, *Borges: esplendor y derrota,* p. 49.

33. The summons was issued in May 1918 by Military District No. 1 of the Federal Capital and sent by diplomatic bag to the Argentine consulate in Geneva; Borges's registration number was 002.049. Information provided by Carlos Alberto Andreola, Buenos Aires.

34. Letter to Godel 5, undated but probably written at the end of October or early November 1918; and Letter to Godel 6, undated but probably written in the early months of 1919.

35. "Paréntesis pasional." See *Textos recobrados, 1919–1929,* pp. 27–29.

36. See Carta 32 in Jorge Luis Borges, *Cartas del Fervor. Correspondencia con Maurice Abramowicz y Jacobo Sureda (1919–1928),* Galaxia Gutenberg-Círculo de Lectores–Emecé: Barcelona 1999, p. 212. This letter was written in French to Jacobo Sureda, who was in Leysin, Switzerland, and then St. Blasien, Höchenschwand, Germany, receiving treatment for tuberculosis. Although Borges was living in Buenos Aires at the time of writing, his family was planning to return to Europe by the end of the year. (See my Chapter 6, p. 104.) Hence Borges's reference in this letter to meeting up with Sureda on New Year's Eve, 1922.

37. *Cartas del fervor,* p. 212.

38. Vázquez, *Borges: esplendor y derrota,* p. 50.

39. Estela Canto, *Borges a contraluz,* Espasa Calpe: Madrid, 1989, pp. 115–16.

40. See unpublished poem reproduced in Donald A. Yates, "Behind 'Borges and I,'" *Modern Fiction Studies,* 19 (1973), pp. 322–23.

41. See Vázquez, *Borges: esplendor y derrota,* p. 50.

42. Canto, p. 117.

43. Vázquez, *Borges: esplendor y derrota,* p. 50.

44. Letter to Godel 5, undated but probably written at the end of October or early November 1918.

45. See Canto, p. 116. According to Donald Yates (interview, St. Helena, California, March 7, 1999), the woman concerned may have been a former mistress of Dr. Borges's.
46. Vázquez, *Borges: esplendor y derrota,* p. 51.
47. Letter to Godel 6, undated but probably written in the early months of 1919.
48. Letter to Godel 6.

Chapter 5: **Spain (1919–1921)**

1. Letter to Godel 6.
2. "An Autobiographical Essay," p. 219.
3. Jorge Guillermo Borges, "Del poema de Omar Jaiyám," *Gran Guignol* (Seville), 1, February 10, 1920. Quoted in Vaccaro, *Georgie,* p. 144.
4. Jorge Guillermo Borges, "El cantar de los cantares," *Gran Guignol* 1, March 10, 1920. Reprinted in Vaccaro, *Georgie,* pp. 148–51.
5. "La llama" was first published in the Seville magazine *Grecia* 41, February 29, 1920. See *Textos recobrados (1919–1929),* p. 36. It was included, with amendments, as "Llamarada" in the first edition of *Fervor de Buenos Aires* (1923) but omitted in subsequent editions of this collection.
6. "An Autobiographical Essay," p. 219.
7. "Himno del mar," *Grecia* 37, December 31, 1919. Reprinted in *Textos recobrados, 1919–1929,* pp. 24–26.
8. "An Autobiographical Essay," p. 220.
9. "Motivos del espacio y del tiempo (1916–1919)," *Gran Guignol* 1, April 24, 1920. Reprinted in *Textos recobrados, 1919–1929,* pp. 40–41.
10. Letter to Abramowicz, December 1, 1919. *Cartas del fervor,* p. 66.
11. Quoted in José María Barrera, "Borges en Sevilla," *Anthropos. Revista de Documentación Científica de la Cultura,* 142–43, (1993), pp. 157–60 (p. 158). This article will be identified in subsequent endnotes as Barrera, *Anthropos.*
12. "An Autobiographical Essay," pp. 220–21.
13. Letter to Abramowicz, January 12, 1920, *Cartas del fervor,* p. 74.
14. Quoted in Barrera, *Anthropos,* p. 158.
15. Ibid.
16. Based on an account given by Adriano del Valle in his review of *Rompecabezas,* a play by Luis Mosquera and Isaac del Vando Villar, published in *El Liberal* (Seville), October 6, 1921. Quoted in Barrera, *Anthropos,* p. 158.
17. "Paréntesis pasional," *Grecia* 38, January 20, 1920. Reprinted in *Textos recobrados, 1919–1929,* pp. 27–29.
18. See Barrera, *Anthropos,* p. 157.
19. "El cantar de los cantares," *Gran Guignol,* 1, March 10, 1920.
20. *Gran Guignol,* 1, February 10, 1920. Reprinted in *Textos recobrados, 1919–1929,* pp. 32–33.
21. "Al margen de la moderna estética," *Grecia* 39, January 31, 1920. Reprinted in *Textos recobrados, 1919–1929,* pp. 30–31.
22. See *Cartas del fervor,* p. 76. The letter appears to have been sent from Madrid shortly after Borges arrived there in March. The poem "Pedro-Luis en Martigny" and the letter to Abramowicz were reproduced in Daniel Mayer, "Sérieux comme

un tigre. Jorge Luis Borges en Suisse," *Écriture* (Lausanne), 28 (1987). The poem is included in *Textos recobrados, 1919–1929*, p. 48.

23. Guillermo de Torre, "Para la prehistoria ultraísta de Borges," *Cuadernos Hispano-americanos*, 169 (1964), pp. 5–15 (p. 9).

24. "An Autobiographical Essay," pp. 221–22.

25. Undated letter to Adriano del Valle. See Jean Pierre Bernès, *Jorge Luis Borges: Oeu-vres complètes*, Bibliothèque de la Pléiade, Gallimard: Paris, 1993, 1999, vol. II, pp. 1105–6. In subsequent endnotes this two-volume edition will be referred to as Bernès, followed by the volume number.

26. "An Autobiographical Essay," p. 222.

27. Ibid., p. 221.

28. Ibid., p. 222.

29. "La traducción de un incidente," *Inquisiciones,* Proa: Buenos Aires, 1925, and Seix Barral/Biblioteca Breve: Buenos Aires, 1994, p. 18. All subsequent references to *Inquisiciones* will be to the 1994 edition.

30. Guillermo de Torre, "Para la prehistoria ultraísta de Borges," *Cuadernos Hispano-americanos* 169, p. 9.

31. The manuscript of this letter is in the Doucet collection at the Bibliothèque Sainte-Genèviève in Paris. See Bernès I, pp. 1712–13, and *Textos recobrados, 1919–1929*, pp. 44–45.

32. "La traducción de un incidente," *Inquisiciones,* p. 17.

33. "Trinchera" was published in *Grecia* 43, June 1, 1920, and reprinted in *Textos reco-brados, 1919–1929*, p. 49.

34. Letter to Abramowicz from Saragossa, May 4, 1920. See *Cartas del fervor*, p. 78.

35. "Rusia" was published in *Grecia* 48, September 1, 1920 and reprinted in *Textos reco-brados, 1919–1929*, p. 57.

36. Undated letter to Abramowicz from Barcelona. See *Cartas del fervor*, p. 82.

37. Information provided by Carlos Alberto Andreola, Buenos Aires.

38. The letters Borges wrote to Guillermo de Torre that I have consulted in the course of my research are held in a private collection in Buenos Aires and are so far un-published. Henceforward I shall refer to this correspondence by date, where given, and by the number accorded to individual items in this collection, viz., in this in-stance, GDT 1.

39. Letter to Abramowicz, early July 1920. See *Cartas del fervor*, p. 90.

40. Letter to Abramowicz, August 20, 1920. See *Cartas del fervor*, p. 92.

41. Undated letter to Guillermo de Torre, GDT 2, on which Torre wrote "11 June 1920." This date, however, is unrealistic, given that the Borges family only arrived in Palma on June 11, as may be deduced from a letter to Abramowicz dated June 8 (see *Cartas del fervor*, pp. 86–87). The letter to Torre indicates that Borges had already been walking in the mountains, but since he did not go to Valldemosa until the be-ginnning of July, I would say the letter was probably written on July 11.

42. Undated letter to Abramowicz. See *Cartas del fervor*, p. 82.

43. Letter to Guillermo de Torre, September 29, 1920; GDT 6.

44. Letter to Guillermo de Torre, September 3, 1920; GDT 3.

45. Letter to Guillermo de Torre, (July 11 ?) 1920; GDT 2.

46. Ibid.

47. Letter to Abramowicz, August 20, 1920. See *Cartas del fervor*, p. 94.

48. Letter to Guillermo de Torre, September 3, 1920; GDT 3.
49. Letter to Abramowicz, undated but almost certainly written in September 1920. See *Cartas del fervor*, p. 100.
50. Letter to Sureda, October 24, 1920. See *Cartas del fervor*, p. 170. "Judería" was first published in *Fervor de Buenos Aires*, 1923. "Gesta soviética" was published in *Ultra* 3, February 20, 1921, with the title "Gesta maximalista," and reprinted in *Textos recobrados, 1919–1929*, p. 89. "Crucifixión" appears not to have been published.
51. Letter to Guillermo de Torre, November 6, 1920; GDT 5.
52. Letter to Sureda, November 13, 1920. See *Cartas del fervor*, p.179. "Guardia roja" was first published in *Ultra* 5, March 17, 1921, and reprinted in *Textos recobrados, 1919–1929*, p. 91.
53. Letter to Guillermo de Torre, who wrote "3 October 1920" on Borges's letter, although from internal evidence it is more likely to have been December 3; GDT 7.
54. Letter to Sureda, October 4, 1920. See *Cartas del fervor*, p. 164.
55. Letter to Sureda, undated. See *Cartas del fervor*, p. 182.
56. Letter to Guillermo de Torre, (December 3?) 1920; GDT 7.
57. "Poema" was first published in *Baleares* 121, September 15, 1920, and reprinted in *Textos recobrados, 1919–1929*, p. 60.
58. Letter to Sureda, October 30, 1920. Bernès II, pp. 1070–71.
59. Letter to Guillermo de Torre, November 17, 1920; GDT 9.
60. Letter to Abramowicz, undated but written in November 1920. See *Cartas del fervor*, p. 126.
61. Letter to Sureda, November 16, 1920. See *Cartas del fervor*, p. 181.
62. Letter to Guillermo de Torre, December 1920; GDT 10.
63. Letter to Abramowicz, undated but written in November 1920. See *Cartas del fervor*, p. 126.
64. Letter to Sureda, undated but written in November 1920. See *Cartas del fervor*, p. 174.
65. Letter to Abramowicz, undated. See *Cartas del fervor*, p. 140.
66. Letter to Guillermo de Torre, (December 3?) 1920; GDT 7.
67. Letter to Guillermo de Torre, December 1920; GDT 10.
68. Letter to Abramowicz, undated. See *Cartas del fervor*, p. 135.
69. See "El arte de Fernández Peña," reprinted in *Textos recobrados, 1919–1929*, p. 78.
70. See "Ultraísmo," reprinted in *Textos recobrados, 1919–1929*, p. 83.
71. See "Manifiesto del Ultra" reprinted in *Textos recobrados, 1919–1929*, pp. 86–87, and the poem on p. 88.
72. Letter to Sureda, February 25, 1921. See *Cartas del fervor*, p. 192.
73. Letter to Abramowicz, probably October 16, 1920. See *Cartas del fervor*, p. 116.
74. See "Esquisse critique" in Bernès I, pp. 842–43, and *Textos recobrados, 1919–1929*, p. 43.
75. See "Anatomía de mi Ultra," *Ultra* 11, May 20, 1921. Reprinted in *Textos recobrados, 1919–1929*, p. 95.
76. Letter to Guillermo de Torre, February 1921; GDT 8.
77. Letter to Abramowicz, March 2, 1921. See *Cartas del fervor*, p. 147.
78. Ibid.
79. Letter to Sureda, March 3, 1921. See *Cartas del fervor*, p. 193.
80. "La nadería de la personalidad," *Inquisiciones*, p. 99.

Chapter 6: **Buenos Aires (1921–1923)**

1. References are, respectively, to a letter to Adriano del Valle, undated, in Bernès II, p. 1107; letter to Guillermo de Torre, March 1921, GDT 14; letter to Godel 7, undated.

2. Unless otherwise indicated, the poems quoted in this chapter were included in the first edition of *Fervor de Buenos Aires,* 1923. Titles will be given in the main text.

3. See, respectively, the following letters to Sureda in *Cartas del fervor:* letter of June 22, 1921 (p. 200); undated letter, circa August 30, 1921 (p. 205); and letter of June 22, 1921 (p. 200).

4. Letter to Sureda, June 22, 1921, in *Cartas del fervor,* p. 199.

5. Letter to Guillermo de Torre, June 1921; GDT 13.

6. *Cosmópolis* 33, October 4, 1921. Reprinted in *Textos recobrados, 1919–1929,* pp. 102–4.

7. See Borges's prologue to "Santiago Dabove: *La muerte y su traje*" in *Prólogo con un prólogo de prólogos, OC* IV, p. 50.

8. Letter to Sureda, June 22, 1921, in *Cartas del fervor,* pp. 198–99. Borges gave a more extensive outline of the novel in "Macedonio Fernández," *Prólogo con un prólogo de prólogos, OC* IV, pp. 58–59.

9. Letter to Sureda, June 21, 1921, in *Cartas del fervor,* p. 198.

10. Letter to Sureda, undated (circa August 30, 1921), in *Cartas del fervor,* p. 205.

11. Letter to Sureda, November 24, 1921, in *Cartas del fervor,* p. 208.

12. "La nadería de la personalidad," first published in *Proa* (primera época), August 1, 1922, and later in *Inquisiciones,* pp. 93–104.

13. "El cielo azul, es cielo y es azul," *Cosmópolis* 44, August 1922. Reprinted in *Textos recobrados, 1919–1929,* pp. 154–58.

14. "La encrucijada de Berkeley," first published in *Nosotros* 43, 1923, and in *Inquisiciones,* p. 117–27.

15. "Proclama," reprinted in *Textos recobrados, 1919–1929,* pp. 122–24.

16. "Ultraísmo," *Nosotros* 39, December 1921. Reprinted in *Textos recobrados, 1919–1929,* pp. 126–31.

17. Letter to Guillermo de Torre, December 3, 1921; GDT 18.

18. Letter to Sureda, undated (circa March 29, 1922), in *Cartas del fervor,* p. 214.

19. Carrizo, p. 124.

20. Letter to Sureda, undated (circa March 29, 1922), in *Cartas del fervor,* p. 214.

21. Letter to Guillermo de Torre, dated "End of April 1922," GDT 22. Also Vaccaro, *Georgie,* pp. 107–99.

22. Letter to Guillermo de Torre, March 9, 1922; GDT 20.

23. Letter to Sureda, May 29, 1922, in *Cartas del fervor,* p. 221.

24. Letter to Sureda, undated (circa March 1922), in *Cartas del fervor,* p. 209.

25. Letter to Sureda, undated (circa March 29, 1922), in *Cartas del fervor,* p. 214.

26. Letter to Sureda, May 26, 1922, in *Cartas del fervor,* p. 221.

27. Letter to Sureda, undated (probably March 29, 1922), in *Cartas del fervor,* p. 215.

28. Letter to Guillermo de Torre, March 1922; GDT 19.

29. Letter to Sureda, July 25, 1922, in *Cartas del fervor,* pp. 223 and 224.

30. Letter to Guillermo de Torre, November 20, 1922; GDT 24.

31. Letter to Sureda, undated (circa September 1922), in *Cartas del fervor,* p. 225.

32. Ibid.

33. Letter to Guillermo de Torre, February 10, 1923; GDT 25.

34. Letter to Sureda, undated (circa March 1923), in *Cartas del fervor,* p. 227.

35. Letter to Sureda, undated, in *Cartas del fervor,* p. 216. From internal evidence I would say it must have been written about April 1923, but the editor of *Cartas del fervor* surmises—erroneously, in my judgment—that it was written a year earlier, in April 1922.

36. Interview with Concepción Guerrero's daughter, Mercedes Gini de Mills, Edinburgh, April 1, 1996.

37. Letter to Sureda, undated, in *Cartas del fervor,* p. 216.

38. Interview with Mercedes Gini de Mills, Edinburgh, April 1, 1996.

39. Letter to Sureda, undated, in *Cartas del fervor,* p. 216.

40. Letter to Guillermo de Torre, June 26, 1923; GDT 28.

41. Carlos García, "La edición *princeps* de *Fervor de Buenos Aires*" in *El joven Borges, poeta (1919–1930),* Corregidor: Buenos Aires, p. 22.

42. Ibid., p. 33.

43. "An Autobiographical Essay," pp. 224–25.

44. Letter to Guillermo de Torre, July–August 1923; GDT 29.

45. Letter to Sureda, undated (circa March 1923), in *Cartas del fervor,* p. 227.

46. Ibid.

47. Vaccaro, *Georgie,* p. 193.

48. Prologue to the first edition of *Fervor de Buenos Aires,* 1923. A much-revised version of this passage would subsequently appear as an epigraph to *Fervor de Buenos Aires* in the *OC* I, p. 15.

Chapter 7: Second Visit to Europe (1923–1924)

1. Letter to Macedonio Fernández, August 20, 1923. See Bernès II, p. 1115.

2. "Alejamiento" first published in *Alfar* 36 (La Coruña), January 1924. See *Textos recobrados, 1919–1929,* p. 181.

3. Letter to Guillermo de Torre, June 1924; GDT 27.

4. See Carlos García, *El joven Borges, poeta,* pp. 24–32.

5. "La traducción de un incidente," *Inicial* 5, May 1924, and *Inquisiciones,* pp. 18–19.

6. "An Autobiographical Essay," p. 139.

7. "La traducción de un incidente," *Inquisiciones,* pp. 20–21.

8. Ibid., pp. 21–22.

9. See his series of "Soleares" in the first edition to his second book, *Luna de enfrente,* Proa: Buenos Aires, 1925. They were omitted in later editions but are reprinted in *Textos recobrados, 1919–1929,* pp. 225–26.

10. Letter to Guillermo de Torre, June 1924; GDT 37.

11. These were the "Romance de la luna de los gitanos," later called "Romance de la luna luna," and "Soneto," *Proa* 11, June 1925.

12. "Los llanos" was first published in *Nosotros* 18, June 1924, and later in *Luna de enfrente* but omitted in the *OC* since 1974. In subsequent endnotes quotations from poems in *Luna de enfrente* will be from the first edition of 1925. Where relevant, the page number will also be given to the corresponding poem in *Luna de enfrente* in the *Obras completas,* although it must be borne in mind that this collection was much revised by Borges.

13. See letter to Borges and Brandán Caraffa, August 1925, in Ricardo Güiraldes, *Obras*

completas, Emecé: Buenos Aires, 1962, p. 780, and also, Carlos García, *El joven Borges, poeta,* p. 86, note 20.

14. See *Martín Fierro,* March 20, 1924, pp. 12–13. This and subsequent page references are to the facsimile edition, *Revista Martín Fierro, 1924–1927. Edición facsimilar,* Fondo Nacional de las Artes: Buenos Aires, 1995.

15. *Martín Fierro,* May 15, 1924, pp. 25–26.

16. *Martín Fierro,* July 25, 1924, p. 47.

17. Interview with Concepción Guerrero's daughter, Mercedes Gini de Mills, Edinburgh, April 1, 1996.

18. It appeared in the first edition of *Luna de enfrente* but was omitted in later editions.

19. Letter to Guillermo de Torre, August 11, 1924; GDT 39.

20. Letter to Guillermo de Torre, October 26, 1924; GDT 40.

21. *Martín Fierro,* August–September 1924, p. 63.

22. Undated note to Norah Lange written shortly before August 11, 1924. Consulted courtesy of Susana Lange, Buenos Aires.

23. "Queja de todo criollo," *Inquisiciones,* pp. 139–46 (pp. 145–46).

24. See the epigraph to "*Dulcia linquimus arva,*" first published in *Revista de América* 4, July 26, 1925, and later in *Luna de enfrente,* 1925, and *OC* I, p. 68.

25. Undated note to Norah Lange written shortly before August 11, 1924. Consulted courtesy of Susana Lange, Buenos Aires.

26. "El *Ulises* de Joyce," *Proa* 6, January 1925, and *Inquisiciones,* pp. 23–28 (pp. 23 and 24.)

27. "Después de las imágenes," *Proa* 5, December 1924, and *Inquisiciones,* pp. 29–32 (p. 31).

28. "Menoscabo y grandeza de Quevedo," *Revista de Occidente* (Madrid), November 17, 1924, and *Inquisiciones,* pp. 43–49 (p. 48).

29. "Ramón y Pombo," *Martín Fierro,* January 24, 1925, p. 93, and as "Ramón Gómez de la Serna" in *Inquisiciones,* pp. 132–35 (pp. 133 and 134).

30. "Ramón y Pombo," *Martín Fierro,* p. 93, and *Inquisiciones,* p. 132.

31. Letter to Guillermo de Torre, October 26, 1924; GDT 40.

32. Information derived from correspondence consulted by courtesy of Susana Lange, Buenos Aires.

33. See *Martín Fierro,* October 9, 1924; prologue, p. 69, and poems, p. 74. The prologue was reprinted in *Inquisiciones,* pp. 83–85 (p. 83).

34. "Norah Lange," *Martín Fierro,* July 25, 1924, p. 48.

35. Ulyses Petit de Murat, *El Correo Literario,* January 1, 1944, quoted in María Esther de Miguel, *Norah Lange: una biografía,* Planeta: Buenos Aires (1991), p. 103.

36. Ulyses Petit de Murat, *Borges Buenos Aires,* Municipalidad de la Ciudad de Buenos Aires: Buenos Aires, 1980, p. 33.

37. See Norah Lange's brief self-portrait for the anthology by Pedro-Juan Vignale and César Tiempo, *Exposición de la actual poesía argentina,* reprinted in *Martín Fierro,* March 28, 1927, p. 320.

38. Letter to Jacobo Sureda, November 27, 1924, in *Cartas del fervor,* p. 234.

39. "Último sol en Villa Ortúzar" in *Luna de enfrente,* 1925, and *OC* I, p. 71.

40. "Casi Juicio Final" in *Luna de enfrente,* 1925, and *OC* I, p. 69.

41. "La última hoja del *Ulises,*" *Proa* 6, January 1925. Reprinted in *Textos recobrados, 1919–1929,* pp. 201–2.

42. The original title of Borges's essay was "Sobre un verso de Apollinaire," *Nosotros* 190, March 1925, but it appeared as "La Aventura y el Orden" in *El tamaño de mi esperanza,* Proa: Buenos Aires, 1926. See *El tamaño de mi esperanza,* Espasa Calpe/ Seix Barral: Buenos Aires, 1993, pp. 69–72. In subsequent endnotes page references will be to the 1993 edition.

Chapter 8: **Adventures in the Avant-Garde (1925)**

1. Alfredo Andrés, *Palabras con Leopoldo Marechal,* Carlos Pérez Editor: Buenos Aires, 1968, p. 24.
2. Ibid.
3. "*Martín Fierro* y yo," *Martín Fierro,* July 25, 1924, p. 46.
4. See Santiago Ganduglia, "Párrafo sobre la literatura de Boedo," *Martín Fierro,* December 29, 1925, p. 190.
5. See "La inútil discusión de Boedo y Florida," *La Prensa,* September 30, 1928. Reprinted in *Textos recobrados, 1919–1929,* pp. 365–68.
6. See Juan Antonio Villoldo, "La revisión fascista," *Nosotros* 190, March 1925, pp. 332–42.
7. "Carta de la dirección de *Proa*," *Nosotros* 191, April 1925. Reprinted in *Textos recobrados, 1919–1929,* pp. 207–8.
8. Letter to Sureda, undated (circa June or July 1925), in *Cartas del fervor,* p. 236.
9. I have consulted the letter in the Archivo Évar Méndez, which is in the collection of Wáshington Pereyra, Buenos Aires.
10. See *Martín Fierro,* May 5, 1925, p. 106.
11. Letter to Guillermo de Torre, May 23, 1925; GDT 43.
12. The "epitaph" in question appeared in *Martín Fierro,* May 17, 1925, p. 118.
13. "Oliverio Girondo: *Calcomanías*," *Martín Fierro,* June 26, 1925, p. 122, and reprinted in *El tamaño de mi esperanza,* pp. 88–90.
14. Letter to Sureda, undated (circa June or July 1925), in *Cartas del fervor,* p. 236.
15. The letter was dated July 1925 but published several months later as "Carta a Güiraldes y a Brandán en una muerte (ya resucitada) de *Proa*," *Proa* 15, January 1926, and reprinted with the title "Carta en la defunción de *Proa*" in *El tamaño de mi esperanza,* pp. 81–83.
16. "El *Fausto* criollo" in *Proa* 11, June 1925, and *El tamaño de mi esperanza,* pp. 15–19.
17. "El *Fausto* criollo" in *El tamaño de mi esperanza,* p. 17.
18. Letter to Guillermo de Torre, December 31, 1925; GDT 44.
19. These were: "Arrabal en que pesa el campo" and "La fundación mitológica de Buenos Aires" in *Nosotros* 204, May 1926, pp. 52–53.
20. See *Martín Fierro,* December 29, 1925, p. 193.
21. Borges would not immediately abandon the "history of Argentina in verse," but in the course of 1926, this project seems to have withered on the vine. In May he would write of "a possible book of poems entitled *Cuaderno San Martín,*" and later that year he would refer to *Cuaderno San Martín* merely as "a book of *porteño* verses." See, respectively, the footnote in *Nosotros* 204, May 1926, p. 53, and Borges's autobiographical note in Pedro-Juan Vignale and César Tiempo, *Exposición de la actual poesía argentina,* which was reprinted in *Martín Fierro,* March 28, 1927, p. 320.

Chapter 9: **The Aleph (1926)**

1. "La pampa y el suburbio son dioses," *Proa* 15, January 1926, and in *El tamaño de mi esperanza*, pp. 21–25 (p. 21).
2. Alifano, *Conversaciones*, pp. 29–30.
3. Sorrentino, p. 82.
4. Alifano, *Conversaciones*, p. 30.
5. Ibid., p. 29.
6. "Carriego y el sentido del arrabal," *La Prensa*, April 4, 1926, later collected in *El tamaño de mi esperanza*, pp. 27–31 (pp. 29–30). Borges still maintained this view in old age; see Carrizo, p. 174.
7. "Invectiva contra el arrabalero," *La Prensa*, June 6, 1926, and in *El tamaño de mi esperanza*, pp. 121–26 (pp. 126 and 125, respectively).
8. See *Martín Fierro*, February 26, 1927, p. 306. It was given the title "Hombres pelearon" when published in *El idioma de los argentinos*, Manuel Gleizer: Buenos Aires, 1928. See *El idioma de los argentinos*, Seix Barral/Biblioteca Breve: Buenos Aires, 1994, pp. 126–28. All subsequent page references to *El idioma de los argentinos* are to the 1994 edition.
9. "Invectiva contra el arrabalero," in *El tamaño de mi esperanza*, pp. 125–26.
10. Ibid.
11. Written in January 1926, "El tamaño de mi esperanza" was first published in *Valoraciones*, March 1926 and later, in the collection of the same title, pp. 11–14.
12. "El tamaño de mi esperanza," p. 14.
13. Ibid., p. 13.
14. Ibid., p. 14.
15. I am quoting the phrase from Borges's endnote to the poem "Muertes de Buenos Aires I" in the first edition of *Cuaderno San Martín*, Cuadernos del Plata: Buenos Aires, 1929, p. 56.
16. Undated letter to an anonymous recipient, now held in the Borges Collection, Alderman Library, University of Virginia.
17. Petit de Murat, *Borges Buenos Aires*, pp. 63–65.
18. Ibid., pp. 74–75.
19. Letter to Guillermo de Torre, May 1926; GDT 46.
20. Carlos Mastronardi, *Memorias de un provinciano*, Ediciones Culturales Argentinas: Buenos Aires, 1967, p. 226.
21. Francisco Luis Bernárdez, "Nora y Norah" in *Clarín*, December 5, 1968.
22. See "Ofrenda" in *Martín Fierro*, December 12, 1926, p. 286.
23. "Profesión de fe literaria," *La Prensa*, June 27, 1926, and in *El tamaño de mi esperanza*, pp. 127–33.
24. See the review of Pedro Leandro Ipuche's *Júbilo y miedo* by "J.L.B." in *Martín Fierro*, September 3, 1926, p. 248.
25. "An Autobiographical Essay," p. 252.
26. "Página relativa a Figari. Leída con motivo de la inauguración de la exposición de cuadros de Pedro Figari realizada en el Convivio de los Cursos de Cultura Católica," *Criterio* 30, September 27, 1928. Reprinted in *Textos recobrados, 1919–1929*, pp. 362–64 (p. 362). See also Chapter 1, p. 15.
27. See the dedication in *Historia universal de la infamia*, 1935, and my Chapter 14, pp. 213–14.

28. "Historia de los ángeles," *La Prensa*, March 7, 1926, and *El tamaño de mi esperanza*, pp. 63–67 (p. 66).

29. See *Martín Fierro*, May 10, 1926, p. 196.

30. "Criollismo y metafísica," *Martín Fierro*, May 10, 1926, p. 197.

31. "Poesía y sentimentalismo," *Martín Fierro*, October 5, 1926, p. 262.

32. Beatriz de Nóbile, *Palabras con Norah Lange*, Carlos Pérez Editor: Buenos Aires, 1968, p. 18.

33. See the item *"Martín Fierro"* in *Martín Fierro*, November 5, 1926, p. 271.

34. Alfredo Andrés, *Palabras con Leopoldo Marechal*, p. 23.

35. *Martín Fierro*, August 4, 1926, p. 239.

36. Carlos Mastronardi, *Memorias de un provinciano*, p. 210.

37. "La felicidad escrita," *La Prensa*, October 24, 1926, and *El idioma de los argentinos*, pp. 41–47 (p. 47).

38. "La felicidad escrita," p. 41.

39. *Martín Fierro*, November 5, 1926, p. 276.

40. *Martín Fierro*, March 28, 1927, p. 322.

41. *Martín Fierro*, December 12, 1926, p. 280.

Chapter 10: **Rejection (1926–1927)**

1. M. E. de Miguel, *Norah Lange*, p. 119.

2. Beatriz de Nóbile, *Palabras con Norah Lange*, p. 14.

3. M. E. de Miguel, *Norah Lange*, p. 120.

4. See "Cómo Dios le alcanzó una soledad," *Martín Fierro*, July 15–August 15, 1927, p. 366.

5. Beatriz de Nóbile, *Palabras con Norah Lange*, p. 14.

6. See J.L.B. [*sic*], *"Voz de la vida. Norah Lange. 'Proa' 1927,"* *Síntesis* 10, March 1928. Reprinted in *Textos recobrados, 1919–1929*, p. 335.

7. Norah Lange, *Voz de la vida*, Editorial Proa: Buenos Aires, 1927, pp. 26–29.

8. *Martín Fierro*, March 28, 1927, p. 322. In its issue of January 20, 1927, *Martín Fierro* announced that Girondo's father had "just died" but gave no date (see p. 298).

9. See "Cómo Dios le alcanzó una soledad," *Martín Fierro*, July 15–August 15, 1927, p. 366.

10. Beatriz de Nóbile, *Palabras con Norah Lange*, p. 14. It may well have been Norah Lange whom Silvina Ocampo had in mind when she talked about a woman Borges admired who was bald and had to wear a wig. See "Image de Borges" in *Cahiers de L'Herne*, p. 27. Silvina, who was a friend of Norah Borges in this period, would already have known Borges quite well.

11. Beatriz de Nóbile, *Palabras con Norah Lange*, p. 14.

12. *Martín Fierro*, August 31–November 15, 1927, p. 376.

13. Borges would publish this text three times: first in *El idioma de los argentinos*, 1928, see the 1993 edition, pp. 123–26; then as part of the title essay of the collection, *Historia de la eternidad*, 1936, see *OC* I, pp. 353–67 (pp. 365–66); and finally as part of the essay, "Nueva refutación del tiempo," first published as a pamphlet by the (apocryphal) Oportet & Haereses: Buenos Aires, 1947, and later incorporated in *Otras inquisiciones* (1952); see *OC* II, pp. 135–49 (pp. 142–43).

14. See *Martín Fierro*, April 28, 1927, p. 332.

15. Ibid., p. 334.

16. "Un soneto de don Francisco de Quevedo," *La Prensa*, May 15, 1927, and in *El idioma de los argentinos*, pp. 68–69. The lines Borges quoted here were precisely those he had cited in the letter he wrote to Jacobo Sureda circa September 1922, while Concepción Guerrero was away from Buenos Aires for two weeks, an absence he felt so acutely that it put him in mind of death, immortality, and such "fundamental things." See my Chapter 6, p. 107-8.

17. "La fruición literaria," *La Prensa*, January 23, 1927, and in *El idioma de los argentinos*, p. 92.

18. The first part of "Indagación de la palabra" appeared in *Síntesis* 1, June 1927, and it was followed by a second part in *Síntesis* 3, August 1927. The full essay was later reprinted in *El idioma de los argentinos*, pp. 11–25.

19. "Indagación de la palabra," *El idioma de los argentinos*, pp. 23–24.

20. See my Chapter 9, p. 143.

21. "Indagación de la palabra," *El idioma de los argentinos*, p. 24.

22. "El idioma de los argentinos" in *El idioma de los argentinos*, p. 149. The lecture, originally entitled "Sobre el idioma de los argentinos," was delivered on September 23 and published in *La Prensa*, September 24, 1927.

23. When Borges published "A la doctrina de pasión de tu voz" in *Cuaderno San Martín*, it was dedicated to the poet Wally Zenner and dated 1927. The extant manuscript in the Borges Collection at the Alderman Library, University of Virginia, is also dated 1927 but has no dedication. Bioy Casares assured me that Borges had never been in love with Wally Zenner but that, on the contrary, he had found her amusing because of her melodramatic style of recitation (interview, Buenos Aires, November 15, 1995). Zenner herself informed me in a telephone conversation that she had never been a "close friend" of Borges's (Buenos Aires, November 13, 1995). It seems highly improbable, therefore, that Wally Zenner was the subject of the poem, especially at this time. I am confident that this is one of the first examples of Borges's many dedications to women friends in which the dedicatee herself was not necessarily the person who inspired the original composition.

Chapter 11: Revenge and Defeat (1927–1930)

1. The manifesto was reproduced in *La Fronda*, September 8, 1930—two days after the military coup that overthrew Irigoyen—in a piece mocking Borges and his supporters' enthusiasm for the deposed president.

2. "Jorge Luis Borges y la revolución literaria de *Martín Fierro*," *El Correo Literario*, January 1, 1944. Cited in Rodríguez Monegal, *Jorge Luis Borges: A Literary Biography*, pp. 229–30.

3. Letter consulted courtesy of Wáshington Pereyra, Buenos Aires.

4. See *Martín Fierro*, August 31–November 15, p. 380.

5. "Jorge Luis Borges y la revolución literaria de *Martín Fierro*," *El Correo Literario*, January 1, 1944. Cited in Rodríguez Monegal, *Jorge Luis Borges: A Literary Biography*, pp. 229–30.

6. These accusations were recalled in an article by the former *martinfierrista* Luis Emilio Soto, published in *La Vida Literaria*, October–November 1930, with the title "La trahison des clercs."

7. *Martín Fierro*, August 31–November 15, 1927, p. 376.

8. Manuscript letter consulted by courtesy of Eduardo Alvarez Tuñón, Buenos Aires.

9. See Borges's endnote to the section called "Muertes de Buenos Aires" in the first edition of *Cuaderno San Martín,* 1929, pp. 56–57.

10. See "La Chacarita" in *Cuaderno San Martín, OC* I, pp. 90–91.

11. "Página relativa a Figari," *Criterio* 30, September 27, 1928. See also *Textos recobrados, 1919–1929,* pp. 362–64. See also my Chapter 1, p. 15.

12. Petit de Murat, *Borges Buenos Aires,* p. 107.

13. Undated postcard written circa 1928 to Ulyses Petit de Murat. Consulted courtesy of Fedra Petit de Murat, Buenos Aires.

14. Ibid.

15. Ibid.

16. "La perpetua carrera de Aquiles y la tortuga," *La Prensa,* January 1, 1929, and reprinted in *Discusión,* Manuel Gleizer: Buenos Aires, 1932. See *Discusión, OC* I, pp. 244–48.

17. The epigraph reads, *"Para el amor no satisfecho el mundo es misterio, un misterio que el amor satisfecho parece comprender,"* Bradley, *Appearance and Reality,* XV. See *El idioma de los argentinos,* p. 7.

18. "La duración del Infierno" *Síntesis* 25, June 1929, and *Discusión, OC* I, pp. 235–38.

19. "El Paseo de Julio," *Criterio* 51, February 21, 1929, and later in *Cuaderno San Martín,* 1929. See a revised version in *Cuaderno San Martín, OC* I, pp. 95–96.

20. See Vaccaro, *Georgie,* p. 336.

21. José Emilio Pacheco, "Borges y Reyes: una correspondencia," *Revista de la Universidad de México* 34, December (1979), p. 4.

22. Ibid., p. 5.

23. Based on the interview with Elsa Astete Millán, "Habla la mujer de Borges," in *Tiempo Argentino,* February 6, 1983, and on information provided by Elsie Rivero Haedo, Buenos Aires, April 2, 1994.

24. Alifano, *Conversaciones,* p. 59.

25. Milleret, p. 191.

26. Alifano, *Conversaciones,* p. 59.

27. Milleret, pp. 189–91.

28. Alifano, *Conversaciones,* p. 60.

29. Milleret, p. 191.

30. Alifano, *Biografía verbal,* p. 161.

31. Carrizo, pp. 64–65.

32. Sorrentino, p. 82.

33. "An Autobiographical Essay," p. 238.

34. Ibid.

35. The original title was "Hombres de las orillas" when it was first published in *Crítica: Revista Multicolor de los Sábados,* September 16, 1933, but it was changed to "Hombre de la esquina rosada" when included in the collection *Historia universal de la infamia,* 1935.

36. Interview with Elsa Astete Millán, "Habla la mujer de Borges," *Tiempo Argentino,* February 6, 1983.

37. José Emilio Pacheco, "Borges y Reyes: una correspondencia," *Revista de la universidad de México* 34, December (1979), pp. 5–6.

38. Carrizo, p. 181.

39. "Nuestras imposibilidades," *Sur* 4, 1931. Reprinted in *Borges en Sur, 1931–1980,* Emecé: Buenos Aires, 1999, pp. 117–20.

Chapter 12: **Experiments in Fiction (1930–1932)**

1. "An Autobiographical Essay," p. 234.
2. Ibid., pp. 238–39.
3. "Cuentos del Turquestán," *La Prensa*, August 29, 1926. Reprinted in *Textos recobrados, 1919–1929*, pp. 260–63.
4. "La postulación de la realidad," *Azul* 10, June 1931, and later collected in *Discusión*, 1932. See also a much-revised edition of *Discusión* in *OC* I, pp. 173–285. The passages from "La postulación de la realidad" quoted in my text can be found in *Discusión, OC* I, pp. 217–18.
5. "El arte narrativo y la magia," *Sur* 5, 1932, and later in *Discusión*, 1932. My quotations from this essay can be found in *Discusión, OC* I, pp. 230–32.
6. "Una vindicación de la cábala" was published for the first time in *Discusión*, 1932. See *Discusión, OC* I, pp. 209–12.
7. "Una vindicación de los gnósticos," *La Prensa*, January 1, 1932, later published as "Una vindicación del falso Basílides" in *Discusión*, 1932. See *Discusión, OC* I, pp. 213–16.
8. *Noticias Gráficas*, September 6, 1955, p. 5. See also my Chapter 23, p. 327.
9. "Borges at N.Y.U.," in "Prose for Borges," *Triquarterly*, 25 (1972), p. 459.
10. "El acercamiento a Almotásim" first appeared as a "Note" in the collection of essays, *Historia de la eternidad*, Viau y Zona: Buenos Aires, 1936. See also *OC* I, pp. 414–18.
11. "Borges at N.Y.U.," in "Prose for Borges," *Triquarterly*, (1972), p. 459.
12. See "El acercamiento a Almotásim," *OC* I, p. 417.
13. Footnote to "El acercamiento a Almotásim," *OC* I, p. 418.
14. Norah Lange, *45 días y 30 marineros*, Editorial Tor: Buenos Aires, 1933.
15. "Entretiens avec Napoléon Murat," *Cahiers de L'Herne*, pp. 375–77.
16. Interview with Olga Orozco, Buenos Aires, November 7, 1995.
17. Beatriz de Nóbile, *Palabras con Norah Lange*, p. 19.
18. My account of this incident is based on information provided by Jorge Calvetti, Buenos Aires, November 17, 1995.
19. "Noticia de los kenningar," *Sur* 6, 1932, pp. 202–8. Reprinted with the title "Las *kenningar*" in *Historia de la eternidad*, 1936. See also *OC* I, pp. 368–81.
20. "Noticia de los kenningar," *Sur* 6, 1932, p. 208. There is a slightly modified version in "Las *kenningar*," *OC* I, p. 380.
21. See the first of the "Two English Poems" published in *El otro, el mismo*, 1969 and *OC* II, p. 239.
22. Some of the essays in the first edition of *Discusión* were later removed by Borges and others added in subsequent editions. For the original contents, see Nicolás Helft, *Jorge Luis Borges: Bibliografía completa*, Fondo de Cultura Económica: Buenos Aires, 1997, p. 256.
23. My account of this episode is based on information in Aldo Pelligrini, *Oliverio Girondo*, Ediciones Culturales Argentinas: Buenos Aires, p. 15, and in Beatriz de Nóbile, *Palabras con Norah Lange*, pp. 19–20.
24. "Almas al desnudo," *La Novela Semanal*, September 19, 1932.
25. "La perpetua carrera de Aquiles y la tortuga," *El Sol* (Madrid), December 4, 1932, and also *Discusión*. See *OC* I, pp. 244–48.

26. "El querer ser otro," *Litoral*, January 1, 1933. Reprinted in *Textos recobrados, 1931–1955*, pp. 32–34.

Chapter 13: **The Rivals (1933–1934)**

1. "Discusión sobre Jorge Luis Borges," *Megáfono* 1, August 1933, Buenos Aires, p. 24.
2. Interviews with Gloria Alcorta de Girondo, Paris, June 3, 1995, and Olga Orozco, Buenos Aires, November 7, 1995.
3. *Las kenningar,* Francisco A. Colombo: Buenos Aires, 1933.
4. See Bernès I, p. 1527.
5. M. E. de Miguel, *Norah Lange,* p. 158.
6. Quoted in ibid., p. 159.
7. See ibid., pp. 159–60.
8. Ibid., p. 157.
9. For an account of Borges's activities as coeditor of the literary supplement of *Crítica,* see Petit de Murat, *Borges Buenos Aires,* pp. 138–49.
10. See the anthology *Borges en Revista Multicolor de los Sábados,* ed. Irma Zangara, Atlántida: Buenos Aires, 1995.
11. "El dragón (Antiguos mitos germánicos)," *Crítica,* September 23, 1933. See Zangara, *Borges en Revista Multicolor,* p. 39.
12. "Las brujas" (Antiguos mitos germánicos)," *Crítica,* October 7, 1933. See Zangara, *Borges en Revista Multicolor,* pp. 42–43.
13. Burgin, *Conversations,*1969, pp. 110–11.
14. "El mito de los elfos," *Crítica,* November 4, 1933. See Zangara, *Borges en Revista Multicolor,* pp. 43–44.
15. *Noticias Gráficas,* November 17, 1933.
16. See "*45 días y 30 marineros,*" *Crítica,* December 9, 1933. See Zangara, *Borges en Revista Multicolor,* pp. 206–7.
17. First published as "El rostro del profeta" in *Crítica,* January 20, 1934, and as "El tintorero enmascarado Hakim de Merv" in *Historia universal de la infamia,* 1935. See *OC* I, pp. 324–28.
18. *Noticias Gráficas,* October 30, 1933.
19. *Noticias Gráficas,* September 10, 1933.
20. *Noticias Gráficas,* October 30, 1933.
21. "Yo, judío," *Megáfono* 3, April 1934. Reprinted in *Textos recobrados, 1931–1955,* pp. 89–90.
22. Undated review later collected in Ramón Doll, *Policía intelectual,* Editorial Tor: Buenos Aires, 1933.
23. "Discusión sobre Jorge Luis Borges," *Megáfono* 1, August 1933, Buenos Aires, p. 17.
24. "Escenas de la crueldad nazi," *Crítica,* May 5, 1934. See Zangara, *Borges en Revista Multicolor,* pp. 348–67.
25. *Noticias Gráficas,* November 4 and December 12, 1933, respectively.
26. The José Tuntar articles are reprinted in Zangara, *Borges en Revista Multicolor,* pp. 151–81.
27. "El lento suicidio de Diocleciano," *Crítica,* September 2, 1933. See Zangara, *Borges en Revista Multicolor,* p. 160.
28. "Ovidio en el país de las flechas," *Crítica,* October 7, 1933. See Zangara, *Borges en Revista Multicolor,* pp. 162–63.

29. "Espías en la Roma imperial," *Crítica*, November 18, 1933. See Zangara, *Borges en Revista Multicolor*, pp. 166–73.

30. "Las grandes orgías romanas," *Crítica*, March 3, 1934. See Zangara, *Borges en Revista Multicolor*, pp. 173–81.

31. "Espías en la Roma imperial," *Crítica*, November 18, 1933. See Zangara, *Borges en Revista Multicolor*, p. 171.

32. Norah Lange, "Un vacilante juego mortal," *Crítica: Revista Multicolor de los Sábados*, April 7, 1934.

33. Interview with Olga Orozco, Buenos Aires, November 7, 1995.

34. Ibid.

35. I owe this information to Susana Lange, letter of November 6, 2001.

36. Ibid.

37. Norah Lange, *Cuadernos de infancia* (1937), quoted in M. E. de Miguel, *Norah Lange*, p. 15.

Chapter 14: **Failure (1934–1935)**

1. "30 pesos vale la muerte," *Crítica*, July 21, 1934. See Zangara, *Borges en Revista Multicolor*, pp. 51–60.

2. "30 pesos vale la muerte" in Zangara, *Borges en Revista Multicolor*, p. 58.

3. "¡No valía la pena!," *Crítica*, September 8, 1934. See Zangara, *Borges en Revista Multicolor*, pp. 60–63.

4. "¡No valía la pena!," in Zangara, *Borges en Revista Multicolor*, p. 63.

5. See "El acercamiento a Almotásim," *OC* I, pp. 414–18 (p. 417). This story first appeared in *Historia de la eternidad*, 1936 and was then reprinted in *El jardín de senderos que se bifurcan*, 1941, which was incorporated in *Ficciones*, 1944. However, Borges omitted it from *Ficciones* in his *Obras completas*, though it would remain in English editions of this collection.

6. "El acercamiento a Almotásim," *OC* I, p. 417.

7. These "Confesiones" first appeared in *Crítica*, September 15, 1934, under the pseudonym Francisco Bustos and were later incorporated in *El hacedor*, 1960. See in *OC* II: "Dreamtigers," p. 161, "Los espejos velados," p. 164, and "Las uñas," p. 163.

8. "Un infierno" appeared in *Crítica*, September 15, 1934, under the pseudonym Francisco Bustos; see *OC* II, p. 238. It had been the postscript to "La duración del infierno," *Síntesis* 25–27, June 1929, and later incorporated in *Discusión*, 1932; see *OC* II, pp. 235–38.

9. See M. de Torre, *Borges: fotografías y manuscritos*, p. 91.

10. Ibid., p. 92.

11. Sorrentino, p. 15.

12. "Commentaries" in *The Aleph and Other Stories*, p. 271.

13. My account is based on Borges's "Commentaries" in *The Aleph and Other Stories*, p. 271, and his interview with Carlos Peralta, "L'électricité des mots" in *Cahiers de L'Herne*, p. 413.

14. "Commentaries" in *The Aleph and Other Stories*, p. 271.

15. "El muerto" was first published in *Sur* 145, November 1946, and then collected in *El Aleph* (1949).

16. These would appear, respectively, in *Ficciones*, 1944, *El Aleph*, 1949, and *El informe de Brodie*, 1970.

17. Petit de Murat, *Borges Buenos Aires,* p. 149.
18. Alifano, *Conversaciones,* p. 255.
19. *Historia universal de la infamia,* Tor: Buenos Aires, 1935.
20. See the prologue to the 1954 edition of *Historia universal de la infamia* reprinted in *OC* I, p. 291.
21. "An Autobiographical Essay," p. 206.
22. "Tlön, Uqbar, Orbis Tertius," *OC* I, p. 433.
23. See *OC* I, p. 293, but here the dedication is to an equally mysterious S.D., a change effected in the 1954 edition of *Historia universal de la infamia.*
24. See José Tuntar, "Ovidio en el país de las flechas" in Zangara, *Borges en Revista Multicolor,* pp. 162–63.
25. See my Chapter 9, pp. 145–46.
26. See my Chapter 13, p. 201.
27. "Historia de la eternidad" first appeared in a collection of essays with that title published by Viau y Zona: Buenos Aires, 1936. See *OC* I, pp. 353–67.
28. See "Historia de la eternidad," *OC* I, p. 364.
29. Information provided by Susana Lange, letter of December 16, 2000.
30. "Examen de la obra de Herbert Quain" was first published in *Sur* 79, April 1941, and later collected in *El jardín de senderos que se bifurcan,* 1941 and *Ficciones,* 1944.
31. See this footnote in "El acercamiento a Almotásim," *OC* I, p. 418.

Chapter 15: **Isolation (1936–1937)**

1. Bioy Casares, *Memorias,* Tusquets: Barcelona, 1994, p. 108.
2. Interview with Bioy Casares, Buenos Aires, March 31, 1994. A slightly different account is given in Bioy's *Memorias,* p. 108.
3. Interview with Bioy Casares, Buenos Aires, March 31, 1994.
4. Bioy Casares, *Memorias,* p. 77.
5. Ibid.
6. Ibid., p. 86.
7. Ibid., pp. 52–58.
8. Review of *La Estatua Casera, Sur* 18, March 1936. See *Borges en Sur,* pp. 130–31.
9. Bioy Casares, *Memorias,* p. 77.
10. Ibid., p. 78.
11. Ibid., pp. 92–93.
12. Ibid., p. 86.
13. Interview with Bioy Casares, Buenos Aires, November 15, 1995.
14. Burgin, *Conversations,* 1969, p. 56.
15. "Examen de la obra de Herbert Quain" was first published in *Sur,* April 1941, and later collected in *El jardín de senderos que se bifurcan,* 1941 and *Ficciones,* 1944. See *OC* I, p. 464.
16. "Examen de la obra de Herbert Quain," *OC* I, p. 464.
17. "Prólogo" to Arturo M. Jauretche, *El Paso de los Libres. Relato gaucho de la última revolución radical (Diciembre de 1933), dicho en verso por el paisano Julián Barrientos, que anduvo en ella* (1934). Corregidor: Buenos Aires, 1992, pp. 23–24 (p. 23).
18. Horacio Salas, *Borges: una biografía,* Planeta: Buenos Aires, p. 148.
19. "Tareas y destino de Buenos Aires" in *Homenaje a Buenos Aires en el cuarto centenario de su fundación* Municipalidad de la Ciudad de Buenos Aires: Buenos Aires,

1936. See *Textos recobrados, 1931–1955,* pp. 140–55. My quotations in this paragraph are from p. 154.

20. This passage formed part of the speech originally published with the title "Página relativa a Figari" in *Criterio* 30, September 27, 1928. See *Textos recobrados, 1919–1929,* p. 363. See also my Chapter 1, p. 15 and Chapter 11, p. 166.

21. "América y el destino de la civilización occidental," *Nosotros* (segunda época), 1, April 1936, pp. 60–61. See *Textos recobrados, 1931–1955,* pp. 350–51.

22. See Rodríguez Monegal, *Jorge Luis Borges. A Literary Biography,* pp. 297–99, and María Esther Vázquez, *Victoria Ocampo,* Planeta: Buenos Aires, 1991, pp. 148–49.

23. "*L'homme blanc* de Jules Romains," *El Hogar,* September 17, 1937. Reprinted in *Textos cautivos, OC* IV, pp. 315–16 (p. 315).

24. Bioy Casares, *Memorias,* p. 78.

25. Ibid., pp. 78–79.

26. Ibid., p. 79.

27. See Bioy Casares's letter in *Macedonio Fernández: Epistolario. Obras completas,* vol. II, Corregidor: Buenos Aires, 2nd edition, 1991, pp. 352–53.

28. Interview with Bioy Casares, Buenos Aires, September 12, 1994.

29. See "El tamaño de mi esperanza" in *El tamaño de mi esperanza,* p. 14.

30. Sorrentino, pp. 63–64.

31. "Una pedagogía del odio," *Sur* 32, May 1937. See *Borges en Sur,* pp. 145–46.

32. "Una exposición afligente," *Sur* 49, October 1938. See *Borges en "Sur,"* pp. 155–57.

33. "Un caudaloso manifiesto de Breton," *El Hogar,* December 2, 1938. Reprinted in *Textos cautivos, OC* IV, pp. 403–4 (p. 404).

34. "Las 'nuevas generaciones' literarias," *El Hogar,* February 26, 1937. Reprinted in *Textos cautivos, OC* IV, pp. 261–63.

35. Interview with Lila Mora de Araujo, Buenos Aires, September 15, 1994.

36. Alifano, *Conversaciones,* pp. 133–34.

37. Interview with Bioy Casares, Buenos Aires, September 12, 1994.

38. A collection of Norah Lange's speeches was published in 1942 with the title *Discursos* and later incorporated in *Estimados congéneres,* Losada: Buenos Aires, 1968.

39. Interview with Alicia Jurado, Buenos Aires, November 10, 1995.

40. Interview with Bioy Casares, Buenos Aires, November 25, 1995.

41. Sorrentino, p. 17.

42. Carrizo, p. 268.

43. Interview with Bioy Casares, Buenos Aires, September 12, 1994.

44. Ibid.

Chapter 16: **The Death of Father (1938–1939)**

1. "El otro" in *El libro de arena,* 1975. See *OC* III, pp. 11–16 (p. 12).

2. "An Autobiographical Essay," p. 241.

3. See "Entretiens avec James E. Irby," *Cahiers de L'Herne,* p. 399, and "An Autobiographical Essay," p. 241.

4. Ibid., p. 398, and ibid., p. 242.

5. "An Autobiographical Essay," p. 241.

6. Ibid., p. 242.

7. See Borges's reply to a questionnaire in *Latitud* 1, February 1945. Reprinted in *Textos recobrados, 1931–1955,* pp. 352–54 (pp. 352–53).

8. Carrizo, p. 20.
9. "An Autobiographical Essay," pp. 219–20.
10. Sorrentino, p. 96.
11. Manuscript held in the Borges Collection, Alderman Library, University of Virginia.
12. See my Chapter 3, p. 48.
13. See "Historia de la eternidad," *OC* I, p. 359.
14. "Franz Kafka: *La metamorfosis*" in *Prólogo con un prólogo de prólogos,* pp. 103–5 (p. 103).
15. Ibid., pp. 104 and 105.
16. See *El Hogar,* May 27, 1938.
17. See *Textos cautivos, OC* IV, pp. 368–69.
18. See "An Autobiographical Essay," p. 243.
19. "Pierre Menard, autor del *Quijote*" first appeared in *Sur* 56, May 1939, and was later collected in *El jardín de senderos que se bifurcan,* 1941 and *Ficciones,* 1944.
20. "La biblioteca total," *Sur* 59, August 1939, pp. 13–16. Reprinted in *Borges en Sur,* pp. 24–27.
21. "La biblioteca total" in *Borges en Sur,* p. 27.
22. Ibid.
23. "Tlön, Uqbar, Orbis Tertius," *Sur* 68, May 1940, and collected in *El jardín de senderos que se bifurcan,* 1941 and *Ficciones,* 1944.

Chapter 17: **The Example of Dante (1939–1940)**

1. Interview with Bioy Casares, Buenos Aires, November 15, 1995. The apartment was bought in 1957 by Borges's friend, the writer Alicia Jurado. I am grateful to her for showing me around on November 10, 1995.
2. *Antología de la literatura fantástica,* Editorial Sudamericana: Buenos Aires, 1940, and *Antología poética argentina,* Editorial Sudamericana: Buenos Aires, 1941.
3. Quotations from Bioy Casares in my account of this matter are based on two interviews with him in Buenos Aires on November 15 and 25, 1995.
4. "An Autobiographical Essay," p. 242.
5. Quotations are from, respectively, Sorrentino, pp. 72 and 73, and Carrizo, p. 118.
6. "El encuentro en un sueño," *Nueve ensayos dantescos,* Espasa-Calpe: Madrid, 1982, and in *OC* III, pp. 367–69 (p. 369).
7. "La última sonrisa de Beatriz," *Nueve ensayos dantescos, OC* III, pp. 370–72 (p. 370).
8. Ibid., p. 372.
9. "El encuentro en un sueño," Ibid., *OC* III, pp 369.
10. Interview with Bioy Casares, Buenos Aires, November 15, 1995.
11. Ibid.
12. Ibid.
13. Ibid.
14. My account of Borges's relations with Haydée Lange at this time is based on an interview with Olga Orozco in Buenos Aires on November 17, 1995.
15. Sorrentino, p. 38 and "Borges at N.Y.U." in "Prose for Borges," *Triquarterly,* 25 (1972), p. 459, respectively.

16. *Noticias Gráficas,* September 6, 1955, p. 5. Reprinted in *Textos recobrados, 1931–1955,* p. 371. (The date of the interview is given here as July 19, 1955.)

17. *El Congreso* was first published in Buenos Aires by El Archibrazo in 1971 and then included in *El libro de arena,* Emecé: Buenos Aires, 1975.

18. See *Martín Fierro,* January 24, 1925, p. 102.

19. See my Chapter 8, p. 134.

20. *Martín Fierro,* April 28, 1927, pp. 334 and 332, respectively. See also my Chapter 10, p. 156.

21. See my Chapter 11, pp. 162–64.

22. See "La Divina Comedia" in *Siete Noches,* Fondo de Cultura Económica: 2nd edition, Buenos Aires, 1993, p. 91.

23. "La noche cíclica" was later published in *Poemas (1922–1943),* Losada: Buenos Aires, 1943, and in *El otro, el mismo,* 1964. See *OC* II, pp. 241–42.

24. See my Chapter 10, p. 155–56.

25. Interview with Olga Orozco, Buenos Aires, September 15, 1994.

26. The text is so far available only in an English translation by Donald A. Yates, which I have paraphrased and condensed here. See his "Behind 'Borges and I,'" *Modern Fiction Studies,* 19 (1973), pp. 317–24 (p. 322).

27. See ibid., p. 323.

28. "Las ruinas circulares," *Sur* 75, December 1940. Later collected in *El jardín de senderos que se bifurcan,* 1941, and *Ficciones,* 1944.

29. "La lotería en Babilonia" was first published in *Sur* 76, January 1941. Later collected in *El jardín de senderos que se bifurcan,* 1941, and in *Ficciones,* 1944.

30. "La biblioteca de Babel" was first published in *El jardín de senderos que se bifurcan,* 1941, and later in *Ficciones,* 1944.

Chapter 18: **The Garden of Forking Paths (1940–1944)**

1. "Ensayo de imparcialidad," *Sur* 61, October 1939, reprinted in *Borges en Sur,* pp. 28–30.

2. *Antología de la literatura fantástica,* Sudamericana: Buenos Aires, 1940. My quotation is from the edition by Edhasa-Sudamericana: Barcelona, 1977, p. 13.

3. Quotations are from Borges's prologue, "Adolfo Bioy Casares: *La invención de Morel,*" reprinted in *Prólogos con un prólogo de prólogos,* pp. 22–24.

4. "Examen de la obra de Herbert Quain," *Sur* 79, April 1941, and collected in *El jardín de senderos que se bifurcan,* 1941, and *Ficciones,* 1944.

5. "Leyes de la narración policial" was first published in *Hoy Argentina,* April 1933, pp. 48–49, and reprinted in *Textos recobrados, 1931–1955,* pp. 36–39; and "Los laberintos policiales y Chesterton" was first published in *Sur* 10, July 1935, pp. 92–94, and reprinted in *Borges en Sur,* pp. 126–29.

6. "El cuento policial" was delivered as a lecture on June 16, 1978, at the Universidad de Belgrano, and collected in *Borges, oral,* Emecé/Editorial de Belgrano, Buenos Aires, 4th edition, 1995, p. 104.

7. *Seis problemas para don Isidro Parodi* was first published by Editorial Sur: Buenos Aires, 1942. See *Obras completas en colaboración,* pp. 13–121.

8. *El jardín de senderos que se bifurcan* was published by Editorial Sur: Buenos Aires, on December 30, 1941, according to the colophon, although the date of copyright is given as 1942.

9. Bioy Casares's review appeared in *Sur* 92, May 1942. See Emir Rodríguez Monegal, *Jorge Luis Borges: A Literary Biography,* pp. 363–64.

10. See Horacio Salas, *Borges: una biografía,* p. 204.

11. This homage was published under the title "Desagravio a Borges," *Sur* 94, July 1942.

12. See "1941," *Sur* 87, December 1941. Reprinted in *Borges en Sur,* pp. 31–32.

13. "La muerte y la brújula" was first published in *Sur* 92, May 1942 and collected in *Ficciones,* 1944.

14. "Commentaries" in *The Aleph and Other Stories,* p. 269.

15. The headline in the December 1942 issue of *Leoplan* read, "Para este escritor el año 1942 no ha sido muy propicio en cuanto a salud se refiere" ("For this writer the year 1942 has not been very propitious as far as his health is concerned").

16. Interview with Olga Orozco, Buenos Aires, September 15, 1994. The quotation is from "Del infierno y del cielo," first published in *Poemas (1922–1943),* Losada: Buenos Aires, 1943, and later in *El otro, el mismo,* 1964. See *OC* II, pp. 243–44.

17. "La forma de la espada" was first published on July 26, 1942, in *La Nación* and later collected in *Ficciones,* 1944.

18. "El milagro secreto" was first published in *Sur* 101, February 1943, and later collected in *Ficciones,* 1944.

19. David Rock, *Authoritarian Argentina: The Nationalist Movement, Its History and Its Impact,* University of California Press: Berkeley, 1993, p. 135.

20. "Poema conjetural" was first published in *La Nación* on July 4 and later in *Poemas (1922–1943).* It then appeared in *El otro, el mismo,* 1964. See *OC* II, pp. 245–46.

21. Interview with Norah Kildal Lange, Buenos Aires, November 23, 1995.

22. "Tema del traidor y del héroe" was first published in *Sur* 112, February 1944, and later collected in *Ficciones,* 1944.

23. They were given the title "Two English Poems" and a dedication "To Beatriz Bibiloni Webster de Bullrich" when they later appeared in *El otro, el mismo,* 1964. See *OC* II, pp. 239–40.

24. Interview with Olga Orozco, Buenos Aires, November 17, 1995.

25. My account of this episode is based on information provided by Olga Orozco in my interviews with her in Buenos Aires on September 15, 1994, and November 17, 1995.

26. I have consulted typescripts of these two letters to Elsa Astete Millán courtesy of Colección Jorge Luis Borges, Fundación San Telmo, Buenos Aires.

27. "Tres versiones de Judas" was first published in *Sur* 118, August 1944, and later collected in *Ficciones,* 1944.

28. David Rock, *Authoritarian Argentina,* p. 137.

29. *Ficciones* was published by Editorial Sur, Buenos Aires. This first edition consisted of the eight stories that had originally appeared in *El jardín de senderos que se bifurcan,* 1941 and six further stories pertaining to *Artificios;* it also retained the prologues to the two collections, respectively. A further three stories, which now form part of the canonical volume of *Ficciones,* would be added in the second edition published by Emecé in 1956.

30. "Agradecimiento a la demostración ofrecida por la Sociedad Argentina de Escritores," *Sur* 129, July 1945. Reprinted in *Borges en Sur,* pp. 300–2.

Chapter 19: The "New Beatrice" (1944–1946)

1. Estela Canto, *Borges a contraluz*, Espasa-Calpe: Madrid, 1989, p. 24. My account of Borges's relations with Estela Canto is based largely on the information provided in the latter's book.
2. See interview with Estela Canto in *La Nación*, October 7, 1990.
3. For a more detailed account of the autobiographical context of "The Aleph," see Chapter 7, pp. 124–29, Chapter 9, *passim*, and Chapter 13, pp. 202–3.
4. "De la alta ambición en el arte. Contesta Jorge Luis Borges," *Latitud* 1, February 1945. Reprinted in *Textos recobrados, 1931–1955*, pp. 352–54 (p. 353). Since this questionnaire was published in February 1945, Borges must have responded in December 1944 or early January 1945, when he was already in love with Estela Canto.
5. Canto, p. 96.
6. See interview with Estela Canto in *La Nación*, October 7, 1990.
7. Ibid.
8. Interview with Dr. Germán García, president of the Argentine Psychoanalytical Association, Buenos Aires, September 24, 1994.
9. See Rita Goldaracena, "Las inhibiciones del joven Borges," an interview with Dr. Miguel Kohan-Miller, *El País* (Madrid), December 23, 1990.
10. Canto, p. 113.

Chapter 20: Humiliation and Anguish (1946–1947)

1. "Historia de los dos reyes y los dos laberintos" was first published as "Una leyenda arábiga" in *El Hogar*, June 16, 1939, and later collected in the 1952 edition of *El Aleph* as "Los dos reyes y los dos laberintos." "Límites" was collected in *El hacedor*, 1960; see *OC* II, p. 227.
2. "El poeta declara su nombradía" was collected in *El hacedor*, 1960; see *OC* II, p. 228.
3. "An Autobiographical Essay," p. 244.
4. Canto, p. 118.
5. Interview with José María Castiñeira de Dios, Buenos Airs, November 8, 1995.
6. Interview with Raúl Salinas, Buenos Aires, November 22, 1995.
7. Ibid.
8. Ibid.
9. "Para las seis cuerdas: milonga con variaciones" was published under the pseudonym "Fidelio" in *Pueblo Entero*, May 1980. I was able to consult this article courtesy of Fermín Chávez, Buenos Aires.
10. "Jorge Luis Borges, inspector de aves," *Democracia*, July 24, 1946.
11. "¿Cuál es cuál?" in *Descamisada*, August 8, 1946.
12. Borges's speech was later published as "Palabras pronunciadas por Jorge Luis Borges en la comida que le ofrecieron los escritores," *Sur* 142, August 1946, and reprinted as "Déle, déle" in *Argentina Libre*, August 15, 1946. See also *Borges en Sur*, pp. 303–4.
13. Interview with Betina Edelberg, Buenos Aires, September 9, 1996.
14. "An Autobiographical Essay," p. 244.
15. Ibid., p. 245.
16. Alifano, *Biografía verbal*, p. 109.
17. "An Autobiographical Essay," p. 245.

18. Interview with Bioy Casares, Buenos Aires, November 25, 1995.
19. "El muerto," *Sur* 145, November 1946, and *El Aleph*, 1949.
20. It was first published with the title "Los inmortales" in *Los Anales de Buenos Aires* 12, February 1947, and as "El inmortal" in *El Aleph*, 1949.
21. "Los teólogos," *Los Anales de Buenos Aires* 14, April 1947, and *El Aleph*, 1949.
22. "La casa de Asterión," *Los Anales de Buenos Aires* 15–16, May–June 1947, and *El Aleph*, 1949.
23. "La busca de Averroes," *Sur* 152, June 1947, and *El Aleph*, 1949.
24. "El Zahir," *Los Anales de Buenos Aires* 17, July 1947, and *El Aleph*, 1949.
25. Carrizo, p. 235.

Chapter 21: **False Hopes (1947–1950)**

1. Silvina Ocampo, "Image de Borges," *Cahiers de L'Herne*, p. 27, and Rodríguez Monegal, *Jorge Luis Borges: A Literary Biography*, p. 271.
2. Interview with Esther Zemborain de Torres, Buenos Aires, November 27, 1995.
3. Interview with Betina Edelberg, Buenos Aires, September 9, 1996.
4. Clark M. Zlotchew, "Jorge Luis Borges: An Interview," in Burgin (ed.), *Jorge Luis Borges: Conversations*, University Press of Mississippi: Jackson, 1998, p. 222.
5. Alifano, *Biografía verbal*, p. 91.
6. Interview with Esther Zemborain de Torres, November 27, 1995.
7. "Emma Zunz" was first published in *Sur* 167, September 1948, and in *El Aleph*, 1949.
8. Carrizo, p. 235.
9. Burgin, *Conversations*, 1969, p. 41.
10. *La Prensa*, September 12, 1948.
11. My account is based on a report in *La Prensa*, October 9, 1948.
12. Sorrentino, p. 59.
13. "La redención" was first published in *La Nación*, January 9, 1949, and dated "December 1948." It was given the title "La otra muerte" when collected in *El Aleph*, 1949.
14. "La escritura del Dios," *Sur* 172, February 1949, and in *El Aleph*, 1949.
15. Canto, p. 216.
16. "Historia del guerrero y de la cautiva" was first published in *Sur* 175, May 1949, and in *El Aleph*, 1949.
17. Canto, p. 146.
18. Undated letter reproduced in Canto, pp. 147–48.
19. Ibid., pp. 149–50.
20. Canto, p. 120.
21. "La espera" was first published in *La Nación*, August 27, 1950, and in the 1952 edition of *El Aleph*.

Chapter 22: **Borges Against Perón (1950–1955)**

1. See Alicia Dujovne Ortiz, *Eva Perón: A Biography*, Little, Brown: London, 1997, p. 258.
2. Sorrentino, pp. 59–60.
3. The letter was written in 1950 but is otherwise undated.

4. Interview with Betina Edelberg, Buenos Aires, September 9, 1996.
5. "An Autobiographical Essay," p. 248.
6. Interview with Luisa Mercedes Levinson in *Análisis*, Buenos Aires, August 17, 1970, quoted in Horacio Salas, *Borges: una biografía*, p. 226.
7. Interview with Betina Edelberg, Buenos Aires, September 9, 1996.
8. *Visión*, March 10, 1979.
9. "La fiesta del monstruo" was eventually published in *Marcha* (Montevideo), September 30, 1955, and in *Nuevos cuentos de Bustos Domecq*, 1977. See *Obras completas en colaboración*, Emecé: Buenos Aires, 1979, pp. 392–402.
10. Interview with Betina Edelberg, Buenos Aires, September 9, 1996.
11. Milleret, p. 91.
12. Interview with Betina Edelberg, Buenos Aires, September 9, 1996.
13. "La secta del Fénix" was first published in *Sur* 215–216, September–October 1952, and in the 1956 edition of *Ficciones*.
14. Ronald Christ, *The Narrow Act: Borges' Art of Allusion*, New York University Press: New York, 1969, p. 190.
15. See Betina Edelberg, "Algunos de los muchos recuerdos," *Proa* (tercera época), 23 (1996), p. 67.
16. "El escritor argentino y la tradición" was published in *Sur* 232, January–February 1955, and was later incorporated in the 1957 edition of *Discusión*. See *OC* I, pp. 267–74 (p. 273).
17. Dujovne, Ortiz, *Eva Perón*, p. 328.
18. Ibid., p. 334.
19. Quoted in John King, *Sur: A Study of the Argentine Literary Journal and Its Role in the Development of a Culture, 1931–1970*, Cambridge University Press: Cambridge, 1986, p. 145.
20. "El Sur" was published in *La Nación*, February 8, 1953, and incorporated in the 1956 edition of *Ficciones*.
21. Jorge Luis Borges, in collaboration with Margarita Guerrero, *El Martín Fierro*, Columba: Buenos Aires, 1953. See also, *Obras completas en colaboración*, pp. 513–65.
22. Jorge Luis Borges and Margarita Guerrero, *Manual de zoología fantástica*, Fondo de Cultura Económica: Mexico, 1957. An enlarged edition would also appear with the title *El libro de los seres imaginarios*, Kier: Buenos Aires, 1967. See also *Obras completas en colaboración*, pp. 569–714.
23. Interview with Betina Edelberg, Buenos Aires, September 9, 1996.
24. Ibid.
25. "Mateo, XXV, 30" was dated 1953, and first published in *La Nación*, November 15, 1953. It was collected in *El otro, el mismo*, 1964. See *OC* II, p. 252.
26. Carrizo, p. 52.
27. *Visión*, March 10, 1979.
28. "An Autobiographical Essay," p. 248.
29. Ibid.
30. Report in *Clarín*, February 1, 1963.
31. "El desafío" was published in *La Nación*, December 28, 1952 and later incorporated into the 1974 edition of *Evaristo Carriego*. See *OC* I, pp. 165–68.
32. "El puñal" was published in the 1955 edition of *Evaristo Carriego* and then collected in the 1969 edition of *El otro, el mismo*. See *OC* I, p. 156, and *OC* II, p. 327, respectively.

33. "Diálogos del asceta y del rey," *La Nación,* September 20, 1953. Reprinted in *Textos recobrados, 1931–1955,* pp. 302–6 (p. 302).

34. See Rodríguez Monegal, *Jorge Luis Borges: A Literary Biography,* pp. 427–28.

35. "El puñal" was subsequently published on June 25, 1954, in *Marcha,* a left-wing magazine edited by Emir Rodríguez Monegal in Montevideo. See Rodríguez Monegal, *Jorge Luis Borges: A Literary Biography,* p. 427.

36. "El fin" was published in *La Nación,* October 11, 1953, and incorporated in the 1956 edition of *Ficciones.*

37. My account of this episode is based on an interview with Bioy Casares, Buenos Aires, November 17, 1995.

38. Interview with Esther Zemborain de Torres, Buenos Aires, November 27, 1995.

39. "*Inferno,* I, 32" was first published in the Havana magazine *Ciclón* (May 1955), and dated "Buenos Aires, 15 February 1955." It was later collected in *El hacedor,* 1960. See *OC* II, p. 185.

Chapter 23: **La Revolución Libertadora (1955–1959)**

1. See Vázquez, *Borges: esplendor y derrota,* p. 200.

2. Canto, p. 242.

3. Ibid., p. 246.

4. The interview is reprinted in *Textos recobrados, 1931–1955,* pp. 367–71 (p. 371).

5. Sorrentino, pp. 60–61.

6. "An Autobiographical Essay," p. 249.

7. Interview with Esther Zemborain de Torres, Buenos Aires, November 25, 1995.

8. "An Autobiographical Essay," p. 249.

9. Interview with Betina Edelberg, Buenos Aires, September 9, 1996.

10. "An Autobiographical Essay," p. 249.

11. Canto, p. 245.

12. Interview with Bioy Casares, Buenos Aires, November 17, 1995.

13. "L'Illusion comique," *Sur* 237, November–December 1955. Reprinted in *Borges en Sur,* pp. 55–57.

14. Canto, p. 245.

15. Ibid.

16. See Vázquez, *Borges: esplendor y derrota,* p. 186.

17. "Una rosa amarilla" was published in *El Hogar,* January 20, 1956, and collected in *El hacedor,* 1960. See *OC* II, p. 173.

18. *La Acción,* Montevideo, June 4, 1956. See Horacio Salas, *Borges: una biografía,* p. 229.

19. *Propósitos,* Buenos Aires, July 10, 1956.

20. "Una efusión de Martínez Estrada" in *Sur* 242, September–October 1956. Reprinted in *Borges en Sur,* pp. 173–75.

21. "Apoyar la obra de la Revolución" in *El Hogar,* November 2, 1956.

22. "An Autobiographical Essay," p. 250.

23. Interview with Betina Edelberg, Buenos Aires, September 9, 1996.

24. Sábato, "Una efusión de Jorge Luis Borges" in *Ficción* 4, November–December 1956. See Horacio Salas, *Borges: una biografía,* p. 230.

25. Interview with Fermín Chávez, Buenos Aires, November 20, 1995.

26. *Ficción* 6, March–April 1957, quoted in Horacio Salas, *Borges: una biografía,* pp. 230–31.

27. "Borges y yo," *La Biblioteca,* vol. 9, no. 1, 1957, and collected in *El hacedor,* 1960. See *OC* II, p. 186.

28. "El hacedor," *La Biblioteca,* vol. 9, no. 3, 1958, and collected in *El hacedor,* 1960. See *OC* II, pp. 159–60.

29. Interview with Borges in *Il Giornale Nuovo,* Parma, Italy, May 3, 1977, reported in *La Nación,* May 4, 1977.

30. "Ragnarök" was first published in *Sur* 257, March–April 1959, and later included in *El hacedor,* 1960. See *OC* II, pp. 183–84.

31. "El otro tigre" first appeared in *Poemas,* a select anthology of Borges's poems that the publisher Federico Vogelius brought out in 1959 in a private edition limited to twenty-five copies. It was later collected in *El hacedor,* 1960. See *OC* II, pp. 202–3.

32. Burgin, 1969, pp. 47–48.

33. Carrizo, p. 280.

34. Alifano, *Biografía verbal,* p. 111. "Poema de los dones" first appeared in *Poemas,* 1959, Federico Vogelius's private edition of Borges's poems. It was later collected in *El hacedor,* 1960. See *OC* II, pp. 187–88.

35. Milleret, p. 133.

Chapter 24: **The Rule of Mother (1958–1963)**

1. Interview with Esther Zemborain de Torres, Buenos Aires, November 27, 1995.

2. Milleret, p. 39.

3. Rodríguez Monegal, *Jorge Luis Borges: A Literary Biography,* p. 468.

4. "Al iniciar el estudio de la gramática anglosajona" in *El hacedor,* 1960. See *OC* II, p. 217.

5. "Arte poética" first appeared in *Límites,* an anthology published in a limited private edition by Frank M. Virasoro and Federico Vogelius, Buenos Aires, 1958, and in *El hacedor,* 1960. See *OC* II, p. 221.

6. Carrizo, pp. 280–81. "A la patria en 1960" was first published in *La Nación,* May 22, 1960, and later as "Oda compuesta en 1960" in *El hacedor,* 1960. See *OC* II, pp. 212–13.

7. For an account of this episode and quotations from Bianco's memoirs, see Rodríguez Monegal, *Jorge Luis Borges: A Literary Biography,* p. 447.

8. Quoted in Rodríguez Monegal, *Jorge Luis Borges: A Literary Biography,* p. 443. This prize is often erroneously referred to as the Prix Formentor, but the confusion arises from the fact that the same international consortium of publishers had created two prizes—the Prix Formentor would reward a single, recently published novel, while the International Publishers' Prize was meant to recognize an established body of work by a major author. In 1961 the Formentor was awarded to the Spaniard, Juan García Hortelano, for his novel *Tormenta de verano* (*Summer Storm*).

9. My account is based on Carlos Barral, *Memorias,* vol. 2: *Los años sin excusa,* Barral: Barcelona, 1978, pp. 273–75.

10. "An Autobiographical Essay," p. 254.

11. See, respectively, "Le monde de José [*sic*] Luis Borges," *Critique* 63–64, August–September, 1952, pp. 675–87, and "Un homme à tuer: Jorge Luis Borges, cosmopolite," *Les Temps Modernes,* 83 (1952), pp. 512–26.

12. *Les Temps Modernes,* 114–15 (1955), pp. 2123–46 and ibid., 119 (1955), "L'Aleph" appeared in *Les Temps Modernes,* 136 (1957), pp. 1833–47.

13. "Jorge Luis Borges" (1984) in *Perché leggere i classici,* Mondadori: Milan (1991), p. 292.

14. See "Entretiens avec James E. Irby," *Cahiers de L'Herne,* pp. 388 and 391.

15. "An Autobiographical Essay," p. 254.

16. Interview with Denah Lida, Concord, Mass., July 14, 1997.

17. "An Autobiographical Essay," p. 255.

18. See "Historia inédita de Borges," *El País* (Madrid), September 26, 1999.

19. *La Razón,* February 1, 1963.

20. Extract from vol. IV of the Minutes of the Edinburgh Spanish Circle 1962–63. Information provided by Fraser Oliver, honorary secretary, 1996.

21. My account of Borges's conversation with Elba de Loizaga is based on Silvina Bullrich, "Por qué Borges es conservador," *Atlántida,* September 1963.

22. Sorrentino, p. 85.

23. My account is based on a report in *Clarín,* July 2, 1963.

24. Silvina Bullrich, "Por qué Borges es conservador," *Atlántida,* September 1963.

25. Milleret, p. 221.

26. Ibid., p. 220.

27. Estela Canto, p. 251.

28. "*Adam cast forth*" [*sic*], *La Nación,* September 20, 1964, and in *El otro, el mismo,* 1964. See *OC* II, p. 312.

29. "Llaneza" in *Fervor de Buenos Aires,* 1923. See *OC* I, p. 42.

30. Interview with Emilio Petkoff in *O Cruzeiro Internacional* (São Paulo), November 1, 1961.

31. Carrizo, p. 77.

32. Burgin, 1969, p. 42.

33. Ibid.

Chapter 25: **Deconstructions (1963–1967)**

1. See James Woodall, *The Man in the Mirror of the Book: A Life of Jorge Luis Borges,* Hodder & Stoughton, London, 1996, p. 184.

2. Vázquez, *Borges: esplendor y derrota,* p. 235.

3. Interview with Esther Zemborain de Torres, Buenos Aires, November 27, 1995.

4. Vázquez, *Borges: esplendor y derrota,* p. 238.

5. Rodríguez Monegal, *Jorge Luis Borges: A Literary Biography,* p. 470.

6. Interview with Esther Zemborain de Torres, Buenos Aires, November 27, 1995.

7. See Woodall, p. 207.

8. Milleret, p. 231, n. 49.

9. Interview with Esther Zemborain de Torres, Buenos Aires, November 27, 1995.

10. Vázquez, *Borges: esplendor y derrota,* p. 257.

11. Ibid., p. 252.

12. *La Nación,* September 30, 1965.

13. See *Para las seis cuerdas,* Emecé: Buenos Aires, 1965, and *OC* II, pp. 331–50.

14. *La Nación,* November 1, 1965.

15. Milleret, p. 47.

16. Interview with Esther Zemborain de Torres, Buenos Aires, November 27, 1995.

17. Ibid.

18. See "Commentaries" in *The Aleph and Other Stories*, p. 278.

19. "La intrusa" was first published in a limited private edition in 1966 and then collected in the 1966 edition of *El Aleph*.

20. Canto, p. 229.

21. Ibid., pp. 231–33.

22. "Commentaries" in *The Aleph and Other Stories*, pp. 278–79.

23. Ibid., p. 279.

24. "El Evangelio según Marcos" first appeared in *La Nación*, August 2, 1970, and collected in *El informe de Brodie*, Emecé: Buenos Aires, 1970.

25. Milleret, p. 39.

26. "El informe de Brodie" first appeared in the collection of that name published in 1970.

27. "La señora mayor" first appeared in *El informe de Brodie*, 1970.

28. "Guayaquil" first appeared in *El informe de Brodie*, 1970.

29. "Juan Muraña" was first published in *La Prensa*, March 29, 1970, and collected in *El informe de Brodie*, 1970.

30. See my Chapter 1, p. 12.

31. "El indigno" was first published in *El informe de Brodie*, 1970.

32. "Historia de Rosendo Juárez" was first published in *La Nación*, November 9, 1969, and collected in *El informe de Brodie*, 1970.

33. "Commentaries" in *The Aleph and Other Stories*, p. 282. This story was called "Hombre de las orillas" when first published in *Crítica* (1933) but given the new title when included in *Historia universal de la infamia*, 1935.

34. Ibid.

35. "El encuentro" was first published in *La Prensa*, October 5, 1969, and collected in *El informe de Brodie*, 1970.

36. "Commentaries" in *The Aleph and Other Stories*, p. 280.

37. "El otro duelo" first appeared in *Los Libros* 2, August 10, 1970, and collected in *El informe de Brodie*, 1970.

38. "El duelo" was first published on April 30, 1970, in a limited private edition of its own and collected in *El informe de Brodie*, 1970.

39. See my Chapter 7, pp. 128–29.

40. Interviews with Olga Orozco and Lila Mora y Araujo, Buenos Aires, September 15, 1994.

41. "Leyenda," *Elogio de la sombra*, 1969. See *OC* II, p. 391.

Chapter 26: **Marriage (1967–1968)**

1. *Crónicas de Bustos Domecq*, Losada: Buenos Aires, and *Introducción a la literatura norteamericana*, Columba: Buenos Aires, were both published in 1967. See *Obras completas en colaboración*, pp. 297–371 and 979–1046, respectively.

2. My account in this chapter of Borges's friendship with María Kodama is based on interviews with the latter in Buenos Aires on April 5, 1994 and November 21, 1995.

3. Letter from W. J. Bate to Franklin L. Ford, September 20, 1966, Harvard University Archives (UAI 15.1060).

4. Rodríguez Monegal, *Jorge Luis Borges: A Literary Biography*, p. 469.
5. This second edition had thirty-four new entries and was published in 1967 under the title *El libro de los seres imaginarios*, Kier: Buenos Aires.
6. As told by Bioy Casares to Alastair Reid. Author's interview with Reid, Edinburgh, August 14, 1997.
7. "Habla la mujer de Borges," *Tiempo Argentino*, February 6, 1983.
8. Ibid.
9. Interview with Esther Zemborain de Torres, Buenos Aires, November 27, 1995.
10. "Habla la mujer de Borges," *Tiempo Argentino*, February 6, 1983.
11. See interview with Fani Úveda, *Oggi*, October 26, 1987, and reproduced in Spanish in *Siete Dias*, November 26, 1987.
12. Interview with Esther Zemborain de Torres, Buenos Aires, November 27, 1995.
13. "Habla la mujer de Borges," *Tiempo Argentino*, February 6, 1983.
14. Interview with Bioy Casares, Buenos Aires, November 25, 1995.
15. Interview with Esther Zemborain de Torres, Buenos Aires, November 27, 1995.
16. Both poems were published in *Siete poemas* in an edition of only twenty-five copies that was privately printed in 1967 by the bibliophile Juan Osvaldo Viviano, with illustrations by Jorge Larco. They were later collected in *Elogio de la sombra*, 1969. See *OC* II, pp. 364 and 365.
17. *La Nación*, August 13, 1967, and collected in *Elogio de la sombra*, 1969. See *OC* II, p. 371.
18. Interview with Esther Zemborain de Torres, Buenos Aires, November 27, 1995.
19. *Clarín*, September 22, 1967.
20. Interview with Esther Zemborain de Torres, Buenos Aires, November 27, 1995.
21. Ibid.
22. This and subsequent information for which Raimundo Lida is named as the source is based on selected quotations from his private journals provided by his widow, Denah Lida, in Cambridge, Mass., July 21, 1997.
23. *The Harvard Gazette*, vol. LXIII, 1967–68, p. 36.
24. When the author applied in person at the Harvard University Archives in July 1997, he was informed that Borges had omitted to send Harvard a text of the lectures and no recording could be found. Fortunately, a tape recording was subsequently discovered, and Borges's six lectures were published with the title *This Craft of Verse* by Harvard University Press in 2000.
25. Interview with Denah Lida, Cambridge, Mass., July 21, 1997.
26. *Harvard Crimson*, October 11, 1967.
27. *Harvard Crimson*, November 17, 1967.
28. Burgin, *Conversations*, 1969, p. 13.
29. Ibid.
30. "Elsa" was published in the first edition of *Elogio de la sombra*, 1969, but omitted in the *Obras completas*, 1974.
31. Interview with Denah Lida, Cambridge, Mass., July 21, 1997.
32. "El otro" was first published in 1972 as a pamphlet by Juan Osvaldo Viviano and César Palui in a limited private edition. It later appeared in *La Opinión*, September 15, 1974, and was finally collected in *El libro de arena*, 1975.
33. "Cambridge" was first published in *Sur* 314, September–October 1968, and then in *Elogio de la sombra*, 1969. See *OC* II, pp. 358–359.

34. "The Unending Gift" (original title in English) was first published in *La Nación*, February 11, 1968, and then in *Elogio de la sombra*, 1969. See *OC* II, p. 362.

35. Burgin, *Conversations*, 1969, p. 14.

36. Interview with María Kodama, Buenos Aires, September 1, 1996.

37. Ibid.

38. "El amenazado" first appeared in *El oro de los tigres*, 1972. See *OC* II, p. 483.

39. Di Giovanni, "Introduction," *In Memory of Borges*, Constable: London, 1988, p. 22.

40. Ibid., p. 20.

41. Ibid.

42. Ibid., p. 24.

Chapter 27: **Iceland (1969–1971)**

1. "La rosa" would be collected in all subsequent editions of *Fervor de Buenos Aires*. See *OC* I, p. 25.

2. These Japanese tankas were published on October 5, 1969, in *La Nación*, and later collected in *El oro de los tigres*, 1972. See *OC* II, pp. 464–65.

3. Di Giovanni, "Introduction," *In Memory of Borges*, p. 25.

4. Di Giovanni, *In Memory of Borges*, p. 28.

5. See Alifano, *Biografía verbal*, p. 126.

6. Interview with Jack Macrae, New York, April 14, 1999.

7. Interview with María Kodama, Buenos Aires, 21 November 1995.

8. Ibid.

9. Interview with Alicia Jurado, Buenos Aires, September 14, 1994.

10. Interview with Alicia Jurado, Buenos Aires, November 10, 1995.

11. Interview with Bioy Casares, Buenos Aires, November 15, 1995.

12. M. E. de Miguel, *Norah Lange*, p. 220.

13. Di Giovanni, *In Memory of Borges*, p. 35.

14. "An Autobiographical Essay," p. 260.

15. Telephone interview with Norman Thomas di Giovanni, January 2, 1997.

16. See "Borges at N.Y.U." in "Prose for Borges," *Triquarterly*, 25 (1972), p. 459.

17. Susana Lange, letter of December 16, 2000.

18. Ibid.

19. "Browning resuelve ser poeta" was first published in *La Nación*, November 1, 1970, and later collected in *La rosa profunda*, 1975. See *OC* III, p. 82.

20. Interview with María Kodama, Buenos Aires, September 1, 1996.

21. Ibid.

22. Alifano, *Biografía verbal*, p. 127.

23. Carrizo, p. 46, and Alifano, *Biografía verbal*, p. 128.

24. Carrizo, p. 46.

25. Alifano, *Biografía verbal*, p. 128.

26. Interview with María Kodama, Buenos Aires, September 1, 1996.

27. Interview with Jack Macrae, New York, April 14, 1999.

28. Ibid.

29. Interview with Alastair Reid, Edinburgh, August 14, 1997.

30. Ibid.

31. Report in *La Razón*, May 7, 1971.

32. John Simon, "The Most Loathsome Film of All?" in *New York Times*, August 23, 1970, quoted in Edgardo Cozarinsky, *Borges In/And/On Film*, Lumen Books: New York, 1988, p. 91.

33. "Ulrica" was first published in *El libro de arena*, 1975. See *OC* III, pp. 17-19.

34. Interview with María Kodama, Buenos Aires, September 1, 1996.

35. See my Chapter 14, pp. 210–11, for the visit to Santa Anna do Livramento, and Chapter 16, pp. 233–34, for a discussion of "The Dead Man."

36. See my Chapter 5, pp. 88–89.

37. "La noche de los dones" was later collected in *El libro de arena*, 1975. See *OC* III, pp. 41–44.

38. *Las obsesiones de Borges. Una entrevista de Dante Escobar Plata*. Editorial Distal, Buenos Aires, 1989, p. 15.

39. See my Chapter 5, p. 69.

Chapter 28: Between Sunset and Dawn (1971–1975)

1. My account of María Kodama's background is based on my interview with her in Buenos Aires, September 1, 1996, and on an interview she gave to *La Semana*, published on May 15, 1986.

2. See interview with María Kodama published in *La Razón*, November 13, 1985.

3. Interview with María Kodama, Edinburgh, October 24, 1999.

4. "A Islandia" in *El oro de los tigres*, Emecé: Buenos Aires, 1972. See *OC* II, p. 509.

5. "Al Triste" was later included in *El oro de los tigres*, 1972. See *OC* II, p. 493.

6. "East Lansing" was first published in *El oro de los tigres*, 1972. See *OC* II, p. 512.

7. "El oro de los tigres" was first published in the collection of that title. See *OC* II, p. 515.

8. "Lo perdido" was first published in *La Nación*, June 18, 1972, and collected in *El oro de los tigres*. See *OC* II, p. 477.

9. Susana Lange, letter of December 16, 2000.

10. Interview with Donald Yates, St Helena, California, March 27, 1999.

11. "Yo" was later collected in *La rosa profunda*, 1975. See *OC* III, p. 79.

12. Reported in *La Razón*, May 26, 1971.

13. Reported in *Clarín*, December 30, 1971.

14. *La Stampa* of Turin, May 29, 1973, reported in *La Prensa*, Buenos Aires, May 30, 1973.

15. *La Nación*, April 8, 1973.

16. Interview with Fermín Chávez, Buenos Aires, November 20, 1995. See also, "Fidelio" (pseudonym of Arturo López Peña), "Para seis cuerdas: milongas con variaciones" in *Pueblo Entero*, Buenos Aires, May 1980.

17. "Avelino Arredondo" was first published in *El libro de arena*, 1975. See *OC* III, pp. 62–65.

18. Interview in *La Nación*, November 24, 1974.

19. "A Manuel Mujica Láinez" was first published in *La moneda de hierro*, Emecé: Buenos Aires, 1976. See *OC* III, p. 133.

20. Interview in *La Nación*, November 24, 1974.

21. Lecture given to the Peña El Ombú at the Plaza Hotel, as reported in *La Nación*, September 9, 1975.

22. Interview in *La Nación*, November 24, 1974.

23. "En memoria de Angélica" in *La rosa profunda*, 1975. See *OC* III, p. 108.
24. See Carlos Burone, *La Opinión*, December 21, 1974.
25. *El libro de arena*, Emecé: Buenos Aires, 1975, and for "Epílogo," See *OC* III, p. 72.
26. *La rosa profunda*, Emecé; Buenos Aires, 1975. For "The Unending Rose," see *OC* III, p. 116.

Chapter 29: **A New Dawn in Iceland (1975–1976)**

1. "El remordimiento" was first published in *La Nación*, September 21, 1975, and collected in *La moneda de hierro*, 1976. See *OC* III, p. 143.
2. Interview with Bioy Casares, Buenos Aires, September 8, 1996.
3. Interview with Elsie Rivero Haedo, Buenos Aires, March 30, 1994.
4. Interview with María Kodama, Buenos Aires, November 21, 1995.
5. "La moneda de hierro" first appeared in the collection of that title published by Emecé in 1976. See *OC* III, p. 160.
6. "A mi padre" was first published in *La moneda de hierro*, 1976. See *OC* III, p. 141.
7. Interview with María Kodama, Buenos Aires, September 1, 1996.
8. Interviews with María Kodama, Buenos Aires, September 1, 1996, and Edinburgh, October 24, 1999.
9. Interview with María Kodama, Buenos Aires, November 21, 1995, and September 1, 1996.
10. "Un Escolio" in *Historia de la noche*, 1977. See *OC* III, p. 176.
11. Interview with María Kodama, Buenos Aires, September 1, 1996.
12. "Endimión en Latmos" was first published in *La Nación* on November 7, 1976, and later in *Historia de la noche*, 1977. See *OC*, p. 175.
13. Interview with Donald Yates, St. Helena, California, March 27, 1999.
14. "A Johannes Brahms" was first published in *La Nación* on November 2, 1975, and both "El ingenuo" and "A Johannes Brahms" were collected in *La moneda de hierro*, 1976. See *OC* III, pp. 137 and 139, respectively.
15. "La clepsidra" was first published in *La moneda de hierro*, 1976. See *OC* III, p. 157.
16. Interview with Donald Yates, St. Helena, California, March 27, 1999.
17. "Elegía de la patria" was published in *La moneda de hierron*, 1976. See *OC* III, p. 129.
18. Ibid.
19. Ibid.
20. "En Islandia el alba" in *La moneda de hierro*, 1976. See *OC* III, p. 147.
21. My account of this visit to Iceland is based on information provided by María Kodama in Edinburgh on October 24, 1999.
22. "Islandia," *Historia de la noche*, 1977. See *OC* III, p. 179.
23. Quoted in Volodia Teitelboim, *Los dos Borges*, Editorial Sudamericana Chilena: Santiago, p. 216.
24. *La Semana*, May 15, 1986.
25. "El enamorado" in *Historia de la noche*, 1977. See *OC* III, p. 190.
26. My account of his daily routine is based on an interview with Borges published in *Siete Días*, June 17, 1977.
27. Interview with Betina Edelberg, Buenos Aires, September 9, 1996.
28. Report in *Cambio 16*, August 25, 1976.
29. Ibid.

30. Quoted in Teitelboim, *Los dos Borges,* p. 213.
31. Teitelboim, *Los dos Borges,* p. 215.
32. Ibid., p. 228.
33. Quoted in Teitelboim, *Los dos Borges,* p. 212.
34. Ibid., p. 213.

Chapter 30: **Blue Tigers (1976–1979)**

1. See interview with Fani Úveda in *Oggi,* October 26, 1987, and reproduced in Spanish in *Siete Días,* November 26, 1987.
2. Ibid.
3. See my Chapter 29, p. 419–20.
4. "Alejandría, 641 A.D." was first published in *La Nación* on June 26, 1977, and included in *Historia de la noche,* 1977. See *OC* III, p. 167.
5. See Borges's endnote on this poem in *Historia de la noche, OC* III, p. 203.
6. See "Epílogo," *OC* III, p. 202.
7. "Las hojas del ciprés" was first published in *ABC* (Madrid), May 15, 1979, and later incorporated in *Los conjurados,* 1985. See *OC* III, pp. 481–82.
8. First published as "Agosto 25, 1983" in *La Nación,* March 27, 1983, but dated "Buenos Aires, 1977." After undergoing some modifications, the title appeared as "Veinticinco de agosto, 1983" when the story was included in *La memoria de Shakespeare, OC* III, pp. 375–78.
9. "La espera" was first published in *Historia de la noche,* 1977. See *OC* III, p. 192.
10. "Historia de la noche" was first published in the collection of that name. See *Historia de la noche,* Emecé: Buenos Aires, 1977, and *OC* III, p. 201.
11. Reported in *La Nación,* May 9, 1977.
12. My account of Borges's visit to Geneva is based on my interview with María Kodama, Edinburgh, October 25, 1999.
13. Ibid.
14. Ibid.
15. Undated letter to Godel 6. See my Chapter 4, p. 67.
16. Interview with María Kodama, Edinburgh, October 25, 1999.
17. Ibid.
18. Ibid.
19. See Clark M. Zlotchew, "Jorge Luis Borges: An Interview" (1984), in Burgin, *Conversations,* 1998, p. 237.
20. "Tigres azules" was first published in *Rosa y Azul,* Sedmay: Barcelona, 1977, and then with the title "El milagro perdido" in *La Nación,* February 19, 1978. It was included in *La memoria de Shakespeare, OC* III, pp. 379–86.
21. There is a photograph of this tiger in Domenico Porzio, *Jorge Luis Borges: Immagini e immaginazione,* Edizioni Studio Tesi: Pordenone, 1985, photograph no. 143, p. 188.
22. "Los tigres del Annam," *El libro de los seres imaginarios, Obras completas en colaboración,* p. 701.
23. "Caja de música" was first published in *Historia de la noche,* 1977. See *OC* III, p. 172.
24. See Rodolfo Braceli, "Con Borges, créase o no, rehaciendo un poema suyo recién parido," in *Borges-Bioy: confesiones, confesiones.* Sudamericana: Buenos Aires, 1997, pp. 179–91, (p.179).

25. "La dicha" was first published in *La cifra*, 1981. See *OC* III, p. 306.
26. "¡ADEMÁS TRAIDOR: BORGES APOYA A CHILE!," *Crónica*, August 31, 1978.
27. "¡BORGES CONTRA EL GOBIERNO, CONTRA EL ESTADO, CONTRA LA LEY, CONTRA ARGENTINA!" *Crónica*, September 2, 1978.
28. "Elegía" was later collected in *La cifra*, 1981. See *OC* III, p. 307.
29. "El go," was first published in *La Nación*, October 8, 1978, and collected in *La cifra*, 1981. See *OC* III, p. 330.
30. "Himno" was first published on April 19, 1979 in *Clarín*, and in *La cifra*, 1981. See *OC* III, p. 305.
31. For a more detailed version of this episode, see Vázquez, *Borges: esplendor y derrota*, pp. 303–4.
32. "*Inferno*, V, 129" was first published in *La Prensa*, May 20, 1979, and collected in *La cifra*, 1981. See *OC* III, p. 321.
33. *The Divine Comedy*, translated by Geoffrey L. Bickersteth, Shakespeare Head Press/Basil Blackwell: Oxford, 1972, p. 39.
34. Susana Lange, letter of October 3, 2000.
35. "El desierto" and "Blake," *Clarín*, July 12, 1979. Both were collected in *La cifra*, 1981. See *OC* III, pp. 327 and 308, respectively.
36. "La fama" was first published in *Clarín*, August 23, 1979, and collected in *La cifra*, 1981. See *OC* III, p. 323.
37. The interview appeared on August 27, 1979, in *La Mañana* with the headline "El Ultimo Adiós de Borges" ("Borges's Last Good-bye"), and reported in *Crónica* on August 28, 1979.
38. See Juan Gasparini, *Borges: la posesión póstuma*, Foca: Madrid, 2000, p. 58.
39. See Vázquez, *Borges: esplendor y derrota*, p. 304.
40. Interview with María Kodama, Edinburgh, October 25, 1999.
41. Ibid.
42. See Guillermo Gasió, *Borges en Japón. Japón en Borges*, Editorial Universitaria de Buenos Aires: Buenos Aires, 1988, p. 14.

Chapter 31: **The Music of Japan (1979–1981)**

1. Guillermo Gasió, *Borges en Japón, Japón en Borges*, pp. 148 and 52. My account of Borges's visit to Japan is based largely on the various texts collected in anthology.
2. "Yo fui con Borges al Japón: diario de viaje escrito por María Kodama," in Gasió, pp. 133–37. Unless otherwise indicated, quotations in my account of Borges's visit to Japan refer to this source.
3. Interview with María Kodama, Edinburgh, October 24, 1999, and Gasió, p. 145.
4. Interview with María Kodama, Edinburgh, October 24, 1999.
5. Interview with María Kodama, Edinburgh, October 24, 1999, and Gasió, p. 98.
6. Interview with María Kodama, Edinburgh, October 24, 1999.
7. Interview with María Kodama, Edinburgh, October 24, 1999, and Gasió, p. 99.
8. Interview with María Kodama, Edinburgh, October 24, 1999.
9. See interview with Mie Uchida in Gasió, pp. 72–81.
10. "El forastero" was first published in *La cifra*, 1981. See *OC* III, p. 332.
11. "Shinto" was first published in *La Prensa*, February 17, 1980, and collected in *La cifra*, 1981. See *OC* III, p. 331.

12. He published "Once haikus" in *Clarín*, January 24, 1980; they were increased to seventeen (the number of syllables of which a haiku is composed) when collected in *La cifra*, 1981. See *OC* III, pp. 333–35. Borges's lecture was entitled "Mi experiencia con el Japón," Gasió, pp. 143–52; for the passages quoted, see pp. 146–47.

13. The quotation is from "Mi experiencia con el Japón," in Gasió, p. 145.

14. First published in *Clarín* on March 20, 1980. It appeared in an English translation by Alastair Reid with the title "The Web" in *Jorge Luis Borges, Selected Poems*, London: Allen Lane, Penguin Press, 1999, pp. 476–77.

15. *Atlas*, Editorial Sudamericana: Buenos Aires, 1984. See *OC* III, p. 427.

16. Ibid.

17. "Correr o ser" was first published in *Clarín* on May 21, 1981, and later in *La cifra*, 1981. See *OC* III, p. 322.

18. First published, with an English title, in *La Prensa* on September 28, 1980, and later in *La cifra*, 1981. See *OC* III, p. 310.

19. This idea had been adumbrated in the poem "The Unending Gift," which Borges wrote while at Harvard in 1967–68, and collected in *Elogio de la sombra*, 1969. See *OC* II, p. 362, and my Chapter 26, pp. 377–78.

20. "The Cloisters" was first published in *La Prensa*, January 11, 1981, and later in *La cifra*, 1981. See *OC* III, p. 300.

21. Interview with María Kodama, Edinburgh, October 24, 1999.

22. Ibid.

23. "El bastón de laca" was first published in *La Prensa*, December 7, 1980, and later in *La cifra*, 1981. See *OC* III, p. 328.

24. "El tercer hombre" was first published in *La cifra*, 1981. See *OC* III, p. 314.

25. See Borges's endnote on "El tercer hombre" in *La cifra*, 1981. See *OC* III, p. 338.

26. "Los justos" was first published in *La cifra*, 1981. See *OC* III, p. 324.

27. "Dos formas del insomnio" was first published in *La Prensa*, 1981 (no date given in Nicolás Helft's bibliography), and later in *La cifra*, 1981. See *OC* III, p. 299.

28. "Eclesiastés, 1, 9" was first published in *La Prensa*, March 29, 1981, and in *La cifra*, 1981. See *OC* III, p. 298.

29. "Aquél" was first published in *Clarín*, May 21, 1981, and later in *La cifra*, 1981. See *OC* III, p. 297.

30. "La cifra" was first published in *La Nación* on March 19, 1978, with the title "La luna," and later in *La cifra*, Emecé: Buenos Aires, 1981. See *OC* III, p. 337.

31. "Inscripción," *La cifra*, 1981. See *OC* III, p. 289.

Chapter 32: **Deconstructing the Nation (1980–1983)**

1. Interview with Patrick Séry originally published in *L'Evènement du Jeudi*, Paris, June 19, 1986, and reprinted in *El otro Borges: entrevistas 1960–1986*, ed. Fernando Mateo, Equis: Buenos Aires, 1997, p. 200.

2. Interview with Agustina Paz Anchorena by Uki Goñi, tape–recorded in Buenos Aires, November 21, 1997.

3. *Buenos Aires Herald*, February 6, 1981.

4. "We Are Not Worthy of Democracy," an interview with Borges by Larry Rohter and Richard Steele, *Newsweek*, January 12, 1981.

5. "Borges: Grotezco Traidor a la Nación." Report in *Pregón*, May 23, 1981.

6. Report in *Clarín*, July 4, 1981.

7. Ibid.

8. Report in *La Razón*, June 11, 1980, of an interview in Paris, where he received the Cino del Duca International Award for Literature.

9. *Buenos Aires Herald*, February 6, 1981.

10. Ibid.

11. Ibid.

12. "The Old Man and the City," *Times Literary Supplement*, August 20, 1999, p. 11.

13. "Juan López y John Ward" was first published in *Clarín*, August 26, 1982, and collected in *Los conjurados*, 1985. See *OC* III, p. 496.

14. "Milonga de un soldado" was collected in *Los conjurados*, 1985, with the title "Milonga del muerto." See *OC* III, p. 493.

15. Interview with Rodolfo Zibell in *Gente*, September 16, 1982.

16. Ibid.

17. Ibid.

18. "The Old Man and the City," *Times Literary Supplement*, August 20, 1999, p. 11.

19. Ibid.

20. *Gente*, September 16, 1982.

21. Interview in *Folha de São Paulo*, reported in *Crónica*, August 16, 1982.

22. Ibid.

23. Report in *La Semana*, January 27, 1983.

24. *La Semana*, February 10, 1983.

25. "The Old Man and the City," *Times Literary Supplement*, August 20, 1999, p. 12.

26. "Un argumento" was published in *Clarín*, April 7, 1983, but was not included in any of his books.

27. "Posesión del ayer" was first published in *La Prensa*, April 10, 1983, and later in *Los conjurados*, 1985. See *OC* III, p. 478.

28. "Todos los ayeres, un sueño" was first published in *Los conjurados*, 1985. See *OC* III, p. 489.

29. "Milonga del infiel" was first published in *ABC* (Madrid), April 23, 1983, and later in *Los conjurados*, 1985. See *OC* III, p. 491.

30. "Lo nuestro" was published in *ABC* (Madrid), June 8, 1983, but not included in any collection.

31. "Los conjurados" was first published in the review *Lyra* 12, no. 250, 1983, p. 12, and subsequently as the title poem of Borges's last collection. See *OC* III, p. 497.

32. Interview with Carlos Ares in *El País* (Madrid), November 3, 1985.

33. Ibid.

34. Ibid.

35. *Clarín*, November 29, 1983.

Chapter 33: The Weaver of Dreams (1984–1985)

1. "Elegía" was first published in *La Nación*, January 29, 1984, and collected in *Los conjurados*, 1985. See *OC* III, p. 462.

2. The conference was organized by Armando Verdiglione, a well-known Italian writer and publisher, who was the director of the Fondazione di Cultura Internazionale, based in Milan.

3. "Cristo en la cruz" was first published in *Los conjurados*, 1985. See *OC* III, p. 453.

4. "De la salvación por las obras," *Atlas*, 1984. See *OC* III, p. 448.

5. "Alguien sueña" was first published in *La Nación,* December 16, 1984, and collected in *Los conjurados,* 1985. See *OC* III, pp. 467–68.

6. "La larga busca" was first published in *Los conjurados,* 1985. See *OC* III, p. 486.

7. "Abramowicz" was first published in *Los conjurados,* 1985. See *OC* III, p. 463.

8. "Alguien soñará" was first published in *Los conjurados,* 1985. See *OC* III, p. 469.

9. "Prólogo," *Atlas,* Sudamericana: Buenos Aires, 1984. See *OC* III, pp. 400–48 (p. 401).

10. "Prólogo," *Los conjurados,* 1985. See *OC* III, p. 452.

11. "Música griega," *Clarín,* April 11, 1985. It was not included in any of Borges's collections of poetry.

12. *Vogue,* March 1986, p. 337.

13. Ibid.

14. *Los conjurados,* Alianza: Madrid, 1985.

15. *La Semana,* July 25, 1985.

16. See *Clarín,* July 26, 1985.

17. Interview with María Kodama, Edinburgh, October 25, 1999.

18. Ibid.

19. Ibid.

20. *Tiempo Argentino,* September 14, 1985.

21. The interview with Patrick Séry was originally published in *L'Evènement du Jeudi,* Paris, June 19, 1986, and later reprinted in *El otro Borges: entrevistas 1960–1986.* ed. Fernando Mateo, 1997, pp. 199–203.

22. Ibid., p. 202.

23. The interview with Secretan was published in the *Tribune de Genève* on May 30, 1986, but my account is based on Gasparini, p. 82.

24. See Gasparini, p. 90.

25. The interview with Barili was first published in the *New York Times Book Review,* July 13, 1986, and reprinted in Burgin, *Conversations,* 1998, pp. 240–47.

26. "1985" was not published in Borges's lifetime, but see *Proa* (tercera época), Buenos Aires, May–June 1996, p. 11.

27. Compare the wills of 1979 and 1985 in Gasparini, pp. 58 and 60–61, respectively.

28. See Alberto Casares, "La última tarde de Borges en Buenos Aires," *Proa* (tercera época), 23 (1996), pp. 169–70.

29. Gasparini, p. 86.

30. Ibid., p. 170.

31. Casares, "La última tarde de Borges en Buenos Aires," p. 170, and Gasparini, p. 166.

32. Gasparini, p. 87.

Chapter 34: **Creating an End (1985–1986)**

1. Interview with María Kodama, Edinburgh, October 25, 1999.

2. Ibid.

3. Ibid.

4. Interview with María Kodama, Edinburgh, October 24, 1999.

5. Gasparini, p. 101.

6. My account is based on a report of a press conference held by Vidaurre on May 14, 1986, and published in *Tiempo Argentino,* May 15, 1986, p. 16.

7. See Vidaurre interview in *La Razón,* May 15, 1986.

8. Interview with Jean Pierre Bernès by Jorge Urien Berri in *La Nación*, August 20, 1989.
9. Ibid.
10. See Vidaurre in *Tiempo Argentino*, May 15, 1986.
11. This letter is reproduced in Gasparini, p. 64.
12. Interview with Jean Pierre Bernès, Oxford, October 22, 1999.
13. Gasparini, p. 103.
14. Ibid., pp. 103–4.
15. *Tiempo Argentino*, May 15, 1986.
16. Report in *La Razón*, May 15, 1986.
17. Report in *La Semana*, May 15, 1986.
18. My account of Alazraki's visit to Borges is based on his book, *Beyond the Kabbalah*, 1988, pp. 177–78.
19. Gasparini, p. 90.
20. Ibid., p. 98.
21. *La Nación*, June 18, 1986, p. 6.
22. For Borges's literary projects mentioned here, see Bernès (ed.), Jorge Luis Borges, *Oeuvres complètes* I, p. xix, and Bernès II, pp. 1443–44.
23. Gasparini, p. 105.
24. Interview with María Kodama, Edinburgh, October 25, 1999.
25. See Hector Bianciotti's "Préface" to Jorge Luis Borges, *Neuf essais sur Dante*, Gallimard: Paris, 1987, p. 18.

Epilogue

1. Interview with Pastor Edouard de Montmollin in Gasparini, p. 109.
2. Report by Sara Gallardo in *La Nación*, June 19, 1986.
3. Report in *La Nación*, June 21, 1986.
4. Ibid.
5. My account of this episode is based primarily on an article by Jorge Mackey that appeared in *La Nación* on July 8, 2003, and also on an earlier report entitled "Borges's Reconciliation with the Church," *La Nación*, September 14, 1986.
6. Interview with María Kodama, Edinburgh, October 25, 1999.

Bibliography

(Unless otherwise indicated, the place of publication is Buenos Aires.)

Works by Borges in Chronological Order of Publication

Fervor de Buenos Aires (poems), privately printed, 1923.

Luna de enfrente (poems), Proa, 1925.

Inquisiciones (essays), Proa, 1925. [Reissued by Espasa Calpe/Seix Barral, 1993.]

El tamaño de mi esperanza (essays), Proa, 1926. [Reissued by Espasa Calpe/Seix Barral, 1993.]

El idioma de los argentinos (essays), Manuel Gleizer, 1929. [Reissued by Espasa Calpe/Seix Barral, 1994.]

Cuaderno San Martín (poems), Proa, 1929.

Evaristo Carriego (biography and essays), Manuel Gleizer, 1930.

Discusión (essays), Manuel Gleizer, 1932.

Las kenningar (essay), Francisco A. Colombo, 1933. (Later included in *Historia de la eternidad.*)

Historia universal de la infamia (stories), Tor, 1935.

Historia de la eternidad (essays), Viau y Zona, 1936.

El jardín de senderos que se bifurcan (stories), Sur, 1941.

Poemas (1923–1943), Losada, 1943. (First edition of collected poems, omitting a number of poems from earlier books and containing numerous variants on the original texts.)

Ficciones (stories), Sur, 1944.

Nueva refutación del tiempo (essay), Oportet & Haereses (a fictitious publisher), 1947. (Later included in *Otras inquisiciones.*)

El Aleph (stories), Losada, 1949.

Aspectos de la literatura gauchesca (originally a lecture delivered at the University of Montevideo, October 29, 1945), Número: Montevideo, 1950.

Otras inquisiciones (1937–1952), (essays), Sur, 1952.

Poemas (1923–1958), Emecé, 1958. (This marks the beginning of Borges's association with the publishers Emecé).

El hacedor (poems and prose), Emecé, 1960.

Antología personal, Sur, 1961.

Obra poética, Emecé, 1964. (New title for collected poems. Includes new poems in a section called *El otro, el mismo*, later published as a separate volume under this title, Emecé, 1969.)

Para las seis cuerdas (lyrics for *milongas*), Emecé, 1965.

Elogio de la sombra (poems), Emecé, 1969.

El informe de Brodie (stories), Emecé, 1970.

El Congreso (novella), El Archibrazo, 1971. (Later included in *El libro de arena.*)

El oro de los tigres (poems), Emecé, 1972.

Obras completas, Emecé, 1974.

El libro de arena (stories), Emecé, 1975.

La rosa profunda (poems), Emecé, 1975.

Prólogos con un prólogo de prólogos (collected prologues to works by other authors), Torres Agüero Editor, 1975.

La moneda de hierro (poems), Emecé, 1976.

Historia de la noche (poems and prose), Emecé, 1977.

Rosa y Azul (first publication of two stories: "La rosa de Paracelso" and "Tigres azules," which were later included in *Veinticinco agosto 1983 y otros cuentos*), Sedmay: Madrid, 1977.

Obra poética (1923–1976), 10th ed., Emecé, 1978. (Last edition with variants on earlier texts. Henceforward new volumes of poetry will be incorporated without change in subsequent editions.)

Borges, oral (lectures delivered at the Universidad de Belgrano), Emecé/Editorial de Belgrano, 1979.

Siete noches (lectures delivered at the Teatro Coliseo, Buenos Aires, in 1977), Fondo de Cultura Económica: Mexico City, 1980.

La cifra (poems), Alianza: Madrid, 1981.

Nueve ensayos dantescos (essays, five of which were first published in 1948, one in 1951), Espasa-Calpe: Madrid, 1982.

"La memoria de Shakespeare" (story). First published in *Clarín,* May 15, 1980, and later as a booklet in a limited edition of thirty-six copies by Dos Amigos, Colección Valle de Las Leñas, no. 1, 1982. Subsequently incorporated as the title story of a collection forming part of the *Obras completas.*

"Un argumento" (story). First published in *Clarín,* April 7, 1983, and later as a booklet in a limited edition of thirty-six copies by Dos Amigos, Colección Valle de Las Leñas, no. 2, 1983. Not included in any of his collections of stories.

Veinticinco agosto 1983 y otros cuentos (four stories), Siruela: Madrid, 1983.

Los conjurados (poems and prose), Alianza: Madrid, 1985.

Obras completas, four volumes, Emecé, 1989.

This Craft of Verse, Harvard University Press: Cambridge, Mass., and London, 2000. (The Charles Eliot Norton Lectures, originally delivered in English at Harvard during 1967–1968.)

Works in Collaboration

With Adolfo Bioy Casares

Seis problemas para don Isidro Parodi (stories under joint pseudonym, H. Bustos Domecq), Sur, 1942.

Dos fantasías memorables (two stories under joint pseudonym, H. Bustos Domecq), Oportet & Haereses (a fictitious publisher), 1946.

Un modelo para la muerte (novella under joint pseudonym, B. Suárez Lynch), Oportet & Haereses, 1946.

Los orilleros. El paraíso de los creyentes (two screenplays), Losada, 1955.
Crónicas de Bustos Domecq (spoof essays), Losada, 1967.
Nuevos cuentos de Bustos Domecq (stories), Ediciones Librería de la Ciudad, 1977.

With Delia Ingenieros
Antiguas literaturas germánicas, Fondo de Cultura Económica: Mexico City, 1951.

With Margarita Guerrero
El Martín Fierro, Columba, 1953.
Manual de zoología fantástica, Fondo de Cultura Económica: Mexico City, 1957. (An expanded version was published as *El libro de los seres imaginarios,* Kier, 1967.)

With Betina Edelberg
La imagen perdida, 1953. (Unpublished script for a ballet; apparently lost.)
Leopoldo Lugones (essays), Troquel, 1955.

With Luisa Mercedes Levinson
La hermana de Eloísa, Ene, 1955.

With María Esther Vázquez
Introducción a la literatura inglesa, Columba, 1965.
Literaturas germánicas medievales, Falbo, 1966.

With Esther Zemborain de Torres
Introducción a la literatura norteamericana, Columba, 1967.

With Alicia Jurado
Qué es el budismo, Columba, 1976.

With María Kodama
Breve antología anglosajona (translations of Anglo-Saxon texts), La Ciudad: Santiago de Chile, 1978.
Atlas, Sudamericana, 1984.

Obras completas en colaboración, Emecé, 1991

Collection of Texts by Borges First Published in Journals, Magazines, or Newspapers

Jorge Luis Borges: textos cautivos (Ensayos y reseñas en El Hogar, 1936–1939) (essays and reviews published in the magazine *El Hogar*), Tusquets: Barcelona, 1986.
Borges en Revista Multicolor de los Sábados (articles, reviews, and translations first published in the literary supplement of the newspaper *Crítica*), Atlántida, 1995.
Borges en Sur, 1931–1980 (articles and reviews first published in the literary journal *Sur*), Emecé, 1999.
Jorge Luis Borges: textos recobrados, 1919–1929 (uncollected essays, poems, and reviews), Emecé, 1997.
Jorge Luis Borges: textos recobrados, 1931–1955, Emecé, 2001.
Jorge Luis Borges: textos recobrados, 1956–1986, Emecé, 2003.

Borges in English

The most readily available editions are the three volumes published by Penguin:

Jorge Luis Borges, *Collected Fictions*, trans. Andrew Hurley, Allen Lane, Penguin Press: London, 1999.

———. *Selected Poems*, ed. Alexander Coleman, Allen Lane, Penguin Press: London, 1999.

———. *The Total Library: Non-Fiction, 1922–1986*, ed. Eliot Weinberger, Allen Lane, Penguin Press: London, 2000.

Before the above trilogy was published, Borges's principal writings were available to English-speaking readers in a variety of translations by different hands:

Ficciones, ed. with an introduction by Anthony Kerrigan, Grove Press: New York, 1962. (In the UK: Weidenfeld and Nicolson: London, 1962.)

Dreamtigers, trans. Mildred Boyer and Harold Borland, University of Texas Press: Austin, 1964. (Translation of *El hacedor*, 1960.)

Other Inquisitions, 1937–1952, trans. Ruth L. C. Simms, University of Texas Press: Austin, 1964.

Labyrinths: Selected Stories and Other Writings, eds. Donald A. Yates and James E. Irby, New Directions: New York, 1964. (In the UK: Penguin: Harmondsworth, 1970.)

The Book of Imaginary Beings, written in collaboration with Margarita Guerrero. Revised, enlarged, and translated by Norman Thomas di Giovanni in collaboration with the author, Dutton: New York, 1969. (In the UK: Jonathan Cape: London, 1970.)

The Aleph and Other Stories (1933–1969), ed. and trans. Norman Thomas di Giovanni in collaboration with the author, Dutton: New York, 1970. (Contains "An Autobiographical Essay" and "Commentaries." See below.) (In the UK: Jonathan Cape: London, 1971.)

Doctor Brodie's Report, ed. and trans. Norman Thomas di Giovanni in collaboration with the author, Dutton: New York, 1971. (In the UK: Allen Lane: London, 1974.)

Selected Poems, 1923–1967, ed. with introduction and notes by Norman Thomas di Giovanni, Delacorte Press: New York, 1972. (In the UK: Allen Lane: London, 1972.)

A Universal History of Infamy, trans. Norman Thomas di Giovanni, Dutton: New York, 1972. (In the UK: Allen Lane, London, 1973.)

In Praise of Darkness, trans. Norman Thomas di Giovanni, Dutton: New York, 1974. (In the UK: Allen Lane: London, 1975.)

The Book of Sand, trans. Norman Thomas di Giovanni, Dutton: New York, 1977. (In the UK: Allen Lane: London, 1977.)

The Gold of the Tigers: Selected Later Poems, trans. Alastair Reid, Dutton: New York, 1977. (Published in the UK as *The Book of Sand; The Gold of the Tigers*, Allen Lane: London, 1979.)

Borges: A Reader, eds. Alastair Reid and Emir Rodríguez Monegal, Dutton: New York, 1981.

With Adolfo Bioy Casares

Six Problems for Don Isidro Parodi, trans. Norman Thomas di Giovanni, Dutton: New York, 1981. (In the UK: Allen Lane: London, 1981.)

Chronicles of Bustos Domecq, trans. Norman Thomas di Giovanni, Dutton: New York, 1982. (In the UK: Allen Lane: London, 1982.)

Evaristo Carriego, trans. Norman Thomas di Giovanni, Dutton: New York, 1984. (In the UK: Allen Lane: London, 1984.)

With María Kodama
Atlas, trans. Anthony Kerrigan, Viking: New York, 1986.

Borges in French

Oeuvres complètes, ed. Jean Pierre Bernès, Bibliothèque de la Pléiade, Gallimard: Paris, 2 vols.: 1993, 1999. (Contains informative notes, many of biographical and bibliographical interest. Volume II includes translations into French of selected letters to Maurice Abramowicz, Jacobo Sureda, Adriano del Valle, Rafael Cansinos-Asséns, and Macedonio Fernández.)

Correspondence

I have studied correspondence from Borges to the following: Maurice Abramowicz, Susana Bombal, Rafael Cansinos-Asséns, Macedonio Fernández, Roberto Godel, Ulyses Petit de Murat, Norah Lange, Alfonso Reyes, Guillermo de Torre, Jacobo Sureda, Adriano del Valle, Elsa Astete Millán.

Many of these letters were held in private collections when I consulted them, but some correspondence has appeared, either whole or in part, in a variety of publications:

To Maurice Abramowicz
Jorge Luis Borges, *Cartas del fervor. Correspondencia con Maurice Abramowicz y Jacobo Sureda (1919–1928)*, ed. Cristóbal Pera, with a prologue by Joaquín Marco and notes by Carlos García, Galaxia Gutenberg, Círculo de Lectores Emecé: Barcelona, 1999. Also, twenty-three letters described in French and partly reproduced in the auction catalog *Précieux manuscrites et autographes*, Salle Vuillard, Paris-Drouot-Montaigne, September 14, 1996. Extracts from these letters in Spanish translation are reproduced in *Jorge Luis Borges: textos recobrados, 1919–1929*, pp. 428–32.

See also Bernès, vol. II, above.

To Susana Bombal
"De Jorge Luis Borges a Susana Bombal," *Letras de Buenos Aires*, 30 (1995), pp. 11–20.

To Rafael Cansinos-Asséns
See, Bernès, vol II, above.

To Macedonio Fernández
García, Carlos, ed., *Correspondencia, 1922–1939./ Macedonio Fernández, Jorge Luis Borges: crónica de una amistad.* Corregidor, 2000. See also, Bernès, vol II, above.

To Alfonso Reyes
Pacheco, José Emilio. "Borges y Reyes: una correspondencia. Contribución a la historia de una amistad literaria," *Revista de la Universidad de México* 34, December (1979), pp. 1–16.

To Jacobo Sureda

Meneses, Carlos. *Jorge Luis Borges. Cartas de juventud (1921–1922)*, Orígenes: Madrid, 1987. See also under Abramowicz above and Bernès, vol. II, above.

To Adriano del Valle

Pellicer, Rosa. "Cartas de Jorge Luis Borges a Adriano del Valle," *Voz y Letra. Revista de Filología* (Málaga), 1 (1990), pp. 207–14. See also Bernès, vol. II, above.

Bibliographies

García, Carlos. "Borges inédito: bibliografía virtual, 1904–1930," in *El joven Borges, poeta*, pp. 327–63 (see below, p. 546, under "Critical Studies of Borges's Work").

Helft, Nicolás. *Jorge Luis Borges. Bibliografía completa*, Fondo de Cultura Económica, 1997.

Loewenstein, C. Jared. *A Descriptive Catalogue of the Jorge Luis Borges Collection at the University of Virginia Library*, University Press of Virginia: Charlottesville, VA, and London, 1993.

Louis, Annick, and Florian Ziche. *Bibliografía de la obra de Jorge Luis Borges*, E.H.E.S.S.: Paris, 1995.

Salvador, Nélida, and Elena Ardissone. *Bibliografía de tres revistas de vanguardia. (Prisma 1921–22, Proa 1922–23, Proa 1924–26)*, Facultad de Filosofía y Letras, Universidad de Buenos Aires, 1983.

Interviews with Borges

Alcorta, Gloria. "Entretiens avec Gloria Alcorta," *Cahiers de L'Herne*, Paris 1964, pp. 404–8.

Alifano, Roberto. *Conversaciones con Jorge Luis Borges*, Torre Agüero Editor, 1994.

———. *Twenty-four Conversations with Borges, Including a Selection of Poems*, Lascaux Publications: Housatonic, MA, 1984.

Barnstone, Willis, ed. *Borges at Eighty: Conversations*, University of Indiana: Bloomington, 1982.

Borges, Jorge Luis, y Osvaldo Ferrari. *Libro de diálogos*, Sudamericana, 1986.

———. *Diálogos últimos*, Sudamericana, 1987.

———. *Diálogos*, Seix Barral: Barcelona, 1992.

Borges en la Escuela Freudiana de Buenos Aires (responses to questions from audience), Agalma, 1993.

Braceli, Rodolfo. *Borges-Bioy: confesiones, confesiones*, Sudamericana, 1997.

Burgin, Richard. *Conversations with Jorge Luis Borges*, Holt, Rinehart, and Winston: New York: 1969.

———, ed. *Jorge Luis Borges: Conversations*, University Press of Mississippi: Jackson, 1998. (Collection of interviews by different authors.)

Carrizo, Antonio. *Borges el memorioso*, Fondo de Cultura Económica: Mexico City, 1983.

Charbonnier, Georges. *Entretiens avec Jorge Luis Borges*, Gallimard: Paris, 1967.

Escobar Plata, Dante. *Las obsesiones de Borges: una entrevista de Dante Escobar Plata*, Editorial Distal, 1989.

Fernández Moreno, César. "Weary of Labyrinths: An interview with Jorge Luis Borges," *Encounter*, 32 (1969), pp. 3–14.

Fontaina, Milton, Juan Carlos Victorica, and Ricardo Wulicher. *Borges para millones,* Corregidor, 1978.

Guibert, Rita. "Jorge Luis Borges" in *Seven Voices,* Knopf: New York, 1973, pp. 77–117.

Irby, James E. "Entretiens avec James E. Irby" in *Cahiers de L'Herne,* Paris 1964, pp. 388–403.

Mateo, Fernando, ed. *El otro Borges: entrevistas 1960–1986,* Equis, 1997.

Milleret, Jean de. *Entretiens avec Jorge Luis Borges,* Pierre Belfond: Paris, 1967.

Murat, Napoléon. "Entretiens avec Napoléon Murat" in *Cahiers de L'Herne,* Paris 1964, pp. 371–87.

Ocampo, Victoria. *Diálogo con Borges,* Sur, 1969.

Peralta, Carlos. "L'électricité des mots" in *Cahiers de L'Herne,* Paris 1964, pp. 409–13.

Rodman, Selden. *Tongues of Fallen Angels,* New Directions: New York, 1974.

Soler Serrano, Joaquín. "Simplemente Borges" in *Escritores a fondo,* Planeta: Barcelona, 1986.

Sorrentino, Fernando. *Siete conversaciones con Jorge Luis Borges,* Casa Pardo: Buenos Aires, 1973.

Vázquez, María Esther. *Borges: imágenes, memorias, diálogos.* Monte Avila: Caracas, 1977.

———. *Borges: sus días y su tiempo,* Javier Vergara: Barcelona, 1984.

Memoirs, Reminiscences, and Items of Biographical Interest

The most valuable sources are:

Borges, Jorge Luis. "An Autobiographical Essay" and "Commentaries" in *The Aleph and Other Stories* (see above).

Other important items are:

Acevedo de Borges, Leonor. "Recuerdos" (unpublished memoirs).

———. "Propos de Mme. Leonor Acevedo de Borges" in *Cahiers de l'Herne,* Paris, 1964, pp. 9–11.

Alazraki, Jaime. "Epilogue. On Borges' Death: Some Reflections" in *Borges and the Kabbalah,* Cambridge University Press: Cambridge, 1988, pp. 176–89.

Andreola, Carlos Alberto. "Borges en la mira del investigador," *Haute Qualité* (Buenos Aires), 2 (1993), pp. 21–27.

———. "Borges Helvético," *Conectándonos* (Bomberos Voluntarios de Matanza), 18 (1994), pp. 18–19, 26–27.

Andrés, Alfredo. *Palabras con Leopoldo Marechal,* Carlos Pérez Editor, 1968.

Astete Millán, Elsa. "Habla la mujer de Borges," *Tiempo Argentino,* February 6, 1983.

Barrenechea, Ana María. "Jorge Luis Borges y la ambivalente mitificación de su abuelo paterno," *Nueva Revista de Filología Hispánica,* 40 (1992), pp. 1005–24.

Bianciotti, Hector. "Preface" to Jorge Luis Borges, *Neuf essais sur Dante,* Gallimard: Paris, 1987.

Bioy Casares, Adolfo. *Memorias: infancia, adolescencia, y cómo se hace un escritor,* Tusquets: Barcelona, 1994.

Borges, Jorge G. *El Caudillo,* Academia Argentina de Letras, 1989. (First published in a private edition in 1921.)

Burone, Carlos. "En un libro que publicará en abril de 1975, Borges se ocupa por primera vez de los ardores de la pasión," *La Opinión,* December 21, 1974.

Canto, Estela. *Borges a contraluz,* Espasa-Calpe: Madrid, 1989.

Casares, Alberto. "La última tarde de Borges en Buenos Aires," *Proa* (tercera época), 23 (1996), pp. 169–70.

di Giovanni, Norman Thomas. "At Work with Borges," *Books Abroad,* July 1971, pp. 434–44.

———. "Introduction," *In Memory of Borges,* Constable: London, 1988.

———. "The Good Reader: Jorge Luis Borges's 'Exclusively Literary Life,'" *The Times Literary Supplement,* April 26, 2002, pp. 13–14.

Edelberg, Betina. "Algunos de los muchos recuerdos," *Proa* (tercera época), 23 (1996), pp. 65–67.

Gasió, Guillermo, ed. *Borges en Japón. Japón en Borges,* Editorial de la Universidad de Buenos Aires, 1988.

Gasparini, Juan. *Borges: la posesión póstuma,* Foca: Madrid, 2000.

Goldaracena, Rita. "Las inhibiciones del joven Borges," *El País,* December 23, 1990, pp. 12–13. (Interview with the psychologist Miguel Kohan-Miller.)

Howard, Mathew. "Stranger Than *Ficción,*" *Lingua Franca,* June/July, 1997, pp. 41–49.

Mastronardi, Carlos. *Memorias de un provinciano,* Ediciones Culturales Argentinas, 1967.

Mayer, Daniel. "Sérieux comme un tigre. Jorge Luis Borges en Suisse," *Écriture* (Lausanne), 28 (1987), pp. 11–34.

Meneses, Carlos. *Borges en Mallorca (1919–1921),* Aitana: Alicante, 1996.

Nóbile, Beatriz de. *Palabras con Norah Lange,* Carlos Pérez Editor, 1968.

Ocampo, Silvina. "Image de Borges" in *Cahiers de L'Herne,* Paris, 1964, pp. 26–30.

Ocampo, Victoria. "Vision de Borges" in *Cahiers de L'Herne,* Paris, 1964, pp. 19–25.

Petit de Murat, Ulyses. *Borges Buenos Aires,* Municipalidad de la Ciudad de Buenos Aires, 1980.

Porzio, Domenico. *Jorge Luis Borges: Immagini e immaginazione,* Edizioni Studio Tesi: Pordenone, 1985.

Reid, Alastair. "Neruda and Borges," the *New Yorker,* June 24 and July 1, 1996, pp. 56–72.

Salas, Horacio. *Conversaciones con Raúl González Tuñón,* La Bastilla, 1975.

Slavuski, Victoria. "The Old Man and the City," *The Times Literary Supplement,* August 20, 1999, pp. 10–12.

Torre Borges, Miguel de. *Jorge Luis Borges: manuscritos y fotografías,* Renglón, 1987.

———. *Un día en la vida de Jorge Luis Borges.* Privately printed, 1995.

Yates, Donald A. "Behind 'Borges and I,'" *Modern Fiction Studies,* 19 (1973), pp. 317–24.

Biographies of Borges

Alifano, Roberto. *Borges: biografía verbal,* Plaza y Janés: Barcelona, 1988.

Barnatán, Marcos Ricardo. *Borges: biografía total,* Ediciones Temas de Hoy: Madrid, 1995.

Jurado, Alicia. *Genio y figura de Jorge Luis Borges,* Editorial Universitaria de Buenos Aires, 1964.

Rodríguez Monegal, Emir. *Jorge Luis Borges: A Literary Biography,* Dutton: New York, 1978.

Salas, Horacio. *Borges: una biografía,* Planeta, 1994.

Savater, Fernando. *Jorge Luis Borges,* Omega: Barcelona, 2002.

Teitelboim, Volodia. *Los dos Borges: vida, sueños, enigmas*, Editorial Sudamericana Chilena: Santiago, 1996.

Vaccaro, Alejandro. *Georgie (1899–1930): una vida de Jorge Luis Borges*, Proa/Alberto Casares, 1996.

Vázquez, María Esther. *Borges: esplendor y derrota*, Tusquets: Barcelona, 1996.

Woodall, James. *The Man in the Mirror of the Book: A Life of Jorge Luis Borges*, Hodder & Stoughton: London, 1996.

Yates, Donald A. *Jorge Luis Borges: Life, Work, and Criticism*, York Press: Fredericton, New Brunswick, 1985.

Critical Studies of Borges's Work

Aizenberg, Edna. *The Aleph Weaver: Biblical, Kabbalistic and Judaic Elements in Borges*, Scripta Humanistica: Potomac, MD, 1984.

———. *Borges and His Successors: The Borgesian Impact on Literature and the Arts*, University of Missouri Press: Columbia, 1990.

Alazraki, Jaime, ed. *Borges. El escritor y la crítica*, Taurus: Madrid, 1976.

———. *Critical Essays on Jorge Luis Borges*, G. K. Hall: Boston, MA, 1987.

———. *Borges and the Kabbalah, and Other Essays on His Fiction and Poetry*, Cambridge University Press: Cambridge, 1988.

Anthropos. Revista de Documentación Científica de la Cultura, 142–43 (1993). (Special number on Jorge Luis Borges.)

Arana, Juan. *El centro del laberinto: los motivos filosóficos en la obra de Jorge Luis Borges*, EUNSA: Navarra, 1994.

Arriguci, Jr., Davi. "De la fama y de la infamia. (Borges en el contexto literario latinoamericano)," *Cuadernos de recienvenido*, Humanitas/FFLCH/Universidade de São Paulo: São Paulo, 1999, pp. 19–55.

Artundo, Patricia. "Entre 'La Aventura y el Orden': los hermanos Borges y el ultraísmo argentino," *Cuadernos de recienvenido*, Humanitas/FFLCH/Universidade de São Paulo: São Paulo, 1999, pp. 57–97.

Ashbery, John. "A Game with Shifting Mirrors." See *Critical Essays*, Alazraki, ed., 1987.

Balderston, Daniel. *Out of Context: Historical Reference and the Representation of Reality in Borges*, Duke University Press: Durham, NC, and London, 1993.

Barrenechea, Ana María. *Borges, the Labyrinth Maker*, New York University Press: New York, 1965.

——— et al. *Borges y la crítica. Antología*, Centro Editor de América Latina, 1992.

Barth, John. "The Literature of Exhaustion." See *Critical Essays*, Alazraki, ed., 1987.

Bastos, María Luisa. *Borges ante la crítica argentina: 1923–1960*, Hispamérica, 1974.

Bell-Villada, Gene H. *Borges and His Fiction: A Guide to His Mind and Art*, University of North Carolina Press: Chapel Hill, NC: 1981.

Bloom, Harold, ed. *Jorge Luis Borges*, Chelsea House Publishers: New York, 1986.

———. "Borges, Neruda and Pessoa: Hispanic-Portuguese Whitman" in *The Western Canon*, Harcourt, Brace: New York, 1994, pp. 463–92.

Blüher, Karl Alfred, and Alfonso de Toro, eds. *Jorge Luis Borges: variaciones interpretativas sobre sus procedimientos y bases epistemológicas*, Vervuert: Frankfurt am Main, 1992.

Bonatti, María. "Dante en la lectura de Borges," *Revista Iberoamericana*, 43, 1977, pp. 737–44.

Cahiers de L'Herne, "Jorge Luis Borges," Éditions de L'Herne: Paris, 1964.

Calvino, Italo. "Jorge Luis Borges," *Perché leggere i classici,* Mondadori: Milan, pp. 292–301.

Champeau, Serge. *Borges et la métaphysique,* Vrin: Paris, 1990.

Christ, Ronald. *The Narrow Act: Borges' Art of Allusion,* New York University Press: New York, 1969.

Cozarinsky, Edgardo. *Borges in/and/on Film,* Lumen Books: New York, 1988.

Cuadernos Hispanoamericanos, "Homenaje a Jorge Luis Borges," 505–7, Instituto de Cooperación Iberoamericana, Madrid, 1992.

Doll, Ramón. "Discusiones con Borges" in *Policía intelectual,* Tor, 1933.

Dunham, Lowell and Ivar Ivask, eds. *The Cardinal Points of Borges,* University of Oklahoma Press: Norman, 1971. (Papers of an international symposium, University of Oklahoma, 1969.)

Echavarría, Arturo. *Lengua y literatura de Borges,* Ariel: Barcelona, 1983.

Farías, Victor. *Borges y la metafísica del arrabal. "El tamaño mi esperanza," un libro desconocido de Jorge Luis Borges,* Anaya & Mario Muchnik: Madrid, 1992.

———. *Las actas secretas. "Inquisiciones" y "El idioma de los argentinos": los libros proscritos de Jorge Luis Borges,* Anaya & Mario Muchnik: Madrid, 1994.

Fishburn, Evelyn, and Psique Hughes. *A Borges Dictionary.* Duckworth: London, 1990.

Fishburn, Evelyn, ed. *Borges and Europe Revisited,* Institute of Latin American Studies, University of London: London, 1998.

Fló, Juan, ed. *Contra Borges,* Galerna, 1978.

García, Carlos. *El joven Borges, poeta (1919–1930),* Corregidor, 2000.

Gass, William H. "Imaginary Borges and His Books." See *Critical Essays,* Alazraki, ed., 1987.

Genette, Gérard. "L'utopie littéraire" in *Figures,* Seuil: Paris, 1966.

Irwin, John T. *The Mystery to a Solution: Poe, Borges and the Analytic Detective Story,* Johns Hopkins Press: Baltimore, 1994.

Kristal, Efraín. *Invisible Work: Borges and Translation,* Vanderbilt University Press: Nashville, 2002.

Lafon, Michel. *Borges ou la réécriture,* Seuil: Paris, 1990.

Louis, Annik. *Jorge Luis Borges: oeuvres et manoeuvres,* L'Harmattan: Paris, 1997.

Macherey, Pierre. "Borges and the Fictive Narrative." See *Critical Essays,* Alazraki, ed., 1987.

Maier, Linda S. *Borges and the European Avant Garde,* Peter Lang: New York, 1996.

Man, Paul de. "A Modern Master." See *Critical Essays,* Alazraki, ed., 1987.

Manguel, Alberto. "An Endless Happiness: How Borges Throws Open the Doors of the Universal Library," *The Times Literary Supplement,* February 18, 2000, pp. 12–13.

Megáfono, 1, (1933), pp. 13–33. "Discusión sobre Jorge Luis Borges."

Modern Fiction Studies, 19 (1973), (Purdue University, West Lafayette, IN). Special number on Borges.

Molloy, Sylvia. *Signs of Borges,* Duke University Press: Durham, NC, 1994.

Nuño, Juan. *La filosofía de Borges,* Fondo de Cultura Económica: Mexico City, 1986.

Olaso, Ezequiel de. *Jugar en serio: aventuras de Borges,* Paidós Mexicana: Mexico City, 1999.

Olea Franco, Rafael. *El otro Borges, el primer Borges,* Fondo de Cultura Económica de Argentina, 1993.

Paoli, Roberto. *Borges: percorsi di significato,* Universtià degl Studi di Firenze: Florence, 1977.

————. "Borges e Dante," *Studi danteschi*, 56, 1984, pp. 189–212.

————. *Tre Saggi su Borges*, Bulzoni: Rome, 1992.

Pellicer, Rosa. *Borges: el estilo de la eternidad*, Universidad de Zaragoza: Zaragoza, 1986.

Piglia, Ricardo. "Ideología y ficción en Borges" in *Borges y la crítica* (see Barrenechea et al., above).

Prieto, Adolfo. *Borges y la nueva generación*, Letras Universitarias, 1954.

Proa (tercera época) 23 (1996). "Jorge Luis Borges: diez años después."

Rodríguez Monegal, Emir. *Borges por él mismo*, Laia: Barcelona, 1984.

Rowe, William, Claudio Canaparo, and Annick Louis, eds. *Jorge Luis Borges: intervenciones sobre pensamiento y literatura*, Paidós: Buenos Aires, 2000.

Running, Thorpe. *Borges's Ultraist Movement and Its Poets*, International Books: Lathrup Village, MI, 1981.

Sarlo, Beatriz. *Borges: A Writer on the Edge*, Verso: London, 1993.

Scholes, Robert. "The Reality of Borges." See *Critical Essays*, Alazraki, ed., 1987.

Shaw, Donald L. *Borges' Narrative Strategy* (Liverpool Monographs in Hispanic Studies 11), Francis Cairns: Leeds, 1992.

Sosnowski, Saúl. *Borges y la cábala: la búsqueda del verbo*, Hispamérica, 1976.

Stabb, Martin S. *Jorge Luis Borges*, St. Martin's Press: New York, 1970.

Stefanini, Ruggero. "Dante in Borges: l'Aleph, Beatriz, e il Sud," *Italica*, 57, 1980, pp. 53–65.

Sturrock, John. *Paper Tigers: The Ideal Fictions of Jorge Luis Borges*, Clarendon Press: Oxford, 1977.

Suárez, María Victoria, ed. *Fuego del aire: homenaje a Borges*, Fundación Internacional Jorge Luis Borges, 2001.

Sucre, Guillermo. *Borges, el poeta*, Monte Avila: Caracas, 1974.

Steiner, George. "Tigers in the Mirror." See *Critical Essays*, Alazraki, ed., 1987.

Tanner, Tony. "Borges and American Fiction 1950–1970." See *Critical Essays*, Alazraki ed., 1987.

Thiem, Jon. "Borges, Dante, and the Poetics of Total Vision," *Comparative Litertaure*, 40 (1988), pp. 97–121.

Toro, Alfonso de and Fernando de Toro, eds. *El siglo de Borges. Homenaje a Jorge Luis Borges en su centenario* (two vols.), Vervuert: Frankfurt am Main; Iberoamericana: Madrid, 1999.

Triquarterly, 25 (1972), (Northwestern University Press: Evanston, IL). "Prose for Borges."

Updike, John. "The Author as Librarian." See *Critical Essays*, Alazraki, ed., 1987.

Variaciones Borges (Journal of the Jorge Luis Borges Center for Studies and Documentation), Aarhus Universitet: Aarhus, 1996.

Woscoboinik, Julio. *El secreto de Borges: indagación psicoanalítica de su obra*. Trieb, 1988.

————. *El alma de "El Aleph": nuevos aportes a la indagación psicoanalítica de la obra de Jorge Luis Borges*, Grupo Editorial Latinoamericano, 1996.

Yates, Donald A. "Behind 'Borges and I,'" *Modern Fiction Studies*, 19 (1973), pp. 317–24 (see above, p. 544, under "Memoirs, Reminiscences, and Items of Biographical Interest").

Principal Other Works Consulted

Artundo, Patricia M. "Los antecedentes españoles de *Proa. Revista de Renovación Literaria*" in *Las artes en el debate del Quinto Centenario,* Facultad de Filosofía y Letras, Universidad de Buenos Aires, 1992, pp. 11–17.

———. *Norah Borges. Obra gráfica, 1920–1930,* Fondo Nacional de las Artes, 1994.

Barral, Carlos. *Los años sin excusa. Memorias,* vol. 2, Barral: Barcelona, 1978.

Buenos Aires, sus alrededores, y costas del Uruguay, Guía Pirelli, Sudamericana, 1993.

Collier, Simon, Artemis Cooper, María Susana Azzi, and Richard Martin. *¡Tango!: The Dance, the Song, the Story,* Thames and Hudson: London, 1995.

Dante Alighieri. *The Divine Comedy,* trans. Geoffrey L. Bickersteth, revised edition, Shakespeare Head Press/Basil Blackwell: Oxford, 1972.

Dujovne Ortiz, Alicia. *Eva Perón: A Biography,* Little, Brown: London, 1997.

Furness, R.S. *Expressionism,* Methuen: London, 1973.

Girondo, Oliverio. *Espantapájaros y otras obras,* Centro Editor de América Latina, 1981.

———. *El periódico "Martín Fierro," 1924–1949,* Francisco A. Colombo, 1949.

Goñi, Uki. *The Real Odessa: How Perón Brought the Nazi War Criminals to Argentina,* Granta: London, 2001.

Hermes Villordo, Oscar. *El grupo SUR: una biografía colectiva,* Planeta, 1994.

Hernández, José. *El gaucho Martín Fierro* [1872, 1879], ed. Eleuterio F. Tiscornia, 8th ed., Losada, 1949.

Ibarra, Néstor. *La nueva poesía argentina. Ensayo crítico sobre el ultraísmo, 1921–1929,* Vda. de Molinari e Hijos, 1930.

Iturburu, Córdova. *La revolución martinfierrista,* Ediciones Culturales Argentinas, 1962.

King, John. *Sur: A Study of the Argentine Literary Journal and Its Role in the Development of a Culture, 1931–1970,* Cambridge University Press: Cambridge, 1986.

Lange, Norah. *La calle de la tarde,* Samet, 1924.

———. *Los días y las noches,* El Inca, 1926.

———. *Voz de la vida,* Proa, 1927.

———. *45 días y 30 marineros,* Tor, 1933.

———. *El rumbo de la rosa,* Proa, 1930.

———. *Cuadernos de infancia,* Viau y Zona, 1937.

———. *Estimados congéneres,* Losada, 1968 (incorporates *Discursos,* 1942).

Lugones, Leopoldo. *El payador* [1916], Centurión, 1961.

Miguel, María Esther de. *Norah Lange: una biografía,* Planeta, 1991.

Mizraje, María Gabriela. *Norah Lange: infancia y sueños de walkiria,* Facultad de Filosofía y Letras, Universidad de Buenos Aires, 1995.

Naipaul, V.S. *The Return of Eva Perón,* André Deutsch: London, 1980.

Page, Joseph A. *Perón: A Biography,* Random House: New York, 1983.

Pellegrini, Aldo. *Oliverio Girondo,* Ediciones Culturales Argentinas, 1964.

Pereyra, Wáshington Luis. *La prensa literaria argentina. Los años rebeldes 1920–1929,* Librería Colonial, 1995.

Randle, Patricio H., et al. "Algunos aspectos de la geografía urbana de Buenos Aires," *Anales de la Sociedad Argentina de Estudios Geográficos,* 13 (1969), pp. 213–71.

Revista Martín Fierro, 1924–1927. Edición facsimilar (Estudio preliminar de Horacio Salas), Fondo Nacional de las Artes, 1995.

Rock, David. *Argentina 1516–1982: From Spanish Colonization to the Falklands War,* University of California Press: Berkeley, 1985.

————. *Authoritarian Argentina: The Nationalist Movement, Its History and Its Impact*, University of California Press: Berkeley, 1993.

Romero, Luis Alberto. *Breve historia contemporánea de la Argentina*, Fondo de Cultura Económica de Argentina, 1994.

Salas, Horacio. *El Tango*, Planeta, 1986.

————. *El Centenario: la Argentina en su hora más gloriosa*, Planeta, 1996.

Sarlo, Beatriz. *Una modernidad periférica: Buenos Aires 1920 y 1930*, Nueva Visión, 1988.

Sarmiento, Domingo F. *Facundo: or, Civilisation and Barbarism* [1845], Penguin: Harmondsworth, 1998.

Scalabrini Ortiz, Raúl. *El hombre que está solo y espera* [1931], Plus Ultra, 1991.

Schwartz, Jorge, ed. *Homenaje a Girondo*, Corregidor, 1987.

————. *Las vanguardias latinoamericanas*, Cátedra: Madrid, 1991.

————. *Vanguardia y cosmopolitismo en la década del veinte: Oliverio Girondo y Oswaldo de Andrade*, Beatriz Viterbo, 1993.

Shumway, Nicolas. *The Invention of Argentina*, University of California Press: Berkeley, 1991.

Torre, Guillermo de. *Literaturas europeas de vanguardia*, Caro Raggio: Madrid, 1925.

————. "Para la prehistoria ultraísta de Borges," *Cuadernos Hispanoamericanos*, 47 (1964), pp. 457–63.

ULTRA. Edición facsimilar de José Antonio Sarmiento y José María Barrera, Visor: Madrid, 1993.

Videla, Gloria. *El ultraísmo*, Gredos: Madrid, 1963.

Vignale, Pedro-Juan, and César Tiempo, eds. *Exposición de la actual poesía argentina (1922–1927)*, Minerva, 1927.

Viñas, David. *Literatura argentina y realidad política*, Centro Editor de América Latina, 1982.

Williamson, Edwin. *The Penguin History of Latin America*, Allen Lane, Penguin Press: London, 1992.

XUL: Revista de poesía (Buenos Aires) 6 (1984). "Apunte sobre Oliverio Girondo" (special number).

Yahni, Roberto, and Pedro Orgambide. *Enciclopedia de la literatura argentina*, Sudamericana, 1970.

Index

ambitions of, 59, 129, 133, 278–79
appearance of, 150, 275, 347
Astete and, 268, 371–72, 373, 374,
   376–79, 387, 389, 390–91
Becher and, 60–61
as bilingual, 34
Bioy Casares and, 217–19, 223–25, 240–41,
   244, 256–57, 258–59, 314, 324, 369, 479
birth of, 32
Cansinos-Asséns and, 77
Canto and, 275–77, 279–91, 295, 296,
   308–10, 326–27, 331–32, 359–60, 479
Carlyle and, 58
Carriego and, 42–44, 48–49, 50, 168,
   170–71, 175, 381
Casares, Alberto, 479
Cecilia Ingenieros and, 301–2, 303, 304
character and personality of, 39–40, 227,
   241, 276, 293, 301, 314–15, 357
childhood of. *See* childhood
Concepción Guerrero and, 102, 103, 104,
   105, 106, 107, 110–11, 113–14, 120, 122,
   127–28, 148, 385, 439
daily life of, 342, 378, 385, 424
Dante's influence on, 241–44, 245, 250–52,
   253, 254–55, 261, 262, 268–69, 278, 281,
   282, 283, 302–3, 319, 325, 429–31, 434,
   435, 438, 444, 446
death of, 489, 490–91
death of J. G. Borges and, 230–36
death of Leonor Acevedo de Borges
   and, 416–18
di Giovanni and, 378, 380, 381, 385–89,
   391–92, 394, 406
eccentrics, weakness for, 77
education of. *See* education
eyesight problems of, ix, 80, 164, 165,
   166, 262, 324–25, 341, 342, 371, 443, 454
Fernández and, 96, 97
Frances Haslam and, 34, 36–37, 56, 212, 213
funeral of, 490–91
Girondo and, 118, 119, 121, 134, 137, 150,
   164, 183–84, 189, 227–29, 367–68
Haydée Lange and, 244–45, 253, 267–68,
   389, 390, 392–93, 438
illnesses of, 439–40, 474–75, 477, 483,
   485, 487
inadequacy, feelings of, 38, 40, 118, 289,
   307, 366, 417. *See also* self-doubt

influence of, vii, 346–47
international reputation of, 346–47,
   349, 357, 378, 392, 396, 397, 459–60
J. G. Borges and, 31, 40, 46, 47–48, 59,
   64–65, 66, 71–72, 73–74, 82–83, 212–13,
   227, 230–36, 250, 268–69, 318, 366,
   401–2, 418, 482, 485
J. G. Borges's library and, 41–42, 341,
   429
jobs of, 230–31, 292–93, 295–96, 299,
   328–29. *See also* editor, Borges as;
   teacher and professor, Borges as
Kodama and, 369–70, 371, 372, 379,
   385–86, 387–88, 390, 392, 393–95, 398,
   405, 418–20, 422, 424, 433–34, 437,
   438, 440, 441–44, 450–51, 468, 469–70,
   477–79, 481–82, 483, 488
Leonor Acevedo de Borges and, 31, 35–36,
   39–40, 66, 105–6, 110, 235–36, 262–63,
   284–85, 286, 287, 307, 323, 324, 329,
   342, 347, 348, 352, 356, 357, 358, 359,
   363, 416–17
Lorca and, 196
Macedonio, Fernández and, 95, 96–98,
   115, 161, 224–25
Margarita Guerrero and, 314, 315, 319–
   20, 371, 372
marriages of. *See* marriages, Borges's
new apartment purchased by, 471
Norah Borges and, 33, 66, 72, 438, 480
Norah Lange and, 124–27, 135, 142, 143,
   144–46, 151, 152, 154, 155–59, 167–68, 172,
   175, 185, 186–87, 189, 192, 193, 195, 201–3,
   210, 213–14, 220, 229, 241, 242, 389–90,
   393, 407–8
police surveillance of, 320
politics of. *See* politics, Borges's
Torre (Guillermo de) and, 76, 80, 81, 82,
   83, 84, 86, 87, 88, 93, 95, 111, 112–13, 117,
   120, 121, 124, 134, 137, 142, 196, 371
Whitman and, 61, 69, 71, 113, 129, 279
Borges, Leonor Fanny. *See* Borges,
   Norah (Borges's sister)
Borges, Norah (Borges's sister), 50, 65, 76,
   263, 371
arrest and imprisonment of, 306–7
as artist, 72, 81, 85, 100, 103, 112
birth of, 33
Borges and, 33, 66, 72, 438, 480, 484

Emilie (girlfriend), 63–67, 72–73, 80, 94

"Emma Zunz" (Borges), 303–4

Emory University, 420

emotional condition, Borges's, 38, 40, 50, 103, 109, 116, 118, 123, 135, 148, 157, 165–66, 185, 187, 207–8, 209, 212, 238, 240, 253–54, 254–55, 258, 265, 278, 281, 291, 296, 352–53, 377, 379, 387, 391, 416, 420–21, 430, 436

"Empty Drawing Room" (Borges), 106

Encounter, 349

"Encounter, The" (Borges), 367, 386, 387

"End, The" (Borges), 323, 341

"End of the Duel, The" (Borges), 388

"Endymion on Latmos" (Borges), 419–20, 429

English language, 276

"English Poem," 186, 201–2

English translations of Borges's work, 350, 378, 379–80, 385, 388, 406

En la masmédula (Girondo), 227

Enlightenment, 7, 266

Entre Ríos, 9, 23, 25, 42

Enzensberger, Hans Magnus, 345

E. P. Dutton, 380, 381, 387, 388, 392, 406

Erfjord de Lange, Berta, 99, 125, 202, 244

Espantapájaros (Girondo), 189, 192

estancieros, 9, 13, 318

Etcheberrigaray, Miguel Angel, 293

eternity, 214–15, 448–49

ethical instinct, American, 412–13

Etruria Literary Prize, 471

Eva Perón Foundation, 311

Evaristo Carriego (Borges), 168, 170–71, 175, 381

"Examination of the Works of Herbert Quain, An" (Borges), 215, 220, 259, 264, 397

expressionism, 60, 71, 79, 81–82, 87, 112, 113, 117, 118, 143

"Extent of My Hope, The" (Borges), 140–41

Extrema Izquierda, 131, 132

eyesight problems

Borges's, ix, 80, 164, 165, 166, 262, 324–25, 341, 342, 371, 443, 454

J. G. Borges's, 51, 53, 79, 212

Facundo: or, Civilization and Barbarism (Sarmiento), 7–8

"Faded Dawn" (Borges), 94

failure

Borges's sense of, 232, 408

to rebel against mother, 66, 110, 114, 235–36, 263, 265, 285, 286, 323

to win awards, 156, 249, 260, 261, 270, 397, 425, 426

with women, 66, 235–36, 289, 324, 390

as writer, Borges's sense of, 232, 257, 340–41

Falkland Islands. *See* Malvinas islands

fame, 346–47, 357, 378, 392, 396, 397, 416, 418–19, 423, 440

lateness of, vii, 346

rebellion against mother and, 353

family honor. *See* dagger and sword, conflict between

fascism, 132, 185, 198, 221, 265, 269, 270, 305, 344, 409, 430

father(s) and patriarchy, 48, 233–34, 249–50, 254, 268–69, 400, 447, 462–63, 465, 482. *See also* trinities and triangles

Fausto (del Campo), 135, 138

"Feeling in Death" (Borges), 155–56, 214, 253, 443

Fellner, Jorge Patricio, 474

Fernández, Macedonio, 26–27, 28, 42, 95–98, 104, 107, 115, 161, 224, 225, 444

Fernández Peña, Manuel, 86

Fervor de Buenos Aires (Borges), 108, 111–12, 116, 118–19, 156, 267, 381, 385

Ficciones (Borges), 270, 271, 275, 300, 312, 315–16, 346, 350

fiction, viii–ix. *See also specific titles*

Borges on, 176–78, 219, 257

Borges's invention of new kind of, 257, 259–60

detective. *See* detective stories

early experiments in, 175

modes of, viii

as *orbe autónomo,* viii, 177–78, 219, 256, 270

self-exploration through, 211–12, 229, 261–62, 304, 315, 359–68, 377, 397–402, 429–31

straightforward storytelling, 360

Figari, Pedro, 166

Filiberto, Juan de Dios, 142, 171

Fillol Day, Gustavo, 359, 360

"Proclama" (Borges), 100
"Profession of Literary Faith, A" (Borges), ix, 143, 157, 176, 177, 178, 181
professor, Borges as. *See* teacher and professor, Borges as
"Prophet, The" (Borges), 62
Prose Edda (Sturlason), 186
"Prose Poems for I.J." (Borges), 267
prostitutes, 64, 88–89, 168, 234, 400
Protestantism, 34–35, 348, 489, 490
pseudonyms, 200, 201, 207, 218, 259
psychological conflicts, Borges's, 38, 40, 264, 286, 287–88, 289, 304, 308, 321
    J. G. Borges's role in, 46–47, 48, 64–65, 73–74, 235, 366, 400, 482
    Leonor Acevedo de Borges's role in, 66, 307, 323, 359, 363, 399
public speaking and lecturing, 270–71, 288, 295–96, 299, 313, 316, 342, 349, 351, 358, 375, 376, 377, 420–21, 432
Pueblo Entero, 293
Puerto Rico, University of, 455
Pueyrredón de Lastra, Raquel, 306

45 días y 30 marineros (Lange), 181–83, 193, 197, 202, 213
Quevedo, Francisco de, 107, 124, 156–57
Quiroga, Facundo, 7, 118, 136, 138
Quiroga, Horacio, 125

radicalism, 408–9, 421
Radical Party, 10, 14, 15, 94, 160, 162, 185, 191, 221, 317, 330, 334, 350, 351, 466, 473
"Ragnarök" (Borges), 339–40, 350
Read, Herbert, 356
reader(s), 236
    author and, interchangeability of, 237
    Borges's lack of connection with, 177–78, 216
reading
    childhood, viii, 34–35, 39, 40, 41, 43–44
    during teenage years, 56, 58, 60–61
realism, vii–viii, 178, 257
reality, 219, 235, 341, 392. *See also* unreality of material world
rebellion
    against authority, 234, 235
    Borges's will as, 478
    against family, 61, 66, 88, 110, 114, 264

literary, 87, 101, 120
    against mother, 44, 66, 110, 114, 235–36, 263, 265, 285, 286, 301, 323, 353, 354, 355, 359
Recoleta Cemetery, 416, 478
"Redemption" (Borges), 307
"Red Guard" (Borges), 83
Reflector, 85
Rega Molina, Horacio, 224
Reid, Alastair, 395
religion, 444, 468. *See also specific religions*
"Remorse" (Borges), 416
"Return, The" (Borges), 93
"Return to Buenos Aires, The" (Borges), 120
Reverdy, Pierre, 75, 119
revisionism, historical, 192, 221, 226
Revista de Occidente, 116, 393n
Revista Oral, 131, 147
Revolución Libertadora, 327–28, 330–40, 351, 410, 423
Revolution of 1890, 10, 19–20
Reyes, Alfonso, 169, 173, 224, 225
Reyes, Salvador, 102
Ricci, Franco Maria, 469, 481
Rinkyu-ji Temple, 443
Rioan-ji Temple, 443
Risso Platero, Ema, 296, 300, 301
river, as symbol
    in *El Caudillo,* 29, 30 31, 251, 401–2
    in Borges's work, 251, 401–2, 420, 492
Rivera, 211
Rivera, Diego, 226
Rivero, Edmundo, 358
River Plate. *See* Plata, Río de la
Roca, Julio Argentino, 9, 10
Roca-Runciman Treaty (1933), 191, 192, 198
Rodríguez Monegal, Emir, 342, 371
Roeg, Nicolas, 396, 397
Rojas Paz, Pablo, 121, 122, 133, 161, 185
Rolland, Romain, 60
Romains, Jules, 222, 223
romantic attachments. *See* love affairs
Rome, ancient, Argentina compared with, 123, 200, 201
Rosas, Juan Manuel de, 5–6, 35, 64, 105–6, 140–41, 225, 263, 265, 283, 305, 317, 352, 362, 460
"Rosas" (Borges), 105